# FUNDAMENTALS OF ORGANIZATIONAL COMMUNICATION

## Knowledge, Sensitivity, Skills, Values

PAMELA SHOCKLEY-ZALABAK

*University of Colorado at Colorado Springs*



**Allyn and Bacon**

Boston ■ London ■ Toronto ■ Sydney ■ Tokyo ■ Singapore

**Series Editor:** *Karon Bowers*
**Editorial Assistant:** *Jennifer Trebby*
**Marketing Manager:** *Mandee Eckersley*
**Editorial-Production Service:** *Omegatype Typography, Inc.*
**Composition and Prepress Buyer:** *Linda Cox*
**Manufacturing Buyer:** *Julie McNeill*
**Cover Administrator:** *Kristina Mose-Libon*
**Electronic Composition:** *Omegatype Typography, Inc.*

Copyright © 2002 by Allyn & Bacon
A Pearson Education Company
75 Arlington Street
Boston, MA 02116

Internet: www.ablongman.com

Between the time Website information is gathered and then published, it is not unusual for some sites to have closed. Also, the transcription of URLs can result in unintended typographical errors. The publisher would appreciate notification where these occur so that they may be corrected in subsequent editions. Thank you.

**Library of Congress Cataloging-in-Publication Data**

Shockley-Zalabak, Pamela.
 Fundamentals of organizational communication : knowledge, sensitivity, skills, values / Pamela Shockley-Zalabak.—5th ed.
  p.  cm.
 Includes bibliographical references and index.
 ISBN 0-205-34076-8 (alk. paper)
 1. Communication in organizations.  I. Title.

HD30.3 .S55  2001
658.4'5—dc21

2001033388

Printed in the United States of America

10  9  8  7  6  5          06  05  04

*To Charles Zalabak*
*and*
*Leatha and Jim Shockley*

# CONTENTS

---

**CHAPTER EIGHT**

# Participating in Organizations: Developing Critical Organizational Communication Competencies    268

---

**CHAPTER ELEVEN**
## Applications of Organizational Communication    395

---

**CHAPTER TWELVE**
## Organizational Communication: Values and Ethical Communication Behaviors    426

We are in one of the most turbulent and exciting periods in human history. The twenty-first century presents unprecedented challenges and opportunities, and the knowledge we bring to bear on our problems seems at best incomplete as we think about the future.

We are in transition from an information to a knowledge age, with rapid change in the institutions and organizations with which we are most familiar. *Fundamentals of Organizational Communication: Knowledge, Sensitivity, Skills, Values* was written to help readers experience twenty-first-century organizational challenges within the context of learning about communication and organizations.

The fifth edition of this book presents the concepts of organizational communication within a unique competency-based approach that incorporates personal knowledge, interpersonal sensitivity, communication skills, and ethical values. It blends theory, practice, and analysis with an emphasis on knowledge, sensitivity, skills, and values.

Why a competency-based approach? The answer is simple: organizing material by competency components is academically relevant and important to contemporary organizations. Favorable responses to earlier editions from both students and faculty support the competency-based mix of theory and application. In addition, studies in the United States and internationally have described both human and technological communication as the key to excellence in the twenty-first century. Numerous employer surveys have found that accurately processing large volumes of information within organizations, although necessary, is not sufficient for excellence; employers need individuals who take personal responsibility for building relationships that contribute to trust, quality communication, innovation, and change.

## THE COMPETENCY FRAMEWORK

### Knowledge

Theoretical concepts important to the study of organizational communication are presented so that students can develop personal knowledge. Knowledge competencies are what we come to know about the theory and principles of a particular field of study, in this case organizational communication. Knowledge competencies support sensitivity in organizational life, guide our development of skills, and assist us in understanding the application of ethical standards and our personal values in organizational settings. To this end, this book examines various frameworks for understanding organizational communication, communication implications of major organizational theories, and communication processes in organizations.

## Sensitivity

The sensitivity component in the competency framework refers to our ability to sense or become aware of a variety of organizational meanings and feelings. It is related to our ability and willingness to understand what others are feeling and doing. To develop the sensitivity competency, this book encourages students to study and analyze various roles and relationships within organizations. Individual sensitivity can be developed by analyzing the impact of personal behaviors in organizational settings, such as individuals in organizations, dyadic relationships (specifically supervisor–subordinate relationships), group processes, conflict, and leadership and management communication, each examined in the text. In addition, the text emphasizes the importance of the sensitivity component for our increasingly diverse, multicultural, and international organizational world.

## Skills

The skills component of the framework focuses on developing important analytical capabilities as well as the ability to communicate effectively in a variety of settings. It is designed to help students develop both initiating and receiving communication skills. Key organizational communication skills (e.g., decision making, problem solving, fact finding, interviewing, communications technologies, and making presentations) are identified, and analysis and practice opportunities appropriate for each are provided. Also, analysis opportunities provided in case studies and research opportunities contribute to students' skill development.

## Values

The values component in the competency framework is key to the integration of knowledge, sensitivity, and skills. To understand the realities of organizational life, we must first examine how individual and organizational values or ethics can shape organizational communication behavior. Students are provided an opportunity to develop values and ethics through case studies that present ethical dilemmas and value issues in organizational settings. Different value positions and ethical perspectives are adopted to analyze cases, recommend courses of action, and predict outcomes.

# FEATURES OF *FUNDAMENTALS OF ORGANIZATIONAL COMMUNICATION*

Each chapter of *Fundamentals of Organizational Communication* attempts to contribute to competency development through the constant interaction of theory, practice, and analysis. Chapters are preceded by a statement of objectives and a short case study illustrating the concepts to be studied. Key terms and concepts are identified in margins, and chapters end with a concept summary and a workshop posing questions and issues in each of the competency areas: knowledge, sensitivity, skills, and values. The appendix provides additional practice and opportunities for analysis.

Chapters 1 through 4 are designed to develop students' knowledge through an understanding of what contributes to comprehensive communication competency and how we can understand this phenomenon called organizational communication. These chapters emphasize major organizational theories and their communication implications.

Chapters 5 through 9 are designed to develop the sensitivity component of communication competency. These chapters describe individuals in organizations and their intrapersonal, interpersonal, and small-group experiences. The increasing diversity and multiculturalism of organizations as well as the study of conflict and leadership are emphasized. Research indicates that conflict and leadership may well be the focal processes for effective communication in organizations. Texts in organizational communication frequently treat these topics mechanically, without emphasizing underlying subtleties such as organizational climate or the complex interactions of individual predispositions, strategies, and tactics. This book supports understanding of individual preferences in these crucial areas of organizational behavior by using self-assessment instruments.

Competency in the skill component is developed in Chapters 10 and 11, in which the chapters identify key applications and career options for organizational communication skills and make specific suggestions for skill development.

The interaction of personal, organizational, and professional ethics and values is the subject of Chapter 12. The values component of communication competency is presented, placing particular emphasis on how organizational values contribute to organizational culture and effectiveness.

Finally, the appendix contributes to the comprehensive development of all four competency components through an interaction of theory, practice, and analysis. Materials in the appendix are to be used as supplements to the other chapters to apply the concepts learned through practical and realistic examples.

## ACKNOWLEDGMENTS

I wrote this book for four primary reasons: my research interests in organizational communication, my experiences with students who appreciate the importance of the study of organizational communication, my twenty-plus years of business experience in both the private and public sectors, and my fundamental belief that organizations and the discipline of organizational communication must undergo significant change as the world around us changes. When taken together, these experiences and beliefs have been invaluable to me in relating theory to practice and in projecting competency needs for the future.

I am grateful for the help and support of many individuals in the development of this manuscript. My colleagues in the communication department at the University of Colorado at Colorado Springs and throughout the country have provided support, ideas, feedback, and contributions important to this book. I want to thank the many special students at the University of Colorado at Colorado Springs who reviewed and critiqued most of the exercises and cases contained in the text.

I am also grateful to the following individuals who reviewed the manuscript and provided helpful suggestions: Michael L. Fahs, Cal Poly State University–San Luis Obispo; Sandy H. Hanson, University of North Carolina–Charlotte; Becky Johns, Weber State University; David Lapakko, Augsburg College; Diane M. Monahan, Keene State College; Beth A. Semic, University of Nevada at Las Vegas.

On a personal note, I wrote this book with the guidance, love, and support of my family. My father and mother, Jim and Leatha Shockley, have provided the foundation for a special pursuit of learning. To my husband, Charles, whose love, support, work, and encouragement have been continuous, I shall always be grateful.

This book was written for students who want to change and improve organizations, who are willing to take risks in striving for excellence, and who love and appreciate human communication. Therefore, to students (past, present, and future) and to my family (most particularly Charles and Mom and Dad), I dedicate this book.

# CHAPTER ONE

# ORGANIZATIONAL COMMUNICATION
## A Competency-Based Approach

**DEVELOPING COMPETENCIES THROUGH . . .**

### KNOWLEDGE

Describing communication in the information-rich society

Defining and describing communication competency

### SENSITIVITY

Understanding communication as a key to organizational excellence

Developing awareness of our personal communication competencies

### SKILLS

Assessing personal development needs

Practicing analysis capabilities

### VALUES

Understanding communication competency as a personal and organizational need

Clarifying a contemporary "good communicator" theme

# THE CHANGING NATURE OF ORGANIZATIONS AND WORK

We are in one of the most turbulent periods in history. This statement is not profound but is real nevertheless. Our twenty-first-century world is more complex and the knowledge we bring to bear on our problems often adds to confusion and disagreement. We are in transition from an information age to a knowledge age with rapid change in familiar institutions and organizations. We have unprecedented opportunities and unprecedented problems. Most of us seek a firm direction that is outmoded. We are unfamiliar with the concept of anticipatory direction; we have learned too well directions borne of past experiences. We need new thinking, new criticisms, new knowledge, new approaches, and new understandings.

Nowhere is the current turbulence more evident than in contemporary organizations. Increased economic pressures, globalization, rapidly diversifying employee and customer bases, changing technology, an increasing awareness of organizational relationships to society in general, and a host of other factors contribute to new organization types, new relationships between organizations and employees, and a growing acknowledgment of the complexity of all organizational life. The virtual organization, e-commerce, high-performing teams, contract employment, increased contact with a culturally diverse world, and home-based work are but a few of the changes with impacts on interpersonal relationships, group interactions, management and leadership, personal and professional ethics, time management, and nonwork life.

What many have called the old social contract—mutual loyalty and support between employees and their employers—has been replaced by frequent shifts from one employer to another, increased global competition, downsizing in work forces, part-time employment, flatter organizations, and a generally changing relationship between management and workers. Critics of the changing nature of our work lives call for increased workplace democracy, whereas advocates defend the changes as necessary for survival.

# THE COMMUNICATIONS ERA

Regardless of the position taken about the changing nature of organizations and work, few disagree that the communications era surrounds us. We live, work, and play in complex communications environments. Sophisticated communications technologies have changed the way we do everything. As students you are being challenged to sort through more sources of available information than students in any other period in human history. Millions of routine jobs have disappeared, and new and more stimulating jobs requiring communications expertise are being created. In every aspect of our lives we are influenced by information generated and distributed by the people and machines of the communications era.

As an individual you are likely to spend most of your working life employed in an "information" job. You are more likely to create, process, or distribute information than you are to be directly involved in the production of goods. There is a greater need for salespeople, teachers, computer programmers, lawyers, financial analysts, secretaries, managers, bankers, consultants, engineers, doctors, architects, information managers, editors, and social workers and a decreased need for manufacturing assembly workers, miners, toolmakers, machinists, builders, and welders. With more than half of America's work force and gross national product already in knowledge industries, most agree that we are in the postindustrial **information society,** and, as Alvin Toffler (1990) suggests, moving into the knowledge age.

**Information society**
Environment in which more jobs create, process, or distribute information than directly produce goods. The environment is characterized by mass production of information, which requires the constant learning of new activities and processes.

One of the most important characteristics of the "information" era is the rapid change associated with mass production of information, change requiring us all to be constantly involved in the learning of new activities and processes. Most of us have already experienced rapid change brought about by new technologies. For example, although checks can still be written by hand, many of us pay our bills with plastic cards and use computer terminals to deposit money in or withdraw money from our bank accounts. We can still go to the movies, or we can bring the movies to our homes through videocassettes, discs, satellites, and Internet connections. We can write letters and memos to send through "regular" mail, or we can use sophisticated electronic systems to send and receive all types of correspondence and files rapidly. Fiber-optic connections, CD-ROM access, and international telecommunications and computer networks have literally changed the ways in which we do research, changed those with whom we can stay in constant contact, and altered notions of time and space. We are connected daily with virtual strangers through electronic bulletin boards and numerous other information-sharing opportunities. Most students reading this book are in traditional classrooms with "live" instructors. For some students now, and for more in the future, however, "live" means that the instructor is located at a remote site equipped with audio, video, and computer interconnects supported by e-books. *Convergence* is the term of the day, with computing, wireless technologies, and more traditional media such as television converging into integrated tools for work, school, family, and leisure environments.

We have so much information that, for both individuals and organizations, the challenge is how to deal with our information alternatives. This daily increase in information (based on innovations in communications and computer technology) brings with it rapid change in activities, processes, and products.

Two interdependent factors—globalization and information technology—are generating power shifts that result in the organizational challenges of today and tomorrow. Toffler (1990) suggests that throughout history, violence, wealth, and knowledge have been the ultimate sources of social power, and in the twenty-first century, knowledge will be the ultimate source of power. Toffler writes, "Power, in the business of tomorrow, will flow to those who have the best information about the limits of information. . . . The new accelerated system for wealth creation is increasingly dependent on the exchange of data, information, and knowledge. It is 'super-symbolic.' No knowledge exchanged, no new wealth created. . . . Conventional factors of production . . . land, labor, raw materials, and capital—become less important as symbolic knowledge is substituted for them." Thomas Friedman (1999) contends "that globalization made possible the change in how we look at the world. I call this change, 'the democratization of information.' Thanks to satellite dishes, the Internet and television we can now see through, hear through and look through almost every conceivable wall."

Workers in the communications era of microelectronics, computers, and telecommunications have an abundance of information for decision making and a growing concern for information overload. We can routinely communicate across both geography and organizational levels. It is not unusual, for example, for employees of an organization in Boston to interact with their counterparts in Los Angeles, whom they have never met, while both groups are preparing a portion of a single report or recommendation. And for a growing number of individuals, this report can be generated without ever leaving their homes as they "telecommute" from automated home workstations to offices around the globe.

The complexity of all organizational life and the rapid increase in communications technologies place increasing demands on our individual communication abilities. These demands are best met with the perspective that becoming and staying competent is an ongoing process requiring lifelong learning.

## COMMUNICATION: THE KEY TO ORGANIZATIONAL EXCELLENCE

**Organizational excellence**
Ability of people to work together and utilize technology for the creative solving of increasingly complex problems.

In this complex and information-rich society, the key to **organizational excellence** is effective communication. Communication systems within organizations—both human and technological—are responsible for solving increasingly complex problems creatively. People using the machines of the communications era must coordinate large volumes of information for the performance of new and dynamic tasks. There is widespread recognition, however, that excellence in organizational problem solving is more than the efficient management of large volumes of facts. [Organizational excellence stems from the dedicated commitment of people, people who are motivated to work together and who share similar values and visions about the results of their efforts.]

Viewing communications as the key to organizational excellence is not new. As early as 1938, Chester Barnard, in his now-famous work *The Functions of the Executive*, described as a primary responsibility of executives the development and maintenance of a system of communication. Research since then has linked organizational communication to managerial effectiveness, the integration of work units across organizational levels, characteristics of effective supervision, job and communication satisfaction, innovation, adaptability, creativity, and overall organizational effectiveness. In fact, numerous scholars have gone as far as to suggest that organizations are essentially complex communication processes that create and change events. For both the industrial society of the past and the information and knowledge societies of today and tomorrow, there is broad agreement about the centrality of organizational communication and that organizational communication plays a significant part in contributing to or detracting from organizational excellence.

With this emphasis on the complex, fast-paced information society and the importance of human communication, questions arise concerning what skills and abilities organizations need from their future employees. How should individuals prepare themselves for the information responsibilities and opportunities that almost inevitably will be a part of the future? What does it take to contribute to organizational communication excellence?

Put simply, organizations of today and tomorrow need competent communicators at all organizational levels. With more complex decisions, rapid change, more information, and less certainty about what the decisions should be, excellence in the information society depends on the abilities, commitment, and creativity of all organizational members. As a result, students, communication teachers and researchers, and active organizational members must work together to understand what contributes to organizational communication competency and how best to develop personal potential.

## EXCELLENCE IN COMMUNICATION: COMMUNICATION COMPETENCY

Quintilian, an early Latin rhetorician, introduced the ideal of the "good man speaking well," an ideal that is not as far removed from contemporary concepts of organizational communication competency as history might suggest. In fact, Michael Hackman and Craig Johnson (2000) identified a contemporary "good communicator" theme when reviewing research from personnel administrators throughout the United States. Today's organizations need people who can speak well, listen, write, persuade others, demonstrate interpersonal skills, gather information, and exhibit small-group problem-solving expertise. The Massachusetts Institute of Technology Commission on Industrial Productivity, in a *Scientific America* report (Berger et al., 1989), lends further support to these findings when it concludes that the effective use of modern technology requires involved and responsible people to develop capabilities for planning, judgment, collaboration, and analysis of complex systems. In other words, organizations in our complex and turbulent society need flexible and creative people who have diverse and well-developed communication abilities. Yet how do we determine if we are competent organizational communicators? Who decides? On what do we base our conclusions?

**Communication competency**
Composed of knowledge, sensitivity, skills, and values. Competence arises from interaction of theory, practice, and analysis.

Researchers differ in how they define **communication competency.** Some believe that a person is competent if he or she knows what is appropriate in a specific situation, whether or not that behavior actually occurs. A student, for example, who realizes that class participation is required for a high grade may choose not to participate, yet the student can be considered competent because of the knowledge or awareness of the appropriate behavior. Other researchers extend the competency concept beyond knowledge of appropriate behaviors to include actual language performance and the achievement of interpersonal goals. The student, from this latter perspective, must not only recognize appropriate participation behaviors but also participate so as to demonstrate communication competency.

Stanley Deetz (1992), in his work on building a communication perspective for organizations, views more open and involved participation as fundamental to expanding a larger set of stakeholders and their values in organizations. He suggests that increasing the political competence of individuals is necessary for increased participation practices. This "political" competence is based on encoding, decoding, interpreting, reflecting upon, evaluating, conceptualizing, synthesizing, and arriving at decisions about all types of information. The range of skills that Deetz and others describe represents a sophisticated description of communication competency.

Fred Jablin and Patricia Sias (2001), in their comprehensive discussion of communication competency, suggest that the concept of communication competency is best understood by an ecological model that revolves around four systems: "(1) the microsystem, which contains the developing organizational member and other persons in the immediate work environment (e.g., supervisors, coworkers, and clients); (2) the mesosystem, which represents the interrelations among various microsystems (e.g., what individuals learn in their project teams may affect their competence in the functional work groups in which they are members); (3) the macrosystem, which does not represent the immediate context in which an individual works, but does impinge on him or her (i.e., major divisions of the organization and the organization itself as a whole); and (4) the exosystem, which represents the overarching cultural belief system, forms of knowledge, social, technological, and political ideologies. . . . In brief, an ecological perspective emphasizes system embeddedness. That is, the actions of one element of the system affect the other elements." They specifically describe how globalization and technology have changed forever notions of what is a competent communicator. It is fair to conclude that Jablin and Sias expand previous notions of communication competency to extend to groups and to the organization as a whole within its broad environment.

Stephen Littlejohn and David Jabusch (1982) have proposed a particularly useful definition of communication competency for the organizational setting. They suggest that communication competency is "the ability and willingness of an individual to participate responsibly in a transaction in such a way as to maximize the outcomes of shared meanings." This definition requires not only knowledge of appropriate behaviors but also motivation to engage in communication that results in mutual understanding. In other words, communication competency involves our personal willingness and ability to communicate so that our meanings are understood and we understand the meanings of others. Finally, this definition can be applied to the group and macroorganizational levels so important in the ecological model proposed by Jablin and Sias. Regardless of differences in perspectives, organizational communication competency relates to message encoding and decoding abilities, the process of communication initiation and consumption.

When we begin to think about our personal communication competency, we quickly realize that we form impressions of our own competency while making evaluations about the competency of others. We try to decide what is appropriate for us as well as for others, and we determine whether that behavior is effective in a particular circumstance. In other words, my impression of my own competency and the competency of others is related to my evaluation of whether we exhibited the "right" behaviors and achieved "desirable" results in a particular situation. Determining what is "right" and "desirable" is not always easy, however. Think for a moment about your personal experiences. Have you ever been in a situation where others thought you did a good job although you were disappointed in yourself? Who was right? Were you competent or incompetent? Can both be correct?

Earlier we said that organizational excellence depends on the communication competencies of all organizational members. Specifically, we described the need for creative problem solving among diverse groups of people who often share little common information. With this emphasis on communication and technology, the real question becomes what individuals should do to prepare themselves to meet the communication needs in their futures. In other words, how do we develop and evaluate our communication competencies?

Our answer begins by returning to the Littlejohn and Jabusch approach to communication competency. Littlejohn and Jabusch (1982) contend that competency arises out of four basic components: process understanding, interpersonal sensitivity, communication skills, and ethical responsibility. Process understanding refers to the cognitive ability to understand the dynamics of the communication event. Interpersonal sensitivity is the ability to perceive feelings and meanings. Communication skills are the ability to develop and interpret message strategies in specific situations. The ethical component of competency is the attitudinal set that governs concern for the well-being of all participants in taking responsibility for communication outcomes. Finally, Littlejohn and Jabusch believe that competence comes from the interaction of three primary elements: theory, practice, and analysis. When applied to the organizational setting, the Littlejohn and Jabusch approach can be modified and expanded to include the competency components this book seeks to develop: knowledge, sensitivity, skills, and values.

# ORGANIZATIONAL COMMUNICATION: A COMPETENCY-BASED APPROACH

This book is designed to help you develop communication competencies for effective organizational communication. The goal of the book is to provide theory, practice, and analysis opportunities that contribute to knowledge, sensitivity, skills, and values important for organizational excellence.

**Knowledge competency**
Ability to understand the organizational communication environment.

*Knowledge:* the ability to understand the organizational communication environment. Knowledge competencies are what we come to know about a particular field. Knowledge is the learning of theory and principles. Knowledge competencies are fundamental to support our sensitivity to organizational life, to guide our skill development, and to assist us in understanding the application of ethical standards and our personal values in a variety of organizational settings. **Knowledge competency** is developed through the exploration of the interactive, process nature of human communication. We examine what organizational communication is and the major theoretical approaches for its study. We explore the roles of individuals in organizations and examine communication implications of major organizational theories. Finally, vital organizational subjects such as conflict, leadership, and strategic communication are discussed.

**Sensitivity competency**
Ability to sense organizational meanings and feelings accurately.

*Sensitivity:* the ability to sense accurately organizational meanings and feelings. It is related to our ability and willingness to understand what others are feeling and doing. **Sensitivity competency** is developed through the examination of our personal "theories-in-use" about communication and organizations. Individual preferences for leadership and conflict, as well as the impact of personal differences and similarities within organizational settings are assessed. Emphasis is placed on how we come to understand our complex organizational environments.

**Skills competency**
Ability to analyze organizational situations accurately and to initiate and consume organizational messages effectively.

*Skills:* the ability to analyze organizational situations accurately and to initiate and consume organizational messages effectively. The skills competency focuses on developing important analytical capabilities as well as the ability to communicate effectively in a variety of settings. **Skills competency** is developed through analysis and practice opportunities. Specifically, analytical skills are developed by applying knowledge and sensitivity to case studies and individual experiences. Problem-solving and conflict-management skills are also presented and practiced.

*Values:* the importance of taking personal responsibility for effective communication, thereby contributing to organizational excel-

**Values competency**
Importance of taking responsibility for effective communication, thereby contributing to organizational excellence.

lence. **Values competency** is developed through discussion of personal responsibility for participation in organizational communication. Ethical dilemmas relating to organizational communication and the importance of values to organizational culture are examined. Finally, case studies are used to illustrate ethical and value issues common in organizations.

## SELF-ASSESSMENT OF PERSONAL DEVELOPMENT NEEDS

The material in the next eleven chapters is designed to help you develop important competencies for organizational communication. Before you begin to study that material, however, please complete Table 1.1. The following chapters will be more meaningful if you approach theory, practice, and analysis opportunities with a personal assessment of your current strengths and weaknesses. You are about to complete the first of several self-assessments contained in your text. Before you proceed, it is important to understand both the strengths and weaknesses of self-assessment. Self-assessments are generated by you about you. They can be helpful guides to understanding behavior, perceptions, and attitudes important for your communication behaviors. Self-assessment, however, is not a complete or final analysis about you. The questions asked determine the profiles developed. Sometimes we tend to answer the way we think we should as opposed to what we really believe or do. Important questions or issues for you as an individual may not be considered in a particular assessment. Also, although assessments can guide development, they should not be used to develop profiles of "this is the way I am," or "this is the way I am not." In other words, the self-assessments in the text should be used to stimulate your thinking about you and your experiences, not to develop rigid categories or self-descriptive labels.

## SUMMARY

The information-rich society is a reality of our lives that places increasing importance on our individual communication competencies. Organizations of today and tomorrow must depend on people and the machines of the communications era to solve problems creatively and to adapt to rapid change. In this fast-paced environment, organizational excellence is directly related to effective communication from all members of the organization. To prepare for the communication responsibilities and opportunities of the future, individuals need to develop broad-based communication competency. Communication competency is best understood as a complex interaction of knowledge, sensitivity, skills, and values. The goal of this book is to develop these competencies through an interaction of theory, practice, and analysis.

**TABLE 1.1   Self-Assessment of Personal Development Needs**

The following organizational communication competencies are presented for your self-evaluation. For each area you are asked to determine whether your present competencies are highly developed, moderately developed, somewhat limited, or needing development.

| As I begin this course I would describe my KNOWLEDGE in . . . | Highly Developed | Moderately Developed | Somewhat Limited | Needing Development |
|---|---|---|---|---|
| 1. defining and understanding organizational communication as . . . | | | | |
| 2. understanding major theories or how organizations work as . . . | | | | |
| 3. determining how an individual experiences organizational life as . . . | | | | |
| 4. describing what organizational conflict is and how it relates to productive organizations as . . . | | | | |
| 5. identifying characteristics of leadership and management communication as . . . | | | | |
| 6. understanding decision making and problem solving as . . . | | | | |
| 7. understanding strategic organizational communication as . . . | | | | |
| 8. locating career opportunities in organizational communication as . . . | | | | |
| 9. distinguishing between values and ethics in organizational communication as . . . | | | | |

**TABLE 1.1** *(continued)*

| As I begin this course I would describe my *SENSITIVITY to . . .* | Highly Developed | Moderately Developed | Somewhat Limited | Needing Development |
|---|---|---|---|---|
| 10. my personal responsibilities for organizational communication as . . . | | | | |
| 11. how "shared realities" are generated through organizational communication as . . . | | | | |
| 12. why and how people work together as . . . | | | | |
| 13. what motivates me and what is likely to motivate others as . . . | | | | |
| 14. the importance of interpersonal relationships with supervisors, peers, and subordinates as . . . | | | | |
| 15. personal preferences for a variety of approaches to conflict as . . . | | | | |
| 16. the influence of the environment of organizations as . . . | | | | |
| 17. personal preferences for leadership and management communication as . . . | | | | |
| 18. organizational influences for decision making and problem solving as . . . | | | | |
| 19. past achievements, values, and skills that can guide career choices as . . . | | | | |
| 20. how values and ethics contribute to organizational effectiveness as . . . | | | | |

*(continued)*

**TABLE 1.1    (continued)**

| As I begin this course I would describe my SKILLS in . . . | Highly Developed | Moderately Developed | Somewhat Limited | Needing Development |
|---|---|---|---|---|
| 21. analyzing a variety of organizational problems as . . . | | | | |
| 22. developing effective organizational messages as . . . | | | | |
| 23. engaging in active listening as . . . | | | | |
| 24. contributing to supportive organizational environments as . . . | | | | |
| 25. participating in productive conflict management as . . . | | | | |
| 26. leadership communication as . . . | | | | |
| 27. leading and participating in effective group meetings as . . . | | | | |
| 28. fact-finding and evaluation as . . . | | | | |
| 29. gathering information for decision making and problem solving as . . . | | | | |
| 30. analyzing data for decision making and problem solving as . . . | | | | |
| 31. developing and making public presentations as . . . | | | | |
| 32. using a variety of communications technologies as . . . | | | | |

**TABLE 1.1** *(continued)*

| As I begin this course I would describe my VALUES for . . . | Highly Developed | Moderately Developed | Somewhat Limited | Needing Development |
|---|---|---|---|---|
| 33. accepting personal responsibility for communication as . . . | | | | |
| 34. relating individual communication behavior to organizational effectiveness as . . . | | | | |
| 35. using conflict for productive outcomes as . . . | | | | |
| 36. professional applications of organizational communication as . . . | | | | |
| 37. determining how leaders and managers should behave as . . . | | | | |
| 38. influencing my career choices as . . . | | | | |
| 39. understanding organizational values, ethics, and dilemmas as . . . | | | | |

After you have completed your self-evaluation, compile a complete list of items for which you rated your competencies as *Highly Developed.* Next compile lists for those competency items rated *Moderately Developed, Somewhat Limited,* and *Needing Development.* Use these lists to help establish personal objectives for the study of this text. All the competencies evaluated in your self-assessment are presented in the following chapters with theory, practice, and analysis opportunities.

# WORKSHOP

1. Review a copy of the Sunday edition of your city's largest newspaper. Identify all the stories that relate to an "information age" and the technologies of the communications era. Bring copies of selected articles to class for group discussion.

2. In small groups, identify the "information industries" in your community. Compare lists among your groups.

3. Either individually or as an entire class, identify as many jobs as you can that are essentially "information" jobs.

4. Interview a professional in your community. Ask this person to describe what it takes to be a competent communicator in his or her particular job. Compare your findings with other class members.

5. Small groups should use The Case against Hiring Karen Groves, which follows, to determine how communication behaviors influenced Hockaday's management team to vote against hiring Karen Groves. (See p. 14.)

6. Make a list of all the changes you can identify in the way people work. Use the last ten years to stimulate your thinking. Next, survey your home, school, work, business, social, and leisure environments for communications technologies. List all the technologies you currently use. Bring your lists to class for group discussion.

7. Visit one of the numerous job-search sites on the Internet. Identify at least fifty job titles that represent information jobs. Bring your list to class for discussion.

■ ■ ■ ■ ■

## THE CASE AGAINST HIRING KAREN GROVES

John Murphy, the head of personnel for Hockaday Corporation, was excited about the application of Karen Groves to become Hockaday's new training director. Karen's educational background in organizational communication and business, her work in the training department of a major competitor of Hockaday's, and her excellent letters of recommendation made her an appealing candidate. John's initial interview with Karen had gone well and he was anxious for her to meet Hockaday's management staff, who approved John's hiring decisions for major company positions.

John was surprised and dismayed when Hockaday's president reported to John that the staff did not favor hiring Karen. According to the president, Karen surprised the group when she said _____ and _____. They did not believe that she would be good for Hockaday because of her _____.

In groups of four to six members, fill in the blanks to account for what might have happened to create the case against hiring Karen. Describe how the communication abilities of all involved may have contributed to the negative decision. Following individual group discussions, each group should present to the class as a whole its members' description of the situation and how they believe communication affected the outcome.

## REFERENCES AND SUGGESTED READINGS

Barnard, C. 1938. *The functions of the executive.* Cambridge, MA: Harvard University Press.
Berger S., M. Dertouzos, R. Lester, R. Solow, and L. Thurow. 1989. Toward a new industrial America. *Scientific American* 260(6): 39–47.

Bostrom, R. N. 1984. *Competence in communication: A multi-disciplinary approach.* Beverly Hills, CA: Sage.

Boyatzsis, R. 1982. *The competent manager: A model for effective performance.* New York: Wiley.

Bronowski, J. 1958. The creative process. *Scientific American* 199(3): 59–64.

Deetz, S. 1992. *Building a communication perspective in organization studies I: Foundations.* Paper presented at the Speech Communication Association Convention, October, Chicago.

Farace, R., P. Monge, and H. Russell. 1977. *Communicating and organizing.* Reading, MA: Addison-Wesley.

Friedman, T. L. 1999. *The Lexus and the olive tree.* New York: Farrar, Strauss, and Giroux.

Goldhaber, G., M. Yates, D. Porter, and R. Lesniak. 1978. Organizational communication: 1978 state of the art. *Human Communication Research* 5(1): 76–96.

Goodall, H. L., Jr. 1982. Organizational communication competence: The development of an industrial simulation to teach adaptive skills. *Communication Quarterly* 30(4): 282–95.

Hackman, M., and C. Johnson. 2000. *Leadership: A communication perspective.* 3d ed. Prospect Heights, IL: Waveland.

Jablin, F., R. Cude, K. Wayson, A. House, J. Lee, and N. Roth. 1989. *Communication competence in organizations: Conceptualization and comparison across multiple levels of analysis.* Paper presented to the Organizational Communication Division of the International Communication Association, May, San Francisco.

Jablin, F., and P. Sias. 2001. Communication competence. In *The new handbook of organizational communication: Advances in theory, research, and methods,* eds. F. Jablin and L. Putnam, 819–64. Thousand Oaks, CA: Sage.

Jabusch, D. M., S. W. Littlejohn, and G. K. Levison. 1981. *Elements of speech communication: Achieving competency.* Boston: Houghton Mifflin.

Johnson, J. R. 1983. A developmental-biological perspective of human communication competency. *The Western Journal of Speech Communication* 47(3): 193–204.

Kennedy, G. 1969. *Quintilian.* New York: Twayne.

Kotter, J. 1982. What effective general managers really do. *Harvard Business Review* 60(6): 156–67.

Likert, R. 1967. *The human organization.* New York: McGraw-Hill.

Littlejohn, S. W., and D. M. Jabusch. 1982. Communication competence: Model and application. *Journal of Applied Communication Research* 10(1): 29–37.

McCroskey, J. C. 1982. Communication competence and performance: A research and pedagogical perspective. *Communication Education* 31: 1–7.

Monge, P. R. 1982. Communicator competence in the workplace: Model testing and scale development. In *Communication yearbook 5,* ed. M. Burgoon, 505–27. New Brunswick, NJ: Transaction Books.

O'Connell, S. 1988. Human communication in the high tech office. In *Handbook of organizational communication,* eds. G. Goldhaber and G. Barnett, 473–82. Norwood, NJ: Ablex.

Pavitt, C., and L. Haight. 1986. Implicit theories of communicative competence: Situational and competence level differences in judgments of prototype and target. *Communication Monographs* 53(3): 221–35.

Peters, T. J., and R. H. Waterman Jr. 1982. *In search of excellence.* New York: Harper and Row.

Redding, W. 1972. *Communication within the organization: An interpretive review of theory and research.* New York: Industrial Communication Council.

Roberts, K., C. O'Reilly, C. Bretton, and L. Porter. 1974. Organizational theory and organizational communication: A communication failure? *Human Relations* 27(5): 501–24.

Rogers, E. 1988. Information technologies: How organizations are changing. In *Handbook of organizational communication,* eds. G. Goldhaber and G. Barnett, 437–52. Norwood, NJ: Ablex.

Rubin, R. B. 1985. The validity of the communication competency assessment instrument. *Communication Monographs* 52(2): 173–85.

Rubin, R. B., and J. D. Feezel. 1986. Elements of teacher communication competence. *Communication Education* 35(3): 254–68.

Rubin, R. B., and S. A. Henzl. 1984. Cognitive complexity, communication competence, and verbal ability. *Communication Quarterly* 32(4): 263–70.

Schall, M. 1983. A communication-rules approach to organizational culture. *Administrative Science Quarterly* 28(4): 557–81.

Snavely, W. B., and E. V. Walters. 1983. Differences in communication competence among administrator social styles. *Journal of Applied Communication Research* 11(2): 120–35.

Spitzberg, B. H. 1983. Communication competence as knowledge, skill, and impression. *Communication Education* 32(3): 323–29.

Spitzberg, B. H., and W. R. Cupach. 1984. *Interpersonal communication competence.* Beverly Hills, CA: Sage.

Staley, C. C., and P. S. Shockley-Zalabak. 1985. Identifying communication competencies for the undergraduate organizational communication series. *Communication Education* 34(2): 156–61.

Stoddard, T. D. 1980. Business communication as a competency based general education course. *Journal of Business Communication* 17(5): 51–60.

Swenson, D. H. 1980. Relative importance of business communication skills for the next ten years. *Journal of Business Communication* 17(2): 41–49.

Toffler, A. 1990. *Powershift.* New York: Bantam Books.

Tubbs, S., and T. Hain. 1979. Managerial communication and its relationship to total organizational effectiveness. In *Communication and productivity,* eds. P. Clampitt and C. Downs. Paper presented at the Speech Communication Association Convention, November 1983, Washington, DC.

Weick, K. 1976. Educational organizations as loosely coupled systems. *Administrative Science Quarterly* 21(1): 1–19.

Wheeless, V., and C. Berryman-Fink. 1985. Perceptions of women managers and their communicator competencies. *Communication Quarterly* 33(2): 137–47.

Wiemann, J. 1977. Explication and test of a model of communicative competence. *Human Communication Research* 3(3): 195–213.

Wiemann, J., and P. Backlund. 1980. Current theory and research in communicative competence. *Review of Educational Research* 50(1): 185–99.

Wiio, O., G. Goldhaber, and M. Yates. 1980. Organizational communication: Time for reflection? In *Communication yearbook 4,* ed. D. Nimmo, 83–98. New Brunswick, NJ: Transaction Books.

# CHAPTER TWO

# FRAMEWORKS FOR UNDERSTANDING ORGANIZATIONAL COMMUNICATION

## DEVELOPING COMPETENCIES THROUGH . . .

**KNOWLEDGE**

Defining and describing the human communication process

Identifying descriptions of organizations

Surveying definitions of organizational communication

**SENSITIVITY**

Understanding human communication as attempting to create shared realities, shared meanings

Distinguishing among interpersonal, small-group, and organizational communication

**SKILLS**

Practicing analysis capabilities

**VALUES**

Understanding communication as fundamental to the process of organizing

Evaluating communication for ethics and effectiveness

■ ■ ■ ■ ■

# THE "WHAT BUSINESS IS THIS OF OURS?" CASE

The following case describes a problem at Quality Engineering, a medium-sized company located in Denver, Colorado. The case is based on a real situation at Quality, although the name of the supplier in question has been changed. You will use this case to think about the human communication process and to begin to understand the concept of organizational communication.

John and Mary were the only two buyers in the purchasing department of Quality Engineering. Both had been with the company for several years and were experienced in handling purchases for the manufacturing, research, finance, and marketing areas of Quality. Mary typically handled purchases for the manufacturing and research areas, and John was the principal buyer for the rest of the organization. At times their individual work loads required that they cross departments and help each other. Their boss, Mike Anderson, the accountant for Quality, believed that they were the best purchasing team with whom he had ever worked. He was proud of their efforts and willingness to cooperate with each other. He frequently commented to Quality management that John and Mary made money for the company by getting the best possible prices for goods and services.

Mike was surprised and concerned to overhear John and Mary in a heated discussion.

**John:**  I can't believe you are still using Anderson Printing as one of our suppliers. I told you last month that their last two orders for my groups were late and part of the printing had to be sent back because of errors. I told them then that I wouldn't accept any more of their bids on our jobs. It makes me look like a fool when I hear from them that you are still ordering their products for manufacturing and research. How can we enforce good quality from our suppliers if we don't present a united front?

**Mary:**  Just a minute. Anderson Printing has been one of our good suppliers for over ten years. I know we have had some problems with them in the past year but I don't think we should drop them flat. They have pulled us out of a lot of jams when we needed printing in a big hurry. I never agreed to dropping them from our supplier list. You just told them they were gone and expected me to support your decision. You should have talked to me about it first. I don't care if you think you looked like a fool. We are in this together and need to make those types of decisions as a team.

**John:**  I'll admit we should have talked about it, but Anderson made me so mad on that last deal that I just told them they were through. I expected you to support me. We both want what is best for Quality. Our reputations are good because we always get the company the best products for the lowest price. I would have supported you.

**Mary:**  Yes, I suspect you would have, but John, you can't lose your temper like that. We need to work together on these decisions. You and I can usually work out a solution when we try hard enough. I don't want to drop any supplier on the spur of the moment, especially when we may have trouble replacing them. John, sometimes I think we have worked together for so long that we take each other for granted. We are friends and I want it to remain that way, but that shouldn't stop us from doing business with each other as true professionals.

**John:** Wait a minute. Are you saying that I don't act like a professional—?

**Mary:** No, see what I mean? You get mad when I even suggest we might improve the way we do things.

**John:** Well, I just think friends should support each other. I know I may not have handled the Anderson thing just right, but as my friend I expected more support from you.

**Mary:** Oh, John, there you go again!

## INTRODUCTION

Are John and Mary engaged in interpersonal or organizational communication, or both? Does the setting make the difference? Can we distinguish between interpersonal and organizational communication? When we talk about developing our personal communication competencies, is it different for our personal and organizational lives? The answers to these questions lie in understanding what human communication is, how it works, and how organizations and human communication relate. In other words, frameworks for understanding organizational communication can be found in descriptions of human communication and organizations.

**Human communication process**
Attempts to construct shared realities through social interaction.

This chapter is designed to contribute to our *knowledge* by defining and describing the **human communication process** and identifying basic characteristics of organizations and organizational communication. *Sensitivity* competencies are developed through understanding human communication as attempts to create shared realities and distinguishing among interpersonal, small-group, and organizational communication. *Skills* are practiced through application of *knowledge* and *sensitivity* competencies in exercises and case analyses. *Values* are developed through an understanding of the importance of communication in the process of organizing and an awareness that all communication is subject to evaluation for ethics and effectiveness.

## BASICS OF HUMAN COMMUNICATION

Although the discussion between John and Mary is typical of human communication exchanges that occur daily in organizations, it also is typical of communication between two people regardless of the setting. In fact, the discussion between

John and Mary illustrates some of the important basics necessary for understanding human communication.

## Defining Communication

Analyzing the exchange between John and Mary will help us describe human communication. John and Mary are engaged in transferring information, they are eliciting responses from each other, and they are engaged in social interaction. Further, it is possible to say that they are using symbols (words) to attempt to create shared meaning (mutual understanding) that will result in an effect on the two of them. Their disagreement about how to handle problems with Anderson Printing will influence not only what happens to Anderson as a supplier to Quality Engineering but their interpersonal relationship as well. Put another way, their exchange is an example of communication behaviors creating and shaping both relationships and events through a culturally dependent process of assigning meaning to symbols.

John wants Mary to share his reality that Anderson has made serious mistakes that disqualify it from providing goods and services to Quality. Furthermore, he expects Mary to accept another reality: that friends and coworkers should support each other's decisions even if decisions are made on the spur of the moment and in anger. Mary has a different set of realities that she wants John to understand. Although she agrees about recent problems with Anderson, part of her reality includes Anderson's past service to Quality and the possible difficulty of replacing its goods and services with another supplier. She also believes that John should have included her in his decision. We do not know from this exchange how open or direct John and Mary intend to be with each other. We do not have enough information to determine if other agendas are influencing their exchange. We do know John and Mary are making conscious choices about the realities they exchange. When John and Mary exchange their individual realities, their communication is an attempt to construct shared realities.

Although they may not agree, their communication enables each to share the realities of the other.

## THE HUMAN COMMUNICATION PROCESS

When John and Mary are constructing their shared realities, they are engaged in what we call the process of communication. Both John and Mary serve as *sources* and *receivers* of messages. Both engage in message *encoding* and *decoding* and in selecting verbal and nonverbal *channels* for message transmission. Both are influenced by their individual *competence* and their perception of the competence of the other. Each brings to the exchange a different set of *experiences*, and each may view the context of their interaction differently. Thus, all their messages are subject to distortion or noise. The *effect*, or what happens between John and Mary, is a result of the complex interaction of all these elements. Figure 2.1 illustrates a basic model of the human communication process in which John and Mary are engaged.

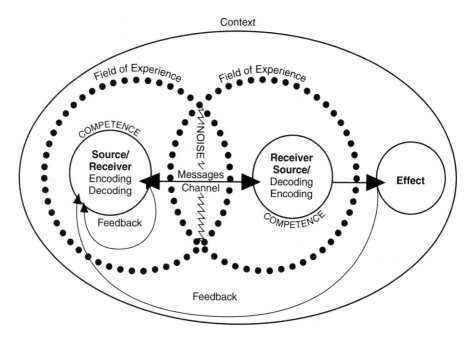

**FIGURE 2.1    A Model of the Human Communication Process**

**Source/Receiver**

Individuals send messages as sources and receive messages as receivers. The process is often so rapid as to appear simultaneous.

## Source/Receiver

Each individual engaged in communication with others is both a message **source** and a message **receiver**. We talk (send messages) while closely monitoring the nonverbal reactions of others (receiving messages). We listen (receive messages) and determine how to respond (send messages). Often message-sending and message-receiving activities occur so rapidly that they seem to be happening simultaneously.

**Encoding/Decoding**

Message encoding is the process of formulating messages, choosing content and symbols to convey meaning. Message decoding is the process of assigning meaning in the role of receiver to message symbols generated by the message source.

## Encoding/Decoding

As a message source and receiver, each individual encodes and decodes messages. Message **encoding** is the process of formulating messages, choosing content and symbols to convey meaning. Message encoding is determining what we want to be understood (content) and how we believe that it can best be presented (choosing symbols). Message **decoding** is the process of assigning meaning in the role of receiver to message symbols generated by the message source. Decoding is taking what we see and hear from others and deciding how it should be interpreted or understood.

Both encoding and decoding are influenced by our communicative competence (knowledge, sensitivity, skills, and values), our specific intentions (desire for clarity, openness, manipulation, deceit, control, and so forth), our past experiences, our perception of the competence of others, and the communication context.

## Message

**Message**
Symbolic attempt to transfer meaning; the signal that serves as a stimulus for a receiver.

The **message** is the symbolic attempt to transfer meaning; it is the signal that serves as a stimulus for a receiver. Sources send messages consisting of auditory, visual, olfactory, gustatory, or tactile stimuli in any combination of these five senses. Sources of messages intend meaning, but messages in and of themselves do not carry meaning. Meanings, or interpretations of messages, are assigned when the receiver decodes the message. Messages serve as symbols for meaning and as such are subject to situational and cultural influences. In other words, to understand a message as a source intends requires an understanding of the source's symbol system (language and actions and intent of language and actions) in a particular situation.

## Channel

**Channel**
Medium through which the message is transmitted.

The **channel** is the medium through which the message is transmitted. It is the link or links between source and receiver. Channels include the five senses and any technological means used for message transmission. Channels are frequently used in combination (verbal and nonverbal, oral and written, face to face, and telemediated), with certain channels generally more credible than others. When verbal and nonverbal messages appear to contradict, for example, researchers tell us that most people will find the nonverbal channel more credible than the verbal one. In other words, most of us believe that it is more difficult to lie nonverbally than verbally. Channels can distort messages both technologically and in sensory reception. Indeed, the very selection of one channel over another may become a message in and of itself. Written channels, for example, are more often used than face-to-face channels for giving bad news. Receiving a memo from your boss—the bad-news channel—may be cause for alarm even before the actual message has been read.

## Noise

**Noise**
Distortion or interference that contributes to discrepancies between the meaning intended by the source of a message and the meaning assigned by the receiver.

**Noise** is the distortion or interference that contributes to discrepancies between the meaning intended by the source and the meaning assigned by the receiver. Noise can be anything: physical distractions, channel interference, communicative competence, communication context, or psychological predispositions. Noise is always present in one form or another, and the type or types of noise contribute to the meanings assigned to messages by receivers and to the encoding of new messages. Think for a moment about your reaction to receiving an important message from a person whose credibility you have reason to doubt. What meaning do you assign to the message based on your prior relationship with this individual? Assume next that you receive the same message from a trusted friend. Is your reaction different? What type of noise was generated by your past experiences with both individuals? How did that noise affect meaning?

## Competence

Each individual brings knowledge, sensitivity, skills, and values to communication interactions. Our ability to understand appropriate behaviors, our specific intentions, our willingness to engage in communication, and our ability to interact with others to generate shared realities all contribute to our impression of our own *competence*. Also, we continually evaluate and form impressions about the competence of those with whom we are communicating. Our impression of our own competence and the impression we have of the competence of others contribute to both the encoding and decoding of messages. Ultimately, competence contributes to communication effects and how we evaluate the effectiveness of our interactions.

**Field of experience**
Set of specific experiences or background that all parties in communication bring to bear on the interaction.

## Field of Experience

All parties in a communication interaction bring a specific set of experiences or background to bear on the interaction. What we do in a particular situation is related to how much we know about the situation from past experiences and whether we share any common past experiences. We may behave very differently in situations in which we have considerable past experience than we would in situations that are new and unfamiliar. The **field of experience** is situation specific and may or may not relate to broader evaluations of self-competence. In other words, although we may feel less competent in situations in which we have little past experience, that impression does not automatically transfer to other circumstances in which we have more background.

Generally, it is believed that the more common the field of experience among those communicating, the easier it is to share similar meanings or to construct shared realities. Have you ever tried, for example, to explain an American sporting event to a visitor from another country where the sport is not played and has never been televised? Did you even know where to begin? Chances are that the lack of any prior experience on the part of your receiver (no common field of experience between you) required you to engage in considerable detail, making it difficult even to begin to describe the event. You can imagine that your approach would be entirely different if you were describing the same event to a longtime fan of the sport.

**Communication context**
Environment for the communication interaction.

## Communication Context

The **communication context** is the environment for the communication interaction. Context includes not only the specific time and place of the interaction but also the roles, relationships, and status of communication participants. Context contributes to our very specific intentions in a given circumstance. Communication intentions, as most of us have experienced, can range from full disclosure, openness, and seeking clarity to deception, ambiguity, manipulation, and control. Most of us recognize that we communicate differently depending on how well we know people, what their formal position is in relation to us, and how visible our communication is to others. The way we express ourselves in the privacy of our own homes may differ from what we will say and do in our work environments. Openly disagreeing with a friend or coworker is different from openly disagreeing with our boss. The way we express ourselves is related to whether we believe others to be more knowledgeable or competent than we are or whether we believe that we possess the best information in a specific setting. The way we express ourselves also reflects the expectations of the particular culture or environment in which we are communicating. We can therefore say that context is both culturally and physically influenced, and as with other elements in the communication process, perception of context can differ from one communication participant to another.

**Effect**

Result, consequence, or outcome of communication exchanges.

## Effect

The communication **effect** is the result, consequence, or outcome of the communication exchange. Effects can be observed to be directly related to communication interactions. When people have an argument and terminate relationships at the end of the argument, we witness what we would call an obvious effect. At other times, the effect is not immediately observable or is, at best, delayed in time and context. A student does not contribute to a group project; the project is completed and all group members receive the same grade. Nothing appears to happen until the next class project begins and members of the group ask the instructor to reassign the student to another team. Although less direct, this effect nevertheless should be understood as an outcome of previous communication exchanges.

In addition to being viewed in terms of results, the effect of an interaction is evaluated by communication participants for effectiveness and ethics. Did the outcomes result from the free, informed choices of all parties? Did one or more parties feel manipulated? Were all parties empathically supported? Were the best alternatives considered as a result of the interaction? It is in this evaluative area—ethics and effectiveness—that future interactions are influenced. Perceptions of whether past interactions were ethical and effective influence perceptions of the desirability of future communication.

## THE CONSTRUCTION OF SHARED REALITIES

Human communication is the process of attempting to construct **shared realities,** to create shared meanings. It is our attempt to have others understand our world as we do or as we want them to understand it and our efforts to comprehend the

**Shared realities**
Meanings resulting from the communication process; attempts to have others understand our world as we do or as we intend for it to be understood and our efforts to comprehend the world of those around us.

world of those around us. The process is culturally and contextually influenced with success or failure in individual communication competencies: knowledge, sensitivity, skills, and values. As a process for the construction of shared realities, human communication is dynamic and ever-changing.

When this process occurs between two individuals with some type of ongoing relationship, we call the process *interpersonal communication*. When the process occurs among several individuals, we are describing *group communication*. When large numbers of people are involved (either personally or through technological channels), we call the process *public* or *mass media communication*. Finally, the human communication process in organizations is referred to as *organizational communication,* the subject of our text. Whether in interpersonal, group, public, mass media, or organizational contexts, the human communication process involves attempts to construct shared realities among people to generate shared meaning. Think back to the "What Business Is This of Ours?" case. What were the shared realities at Quality Engineering? Describe the fields of experience and the context of the interaction between John and Mary. What were the noise factors? Can you predict the effect of their interaction? Will they be able to work together in the future?

A word of caution is appropriate at this point. Although we continue to describe human communication as the process of constructing shared realities, creating shared meanings, we must remember that shared meanings can be representative not only of openness and clarity but also of manipulation, control, or deceit. I can deliberately attempt to have you understand a situation as I understand it, hoping for a shared reality characterized by openness, but I can also deliberately attempt to have you understand a situation very differently from what I know the facts to be. Suppose that I want you to share with me a reality that I choose but not one based on my more complete knowledge, experience, or awareness. My messages then generate a shared reality between us that is characterized by deceit. The important concept here is that the construction of meaning is an intentional process between us related to our knowledge, sensitivity, skills, and values.

## CONCEPTS OF ORGANIZATIONS

We have been defining and describing the human communication process in a variety of possible contexts. Our particular interests are, of course, communication and organizations and how communication influences organizational processes and events. We begin to explore the relationship between communication and organizations by first identifying what an organization is and what it does.

**Organization**
Result of the process of organizing; dynamic system in which individuals engage in collective efforts for goal accomplishment.

The term **organization** is applied to the results of the process of organizing. Organizing is an attempt to bring order out of chaos or establish organizations, entities in which purposeful and ordered activity takes place. Organizing is accomplished through purposeful activities generated as a result of communication behaviors. In other words, the process we call organizing is accomplished through human communication as individuals seek to bring order out of chaos and establish entities for purposeful activities.

Amitai Etzioni (1964) has described organizations as social units or groupings of people deliberately constructed and reconstructed to strive for specific goals. As such, organizations are characterized by divisions of labor for goal achievement. These efforts also are directed by relatively continuous patterns of authority and leadership. Interdependence exists among organizational components as well as with the external environment. This complex interdependence requires coordination achieved through communication.

Consistent with the Etzioni view, Richard Farace, Peter Monge, and Hamish Russell (1977) have provided a description of organizations that reflects much of modern organization theory. They suggest that organizations can be best understood as

> two or more individuals who recognize that some of their goals can be more readily achieved through interdependent (cooperative) actions, even though disagreement (conflict) may be present; who take in materials, energy, and information from the environment in which they exist; who develop coordinative and control relationships to capitalize on their interdependence while operating on these inputs; and who return the modified inputs to the environment in an attempt to accomplish the goals that interdependence was meant to make possible. (p. 16)

This definition focuses on organizations as dynamic systems in which individuals engage in collective efforts for goal accomplishment. To remain dynamic, organizations must adapt to continually changing environments, both internally and externally. From this perspective of adaptation and change, organizations can be understood as active and dynamic mergers of human behaviors and technological operations. Gerald Goldhaber (1993) describes an organization as "a living, open system connected by the flow of information between and among people who occupy various roles and positions" (p. 11). R. Wayne Pace and Don Faules (1994) draw the most common distinction between the notions of organization and organizing:

> How one orders people, things, and ideas in an organized fashion is affected by whether one begins from an objectivist's or a subjectivist's point of view. The objective approach suggests that an organization is a physical, concrete thing, that it is a structure with definite boundaries. The term "the organization" implies that something is tangible and actually holds people, relationships, and goals. Some people refer to this approach as the container view of organizations. The organization exists like a basket, and all the elements that make up the organization are placed in the container.
>
> A subjective approach looks at an organization as activities that people do. Organization consists of the actions, interactions, and transactions in which people engage. Organization is created and maintained through the continually changing

contacts people have with one another and does not exist separately from the people whose behavior constitutes the organization.

From the objective view, organization means structure; from the subjective view, organization means process. (p. 7)

Katherine Miller (1995) identifies five critical features she believes are possessed by all organizations: two or more people (a social collectivity), goals, coordinating activity, structure, and environmental embeddedness. Gerald Pepper (1995) provides a communication-based definition when he describes organizations as consisting of the organizing activities of its members. Pepper argues: "Though this definition may seem circular, it really is quite descriptive of a communication explanation of organizations. The definition accounts for traditional, pyramidal organizational form just as easily as it accounts for nontraditional democratic, 'feminist' organizational forms, because the key to the definition is the communicative relationships among the members, rather than arbitrary components assumed to define the organization" (pp. 17–18).

Stanley Deetz (1994a) emphasizes the importance of the modern organization for all society and in particular for public decision making:

> In most modern societies corporations make crucial decisions for the public regarding the use of resources, development of technologies, products made, and working relations among people. While state political processes are significant, the shaping of these central decisions through regulation and incentives is considerably less important than the central decision-making processes within corporations themselves. Corporate practices pervade modern life by providing personal identity, structuring time and experience, influencing education and knowledge production, directing artistic expression, and instituting particular structures of family life. (p. 217)

Taken as a whole, these definitions and issues help us understand organizations from their structure and from the ways they continually create and change what they do and how they do it. This process occurs through communication behaviors. Put another way, understanding what an organization is and how it works requires an understanding of the process of organizational communication.

Throughout the next several chapters we explore many different types of organizations. Organizations with which you have personal contact and involvement are examined. We discuss traditional hierarchical organizations, profit-making organizations, and nonprofit groups. We describe organizations in which hierarchy is replaced by flatter forms and the use of technology to create virtual groups or entire organizations. We explore partnerships, entrepreneurial opportunities, and home-based work as well as global ventures. For all these "types" of organization, you will come to understand human communication behaviors as creating and shaping both relationships and events.

# DEFINITIONS OF ORGANIZATIONAL COMMUNICATION

**Organizational communication**
Process through which organizations are created and in turn create and shape events. The process can be understood as a combination of process, people, messages, meaning, and purpose.

**Organizational communication** is both similar to and distinct from other types of communication. Organizational communication has sources and receivers who are engaged in the encoding and decoding of messages. Messages are transmitted over channels distorted by noise. As with other forms of communication, organizational communication is related to the competencies of individuals, their fields of experience, the communicative context, and the effects or results of interactions. Yet organizational communication is more than the daily interactions of individuals within organizations. It is the process through which organizations create and shape events.

Miller (1995) identifies five critical features of human communication important for understanding communication processes within organizations: (1) communication occurs between or among two or more people, that is, communication occurs in a social collectivity; (2) communication is a process suggesting that it is continuous and complex, and it cannot be arbitrarily isolated; (3) communication is transaction; (4) communication is symbolic; and (5) communication is intentional. Miller concludes:

> Studying organizational communication requires looking at how communication processes contribute to the coordination of behavior in working toward organizational and individual goals. Such a study also points our attention to the impact of structure and power on communication and to influences both within and outside organizational boundaries. Studying organizational communication also highlights the multiple interpretations that symbols might manifest as well as the impact of history and various organizational constituents on the communication process. (p. 19)

Eric Eisenberg and H. L. Goodall Jr. (1997) suggest four overall approaches to defining organizational communication: communication as information transfer, communication as transactional process, communication as strategic control, and communication as balancing creativity and constraint. Specifically, the communication as information transfer perspective uses a pipeline or conduit metaphor to transmit a message from a sender to a receiver or one part of the organization to another. Communication is used to accomplish specific objectives with scant concern for distortion of information. Although generally considered an inadequate and overly simplistic approach by organizational communication researchers, this "I-sent-the-message-and-everyone-understands" approach is common in organizational practice.

The communication as transactional-process approach as described by Eisenberg and Goodall more closely matches our discussion to this point. The metaphor they use for this perspective is: "Process; communication is a process that creates relationships; 'You cannot not communicate.'" Meanings are in receivers, and shared meaning becomes the measure of effectiveness. In a basic departure from the perspective we have been discussing, Eisenberg and Goodall believe that the transactional-process perspective does not account for ambiguity, deception, or diversity in points of view. Regardless of the perspective taken, anyone working in organizations can describe numerous examples when organizational transactions (messages) have resulted in improved understandings and other examples when organizational transactions have been variously interpreted with confusing results.

The communication-as-strategic-control perspective uses the metaphor of individuals attempting to control their environments through the use of strategic ambiguity that allows for the organizational members' unified diversity while generally preserving their privileged positions. Mission statements, visions, goals, and strategic planning are all current organizational examples of communications that result in varying ways of identifying with messages and varying interpretations of desired outcomes. Eisenberg and Goodall suggest that the measure of effectiveness for this perspective is coordinated actions accomplished through diverse interpretations of meanings. As they state, "If we accept the idea that the meaning one person creates may not correspond to the meaning that another person gives to the same communication, it is less important that the two people fully understand or agree with each other than it is that they act in mutually satisfying ways." Although the approach admittedly minimizes some of the ethical considerations discussed later in this book, it emphasizes the notion that organizational messages are received by diverse populations, an important concept for understanding how organizations create and shape events. The strategic-control perspective should be viewed, however, as an extension of the information-transfer and transactional-process perspectives and not as a unique description of organizational communication.

Finally, Eisenberg and Goodall provide their preferred perspective for defining organizational communication, communication as balancing creativity and constraint. According to Eisenberg and Goodall, organizational

> communication is the moment-to-moment working out of the tension between individual creativity and organizational constraint. By the phrase "moment-to-moment working out of the tension" we refer specifically to the balance of creativity (as a strategic response to organizational constraints) and constraints (as the constructions of reality that limit the individual's choice of strategic response). (pp. 29-30)

The metaphor for this perspective is balance, but the basic assumption is duality of structure: "Individuals are molded, controlled, ordered, and shaped by society and social institutions; individuals also create society and social institutions" (Eisenberg and Goodall, 1993). This approach will be particularly meaningful when we discuss organizational culture, values, and individual congruence between organizational and individual expectations.

These four perspectives—communication as information transfer, communication as transactional process, communication as strategic control, and communication as balancing creativity and constraint—are more similar than different in emphasizing the importance of organizational communication. They all return, however, in one way or another to our basic description of human communication as behaviors that create and shape both relationships and events through a culturally dependent process of assigning meaning to symbols. Organizational communication as a complex interaction of process, people, messages, meaning, and purpose, is described next.

## Organizational Communication as Process

As with other forms of communication, organizational communication is best understood as an ongoing process without distinct beginnings and ends. The process includes patterns of interactions that develop among organizational members and those external to the organization and how these interactions shape organizations.

Because the process is ever-changing, it can be described as evolutionary and culturally dependent. In other words, the ongoing process of creating and transmitting organizational messages reflects the shared realities resulting from previous message exchanges and evolves to generate new realities that create and shape events.

The process occurs in developing strategy, planning, decision making, and executing the work of the organization. The process also occurs, however, during the unexpected crisis, changes in the external environment, encounters with competitors, and a host of less visible ways. The process occurs between individuals performing daily work and includes messages to large numbers of employers, customers, and stakeholders. All these interactions taken together create and shape the ongoing organization.

## Organizational Communication as People

Individuals bring to organizations sets of characteristics that influence how information is processed. Organizational communication contributes to creating relationships and assists both individuals and organizations in achieving diverse purposes. Organizational communication occurs between and among people who share both work and interpersonal relationships. Organizational communication also occurs between and among people who are geographically separated and who may speak different languages and have widely differing cultural perspectives. It is fair to say that organizational communication occurs across networks of people who are seeking to obtain a variety of objectives requiring communication interactions.

## Organizational Communication as Messages

Organizational communication is the creation and exchange of messages. It is the movement or transmission of verbal and nonverbal behaviors and the sharing of information throughout the organization. Communicators are linked together by channels, and messages are described with such terms as *frequency, amount,* and *type.* Concern is expressed for message fidelity, or the extent to which messages are similar or accurate at all links through the channels. Organizational messages increasingly are telemediated (via the use of complex technologies to exchange messages), extending their geographic reach, changing notions of time and space, and altering who participates in communication processes.

## Organizational Communication as Meaning

Organizational communication creates and shapes organizational events. Role taking occurs as individuals engage in social interaction within the ever-changing organizational context. Organizational communication is the symbolic behavior of individuals and organizations that, when interpreted, affects all organizational activities. Organizational communication does not create a singular set of meanings for organizational members and activities. The interactions of ever-changing behaviors often create multiple perceptions of events and multiple realities that become the process through which organizational meanings are generated.

## Organizational Communication as Purpose

Organizational communication is organizing, decision making, planning, controlling, and coordinating. Organizational communication seeks to reduce environmental uncertainty. It is people, messages, and meaning. It is intentional and unintentional messages explaining the workings of the organization. It is the process through which individuals and organizations attempt goal-oriented behavior in dealing with their environments.

Deetz (1994b) provides an important summary perspective to our discussion of definitions for organizational communication. Deetz suggests:

> Communication, in the view I am suggesting, refers to the social processes by which meanings, identities, psychological states, social structures, and the various means of the contact of the organization with the environment are both produced, reproduced, or changed. In both its constitutive and reproductive modes, communication processes are central to how perceptions, meanings, and routines are held in common. In all interactions, including those in organizations, perception, meaning, and data transmission are all complex, multileveled phenomena produced out of and producing conflicting motives and structures. (p. 90)

Can you now answer the question we asked at the beginning of the chapter about the differences between organizational and other types of communication? You should be able to do so. Whereas interpersonal and group communication occur in organizations, organizational communication is a more comprehensive process including, but not limited to, one-on-one and group exchanges. Competencies for organizational communication include interpersonal abilities, but organizational communication competencies also require effectiveness in complex and changing environments where diverse groups of people join in purposeful activity. The goal of this book is to help you identify and develop important competencies for organizational communication. The next several chapters concentrate on knowledge, sensitivity, skills, and values important in interpersonal, group, and organization-wide contexts.

Let us return to our case study. Describe the interaction between John and Mary from an organizational communication perspective. Can you identify organizational factors influencing their exchange? Do John and Mary have a work relationship, or are they communicating as friends? Can they be both? Is this an example of organizational goal-directed behavior? How might their exchange affect Quality Engineering?

It is difficult to be certain about our answers for this case. The chances are that most of us feel the need for additional information about John and Mary and Quality Engineering. Yet the lack of complete information is very characteristic of many, if not most, of our organizational experiences. In fact, it is probable that even with more information we can never be certain of all the shared realities between John and Mary. Indeed, as we begin our study of organizational communication, a key to our personal development rests with our ability to analyze thoughtfully while recognizing the limits of our understanding.

## SUMMARY

Human communication is the process through which we attempt to construct shared realities. The human communication process includes sources and receivers, message encoding and decoding, channels, noise, communicative competence, participant fields of experience, contexts, and effects. The process is evaluated for effectiveness and ethical behaviors, with these evaluations influencing future interactions. Organizations are the products of organizing activities and can be described as deliberately constructed social units designed to strive for specific goals. As such, organizations are dynamic mergers of human behaviors and technological operations. Organizational communication includes all the descriptors in the human communication process. It is also the process through which organizations are created and in turn create and shape events. As such, organizational communication can be understood as a combination of process, people, messages, meaning, and purpose.

## WORKSHOP

1. Identify all the organizations of which you are a member. Include the school you are currently attending. Describe shared realities for each organization. Discuss as a class the shared realities of your school.

2. Shared meanings or shared realities are what organizational communication is all about. My Meaning, Your Meaning, Our Meanings, an exercise to illustrate the importance of meanings and shared realities, is found below. Divide the class into groups of six members each and complete the exercise. Discuss what you have learned about meanings and shared realities. (See p. 33.)

3. The following case, "What Do You Mean I'm Not Getting a Raise?" illustrates organizational messages with multiple meanings. Study the case and attempt to understand how people receiving the same message can arrive at very different meanings. (See p. 34.)

## My Meaning, Your Meaning, Our Meanings

Read each of the following four statements and write your response. You may agree, disagree, or take no position on the statement. Your response should accurately reflect the statement's meaning to you.

1. Oral skills are more important than written communication skills for most jobs. I (agree with, disagree with, don't know about) this statement. It means to me . . .

2. People who are the most intelligent make the best grades and are the most successful. I (agree with, disagree with, don't know about) this statement. It means to me . . .

3. The successful organizational member must be competitive and persuasive. I (agree with, disagree with, don't know about) this statement. It means to me . . .

4. The successful organizational member is more analytical than others and believes technical skills are more important than communication abilities. I (agree with, disagree with, don't know about) this statement. It means to me . . .

Discuss your responses and compare similarities and differences in groups of six. What influenced the similarities and differences in your answers? How do these influences contribute to the meanings we assign to messages?

Next, consider the following four professions: minister, salesperson, lawyer, television executive. As a group, attempt to determine how you think that most people in these professions would react to the four statements. Again, what does that tell us about how meanings are influenced? How accurate can you be about your perceptions of the meanings others might assign?

Finally, as a group, attempt to develop a response to each statement that all group members can support. (Total agreement is not necessary, only general support.) How do these group statements differ from your individual statements? Did your statements become a shared reality for your group? If so, why? If not, why not? (If time permits, compare your group's statements with other groups in your class. What are the similarities and differences? Are there any surprises?)

■ ■ ■ ■ ■ ▬▬▬▬▬▬▬▬▬▬▬▬▬▬▬▬▬▬▬▬▬▬▬▬

# THE "WHAT DO YOU MEAN I'M NOT GETTING A RAISE?" CASE

Jane Jackson, division manager of AMC, Inc., had spent the day in the cafeteria meeting with each of AMC's three manufacturing shifts. She had good news and had been eager to make the announcement that the company would not begin the layoffs rumored to occur at the end of the present round of contracts. Instead of layoffs, management had decided to freeze wages and evaluate in six months when cost-of-living and merit increases could resume. Jane had been careful with the announcement, reading the press release exactly as it was written from corporate headquarters.

Following her cafeteria meetings, Jane asked her section managers to meet with individual supervisors on each of the three shifts to determine how the news was being received. Jane had been concerned about the layoff rumors and expected a generally favorable response to the announcement. She was not prepared for her section managers' feedback. Several supervisors reported that although there was considerable relief that layoffs were not imminent, many workers did not understand that they would not receive their annual increases at performance appraisal time. Numerous workers believed management intended to consider layoffs again at the end of the six-month freeze period, and others thought that the wage freeze meant no new people were being hired. Jane could not understand how all this confusion was possible. After all, everyone got exactly the same message.

What would you tell Jane about messages and meanings? What are the probable reasons for this confusion? What would you do if you were Jane and her section managers?

# REFERENCES AND SUGGESTED READINGS

Byers, P. B. 1996. *Organizational communication: Theory and behavior.* Boston: Allyn and Bacon.

Deetz, S. A. 1992. *Democracy in an age of corporate colonization.* Albany: State University of New York Press.

Deetz, S. 1994a. Representative practices and the political analysis of corporations: Building a communication perspective in organization studies. In *Organizational communication: New perspectives,* ed. B. Kovacic, 209–42. Albany: State University of New York Press.

Deetz, S. 1994b. *Transforming communication, transforming business: Building responsive and responsible workplaces.* Cresskill, NJ: Hampton Press.

Eisenberg, E. M., and H. L. Goodall Jr. 1997. *Organizational communication: Balancing creativity and constraint.* 2d ed. New York: St. Martin's.

Etzioni, A. 1964. *Modern organizations.* Englewood Cliffs, NJ: Prentice Hall.

Farace, R., P. Monge, and H. Russell. 1977. *Communicating and organizing.* Reading, MA: Addison-Wesley.

Fisher, D. 1993. *Communication in organizations.* Minneapolis/St.Paul: West.

Goldhaber, G. 1993. *Organizational communication.* 6th ed. Dubuque, IA: Brown.

Krone, K., F. Jablin, and L. Putnam. 1987. Communication theory and organizational communication: Multiple perspectives. In *Handbook of organizational communication,* eds. F. Jablin, L. Putnam, K. Roberts, and L. Porter, 18–40. Newbury Park, CA: Sage.

Miller, K. 1995. *Organizational communication: Approaches and processes.* Belmont, CA: Wadsworth.

Pace, R. W., and D. F. Faules. 1994. *Organizational communication.* 3d ed. Englewood Cliffs, NJ: Prentice Hall.

Pepper, G. 1995. *Communicating in organizations: A cultural approach.* New York: McGraw-Hill.

Putnam, L. 1983. The interpretive perspective: An alternative to functionalism. In *Communication and organizations: An interpretive approach,* eds. L. Putnam and M. Pacanowsky, 31–54. Beverly Hills, CA: Sage.

Wilson, G., H. Goodall, and C. Waagen. 1986. *Organizational communication.* New York: Harper and Row.

■ ■ ■ ■ ■

# CHAPTER THREE

# THEORETICAL PERSPECTIVES FOR ORGANIZATIONAL COMMUNICATION

## DEVELOPING COMPETENCIES THROUGH . . .

### KNOWLEDGE

Describing the Functional approach to organizational communication

Describing the Meaning-Centered approach to organizational communication

Describing Emerging Perspectives for organizational communication

Distinguishing among the Functional approach, the Meaning-Centered approach, and Emerging Perspectives

### SENSITIVITY

Understanding the importance of meaning generation for organizational communication

Identifying how organizational communication creates and shapes organizational events

### SKILLS

Developing analysis abilities using the Functional approach, the Meaning-Centered approach, and Emerging Perspectives

Practicing analysis abilities

### VALUES

Viewing communication as the fundamental organizational process

Relating organizational communication to a variety of value and ethical issues

■ ■ ■ ■ ■

## THE CORONADO COMPANY'S QUALITY DEFECTS CASE

Coronado Manufacturing Company, located in Trenton, New Jersey, is a small-appliance manufacturer providing house brand products to a series of major chain stores. The situation you are about to examine was once a major issue for Coronado, threatening their long-term survival. We use their quality defects problem to assist in understanding major theoretical perspectives for organizational communication.

Bill Drake, president of Coronado Manufacturing Company, could hardly believe the conclusions in the consultant's report. Product quality had always been a strength of Coronado Manufacturing, and now defective products were being blamed for declining sales in the company's small-appliance line. The report went on to say that the sales department for Coronado was not passing along customer complaints to anyone in manufacturing. Furthermore, Drake was confused by his own lack of personal knowledge about customer dissatisfaction and about problems in manufacturing. After all, he met weekly with the management team responsible for spotting these problems, and they all knew that he felt that the customer was number one.

Drake thought about the history of Coronado Manufacturing. Coronado had been founded some fifty years ago by Drake's father and uncle. Both men had worked most of their lives for a major manufacturer of small appliances well known for its quality products and customer concern. In founding Coronado both men had hired people who cared about quality and understood customers. In fact, stories were told about the founders personally emphasizing quality to newcomers on the manufacturing line and making "surprise" visits to customers to check on how "their" products were working. When Bill Drake's father retired, he had admonished Bill not to forget the basics that had made the business successful.

Bill Drake had assumed he was successfully carrying on Coronado's quality and customer traditions. Was the report accurate? Was his management team withholding information? How could he determine what to do?

Bill Drake is confronted with a management problem requiring immediate action. The decisions he makes, the action he takes, and what ultimately happens to Coronado Manufacturing provide examples of how organizational communication creates and shapes events.

## INTRODUCTION

In Chapter 2 we defined organizational communication as the process through which organizations create and shape events. This chapter is designed to help us understand this process and to develop our competencies in determining how Bill Drake might approach his problem. Three different approaches—Functional, Meaning-Centered, and Emerging Perspectives—are presented as ways to understand the processes of organizational communication and are used as frameworks to help analyze specific organizational situations, experiences, and problems.

The Functional and Meaning-Centered approaches ask different questions about organizational communication. The Functional approach asks how and why communication works, whereas the Meaning-Centered approach asks what communication is. The Functional approach asks what purpose communication serves within organizations and how messages move. The Meaning-Centered approach asks if communication is the process through which organizing, decision making, influence, and culture occur. The Functional approach describes organizational reality in such terms as chains of command, positions, roles, and communications channels, whereas the Meaning-Centered approach defines as reality the symbolic significance of these terms. The Functional approach subordinates the importance of the individual to his or her organizational position and function, whereas in the Meaning-Centered approach the significance of the individual is the key focus.

The Emerging Perspectives we discuss ask questions about communication as a constitutive or basic process of social construction. Emerging Perspectives focus attention on power and control and on the marginalization of voices other than those of the dominant control structure.

After studying this chapter you will be able to answer several questions about the Functional approach, the Meaning-Centered approach, and Emerging Perspectives.

### THE FUNCTIONAL APPROACH

1. What are different types of organizational messages?
2. How do organizing, relationship, and change messages differ?
3. How can communication networks be described?
4. How do different communications channels affect messages?
5. What is communication load?
6. What is distortion in organizational communication?

### THE MEANING-CENTERED APPROACH

1. How is "reality" generated through human interaction?
2. Why are communicating and organizing almost synonymous processes?
3. How does communication contribute to decision making?
4. What is meant by sensemaking?
5. What are influence processes in organizations?
6. What are communication rules?
7. What is the difference between treating culture as something an organization has versus something an organization is?
8. What is meant by communication climate?

### EMERGING PERSPECTIVES

1. What is meant by communication as constitutive processes?
2. What are the issues for organizational communication when adopting a postmodern viewpoint?
3. What is the emphasis of critical organizational communication theory?
4. What is feminist organizational communication theory?
5. How do the values evidenced in Emerging Perspectives differ from the Functional and Meaning-Centered approaches?
6. What is the common ground among the three perspectives? What are the most important differences?

Think back to the Coronado Quality Defects case. Which of these questions should Bill Drake be asking? As you study the material in this chapter, try to determine how the Functional approach, the Meaning-Centered approach, and Emerging Perspectives can help Bill Drake solve his problem at Coronado Manufacturing.

This chapter contributes to *knowledge* competencies by describing and contrasting three approaches to organizational communication. Individual *sensitivity* competencies are developed by examining the development of meaning in organizations and individual communication behaviors that shape and change organizational events. *Skills* are developed and practiced by applying Functional, Meaning-Centered, and Emerging Perspectives approaches to cases and exercises. Finally, *value* competencies are encouraged by examining organizational communication as the fundamental organizational process reflective of multiple ethical issues and concerns.

## THE FUNCTIONAL APPROACH

**Functional approach**
Way of understanding organizational communication by describing what messages do and how they move through organizations.

The **Functional approach** helps us understand organizational communication by describing what messages do and how they move through organizations. This perspective describes communication as a complex organizational process that serves organizing, relationship, and change functions: what messages do. The way messages move through organizations is described by examining communication networks, channels, message directions, communication load, and distortion. The Functional approach suggests that communication transmits rules, regulations, and information throughout the organization. Communication establishes and defines human relationships, helps individuals identify with goals and opportunities, and is the process by which the organization generates and manages change. These functions occur during the repetitive patterns of communication interactions in which organizational members engage.

In Chapter 2 we described organizations as dynamic systems in which individuals engage in collective efforts to accomplish goals. We found that organizations can be understood not only in terms of their structure but also by the way they continually create and change what they do and how they do it. We claimed that, as such, organizations emerge and evolve through communication behaviors. The Functional approach describes organizations as dynamic communication systems with the various parts of the system operating together to create and shape organizational events.

### Organizational Communication Systems: Component Parts

Before we can examine what messages do and how they move in organizations, we need to understand the concept of an **organizational communication system** on

**Organizational communication system**
Number of related units and processes that operate together within the organization and with its environment to create and shape organizational events. Information processing is the primary function of the communication system.

which the Functional approach is based. What are the main parts of the system? What parts work together to create and shape organizational events? How does communication contribute to keeping a system dynamic? What role did communication play in organizations that cease to exist?

In the Functional approach, information processing is seen as the primary function of organizational communication systems. It takes place in a number of related units that when taken together are called organizations or suprasystems. The individual units, sometimes called subsystems, are related by some degree of structure and when described as a whole can be distinguished from other organizations in the environment by their boundary. The individual units are interdependent and permeable to other units and the external environment.

The Coronado Manufacturing Company provides an example of an organizational communication system with its manufacturing and sales units; Bill Drake as president represents a management unit. These units relate to each other to produce a product that customers in the external environment, outside the Coronado boundary, will buy. Coronado Manufacturing Company is the suprasystem with management, manufacturing, and sales subsystems. The external environment, however, is important to Coronado. Sales are slipping. Bill Drake needs external information (from the consultant and customers) to make decisions about internal operations, decisions that in turn will influence future sales.

**Communication inputs**
Information in the external environment that may influence the decision making of the organization.

## Communication Inputs

This relationship between external environment information and internal information processing is important for understanding organizational communication systems. Information in the external environment, commonly known as **communication inputs,** is any information that can potentially influence the decision making of the suprasystem (organization). It is crucial for an organization to have accurate and timely information inputs to adapt and change. Bill Drake realizes that the future of Coronado Manufacturing is related to the accuracy of the inputs about quality defects from his customers. Without this information his understanding of the sales problem is incomplete. Only with accurate information about quality problems can he make informed decisions.

**Communication throughput**
Transforming and changing of input information for internal organizational use and the generation and transmission of internal information throughout the organization.

## Communication Throughput

When information enters the organization, the communication system begins a process known as **communication throughput,** or the transforming and changing of input information for internal organizational use. Bill Drake, in taking the consultant's report and evaluating what to do, is taking inputs and transforming them into organizational action. His decisions and the decisions of people in sales and manufacturing can be described as throughput communication. In other words, the internal subsystems (management, sales, manufacturing) of Coronado are moving messages through the organization that will influence the production of products and ultimately customer satisfaction. The quality of throughput communication will determine whether or not the defects problem is solved. Even with accurate and timely inputs, the subsystems of Coronado require effective internal communication to increase sales. Bill Drake has reason to question the throughput communication of his organization when he realizes that despite weekly staff meetings, he was unaware of the quality problem.

## Communication Output

**Communication output**
Messages to the external environment from within the organization.

Messages to the external environment from within the organization are known as **communication output.** Outputs can be thought of as the results of the input and throughput process and are both intentional and unintentional. Coronado Manufacturing, through its sales force and advertising, generates intentional output communication. The defects in its products, however, have become unintentional output messages with important consequences. The low-quality message from the defective products is a potentially more powerful message than positive messages from advertising and sales campaigns.

## Open versus Closed Systems

**Open systems**
Organizations that continually take in new information, transform that information, and give information back to the environment.

**Closed systems**
Organizations that lack input communication, making it difficult to make good decisions and stay current with the needs of the environment.

**Equifinality**
Potential for the use of a variety of approaches to reach system goals.

The response of the environment (in Coronado's case, the customers) to organizational communication is feedback that in turn becomes new inputs to the system. The way the organization responds to these new inputs with throughput efforts and new outputs determines whether it has an open or closed system. **Open systems** continually take in new information, transform that information, and give information back to the environment. By contrast, **closed systems** are characterized by a lack of input communication, making it difficult to make good decisions and stay current with the needs of the environment. Open systems use a variety of problem-solving approaches. There is no one best way to do things. This ability to use a variety of approaches is called **equifinality**, meaning that there are many ways to reach system goals.

Bill Drake wants Coronado Manufacturing to operate as an open system. He is listening to customer complaints and trying to decide what to do. He can consider a new advertising campaign or new approaches from his sales staff. He knows, however, that he is unlikely to be successful until the defects problem is solved. In the long term, if Bill Drake pays no attention to sales or quality problems, he increases the likelihood that Coronado Manufacturing will go out of business. As we can see from studying the Coronado case, however, Bill Drake has more than one way to approach his problems. He can work with both manufacturing and sales, he can work only with manufacturing, he can assign responsibility to others, he can retain much of the responsibility himself, and he has other options. There are a number of ways (equifinality) to solve Coronado's problems. Figure 3.1 illustrates the Coronado Manufacturing communication system.

**Message functions**
What communication does or how it contributes to the overall functioning of the organization.

## Message Functions

When we talk about **message functions** within organizations we are talking about what communication does or how it contributes to the overall functioning of the organization. Numerous researchers have described message functions in attempts to understand how communication systems work. Daniel Katz and Robert Kahn (1966), for example, provide a message-function classification that includes production, maintenance,

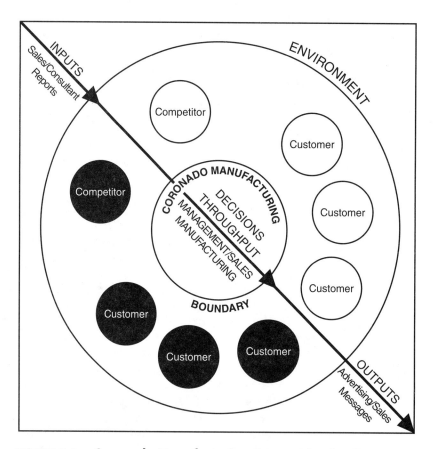

**FIGURE 3.1    Coronado Manufacturing Communication System**

adaptation, and management communication. Howard Greenbaum (1976) talks about regulative, integrative, innovative, and informative-instructive networks. W. Charles Redding (1972) suggests that message flow can be classified by task, maintenance, and human concerns, and Leo Thayer (1968) identifies functions that inform, persuade, command, instruct, and integrate.

In an attempt to understand organizational communication from the Functional approach, message functions in three broad categories—organizing functions, relationship functions, and change functions—are described. Each function is seen as necessary for an open communication system, although the exact balance among message functions will vary by organizational type and circumstance.

**Organizing functions**
Messages that establish the rules and regulations of a particular environment.

## Organizing Functions

People who work together talk more about doing tasks than any other subject. This finding is not surprising. To engage in organized activity in pursuit of goals, people in organizations must develop and exchange messages about rules, regulations, policies, and tasks.

**Organizing functions** establish the rules and regulations of a particular environment. Policy manuals, employee handbooks, orientation training, newsletters, and a variety of other sources convey information about how the organization expects to work and what it requires of its members. These organizing messages define and clarify tasks, develop work instructions, and evaluate task accomplishment.

Organizing messages can be found in every aspect of our lives. The school you attend publishes standards for admissions and requirements for specific majors and degrees. Instructors establish requirements and define performance expectations. You converse with teachers and peers about assignments and responsibilities. All these messages and many more describe how your school is organized, how it is supposed to work, and how you fit into that process.

The adequacy and effectiveness of organizing messages can be evaluated by how well organizational members understand and perform tasks, how rules and regulations are understood and followed, and how adequately daily operations support organizational goals. In sum, the organizing function of communication guides, directs, and controls organizational activity.

**Relationship functions**
Communication that helps individuals define their roles and assess the compatibility of individual and organizational goals.

## Relationship Functions

The **relationship function** of organizational communication helps individuals define their roles and assess the compatibility of individual and organizational goals. Relationship communication contributes to individuals' identification with an organization or sense of "belonging" in their work environment. Frequently referred to as integrative or maintenance messages, relationship communication contributes to employee morale and maintains or integrates individuals with their work environments.

Communication establishes relationships between supervisors and subordinates and within peer groups. Relationship messages range from informal conversations to visible symbols of status such as large offices and reserved parking spaces. Job titles, awards, and promotions are other examples of relationship communication that determine how individuals identify or relate to the organization.

Whereas organizing messages communicate how the organization operates, relationship messages establish the human interactions that make such operation possible. Chances are, for example, that your sense of belonging with your school or lack of it is closely related to your interpersonal interactions with teachers and other students. In fact, your ability to meet performance expectations successfully may be influenced by your relationships with your instructors and how comfortable you are in exchanging ideas with them. The same may be true of your relationships with other students. The quality of your work on a team project is probably influenced by how much you feel a part of—or integrated with—your group. The effectiveness of relationship messages is reflected in individual satisfaction with work relationships, productivity, employee turnover, overall support for organizational practices, and a variety of other less obvious ways.

**Change functions**
Messages that help organizations adapt what they do and how they do it; viewed as essential to an open system.

## Change Functions

**Change functions** help organizations adapt what they do and how they do it and are essential to an open system. Change messages occur in organizational problem solving, individual decision making, feedback from the environment, and numerous other choice-making situations. Change communication is the processing of new ideas and information as well as the altering of existing procedures and processes. It is essential for continual adaptation to the environment and for meeting the complex needs of individuals working together.

Experiences in decision-making groups help illustrate how change messages function. When working with a group of students to develop a class presentation, chances are you can recall messages speculating about the best approach and who should take what type of responsibility. Furthermore, you probably attempted to reduce the ambiguity of the assignment by determining what the instructor wanted and what would be appropriate for the time you had. Your group's ability to exchange innovative messages and adapt to the requirements of the assignment influenced your effectiveness and final grade. In the Coronado case Bill Drake became aware of his quality problem through change messages, specifically through declining sales and a consultant's report. His attempt to correct the problem will require change messages with his sales and manufacturing staffs and new approaches to reverse the negative reactions of his customers.

The ultimate effectiveness of change communication is the survival of the organization. Without appropriate change, organizational systems stagnate and die. Change communication is necessary for innovation and adaptation and is the process through which the organization obtains new information, chooses among various alternatives, and weighs current practices against emerging needs. Timely and creative change communication is required for a dynamic and open system. The effectiveness of change messages can be determined by whether the organization gathers information from the best available sources and acts on that information with a timely, quality decision. Figure 3.2 illustrates organizing, relationship, and change functions.

**Message structure**
Movement of organizing, relationship, and change messages throughout the organization and between the organization and its external environment.

## Message Structure

The movement of organizing, relationship, and change messages throughout the organization and between the organization and its external environment is the **message structure** of organizational communication. The Functional approach to structure asks questions about the repetitive patterns of interactions among members of the organization (networks), the use of a variety of channels for communication, message directions, and the amount of messages and the types of distortions that can be expected to occur in organizational communication. In other words, the structure of organizational communication can be understood in terms of networks, channels, message directions, load, and distortion.

### FIGURE 3.2    The Functional Approach

*Organizing Messages*

Rules and regulations
Organizational policies
Task definition
Task instruction
Task evaluation

*Relationship Messages*

Individual role definition
Individual/organizational goals
Status symbols
Integration among supervisor/subordinates, peers

*Change Messages*

Decision making
Market analysis
New idea processing
Environmental inputs
Employee suggestions
Problem solving

**Networks**
Formal and informal patterns of communication that link organizational members together.

# Communication Networks

Communication **networks** are the formal and informal patterns of communication that link organizational members together. Networks can be described by how formally or informally they are organized, by the links between people, and by the roles people perform as they link.

Communication networks develop as a result of both formal organization and informal social contact. Organizations divide work by function and task. Organization charts that map out who reports to whom and in what area of responsibility can be described as blueprints for the way decisions are to be made, the way conflicts are to be resolved, and which groups are responsible for "networking" to reach organizational goals. The formal organization (as illustrated by the organization chart just mentioned) prescribes who has the right to tell others what to do, who is to work together as a unit or team, and who has the final authority in disagreements. In other words, the formal act of organizing creates organizational communication networks or the formal communication system.

As individuals work together, interpersonal relationships develop and extend beyond the specific requirements of the work group. Informal networks emerge, with individuals exchanging diverse types of information related both to the organization and to their social relationships. The organizational grapevine is perhaps the most frequently discussed example of an informal network.

Supervisors and subordinates, task forces, committees, quality circles, and other types of decision-making bodies are examples of formal communication networks. Formal networks also are established with various forms of technology such as computers and video systems. Generally speaking, these telemediated networks are used to establish communication links that geographic separation would otherwise make difficult and costly. In our shift to an information-rich society, these technological networks are of increasing importance and are projected to change the way we establish networks and broaden the scope of our network involvement.

Informal networks emerge as a result of formal networks and are formed by individuals who have interpersonal relationships, who exchange valuable information across reporting chains, and who disregard formal status and timing. Typically, informal networks exclude numerous individuals who are designated for network inclusion by the formal chain of command.

Formal and informal networks exist side by side; individuals maintain membership in both. Formal and informal networks contribute to organizational reality, and both networks change and shape organizational events. Message structure within organizations cannot be understood without evaluating how both formal and informal patterns of interaction take place.

Think about your own personal networks. What formal networks exist in the organizations of which you are a member? What types of networks exist in your school? How do you establish your informal networks? Which type of network is more meaningful to you? We are all involved in both formal and informal networks. When we evaluate our personal experiences we can better understand how organizational networks function and how they contribute to the movement of organizing, relationship, and change messages. In Chapters 5 and 6 the discussion of networks is expanded and implications for individuals and groups are described.

**Channels**

Means for the transmission of messages. Common means are face-to-face interaction, group meetings, memos, letters, computer-mediated exchanges, web sites, presentations, and teleconferencing.

## Communication Channels

**Channels** are the means for transmission of messages. Organizations typically have a wide variety of channels available for transmitting oral and written messages. Face-to-face interaction, group meetings, memos, letters, computer-mediated exchanges, web sites, presentations, and teleconferencing are among the channels commonly used in contemporary organizations. Increasing emphasis is placed on developing new and improved technical channels that speed information transfer and shorten decision-making response time. Indeed, it is fair to say the choice and availability of communication channels influence the way the organization can and does operate.

Questions arise as to the effectiveness of various channels and what is communicated by channel selection. Although most of us take channel use for granted, selecting one channel over another can communicate subtle and important attitudes about both the message receiver and the message itself. For example, most of us like to communicate good news in face-to-face interaction. We enjoy the reactions of others and deliberately choose channels that permit close, immediate contact. If the news is not positive, we may prefer another channel. Negative messages, more than good news, are likely to be transmitted in a less immediate channel such as letters or memos, the telephone, e-mail, or a third-party announcement. In fact, research suggests that our attitude about the message and our willingness to have contact with the receiver significantly influence the channels we use for communication.

Attitudes about messages and receivers are not the only factors that influence channel selection. Power and status, work requirements, technical capability, and judgments about channel effectiveness all contribute to the mode or modes we use. High-status organizational members, for example, can determine what channels they personally want to use and what modes others must use in communicating with them. The president of the company can initiate face-to-face interaction with just about anyone in the organization. The chances are good, however, that not all organizational members can walk into the president's office for an unscheduled visit. In the Coronado case, Bill Drake can require the consultant to submit a report and recommendations in writing. Drake can require his sales and manufacturing people to meet with him and make detailed presentations of their ideas. It is unlikely that the consultant or the sales and manufacturing managers could make the same requirement of Bill Drake.

Judgments about channel effectiveness also guide organizational members in making communication choices. Face-to-face interaction has the strength of immediacy and the capacity to monitor nonverbal as well as verbal behavior. Face-to-face interaction also permits questions and immediate clarification of ambiguous messages. The face-to-face channel, however, does not provide support for complicated instructions requiring considerable technical detail. A financial report presented orally may be much less effective than if the same material had been summarized in writing. On the other hand, delivering an employee reprimand via the company's e-mail system may be destructive and fail to gain the desired outcome.

Research on the effectiveness of channels supports what many organizational members know about the importance of the immediate mode of oral communication. Oral messages accompanied by supporting written messages have been described as the most effective method for transmitting information from management throughout the organization. Face-to-face oral methods without written accompaniment have been found to be effective for employee reprimands and in settling work disputes. Written channels are more effective when communication requires future employee action or is of a general nature. Directives, orders, important policy changes, and the need for immediate action are best communicated orally and accompanied by written support.

Judgments about channel effectiveness also are based on financial cost and individual skill levels. The cost of telemediated channels and the skills necessary to use computers and teleresources are important factors governing their selection as organizational channels. Access and availability of channels and the type of response needed also influence which channel or channels are effective in particular situations.

Bill Drake will be confronted with channel selection as he works on the defects problem. He will use internal channels, and once the problem is solved he must consider how to communicate to his customers. How would you advise Drake? Are particular channels more appropriate than others as he seeks to regain lost sales? Attempt to describe the criteria Drake should use for channel selection.

**Direction**
Description of the movement of messages in organizations based on authority or position levels of message senders and receivers; typically described as downward, upward, and horizontal communication.

## Message Direction

As messages move through channels, we begin to think about that movement in terms of **direction.** Researchers typically describe three primary message directions in organizations: downward, upward, and horizontal. Downward communication describes message movement from a person in a position of authority to a subordinate or subordinate group. It is characterized by those with higher authority developing messages to transmit to those lower in authority, with authority being defined by the chain of command or the formal structure of the organization. We have downward communication, for example, when the board of regents for the university votes to raise tuition for the upcoming semester. The board formally informs the school's president, who in turn informs officials in admissions and records; finally, students, who will pay the new fees, are advised of the bad news.

Upward communication describes message movement that begins with lower organizational levels and is transmitted to higher levels of authority. As with downward communication, authority levels are defined by the formal organization. Subordinates are engaging in upward communication when they complain about working conditions to a supervisor, who in turn reports their concerns to higher management.

Horizontal communication moves laterally across the organization among individuals of approximately the same level and without distinct reporting relationships to one another. In other words, there is horizontal flow when various department heads come together to discuss common problems from their respective groups. This communication generally moves messages more quickly across the organization than if the messages were to follow the vertical chain of command.

Information flow cannot always be described in terms of specific direction. Informal network flow such as the grapevine and flow between organizational members and the organizational environment (i.e., customers, vendors, stockholders, regulators) may move both vertically and horizontally, all within the transmission of a single message. Messages may move among people of different organizational authority levels and different organizations without the message having anything to do with authority or reporting relationships. When the research engineer speculates about the feasibility of a new product with the head of the marketing department, different authority levels are represented. One is a manager and one is not. The call a salesperson makes to a customer does not specify a place in a single organizational hierarchy for either individual with regard to the other. We do not, however, label that flow as up or down the chain of command because the exchange is about a subject not related to the authority of the two individuals. R. Wayne Pace (1983) has described this interaction as cross-channel communication. Whether cross-channel or grapevine, informal network flow is not dependent on formal organizational structure and is more difficult to describe in terms of specific message directions.

**Load**
Number of messages moving through the communication system; commonly referred to as load, overload, and underload.

## Communication Load

The number of messages moving through the communication system is yet another important variable for describing the message structure of organizational communication. We commonly refer to the number of messages as communication **load,** or the volume, rate, and complexity of messages processed by an individual or the organization as a whole.

Load is a common term for most of us. In fact, it is a rare student who has not proclaimed himself or herself to be in information overload during midterms or final examinations. The concept of load, however, is not limited to the overload state. Load, for example, can be defined as the optimum or ideal volume, rate, and complexity of messages for a particular individual or organization. Underload is present when the volume, rate, and complexity of messages to an individual or organization are lower than the capacity of the individual or system. Underload is frequently found when individuals engage in routine, repetitive tasks that have been thoroughly learned and no longer present challenges. This situation leads to boredom and the underutilization of human potential. Overload, on the other hand, occurs when the volume, rate, and complexity of messages exceed the system's capacity. It generates stress and strains the capacity of individuals to deal with information. In fact, one of the continuing concerns of the information-rich society is that the ease with which we can use new technologies to process large volumes of messages is generating a permanent overload in many jobs, a situation that actually impairs rather than strengthens the decision-making process.

**Distortion**
Anything that contributes to alterations in meaning as messages move through the organization.

## Message Distortion

Closely related to the concept of load are the types of communication problems, or **distortions,** that occur as messages move throughout the organization. These distortions occur because of load, message direction, channel usage, and the very composition of the networks themselves. Put simply, distortions are those things that contribute to alterations in meaning as messages move through the organization. Distortions are noise in the organizational communication system.

Organizational communication is characterized by the serial transmission of messages. Messages pass first to individuals as receivers, who then become senders of information. Supervisors learn of changes in policies and have the responsibility to transmit those changes to a subordinate group. Messages are influenced by the numbers of people involved (the network), the channels for transmission (oral, written), and the direction of flow (vertical, horizontal, informal). Research consistently finds that original messages change or are distorted in the serial transmission process. Information is lost from or added to the message, the interpretation of facts changes, and new interpretations develop. Researchers Gordon Allport and Leo Postman (1947) have described systematic serial transmission distortions as leveling, dropping or minimizing part of the message; assimilating, altering the message to fit individual or group attitudes, beliefs, and expectations; and sharpening, making some parts of the message more important than originally intended.

These distortions in serial transmission are brought about in part by perceptual differences among people, differences influenced by role and status. A manager may view a change in work hours as much less important than do the subordinates, who believe that no one was concerned about them when making the decision. The manager sees the change as necessary to accommodate a new schedule, whereas the workers are convinced the company never takes them into consideration. These perceptual differences affect the amount of attention given to the message and the interpretation of its meaning. They also influence the ability of the manager and members of the group to transmit the message to others. In addition to role, status, experience, values, and personal style, numerous other influences contribute to perception and how individuals knowingly or unknowingly distort organizational messages.

Finally, the very language of the message is subject to distortion. Definitions of terms and concepts vary throughout the organization. An excellent example of this phenomenon occurred in a small East Coast manufacturing company involved in introducing computer-assisted manufacturing processes. The president of the company announced the "entry of Cooper Manufacturing into the information age."

Training classes were scheduled for all personnel working in areas where the new systems were being installed. Instead of the expected positive response, management was amazed when the director of personnel reported employee concern that the training programs were designed for people to fail and were really a way to push them out of jobs.

## The Functional Approach: Summary of Essential Characteristics

The Functional approach helps us understand organizational communication by describing message function and structure. Based on a view of organizations as complex communication systems, the Functional approach identifies organizing, relationship, and change functions for messages and describes message structure as the movement of messages through formal and informal networks. Network members use diverse channels that transmit messages in lateral, vertical, and less structured directions. The load of these messages on the networks is the capacity measure of the organizational communication system. Finally, the Functional approach suggests that all messages are subject to numerous and predictable types of distortions, distortions that affect both message movement and meaning.

Can you now answer the questions asked at the beginning of the chapter? Could you use the Functional approach to help advise Bill Drake about Coronado Manufacturing? More important, can you describe your school as an organizational communication system? The case that follows gives you an opportunity to describe an organizational communication system from a Functional perspective and to suggest improvements by using the concepts of the Functional approach.

■ ■ ■ ■ ■ ▬▬▬▬▬▬▬▬▬▬▬▬▬▬▬▬▬▬▬▬▬▬▬▬▬▬▬▬▬▬▬▬▬▬▬▬▬▬▬▬▬

## THE UNITED CONCEPTS ADVERTISING AGENCY DILEMMA CASE

Jane Peters was having the best morning of her career. Since coming to United Concepts Advertising as an account executive, she had been successful in acquiring new business, but nothing as big as the Raven Furniture account. Raven was the largest chain of furniture stores in the West, and landing the account meant something not only in the West Coast offices of United Concepts but in Chicago and New York as well.

Jane knew that her creative team, John and Chris, was largely responsible. The close working relationship among the three was the best Jane had experienced in her fifteen years in the advertising industry. In fact, Jane began to think of ways to make John and Chris more visible to her boss, Frank Donnell. After all, Frank was pleased that the agency got the Raven account. Perhaps he could be persuaded to promote John and Chris to senior creative positions.

*(continued)*

**THREE WEEKS LATER**

Jane was exhausted. Getting the Raven account up and going was not only requiring long hours but was also complicated by the resistance of some of the top management at Raven. She had never imagined there would be resistance at Raven to changing agencies and considerable disagreement about the United Concepts proposal. In fact, dealing with the various people at Raven was taking too much time. Her other accounts were not getting the service they needed, and Chris had just made a major error in the Raven ad scheduled to run this weekend. Jane caught the mistake as it was about to go to the printer. Although it was costly to adjust the error at that point, she was relieved but shaken at how close they had come to a major problem. Jane considered approaching Frank Donnell for more help on the account.

**ONE WEEK LATER**

The creative meeting wasn't working. John and Chris were angry with each other and could not agree on an approach for Raven's Christmas promotion. They complained that Jane was too busy to work with them the way she used to and blamed her for rushing the creative process. Jane was sympathetic but told John and Chris that they did not understand her current pressure. The meeting ended with the first real tension the group had experienced. Jane went to see Frank Donnell and asked for help, additional people and promotions to recognize the real efforts of John and Chris.

**TWO WEEKS LATER**

Jane was angry as she read her memo from Frank Donnell. Yes, her request for one additional staff person would be honored, but no promotions for Chris and John. Company policy prohibited the creation of additional senior creative positions in the West Coast office. Jane began to draft an angry response. Raven people were just beginning to appreciate their work. How was she going to continue to motivate Chris and John? Would they resent the new person? Was the Raven account worth all this trouble?

1. Describe the United Concepts Agency as a communication system.
2. What are the communication inputs, throughputs, and outputs?
3. Can you find examples of organizing, relationship, and change communication?
4. Describe Jane's communication links or networks.
5. Are communication channels and direction of message flow appropriate?
6. What about communication load?
7. How would you advise Jane? What would you tell Chris and John? What would you tell Frank Donnell?

# THE MEANING-CENTERED APPROACH

The second major approach for understanding organizational communication is the **Meaning-Centered approach.** This approach asks what communication is, not how and why it works. The Meaning-Centered perspective is concerned with how organizational reality is generated through human interaction. As such, message purposes (functions) and message movement (structure) are secondary to understanding communication as the construction of shared realities (human interac-

**Meaning-Centered approach**
Way of understanding organizational communication by discovering how organizational reality is generated through human interaction. The approach describes organizational communication as the process for generating shared realities that become organizing, decision making, sense making, influence, and culture.

tion). Specifically, the Meaning-Centered approach describes organizational communication as the process for generating shared realities that become organizing, decision making, sense making, influence, and culture. Figure 3.3 summarizes key assumptions of the Meaning-Centered perspective.

Think back to Coronado Manufacturing. Proponents of the Meaning-Centered approach would have Bill Drake ask questions about which human interactions contributed to the shift away from the company's quality culture. They would encourage him to discover why his perception of the values of the company seem not to be shared in either manufacturing or sales. They would advise him to understand his present problem by reviewing Coronado's organizing and decision-making activities.

## Communication as Organizing and Decision Making

**Organizing**
Bringing order out of chaos with organizations as the products of the organizing process; described as almost synonymous with the communication process.

### Organizing

In Chapter 2 we described **organizing** as bringing order out of chaos and organizations as the products of the organizing process. The Meaning-Centered approach to organizational communication describes communicating and organizing as almost synonymous processes. Decision making, or the process of choice from

---

**FIGURE 3.3    Key Assumptions of the Meaning-Centered Approach**

1. All ongoing human interaction is communication in one form or another.
2. Organizations exist through human interaction; structures and technologies result from the information to which individuals react.
3. Shared organizational realities reflect the collective interpretations by organizational members of all organizational activities.
4. Organizing and decision making are essentially communication phenomena.
5. Sensemaking combines action and interpretation.
6. Identification, socialization, communication rules, and power all are communication processes that reflect how organizational influence occurs.
7. Organizing, decision making, and influence processes describe the cultures of organizations by describing how organizations do things and how they talk about how they do things.
8. Organizational cultures and subcultures reflect the shared realities in the organization and how these realities create and shape organizational events.
9. Communication climate is the subjective, evaluative reaction of organization members to the organization's communication events, their reaction to organizational culture.

among uncertain alternatives, also is viewed as essentially a communication phenomenon and part of the organizing process.

What do we mean when we say that communicating, organizing, and decision making are essentially similar processes? Karl Weick, in his important book *The Social Psychology of Organizing* (1979), provides helpful insight for answering our questions. Weick proposes that organizations as such do not exist, but rather are in the process of existing through ongoing human interaction. In other words, there is no such thing as an organization; there is only the ongoing interaction among human activities, interaction that continually creates and shapes events. As previously discussed, all ongoing human interaction is communication in one form or another.

The Weick perspective suggests that Coronado Manufacturing can be better understood as fifty years in the process of evolution rather than as an organization that was founded and structured fifty years ago. Bill Drake's father and uncle initiated the ongoing process, and Drake is part of the continuing stream of interactions. Put another way, the Weick model contends that organizations do not exist apart from the human interactions of members. As Weick has described, communication is "the substance of organizing."

Weick focuses on the organizational environment as the communication links and messages that are the basis of human interaction. He is not as concerned with the physical or technical structure of organizations as he is with the information to which individuals react. Weick contends that human reactions "enact" organizational environments through information exchanges and the active creation of meanings. This creation or enactment of organizational environments differs among individuals, resulting in multiple and diverse meanings and interpretations. Weick explains that organizational members use rules and communication cycles to continually process what he calls "equivocal" messages or messages susceptible to varying interpretations. Organizational rules are the relatively stable procedures or known processes that guide organizational behavior. In Coronado's case, the processing of a sales request has some fairly specific procedures for internal communication response. These rules (procedures) can be used as guidance for most inquiries. The defects problem is not as well defined. Communication cycles—conversations among those involved with the problem—become important to reduce the equivocality of the Coronado problem. Weick describes the use of rules and communication cycles as "selection" processes or the use of selected information to reduce uncertainty. Selected rules and communication cycles, however, will vary in their effectiveness for actually reducing equivocality. When the selection process is effective, Weick proposes individuals engage in "retention" to literally save rules and cycles for future guidance. Weick describes this retained information as causal maps used to make sense of future equivocality. Weick concludes the main goal of the process of organizing is an attempt to reduce equivocality—ambiguity—in order to predict future responses to organizational behaviors.

Supervisors reduce equivocality for their subordinates by the organizing of work assignments and the communication of task requirements. The supervisor gives a subordinate an assignment (desired action); the subordinate attempts the assignment (response); the supervisor evaluates the assignment (feedback). This interaction reduces equivocality for both the supervisor and subordinate. The supervisor understands what the subordinate believed the assignment to be by evaluating what was accomplished. The feedback to the subordinate (often in the form of rewards or punishment) reduces uncertainty about the adequacy of the performance. This cycle—repeated at all organizational levels—is the organizing process. As Phillip Tompkins and George Cheney (1983b) have pointed out, "This double interact of control—directing, monitoring, and reward/punishing—simultaneously provides us with the basic act of organizing and demonstrates why communicating and organizing are nearly synonymous."

Bill Drake is processing equivocal messages. He is attempting to determine if the consultant's report is accurate. He is more concerned with the effect of quality defects than specific technical problems. Even if assembly-line improvements are needed, it is through human communication that problems will be identified and solved. Drake does not understand how the company values of quality and customer service have changed. He is uncomfortable with the equivocality (ambiguity) of his interactions with sales and manufacturing management. He needs to figure out what his alternatives are and what to do next.

## Decision Making

segment type="">**Decision making**
Process of choosing from among numerous alternatives; the part of the organizing process necessary for directing behaviors and resources toward organizational goals.

The process of choosing from among numerous alternatives (decision making) is the organizing process of directing behaviors and resources toward organizational goals. Decision making, as with other organizing efforts, is accomplished primarily through communication. **Decision making** is the process in which Bill Drake and his staff must engage.

A practical example helps to illustrate decision making as an organizing process. When you work with a group of students on a major class project, one of your goals may be a high grade from your instructor. There are numerous ways to approach this goal. Choosing from among these alternatives (decision making) is the first step toward assigning individual responsibilities within the project and deciding what resources the group will need (organizing). This choosing or decision making results from the communication interactions of the group. The quality of the group's decisions will influence the quality of the project and whether the group reaches its goals.

What influences the way this decision making occurs? Each member of the group brings different experiences, abilities, and expectations to the group. Each member is operating with a set of premises or propositions about what he or she believes to be true. Decision making is the attempt to merge these individual premises into more general ones (shared realities) that most members of the group can accept.

Think for a moment about a group of students working on an assignment. One student may be operating from the premise that group projects are not worth much time and effort. Others may believe that the project is important for the course grade and needs careful planning and attention. Another may believe that his or her idea for the topic is superior. These premises (propositions about what is true) influence individual behavior and the types of alternatives the group will consider. Also, some members may identify (experience a sense of "we") with the efforts of the group, whereas others may feel no sense of belonging or commitment. Those individuals who identify with each other are more likely to attempt a decision that most members of the group believe is appropriate than are those members who identify elsewhere.

Organizational decision making is the process that sets in motion much of the "doing" of the organization. Decision making reduces message equivocality by choosing from among numerous alternatives. These choosing activities occur through human communication.

## Communication as Influence

**Influence**
Organizational and individual attempts to persuade; frequently seen in organizational identification, socialization, communication rules, and power.

The Meaning-Centered approach proposes that **influence** is a necessary process for creating and changing organizational events. In other words, this approach considers who and what are viewed as influential, the way people seek to influence others, and how people respond to influence all contribute to organizing and decision making. Questions about the influence process in organizations focus on how individuals identify with their organizations, how organizations attempt to socialize members, how communication rules emerge to direct behavior, and how power is used. Identification, socialization, communication rules, and power all are essentially communication processes that help us understand how organizational influence occurs. From the Meaning-Centered perspective, the influence process is fundamental to the development of shared organizational realities and ultimately to creating and shaping organizational events. Indeed, it is fair to say that from a Meaning-Centered approach organizational communication is the process through which organizational influence takes place.

## Identification

**Identity**
Relatively stable characteristics, including core beliefs, values, attitudes, preferences, decisional premises, and more that make up the self.

We all come to organizational experiences with a sense of self or our personal **identity** or identities. Our identity can be described as relatively stable characteristics that include our core beliefs, values, attitudes, preferences, and decisional premises. Craig Scott, Steven Corman, and George Cheney (1998) explain **identification:** "Each identity references certain norms and other ideas about who we are, how we are to act, and what is important to us. An identity makes further sense in terms of defining who we are and who we are not on the basis of social memberships. . . . Identification is the process of emerging identity. Identification, especially as expressed in symbolic terms, represents the forging, maintenance, and alteration of linkages between persons and groups. . . . Identification represents the dynamic social process by which identities are constructed, through which they guide us, and by which they order our world."

**Identification**
Dynamic social process by which identities are constructed; includes perceptions of a sense of belonging. Usually associated with the belief that individual and organizational goals are compatible.

We are more likely to be receptive to influence attempts in organizations with which we identify or have a sense of "we" or belonging. Identification or the lack of it results from the identity or identities we bring to our organizational experiences and from a variety of organizational relationships (supervisors, peers, subordinates). As such, identification can be understood as an active process to which both individuals and organizations contribute. Tompkins and Cheney (1983b) have described organizational identification as part of the unobtrusive control processes of organizations. According to Cheney (1983): "Identifications are important for what they do for us: they aid us in making sense of our experience, in organizing our thoughts, in achieving decisions, and in anchoring the self. Perhaps most important for students of communication, identifying allows people to persuade and to be persuaded."

Most organizations encourage members to identify with the organization. Chances are that when you entered school you were encouraged to join various organizations, attend sporting functions, and oppose your school's most important rivals. Although most of these activities are enjoyable in and of themselves, they also develop a sense of "we" with the school. This sense of "we" means that our school's interests become our own and are influential in choices.

It is this relationship between identification and choices that illustrates the relationship that identification has to organizing and decision making. Tompkins and Cheney (1983b) describe this relationship: "A person identifies with a unit when, in making a decision, the person in one or more of his/her organizational roles perceives that unit's values or interests as relevant in evaluating the alternatives of choice."

It is likely that when people perceive the goals of an organization as compatible with their individual goals, they are identifying with the organization. The person who identifies is likely to accept the organization's decisional premises or reasoning. We can therefore say that the person who identifies is more likely to be positively influenced by the organization. A subordinate, for example, is more likely to be persuaded that a need for operating changes is favorable if the subordinate identifies with the organization and his or her supervisor. On the other hand, the subordinate who does not identify with the organization may view the same decision with resistance and suspicion. As organizations are faced with increasing challenges to change, the issue of identification as influence takes on particular importance. Specifically, all organizational members must be concerned not only with the positive aspects of identification but also with the potential limitations of identification if influential relationships contribute to a suspension of critical thinking. Practically speaking, we can all see how identification works by looking at our personal and organizational lives. The chances are that we are more likely to be influenced by individuals and groups with whom we feel a strong sense of "we" than by those with whom we feel no such relationship.

**Socialization**

Active organizational attempts to help members learn appropriate behaviors, norms, and values.

## Socialization

Closely associated with identification is the influence process of **socialization,** or active organizational attempts to help members learn appropriate behaviors, norms, and values. The socialization process attempts to help new members understand how their interests overlap with those of the organization. Gerald Pepper (1995) describes socialization as involving "the formal and informal practices of bringing new members into a group and the efforts of the newcomer to make sense of the experience." Socialization efforts provide job or task information, describe how the individual's position fits in the hierarchy of the organization, and establish social or interpersonal relationships within the organization.

Socialization efforts frequently are categorized in phases or stages. Raymond Falcione and Charmaine Wilson (1988), in reviewing recent research on socialization and the work of Frederick Jablin in particular, describe stages or phases of socialization, namely, **anticipatory socialization, encounter socialization,** and **metamorphosis socialization.** Anticipatory socialization begins before individuals enter organizations and results from past work experiences and interactions with family, friends, and institutions such as schools, churches, or social organizations. Anticipatory socialization is shaped by pre-entry information about the organization and the anticipated work role. Anticipatory socialization is the readiness an individual brings to the "reality shock" of organizational entry. Anticipatory socialization also includes what individuals learn about particular organizations prior to entry. The employment interview is an important example. Organizational representatives conducting interviews provide important socialization information while assessing the potential fit of the candidate to the organization. In addition, interviews are important opportunities for individuals to determine whether their expectations match their perceptions of the expectations of the organization.

**Anticipatory socialization**
Pre-entry information about the organization and the anticipated work role.

**Encounter socialization**
Early organizational experiences reducing uncertainty about all aspects of organizational life.

**Metamorphosis socialization**
Initial mastery of basic skills and information and adjustments to organizational life.

The encounter stage for socialization involves new employee training, supervisor coaching, peer groups, and formal organizational documents. Newcomers learn tasks, develop relationships, and reduce uncertainty about most aspects of organizational life. Finally, the metamorphosis phase of socialization occurs when the newcomer begins to master basic organizational requirements and adjusts to the organization. The phases, however, should be considered only general descriptions of the socialization process with full realization that differences in individuals and influence attempts generate very different socialization experiences.

Meryl Reis Louis (1980) offers a somewhat different model of the newcomer experience. Louis argues that newcomers initially experience change, contrast, and surprise during organizational entry. Louis describes "change" as the differences between past experiences and the current new environment. Based on past experiences, individuals identify what is uncertain in the new environment. Louis contends that difficulty of adjustment is related to similarities or differences with the old or other past experiences. In other words, if the new environment is completely different from other past experiences, Louis would predict more difficulty because of more uncertainty and the need for more learning. Louis's concept of "contrast" is more individually based. Contrast is the perception by an individual of differences between old and new ways and the assignment of importance to these perceptions. Perceptions of contrast assist the individual in selecting what he or she believes are important differences needing attention and adjustment. Finally, surprise is described as any difference between an individual's anticipations about a new setting and subsequent experiences in the new setting. Surprise can be positive or negative, with individuals continually trying to "make sense" of the surprises they encounter. Think for a moment about your newcomer days in your school. Try to describe your experiences in terms of anticipatory socialization, encounter socialization, and metamorphosis socialization. Were there surprises? How did you make sense of them?

A broad range of potential strategies are available to organizations as they attempt to socialize newcomers. John Van Maanen and Edgar Schein (1979) have described six dimensions of socialization in terms of contrasts regarding socialization targets, processes, and values. The six dimensions are (1) collective versus individual, (2) formal versus informal, (3) sequential versus random, (4) fixed versus variable, (5) serial versus disjunctive, and (6) investiture versus divestiture. Collective socialization efforts put groups of newcomers through experiences as a group, whereas individual efforts focus on newcomers singly in isolation from others. Formal efforts occur when organizations provide special and defined experiences for newcomers, whereas informal efforts do not separate newcomers from longer-term organizational employees. Sequential socialization describes a series of discrete and identifiable steps in the socialization process. Random socialization is not specifically defined and is ambiguous and continually changing. Fixed socialization refers to efforts with a precise and known timetable. Variable socialization has a process, but the timing of events is unknown. Serial socialization is described as a process with experienced organizational members serving as role models. Disjunctive socialization provides no role models for newcomers. Finally, investiture socialization refers to processes in which personal characteristics of newcomers are valued. Divestiture socialization attempts to strip newcomers of personal characteristics.

Fred Jablin (2001), in a comprehensive review of socialization research, challenges the Van Maanen and Schein descriptions as focusing too completely on one-way organizational attempts at socialization without evaluating the importance of two-way interactions during individuals' entry and assimilation into the organization. Jablin goes on to discuss important interaction processes occurring during training, formal mentoring, and informal mentoring and as individuals engage in information seeking.

Jablin, referring to his earlier work with Vernon Miller, describes specific tactics newcomers use: *overt questions,* or asking for information in a direct manner; *indirect questions,* or getting others to give information by hinting and use of noninterrogative questions; *third-party questions,* or asking someone else rather than the primary information target; *disguising conversations,* or the use of jokes, verbal prompts, and self-disclosure to ease information without the other person's awareness; *observing,* or watching another's actions to model behavior or discern meanings associated with events; and *surveillance,* or indiscriminately monitoring conversations and activities to which meaning can be attributed retrospectively. Based on numerous research studies, Jablin (2001, 770–71) suggests the following tentative conclusions:

1. As newcomers' perceptions of the social costs of seeking information increase, their use of overt/direct information seeking decreases and their use of covert tactics increases.
2. The most frequent kinds of information sought by newcomers concern referent/task/technical issues, and they tend to seek such information through overt/direct information seeking.
3. In general, the most frequent information-seeking tactics used by newcomers are overt/direct and observing, with some studies reporting over/direct as the most frequent approach and other studies reporting monitoring.
4. Supervisors and coworkers are the most common targets of newcomers' information seeking.
5. When seeking relational/social information, newcomers most frequently employ observation and monitoring, whereas when seeking appraisal information, they most often use overt and monitoring tactics.
6. The frequency and use by newcomers of particular information-seeking behaviors are associated with outcomes such as role ambiguity, role conflict, task mastery, role orientation, organizational commitment, job involvement, intent to leave, performance, and job satisfaction.
7. Newcomers' perceptions of target social support, levels of self-esteem, tolerance for ambiguity, value of feedback, and organizational domain/field of study are related to their information-seeking behavior.
8. Newcomers' information-seeking behaviors vary with their experience of institutional, as compared with individualized, organizational socialization.

Pepper (1995) describes socialization attempts as strategic organizational efforts to reproduce or perpetuate culture. Supporting this position is the work of Mary Helen Brown (1985). She found that organizational stories were an important part of the process and that as members were more socialized into the organization, story use became more associated with organizational values and cultures. In other words, the more individuals were exposed to organizational socialization attempts and the more they identified with the organization, the more likely they were to tell stories supporting overall organizational values.

Generally speaking, during socialization processes individuals are learning what Louis (1980) has described as role-related information and organizational culture information. Presumably, as with the identification process, the greater the degree of socialization, the more likely individuals will respond favorably to organizational persuasion. In fact, little doubt remains that socialization is related to organizational commitment, decision making, perceptions of communications climate, and overall job satisfaction.

## Communication Rules

**Communication rules** are general prescriptions about appropriate communication behaviors in particular settings. Rules operate to influence behavior, are spe-

**Communication rules**
General prescriptions about appropriate communication behaviors in particular settings. Thematic rules are general prescriptions of behavior reflecting the values and beliefs of the organization, whereas tactical rules prescribe specific behaviors as related to more general themes.

cific enough to be followed, and occur in particular contexts. In other words, communication rules are informal norms about what type of communication is desirable in a particular organization. Rules tell us, for example, whether disagreement is encouraged or discouraged, how we are expected to contribute our ideas, and whether we should ask for a raise or never mention the subject of salary in a particular situation. Rules aid in socialization and are therefore likely to be used by those high in organizational identification, those who want to exhibit a sense of "we" with the organization. Generally, rules are learned through informal communication such as organizational stories, rituals, and myths.

Communication rules are of two general types, thematic and tactical. Thematic rules are general prescriptions of behavior reflecting the values and beliefs of the organization. Tactical rules prescribe specific behaviors as related to more general themes. Several tactical rules may evolve from one general thematic rule. A major Midwest computer company has a strong thematic rule of "Communicate your commitment to the company." Several tactical rules have developed that relate to that theme, such as "Come in on Saturday to finish up, but make sure you tell someone," "Complain about how tough the challenge really is," and "Use the term *family* to refer to the company." These examples illustrate the contextual nature of thematic and tactical rules. Although the preceding statements are not only acceptable but also desirable in one particular company, they make little or no sense outside that context. Compliance with thematic and tactical rules indicates that an individual has received socializing information and identifies, at least to some extent, with the organization.

Maryan Schall (1983) suggests that communication rules help us understand the shared realities and values that influence organizational expectations. Donald Cushman, Sarah King, and Ted Smith (1988) have characterized her view as a contingency-rules perspective that permits various subcultures based on rule sets and images both similar to and divergent from the formal culture espoused by management. Marshall Scott Poole and Robert McPhee (1983) and

**Structuration**
Production and reproduction of social systems via the application of generative rules and resources in interaction.

Poole, David Seibold, and McPhee (1985) add the dimension of **structuration** when they contend that structurational rules theory provides a dynamic view of communication rules where diverse rule sets emerge through complex formal and informal interactions. Structurational theory further proposes that rules not only influence behavior but are influenced by members' conceptions of appropriate behaviors. Poole and McPhee (1983) explain:

Structuration refers to the production and reproduction of social systems via the application of generative rules and resources in interaction. For example, the status hierarchy in a work group is an observable system. The structure underlying this system consists of rules, such as norms about who takes problems to the boss, and resources, such as a special friendship with the boss or seniority. The status system exists because of the constant process of structuration in which rules and resources are both the medium and outcome of interaction. Members use rules and resources to maintain their places or to attempt to rise in the hierarchy; the structure of rules and resources thus produces the status system. (p. 210)

We will expand our understanding of communication rules when we discuss communication as culture.

## Power

**Power**
Attempts to influence another person's behavior to produce desired outcomes. The process occurs through communication and is related to resources, dependencies, and alternatives.

An additional communication dynamic that influences behavior is the use of power. In its most general sense, **power** has been defined as an attempt to influence another person's behavior to produce desired outcomes. As such, power is a neutral term subject to positive use as well as abuse. The power process occurs through communication and is related to resources, dependencies, and alternatives.

A resource is something owned or controlled by an individual, group, or entire organization. Resources are materials, information, knowledge, money, and a variety of other possible assets. Either owning or controlling resources allows individuals or organizations to influence interactions with others. A manager may control budget allocations within a department. Individual department members control important technical information not known to the manager. Both are resources influential in interactions between the manager and subordinates. Resources are closely linked to alternatives: A resource is more valuable if few alternatives to the use of the resource are available. Generally speaking, the individual controlling scarce resources is in a more influential (higher-power) position than the individual who controls resources with ample alternatives.

Although it is an outmoded notion, many believe power is a fixed commodity rather than a process of human interaction. In other words, many individuals behave as if the more power they have, the less is left for others. In reality, power is not a commodity but an influence process that permits all involved to gain more power, lose power, or share power. Therefore, when influence attempts result in abuse, evidence suggests that we will seek other alternatives and lessen our dependency on the power abuser. Communication between supervisors and subordinates can illustrate this phenomenon. Supervisors and subordinates both have resources. The supervisor has the formal authority established by the chain of command. The supervisor controls information flow and performance evaluation. Subordinates control technical performance and have vital firsthand information about the progress of work. Both are dependent on each other; the supervisor directs, but without compliance and performance, no work is accomplished. If the supervisor becomes abusive in directing the work, a subordinate group may seek other alternatives by withdrawing from interaction with the supervisor or withholding information the supervisor needs to make good decisions. At an extreme the subordinate group may complain to others in management, transfer to other departments, or leave the organization. Power is one of the central issues we will discuss in the Emerging Perspectives section of this chapter.

**Culture**
Unique sense of the place that organizations generate through ways of doing and ways of communicating about the organization; reflects the shared realities and shared practices in the organization and how they create and shape organizational events.

# Communication as Culture

Organizing, decision making, and influence processes, when taken together, help us describe the **culture** of organizations by describing how organizations do things and how they talk about how they do things. Put another way, organizational culture is the unique sense of the place that organizations generate through ways of doing and ways of communicating about the organization. Organizational culture reflects the shared realities and shared practices in the organization and how these realities create and shape organizational events. Organizational culture is the unique symbolic common ground that becomes the self-definitions or self-images of the organization.

Metaphors help us understand the differences between the Functional and Meaning-Centered approaches to organizational cultures. Metaphors are ways of describing the likeness of one concept or person to another concept or person by speaking of the first as if it were the second. We say "She is the life of the party" or "He is the salt of the earth." Managers are referred to as quarterbacks, coaches, or lions in battle, with organizational decisions described as game or battle plans. These metaphors give us underlying assumptions for understanding behavior or concepts based on our knowledge of what we say something is like. We use our knowledge of what quarterbacks do, for example, to understand what managers do (a common metaphor supporting a bias toward male managers). We use the metaphor of a string quartet to explain excellence in teamwork based on the varying talents of individual contributors. Organization-wide metaphors used for the Functional and Meaning-Centered approaches work in much the same way.

When we described the Functional approach to organizational communication we talked about communication systems with inputs, throughput, and outputs. We described subsystems, suprasystems, and boundaries to external environments. We were using the organic metaphor of the dynamic system taken from the study of biology for conceptualizing or understanding organizational communication. The systems metaphor gave a distinct and descriptive set of assumptions about the way organizational communication works. Culture, in the systems metaphor, is one of many organizational variables.

The Meaning-Centered and Functional approaches differ in the metaphors used to understand organizational communication. The systems metaphor of the Functional approach is replaced in the Meaning-Centered perspective with the cultural metaphor. This culture metaphor describes communication as culture rather than describing culture and communication as separate entities. The culture metaphor promotes understanding communication as a process for generating shared realities and practices that in turn we call organizational culture.

When culture is used as a metaphor for organizational communication, we attempt to understand communication by understanding the uniqueness or shared realities in particular organizations. We explore how organizations use language, the symbols, jargon, and specialized vocabulary used by people working together.

We examine behaviors exhibited in rituals and rites of organizational life and listen for the general standards or values of the organization as described in stories, legends, and reminiscences. We focus on how communication activities generate uniqueness or symbolic common ground. There is a danger, however, in oversimplifying culture as a single set of commonly held values, beliefs, actions, practices, rules, and dialogues mutually supported by all organizational members. In reality, organizations commonly reflect subcultural consensus and even lack of consensus about values, beliefs, actions, practices, rules, and dialogues. Embedded in this notion of culture as a metaphor for organizational communication is a view of organizations as dynamic, continually changing, and meaning-producing bodies.

Eric Eisenberg and Patricia Riley (2001) suggest, "a communicative view of organizational culture sees communication as constitutive of culture. The process that we wish to label organizational culture consists solely of patterns of human action and its recursive behaviors (including talk and its symbolic residues) and meaning." As Charles Conrad (1994) describes,

> Cultures are communicative creations. They emerge through communication, are maintained through communication, and change through the communicative acts of their members. Simultaneously, communication is a cultural creation. Persons' perceptions of the cultures in which they live (both their overall culture and their organizational cultures) form the situations that guide and constrain their communication. (p. 31)

Members of organizations working together communicate to create the activity and practice of the organization and to interpret the meaning of that activity and practice. Observing who is involved in important decisions, how influence takes place, and how people treat each other helps in understanding the "uniqueness" of an organization. Words, actions, artifacts, routine practices, and texts are the regular communication interactions among organizational members that generate uniqueness or culture(s). Communication provides organizational members with similar experiences and realities (if not similar levels of agreement and values about experiences and realities). In this dynamic view of culture as communication, these realities are constantly subject to change as organizational members react to new information and circumstances.

Michael Pacanowsky and Nick O'Donnell-Trujillo (1983) contend that rituals are an important cultural performance contributing to shared reality. Whether personal, task, social, or organizational, rituals help define what is important or the values of the culture and provide a communication process to transmit those values. Awards ceremonies, Friday afternoon get-togethers, graduation, and numerous daily routines are all rituals that both provide regularity and signify importance in organizational life.

Organizational storytelling is described as a way to infuse passion or interest into everyday activities. Stories generate a sense of history about organizational existence and identify values through descriptions of success and failure. In the Coronado case, stories about the founders transmitted important information about the Coronado values of quality and customers. The Meaning-Centered approach suggests that Coronado's manufacturing problem partly can be described in terms of a shift in culture or values.

Disagreement exists about the importance of shared values and attitudes as reflective of organizational culture. Eric Eisenberg and H. L. Goodall (1993), for example, contend

> practices are primary in defining organizational culture—what people do, where they do it, whether they are rewarded or punished for doing it. Attitudes and values sometimes follow from practices, but even if they don't, most cultures show considerably more alignment in practice than they do in the attitudes, opinions, or beliefs of individual members. (p. 52)

Work that Don Morley and I have conducted (Morley and Shockley-Zalabak, 1991; Morley, Shockley-Zalabak, and Cesaria, 1997; Shockley-Zalabak and Morley, 1989, 1994) supports the practice perspective but places more emphasis on values as related to rules and behaviors. Specifically, Morley and I have examined relationships among organizational founders' values, individual organizational member values, organizational communication rules (rules are discussed earlier in this chapter), organizational communication activities, and perceptions of organizational outcomes. Our work was based on the argument that a communication rule-based approach is particularly appropriate for the study of shared realities and the values that influence organizational practices and expectations. We found that management and employee values and perceptions of communication rules are related over time. Management values were directly related to employee values, and management values directly influenced employee perceptions of communication rules. Employee values indirectly influenced management communication rule perceptions. Over time, management and employee values both contributed to the emergence of new communication rules about expected organizational behaviors and practices. Knowing the rules was related to organizational and work satisfaction, levels of communication participation, and predictions of the overall effectiveness of organizations. Those less in agreement with and less aware of the rules indicated less communication participation and less work satisfaction and exhibited less optimism about overall organizational effectiveness. Differing rule sets were evidenced in various functional areas of organizations, indicating the presence of subcultures. Over time, rules emerged and died, supporting previous conceptualizations of culture as dynamic and changing. This work and the work of many others establishes the communication-as-culture view as central to understanding or interpreting our organizational lives.

Bill Drake is faced with understanding the communication interactions that have contributed to a change at Coronado in what is considered quality. Stories about his father and uncle have not been sufficient to maintain the earlier focus on customers. Bill Drake needs to understand what the new unique sense of Coronado really is. Can you suggest ways he might find out? How can his perception of the values of Coronado be different from that of others in the company? What should Drake do to determine what the culture of Coronado Manufacturing really is?

**Communication climate**

Reaction to the organization's culture; consists of collective beliefs, expectations, and values regarding communication that are generated as organizational members continually evaluate their interactions with others.

# Communication Climate

The culture of an organization describes the unique sense of the place, its practices, and how that organization describes itself. The reaction to an organization's culture is the organization's **communication climate.** Marshall Poole (1985) suggests that a communication climate consists of "collective beliefs, expectations, and values regarding communication," which are generated as a result of organizational members continually evaluating their interactions with others.

We are used to thinking of climate in geographic terms. We think about temperature, humidity, winds, and rainfall and react somewhat subjectively to what we believe is a desirable climate. So it is with a climate for communication. The climate is a subjective reaction to organization members' perception of communication events. The subjective reaction is shared to a great extent either by individual groups or the entire organization.

Redding (1972) proposed that the collective beliefs that become the communication climate are associated with five communication factors: supportiveness; participative decision making; trust, confidence, credibility; openness and candor; and high performance goals. In other words, the more supportive the communication environment—the more people participate in decision making, have trust and confidence in their coworkers, can be open, and understand organizational goals—the more likely there will be positive collective attitudes about the communication climate. Underlying this notion is the assumption that the more positive the climate, the greater the satisfaction of individual employees.

Research has related communication climate to morale, job satisfaction, perceptions of organizational effectiveness, and actual organizational effectiveness. Critics of this research, however, suggest that the subjective nature of climate makes it a difficult concept to relate definitively to organizational outcomes.

Think for a moment about the culture of your school. By now you probably have learned the ropes and know how things are supposed to work. You know who holds power, what some of the rituals are, and how socializing generally takes place. You can describe the unique sense of the place to others, but your description does not necessarily tell whether you think it is a good place. Your attitude—climate evaluation—is your reaction to the culture, not a description of the culture itself.

Identify the organizations of which you are a member. How would you describe their climate? How does a positive view of climate influence your behavior? What are the differences when your view is negative?

## The Meaning-Centered Approach: Summary of Essential Characteristics

The Meaning-Centered approach to organizational communication understands communication as a complex process that creates and shapes organizational events. As such, communication is organizing, decision making, influence, and culture. Organizing is viewed as an ongoing process of human interactions attempting to reduce message equivocality. Decision making is part of organizing and is the process responsible for moving individuals and resources toward accomplishment of organizational goals. Influence is the process in which individuals and organizations engage to generate desired behaviors and is therefore closely related to organizing and decision making. Culture, as a metaphor for organizational communication, is the unique sense of a place that reflects the way things are done and how people talk about the way things are done. Finally, communication climate is the subjective reaction to the communication events that contribute to uniqueness or culture. The Meaning-Centered approach makes only limited distinctions among organizing, decision making, influence, and culture. All are seen as processes of communication, and all help us understand how organizations create and shape events through human interaction.

Now return to the beginning of the chapter. Can you answer each of the questions about the Meaning-Centered approach? How does it differ from the Functional approach? What are the similarities? Earlier you described the communication system of your school. Now describe the culture of your school. Are there particular stories or rituals that come to mind? What are the communication rules? The following case gives you an opportunity to apply the Meaning-Centered approach to an organizational problem and to suggest improvements from the Meaning-Centered perspective.

■ ■ ■ ■ ■ ▬▬▬▬▬▬▬▬▬▬▬▬▬▬▬▬▬

## THE "NEWCOMERS AREN'T WELCOME HERE" CASE

Joe and Henry have worked for Temple Air Conditioning and Heating for over twenty years. Both men are competent workers who were hired by Temple's founder, Bernie Jones. In fact, Joe, Henry, and Bernie still have an occasional beer together on Friday nights after work. Bernie is always complaining that the good old days are over and that nobody should have so much paperwork to run a heating and air-conditioning business. Joe and Henry don't think things have really changed all that much except that the houses keep getting bigger and fancier. Joe and Henry have worked as a team for the last fifteen years without a supervisor. They are part of the reason Temple has a good reputation for quality work and fast service. Joe and Henry don't spend time with other installation teams and don't see any reason why they should.

### EARLY MONDAY MORNING

Bernie's announcement was a blow. He was bringing in a college-educated person to supervise the installation teams. Joe and Henry could hardly believe what they were hearing. They should have known something was up when Bernie called everyone together before the trucks went out one Monday morning.

> **Joe:**  Who does he think he is, bringing in some college guy—what do we need another guy for?
>
> **Henry:**  Yeah, Bernie is losing it. He knows how this place got built—off our backs. I am not going to work for anybody, let alone somebody with a fancy degree.

*(continued)*

**Joe:** I always looked up to Bernie—and I thought he felt the same way about us. Obviously we were wrong. After twenty years, to be wrong about a guy makes you feel stupid.

**Henry:** What do you think we should do?

**Joe:** How would I know?

**Henry:** Well, I'm not going to take this lying down. Are you with me?

**Joe:** Sure, we can make Temple fall apart.

1. How would you describe Temple's culture?
2. How would you describe the identification of Joe and Henry with Temple? Before the announcement? After the announcement?
3. What are Joe and Henry's communication rules? Are they the same as for the rest of the organization? Do we know?
4. Can you identify any shared realities for Joe and Henry?
5. What should Joe and Henry do?
6. Could Bernie have handled the announcement in a manner that would not have alienated Joe and Henry?
7. What do you think is going to happen?

## EMERGING PERSPECTIVES

Emerging Perspectives for organizational communication critique and challenge many of the basic assumptions and interpretations found in the Functional and Meaning-Centered approaches and provide important value propositions for our consideration. In the next section of this chapter, the concept of communication as a constitutive process is introduced and three approaches—postmodernism, critical theory, and feminist theory—are described as important perspectives for the study of organizational communication.

The rising interest in postmodernism, critical theory, and feminist theory can be understood when we consider the magnitude and rate of change in almost all aspects of our lives and the failure of more traditional approaches to guide our uncertainty. Organizations are increasing in size and complexity, with communications technologies changing even the most basic of organizational processes. Globalization both influences organizing processes and changes the very nature of work itself. Almost simultaneously we experience the influence of mass culture and the fact that fewer and fewer of us use similar information sources. In addition, our awareness of issues of diversity, difference, and marginalization grows. Put simply, this current time of turbulence and rapid change has given rise to a contemporary context where new questions and new challenges are important for understanding our organizational lives.

### Communication as Constitutive Process

Stanley Deetz (1992) helps us understand the concept of communication as **constitutive process** when he suggests: "Communication cannot be reduced to an infor-

**Constitutive process**
Communication seen as a process of meaning development and social production of perceptions, identities, social structures, and affective responses.

mational issue where meanings are assumed to be already existing, but must be seen as a process of meaning development and social production of perceptions, identities, social structures, and affective responses. The core issues in 'communication' research, rather than research on communication, center on process of open participation in perception and meaning construction rather than on effective processes of expression and influence" (p. 4). Deetz is suggesting that we move beyond Functional concerns for message production and transfer and the Meaning-Centered issues of "realities" and cultures to a fundamental view of communication that constitutes or brings about self and social environments. Communication is not synonymous with organizing, decision making, and influence but is better understood as the process that literally produces organizing, decision making, and influence. Deetz (1994) believes this constitutive view is fundamental because of four conditions:

1. Group and social structure role identities are no longer stable.
2. Multiculturalism is a reality and will not disappear.
3. Mediated experience will increasingly exceed direct sensory experience.
4. Social and political policies related to communication increasingly will have to consider the process of meaning construction rather than simply transmission and expression.

The value and ethical dimensions of his position are clear when Deetz (1994) states:

> Open participatory democracy supersedes all other goals of communication. From a communication perspective, efficiency, effectiveness, and information transfer cannot stand alone, but are interpreted within the promotion or demise of participation. Communication research thus is about the creation of more participatory communication practices and the critique and/or deconstruction of control processes. (p. 108)

This view of communication as constitutive process and the call for more participative communication processes can be seen in each of the three approaches to the study of organizational communication that follow. We begin with the postmodern perspective.

**Postmodernism**
Theoretical perspectives representing an alienation from the past, skepticism about authority structures, ambiguity of meanings, and mass culture.

# Postmodernism and Organizational Communication

The term **postmodernism** has been variously defined and hotly debated in fields as diverse as architecture, film, education, philosophy, sociology, and communication. Generally referring to perspectives that reject former notions of authority and power, stability of meanings, and concepts of effectiveness, postmodernism has become known as theoretical perspectives that represent an alienation from the past, skepticism about authority structures, ambiguity of meanings, and mass culture. Historical modernism is viewed as preceding postmodernity in time and experience, with postmodernism presenting challenges to the established traditions of modernism.

Modernist assumptions have been well summarized by Eisenberg and Goodall (1993):

1. Divisions of labor and hierarchy lead to increased efficiency.
2. Communication is instrumental to the accomplishment of tasks and goals; meanings should be consensual among workers.
3. Effectiveness can be measured and rewards linked to achievement; work and home are separate.
4. Meanings are in people giving importance to language as a symbolic system.

Eisenberg and Goodall (1993) describe the postmodern challenge to modernist assumptions:

1. Flattening of hierarchies contributes to greater flexibility and efficiency.
2. Communication is both instrumental and expressive; shared meanings are rare.
3. Group achievements and rewards are more viable than individual recognition, effectiveness is only partially measurable, and home and work are not separate concerns.
4. Ambiguity is pervasive, choice making is an illusion, and symbols are open to multiple interpretations.

Postmodern theorists reject the claims of the Functional and Meaning-Centered perspectives as overly simplistic and lacking in understanding of a world characterized by rapid change, multiple meanings, and pervasive ambiguity. The notion of grand master narratives (stories with broad application and explanatory power, i.e., principles of scientific management or prescriptions for strong cultures) are replaced by the micronarratives of individual organization members. Postmodern theorists look at individual behaviors without implying relationships to underlying values, assumptions, and rationales. In particular, postmodern organizational communication seeks to understand how multiple meanings and multiple interpretations of organizational events influence multiple and diverse behaviors.

**Deconstruction**
Refers to the examination of taken-for-granted assumptions, the examination of the myths we use to explain how things are the way they are, and the uncovering of the interests involved in socially constructed meanings.

**Deconstruction** is the method of postmodern analysis. Put simply, deconstruction refers to the examination of taken-for-granted assumptions, the examination of the myths we use to explain how things are the way they are, and the uncovering of the interests involved in socially constructed meanings. The value base of postmodern organizational communication rests with shared power, concepts of empowerment and interdependence, and multiple interpretations of everyday events.

Postmodern analysis challenges traditional notions of rationality and, as such, rejects many of the tenets of the Functional approach as well as the emphasis on shared realities in the Meaning-Centered perspective. As Dennis Mumby and Linda Putnam (1992) suggest:

> Although traditional epistemological thought construes rationality in terms of a set of principles that reflect an objective reality, postmodernists treat rationality as relative, or as a product of a given set of historically situated institutional practices. Proponents of poststructuralism, one of the many schools of postmodernism, focus on discourse and linguistic patterns as the institutional practices that shape rationality, construct power relationships, and enact member identities. (p. 467)

Although admittedly complex in its propositions and concepts, postmodern organizational communication analysis provides additional useful ways to ask questions about organizational communication.

## Critical Theory and Organizational Communication

**Critical theory**
Focuses attention to studies of power and abuses of power through communication and organization.

**Critical theory** focuses our attention to studying power and abuses of power through communication and organization. As Deetz (9001) explains:

> The central goal of critical theory in organizational communication studies has been to create a society and workplaces that are free from domination and where all members can contribute equally to produce systems that meet human needs and lead to the progressive development of all. (p. 26)

The critical theory approach depicts organizations as systems where power is hidden from ready observation and examination and is maintained through legitimate controls over employees. This notion of pervasive power that is not visible or overt and is generally accepted based on our myths of "how things came to be" is called **hegemony**. Hegemony is a process of control based on a dominant group leading others to believe that their subordination is normal or the norm. Hegemony implies to some (but not all) critical theorists that certain people in organizations are oppressed even when they do not recognize their experience as such. This perspective is in direct contradiction to both the Functional and Meaning-Centered approaches, which rely heavily on overt communication actions and practices.

**Hegemony**
Process of control based on a dominant group leading others to believe that their subordination is the norm.

For critical theorists, power and communication are closely intertwined. Power is exercised through communication and power influences communication rules and structures. Dennis Mumby (1987) has characterized organizational power controls as domination based on getting people to organize their behavior around particular rule systems. Legitimate control emerges through stories, myths, rituals, and a variety of other symbolic forms. These forms in turn become the rules that prescribe appropriate behavior. This "legitimate" yet hidden exercise of power can contribute to the suspension of critical thinking.

With roots in the work of Karl Marx, critical theory (sometimes referred to as critical interpretative perspectives) depicts organizations as political sites making increasingly important decisions about the public good. As Deetz (1994) explains:

> Public decision making in corporate sites is increasing and deserves much more of our attention. Corporations make most proactive decisions regarding use of public natural resources, product development, income distribution, the nature of work and leisure, technological development, working relations among people, and the contents of public knowledge. The state has increasingly been relegated to the creation of a stable environment for corporations and reactive policing and regulation. (p. 30)

Dennis Mumby (1993) concludes:

> One of the principal tenets of the critical studies approach is that organizations are not simply neutral sites of meaning formation; rather, they are produced and reproduced in the context of struggles between competing interest groups and systems of representation. Organizations are thus political in that the complex system of discursive and nondiscursive practices that make them up reflect the struggle to fix and institutionalize the dominance of certain groups and meaning structures over others. (p. 21)

As Deetz (2001) describes:

> While organizations could be positive social institutions providing forums for the articulation and resolution of important group conflicts over the use of natural resources, distribution of income, production of desirable goods and services, the development of personal qualities, and the direction of society, various forms of power and domination have led to skewed decision making and fostered social harms and significant waste and inefficiency. (p. 26)

Critical theory helps us ask questions about how we can change and reform organizational practices to better represent a variety of stakeholders with competing interests. Deetz (1994) describes both domination and codetermination as potential decision processes and makes the claim for reform based on codetermination. He writes:

> Whether we consider expression or constitutive practices, the decision practices can be relatively open and participatory or closed and exclusive. Habermas provided the most complete modern conception of this difference in his analysis of difference between strategic action aimed at control and communicative action aimed at reaching understanding. The open inclusionary practices will be called political codetermination directed by coordination and the closed exclusionary ones will be called political domination directed by control. (p. 99)

Distinctions between postmodern and critical approaches generally focus on differences in approach to organizational understandings. Specifically, postmodern approaches emphasize deconstruction and the unmasking of myths and assumptions to open the possibility of new understandings and new processes. Critical approaches, on the other hand, use value-laden ideological critique to demonstrate domination and to produce opposition. As Mats Alvesson and Stanley Deetz (1996) conclude:

> Both critical theory and postmodernism see their work as responses to specific social conditions. Contemporary society as a result of science, industrialization, and communication/information technologies has developed positive capacities but also dangerous forms of domination. Both critical theory and postmodernism describe Western development as one where a progressive, instrumental modernism gradually eclipsed traditional society with fairly clear payoffs but also great costs. They agree that something fundamental has gone awry and that more technical, instrumental "solutions" will not fix it. (pp. 194–95)

**Feminist theory**
Focuses on the marginalization and domination of women in the workplace and the valuing of women's voices in all organizational processes.

# Feminist Perspectives and Organizational Communication

**Feminist theory** focuses on the marginalization and domination of women in the workplace and the valuing of women's voices in all organizational processes. Although diverse in perspective and approaches, feminist theory generally attempts to move our society beyond patriarchal forms and social practices by critiquing power relationships that devalue women.

Judi Marshall (1993) describes male forms as the norms to which organizational members adapt. She proposes that the male principle can be characterized as self-assertion, separation, independence, control, competition, focused perception, rationality, analysis, clarity, discrimination, and activity. The female principle is described as interdependence, cooperation, receptivity, merging, acceptance, awareness of patterns, wholes, and synthesizing. Although males and females can access both types of values, evidence exists that females in organizations adapt to male norms while being evaluated against female stereotypes. Marshall concludes, "The male domination of cultures goes largely unrecognized in organizational life and in mainstream organizational theory." Marshall further discusses primary communication issues that she categorizes as communication of difference, risk, marginality, potential disruption, status, man-made language, exclusion from informal networks and communication, gender-differentiated discourse, and different patterns of thinking and valuing. She goes on to revision theories of organizational communication with an emphasis on integrating high forms of female and male values in communication within a framework that honors both with equality for difference rather than the equality of sameness that has been characteristic of the Functional and Meaning-Centered approaches.

Patrice Buzzanell (1994) describes feminist organizational communication theorizing as discussing "the moral commitment to investigate the subordinated, to focus on gendered interactions in ordinary lives, and to explore the standpoints of women who have been rendered invisible by their absence in theory and research." Buzzanell discusses how gender is socially constructed and enacted in organizations with messages, structures, and practices becoming the contexts for gender construction and negotiation. Organizational communication is therefore the focal process for this construction and negotiation.

Buzzanell examines three traditional themes in organizational writings—competitive individualism, cause-effect/linear thinking, and separation or autonomy—and contrasts them to feminist organizational communication theory. The ethic of competitive individualism creates organizational winners and losers based on competition and a need to excel over others. This competitive ethic typically casts women in the role of the "other," whereas stereotypical expectations and behaviors cast women as "losers." Buzzanell contrasts the competitive ethic with the cooperative enactment of organizations in which opportunities exist to understand how women translate the cooperative ethic into talk and behavior. She calls for understanding how people communicate in cooperative-oriented and feminist-based organizations and contrasting that talk with how people communicate in competitively driven groups.

The second theme, cause-effect/linear thinking, is based on the superiority in traditional society of the rational, direct, and solution-oriented. Feminist organizational communication theory asks questions about alternatives and explores the double binds created for women who are negatively sanctioned for adopting the scientific male style and who also are devalued for choosing stereotypical feminine communication patterns.

The third theme, separation and autonomy, is based on socialization practices that urge men to become separate and autonomous through action, work, and status; women, by contrast, are socialized for nurturing, being attractive, following authority, and being well liked. Feminist organizational communication theory offers the potential to examine the consequences of these socialized differences for both men and women. Feminist theory explores the importance of integrating emotion in communication theory while promoting discussions of developing the authentic self.

When discussing the Meaning-Centered approach, we discussed organizational socialization or attempts by organizations to help members learn appropriate behaviors, norms, and values. Connie Bullis (1993) uses feminist theories to develop an alternative perspective. Bullis describes why it is important to consider how socialization practices can construct women as marginalized others. Bullis challenges us to think about voices marked as outsiders, unsocialized, uncommitted, disloyal, absentee, unemployable, or dropouts. In later work, Bullis and Karen Stout (1996) raise important questions about socialization processes that function both to marginalize as well as socialize. Think for a moment about your own experiences. Have you ever considered yourself marginalized? If so, what were the communication experiences contributing to this feeling? If not, can you identify examples where others may have been excluded during socialization communication? We will continue our discussion of important emerging perspectives in Chapter 4.

## Emerging Perspectives: Summary of Essential Issues

Emerging Perspectives for organizational communication describe communication as a constitutive process and critique and challenge basic assumptions of message meaning and transfer, power and domination, and notions of rationality associated with hierarchical and patriarchal systems. Communication as constitutive process brings about self and social environments. Communication literally produces organizing, decision making, and influence. Postmodernism rejects former (modern) notions of authority and power, stability of meanings, and concepts of effectiveness. Postmodernism is represented in flattening of hierarchies, instrumental and expressive communication with multiple meanings, group as contrasted to individual achievements, and pervasive ambiguity. Deconstruction is the method of postmodern analysis with its emphasis on the exposure of the myths we use to explain the way things are and the uncovering of interests involved in socially constructed meanings.

Critical theory shifts our attention to power and abuses of power through communication and control in organizations. Organizations are depicted as political decision-making sites with potential for both domination and codetermination. Finally, feminist perspectives focus on the marginalization and domination of women in the workplace and how the valuing of women's voices contributes to an equality for differences rather than the equality of sameness characteristic of the Functional and Meaning-Centered approaches.

Return to the three cases presented thus far in this chapter. Ask questions about the cases using postmodern, critical, and feminist perspectives. Contrast your answers to those generated when using the Functional and Meaning-Centered approaches. What are the differences? Where can you find similarities?

## SUMMARY

The Functional approach, the Meaning-Centered approach, and Emerging Perspectives for understanding organizational communication help us ask questions important for analyzing problems. You should now review summary sections for each perspective. Figure 3.4 identifies key questions from each perspective. These questions can be used throughout the text as we analyze a variety of organizational problems.

## WORKSHOP

1. Form groups of four to six members each. Using your school as an organization with which all class members are familiar, identify organizing, change, and relationship messages. Groups should compare lists. How much agreement and disagreement exist? What accounts for the differences?

**FIGURE 3.4 Analyzing Organizational Problems**

*The Functional Approach*

1. How effective are organizing, relationship, and change messages?
2. What types of formal and informal communication networks exist? What network roles can you identify? Are they adequate?
3. Is channel use appropriate for effective communication?
4. Is the load on the communication system part of the problem?
5. What types of communication distortion exist?
6. Does the organization get good input communication from its environment? How effective is throughput and output communication?
7. Is the system open or closed?

*The Meaning-Centered Approach*

1. Do organizing activities help reduce message equivocality?
2. How effective is decision-making communication?
3. Do most organizational members identify with the organization? How do you know?
4. What attempts are made at organizational socialization? Are they appropriate and effective?
5. How does power relate to the problem?
6. Do organizational stories, rituals, and events provide important information?
7. What type of culture exists? Is it effective? How do you know?
8. How can the communication climate be characterized? Is that appropriate? What should change?

*Emerging Perspectives*

1. What are the hidden power relationships?
2. Are women and others marginalized?
3. Describe abuses of power.
4. Do stories, rituals, and events sustain hierarchical and patriarchal systems?
5. Is decision making characterized by domination or codetermination? How can change occur?
6. How is rationality conceptualized and presented?

2. The Meaning-Centered approach to organizational communication describes communication as culture. The following process should be undertaken to develop a cultural story about a familiar organization. Students can work individually or in groups. An organization in which access and appropriate approvals for observations and interviews can be obtained should be selected. Guidelines for this project should be discussed and understood by all members of the class. Based on the

scope of the assigned project you should (a) spend time observing interactions in the organization and taking notes about your observations; (b) review published materials such as mission statements, policy manuals, goals, and training programs; (c) talk with employees and ask questions about their values, stories, rules about how the organization operates and how they are expected to behave, and perform, and so forth; and (d) observe the physical aspects (dress, technology, offices, etc.) of the work environment. Using notes and observations write a story to explain the organization to others. If possible, share your story with organizational members and ask them to react to your observations. Be prepared to present your findings to the class both orally and in writing.

3. Emerging Perspectives challenge modern notions of organizational communication. Add to the following myths list any common assumptions you can identify about organizational life.

Myth List:    Men are stronger leaders during organizational crisis.
              Women are more nurturing managers than men.
              Management must exercise control for organizations to succeed.

For each myth on the list, discuss the following questions:

1. How do notions of power contribute to this statement?
2. Does this statement marginalize men or women? What does it mean for other important differences people exhibit?
3. Describe abuses of power related to this statement.
4. How much genuine participation occurs in decision making if this statement is true?
5. What is the basis of rationality for the statement?

Listen to the discussion. Is it difficult to deconstruct or critique myths of how things happen? Why? Why not?

4. Maryanne Wanca-Thibault offers insight into feminist perspectives in her essay, "Taking a Feminist Perspective in Organizational Communication." How do the three perspectives she describes differ, and what implications do they suggest for the organizational communication experiences of women and men? (pp. 77–81).

## Taking a Feminist Perspective in Organizational Communication

### Maryanne Wanca-Thibault, Ph.D.[1]

The impact of gender in the workplace is a topic of continuing interest as more women enter the workforce and vie for positions that have traditionally gone to white males. In the 1960s virtually all white-collar employees in the United States

[1]Maryanne Wanca-Thibault is an assistant professor of communication at the University of Colorado at Colorado Springs. Her research interests include feminist perspectives for organizational communication and health communication. Wanca-Thibault teaches organization communication and has extensive experience in business and industry.

were male. Over the last three decades women have gained ground as supervisors and managers, yet their numbers are still substantially outpaced by men. For example, in 1992 women accounted for 37 percent of all managers, reflecting a 76 percent increase in the nine years from 1983 to 1992. Virtually all these positions, however, were concentrated in lower levels of management. By 1995, only 3 percent of all senior managers in the top 1,500 largest U.S. corporations were women, and less than one half of one percent were among the highest paid officers of the nation's 1,000 largest industrial and service companies. Moreover, during that period women's earning power only increased from 60 to 70 cents compared with the dollar that men earned, with the greatest monetary disparity in white-collar jobs. So although there has been a significant increase in the numbers of women entering the ranks of working Americans, representation in management and wage parity are two important areas where women are yet to be treated as equal.

A fundamental reason that women and other minorities have continued to lag behind has much to with social structure. Our culture is traditionally patriarchal, which means that the dominant social values and institutional structures are defined by a male-centered viewpoint. Male stereotypes are held as the ideal to which all individuals should aspire, which suggests that white males are the only legitimate meaning makers and that other notions of reality are devalued and less likely to be expressed. Feminism provides a method for critically uncovering and responding to the marginalized voices of women and other minorities. To this end, in the remainder of this essay I define feminism as it relates to the study of organizational communication and discuss several feminist perspectives or theories that provide another distinct viewpoint of organizational reality. Finally, I present a rationale for the importance of adopting a feminist perspective when viewing organizations.

### Defining a Feminist Perspective in Organizations

Feminism is a fairly young research tradition in organizational communication. In fact, feminism was virtually nonexistent in the field until the mid-1980s. Up to that time, research was conducted primarily by white male professors for white male managers. It was only in the mid-1970s, as more women entered academe and the workforce, that women's issues emerged in the organizational and management research literature.

Most of the scholarship through the 1980s concentrated on possible gender differences in the workplace; a feminist perspective began to appear more frequently in the research during the mid-1980s.

Today there are a growing number of academics (men and women alike) who are exploring organizational issues using a feminist perspective (see Bullis 1993; Buzzanell 1994; Marshall 1993).

### What Is a Feminist Perspective?

A feminist perspective explores the marginalization and domination of women in the workplace and the significance of women's voices in all organizational processes. This perspective encompasses a variety of theories and approaches, all of which attempt to uncover, critique, and change the power relationships that devalue women and their viewpoints in our culture. More specifically, Buzzanell (1994) offers a comprehensive explanation of what a feminist perspective offers our field.

> Feminist organizational communication theory explores: how language creates gendered relationships; how communication reaffirms hierarchies that subordinate organization members and alternate views; and how women express and interpret organizational experiences. Feminist organizational communication theorizing includes, as its aim, the utilization of different premises and solutions for oppression found in the numerous feminist perspectives to create theory and research that enhance awareness of women's subordination in organizational life, and that direct individual, organizational, and societal change. (p. 343)

Three of these perspectives seem to have the most promise for studying communication in organizations: liberal feminism, standpoint feminism, and postmodern feminism.

## Liberal Feminism

Liberal feminism has provided the dominant perspective for feminists in the United States, and much of the early work in organizational communication reflects this viewpoint. Liberal feminists argue that all human beings possess natural rights but only men have been legitimately granted these rights. Men freely operate in the public domain (the workplace), which offers them the power, prestige, and money that allow their full participation in a capitalist democracy. Until recently, women have been excluded from this realm (or given a minor role in it). Instead, their role is defined in terms of the private domain (home and family) where traditional, domestic roles are played out. This view suggests that gender stereotyping must be eliminated. Women must be allowed to fully participate in institutions if they are to achieve their rightful, equal status with men. Thus, the broad question of equality in organizations is a concern for liberal feminists and the frame they use to critique current organizational structure and practices.

## Standpoint Feminism

Standpoint feminism is another potentially useful way from which to view organizational issues. Unlike liberal feminism, which values equality based on universal experiences, objective reality, order, and unity, standpoint feminists value equality based on multiple realities and the complexity that richness and diversity bring to any experience. Initially, standpoint feminists assumed that all women experienced marginalization or exclusion from groups in power similarly. Over time, however, this unified women's standpoint was largely dismissed by black and minority feminists who pointed out that their view of the world certainly was not the same as that of first-world, middle-class, white women (Bullis, 1994). They argued that women's standpoints are not neutral; they are dictated by a variety of individual experiences, preferences, and demographic and socioeconomic factors. The evolution of this perspective calls for a multiplicity of different voices and stories (both men's and women's) that represent different and equally valid sources of knowledge. Standpoint feminism does not strive for a single unified voice, but rather privileges a unified order that challenges and works to transform the status quo.

As with other feminist perspectives, feminist standpoint theory is concerned with revealing a set of alternative views that could uncover alternate meanings, processes, and outcomes. It is distinctive, however, in that it privileges the specific accounts of individuals, each of whom has unique experiences and perspectives. It is that diversity that helps to add a complexity and richness to an understanding of the values and practices at work in a community.

*Postmodern Feminism*

Postmodern feminism is presented as a third perspective that can be helpful for understanding individuals and organizations. Unlike the other two viewpoints, it assumes that there can be no single, unified feminist perspective. Individuals come to comprehend their social reality based on their everyday discourse or talk with others, and language is the key tool used to understand the self and others. Because an individual's reality is based on language and not merely defined by biological differences, postmodern feminists argue that this "social construction of reality" is neither universal nor stable.

For example, postmodern feminists would argue that an individual's sex is biologically determined; one is either male or female. The behaviors, norms, and gender roles that one takes on, however, are social constructions based on our experiences and perceptions of how males and females should act. Thus, gender is not a stable concept as is one's sex. Because women have traditionally been defined as "other" in our social institutions, postmodern feminists attempt to deconstruct patriarchal discourse in an attempt to show that women's viewpoints have been systematically excluded (Mumby, 1992). They search for different explanations and alternative ways of using language as a means of transforming the status quo.

*The Value of Adopting a Feminist Perspective in Organizations*

Historically, women in the workforce have been excluded from the patriarchal system that defines contemporary organizations. Moreover, women's experiences produce organizational perspectives, values, and ideas that have been overlooked or are noticeably absent in much of the organizational communication literature (Bullis 1994). For the most part, this male domination of our social institutions has largely gone unchallenged (Marshall, 1993).

A feminist perspective offers a different set of viewpoints for understanding organizations and their members. It exposes differences that have purposely been made invisible by those in power. Feminist research provides an opportunity to question the basic premises we hold as a society. In addition, it portrays the extent to which the public and private domains are constructed to privilege one particular cultural perspective over another. For example, Marshall (1993) proposes that males and females privilege different standards of organizational behavior. Males are typically characterized by self-assertion, separation, independence, control, competition, focused perception, rationality, analysis, clarity, discrimination, and activity. Females, on the other hand, value interdependence, cooperation, receptivity, merging, acceptance, awareness of patterns, wholes, and synthesizing. Although both sets of values are accessible, evidence suggests that females in organizations adapt to male norms while being evaluated against female stereotypes. Thus, women face the daunting task of having to live up to a double standard in organizations if they are to be successful. In the end, a feminist perspective perhaps has the potential to help individuals "re-vision" the best of both realities, thereby changing the reality of organizational life.

# REFERENCES AND SUGGESTED READINGS

Albrecht, T. L., and B. Hall. 1991. Relational and content differences between elites and outsiders in innovation networks. *Human Communication Research* 17: 535–61.

Allport, G., and L. Postman. 1947. *The psychology of rumor.* New York: Holt.

Alvesson, L. M., and S. Deetz. 1996. Critical theory and postmodern approaches to organizational studies. In *Handbook of Organizational Studies,* eds., S. R. Clegg, C. Hardy, and W. R. Nord, 191–217. London: Sage.

Barnett, G. 1988. Communication and organizational culture. In *Handbook of organizational communication,* eds G. Goldhaber and G. Barnett, 101–30. Norwood, NJ: Ablex.

Brown, M. H. 1985. That reminds me of a story: Speech action in organizational socialization. *Western Journal of Speech Communication* 49: 27–42.

Bullis, C. 1993. Organizational socialization research: Enabling, constraining, and shifting perspectives. *Communication Monographs* 60: 10–17.

Bullis, C., and K. Stout. 1996. *Organizational socialization: A feminist standpoint approach.* Paper presented at the National Speech Communication Association Convention, November, San Diego, CA.

Buzzanell, P. M. 1994. Gaining a voice: Feminist organizational communication theorizing. *Management Communication Quarterly* 7(4): 339–82.

Cheney, G. 1983. On the various and changing meanings of organizational membership: A field study of organizational identification. *Communication Monographs* 50: 342–62.

Conrad, C. 1994. *Strategic organizational communication: Toward the twenty-first century.* New York: Holt, Rinehart and Winston.

Corman, S. R., and M. S. Poole, eds. 2000. *Perspectives on organizational communication: Finding common ground.* New York: Guilford Press.

Cushman, D., S. King, and T. Smith. 1988. The rules perspective on organizational communication research. In *Handbook of organizational communication,* eds. G. M. Goldhaber and G. A. Barnett, 55–94. Norwood, NJ: Ablex.

Dahle, T. L. 1954. An objective and comparative study of five methods of transmitting information to business and industrial employees. *Speech Monographs* 21: 21–28.

Davis, K. 1967. *Human behavior at work.* New York: McGraw-Hill.

Deetz, S. 1992. *Building a communication perspective in organization studies I: Foundations.* Paper presented at the Speech Communication Association, October, Chicago.

Deetz, S. 1994. *Transforming communication, transforming business: Building responsive and responsible workplaces.* Cresskill, NJ: Hampton Press.

Deetz, S. 2001. Conceptual foundations. In *The new handbook of organizational communication: Advances in theory, research, and methods,* eds. F. M. Jablin and L. L. Putnam, 3–46. Thousand Oaks, CA: Sage.

Donnellon, A., B. Gray, and M. Bougon. 1986. Communication, meaning and organized action. *Administrative Science Quarterly* 31: 43–55.

Eisenberg, E., and H. L. Goodall. 1993. *Organizational communication: Balancing creativity and constraint.* New York: St. Martin's.

Eisenberg, E., and P. Riley. 1988. Organizational symbols and sense-making. In *Handbook of organizational communication,* eds. G. Goldhaber and G. Barnett, 131–50. Norwood, NJ: Ablex.

Eisenberg, E. M., and P. Riley. 2001. Organizational culture. In *The new handbook of organizational communication: Advances in theory, research, and methods,* eds. F. M. Jablin and L. L. Putnam, 291–322. Thousand Oaks, CA: Sage.

Falcione, R., L. Sussman, and R. Herden. 1987. Communication climate in organizations. In *Handbook of organizational communication,* eds. F. Jablin, L. Putnam, K. Roberts, and L. Porter, 195–227. Newbury Park, CA: Sage.

Falcione, R., and C. Wilson. 1988. Socialization processes in organizations. In *Handbook of organizational communication,* eds. G. Goldhaber and G. Barnett, 151–69. Norwood, NJ: Ablex.

Farace, R. V., P. R. Monge, and H. M. Russell. 1977. *Communicating and organizing.* Reading, MA: Addison-Wesley.

Ferguson, K. 1984. *The feminist case against bureaucracy.* Philadelphia: Temple University Press.

Goldhaber, G. M. 1986. *Organizational communication.* 4th ed. Dubuque, IA: Brown.

Greenbaum, H. H. 1976. The audit of organizational communication. In *Communication in organizations,* eds. J. L. Owen, P. A. Page, and G. I. Zimmerman, 271–89. St. Paul, MN: West.

Jablin, F. 1982. Formal structural characteristics of organizations and superior-subordinate communication. *Human Communication Research* 8(4): 338–47.

Jablin, F. M. 2001. Organizational entry, assimilation, and disengagement/exit. In *The new handbook of organizational communication: Advances in theory, research, and methods,* eds. F. M. Jablin and L. L. Putnam, 732–818. Thousand Oaks, CA: Sage.

Jablin, F. M., and L. L. Putnam, eds. 2001. *The new handbook of organizational communication: Advances in theory, research, and methods.* Thousand Oaks, CA: Sage.

Katz, D., and R. Kahn. 1966. *The social psychology of organizations.* New York: Wiley.

Koehler, J. W., K. W. Anatol, and R. L. Applbaum. 1976. *Organizational communication: Behavioral perspectives.* New York: Holt, Rinehart and Winston.

Kreps, G. L. 1986. *Organizational communication.* White Plains, NY: Longman.

Level, D. A., and W. P. Galle. 1980. *Business communications: Theory and practice.* Dallas, TX: Business Publications.

Louis, M. R. 1980. Surprise and sense making: What newcomers experience in entering unfamiliar organizational settings. *Administrative Science Quarterly* 25: 226–51.

Marshall, J. 1993. Viewing organizational communication from a feminist perspective: A critique and some offerings. In *Communication yearbook/16,* ed. S. Deetz, 122–43. Newbury Park: Sage.

McPhee, R. D., and P. K. Tompkins, eds. 1985. *Organizational communication: Traditional themes and new directions.* Beverly Hills, CA: Sage.

Miller, K. 1999. *Organizational communication: Approaches and processes.* 2d ed. Belmont, CA: Wadsworth.

Mintzberg, H. 1973. *The nature of managerial work.* New York: Harper and Row.

Monge, P. 1990. Theoretical and analytical issues in studying organizational processes. *Organization Science* 4: 406–30.

Monge, P., and E. Eisenberg. 1987. Emergent communication networks. In *Handbook of organizational communication,* eds. F. Jablin, L. Putnam, K. Roberts, and L. Porter, 304–42. Newbury Park, CA: Sage.

Morley, D. D., and P. Shockley-Zalabak. 1991. Setting the rules: An examination of the influence of organization founders' values. *Management Communication Quarterly* 4: 442–49.

Morley, D. D., P. Shockley-Zalabak, and R. Cesaria. 1997. Organizational communication and culture: A study of 10 Italian high-technology companies. *Journal of Business Communication* 34: 253–68.

Mumby, D. 1987. The political function of narratives in organizations. *Communication Monographs* 54: 113–27.

Mumby, D. K. 1993. Critical organizational communication studies: The next 10 years. *Communication Monographs* 60: 18–25.

Mumby, D. K., and L. L. Putnam. 1992. The politics of emotion: A feminist reading of bounded rationality. *Academy of Management Review* 17: 465–86.

Pacanowsky, M., and N. O'Donnell-Trujillo. 1983. Organizational communication as cultural performance. *Communication Monographs* 50: 126–47.

Pace, R. W. 1983. *Organizational communication: Foundations for human resource development.* Englewood Cliffs, NJ: Prentice Hall.

Pepper, G. 1995. *Communicating in organizations: A cultural approach.* New York: McGraw-Hill.

Poole, M. S. 1985. Communication and organizational climates: Review, critique, and a new perspective. In *Organizational communication: Traditional themes and new directions,* eds. R. D. McPhee and P. K. Tompkins, 79–108. Beverly Hills, CA: Sage.

Poole, M. S., and R. D. McPhee. 1983. A structural analysis of organizational climate. In *Communication and organizations: An interpretive approach,* eds. L. Putnam and M. Pacanowsky, 195–219. Beverly Hills, CA: Sage.

Poole, M. S., D. R. Seibold, and R. D. McPhee. 1985. Group decision-making as a structurational process. *Quarterly Journal of Speech* 71: 74–102.

Putnam, L. 1983. The interpretive perspective: An alternative to functionalism. In *Communication and organizations: An interpretive approach,* eds. L. Putnam and M. Pacanowsky, 31–54. Beverly Hills, CA: Sage.

Putnam, L., and M. Pacanowsky, eds. 1983. *Communication and organizations: An interpretive approach.* Beverly Hills, CA: Sage.

Redding, W. C. 1964. The organizational communicator. In *Business and industrial communication: A source book,* eds. W. C. Redding and G. Sanborn, 29–58. New York: Harper and Row.

Redding, W. C. 1972. *Communication within the organization.* New York: Industrial Communication Council.

Redding, W. C. 1983. Stumbling toward identity: The emergence of organizational communication as a field of study. In *Organizational communication: Traditional themes and new directions,* eds. R. D. McPhee and P. K. Tompkins, 15–54. Beverly Hills, CA: Sage.

Riley, P. 1983. A structurationist account of political culture. *Administrative Science Quarterly* 28: 414–37.

Rogers, E., and R. Agarwala-Rogers. 1976. *Communication in organizations.* New York: Free Press.

Schall, M. S. 1983. A communication rules approach to organizational culture. *Administrative Science Quarterly* 28(4): 557–81.

Scott, C. R., S. R. Corman, and G. Cheney. 1998. Development of a structurational model of identification in the organization. *Communication Theory* 8(3): 298–336.

Shockley-Zalabak, P., and D. D. Morley. 1989. Adhering to organizational culture: What does it mean, why does it matter? *Group and Organization Studies* 14: 483–500.

Shockley-Zalabak, P., and D. D. Morley. 1994. Creating a culture: A longitudinal examination of the influence of management and employee values on communication rule stability and emergence. *Human Communication Research* 20(3): 334–55.

Smircich, L. 1983. Concepts of culture and organizational analysis. *Administrative Science Quarterly* 28: 339–58.

Smircich, L., and M. Calás. 1987. Organizational culture: A critical assessment. In *Handbook of organizational communication,* eds. F. Jablin, L. Putnam, K. Roberts, and L. Porter, 228–57. Newbury Park, CA: Sage.

Smith, R. C., and P. K. Turner. 1993. *A metaphor analysis of organizational socialization theorizing: A call to move beyond formulaic, containment, and dualistic grounds.* Paper presented at the Speech Communication Association Convention, November, Miami.

Stohl, C. 2001. Globalizing organizational communication. In *The new handbook of organizational communication: Advances in theory, research, and methods,* eds. F. M. Jablin and L. L. Putnam, 323–75. Thousand Oaks, CA: Sage.

Thayer, L. 1968. *Communication and communication systems.* Homewood, IL: Irwin.

Tompkins, P., and G. Cheney. 1982. *Toward a theory of unobtrusive control in contemporary organizations.* Paper presented at the Speech Communication Association Convention, November, Louisville, KY.

Tompkins, P., and G. Cheney. 1983a. Account analysis of organizations: Decision making and identification. In *Communication and organizations: An interpretive approach,* eds. L. Putnam and M. Pacanowsky, 123–46. Beverly Hills, CA: Sage.

Tompkins, P., and G. Cheney. 1983b. Communication and unobtrusive control in contemporary organizations. In *Organizational communication: Traditional themes and new directions,* eds. R. D. McPhee and P. K. Tompkins, 179–210. Beverly Hills, CA: Sage.

Weick, K. 1979. *The social psychology of organizing.* 2d ed. Reading, MA: Addison-Wesley.

Van Maanen, J., and E. Schein. 1979. Toward a theory of organizational socialization. In *Research on organizational behavior,* eds. B. M. Straw and L. L. Cummings, 209–64. Greenwich, CT: JAI Press.

**. . . . .**

# CHAPTER FOUR

# COMMUNICATION IMPLICATIONS OF MAJOR ORGANIZATIONAL THEORIES

## DEVELOPING COMPETENCIES THROUGH . . .

### KNOWLEDGE

Describing Scientific Management theories for organizations

Describing Human Behavior theories for organizations

Describing Integrated Perspectives theories for organizations

Describing Postmodern, Critical, and Feminist theories for organizations

### SENSITIVITY

Awareness of communication implications of Scientific Management theories

Awareness of communication implications of Human Behavior theories

Awareness of communication implications of Integrated Perspectives theories

Awareness of communication implications of Postmodern, Critical, and Feminist Perspectives

### SKILLS

Applying theory to familiar organizations

Practicing analysis capabilities

## VALUES
Understanding Scientific Management, Human Behavior,
Integrated Perspectives, and Postmodern, Critical, and Feminist
Perspectives in contemporary organizations
Clarifying the importance of values in organizations

■ ■ ■ ■ ■

# THE DAVIS INSTRUMENT COMPANY'S MANUFACTURING CRISIS

Pam Martin was not surprised that the three supervisors in her section were disagreeing about how to train on the new MCF system. Joan, Henry, and Frank rarely agreed on how to solve section problems. Even though Pam had been their manager for over two years and knew each of them to be highly competent, the three seemed to view their work at Davis very differently. The problem for today's staff meeting was no exception. The new MCF system was being installed throughout all Davis Instrument Company's manufacturing areas to computer-automate and control assembly work previously done by highly skilled workers. The system would not replace any existing employees but would require training on new machines and computer controls. Over time, productivity would be expected to increase, and those employees who had early training on the system would be in positions for rapid advancement. All three of Pam's subordinates had supported acquiring the new system and thought that it was in the best long-term interests of Davis, but Joan, Henry, and Frank did not agree on how to select employees for training on the MCF and how to restructure work teams to implement the new process.

Joan argued that Pam and the supervisors should just decide. After all, early training on the system should fit the best workers with the highest aptitudes for computers to the new jobs. Yes, of course that means that other good workers would not have as much chance for advancement, but tough decisions are what management gets paid to make. Joan contended that the supervisors were in the best position to judge how to restructure the work teams. She proposed that the supervisors draw up a list of new job assignments, announce them to the group, and develop a timetable for system implementation.

Henry strongly disagreed. He voiced concern that his work team was worried about the new assignments. Henry believed that the affected workers should have some say in the assignment decisions. He supported letting each work team give their supervisors a plan for reassignment that the supervisors would then use for final decisions. He contended that individuals were more likely to be motivated and accept the changes willingly if they had a part in determining how the changes were to be implemented.

Frank thought that both Joan and Henry represented extreme positions that really did not serve the best interests of Davis. He proposed that the three supervisors draw up overall criteria for the new positions and the job assignments needed for each work team. They should then present the reorganization plan to their work teams and have individual meetings with each worker to determine interest and skill fit for each of the new positions. Frank agreed with Joan that some tough decisions about particular individuals would have to be made. He also agreed with Henry that better motivation would result if each individual had some input about the future assignment.

Pam knew all three wanted the project to succeed. The question was how to get Joan, Henry, and Frank to agree on an approach.

1. Joan, Henry, and Frank are all competent supervisors. What accounts for their differences?
2. Is it possible that they have different types of people in their work teams?
3. Can you describe how each of the three views the role of supervisor?
4. How do you think they view their work groups?
5. Do they have different theories of how organizations work?

## INTRODUCTION

The disagreement of Joan, Henry, and Frank is a good example of individuals with different views about how organizations should operate. Joan, Henry, and Frank all agree that the MCF system is a needed change but disagree about how that change should be made. Their disagreement can be traced, at least in part, to the differing ways in which they view workers and organizations.

In Chapter 3 we established three major perspectives for studying organizational communication: the Functional approach, the Meaning-Centered approach, and Emerging Perspectives. In this chapter we identify and describe major organizational theories and evaluate their communication implications from these three approaches. We will look at how researchers describe the ways in which organizations should work, what types of assumptions are made about people in organizations, and what these descriptions and assumptions mean for organizational communication.

We examine four major perspectives or schools of organizational thought: the Scientific Management, Human Behavior, Integrated, and Postmodern, Critical, and Feminist Perspectives schools. The four can be distinguished from one another by the questions researchers representing each viewpoint ask about organizations. Theorists representing the Scientific Management school ask questions about how organizations should be designed, how workers can be trained for maximum efficiency, how the chain of command works, and how division of labor should be determined.

Human Behavior theorists are concerned about the influence of individuals in organizations, what motivates workers, and how motivation affects the organization. These theorists believe organizational design and structure reflect basic assumptions about human behavior. They describe organizational relationships and people as resources. Human Behavior approaches are frequently discussed as human relation and human resource theories.

The development of what we call the Integrated Perspectives school can be traced to criticisms of Scientific Management and Human Behavior approaches. In the Integrated Perspectives approach, researchers ask questions about how structure, technology, and people relate to their environments. They are concerned with relationships among organizational design, employee motivation, communication participation, and organizational values, because these factors relate to the organization's ability to function in its environment. In some respects, the Integrated Perspectives approach reflects a merger of much of the thinking developed by Scientific Management and Human Behavior researchers. Finally, Postmodern, Critical, and Feminist Perspectives present a critique of power and domination in organizations, and of rationality as described by the Scientific Management perspective and seek to examine the privilege of certain organizational members and the marginalization of others.

This chapter is designed to contribute to *knowledge* competencies by describing major organizational theories representing Scientific Management, Human Behavior, Integrated, and Postmodern, Critical, and Feminist Perspectives. *Sensitivity* competencies are fostered by examining communication implications found in theory. Analysis *skills* are developed by combining knowledge and sensitivity competencies for application to familiar organizations and case studies. Finally, knowledge, sensitivity, and skill competencies influence *values* through evaluation of Scientific Management, Human Behavior, Integrated, and Postmodern, Critical, and Feminist Perspectives theories in contemporary organizations and by examining the importance of values for successful organizations.

## THE SCIENTIFIC MANAGEMENT SCHOOL

The Scientific Management school was well described by Frederick Taylor when, in his classic work *Principles of Scientific Management* (1913), he attempted to convince readers that the inefficiency in most organizations is caused by a lack of systematic management and that "the best management is a true science, resting upon clearly defined laws, rules, and principles, as a foundation." This foundation, from the Scientific Management point of view, rested on "scientifically" designed organizations characterized by carefully developed chains of command and efficient division of labor.

Three men—Frederick Taylor, Henri Fayol, and Max Weber—were largely responsible for developing the major concepts of the Scientific Management approach. All three were contemporaries living and writing during a period from the middle of the nineteenth century to World War I. The approaches of Taylor, Fayol, and Weber are used to describe the **Scientific Management perspective.**

### Major Scientific Management Theories

#### Principles of Scientific Management: Frederick Taylor (1856–1915)

Frederick Taylor is often referred to as the father of Scientific Management. Taylor's work experience, ranging from common laborer to chief engineer, served as the basis for the development of the four essential elements he viewed as the foun-

**Scientific Management perspective**
Theoretical approach to organizations that emphasizes organizational design, worker training for efficiency, chains of command, and division of labor. The perspective rests on the assumption that work and organizations can be rationally or "scientifically" designed and developed.

**Time and motion**
Technique for determining the efficiency of production through work observation and time measurements; used to develop work standards that can be measured for efficiency.

dation of scientific management: (1) careful selection of workers, (2) inducing and training the worker by the scientific method, (3) equal division of work between management and workers, and (4) discovering the scientific method for tasks and jobs.

Taylor (1913) held management responsible for devising the scientific method of work. He contended that inefficiency is fostered by allowing workers to determine how tasks should be performed. Furthermore, he believed that management is responsible for identifying "one best way" to perform tasks and that management should be exacting in teaching workers this scientific method for task performance. Taylor advised managers that "each man should daily be taught by and receive the most friendly help from those who are over him, instead of being, at the one extreme, driven or coerced by his bosses, and at the other left to his own unaided devices. This close, intimate, personal cooperation between the management and the men is the essence of modern scientific or task management." Taylor believed close contact between management and workers would eliminate the necessity for peer communication and what he called "soldiering," the unhealthy influence of the peer group.

Taylor is famous for his introduction in industry of the **time and motion** study. Taylor believed that if tasks were scientifically designed and workers extensively trained, the efficiency of production could be determined by timing the amount of work (motion) performed by individuals and teams. His "one best method" of task design was intended to produce the adoption of work standards that could be measured to increase efficiency and overall productivity.

To implement scientific task design and measurement in the workplace, Taylor recommended that management have sole responsibility for adopting and enforcing work standards. Taylor (1913) underscored the importance of the relationship between supervisor and subordinate when he suggested having "an inflexible rule to talk to and deal with only one man at a time, since each workman has his own special abilities and limitations, and since we are not dealing with men in masses, but are trying to develop each individual man to his highest state of efficiency and prosperity." He also considered the possibility that workers might propose improvements in how to complete tasks. When this occurred, Taylor advised management to conduct careful analysis of the new methods, conduct experiments to determine their accuracy, and then revise the existing standard if the new method should prove superior.

Taylor believed scientific management could only be accomplished with a well-defined chain of command and very specific division of labor. He held management responsible for developing the chain of command and organizing a division of labor based on well-defined work standards and measurement of standards to increase efficiency. Taylor's concepts were extremely influential in the early 1900s and continue to influence how organizations are designed, how performance standards are established, and how work efficiency is measured today.

## Principles of Management: Henri Fayol (1841–1925)

Henri Fayol is credited with the first known attempt to describe broad principles of management for the organization and conduct of business. A French mining engineer, Fayol spent his working career as an engineer and later managing director of the Comambault, a mining company that was floundering before Fayol assumed leadership. Fayol enjoyed enormous success as director of Comambault and was widely credited with turning a financially troubled company into a stable and thriving institution. Fayol founded the Center for Administrative Studies and, as a leading industrialist, attempted to influence the French government to apply his principles of administration. His early papers on general administrative theory became the influential text *General and Industrial Management*, first published in 1916.

In *General and Industrial Management* (1949), Fayol proposed fourteen principles of administration or management that he viewed as essential for effective organization: division of work, authority, discipline, unity of command, unity of direction, subordination of individual interests to the general interest, remuneration, centralization, scalar chain (line of authority), order, equity, stability of tenure of personnel, initiative, and esprit de corps.

1. *Division of work.* Fayol argued that specialization is the natural order in the universe and as such should be applied to organizations. Specifically, he proposed a division of labor based on task specialization, with individuals having specific and well-defined assignments.

2. *Authority.* Fayol defined authority as "the right to give orders and the power to exact obedience." As did Taylor, Fayol placed responsibility for the exercise of authority with management. He also emphasized a difference between authority as a result of job title versus what he called "personal" authority. He preferred personal authority based on intelligence, experience, moral worth, ability to lead, and past service. Although he did not describe it as such, Fayol was recognizing the importance of what is now called credibility in leadership.

3. *Discipline.* Discipline can be observed, according to Fayol, in the agreed-upon behavior and the evidence of that behavior between individuals and the organization. In other words, discipline is present when the behavior desired by management is exhibited by the work force. Fayol held management responsible for discipline, although he made no mention of a specific implementation process.

4. *Unity of command.* Fayol's principle of unity of command carried specific recommendations for communication. He contended that orders should come from only one superior and that a bypass of the chain of command would be a source of organizational problems. He believed messages should move from supervisors to subordinates as prescribed by the formal organization chart.

5. *Unity of direction.* Unity of direction was expressed by Fayol as "one head and one plan for a group of activities having the same objective." Unity of

direction was achieved by sound structuring of the organization. Unity of direction represented the formal organizational structure, whereas unity of command referred to people functioning within the structure.

6. *Subordination of individual interests to the general interest.* Individual interests were to be secondary to the overall good of the group or the organization, according to Fayol. Specifically, Fayol suggested that this subordination should be brought about by "(1) firmness and good example on the part of superiors; (2) agreements as fair as is possible; (3) constant supervision."

7. *Remuneration.* Fayol called for a fair price for services rendered. He believed that pay scales should be just and should motivate workers, but should not overcompensate.

8. *Centralization.* In his principle of centralization, Fayol recognized the need for flexibility in management principles. He advised: "Centralization is not a system of management good or bad of itself, capable of being adopted or discarded at the whim of managers or of circumstances; it is always present to a greater or lesser extent. The question of centralization or decentralization is a simple question of proportion."

9. *Scalar chain.* In his discussion of the scalar chain, Fayol directly referred to messages moving vertically and horizontally throughout the organization. In fact, his discussion of the scalar chain is the only known treatment of horizontal communication found in organizational literature until the writings of Chester Barnard in 1938. Fayol defined the scalar chain as "the chain of superiors ranging from the ultimate authority to the lowest ranks. The line of authority is the route followed—via every link in the chain—by all communications which start from or go to the ultimate authority." Fayol described the chain as carrying messages in vertical directions. As such, the chain would have an equal capacity to carry messages vertically, both downward and upward. Fayol admitted that at times the chain required too much time for messages to travel effectively through all the links. He suggested that when the necessity for rapid message exchange occurred, it would be advisable to use a "gang plank" whereby peers communicated directly without regard to the scalar chain (see Figure 4.1). This "gang plank" has become known in organization and communication literature as **Fayol's bridge**. Fayol says, "Use of the 'gang plank' is simple, swift, sure." He warned that the gang plank should be used sparingly and only in cases in which it would serve the general interest. Fayol viewed horizontal communication as task-related and as not carrying the potentially negative influences of "soldiering" as described by Taylor.

**Fayol's bridge**
Horizontal communication between peers.

10. *Order.* Fayol contended that both material and social order should be interpreted so that everything and everybody had a specific place and responsibility. As a principle of administration, the concept of order was to be put into effect through an organization's structure.

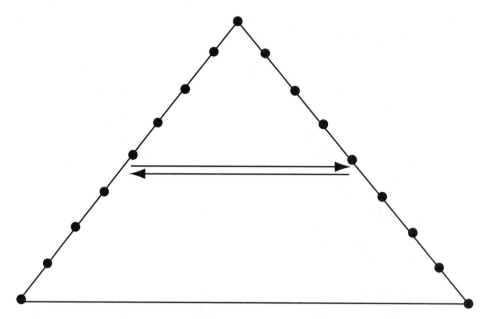

**FIGURE 4.1 Fayol's "Gang Plank," or Horizontal Communication between Peers**

11. *Equity.* Fayol valued what he called equity, or a combination of kindliness and justice toward all members of the scalar chain. He viewed equity as necessary to encourage workers to carry out duties with devotion and loyalty.

12. *Stability of tenure of personnel.* Fayol recognized the cost to organizations of training workers and the amount of time it took for a person to become competent in a given position. Thus, he believed that a work force that was relatively stable across time was in the best interests of the organization.

13. *Initiative.* Fayol saw initiative, as a principle of administration, as the ability to think through and execute plans. Furthermore, initiative was needed at all organizational levels, according to Fayol. He considered the manager who permitted the exercise of initiative within a work group to be superior to the one who could not.

14. *Esprit de corps.* Fayol's concept of esprit de corps was based on his belief that the strongest organization exhibited union of purpose. Fayol suggested that esprit de corps could be achieved by implementing his principle of unity of command. In advising managers about establishing esprit de corps, he warned against dividing and ruling and the abuse of written communication. Fayol suggested that when giving an order that required explanation, "usually it is simpler and quicker to do so verbally than in writing. Besides, it is well known that differences and misunderstandings which a conversation could clear up, grow more bitter in writing."

In addition to his fourteen principles of administration, Fayol identified five basic activities of management. These activities—planning, organizing, commanding, coordinating, and controlling—encompassed all fourteen principles of administration and served as a summary of Fayol's view of the overall responsibility of management.

Planning was described by Fayol as the development of operational strategies for the organization and the forecasting of future needs. Organizing was the use of people and materials to implement the organizational plan or goals. Commanding was the management function of obtaining maximum or optimum return for the organization from human and material resources. Coordinating was the function of integrating the efforts of all organizational members. Finally, controlling required management to establish how closely to its plan the organization was operating. To accomplish these five activities of management successfully, managers were to use all fourteen of Fayol's principles of administration. Although Fayol was writing early in the 1900s, his activities of management and principles of administration continue to receive extensive attention and are influential in the operation of contemporary organizations.

## Principles of Bureaucracy: Max Weber (1864–1920)

**Bureaucracy**
Organizations based on formalized rules, regulations, and procedures, which make authority rational as opposed to charismatic or traditional.

Max Weber, a German sociologist, is frequently referred to as the father of **bureaucracy**. Heavily influenced by socialist philosophy, Weber developed his theory of bureaucracy as a response to the abuses of authority he believed to be present in early patrimonial (advancement by inheritance) systems. To Weber, the bureaucratic model for organizations should be based on authority relationships that emphasize depersonalization and task competence.

Weber (1947) identified three types of authority: charismatic, traditional, and bureaucratic. Charismatic authority is based on the specific characteristics of the person exerting authority. Personal attributes of the individual inspire others to follow. This authority is nonstructural (does not go with specific jobs) and usually nontransferable from person to person. In other words, charismatic authority is individually based, and when the charismatic leader leaves the organization, the authority or ability to influence leaves with him or her. Weber believed charismatic authority contributed to unstable organizations and disorderly transition of power from one person to another.

Traditional authority, according to Weber, is associated with the customs of a group or society. Although generally more stable than charismatic authority, traditional authority passes from individual to individual based on custom or tradition rather than ability or task competence. A family-owned company, for example, traditionally remains in the family from one generation to another, regardless of the abilities of others who might want to head the organization. Outsiders are simply not members of the family.

Weber believed bureaucratic authority represented the ideal for organizations. Bureaucratic authority was to rest on formalized rules, regulations, and procedures that made authority "rational-legal," not based on personal charisma or tradition. Bureaucratic leaders were to be selected according to rules and regulations designed to promote the most competent for the particular job. This ideal bureaucracy, with its rational-legal authority mode, was designed to counteract nepotism, favoritism, and unbalanced decision making. As did Taylor and Fayol, Weber called for division of labor and for task specialization. He supported a formal **chain of command** and hierarchical structure. Impersonality in interpersonal relations was valued, and employment selection and promotion were to be based on competence.

**Chain of command**
Formal authority and reporting structure of an organization.

Weber's ideal bureaucracy can be described as having a hierarchy of authority with a scalar chain of command. This chain of command would be organized according to task specialization and should represent division of labor appropriate to the required tasks. Also, the chain of command should operate with standardized rules and procedures designed to emphasize "rational" decision making and task competence. The rules and procedures of the bureaucracy should emphasize the employment of qualified personnel, not necessarily those who have family or personal connections or whom tradition might select, but personnel with the best task competencies for a particular job. To secure qualified personnel, detailed definitions of job expectations and responsibilities would have to be developed in accordance with the rules and procedures of the organization. Communication in the bureaucratic system should be formal and follow the chain of command. According to Weber, the ideal bureaucracy should place primary emphasis on the goals of the organization and put individual interests secondary to organizational productivity.

## COMMUNICATION IMPLICATIONS OF SCIENTIFIC MANAGEMENT THEORIES

Communication, from the Scientific Management point of view, was to be a tool of management designed to facilitate task completion and as such was to operate as one of many organizational variables. Communication activities were to be specialized, as were tasks and jobs. Specifically, communication was required to train workers and give daily instructions concerning job requirements. Communication activities were to be formal, and interpersonal communication of a social or personal nature was to be discouraged, particularly among peers. Horizontal communication was to occur infrequently and only when following the chain of command was too time-consuming and cumbersome. Scientific Management theorists envisioned more messages flowing from supervisors to subordinates than from subordinates to supervisors. Status differences between managers and workers were to be encouraged and were believed essential for enforcing organizational rules and regulations.

Taylor, Fayol, and Weber all viewed communication as rational and functioning to reduce uncertainty about task expectations and measurement. Thus, the communication activities of the organization were developed and implemented by management as a natural reflection of their planning, organizing, commanding, coordinating, and controlling responsibilities.

The Functional approach to organizational communication can be used to describe communication implications from the Scientific Management viewpoint. Specifically, Taylor, Fayol, and Weber viewed organizational communication as functioning to organize task performance and to clarify rules and regulations. The relationship function of communication was relatively unimportant, although managers were advised to treat subordinates fairly and justly. Social or personal messages were to be discouraged. Although the Scientific Management theorists did not emphasize organizational change, management was to be responsible when change was necessary. Thus, any change in communication would result from management decisions and would be initiated and implemented by management. Worker involvement in change messages was to be minimal.

In terms of message structure, Scientific Management theorists described messages as flowing via the chain of command primarily in a downward direction. Limited upward communication was desirable, and only in particular types of situations should horizontal "bridge" communication occur. Communication networks were formal and prescribed to follow the chain of command, with the supervisor/subordinate communication link of particular significance. Informal networks were described as undesirable, and load in the system was expected to be moderate with minimal distortion.

The Meaning-Centered approach to organizational communication provides yet another way to analyze and evaluate communication implications from the Scientific Management viewpoint. Taylor, Fayol, and Weber did not describe communication as processes of organizing, decision making, influence, and culture. Rather, communication was described as a variable of the organization controlled by management. Organizing and decision making were management responsibilities that were to be carried out with bureaucratic authority. Culture was not a primary consideration, although culture contributed to the undesirable customs (traditions) of Weber's traditional authority mode or Taylor's concept of soldiering.

Even though Taylor, Fayol, and Weber did not envision communication as organizing, their works have implications for message equivocality. Specifically, the Scientific Management theorists prescribed messages low in equivocality with high degrees of definition in both task expectations and performance measurement.

The Scientific Management theorists viewed decision making as an organizational variable. They did not envision decision making as an ongoing process, much less a communication process. The decision-making variable was management controlled, with the primary premise for all decisions the efficient use of both human and material resources for goal achievement. Influence was also described as management controlled and executed. Management was responsible for organizational identification and the use of power to direct the organization. Ideally, power was the bureaucratic power of the Weber description rather than influence of personal characteristics (charisma) or the authority of tradition and custom. Scientific Management theorists did not consider abuses of power, as evidenced in Emerging Perspectives, and readily supported a legitimate power within the control of management. Although culture was not directly considered in the Scientific Management point of view, the emphasis on management responsibility and control implied a "management" culture that established the norms of the organization. Scientific management was not concerned with the Emerging Perspectives issues of domination and control except as evidenced in the abuses Weber considered from "nonrational" charisma-based systems. Hierarchy, control, patriarchy, and top-down decision making were viewed as appropriate and effective. Objective rationality was valued and important for organizational effectiveness. Women and other marginalized voices were not considered.

## SCIENTIFIC MANAGEMENT THEORIES IN CONTEMPORARY ORGANIZATIONS

By looking at the dates of the writings of Taylor, Fayol, and Weber, we are tempted to believe that the Scientific Management viewpoint is outdated and may provide limited usefulness in understanding today's organizations. Dates, however, can be misleading. A careful examination of most contemporary organizations reveals numerous Scientific Management principles still in operation. The Davis Instrument Company from the beginning of this chapter is a prime example. Davis has a chain of command for its manufacturing units. Pam is a manager responsible for three supervisors, who in turn each direct a team of workers. Davis can be described as having a division of labor that is in the process of change because of the introduction of the new MCF system. This change will require extensive task instruction and the careful selection of the "best" workers for the new jobs. Davis holds management responsible for determining how the system is to be implemented. Furthermore, Joan is exhibiting a Scientific Management perspective when she argues that Pam and the supervisors should decide about job assignments without worker input. She believes that managers should be responsible for work design and for structuring their teams for maximum efficiency. Based on what we have learned about the principles of administration proposed by the Scientific Management theorists, Joan's proposal represents their views.

Local, state, and national governments have been organized with many of the principles from the Scientific Management school. Not only do these organizations have hierarchies and chains of command, but also the transfer of power is governed by rules and regulations similar to those proposed by Weber. Although votes for officials may be based on their personal charisma, the successful candidate assumes office only after following the prescribed election rules. Both state and federal civil service have detailed job descriptions for most positions, with promotions governed by rules and regulations designed to eliminate favoritism and emphasize overall ability. Obviously, one can argue with how well these principles work in actual practice, but their design is a distinct legacy from the Scientific Management theorists.

Think about your school from the Scientific Management viewpoint. Are scientific principles reflected in admission policies and the rules and regulations that govern the granting of degrees? How would you characterize the division of labor between students and teachers? Is there a chain of command? Do scientific principles influence communication? Attempt to characterize the effectiveness of the scientific principles you identify and extend your analysis to other organizations to which you belong. For most organizations, you will be able to identify at least some of the principles first described by Taylor, Fayol, and Weber.

## THE HUMAN BEHAVIOR SCHOOL

The Human Behavior school shifts the emphasis from the structure of organizations, work design, and measurement to the interactions of individuals, their motivations, and their influence on organizational events. The **Human Behavior perspective** assumes that work is accomplished through people and emphasizes cooperation, participation, satisfaction, and interpersonal skills. Theorists representing this viewpoint see organizational design and function as reflections of basic assumptions about human behavior. The work of Mary Parker Follett, Elton Mayo, Douglas McGregor, and Rensis Likert is used to describe important characteristics of the Human Behavior approach to organizations.

**Human Behavior perspective**
Theories of organizations that emphasize the interactions of individuals, their motivations, and their influence on organizational events.

### Major Human Behavior Theories

#### Principles of Coordination: Mary Parker Follett (1868–1933)

Mary Parker Follett was ahead of her time in proclaiming that productive organizations must be concerned with the desires and motivations of individuals and groups. An honor graduate of Radcliffe College, Parker Follett was not a businessperson in the usual sense, but came to her interest in profit-making organizations from her work in political science, government, and social administration. A prolific lecturer in both Europe and the United States, Parker Follett is best known for her true principles of organizations based on a stable foundation for the steady, ordered progress of human well-being. Years ahead of other theorists, Parker Follett characterized conflict as potentially constructive, and described collective responsibility and integration as supportive of business excellence. Parker Follett is famous for her psychological foundations of the smoothly operating organization. Specifically, Parker Follett's four active principles are (1) coordination by direct contact of the responsible people concerned, (2) coordination in the early stages, (3) coordination as a reciprocal relation of all the features in a situation, and (4) coordination as a continuing process. Although less well known than Scientific Management theorists, Parker Follett, in her shift to the psychological and motivational processes of workers, made significant contributions to the emergence of behavior theories for understanding organizational life.

### The Hawthorne Effect: Elton Mayo (1880–1949)

Elton Mayo (1945) did not expect to be credited with beginning the Human Behavior point of view. As an influential Harvard professor, he was interested in expanding the understanding of the work environment as described by Frederick Taylor. When the famous Hawthorne studies began, he was experimenting with the alteration of physical working conditions to increase productivity.

The Chicago Hawthorne plant of the Western Electric Company was the site of the research. In 1927, Mayo led a research team from the Harvard Graduate School of Business Administration in a series of experimental studies designed to improve the physical working environment for increased productivity. Management at the Hawthorne plant was aware that severe dissatisfaction existed among workers, and previous efforts by efficiency experts had failed both to reduce tension and to increase productivity. Mayo and his colleagues began to experiment with altering physical conditions to determine a combination of conditions that would increase productivity. They worked with factors such as lighting, noise, incentive pay, and heating. As the studies progressed, they found little support for the expected relationship between improved working conditions and improved productivity. They became aware that other unexpected factors were interacting with physical factors to influence work output. During their study of changes in lighting intensity, Mayo and his colleagues observed that work output increased when lighting intensity increased. That was a result that could be interpreted in terms of Taylor and the Scientific Management viewpoint. Yet they also observed that work output increased when they decreased lighting intensity. That was a result that was counter to not only Taylor but also any previously established principles of Scientific Management. In fact, output increased no matter how the physical variables were changed. Mayo and his colleagues came to understand that a powerful and previously unrecognized influence in the experimental setting was the attention the researchers were paying to the workers. The attention encouraged a group norm that emphasized increased production no matter how the physical environment was altered. This effect, widely known as the **Hawthorne effect,** was the first documentation in industrial psychological research of the importance of human interaction and morale for productivity. The Hawthorne studies became the first organized attempts to understand the individual worker as key to the overall production process. As a result of the Hawthorne research, production could no longer be viewed as solely dependent on formal job and organizational design.

**Hawthorne effect**
Group norms that influence productivity apart from the physical production environment.

### Theory X and Theory Y: Douglas McGregor (1906–1964)

In his famous work *The Human Side of Enterprise* (1960), Douglas McGregor proposed his **Theory X–Theory Y** concept as a way to distinguish between the Scien-

**Theory X–Theory Y**
McGregor's description of management assumptions about workers. Theory X characterizes assumptions underlying Scientific Management theory, and Theory Y is associated with assumptions common to Human Behavior perspectives. Theory X managers assume that workers dislike work and will avoid responsible labor. Theory Y managers believe that workers can be self-directed and self-controlled.

tific Management and Human Behavior perspectives. A former president of Antioch College and a Massachusetts Institute of Technology professor of management, McGregor was interested in the basic assumptions about human nature inherent in both scientific and humanistic theories of management and organization.

McGregor presented Theory X as a summation of the assumptions about human nature made by those favoring the Scientific Management ideas of Taylor, Fayol, and Weber. McGregor believed that hierarchical structure, management control of influence and decision making, close supervision, and performance measurement were based on assumptions about how to motivate human behavior. Specifically, McGregor proposed that Theory X managers believe that the average person dislikes work and will avoid responsible labor whenever possible. Management must respond to this dislike of work with controls that are supported by punishments if workers fail to perform adequately. Theory X managers also assume that most people actually prefer to be directed so as to avoid responsibility for their actions. This direction allows workers to maintain job security without having to exhibit personal ambition.

Although McGregor believed that Theory X accurately characterized the assumptions underlying Scientific Management theory, he doubted that these assumptions provided the best evidence of how to motivate workers, contribute to employee satisfaction, or stimulate high levels of productivity. Building on the work of Mayo and others, he proposed Theory Y as an alternative to Theory X and as a way to understand individual motivation and interaction within organizations.

Theory Y managers assume a very different type of worker. The worker characterized by Theory Y finds work as natural as play and as such is self-directed and self-controlled. Employees are personally committed to organizational objectives and do not need close supervision or the threat of punishment to be productive. Individual commitment is a function of feeling rewarded through personal achievement. Unlike workers depicted in Theory X, Theory Y workers actually seek responsibility and have a high degree of innovativeness and creativity for solving organizational problems. McGregor contended that most modern organizations do not realize the Theory Y potential of their work force and therefore only partially use the intellectual potential of their employees.

McGregor has been criticized for what some have called a polarized either/or approach to human nature. McGregor has responded that Theory X and Theory Y are assumptions that may be better understood as ranges of behaviors from X to Y. Managers, as such, can draw on both sets of assumptions, depending on the situation and specific people involved (Figure 4.2).

McGregor and also Likert are sometimes associated with both the Human Behavior and Human Relations perspectives. Although similar in most respects, Human Relations views extend the focus beyond the specific behaviors of workers to evaluating how the entire organization can encourage the productive and effective use of people as resources, thereby supporting organizational productivity.

**FIGURE 4.2    Douglas McGregor: Theory X and Theory Y**

| THEORY X ASSUMPTIONS | THEORY Y ASSUMPTIONS |
|---|---|
| 1. People dislike work and will avoid work when possible. | 1. People view work as natural as play. |
| 2. Workers are not ambitious and prefer direction. | 2. Workers are ambitious and prefer self-direction. |
| 3. Workers avoid responsibility and are not concerned with organizational needs. | 3. Workers seek responsibility and feel rewarded through their achievements. |
| 4. Workers must be directed and threatened with punishment to achieve organizational productivity. | 4. Workers are self-motivated and require little direct supervision. |
| 5. Workers are not highly intelligent or capable of organizational creativity. | 5. Workers are creative and capable of organizational creativity. |
| 6. Organizations have difficulty in using human resources. | 6. Organizations have difficulty in using human resources. |

### Participative Management: Rensis Likert (1903–1981)

As a professor of sociology and psychology and director of the Institute of Social Research at the University of Michigan, Rensis Likert conducted extensive research to determine how management differed between successful and less successful organizations. His classic work, *New Patterns of Management* (1961), advanced his theory of **participative management** based on comparisons between productive and less productive work groups.

**Participative management**
Likert's theory of employee-centered management based on effectively functioning groups linked together structurally throughout the organization.

Likert, in *New Patterns of Management,* set forth a new theory—participative management—that rejected many of the assumptions on which Scientific Management was founded. His employee-centered management was based on effectively functioning groups linked together structurally throughout the entire organization. In other words, Likert proposed that the management process should depend on participative groups formed to have overlapping individual membership among groups. Figure 4.3 illustrates how an organizational chart using the Likert concept might look.

Likert supported his participative management theory with extensive research in high- and low-production situations. He believed that proper understanding of the differences or variability in human performance could help build productive organizations. Taylor had interpreted variability in performance as a need to establish specific procedures and production standards; Likert's interpretation called for an increase in participation by organizational members at all levels.

In an attempt to demonstrate the importance of participative management, Likert offered an extensive comparative analysis of management systems, which he identified as Systems I–IV. System I (exploitive authoritative) is similar to McGregor's Theory X assumptions. System I finds management closely control-

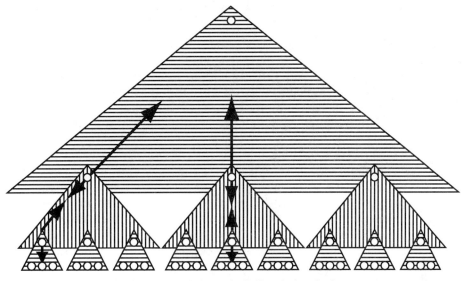

(The arrows indicate the linking pin function.)

**FIGURE 4.3    Likert's Linking Pin Concept**

R. Likert, *New Patterns of Management*, 1961, p. 113. Reproduced with permission of The McGraw-Hill Companies.

ling and directing work with little reliance on workers for problem solving. A general atmosphere of distrust discourages communication from flowing freely in all directions. System II (benevolent authoritative) is still characterized by hierarchical management control. Some trust and confidence, however, is placed in workers. A System II organization generally has more communication from employees than its System I counterpart. System III (consultative) finds management actively seeking input from employees. Important decisions still are made at the top but with much greater worker involvement than in Systems I and II. System III even permits some decisions to be made at lower levels within the organizations.

System IV, Likert's ideal of participative management, is characterized by trust between management and employees and by decisions being made throughout the organization. Accurate communication flows in all directions, and people are motivated because of their participation in organizational events and in shaping their own futures. Goal setting, as well as appraisal of how well goals are being met and the overall effectiveness of the organization, takes place at all organizational levels.

To support his participative management theory, Likert conducted extensive research comparing high- and low-performance groups. He contended that advances in the behavioral sciences made it possible to measure organization dimensions such as motivation, communication, and decision making. On the basis of this work, Likert contended that general supervision produces better results than close supervision and that employee-centered versus job-centered groups were more productive. Both findings are in direct contrast to basic principles from the Scientific Management school.

As had Mayo and his colleagues, Likert believed that the influence of the peer group was important. Unlike Taylor, who called for the elimination of peer-group influence, Likert believed that the peer group could assist in building an effective organization. Furthermore, Likert's research indicated that higher productivity came from groups with high peer loyalty and a group sense of responsibility for getting work done.

Likert's (1961) attitude toward communication was clear when he stated: "Communication is essential to the functioning of an organization. It is viewed widely as one of the most important processes of management." Likert believed that confidence and trust throughout the organization were essential for effective communication. He also commented on research indicating that most managers view downward messages as the greatest communication problem in organizations. He contended that deficiencies in upward communication were probably more serious than those in downward messages.

Likert's research also revealed that productivity was high in groups in which the supervisor and subordinate shared reasonably accurate perceptions of each other. Likert concluded from this finding that good communication and high performance go together.

Likert's participative management system was based on cooperation and motivation. Participative management was considered most appropriate when the work was varied, thereby creating a greater need for decision making throughout the organization. (Likert admitted that worker attitude was not as highly correlated to productivity in highly mechanized and routine work situations.) To disperse decision making throughout the organization, supportive relationships had to exist. Leadership and all other processes of the organization were to be exercised so that individuals would feel supported and affirmed in their personal worth and importance. This supportive climate could only be achieved, according to Likert, through the interlocking of effectively functioning groups.

Likert's theory of participative management was based on his research and assumptions about what happens in groups. Specifically, he contended that groups with high loyalty and attraction communicated more and were more receptive to communication from others than groups in which loyalty and attraction were not high. Members of effective groups also tended to communicate more accurately and relevantly than did individuals using the scalar chain.

Likert's participative management system was put into practice through a structure of interlocking groups, with members having multiple group memberships. These multiple group memberships provided links among groups, or what is now known as the famous "linking pin" function. This system of organization underscored Likert's commitment to broad participation at all organizational levels. Likert (1961), in describing the benefits of linked groups, predicted "fuller and more candid communication throughout the organization—upward, downward, and between peers." In sum, Likert's concept of participative management rested on his contention that the supportive atmosphere of the effective group promoted creativity, motivated people to use the communication process as both senders and receivers, and exerted more influence on leadership than in other types of systems.

## COMMUNICATION IMPLICATIONS OF HUMAN BEHAVIOR THEORIES

Effective communication was a cornerstone of the Human Behavior perspective. Management was to trust employees, and employees were to feel free to discuss job-related concerns with their supervisors. Peer-group interaction was not only recognized but was also viewed as a potentially positive influence for productivity. The human behavior theorists recognized both formal and informal communication networks carrying task and social support messages. Interactions at all levels were expected to be extensive and friendly, with substantial cooperation throughout the organization. From the Human Behavior viewpoint, communication was vital to the use of human resources and good organizational decision making.

When we use the Functional approach to describe communication implications from the Human Behavior viewpoint, we see a more complex role for communication than the Scientific Management theorists envisioned. As in the Scientific Management viewpoint, communication was seen as performing an organizing function providing task instruction, information, rules, and regulations. Unlike the Scientific Management viewpoint, the relationship function of organizational communication was considered significant. Mayo and Likert, in particular, recognized the importance of peers and how peer interactions contributed to integration within the organization. Also, Likert believed supportive relationships developed through effective communication were crucial for organizational productivity. Finally, the change function of communication was everyone's responsibility. Human Behavior researchers believed that employees at all levels were capable of participation in decision making and creating new directions for the organization.

The Human Behavior theorists described messages moving in all directions, through both formal and informal networks. These theorists emphasized oral channels, with little emphasis on written modes of communication. With both formal and informal messages moving in multiple directions, Human Behavior theorists described a communication load that was moderate to high and predictably distorted.

When we use the Meaning-Centered approach to identify the communication implications of Parker Follett, Mayo, McGregor, and Likert, we again come to the conclusion that communication was better understood in the Human Behavior perspective than in the Scientific Management approach. For example, communication was described by Likert as part of the organizing process. Likert also encouraged increased communication participation throughout the organization. Decision-making responsibility rested with all organizational members based on the belief that individual workers were capable of creative organizational input and that organizations were more productive with broad participation.

Culture was not specifically considered by Parker Follett, Mayo, McGregor, and Likert, although Likert did talk about supportive climates and described the types of groups he believed contributed most to productivity. Culture, however, was alluded to by the Human Behavior theorists when they discussed influence and power. They described the influence processes of identification and socialization as occurring primarily within peer groups, with power dispersed widely throughout the organization.

The Human Behavior perspective exhibits more concern with worker participation and satisfaction than do Scientific Management theories. Despite this concern for participation, Human Behavior theorists pay little attention to the concerns of power and how communication constitutes organizing, decision making, and influence. Women and other marginalized voices are not included as concerns. Although the Human Behavior perspective understands informal communication interactions and the potential for multiple meanings, the perspective generally emphasizes the importance of communication to reduce ambiguity and increase shared meanings.

## HUMAN BEHAVIOR THEORIES IN CONTEMPORARY ORGANIZATIONS

Most contemporary organizations include not only Scientific Management ideas but also much of the thinking generated from the Human Behavior theorists. The Davis Instrument Company is an example. Davis is structured according to many of the principles of Scientific Management, but Davis also exhibits the influence of Parker Follett, Mayo, McGregor, and Likert. Pam Martin is making decisions about the new MCF system with participation from her subordinates. She is using a group process to address issues and solve problems. Earlier we identified Joan as articulating a Scientific Management approach. We can expand our analysis and describe Henry as representing the Human Behavior viewpoint when he calls for extensive involvement from the various work teams in determining their new training and job assignments. Both Henry and Frank reflect Theory Y assumptions about people when they contend that workers are more motivated when involved in decisions that directly affect them. In fact, when we thoughtfully analyze the Davis case, it is possible to conclude that both Scientific Management and Human Behavior ideas are in evidence and that both will contribute to the success or failure of the new MCF system.

Most contemporary organizations are similar to Davis in their combined usage of Scientific Management and Human Behavior ideas. Committees, project teams, and work units all are examples of the use made of groups in modern organizations. Training for managers and supervisors emphasizes developing interpersonal skills for working effectively with subordinates. New employees attend orientations designed to help them understand and become a part of the organization. Awards honor a variety of creative contributions, and profit-sharing and merit-pay plans attest to the importance of employee involvement for organizational success. These examples and many others exist side by side in today's organizations with hierarchical structures, division of labor, chains of command, and final management responsibility in decision making.

Earlier you described your school from a Scientific Management point of view. Now think about that same organization from the Human Behavior viewpoint. What assumptions are made about the basic nature of students? Is there an honor code for academic achievement, or are exams tightly monitored and cheating vigorously punished? Is creativity expected from students? Is there a supportive atmosphere that contributes to effective communication among students and with teachers? Attempt to characterize your school in terms of Theory X and Theory Y. Does one work better than the other? If so, why? If not, how do they work in combination? Finally, describe which of the Human Behavior concepts you believe to be the most influential for effective communication.

## THE INTEGRATED PERSPECTIVES SCHOOL

Both Scientific Management and Human Behavior approaches have been criticized for their failure to integrate organizational structure, technology, and people with the larger environment in which organizations exist. The Scientific Management theorists concentrated on organizational structure and work design with little attention to people and organizational environments. The Human Behavior theorists were concerned with people but also tended to ignore influences beyond organizational boundaries. In reaction to these criticisms, a number of organizational researchers have developed the **Integrated Perspectives** viewpoint. These theorists attempt to explain how people, technologies, and environments integrate to influence all that happens in organizations. Specifically, we examine the process and environmental approaches of Herbert Simon, Eric Trist, Kenneth Bamforth, Joan Woodward, Paul Lawrence, Jay Lorsch, Daniel Katz, Robert Kahn, Gareth Morgan, Margaret Wheatley, and Peter Senge and the cultural approaches of Terrence Deal, Allen Kennedy, William Ouchi, Thomas Peters, Robert Waterman, Edgar Schein, and Karl Weick.

**Integrated Perspectives**
Theories that attempt to explain how people, technologies, and environments integrate to influence goal-directed behavior.

### Major Integrated Perspective Theories: Process and Environmental Approaches

Process and environmental approaches to organizational theory attempt to describe how complex processes such as decision making influence the internal operation of organizations and are influenced by external environments. Researchers using these perspectives seek to explain how human and technical systems interact with the broader environments in which organizations operate and in so doing seek to test basic assumptions from both Scientific Management and Human Behavior viewpoints. To describe process and environmental approaches, we will discuss the decision-making approach of Simon, sociotechnical integration as described by Trist and Bamforth, contingency theory as introduced by Woodward, Lawrence and Lorsch, and Katz and Kahn's systems theory. Finally, we will explore what is described as the new organization science and learning organizations using the work of Wheatley, Senge, Morgan, and others.

### Decision-Making Approach: Herbert Simon (1916– )

In 1947, Herbert Simon offered a description of organizations that differed from both the Scientific Management and Human Behavior viewpoints. Simon (1957) proclaimed that organizational behavior is a complex network of decisions with decision-making processes influencing the behavior of the entire organization. According to Simon, organizations can be understood in terms of what types of decisions are made at various organizational levels and with what types of information. As such, Simon viewed the **decision-making approach** as the essential organizational process.

**Decision-making approach**
Simon's concept that organizational behavior is a complex network of decisions, with decision-making processes influencing the behavior of the entire organization.

**Bounded rationality**
Assumption that people intend to be rational, but with limited information-processing capacity, human decision making is based on selective perception and therefore exhibits "limited" rationality.

Understanding the limitations of human decision making was important to Simon's model. Along with Richard Cyert and James March (Cyert and March, 1963), Simon introduced the concept of **bounded rationality** as a way to understand information processing and decision making. Specifically, the concept of bounded rationality assumed that people intend to be rational, but with limited information-processing capacity, human decision making is based on selective perception and therefore exhibits "limited" rationality. Simon argued that individuals often make organizational decisions while realizing that their decisions are based on partial information. Simon called this process "satisficing," or the making of decisions with partial information in the hope the decision will be good enough, if not the best.

Simon clearly challenged the "one best way" of the Scientific Management theorists. He also largely ignored the descriptions of human behavior as offered by Human Behavior theorists in favor of an explanation of human behavior based on the concept of bounded rationality. He described decision making as the fundamental organizational process. Decision making, he said, occurs through the communication behaviors of individuals who intend rationality but can only approach rationality because of limited information-processing capacity.

### Sociotechnical Integration: Eric L. Trist (1909–1993) and Kenneth W. Bamforth[1]

The concept of **sociotechnical integration** rested on two assumptions first described by Eric Trist and his student Kenneth Bamforth (1951) as a result of their

---

[1]Birthdate unknown.

**Sociotechnical integration**
Theoretical attempt to balance human social-psychological needs with organizational goals; an assumption that organizational production is optimized through optimizing social and technical systems.

work with a British coal-mining operation: (1) organizational production is optimized through optimizing social and technical systems, and (2) a constant interchange exists between the work system and the broader environment.

The sociotechnical approach attempted to balance human social-psychological needs with organizational goals. Communication in the sociotechnical approach related to work, to the needs of the environment, and to the personal needs of workers. Trist and Bamforth tested the sociotechnical concept in a British coal-mining operation. Workers were trained to rotate as necessary through all the tasks required by new machines. This cross-training was designed to introduce variety and interest into the work environment. Also, each work team was permitted to set its own rate of production and was responsible for handling its own problems and conflicts. The output of these autonomous groups was compared with groups with more traditional and "scientifically" designed assignments. In the Trist and Bamforth experiment, the sociotechnical groups outperformed their scientific group counterparts by approximately 34 percent, or 1.8 tons per shift.

These experiments led Trist and Bamforth to conclude that meaning in work could be established through group assignments that permit individuals to be included in entire task cycles rather than working on isolated parts of a job. The autonomy of groups in setting their own standards and making decisions about their own problems could give individuals a sense of self-determination that closer supervision and control could not achieve. This emphasis on group-set goals and responsibilities could contribute to a solidarity of purpose that could help integrate individual and organizational goals. This integration would be productive for both individuals and organizations.

**Contingency theory**
Approach that rejects the "one best way" to organize in favor of the view that no specific set of prescriptions is appropriate for all organizations. As such, organizations must adapt to changing circumstances and the needs of individuals and the environment in which the organization operates.

## Contingency Theory: Joan Woodward (1916–1971), Paul Lawrence (1922– ), and Jay Lorsch (1932– )

The **contingency theory** began when Joan Woodward (1965) researched one hundred British manufacturing firms in an effort to develop a list of characteristics that would indicate differences in organizational structure. Her classification included organizations with little technological complexity and those with extensive reliance on complicated technologies. Her findings relating differences in technology to differences in organizational structure became the foundation of modern contingency theory, or the realization that differences in organizations are due to differences in goals and environments.

Contingency theory rejects the "one best way" to organize as described by Scientific Management's theorists. Contingency theory also finds the Human Behavior approach lacking an explanation of the complex relationships among units within the organization and the larger environment in which the organization operates.

Lawrence and Lorsch (1969) describe contingency theory as the establishment of internal organizational operations contingent or dependent on external environmental needs and individual needs. Lawrence and Lorsch view organizations as having three primary relationships that determine how organizations operate and respond to their environment. Specifically, organizations have what Lawrence and Lorsch call "interfaces" at the organization-to-environment, group-to-group, and individual-to-organization levels. They suggest that organizational design and operation should be based on these three "interfaces," which differ for all organizations.

Proponents of the contingency view suggest that there is no specific set of prescriptions appropriate for all organizations. Organizations must adapt to changing circumstances and the needs of individuals and the environments in which the organizations operate. As such, organizational designs based on Scientific Management concepts may be appropriate in certain circumstances. The concerns of the Human Behavior theorists also can be valuable when matched to specific situations. In other words, contingency theory suggests that considerable judgment is required to understand effective organizational operation because that operation "all depends on the situation."

**Systems theory**
Describes organizations as made up of subsystems that take in materials and human resources, process materials and resources, and yield a finished product to the larger environment.

## The Systems Approach: Daniel Katz (1903–1998) and Robert Kahn (1918–  )

Closely related to contingency theory, **systems theory** grew in direct response to criticisms of both Scientific Management and Human Behavior philosophies. The systems approach emphasizes interaction with the larger environment, and as Katz and Kahn (1966) suggest, "is basically concerned with problems of relationships, of structure, and of interdependence rather than the constant attributes of objects."

Katz and Kahn contend that most formal organizations operate with five basic subsystems: productive subsystems dealing with work accomplished, supportive subsystems dealing with relationships and needed materials support, maintenance subsystems to integrate people into their functional role; adaptive subsystems geared for change, and managerial subsystems for coordination and control of the various subsystems.

In systems theory, the organization takes in materials and human resources (input), processes materials and resources (throughput), and yields a finished product (output) to the larger environment. Along with input, throughput, and output, the ideal system should have a self-corrective mechanism whereby feedback or input from the environment can be processed into adaptation of throughput and, potentially, output. The system's self-corrective mechanism is called the system's cybernetic, which in the ideal system is the management team. In systems theory, the law of equifinality attests to the multiple-action courses possible for the achievement of a goal. Equifinality rejects the concept of a single course of action to reach a single goal.

Katz and Kahn and other systems theorists advance a principle of optimization, or looking for maximum output in return for minimum input. Maximum return for minimum input is affected by feedback from the environment and management's ability to adjust. Thus, systems may be described as open or closed, mechanistic or organic. An open system exchanges information with its larger environment. A closed system limits exchange with the environment and seeks to operate as a self-contained unit. Systems theorists relate the closed organizational system to a closed thermodynamic system, contending that they both will approach a condition of maximum entropy with no further possibility of useful work. The open system, on the other hand, fights entropy and seeks a dynamic equilibrium among input, throughput, and output. The open system exhibits the law of equifinality and has a sound self-corrective mechanism.

The organic system is suited to change, whereas the mechanistic system functions best in stable conditions. The mechanistic system frequently exhibits much of the prescriptive structure of Scientific Management with its rigid hierarchy and specialized differentiation of tasks. The organic system is characterized by greater emphasis on individuals and their capacities for unique contributions. Hierarchy may exist in the organic system, but authority is exercised more by consent than coercion or legitimate right of office. The organic system compares favorably with descriptions of open systems, whereas the mechanistic system may be compared with closed systems.

## The New Systems Approaches—Flux, Transformation, Quantum Physics, Self-Organizing Systems, and Chaos Theory: Gareth Morgan (1943–   ) and Margaret Wheatley (1944–   )

Systems theory as described by Katz and Kahn (in the section above) is currently undergoing an important transformation brought about by rethinking the basic nature of systems and system relationships to the environment. Gareth Morgan (1997), in his important book, *Images of Organizations*, explains:

> Traditional approaches to organization theory have been dominated by the idea that change originates in the environment. . . . The organization is typically viewed as an open system in constant interaction with its context, transforming inputs into outputs as a means of creating the conditions necessary for survival. Changes in the environment are viewed as presenting challenges to which the organization must respond. (p. 253)

**Autopoiesis**
Process describing each element in a system simultaneously combining the maintenance of itself with the maintenance of the other elements of the system.

Morgan describes the work of two Chilean scientists, Humberto Maturana and Francisco Varela, who are credited with a new approach to systems theory—**autopoiesis**—a perspective that supports rethinking organizational relationships to the environments in which they are embedded. Autopoiesis refers to what Morgan (1997) describes as

> all living systems are organizationally closed, autonomous systems of interaction that make reference to themselves. The idea that living systems are open to an environment is, (in the view of Maturana and Varela) the product of an attempt to make

sense of such systems from the standpoint of an external observer. Their theory challenges the validity of distinctions drawn between a system and its environment and offers a new perspective for understanding the processes through which living systems change. (p. 253)

Morgan takes an example from a biological organism to explain:

> The bee as an organism constitutes a chain of self-referring physiological processes with their own circular organization and lives within a society of bees where relations are also circular. In turn, the relationship between the society of bees and the wider ecology is also circular. Eliminate the bees and the whole ecology will change, for the bee system is linked with the botanical system, which is linked with insect, animal, agricultural, human, and social systems. All these systems are self-referential and turn back on each other. A change in any one element can transform all the others. . . . An understanding of the autopoietic nature of systems requires that we understand how each element simultaneously combines the maintenance of itself with the maintenance of the others. (p. 254)

Management theorist Margaret Wheatley (1992) describes autopoietic structures as each having a unique identity, a clear boundary, yet merged with its environment.

Supporting a transformation in systems thinking, Wheatley uses insights from quantum physics, self-organizing systems, and chaos theory to present a view of systems theory with new possibilities for connections and change. Wheatley argues, as do many physicists, that the relationships in the quantum world are not just interesting but are all there is to reality.

This notion of complex, fluid, ever-changing relationships answers conceptual questions about influences for organizational behavior. We no longer have to attempt to decide whether the individual or the system is more influential; relationships continually shift and change depending on individuals and the moment. This notion of pervasive relationships—a relational universe—as described in quantum theory suggests that we do not create reality but that we evoke potentials that are already present. Wheatley (1992) identifies this notion as closely related to Weick's concept of enactment in organizations: how we participate in the creation of organizational realities. As Wheatley concludes:

> To live in a quantum world, to weave here and there with ease and grace, we will need to change what we do. We will need to stop describing tasks and instead facilitate process. We will need to become savvy about how to build relationships, how to nurture growing, evolving things. All of us will need better skills in listening, communicating, and facilitating groups, because these are the talents that build strong relationships. It is well known that the era of the rugged individual has been replaced by the era of the team player. But this is only the beginning. The quantum world has demolished the concept of the unconnected individual. More and more relationships are in store for us, out there in the vast web of universal connections. (p. 38)

**Dissipative structures**
Descriptions of structures when a loss of energy and form contributes to disequilibrium, which in turn contributes to growth and new structures and forms.

Wheatley discusses the chemistry theory of **dissipative structures** to illustrate her contention that the new science helps us understand that disorder can be the source of new order. As Wheatley (1992) explains:

Dissipation describes a loss, a process by which energy gradually ebbs away. Yet Priogogine discovered that such dissipative activity could play a constructive role in the creation of new structures. Dissipation didn't lead to the demise of a system. It was part of the process by which the system let go of its present form so that it could reemerge in a form better suited to the demands of the present environment. . . . Dissipative structures demonstrate that disorder can be a source of order, and that growth is found in disequilibrium, not in balance. The things we fear most in organizations—fluctuations, disturbances, imbalances— need not be signs of an impending disorder that will destroy us. Instead, fluctuations are the primary source of creativity. Scientists in this newly understood world describe the paths between disorder and order as "order out of chaos" or "order through fluctuation" (Prigogine, 1984). These are new principles that highlight the dynamics between chaos and creativity, between disruptions and growth. (pp. 19–20)

The theory of dissipative structures helps explain how dissipating energy is used to recreate structures into new forms of organization. When levels of disturbance amplify, dissipative structures possess innate properties for reconfiguration to deal with new information. This capacity is frequently called

**Self-organizing or self-renewing systems**
Processes occurring when disturbances amplify stimulating reconfigurations to deal with new information.

**self-organizing** or **self-renewing systems.** A key feature is resiliency as contrasted to stability. Wheatley (1992) describes adaptive organizing as tapping into this property of self-organizing or self-renewing systems. She further contends that information is the creative energy both for organizations and the universe. As she explains:

But an organization can only exist in such a fluid fashion if it has access to new information, both about external factors and internal resources. It must constantly process this data with high levels of self-awareness, plentiful sensing devices, and a strong capacity for reflection. Combing through this constantly changing information, the organization can determine what choices are available, and what resources to rally in response. This is very different from the more traditional organizational response to information, where priority is given to maintaining existing operating forms and information is made to fit the structure so that little change is required. (p. 91)

**Chaos theory**
Description of systems disturbed from stable states to states of unpredictability.

**Chaos theory** is the final construct from the new science that Wheatley describes. Put simply, chaos is the last stage as a system of any type moves away from order. When systems are disturbed from their stable states, they begin a process of swinging back and forth (oscillating) and, for some, the move to the next state is chaos or total unpredictability. During this point of chaos, instead of everything coming apart, the strange attractor comes into play, pulling the system to a new shape and form. Wheatley (1992) believes that attractors are at work in organizations and that

> one of the most potent shapers of behavior in organizations, and in life, is meaning. . . . When a meaning attractor is in place in an organization, employees can be trusted to move freely, drawn in many directions by their energy and creativity. There is no need to insist, through regimentation or supervision, that any two individuals act in precisely the same way. We know they will be affected and shaped by the attractor, their behavior never going out of bounds. We trust that they will heed the call of the attractor and stay within its basin. We believe that little else is required except the cohering presence of a purpose, which gives people the capacity for self-reference. (pp. 134–136)

Although admittedly somewhat complex, principles from quantum physics, self-organizing systems, and chaos theory provide important perspectives for understanding systems theory. Of particular importance in this new science conceptualization of organizations are the information and communication processes in which individuals engage.

**Learning organizations**
Organizations gaining knowledge from continuous processes of information exchange between the organization and its environments.

## Learning Organizations: Peter Senge[2] and Gareth Morgan (1943– )

The concept of designing organizations to learn in a brainlike way is another important extension of systems theory (Morgan, 1997). Early research focusing on **learning organizations** was conducted by information theorists under the umbrella of what is now called cybernetics. As Gareth Morgan describes:

> Cybernetics thus leads to a theory of communication and learning stressing four key principles: (1) Systems must have the capacity to sense, monitor, and scan significant aspects of their environment. (2) They must be able to relate this information to the operating norms that guide system behavior. (3) They must be able to detect significant deviations from these norms. (4) They must be able to initiate corrective action when discrepancies are detected. If these four conditions are satisfied, a continuous process of information exchange is created between a system and its environment, allowing the system to monitor changes and initiate appropriate responses. . . . This is fine so long as the action defined by those standards is appropriate for dealing with the changes encountered. But when this is not the case, the intelligence of the system breaks down, for the process of negative feedback ends up trying to maintain an inappropriate pattern of behavior. (pp. 85-86)

Learning using these four basic principles is called single-loop learning. This definition of single-loop learning helps to draw a distinction between the process of learning and process of learning to learn. More complex systems such as the human brain and some types of computers have the capacity to detect and correct

[2]Dates not released.

mistakes in operating norms and principles and thus influence the standards for future action. This ability to question and influence change in operating norms is called learning to learn or double-loop learning. Chris Argyris of Harvard and Donald Schon of MIT first brought the learning to learn concept to managerial attention. Peter Senge of MIT popularized the concept of the learning organization in his now famous work, *The Fifth Discipline* (1990).

Senge (1990) provides five new "component technologies" that he claims are gradually converging to innovate learning organizations. Senge contends that the five disciplines must develop as an ensemble. He goes on to describe systems thinking as the fifth discipline because

> it is the discipline that integrates the disciplines, fusing them into a coherent body of theory and practice. It keeps them from being separate gimmicks or the latest organization change fads. Without a systemic orientation, there is no motivation to look at how the disciplines interrelate. By enhancing each of the other disciplines, it continually reminds us that the whole can exceed the sum of its parts. (p. 12)

#### SENGE'S FIVE DISCIPLINES ARE:

1. *System thinking:* the ability to think about connections and patterns and to view systems as wholes, not individual parts of the patterns.
2. *Personal mastery:* developing special levels of proficiency. Personal mastery is the discipline of continually clarifying and deepening our personal vision, of focusing our energies, of developing patience, and of seeing reality objectively. As such, it is an essential cornerstone of the learning organization, the learning organization's spiritual foundation. An organization's commitment to and capacity for learning can be no greater than that of its members. The roots of this discipline lie in both Eastern and Western spiritual traditions and in secular traditions as well.
3. *Mental models:* deeply ingrained assumptions, generalizations, or even pictures or images that influence how we understand the world and how we take action.
4. *Building shared vision:* the capacity to hold a shared picture of the future we seek to create. When there is a genuine vision, people excel and learn, not because they are told to but because they want to.
5. *Team learning:* learning that starts with dialogue, the capacity of members of a team to suspend assumptions and enter into genuine "thinking together." The discipline of dialogue also involves learning how to recognize the patterns of interaction in teams that undermine learning.

Senge (1990) concludes his identification of the five disciplines,

> systems thinking makes understandable the subtlest aspect of the learning organization—the new way individuals perceive themselves and their world. At the heart of a learning organization is a shift of mind—from seeing ourselves as separate from the world to connected to the world, from seeing problems as caused by

someone or something "out there" to seeing how our own actions create the problems we experience. A learning organization is a place where people are continually discovering how they create their reality. And how they can change it. (pp. 6-13)

**Cultural approaches**
Theories that describe how organizational members collectively interpret the organizational world around them to define the importance of organizational happenings. Approaches to theory that explain organizational behavior in terms of the influence of cultures that exist both internally and externally to the organization.

# Integrated Perspectives Theories: Cultural Approaches

**Cultural approaches** to organizational theory describe how organizational members collectively interpret the organizational world around them to define the importance of organizational happenings. In other words, cultural approaches to organizational theory explain organizational behavior in terms of the influence of cultures that exist both internally and externally to the organization. Cultural research attempts to identify how a unique sense of the place (culture) contributes to individual behavior and organizational effectiveness.

Cultural theories are the newest additions to the Integrated Perspectives approach, although the importance of culture has been recognized for many years. Deal, Kennedy, Ouchi, Peters, and Waterman provide prescriptive approaches to how cultures influence organizational effectiveness. Schein and Weick provide more theoretically oriented perspectives.

## Elements of Culture: Terrence Deal (1939– ) and Allen Kennedy (1943– )

Terrence Deal and Allen Kennedy, in their book *Corporate Cultures: The Rites and Rituals of Corporate Life* (1982), identify five basic elements of organizational culture: business environment, values, heroes, rites and rituals, and the cultural network. Each contributes to managing behavior and, according to Deal and Kennedy (1982), "helps employees do their jobs a little better." Essentially, a strong culture contributes to managing the organization by spelling out in general terms how people are to behave while helping people feel better about what they do, enabling hard work and excellent productivity.

Deal and Kennedy (1982) suggest that the business environment is "the single greatest influence in shaping a corporate culture." What companies do in their competitive environments shapes the reality of how organizations manage activity and whether or not they are successful. Values emerge that help individuals determine where the emphasis of their efforts should be placed. In other words, organizational values help people become dedicated to a cause, which in turn guides decisions about all types of behaviors. These strong values are not, however, without their dangers. Strong organizational values may limit change and encourage obsolescence when organizational values come in conflict with changing environments requiring new decisions and approaches. Regardless of whether their impact is positive or negative, values, according to Deal and Kennedy, are the core of corporate culture.

Deal and Kennedy contend that heroes are the real live human successes who become role models for the culture's values. Stories and myths about the behaviors of heroes help organizational members determine what they have to do to succeed and what is valued by the organization. Rites and rituals also serve this function. Deal and Kennedy identify management rituals such as formal meetings in which rituals develop about the number held, the setting, the table's shape, who sits where, and who is in attendance. Recognition rituals, ranging from formal events honoring outstanding service to informal traditions, also identify what the organization holds to be important and help to integrate individual and organizational goals. Finally, Deal and Kennedy suggest that informal organizational communication is the cultural network and as such is the only way to understand what is really going on. From the Deal and Kennedy perspective, culture is the organizational process that most contributes to shaping organizational outcomes. The communication of culture therefore both shapes behavior and reflects the operating reality of the organization.

## Theory Z

Ouchi's theory derived from comparisons between Japanese and American organizations. Theory Z organizations retain individual achievement and advancement as a model but provide a continuing sense of organizational community not typical of many U.S. organizations.

## Theory Z: William Ouchi (1943– )

Among the more popular of the new cultural approaches is William Ouchi's **Theory Z** (1981). As McGregor characterized human behavior with Theory X and Theory Y, Theory Z proposes that organizations must adapt to the key elements of the culture in which they operate. In other words, Theory Z makes assumptions about culture as Theory X and Theory Y made assumptions about individuals.

Ouchi's work begins by contrasting what he calls Type A American with Type J Japanese organizations. He contends that the two types differ in seven defining characteristics appropriate to each culture. Type A American organizations are characterized by short-term employment, individual decision making, individual responsibility, rapid promotion, formal control, specialized career paths, and segmented concerns. Type A organizations reflect cultural values of individuality over group membership and assume that broad social needs are supported by institutions such as churches, schools, and neighborhood groups rather than formal employment groups.

On the other hand, Type J Japanese organizations can be characterized by lifetime employment, consensual decision making, group or collective responsibility, slow advancement, informal control, generalized career paths, and holistic concerns. The Type J organization reflects a culture in which loyalty to groups is more important than individual achievement and in which individuals gain identity from long-term affiliations with the companies for which they work. Japanese culture supports an organizational structure that actually reduces employees' incentives to leave the work group and does not reward desires for rapid advancement.

Ouchi argues that American culture is changing, requiring a rethinking of some of the elements of the Type A organization. Although individuality is still valued, increased geographic mobility has generated a void in the social needs of workers who previously could have been expected to have those needs met from long-term, stable affiliations in their home communities. Ouchi proposes a Theory Z organization that retains individual achievement and advancement as a model but provides a continuing sense of organizational community not typical of Type A organizations. He sees the Theory Z organization as adapting to the changing needs of a mobile society and adapting to those needs in ways that support important cultural values—individuality—while adjusting to the evolution of new values, beliefs, and needs.

### In Search of Excellence: Thomas Peters (1942– ) and Robert Waterman (1936– )

In their famous best-seller *In Search of Excellence* (1982), Thomas Peters and Robert Waterman report the results of their study of sixty-two successful representatives of U.S. industry. Peters and Waterman attempted to understand how these large, successful companies were adapting to their changing environments. They worked from the premise that organizational structure cannot be understood apart from people. Indeed, Peters and Waterman (1982) suggest that "any intelligent approach to organizing had to encompass, and treat as interdependent, at least seven variables: structure, strategy, people, management style, systems and procedures, guiding concepts and shared values (i.e., culture), and the present and hoped-for corporate strengths or skills."

Peters and Waterman studied Hewlett-Packard, Digital Equipment, Frito-Lay, Delta Airlines, McDonald's, Boeing, Exxon, and numerous other companies selected because of their prestige in the business world, overall financial performance, industry position, and innovativeness as measured by their ability continually to bring new products and services to changing markets. Peters and Waterman (1982) were testing their assumption that excellent companies "not only are unusually good at producing commercially viable new widgets: innovative companies are especially adroit at continually responding to change of any sort in their environments."

As a result of their work, Peters and Waterman have identified eight cultural themes that most nearly characterized excellent, innovative companies. These themes suggest that "excellent companies were, above all, brilliant on the basics." The eight themes as identified by Peters and Waterman are as follows:

1. *A bias for action.* Excellent companies made decisions. They were analytical but not paralyzed by too much information. When they had a problem, they took action.
2. *Close to the customer.* Service, reliability, innovative products, and continual concern for customer needs were fundamentals for the excellent companies. The close-to-the-customer value also resulted in new product ideas and served as the basis for innovation.
3. *Autonomy and entrepreneurship.* Excellent companies wanted leaders in all types of organizational activity. They encouraged risk taking and innovation

and gave people responsibility for their own ideas. People were not so tightly controlled as to lose creativity.

4. *Productivity through people.* Workers at all organizational levels were the source of quality and the source of productivity. Excellent companies fought against a we/they management/labor attitude.

5. *Hands-on, value-driven.* The basic philosophy and values of the organization contributed more to achievement than did any specific technology or material resource. Values were seen to influence behavior and were considered the core of excellence.

6. *Stick to the knitting.* Excellent companies stayed in the businesses they knew. They did not diversify beyond what they understood in terms of either technology and service or customers. They grew by doing what they did extremely well.

7. *Simple form, lean staff.* None of the excellent companies was run with complicated organizational structures. In fact, many of the top corporate staffs were running multibillion-dollar organizations with fewer than a hundred people.

8. *Simultaneous loose-tight properties.* These companies were both centralized and decentralized. Autonomy and entrepreneurship were encouraged at all levels within the organizations. Decision making was often decentralized, yet core values were very centralized and rigidly supported.

As Peters and Waterman (1982) suggest, "The excellent companies live their commitment to people, as they also do their preference for action—any action—over countless standing committees and endless 500-page studies." Above all, though, "the intensity itself, stemming from strongly held beliefs, marks these companies."

As Ouchi discusses the broad influence of culture, Peters and Waterman describe how specific cultural themes contribute to excellence and organizational abilities to adapt to changing markets. Interestingly enough, much of what Peters and Waterman suggest that the excellent companies do in terms of people support and encouragement is similar to what Ouchi suggests that the Theory Z organization does in providing recognition for individual achievement while still meeting social support needs.

## Organizational Culture Formation: Edgar Schein[3]

Edgar Schein (1985b) defines organizational culture as "a pattern of basic assumptions—invented, discovered, or developed by a given group as it learns to cope with its problems of external adaptation and internal integration—that has worked well enough to be considered valid and, therefore, to be taught to new members as the correct way to perceive, think, and feel in relation to those problems." In support of this definition, Schein provides a model of culture with three distinct levels: (1) artifacts and creations, (2) values, and (3) basic assumptions. Artifacts and creations are the most visible level of culture consisting of the physical and social environment

---

[3]Dates not released.

created by organizational members. Artifacts and creations are observable not only by members of the culture but by observers as well. Artifacts and creations include architecture, technology, furniture, dress, and a variety of written documents. Behaviors such as decision making, meetings, and networks also are included. The second level, values, refers to both individual and group preferences for the way it should be in the organization. Values are less observable, although relationships between values and behaviors have been established by a variety of scholars. Finally, Schein describes as his third level, basic assumptions. Basic assumptions are the core of what individuals believe to be true about the world and how it works. Basic assumptions form around humanity's relationship to nature, the nature of reality and truth, the nature of human nature, the nature of human activity, and the nature of human relationships.

Schein (1983) also provides a model of how organizational cultures begin. According to Schein, the history of new organizations suggests they share the following initial steps: (1) the founder (or founders) has an idea for a new enterprise; (2) a founding group is created with members who have initial consensus about the idea; (3) a founding group acts to bring structure and resources to the idea; and (4) the initial functioning of the group is based on the idea, that is, the group begins to develop a history. Schein (1983) suggests:

> In this process the founder will have a major impact on how the group solves its external survival and internal integration problems. Because the founder had the original idea, he or she will typically have biases on how to get the idea fulfilled—biases based on previous cultural experiences and personality traits. (p. 17)

In later work, Schein (1985a) suggests that the functions of culture differ by growth stages of organizations. During the birth and early growth stages of organizations, for example, the founder or family dominates the organization and culture functions to hold the organization together, emphasize socialization, and develop commitment. Organizational midlife is characterized by the spawning of subcultures and loss of key goals, values, and assumptions. Organizational maturity brings cultural constraint on innovation with an emphasis on preservation of the past.

Warren Bennis (1986) also supports the importance of the powerful actor influence on culture. He states:

> I believe that the single most important determinant of corporate culture is the behavior of the chief executive officer. He or she is the one clearly responsible for shaping the beliefs, motives, commitments, and predispositions of all executives—from senior management to the operators of the organization. (p. 64)

### Sensemaking Model: Karl Weick (1936– )

The work of Karl Weick (1995) is an excellent example of what we mean by integrated perspectives. Many familiar with Weick's work would argue that he should be characterized as writing from a systems perspective, whereas others contend he more readily advances concepts aligned with culture studies. The discussion in

Chapter 3 of his views of enactment of organizations carries a distinctively "systems" flavor. Here, however, his sensemaking model is placed in the cultural perspectives section because of its focus on the intersection of simultaneous interpretation and action. Weick's provocative statement, "The outcome comes before the decision," helps us understand the dynamic nature of his sensemaking model, which includes authoring as well as interpretation. Weick (1995, 8–11) explains:

> The process of sensemaking is intended to include the construction and bracketing of the textlike cues that are interpreted, as well as the revision of those interpretations based on action and its consequences. Sensemaking is about authoring as well as interpretation, creation as well as discovery. . . . A crucial property of sensemaking is that human situations are progressively clarified, but this clarification often works in reverse. It is less often the case that an outcome fulfills some prior definition of the situation, and more often the case that an outcome develops that prior definition.

Weick is referring to the central role an individual's own actions play in determining what is the "sense of situations." He is arguing that it is a mistake to think that we make decisions in organizations according to well-developed plans. He proposes that we make decisions and then render them sensible by explaining the meaning of our decisions. Weick (1995, 61–62) identifies sensemaking as having seven distinguishing characteristics and provides a recipe for understanding each of the characteristics:

1. *Grounded in identity construction.* The recipe is a question about who I am as indicated by discovery of how and what I think.
2. *Retrospective.* To learn what I think, I look back over what I said earlier.
3. *Enactive of sensible environments.* I create the object to be seen and inspected when I say or do something.
4. *Social.* What I say and single out and conclude are determined by who socialized me and how I was socialized, as well as by the audience I anticipate will audit the conclusions I reach.
5. *Ongoing.* My talking is spread across time, competes for attention with other ongoing projects, and is reflected on after it is finished, which means that my interests may already have changed.
6. *Focused on and by extracted cues.* The "what" that I single out and embellish as the content of the thought is only a small portion of the utterance that becomes salient because of context and personal dispositions.
7. *Driven by plausibility rather than accuracy.* I need to know enough about what I think to get on with my projects, but no more, which means sufficiency and plausibility take precedence over accuracy.

Individual and organizational sensemaking activities illustrate the intersection of interpretation and action. Sensemaking can therefore be understood as part of the cultural web of the organization as well as a highly individual process.

Weick (1995) relates organizations and sensemaking processes: "Both organizations and sensemaking processes are cut from the same cloth. To organize is to impose order, counteract deviations, simplify, and connect, and the same holds true when people try to make sense."

Taken as a whole, these descriptions of cultural development, transmission, and sense making reflect basic assumptions about the dynamic nature of culture and its propensity to change across time.

## COMMUNICATION IMPLICATIONS OF INTEGRATED PERSPECTIVES THEORIES

The Integrated Perspectives theories present a diverse set of implications for organizational communication. The systems theorists all describe organizations with changing needs and environments, even though descriptions of the relationship to environments vary. Thus, the effectiveness of communication is related not only to what happens within the organization, but also to how the organization communicates with its environment, its customers and community. The cultural approaches, on the other hand, are more specific about the importance of communication in carrying messages about the culture and influencing behavior through cultural expectations.

When we examine the communication implications of the Integrated Perspectives ideas from the Functional framework, we see a different picture from either the Scientific Management or Human Behavior approaches. The rejection of the "one best way" concept and the emphasis on the external environment require a communication system in continual adaptation to changing circumstances. Communication fulfills organizing, relationship, and change functions, yet the balance among these functions depends on the needs of the specific organization based on its goals and environment. Likewise, message structure depends on what the organization does, who its members are, and how the organization relates to its public. Message direction, load, channels, networks, and distortion all can be described as contingent or dependent on specific circumstances.

The decision-making and cultural concepts of the Integrated Perspectives viewpoint take on particular significance when viewed from a Meaning-Centered approach to organizational communication. Both these concepts are based on how organizational members generate shared meanings and how these meanings influence behavior and organizational effectiveness. Although Integrated Perspectives theorists do not describe communication as synonymous with organizing, decision making, and culture, they do view rich, intense, informal communication as the foundation for influence and for the network that carries organizational culture. The major premises underlying the prescriptive and popularized cultural approaches are that organizations are more effective with strong cultures and that strong cultures require effective communication. Organizational identification and socialization are fundamental to a strong culture and as such are important managerial responsibilities.

The cultural theorists also underscore the importance of values for excellent organizations and the need for values to become part of the shared realities of organizational members. This concept of developing shared realities is the essence of the Meaning-Centered approach to organizational communication. Thus, cultural theorists can be said to understand that the generation of shared realities contributes to creating and shaping organizational events.

The Integrated Perspectives theories do not generally consider communication as a constitutive process but portray communication as symbolic processes enabling the construction of shared realities. Cultural theorists focus less on objective rationality than do other approaches but do not extend their concepts to critiques of power and the marginalization of women's voices. Multiple meanings, ambiguity, and continual change all are described in Integrated Perspectives theories. As such, this diverse group of theories begins to reflect some of the tenets of critical and postmodern organizational communication approaches.

## INTEGRATED PERSPECTIVES THEORIES IN CONTEMPORARY ORGANIZATIONS

With the contributions of theorists such as Simon, Woodward, Lawrence, Lorsch, Katz, Kahn, Trist, and Bamforth, we talked about the importance of the external environment and began to merge much of the thinking from the Scientific Management and Human Behavior approaches. Also, with the advent of the cultural approaches proposed by Integrated Perspectives theorists, communication was described as the process through which shared realities are generated and through which values, identification, and socialization occur.

There are numerous examples of the importance of organizations adjusting to their external environments. Big American cars of the 1950s and 1960s lost their competitive market position to foreign competition. The introduction of personal computers for a home market found several hundred companies scrambling to introduce new and better products in an attempt to gain market share. The back-to-basics emphasis in education has been in response to concerns that students are not developing competencies needed for an information society. The list could go on. The contribution of Integrated Perspectives theorists in describing the need to acknowledge the influence of the external environment has improved our ability to think comprehensively about organizations and how people and technology relate to larger environments.

Concern for organizational culture is readily apparent in contemporary organizations. Organizations publish vision and mission statements, conduct training programs that identify the values of the organization, and hold annual events of special cultural significance. Schools have graduation ceremonies; sales organizations have annual awards banquets; and special traditions emerge to celebrate promotions, achievements, and a variety of other organizational events.

The significance of the Integrated Perspectives approaches can be seen in a return to the Davis Instrument Company's manufacturing changes. The introduction of the new MCF system is in response to market pressure to remain cost competitive. The concern for how to reassign and train workers illustrates essential sociotechnical relationships among environmental needs for change, human needs during change, and the changing requirements of new technology. What happens next at Davis will depend on some factors not readily apparent in the case. What are the general expectations of the Davis work force regarding change? What does the "culture" suggest is going to happen? The decisions Pam Martin's supervisors make will be accepted or resisted, at least in part, based on their cultural fit to the shared realities of Davis and to the organizational values held by Davis employees. To advise Pam Martin and the supervisors effectively, we would need to know more about how things really work at Davis.

Think for a moment about organizations with which you are familiar. How have they adjusted to their environments? Is your school state-funded or dependent on private revenue? For either case, think about environmental influences school administrators must consider when planning programs and asking for monetary support. Now describe the shared values of your school. How are they communicated? Can you identify some of the rites and rituals that influence student identification and socialization? Finally, attempt to define what you would say to a new student about what it takes "to be successful around here."

# POSTMODERN, CRITICAL, AND FEMINIST PERSPECTIVES

Although all the perspectives discussed describe power relationships within organizations and although Integrated Perspectives place considerable emphasis on the subjective and interpretative dynamics in organizations, little attention is paid to power as domination or the challenging of traditional hierarchical and patriarchal systems of authority. Postmodern, Critical, and Feminist theory provide that critique and examine alternatives for organizational life.

**Postmodern and Critical Perspectives**
Theories that focus on power and domination and on challenges to hierarchy, bureaucracy, and management control.

**Postmodern and Critical Perspectives** focus on power and domination and on challenges to hierarchy, bureaucracy, and management control. In this section the postmodern organization as described by Stewart Clegg is discussed and the critical perspectives of Jurgen Habermas are explored. Next come commentaries from a diverse set of authors on postmodernism and critical theory. Finally, to understand the historical and present marginalization, discrimination, and oppression of women in the workplace, Feminist theory as described by Marta Calás and Linda Smircich is discussed.

## Postmodern Perspectives: Stewart Clegg (1947– )

Stewart Clegg (1990), in his work *Modern Organizations*, builds on the concepts of French philosophers such as Jean-François Lyotard (1984) and Jean Baudrillard (1983), who describe the postmodern condition as highly ordered, technologically specialized, mass-mediated, and demanding of precision, speed, flexibility, and adaptability in individual performance. These continuous and often conflicting demands promote numerous constructions of reality, foster ambiguity, raise distrust of traditional authority, and stimulate alternative sensemaking. Baudrillard has termed the postmodern condition of converting empirical and symbolic reality into mass-mediated signs, experiences, and objects the simulacrum. Although the literature of postmodernity (the historical period) and the philosophical tenets of postmodernism are extensive and important, we will focus on Clegg's description of the postmodern organization to assist our understanding of the ever-evolving ways in which we come to know organizational life.

Scientific Management, and to some extent the other organizational perspectives discussed, called for task specialization, mass consumption, and specialized jobs for which workers were thoroughly and completely trained. Clegg contends that postmodernism rejects these concepts when he characterizes postmodern organizations as flexible structures needing workers with multiple skills who are capable of continual learning. Market niches replace mass consumption, and smaller is better if organizations are doing what they do best. Bureaucracy is replaced by workplace democracy in which all employees are valuable sources of decision making. Market needs are primary, and teams replace the emphasis on the individual contributor. Top-down management is made obsolete by self-managing teams and quality is a part of all processes, not the "inspected-for-quality" mentality of the past. Management is a responsibility fulfilled at a point in time rather than a permanent occupation, and rewards are more group- or team-based than based on the individual. Trust is fundamental among all managers and employees, with an emphasis on broad support for planning and decision making. Eric Eisenberg and H. L. Goodall (1993) have described five principles of the postmodern organization: decentralization of power, changes in markets and commodity values, flattening of hierarchies, cultures based on trust and respect for differences, and the use of groups. Many of the principles of self-managing teams are described in Chapter 6.

## Critical Theory: Jurgen Habermas (1929–  )

Critical theory is what the name implies: a criticism, a critique of society, organizations, and social constructions. Tracing its roots to the work of Karl Marx and others, Critical theory today takes as a central theme the issues of power and power abuse in organizations and society as a whole. Although Critical theory continues, as Marx did, to look at problems with capitalism and oppression in society, current theorists are not expecting revolution but are seeking ways to generate a more genuinely participatory and democratic order. Jurgen Habermas, along with theorists such as Michel Foucault (see References and Suggested Readings for more information), rejects the concept of rational science as the basis of valid knowledge on which arbitrary capitalism is constructed. Habermas calls for the use of Critical theory (criticism, critique, and so forth) to reconstitute reason and rationality as processes for positive social change. According to Habermas, communicative process is the basis for change and, as discussed in Chapter 3, carries a notion of constitutive process, literally foundational to all organizing, influence, and decision making.

The concepts of Habermas and other Critical theorists challenge notions that management exists as a naturally emergent, value-free set of practices and persons. Critical theorists call for a third paradigm in contrast to scientific and interpretative approaches to management and organization. Specifically, Critical theorists seek understanding of organizational life nested in the broader context of society through understanding of power and political relationships.

### Commentaries on Critical Theory and Postmodernism: Mats Alvesson (1956– ) and Stanley Deetz (1948– ), Martin Kilduff (1949– ) and Ajay Mehra (1968– ), and Gareth Morgan (1943– )

The scholars in this section further our understanding of the importance of Postmodernism and Critical Perspectives. Unlike Clegg and Habermas, who are identified specifically with their respective theoretical approaches, Mats Alvesson, Stanley Deetz, Martin Kilduff, Ajay Mehra, and Gareth Morgan provide commentaries to identify key concepts and connections across the vast literatures of postmodernism and Critical theory. In other words, the explanations that follow help to understand broad concepts without focusing as much on the specific contributions to postmodernism and Critical theory of each of these scholars.

Alvesson and Deetz (1996) characterize the rise of both Critical theory and postmodernism as responses to social conditions. The current complex society has many positive capacities but also dangerous forms of domination. Both postmodernism and Critical theory identify significant problems that traditional, modern, technical, instrumental solutions will not address. The goal of Critical theory is to create societies and workplaces free of domination, with all members having equal opportunities to contribute. Critical theory pays particular attention to ideological critique. Critical theory calls into question the illusion that organizations and their processes are natural and self-evident, the universalization of managerial interests, the primacy of instrumental reasoning, and hegemonic practices.

Kilduff and Mehra (1997) describe Postmodern perspectives as championing many different theoretical positions while encouraging the continual challenging of underlying assumptions of how we view organizations and organizational life. Second, Kilduff and Mehra suggest postmodernism sees "truth" as problematic and focuses instead on how individuals construct their social worlds and how this construction takes on the nature of certainty or truth. Finally, postmodernism views the objective as subjective and challenges notions that we truly can generalize from one experience to another.

Morgan (1997), using an organization as domination metaphor, describes what he calls the ugly face of domination. Specifically, Morgan identifies examples of how organizations establish class structures (i.e., management and working classes) that provide forms of control over work, behavior, and even the continuation of employment. Examples of work hazards, occupational disease, and industrial accidents can also be viewed as resulting from domination. Children working sixteen-hour shifts, employees exposed to toxic chemicals without their knowledge, and equipment only marginally safe are but a few examples of concerns raised by Critical theorists. Workaholism and social and mental stress can be traced to the demands and norms established with today's high-pressured organizations. In addition, Morgan and others contend that the world economy is dominated more by multinational organizations than by governments or national alliances. Critical theorists view these multinational organizations as primary sites for domination and abuses of power.

### Feminist Organization Theories: Marta Calás (1942– ), and Linda Smircich[4]

Marta Calás and Linda Smircich (1992) have helped expand the realm of issues discussed by critical theorists through their application of feminist approaches to the critical study of organizations. Calás and Smircich, along with others, have moved beyond treating gender as one of many variables important to organizational and management studies to critique basic assumptions in organizational research. Specifically, **Feminist Perspectives** require that organizational theory be examined for its promotion of patriarchy as a particular understanding of power and gender relationships. A male-world view is examined, with particular attention to considerations of valuing the man as rational and the woman as supportive and nurturing. As such, women's experiences and voices are marginalized; they are of value, but less than centrally important to organizational power relationships.

**Feminist Perspectives**
Theories that critique the gendered assumptions of modern organizations and call for the recognition and valuing of multiple voices and perspectives.

Calás and Smircich (1996) identify seven approaches to Feminist theory: (1) liberal, (2) radical, (3) psychoanalytic, (4) Marxist, (5) socialist, (6) poststructuralist/postmodern, and (7) third world/postcolonial. The following descriptions help to see the distinctions among the seven and overall considerations of feminist organizational theories.

*Liberal feminist theory* provides evidence of inequities, particularly economic inequities, using a symbol (statistics) that carries strong social and academic credibility. Liberal Feminist theory initially countered the claims that feminism has gone too far and currently counters the thesis that "more women will make it better."

*Radical-cultural feminism* portrays possibilities and visions of an alternative world outside of patriarchy, offers "consciousness raising" as a unique form of organizational research and practice, documents alternative practices and alternative organizations, and provides specific examples of successful non-bureaucratic organizations.

*Psychoanalytic feminism* highlights the importance of psychosexual development in the formation of patriarchal social structures; fosters changes in gender relations and child-rearing practices as a step toward reducing gendered social inequality; and in intersection with cultural feminism, documents the

---

[4]Dates not released.

possibility of positive organizational practices located in women's unique psychosexual orientations and experiences, particularly those associated with caring, nurturing, and relating to others.

*Marxist feminist theory* is a reaction to and critique of capitalism. The class struggle between labor and capital is the central analysis of this perspective. Feminist perspectives identify "gender" as similar to "class," a social category, characterized by relations of domination and oppression.

*Socialist feminism/gendering of organizations and organizing* incorporates insights from Marxist, radical, and psychoanalytic feminism and focuses on gender relations and sex-gender systems.

*Poststructuralist feminism/postmodern perspectives* focus on the discursive nature of "social reality" and "subjectivity" and provides a complex view of social structures and oppression.

*Third-world/postcolonial feminism* critiques the concept of "gender" as constituted in the West and opens the possibility of other gendered configurations and more complex relations between women and men.

# COMMUNICATION IMPLICATIONS OF POSTMODERN, CRITICAL, AND FEMINIST PERSPECTIVES

The Postmodern, Critical, and Feminist approaches discussed focus on the centrality of organizational communication for understanding organizational relationships and the construction of broader social relationships. When we examine Postmodern and Critical Perspectives from the Functional framework, we quickly understand that the Functional framework is the focus of critique of those supporting a Postmodern and Critical Perspective. Although organizing, relationship, and change messages are acknowledged in Postmodern and Critical Perspectives, message functions are examined relative to power relationships, abuses of power, and the capacity of all messages to incorporate multiple meanings and ambiguity. Hierarchy with its control of networks, exclusion of voices other than the dominant power structure, and deliberate distortions through mediated channels should be exposed so as to support more participative and democratic practices in organizations.

The Meaning-Centered approach to organizational communication is reflected in Postmodern, Critical, and Feminist Perspectives of power, communication rules, and organizational attempts to manage socialization and culture. Postmodern and Critical Perspectives discount interpretative notions of the Meaning-Centered approach that focus on shared realities.

The Emerging Perspectives approach to organizational communication is most closely associated with Postmodern and Critical Perspectives theory. Emerging Perspectives describe communication as a constitutive process, a description closely aligned with the concepts of Habermas and others. Emerging Perspectives, along with Feminist Perspectives, also examine the ways in which power is abused and dominant voices marginalize women and others. The Emerging Perspectives approach to organizational communication criticizes Functional and Meaning-Centered perspectives in much the same manner as Postmodern and Critical Perspectives theorists discredit other schools of organizational behavior. Both the Emerging Perspectives approach and Postmodern and Critical Perspectives theories propose a value of increased participation and democracy among workers with an emphasis on the value of all organizational voices.

## POSTMODERN, CRITICAL, AND FEMINIST PERSPECTIVES IN CONTEMPORARY ORGANIZATIONS

The delayering of organizations—reduced numbers of hierarchical levels and managers—is evident in numerous organizations, with self-managing and high-performance teams replacing traditional notions of supervision. Postmodern and Critical Perspectives describe these changes in terms of power shifts, interdependence, and increased needs for flexibility and adaptation as contrasted with task specialization and shared meanings. Organizations of today and tomorrow are populated with increasingly diverse workers. Customers and markets are both diverse and specialized. Adaptation, flexibility, and change are more common than unusual, and organizations regularly examine new approaches requiring increased and changing skills from the work force. Hierarchy is challenged, ambiguity increased, and shared practices are required among those with fewer and fewer of the same messages or interpretations. Feminist issues affecting women and minorities struggle to come to the forefront of organizational concerns. Internationalization, global markets, and the changing work force all evidence postmodern and critical challenges in organizational life.

The Davis Instrument Company's problems can be viewed from both Postmodern and Critical approaches. Davis needs to change. The old relationships are not working as effectively as in the past. Assumptions about shared realities and how power relationships should contribute to decisions are reflected in the practices of Davis. Multiple meanings, ambiguity, and flexibility are issues facing management and the entire organization. To understand the Davis problem requires thinking about the assumptions that guide Davis decision making. In addition, consideration can be given to whether worker voices are marginalized as contrasted to the concerns of managers and supervisors.

## SUMMARY

In this chapter Scientific Management, Human Behavior, Integrated Perspectives, and Postmodern, Critical, and Feminist Perspectives for studying organizations and their communication implications were discussed. The Scientific Management stance was described by Frederick Taylor, Henri Fayol, and Max Weber as a "scientific" approach to the design of organizations. Organizational design was based on a carefully developed chain of command and efficient division of labor. Taylor described how the scientific method of work was to be established and became famous for the introduction of time and motion studies. Fayol organized the first general set of principles for management and identified five basic activities of management: planning, organizing, commanding, coordinating, and controlling. Fayol also introduced the concept of horizontal communication with the use of his famous "bridge." Weber, the father of bureaucracy, established criteria for evaluating an organization based on merit and productivity. Weber's system included bureaucratic authority, standardized rules and procedures, "rational" decision making, task competence, and qualified personnel. In the Scientific Management point of view, communication was viewed as management's responsibility, with task- and rule-related messages moving along formal networks in a downward direction. As such, messages were expected to be low in equivocality. Decision making was a management-controlled variable of the organization, as was influence. Culture was not considered and probably would have been viewed as inappropriate.

The Human Behavior viewpoint shifted the emphasis away from the structure of organizations, work design, and measurement to the interactions of individuals, their motivations, and influence on organizational events. The work of Mary Parker Follett, Elton Mayo, Douglas McGregor, and Rensis Likert was used to describe this viewpoint. Parker Follett urged that productive organizations must be concerned with the desires and motivations of individuals and groups. Mayo's famous Hawthorne studies demonstrated the importance of peer influence for productivity. McGregor described the assumptions we make about human nature and how they contribute to what we view as appropriate organizational behavior. McGregor proposed that Theory X managers believe the average person dislikes work and will avoid responsible labor whenever possible; the Theory Y worker, on the other hand, was characterized as self-directed and self-controlled and as finding work as natural as play. Likert, as Weber had done for the Scientific Management viewpoint, described systems of management and proposed a new theory, participative management. Likert's systems—exploitive authoritative, benevolent authoritative, consultative, and participative—reflect how management uses information from employees. Likert's ideal of participative management was based on trust between management and employees, with decisions made throughout the organization. Groups and links among groups were a central focus of his approach. The Human Behavior theorists described communication as performing organizing, relationship, and change functions, with all organizational members participating. Networks were both formal and informal, and message equivocality could be characterized as higher than the Scientific Management theorists envisioned. Decision making occurred throughout the organization, particularly if the organization demonstrated a supportive climate. The peer group was viewed as a primary source of influence.

The approaches of Herbert Simon, Eric Trist, Kenneth Bamforth, Joan Woodward, Paul Lawrence, Jay Lorsch, Daniel Katz, Robert Kahn, Gareth Morgan, Margaret Wheatley, Peter Senge, Terrence Deal, Alan Kennedy, William Ouchi, Thomas Peters, Robert Waterman, Edgar Schein, and Karl Weick grew out of criticisms of both the Scientific Management and Human Behavior viewpoints. These viewpoints, according to their critics, had failed to integrate organizational structure, technology, and people with the larger environments in which organizations exist. The Integrated Perspectives approaches attempted to explain how people, technology, and environment interact to influence goal-directed behavior. Simon introduced the concept that decision making could be viewed as the essential organizational process. To Simon, organizational behavior was a complex network of decisions that created and shaped organizational events. The process was "bounded" in rationality by the limits of human information processing. Trist and Bamforth described the necessity for integrating social and technical systems to maximize productivity, and Woodward and Lawrence and Lorsch rejected any "one best way" to organize in favor of what they called contingency theory. Contingency theory was described as the establishment of internal organizational processes and states contingent on external environmental and individual member needs. Although closely related to contingency theory, the systems approach, as described by Katz and Kahn, emphasized the relationships among subsystems of the organization for the taking in of materials and resources (input), the processing of materials and resources (throughput), and the yielding of a finished product (output) to the larger environment.

Cultural approaches attempted to explain organizational behavior in terms of the influence of culture. Deal and Kennedy identified five basic elements of organizational culture: business environment, values, heroes, rites and rituals, and cultural network. Ouchi described a new Theory Z organization that adapts to the American culture through emphasis on both individual achievement and social support, and Peters and Waterman identified eight cultural themes dominant in successful U.S. organizations. These themes, according to Peters and Waterman, emerge from the strongly held beliefs or values that mark successful companies. Schein provided a model of how organizational cultures begin by describing the importance of founders or founding groups and extending that discussion to differences in cultures by growth stages of organizations. The communication implications resulting from the work of the Integrated Perspectives theorists are diverse, with communication viewed both as a central process for organizational effectiveness and as dependent on the needs of a particular organization.

The Postmodern and Critical Perspectives theories discussed focus on power as domination or the challenging of traditional hierarchical and patriarchal systems of authority. Postmodern and Critical Perspectives provide critique and examine alternatives for organizational life. Stewart Clegg, representing the postmodern view, characterized postmodern organizations as flexible structures needing workers with multiple skills who are capable of continual learning. Market niches replace mass consumption, and bureaucracy is replaced by work place democracy. Teams replace the emphasis on the individual contributor. Critical theory is what the name implies: a criticism, a critique of society, organizations, and social constructions. Jurgen Habermas rejected the concept of rational science as the basis of valid knowledge on which arbitrary capitalism is constructed. He used concepts of communication and criticism to reconstitute reason and rationality as processes for positive social change. Finally, Feminist Perspectives as described by Marta Calás and Linda Smircich critiqued the gendered assumptions of modern organizations and called for the recognition and valuing of multiple voices and perspectives.

## WORKSHOP

1. Form groups of four to six members each. Identify organizations in your community with which group members have some familiarity. Discuss whether these organizations represent Scientific Management, Human Behavior, Integrated Perspectives, or Postmodern, Critical, and Feminist Perspectives viewpoints. Do any of the organizations represent combined approaches? How effective is communication in the various organizations?

2. A Guide to Case Development and Analysis should be used as you begin to examine increasingly complex organizational cases and prepare cases from personal interviews and experiences. (See pp. 130–131.)

3. Using the Guide to Case Development and Analysis, analyze the "What Do You Mean I'm Not Going to Graduate?" and the "We Never Had to Advertise Before" cases and propose ways to approach the problems identified in the cases. (See pp. 131–133.)

### A Guide to Case Development and Analysis

Case studies help close the gap between reading about organizations and theory and knowing what to do in an actual organizational situation. Cases are examples or illustrations of organizational problems to which we apply the theory we study to determine how best to solve problems.

A case gives information about the organization, its people, and its problems. Information is used to analyze what contributed to the problems and determine how the problems presented in the case might be treated. When preparing an original case, your personal business experiences or interviews with organizational members can be used to identify interesting communication problems. Problems are usually presented (either orally or in writing) in story or narrative forms with enough clarification so others can generate solutions. Case development and analysis can be approached by a three-step process. The process begins by asking questions and developing answers in each of our competency areas: knowledge, sensitivity, skills, and values.

#### 1. IDENTIFY AND DESCRIBE THE SITUATION OR PROBLEM
*Knowledge*
What are the major and minor problems in the case?
What communication theories apply to these problems?
What organizational theories or perspectives are apparent?
What information is missing?

What assumptions are we making about the organization, its people, and their problems?

### Sensitivity
Who or what appears to be most responsible for the communication problems?
What are the shared realities in the organization?
Are the principal individuals good communicators? If not, what are their limitations?
Are the principals in the case assuming responsibility for their communication behaviors?

### Skills
What skills do the case principals exhibit?
What additional skills are needed?
How could these skills be developed?
What overall organizational skills are lacking?
What are the major organizational strengths?

### Values
What is important or valuable to the involved individuals?
Do they share similar values?
How would you describe the culture of the organization?
Are individual and organizational goals compatible?

### 2. DEVELOP ALTERNATIVES AND TEST THE "REALITY" OF POSSIBLE SOLUTIONS
What should be done?
How many alternatives can be generated?
Can alternatives be combined?
What can be done?
Are the people involved willing to change?

### 3. PROPOSE SOLUTIONS AND SUGGEST IMPLEMENTATION PLANS
Explain your reasoning for solution selection.
Identify who is responsible for what.
Determine a timetable for implementation.
Suggest how your solution might be evaluated.

■ ■ ■ ■ ■ ▬▬▬▬▬▬▬▬▬▬▬▬▬▬▬▬▬▬▬▬▬

## THE "WHAT DO YOU MEAN I'M NOT GOING TO GRADUATE?" CASE

Central University is a large midwestern school noted for its fine undergraduate liberal arts programs. All students entering the university are required to complete humanities, social science, mathematics, natural science, and foreign language requirements. The foreign language requirement has been strengthened in the last two years, and all students are required to complete four semesters of a language or pass a competency examination.

*(continued)*

The foreign language requirement has not been received favorably by the student body. Petitions to the university's committee on academic progress are often requests for exceptions to the requirement so as to graduate in a desired semester. To minimize these complaints and better inform the student body about the nature of the requirements, the committee has asked that admissions and records revise Central's bulletin to place the requirements section in a more prominent position. The advising service also has been asked to name all juniors and seniors who have not completed the requirement.

Jane Jordan is one of the students who, in her second semester of her senior year, has received a notice from the advising office that she will not graduate on schedule because of a one-semester deficiency in Spanish. Jane is furious and goes to the head of the committee on academic progress with her complaint. Jane claims that she was admitted to Central before the requirement was put in place and that although she had to drop out for two semesters to work, she should be graduated under her original admission requirements. Jane admits that she was advised of the new requirement when she returned to Central but was assured by an advisor that she could get out of it because of her original admission date and generally good academic record. Jane further contends that she has a job waiting at the end of the semester and will be harmed if required to stay at Central another term. The head of the committee on academic progress ponders what to do.

### QUESTIONS FOR DISCUSSION
1. What are the communication problems in this case?
2. Who is responsible?
3. Is Jane approaching the problem correctly?
4. What should the head of the committee do?

## THE "WE NEVER HAD TO ADVERTISE BEFORE" CASE

John Murphy and his father, Al, are arguing again. In fact, it seems they argue most of the time now. Today's argument is over whether or not to begin radio advertising for their appliance repair shop.

Al Murphy founded Murphy's Appliance Repair some twenty-five years ago. John literally grew up in his father's business and had been eager to finish college and prepare to take over daily operation when his father retired. Neither man had anticipated their numerous differences of opinion.

Al believed that he knew the business better than anyone and that John's ideas were too new and costly for any successful operation. John, on the other hand, believed there was increasing competition in their part of town and that resting on past success was dangerous. John wanted to add additional automated machinery and advertise, as two of their competitors were doing. John saw the changes as progressive and necessary to the long-term survival of the business.

John had never had trouble communicating with his father before. He wondered what he could say to make his point. After all, the business had to support not only his father and mother but John's family as well. He had every right to make decisions if he was to have so much responsibility. Al felt much the same way. How could this disagreement be happening? He had looked forward to John's entrance into the business. Had college ruined his understanding of business? Wasn't it supposed to be just the other way around?

### QUESTIONS FOR DISCUSSION

1. What is happening between John and Al?
2. Is advertising the real issue?
3. Are their values different?
4. What would you suggest that John do?
5. What can Al do?

# REFERENCES AND SUGGESTED READINGS

Alvesson, M., and S. Deetz. 1996. Critical theory and postmodernism approaches to organizational studies. In *Handbook of organization studies*, eds. S. Clegg, C. Hardy, and W. R. Nord, 191-217. Thousand Oaks, CA: Sage.

Alvesson, M., and H. Willmott, eds. 1992. *Critical management studies*. London: Sage.

Barnard, C. 1938. *The functions of the executive*. Cambridge, MA: Harvard University Press.

Baudrillard, J. 1983. *Simulations*. New York: Semiotext.

Baudrillard, J. 1990. *Cool memories*. London: Verso.

Bennis, W. G. 1986. *Leaders and visions: Orchestrating the corporate culture*. New York: The Conference Board.

Calás, M. B., and L. Smircich. 1992. Using the F word: Feminist theories and the social consequences of organizational research. In *Academy of management proceedings*, ed. F. Hoy, 335-39. Washington, DC: Academy of Management.

Calás, M. B., and L. Smircich. 1996. From "the woman's" point of view: Feminist approaches to organization studies. In *Handbook of organization studies*, eds. S. Clegg, C. Hardy, and W. R. Nord, 218-257. Thousand Oaks, CA: Sage.

Clegg, S. 1990. *Modern organizations*. Newbury Park, CA: Sage.

Cyert, R. M., and J. G. March. 1963. *A behavioral theory of the firm*. Englewood Cliffs, NJ: Prentice Hall.

Deal, T., and A. Kennedy. 1982. *Corporate cultures: The rites and rituals of corporate life*. Reading, MA: Addison-Wesley.

Eisenberg, E., and H. L. Goodall. 1993. *Organizational communication: Balancing creativity and constraint*. New York: St. Martin's.

Fayol, H. 1949. *General and industrial management*, trans. C. Storrs. London: Pitman and Sons.

Foucault, M. 1972. *The archaeology of knowledge*. London: Tavistock.

Foucault, M. 1979. *The birth of the prison*. Hammondsworth, Eng.: Penguin.

Katz, D., and R. Kahn. 1966. *The social psychology of organizations*. New York: Wiley.

Kilduff, M. and A. Mehra. 1997. Postmodernism and organizational research. *Academy of Management Review* 22 (3): 453-81.

Lawrence, P., and J. Lorsch. 1969. *Developing organizations: Diagnosis and action*. Reading, MA: Addison-Wesley.

Likert, R. 1961. *New patterns of management*. New York: McGraw-Hill.

Lorsch, J., and P. Lawrence. 1970. *Studies in organization design*. Homewood, IL: Irwin.

Lyotard, J. 1984. *The postmodern condition: A report on knowledge*, trans. G. Bennington and B. Massumi. Minneapolis: University of Minnesota Press.

March, J. G., and H. A. Simon. 1958. *Organizations.* New York: Wiley.

Mayo, E. 1945. *The social problems of an industrial civilization.* Boston: Graduate School of Business Administration, Harvard University.

McGregor, D. 1960. *The human side of enterprise.* New York: McGraw-Hill.

Metcalf, H. C., and L. Urwick. 1940. *Dynamic administration: The collected papers of Mary Parker Follett.* New York: Harper and Row.

Morgan, G. 1997. *Images of organizations.* Thousand Oaks, CA: Sage.

Ouchi, W. 1981. *Theory Z.* Reading, MA: Addison-Wesley.

Pasmore, W. A., and J. J. Sherwood. 1978. *Sociotechnical systems: A sourcebook.* San Diego, CA: University Associates.

Peters, T. J., and R. H. Waterman Jr. 1982. *In search of excellence.* New York: Harper and Row.

Roethlisberger, F. J., and W. J. Dickson. 1939. *Management and the worker.* Cambridge, MA: Harvard University Press.

Schein, E. H. 1983. The role of the founder in creating organizational culture. *Organizational Dynamics,* summer, 13-28.

Schein, E. H. 1985a. How culture forms, develops, and changes. In *Gaining control of the corporate culture,* eds. R. H. Kilmann, M. J. Saxton, and R. Serpa, 17-43. San Francisco: Jossey-Bass.

Schein, E. H. 1985b. *Organizational culture and leadership.* San Francisco: Jossey-Bass.

Senge, P. 1990. *The fifth discipline.* New York: Doubleday/Currency.

Simon, H. A. 1957. *Administrative behavior.* New York: Macmillan.

Smith, A. 1937. *The wealth of nations* (Cannon ed.). New York: Modern Library.

Taylor, F. W. 1913. *Principles of scientific management.* New York: Harper and Brothers.

Trist, E. L., and K. W. Bamforth. 1951. Some social and psychological consequences of the long-wall method of coal-getting. *Human Relations* 4: 3-38.

Weber, M. 1947. *The theory of social and economic organization,* trans. A. Henderson and T. Parsons. New York: Free Press.

Weick, K. 1995. *Sensemaking in organizations.* Thousand Oaks, CA: Sage.

Weick, K., and S. Ashford. 2001. Learning in organizations. In *The new handbook of organizational communication: Advance in theory, research, and methods,* eds. F. Jablin and L. Putnam, 704–31. Thousand Oaks, CA.: Sage.

Wheatley, M. 1992. *Leadership and the new science.* San Francisco: Berrett-Koehler.

Woodward, J. 1965. *Industrial organization: Theory and practice.* London, New York: Oxford University Press.

■ ■ ■ ■ ■

# CHAPTER FIVE

# INDIVIDUALS IN ORGANIZATIONS

---

## DEVELOPING COMPETENCIES THROUGH . . .

### KNOWLEDGE

Describing the diversity in the work force

Describing intrapersonal and interpersonal experiences of individuals in organizations

Describing theories of motivation

### SENSITIVITY

Relating motivation to communication behaviors

Being aware of communication apprehension in organizational experiences

Understanding how perceptions of communication competencies affect work satisfaction

Describing the importance of trust for interpersonal relationships

Distinguishing between barriers and positive attitudes for valuing diversity

### SKILLS

Valuing diversity

Practicing active listening

Practicing analysis capabilities

**VALUES**

Relating individual communication experiences to organizational identification, work performance, communication, and job satisfaction

Identifying personal needs in work settings

Relating valuing diversity to interpersonal effectiveness

■ ■ ■ ■ ■ ▬▬▬▬▬▬▬▬▬▬▬▬▬▬▬▬▬▬▬▬▬▬

## DAVE GREEN'S FIRST REAL JOB

Dave Green was excited. Today was his first day in the Human Resource Department of AMX Corporation, one of the best-known management training firms in the country. Landing a job with AMX had not been easy. On his campus alone, ten candidates had interviewed with the AMX recruiter. He had been told AMX had over 200 total applications from which to choose.

Dave knew that his degree in organizational communication was a good choice. Even so, he had been apprehensive about finding just the right job. The training position in the Human Resource Department was perfect, and working for Sally Johnson—one of the best trainers in the Midwest—was a real opportunity. Of course, he still worried about exactly what would be expected and whether he really was ready.

Dave's initial assignment was to work with a team of three experienced researchers and trainers to locate materials for a new training program Sally was developing. Although Sally had assured him that the three wanted more help, Dave wondered about his reception into the group. After all, they had been with AMX for several years and had worked together for Sally for more than two years. How would they feel about his becoming a member of the team?

As Dave prepared for his first meeting with Sally and the group, he began to think about what he might say and ask. How should he describe his skills? What techniques could he use to best understand their expectations of him? What were his goals in this job?

In this chapter we follow Dave's experiences with AMX Corporation. We try to understand his experiences as they might relate to our attempts to develop communication competencies important for working with supervisors, subordinates, and peers.

## INTRODUCTION

It is not unusual to be both excited and apprehensive when beginning a new semester, starting a new job, or joining a new volunteer group. We aren't completely sure what to expect. What will the people be like? Will our competencies meet the expectations of others? As individuals, we bring skills and abilities to organizations and expectations about what we hope will happen. We want to be successful, but like Dave Green, we wonder if our communication competencies are appropriate to the task.

Think for a moment about the organizations of which you are a member. How did you feel when you first enrolled in your school, were hired for your job, or joined a new church? How do you feel now? How would you describe your organizational experiences? Which give you the most satisfaction?

In previous chapters perspectives for understanding organizational communication have been described and major organizational theories have been studied. Now we will relate what we know about organizations as a whole to how individuals experience organizational life. Although we view organizations as entities in which many people work together for goal achievement, we all experience organizations as individuals. Understanding our individual experience is important for developing communication competencies that contribute to personal satisfaction as well as to overall organizational effectiveness.

This chapter is designed to contribute to *knowledge* by defining and describing concepts of motivation and identifying the primary characteristics of a diverse work force, including supervisor, subordinate, and peer relationships. *Sensitivity* competencies are developed through awareness of individual predispositions for organizational communication behaviors and by identifying effective and ineffective message strategies and tactics. *Skills* are developed by applying knowledge and sensitivity competencies to case and transcript analysis and practicing active listening. Finally, *values* are developed through awareness of the relationship of communication and organizational identification, work performance, and communication and job satisfaction.

## INDIVIDUALS IN ORGANIZATIONS

Working in organizations is an important fact of life for almost everyone, so important, in fact, that for most people, organizational experiences influence how we evaluate our individual self-worth and achievements. Yet how do we understand these experiences? How do they relate to developing communication competencies for organizational excellence?

An individual's organizational experiences result from the attitudes, beliefs, preferences, and abilities the individual brings to the organization; how the organization seeks to influence the individual; and what types of organizational relationships the individual develops. Each person brings to an organization his or her personal needs, predispositions for behavior, communication competencies, expectations, and skills. Individuals also develop relationships with supervisors, peers, subordinates, customers, and vendors that become primary information sources about all aspects of organizational life. The organization in turn establishes goals, policies, procedures, and reward systems that influence individual expectations and job experiences.

An individual's relationship with his or her supervisor is one of the most important of the primary communication experiences in organizational life. It is so important, in fact, that the quality of this relationship usually determines how the individual identifies with the organization as well as the individual's job and organization satisfaction. Peers also are an important source of information and support. Communication experiences with supervisors and peers are so influential that they contribute to the quality and quantity of an individual's work. The research of J. David Pincus (1986) has related quality and quantity of work—job performance—to perceptions of organizational communication experiences. In particular, quality of supervisory communication and information exchange within peer groups has been significantly related to revenue and work load measures of the overall organization.

An individual's communication satisfaction, according to Cal Downs and Michael Hazen (1977), is really a summing up of individual experiences in organizations, particularly experiences with information flow and relationships. Communication satisfaction is important to individuals, as evidenced by numerous studies that have linked communication satisfaction to job performance and job satisfaction. In other words, individuals who are satisfied with organizational communication experiences are more likely to be effective performers and to be satisfied with their jobs than those who have less positive communication relationships.

Figure 5.1 illustrates the primary communication experiences of individuals in organizations and relates these experiences to organizational outcomes such as communication and job satisfaction. The next sections of this chapter explore intrapersonal and interpersonal experiences in organizations and identify strategies and tactics for increasing individual communication effectiveness. Chapter 6 discusses individuals and small-group experiences.

## THE INTRAPERSONAL EXPERIENCE

Most of us want to identify with the organizations for which we work. We want to be thought of as good performers with high work standards. Certainly, most of us want to be satisfied with organizational communication as well as other aspects of our jobs. Earlier we found that people's work satisfaction is related to a variety of organizational relationships. If true for us, it becomes important to understand what contributes to these relationships. Among the primary influences on our relationships with supervisors, peers, and subordinates are the individual characteristics we possess, characteristics that can be described as our **intrapersonal experience.** The intrapersonal experience is based in part on self-concept, which in turn is influenced by a variety of past experiences, including various group affiliations. Our intrapersonal experience is composed of our personal needs, predispositions for behavior, communication competencies, and expectations. We quickly recognize that the intrapersonal experi-

**Intrapersonal experience**
Composed of our personal needs, predispositions for behavior, communication competencies, and expectations.

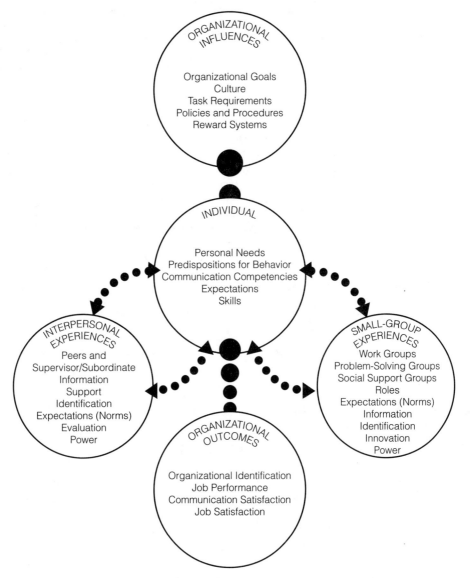

**FIGURE 5.1    Individuals in Organizations: Primary Communication Experiences**

ence is complex and differs from individual to individual. Understanding and appreciating these differences becomes central to building effective and satisfying organizational relationships. Before we discuss ways of understanding the intrapersonal experience, we return to Dave Green and his first real job. We will look at what Dave brings to AMX as a way of understanding individual intrapersonal experiences within organizations.

■ ■ ■ ■ ■

## DAVE GREEN: THE INTRAPERSONAL EXPERIENCE

Dave knows that the AMX job will be a test of what he has learned. He has always been a top student. He was proud to be listed on honor rolls, and he graduated in the top 10 percent of his class. He has thought a lot about the AMX interview questions concerning his strengths and weaknesses and ultimate career goals.

Dave knows he has good verbal skills and has been able to work effectively in groups. In fact, on most group projects during his university days he volunteered to do the oral presentations, something many of his fellow students dreaded. In return, Dave has not always done his share of the research and writing. He remembers describing himself to the AMX interviewer as a leader, yet he wonders if that will be at all appropriate when he is the new member of an experienced work team. As Dave thinks about his new job, he is inclined to wait and let others take the lead until he has more experience. After all, he wants the people at AMX to think that he is competent and worthy of their decision to hire him.

As Dave begins his new job, he expects his work to be very different from his four years of college. He believes that AMX is a top company with highly competent people. He is somewhat apprehensive about his ability to produce in a team of experienced researchers and trainers. Also, he believes his new boss will have high expectations of his abilities, abilities that as yet have not been thoroughly tested. As learned in Chapter 3, Dave is in the anticipatory phase of socialization.

**Motivation**
Term to describe intrapersonal experiences that influence behavior.

## Motivation

Dave Green would say that he is beginning his new job at AMX with high **motivation.** He wants to succeed and looks forward to the chance to demonstrate his abilities. Chances are the AMX interviewers offered him the job because they also believed that he was motivated to achieve. What exactly is motivation, and how does motivation relate to intrapersonal experience and communication competency?

Put simply, motivation is the term used to describe intrapersonal experiences that influence behavior. We don't see the motivation, but we see behavior. We infer that unseen internal reactions have motivated that behavior. Dave Green, for example, tells the interviewer that he is eager to work for such a well-respected management training firm. Dave's statement is observable behavior. The interviewer, however, infers that Dave's statement of eagerness reflects his motivation to succeed at AMX. Taking the interview and Dave's qualifications as a whole, the interviewer decides that Dave is positively motivated to behave in a way desirable to AMX. As a result, Dave gets the job.

Chances are that we can all recall times when we were highly motivated to do a good job and other times when we were not motivated at all. We recognize what feeling motivated is and can understand that in some way that feeling influenced our behavior. What causes that internal experience? What happens to motivate us?

Social scientists take many different approaches to describe the somewhat ambiguous concept of motivation for behavior. Abraham Maslow, for example, contends that behavior is influenced by internal needs. He thinks that needs such as safety and security, prestige, and self-actualization are more important in understanding an individual's behavior than influences in the external environment. Frederick Herzberg, on the other hand, describes behavior as a result of both internal and external motivators, and B. F. Skinner views reinforcement from the external environment as the primary influence for behavior. In their criticism of need satisfaction theories, Gerald Salancik and Jeffrey Pfeffer provide an important link between motivation and communication theory when they propose that workers' job attitudes are a function of their communication activities.

**Hierarchy of Needs**
Maslow's description of human behavior based on an ascending order of physiological, safety and security, love and social belonging, esteem and prestige, and self-actualization needs.

## Abraham Maslow (1908–1970)

Abraham Maslow (1954) is famous for what has been described as his **Hierarchy of Needs** theory, which proposes that human behavior seeks either to increase need satisfaction or to avoid a decrease in need satisfaction. According to Maslow, individuals focus attention on needs that are not met and are motivated to seek satisfaction of those needs. Maslow describes needs in an ascending hierarchy beginning with physiological needs, followed by safety and security needs, love and social belonging, esteem and prestige, and self-actualization (see Figure 5.2).

Physiological needs are the basic body needs of food, sleep, sex, and survival. Although these needs vary from individual to individual, Maslow contends that until these needs are reasonably well met, individuals do not focus their behavior on higher-level needs. From an organizational perspective, many physiological needs are met by the regularity of a paycheck, which provides food and basic physical survival.

Maslow believed that the satisfaction of safety and security needs also varies from individual to individual. What constitutes freedom from physical harm and security to one individual may not represent that same safety to another. Individuals in organizations satisfy their safety and security needs when they believe their jobs are relatively secure and when working conditions are free of physical harm.

Love and social belonging needs are met through family affiliations, friendships, and a variety of peer groups that provide social support and affection. As with all other needs, the degree to which individuals seek love and social belonging varies. Social belonging needs in organizations are generally thought of as being satisfied through peer and supervisory and subordinate relationships and through similarities between the organization's values and the values of individual members.

Maslow describes esteem and prestige needs as the desire for self-respect and the respect of others. Esteem and prestige are both internally defined and influenced by perceptions of what is prestigious to others. In organizations, esteem and prestige needs are satisfied through performance evaluation, job titles, status symbols, and the pride individuals feel in their work contributions.

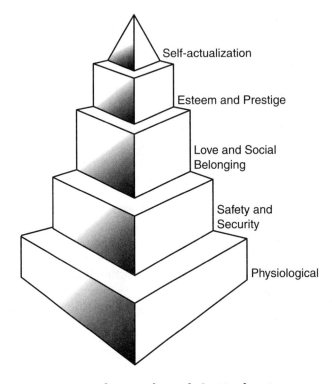

Self-actualization

Esteem and Prestige

Love and Social
Belonging

Safety and
Security

Physiological

**FIGURE 5.2    The Need Levels in Maslow's
Hierarchy of Needs**

Self-actualization is at the top of Maslow's hierarchy. According to Maslow, self-actualization is the belief that one has satisfied his or her full potential and is engaged in activities for which he or she is uniquely suited. As such, self-actualization cannot be explained in terms of a specific organizational responsibility or recognition but in terms of how an individual believes his or her abilities are used within the organizational setting.

Maslow's Hierarchy of Needs has several important implications for communication behavior. The theory implies that individual communication behavior in some way reflects an assessment of need satisfaction. Observation of individual communication behavior can therefore provide important evidence about what is motivational to an individual at a given time. The individual who communicates an insecurity about his or her acceptance in a work team may be focusing on low fulfillment of love and social belonging needs. A supervisor, according to Maslow, is unlikely to be able to motivate this individual by describing the prestige associated with a new job assignment that further removes the individual from peer approval.

Maslow's theory implies that it is not motivational to communicate about needs that are reasonably well met. Although money and fringe benefits are important, communication designed to motivate at these lower-level needs frequently does not accurately assess the love and social belonging, esteem and prestige, and self-actualization needs of individuals. Maslow's theory also suggests that if communication behavior in the organization does not meet the perceived needs of the individual, the individual will continue, in what is essentially healthy behavior, to seek need satisfaction. Thus, complaints and conflict that are often viewed as counterproductive organizational behaviors may be healthy individual behavior in pursuit of personal need satisfaction.

As Dave Green begins his job at AMX, he is concerned about his acceptance in an experienced work team. Using Maslow's concepts we would say that Dave is concerned about his love and social belonging needs. He is therefore likely to pay particular attention to communication with his peers and to behave in ways he believes appropriate for their acceptance.

**Motivation-Hygiene theory**
Herzberg's description of human behavior based on the influence of both internal and external factors. The theory proposes that satisfaction and dissatisfaction are not polar opposites and that what produces dissatisfaction with work when corrected will not necessarily produce motivation.

## Frederick Herzberg (1923–2000)

The **Motivation-Hygiene theory** of Frederick Herzberg (1966) emphasizes the influence of both internal and external factors in explaining human behavior. Herzberg's theory proposes that satisfaction and dissatisfaction are not polar opposites. In other words, what produces dissatisfaction in the work environment, if corrected, will not necessarily produce satisfaction or motivation. His research suggested that environmental factors (hygiene factors) such as status, interpersonal relations, supervision, policies, working conditions, and salary all influenced whether workers were dissatisfied. For example, if salaries were too low, dissatisfaction was predictable. If salary adjustments were made, however, satisfaction or motivation would not necessarily occur, although dissatisfaction might be lessened. The factors he found to be motivational were work itself, achievement, growth and responsibility, recognition, and advancement.

Herzberg concluded that many organizations attempt to motivate workers through hygiene factors, when hygiene factors can only be expected to relate to whether workers are dissatisfied, not whether they are truly motivated. From a communication perspective, Herzberg's Motivation-Hygiene theory suggests that dissatisfaction can be relieved by satisfactory communication and action directed toward hygienic work factors. Motivation, however, will not be achieved by such communication. Motivational communication is more likely to be effective when directed to achievement, recognition, challenging work, increased responsibility, and growth and development.

Herzberg's concept of motivation, applied to Dave Green, suggests that Dave will be motivated by his desire to be competent (to achieve) in his new work setting. From the Herzberg perspective, Dave's apprehension about joining an experienced work team is based on his motivation for challenging work and growth and development.

**Rewards**
Positive feedback or tangible reinforcements for organizational behaviors.

## B. F. Skinner (1904–1990)

B. F. Skinner, in contrast to both Maslow and Herzberg, proposed that human behavior can be motivated and is influenced by **rewards** in the individual's environment. According to Skinner

(1953), behavior reinforced through positive feedback or tangible rewards will be perpetuated, whereas behavior that does not receive positive reinforcement will be unlikely to continue. When applied to the organizational setting, the paycheck is a form of feedback that reinforces behavior expectations. Supervisors provide feedback on behavior to subordinates, and peer groups develop norms of expected behaviors that when exhibited by individuals are rewarded with continued group membership. Skinner's theory does not take into account individual needs, as Maslow's does, nor admit to complex relationships between satisfaction and dissatisfaction, as does Herzberg's Motivation-Hygiene theory. Skinner's theory does suggest that communication about rewards will be motivational only as long as rewards are linked to specific behaviors. In other words, if behavior is to be influenced, communication must be directed at specific behaviors and linkages must be understood by people the organization seeks to influence.

Skinner's theory of what motivates behavior suggests that Dave is joining AMX because of what he knows about the organization and his belief that he has landed a prize job. His reward in obtaining the job will probably influence his attempts to exhibit behaviors that support the norms of his new work team. According to Skinner, these norm-conforming behaviors, if supported by positive feedback or tangible rewards from his peers and supervisor, will motivate Dave to perpetuate their use and become one of the group.

## Gerald Salancik (1943–1996) and Jeffrey Pfeffer (1946– )

**Social Information Processing**
Theory that proposes that a person's needs and attitudes are determined by the information available at any given time.

Gerald Salancik and Jeffrey Pfeffer (1978), in criticizing need satisfaction theories, propose that a person's needs and attitudes can be understood in terms of the **Social Information Processing** theory. This theory proposes that people's needs and attitudes are determined by the information available to them at any given time. Salancik and Pfeffer suggest three basic determinants of attitudes or needs, (1) the individual's perception of the job or task characteristics, (2) information the social environment provides to the individual about what attitudes are appropriate (i.e., social information), and (3) the individual's perception of the reasons for his or her past behaviors. Thus, Salancik and Pfeffer describe needs differently from the internal-drives portrayal of Maslow. Salancik and Pfeffer conceptualize needs as the results or outcomes produced by an individual's perceptions and by the social information available in the work environment.

Salancik and Pfeffer identify four ways in which social information influences attitudes: (1) overt, evaluative statements of coworkers directly shape individual worker attitudes; (2) frequent talk among coworkers about certain dimensions of the job and work environment focuses attention on what is considered to be important or salient in the work setting; (3) information from coworkers, or social information, helps interpret and assign meaning to environmental cues and events in the work setting; and finally, (4) social information influences the way an individual interprets his or her own needs. Thus, Salancik and Pfeffer argue that job attitudes are a result of social information in the work setting coupled with the consequences of past individual choices. The organization, then, can be viewed as having influence on attitudes by contributing information to the attitude formation process. The Social Information Processing theory challenges notions that individuals have stable, relatively unchanging internal needs. Salancik and Pfeffer propose that the communication activities of an organization act as a primary influence on attitude formation, which in turn is influential in understanding human behavior.

Dave Green's transition from school to AMX helps us understand the somewhat complex relationships proposed by Salancik and Pfeffer. Dave Green expresses a positive attitude about his experiences during college. The same Dave Green also expresses uncertainty about his ability to meet the expectations at AMX. Salancik and Pfeffer contend that the individual's perception of the job or task characteristics shapes attitudes or needs. Thus, it is expected that Dave's perception of his competency will differ based on his understanding of the differences between college and AMX.

During college Dave made effective use of his verbal skills and ability to work in groups by volunteering to organize and make oral presentations researched and written by other classmates. Chances are Dave considered these tasks an appropriate use of his abilities (the approach met his needs), at least in part because his classmates approved of his efforts in the group and made known their dread of doing the presentations themselves. In other words, they influenced Dave with social information (1) overt, evaluative statements about Dave's positive contributions and (2) frequent talking about certain important dimensions of the project (oral presentations).

Also, Dave told the AMX interviewer that he was a leader, yet we see that he is inclined to let others take the lead until he has more experience at AMX. From the Salancik and Pfeffer perspective, Dave's attitude is probably shaped by his assignment of meaning to environmental cues, specifically the competence of the experienced team he is joining as a junior member. The Social Information Processing concept suggests that Dave does not have a stable need to lead and that the difference in this need between college and AMX is based on the social information available to him about the differences in the expectations and realities of the two environments.

## Relating Communication and Motivation

Regardless of their differences in perspective, the theories of Maslow, Herzberg, Skinner, Salancik, and Pfeffer relate motivation and attitudes to communication experiences and behaviors. Research conducted by H. Wayland Cummings, Larry Long, and Michael Lewis exploring the relationship between communication and motivation also supports this strong link. Specifically, Cummings, Long, and Lewis (1983) found that individuals have a complex mix of intrinsic (internal) and extrinsic (external) motivators that, depending on their importance in a particular situation, influence how the individual responds to managing information, problem and solution identification, conflict management, and behavior regulation. Cummings,

Long, and Lewis go so far as to suggest "that a highly motivated worker will be productive when the worker's communication preference (associated with the worker's motivational patterns) matches the managerial communication environment of the organization."

Earlier we inferred from Dave Green's communication behavior that he was highly motivated as he began his new job at AMX. To illustrate the communication and motivation relationship further, the statements in Figure 5.3 have been taken from transcripts of conversations with workers asked to describe what motivates them in their work. The statements have been categorized as they reflect the motivational theories of Maslow, Herzberg, Skinner, and Salancik and Pfeffer.

## Predispositions for Organizational Communication Behaviors

Predispositions or preferences for organizational communication behaviors are an important part of an individual's intrapersonal organizational experience. Predispositions are personally held preferences for particular types of communication situations or behaviors. These preferences are a result of intrapersonal needs (motivation), past experiences, current information, and self-perception of communication competency. Predispositions for oral communication, for example, have been found to be related to our occupation choice, job satisfaction, productivity, advancement, and job retention. Thus, we infer that communication predispositions and preferences influence behavior and are therefore important for individual organizational experiences.

**Communication apprehension**
Predisposition for behavior described as an individual's level of fear or anxiety associated with either real or anticipated communication with others.

### Communication Apprehension
One of the most frequently researched of all communication predispositions is what James McCroskey (1982) has described as **communication apprehension** (CA). Generally defined as an individual's level of fear or anxiety associated with either real or anticipated communication with others, CA has been found to be meaningfully associated with such important organizational outcomes as occupation choice, perception of competence, job satisfaction, advancement, and job retention. In other words, individuals with high communication apprehension are more likely than others to be in jobs with low communication requirements, to believe themselves less competent than others, to exhibit lower job satisfaction than their counterparts, and to not advance in their organization as their technical skills might suggest they could. They will also spend less time than others with the organization.

Dave Green does not appear to be high in communication apprehension. His past experiences in groups suggest that he will volunteer for public speaking situations and is generally comfortable with his verbal skills. He can be expected, more than a person with higher communication apprehension, to integrate with his work group and successfully use his abilities at AMX.

**FIGURE 5.3    Worker Examples of Personal Motivation**

### MASLOW'S HIERARCHY OF NEEDS THEORY

1. Physiological needs. "I work because I have to put food on the table."
2. Safety and security needs. "I like to work here because there is a real commitment to no layoffs. The last place I worked wasn't like that."
3. Love and social belonging. "The people I work with are my best friends; we would do anything for each other."
4. Esteem and prestige. "This job has given me the visibility I need to advance."
5. Self-actualization. "My work is ideally suited for my talents. In some ways it doesn't seem right to take money for doing what I love to do."

### HERZBERG'S MOTIVATION-HYGIENE THEORY

*Hygiene Factors:*

1. Salary. "The pay here is good, and I give them a good return on their money."
2. Supervision. "I like my supervisor. We were really unhappy with the previous guy."
3. Status. "I like having my own office and a secretary. I've never had that before."

*Motivation Factors:*

1. Achievement. "I really feel a sense of accomplishment in this job."
2. Work content. "The work is challenging, and I think we are putting out a good product."
3. Responsibility. "They let us take real responsibility here. People expect the best but they don't always look over your shoulder."

### SKINNER'S POSITIVE REINFORCEMENT THEORY

1. Rewards. "We get a bonus if we outproduce our quota."
2. Rewards. "My supervisor was really complimentary about the design of the new system. I believe that my efforts are recognized."

### SALANCIK AND PFEFFER'S SOCIAL INFORMATION PROCESSING THEORY

1. Social information. "My boss really helped me identify what was important for this job. I think that I have responded with efforts that are recognized by the organization."
2. Social information. "My coworkers really helped me learn the ropes. You can make a lot of mistakes in this job if you don't learn what your work team needs and wants."

## Leadership and Conflict Preferences

In addition to differing levels of apprehension, individuals differ in their desire to lead others and in their perception of what is effective leadership. Individuals also differ in how they approach conflict. Leadership and conflict preferences have been theorized to influence choice of communication strategies and tactics in leadership and conflict situations. Numerous researchers have described both leadership and conflict predispositions or preferences in terms of an individual's combined concern for tasks or goals and people relationships. These two concerns combine with past experiences and an assessment of the present situation to influence behavior. Various predispositions for leadership and conflict behaviors are generally described as preferences for collaboration, compromise, avoidance, competition, or accommodation. For example, an individual with a strong competitive predisposition may not cooperate with the ideas of others in the same manner as an individual with a collaborative or accommodative predisposition. The individual with strong avoidance predispositions may attempt to avoid leadership responsibilities and conflict situations, as would the person with high communication apprehension. These preferences are described in detail in later chapters, and you will be provided with an opportunity to assess your individual predispositions for leadership and conflict.

## Communication Competency

Individuals' perceptions of their communication competencies—knowledge, sensitivity, skills, and values—influence their organizational experiences. When individuals believe their competencies are lower than others, that fact may well limit the responsibilities they will accept. On the other hand, individuals who assess their competencies as comparable to others may willingly accept new responsibilities as challenging and worthwhile. Perception of competency is, of course, related to communication apprehension and leadership and conflict preferences, but it is also related to past experiences, the presence or absence of particular skills, and deliberate attempts to improve competencies. As such, perception of competency can be described as a summing up of preferences and predispositions for organizational communication behavior.

# INTERPERSONAL EXPERIENCES

Much of our time in organizations is spent interacting with other people. A variety of interpersonal communication relationships is important for individual job involvement, satisfaction, identification, commitment, and productivity. This variety is important in understanding yet another dimension of how individuals experience organizations. As you might expect from the discussion of the intrapersonal experience, predispositions and preferences influence the types of interpersonal relationships that individuals establish. Preferences, however, are inadequate to

**Interpersonal experiences**
Descriptions of important one-on-one organizational relationships such as supervisors and subordinates and peer to peer.

explain fully what happens in what are called primary dyadic relationships in organizations. The relationships supervisors and subordinates and peers establish are governed not only by individual predispositions, but also by important task and social considerations as well as increasing diversity in the workplace. Before we explore the primary interpersonal relationships of supervisors and their subordinates and individual peer interactions, we return to Dave Green and observe some of his early **interpersonal experiences** at AMX.

■ ■ ■ ■ ■

## DAVE GREEN: INTERPERSONAL EXPERIENCES

Dave was pleased that John, the senior writer on the team, had asked him to lunch. Dave had worried that John might treat him like a kid because John did remind Dave a bit of his own father. He could learn a lot from John and certainly wanted John to think he was doing his job. Maybe John could fill him in on what his boss, Sally Johnson, really expected. The first few weeks of Dave's job at AMX had left him both elated and confused. Sally was friendly and seemed anxious for him to succeed, yet he wasn't sure what her expectations were. She had assigned him to do some research for part of the new project, but organizing and presenting the material was left up to Dave. Dave wasn't comfortable with asking her just what she wanted for the end product. He wasn't sure if Sally wanted a particular approach or didn't care as long as the material was good. John had told him yesterday that Sally would listen to a variety of approaches if the information was interesting and important. Dave was somewhat apprehensive about what Sally would find interesting. This lunch with John was timely. Maybe he could run some ideas past him and get a better feel for what he should do.

Dave's dilemma about his assignment is not unusual. Establishing expectations in supervisor-subordinate relationships can be difficult, especially in the beginning of a job. Dave is fortunate to have a peer like John who can help him define Sally's expectations and give him support as he adjusts to new challenges and ways of doing things. Dave is experiencing what was described in Chapter 3 as encounter socialization.

Dave is fortunate to have John's support because research reveals that primary dyadic relationships are important to overall job satisfaction. Successfully meeting Sally's expectations will influence not only how Sally feels about Dave, but also Dave's entire organizational experience. As researchers Sue DeWine and Frank Barone (1984) have suggested, "perceived organizational communication relationships are considered to be the most important contributor to job satisfaction as an organizational outcome." In addition Gerald Goldhaber, Michael Yates,

D. Thomas Porter, and Richard Lesniak (1978) reported that the most important organizational relationships are those closest to the individual and that "maintaining an effective relationship with an employee's immediate supervisor is, thus, the most important correlate of job satisfaction." Gail McGee, Jane Goodson, and James Cashman (1987) contrasted employees reporting themselves to be high in stress but high in job satisfaction, with employees reporting high stress but low job satisfaction. Their findings support the importance of interpersonal relationships when they report that employees with high stress and high job satisfaction (more than their less satisfied counterparts) found their jobs challenging and interesting, perceived organizational communication as timely and useful, perceived fewer supervisory problems, and worked with managers whom they perceived to be high in referent power.

## Communication Networks

The concept of communication networks (formal and informal patterns of communication that link organizational members together) was introduced in Chapter 3. Dave's experiences help expand on the earlier discussion and explain the various networks we can expect in most any type of organization. Cynthia Stohl (1995) suggests that networks can be described at four interdependent levels: personal, group, organizational, and interorganizational. Peter Monge and Noshir Contractor (2001) explain: "Communication networks are the patterns of contact between communication partners that are created by transmitting and exchanging messages through time and space. These networks take many forms in contemporary organizations, including personal contact networks, flows of information within and between groups, strategic alliances between firms, and global network organizations, to name but a few." Dave will participate in all levels as he links not only with his primary work team and supervisor but with others throughout the organization and with other organizations.

Richard Farace, Peter Monge, and Hamish Russell (1977) have identified three general properties of the links found in organizational networks: symmetry, strength, and reciprocity. They describe a symmetrical link as persons equally exchanging information during an interaction. In other words, the network is symmetrical when both parties have approximately the same amount of give and take. Symmetrical links are common among peers when interacting about work problems or social interests.

The opposite of the symmetrical link is the asymmetrical link, in which one individual gives more information than another. Common organizational examples of asymmetrical links are supervisors giving directions to subordinates or instructors lecturing to students. In most cases, more information is sent from supervisors to subordinates and from instructors to students than the other way around.

The network property of strength refers to the frequency and length of interactions among linked individuals. Strong links communicate more frequently than weak links and usually have longer periods of interaction. The strength of communication links predicts who is influential among organizational members. The stronger the communication link among people the greater the chances of linked individuals influencing each other's behavior.

The final property, reciprocity, describes the level of agreement among organizational members about their network links. In other words, do individuals agree or disagree about the type of link they have with one another? Disagreement about whether or not individuals are linked frequently can be understood in terms of the differing perceptions individuals bring to communication relationships. For example, a subordinate may perceive a symmetrical link to his or her supervisor, whereas the supervisor would describe the link as somewhat weak and certainly asymmetrical. Independent observation could help to understand the discrepancy, but the perceptions of each individual would still influence their overall relationship.

Individuals perform diverse roles in networks. Common roles such as liaisons, bridges, gatekeepers, participants, nonparticipants, and isolates all function differently in communication networks. Liaisons link or connect groups with common information without being members of either group. Bridges link groups together by having membership in two or more groups. Both liaisons and bridges engage in what is described as boundary spanning. Boundary spanning occurs when one holds a role in a particular organization and is also responsible for linking or representing that organization to the external environment and to other organizations. Boundary spanning also occurs when individuals have multiple group memberships, requiring them to represent one group or groups to others.

Gatekeepers are positioned in networks to control the flow of information through a communication chain. Gatekeepers routinely receive information and determine whether or not to transmit that information to the next link or links in the chain. Managers are gatekeepers in relation to their subordinates. Secretaries are gatekeepers because they filter messages and may even determine who can reach their bosses. Subordinates can keep problems from their managers in a gatekeeper role. Anyone in the network can function in this role.

A network isolate can be described as an individual with few or no communication links throughout the organization. Isolates often are apprehensive about communication and deliberately avoid interaction with others. Few organizational members are complete isolates, however. Individuals or groups may be isolates from other groups. Competition between groups, for example, may weaken communication links and contribute to isolation, and individuals or groups may be isolated from certain communication functions while participating in others. An individual or group may be involved in the sending and receiving of organizing and relationship messages without being connected or linked (i.e., involved) in change messages or the innovative function.

Finally, there are the network participants and nonparticipants. Participants are individuals who participate in linked communication behaviors but who are not usually in liaison or bridge roles. They are typically seen as members of the group but not influential to other groups. Nonparticipants are formal members of groups but do not affiliate with others in the group to the extent that participants do. According to Gerald Wilson, H. Lloyd Goodall, and Christopher Waagen (1986), nonparticipants differ from isolates in that nonparticipants have demonstrated more communication and relationship abilities. Nonparticipants refrain from communication out of choice, not out of inability or fear.

Perceptions of various network roles differ. Although liaisons and nonliaisons are often similar in background, liaisons routinely enjoy higher organizational status than their nonliaison counterparts. Liaisons believe they have and are perceived by others to have more communication contacts and opportunities. Isolates, on the other hand, tend to withhold information and are less likely than others to facilitate communication flow. Isolates depend more than others on technology rather than interpersonal contact and in general have a lower self-concept and a higher need for security than their more communicatively linked counterparts. Figure 5.4 illustrates the communication links.

Network roles influence whom organizational members use as references to manage the uncertainty of organizational environments. Priti Shah (1998) explains that individuals select social referents to help them evaluate and comprehend their performance, compensation, career trajectories, and work responsibilities. These social referents are particularly important during times of uncertainty. Shah describes two general types of network relationships used as social referents: cohesive links and structurally equivalent links. Cohesive links are individuals with close interpersonal ties, or friends. Structurally equivalent links are individuals who share a similar pattern of relationships with others and therefore occupy the same overall position in a network. Shah's research demonstrated that both types of network relationships are used to reduce organizational uncertainty and to understand the complexities of daily organizational life.

In recent work, Terrance Albrecht and Bradford Hall (1991) studied the relationship and content differences between what they termed elites and outsiders in innovation networks. Elites were defined as "those who appeared as members of the dominant dense cluster in a communication network based on talk about innovation." Albrecht and Hall suggest that the influence of elites who cluster together may be explained in part by an uncertainty-reduction perspective. People communicate in organizations to reduce uncertainty and make their environments more understandable or predictable. Innovation, on the other hand, fosters change and introduces turbulence. The close personal relationships of elites potentially produce a personal and professional security that provides support for change and risk.

Albrecht and Hall (1991) conclude that "personal relationships play an important role in the development of new ideas in organizations, creating a discernible social structure in the workplace that divides people along relational and content domains. Each of the three innovation networks in this study comprises a central group of relatively dense, interactive elites either a peripheral, isolated, or less dominant group of outsiders." Innovation networks were dominated by elite groups of individuals as opposed to individuals, and outsiders viewed elites as more trustworthy, supportive, influential, and receptive to new ideas than other outsiders. Eileen Berlin Ray (1993) adds a word of caution when she suggests that

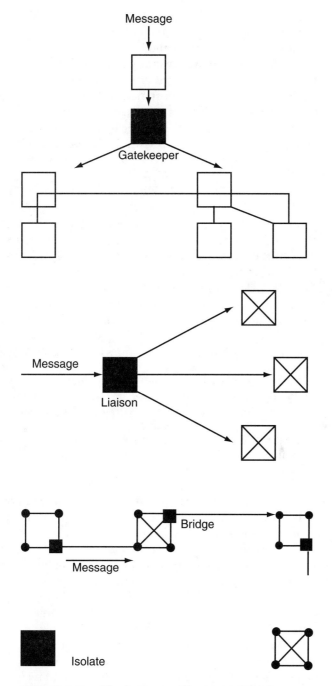

**FIGURE 5.4    Black Boxes Illustrate Gatekeeper, Liaison, Bridge, and Isolate Communication Links**

the power of supportive communication potentially can be used to manipulate and control rather than generate broad participation practices.

The final type of link discussed here is called "weak ties" or our communication links that are less developed and are generally more limited in space, place, time, and strength of emotional bonding. Beginning with the work of Mark Granovetter (1973), the notion of weak ties is important in organizations because individuals with many weak ties have increased access to information primarily because of the diverse nature of those links. In other words, individuals who are closely linked have the potential to all end up with the same information. Information coming from diverse sources provides the potential for different perspectives and new ideas.

In addition to the focus on individual network roles, communication networks are described in terms of their overall size (numbers of members), inclusiveness (numbers of individuals in the network as contrasted to the numbers of isolates), density (ratio of pairs of nodes that are mutually reachable to total number of pairs of nodes), centralization (comparison of the links of the most central network individual with other network members), and a host of other features. Monge and Contractor (2001) describe the importance of understanding that both formal and emergent networks exist side by side in organizations, with individuals having membership in multiple networks. They suggest that

> the distinction between formal and informal structures in organizations has diminished significantly in recent years and may become increasingly irrelevant in the coming decade. Reasons for this center on shifts in organizational structure and management philosophy. Prominent among these are changes to more team-based forms of organizing, the adoption of matrix forms of organizational structure, and shifts to network forms of organizing. At the core of these changes has been the explosion of lateral forms of communication made possible by new information technologies that facilitate considerable point-to-point and broadcast communication without regard for traditional hierarchy. (p. 446)

Regardless of the positive or negative nature of interactions, the importance of interpersonal experiences for organizational life is well established. Whether a newcomer to the organization, a transferred or relocated worker, or a long-time member of a work group, we can see why it is important to understand how we form relationships in a diverse work force and in particular how supervisor and subordinate and peer-to-peer relationships influence our organizational experiences.

## A Diverse Work Force

Most organizations employ men and women of differing ages, ethnicity, race, and values. The paid work force of today and tomorrow is characterized by a diversity of people that is rapidly increasing in the twenty-first century. Most of us will form as many interpersonal relationships in organizations with people who are different from us as with those with whom we have much in common. William Johnston (1987), in the Hudson Institute's famous Workforce 2000 report, described **work force**

**Work force diversity**
Description of workers that emphasizes differences in age, gender, race, ethnicity, and values.

**diversity** by five demographic facts: (1) The population and overall work force are growing more slowly than at any time since 1930, (2) the number of younger workers is declining as the average age of the work force and population rises, (3) women will continue to enter the work force in record numbers, (4) minorities will be a larger proportion of the new labor force, and (5) immigrants will increase their participation as workers at the highest level since World War I. Johnston referred to these trends as facts based on the globe's known demographic profile.

Sandra Ketrow (1992) provides an additional perspective:

> According to Worldwatch Institute (September 12, 1992), women rather than men are the family breadwinners in most of the world, where sex discrimination against them is a major cause of poverty. If such discriminatory attitudes prevail through overt or implicit interaction in organizations, attention to sex and gender as they relate to work performance and work- or task-related communication is crucial as we watch the balance of numbers shift in our workplaces. (p. 3)

Lea Stewart (1993) puts global population statistics in perspective:

> By 2050, half of the U.S. population will be African American, Hispanic American, Native American, and Asian American. These demographic changes are a clear motivation for embracing cultural diversity in organizations. Although organizational cultures tend to try to reproduce themselves . . . , the culture of the past can no longer be replicated. The Organization Man no longer exists to fill middle management jobs in the same way as his predecessors did. . . . Thus, accepting cultural diversity is a necessity. (p. 2)

Philip Harris and Robert Moran (1996) describe six trends in the work force that futurists believe are of critical importance to the new work culture.

1. *Diversity of personnel.* Women, minorities, and migrants constitute the majority of new entrants to the labor force. Based on current population demographics, this trend will accelerate over the next several decades. In addition, the work force is aging and is more mobile and diverse in attitudes and lifestyles.
2. *Expansion of worker support services.* Based on an expansion of women in the work force and dual career families, employer programs to facilitate integration between work and home (e.g., family leave to cope with sick dependents and elder care, day care for children) will need to increase.
3. *Flexible work arrangements.* Efforts to get more work done at lower costs will focus on varying work schedules, job sharing, temporary and contract work, home-based work, and satellite work centers.
4. *Focused human resource development.* Based on the need for new and critical knowledge and technological skills, training and education efforts for workers on the job, as well as cooperative relationships with schools to prepare future employees, are increasing.

5. *Competing in the global talent pool.* Changes in the world economy have contributed to organizations restructuring and engaging in mergers and acquisitions. Knowledge workers are increasingly recruited across geographic borders, with work performed locally and globally all within a given organization.

6. *Creating virtual corporations and communities.* New computer networks, telecommunications, and virtual reality technologies are creating new electronic relationships as well as new commercial ventures. Embedded in these trends is the concept that by valuing differences, companies are acknowledging the historic shifts in the makeup of the labor market, suppliers, and customers.

The work force is increasingly diversified by women, minorities, immigrants, the overall aging of workers, and the increased participation by the physically challenged. The resulting differences in communication styles, needs for social support, languages, and values all stimulate our abilities to form effective interpersonal relationships. Diverse people bring different intrapersonal attitudes, experiences, expectations, and competencies to organizations. These differences can contribute to organizational effectiveness when those with differing styles and values work together in interpersonal relationships characterized by mutual understanding and satisfaction. Differences, however, can produce conflict, tension, stereotyping, harassment, discrimination, abusive control, and exclusion, which all contribute to a variety of negative organizational outcomes. Evidence exists that these negative outcomes continue with sex and racial/ethnic segregation of occupations, salary differences for women and minorities not explained by performance or education differences, and differing evaluations of behaviors for women, minorities, and white males. Patricia Amason, Myria Allen, and Susan Holmes (1999) underscore the importance of the communication of social support as organizations adapt to multicultural issues such as cultural stereotyping, language barriers, and employee attempts to acculturate. In a study of Hispanic employees' acculturative stress and social support, Amason, Allen, and Holmes reported that for both Hispanics and Anglo Americans, perceptions of support from supervisors did not differ but social support communication was more likely to occur between members of the same racial/ethnic group. Of particular importance was the finding that praise and help with personal problems from Anglo American to Hispanic peers was highly valued and significant in contributing to positive acculturation.

As Dave Green enters AMX, he will experience what diversity can contribute in generating new and better training designs. Part of his experience will come from understanding how interpersonal relationships are formed.

## FORMING INTERPERSONAL RELATIONSHIPS

Most relationships in organizations begin on a relatively impersonal basis. We base our understanding of people on what we know about their membership in a specific group, culture, or role and make predictions about communication on general versus individual, specific information. Our effectiveness in interpersonal relationships is related to our awareness of differences and similarities in groups and our willingness to test the accuracy of our understanding. In addition, effectiveness is related to our ability to accept differences as legitimate and important for organizational effectiveness. Dave Green begins his relationship with Sally Johnson based on his understanding of professional women and his expectations of what managers do. As Dave becomes acquainted with Sally, the relationship becomes more interpersonal, with Dave and Sally responding to each other not just as members of groups but also as unique individuals. Joseph DeVito (1988) describes this process of relationship development: "In impersonal encounters the social or cultural role of the person tells us how to interact, while in personal or interpersonal encounters the psychological role of the person tells us how to interact." In general we can say that as relationships develop we gather information that helps us establish the general norms or rules of how our interactions will progress.

Interpersonal relationships in organizations are formed for important task and social considerations. Unlike our personal relationships, the organization actually structures for us many interpersonal encounters necessary for task accomplishment. To become effective in these diverse relationships, it is important to understand how we are attracted to others and how the impressions we form influence our communication behaviors.

We are attracted to others by physical and personality characteristics. We attribute, for example, more positive characteristics to those we identify as physically attractive than to their less attractive counterparts. Research also indicates that we are most likely to find as attractive those individuals who are similar to us in attitudes and beliefs and in relatively close physical proximity. The influences of similarity and physical proximity often prove problematic when establishing interpersonal relationships in organizations. The organizational requirement to work with those very different from us and in both close and distant proximity challenges us to examine how we form impressions and how we evaluate the competencies of others. In other words, do we evaluate as more competent and worthy of trust those organizational members who are most like us and with whom we have frequent contact? What are the implications of such an evaluation?

In addition to evaluations based on similarity and physical proximity, we tend to like most those individuals who reward or reinforce us. We prefer people who compliment rather than criticize. Again this pattern of impression formation, although certainly understandable, can limit the amount of developmental feedback we solicit or accept from diverse organizational members. Positive feedback, although comforting, does not always stimulate the growth necessary to increase our competency.

Although research does suggest that we are most comfortable with those similar to us and those who reinforce us, for certain of our characteristics we form positive impressions of those who have complementary rather than similar characteristics. For example, talkative individuals may form their most satisfying relationships with less talkative peers, and some supervisors may prefer submissive to more dominant subordinates. In general, however, research suggests that we are most likely to form positive impressions of those whom we find physically attractive; have similar attitudes to ours; and are of the same race, religion, age, and general social class.

We are more likely to establish satisfying interpersonal relationships based on similarity than relationships characterized by diversity. The implications for organizational effectiveness are obvious. Fully competent organizational members must not limit themselves only to the familiar but must be open to establishing satisfying and effective interpersonal relationships with both similar and dissimilar others. Dave Green will face this challenge as he joins members of a team differing in age, sex, and ethnicity.

## Supervisors and Subordinates

The supervisory-subordinate relationship can be described as the primary interpersonal relationship structured by the organization. Because it is formed to support task and job requirements, almost everyone in an organization—except perhaps at the very top of the hierarchy—is involved in such a dyad. Dave Green and Sally Johnson form the supervisor-subordinate dyad of our AMX case.

Both supervisors and subordinates bring a wide variety of personal characteristics and predispositions to their relationships. The interaction of these characteristics influences the satisfaction each person has with the other and helps determine the overall effectiveness of the relationship. A supervisor, for example, who thinks a subordinate shares similar values is more likely to view that subordinate as competent. Subordinates, on the other hand, are more likely to be satisfied with both work and supervision if they perceive a high degree of communication competency in the relationship. Specifically, the work of Anthony Smith and Susan Hellweg (1985) found that "a subordinate's satisfaction with his work and supervision is correlated with the communication competence of both the subordinate and supervisor as perceived by the subordinate." A subordinate's perception of the supervisor's ability to listen, respond quickly to subordinate messages, and be sensitive and understanding was the strongest predictor of satisfaction with both work and supervisor. Subordinates' satisfaction with their supervisors also was found to be directly related to their perception of their own personal communication competence. Vincent Waldron and Marilyn Hunt (1992) found that individuals reporting high-quality relationships with their supervisors were more likely to engage in informal, friendly interactions with their supervisors, to conform to formal and informal requests, to attempt to clarify expectations, and to accept criticism from supervisors than were individuals reporting lower-quality relationships.

Supervisor-subordinate relationships frequently have been described in terms of Leader-Member Exchange (LMX) theory. LMX theory suggests that leaders have limited time and resources and share both their personal and positional resources differently with their subordinates. Jaesub Lee (1997), in synthesizing much of this research, suggests that

> leaders tend to develop and maintain LMXs with their subordinates that vary in quality, ranging from high (in-group) to low (out-group). In-group exchange is a high quality relationship characterized by high levels of information exchange, mutual support, informal influence, trust, and greater negotiating latitude and input in decision influence. At the other extreme is out-group exchange, a low quality relationship in which the opposite is observed (e.g., more formal supervision, less support, and less trust and attention from the superior). (p. 269)

LMX has been linked to a variety of communication behaviors both with supervisors and with peers.

Related to this notion of LMX is what has been called the "Pelz effect" or the supervisor's upward LMX with his or her own boss. As early as 1952, Donald Pelz found that supportive communication from supervisors perceived to have high upward influence was more satisfying to subordinates than supportive communication from supervisors perceived to be low in the ability to influence their own supervisors. Relating the Pelz effect to LMX, Jaesub Lee (1997) concluded that subordinates who perceived a positive LMX with their supervisors and who perceived their supervisors to have high upward influence were more likely to engage in cooperative communication as contrasted to competitive communication within the work group.

Other studies support the importance of communication competency for the supervisor-subordinate relationship. Numerous studies report that supervisors who are high in communication apprehension are not as well liked as those lower in apprehension, and highly apprehensive subordinates are not as likely as others to seek supervisory positions. Furthermore, Gary Richetto (1969) has found that the credibility of the supervisor is more important than organizational status in determining who is approached for task, political, and social information.

What is the nature of communication between supervisors and subordinates? For one thing, it is frequent and time consuming. Supervisors may spend from one-third to two-thirds of their time communicating with subordinates. These interactions are face to face for the most part, with supervisors initiating mostly discussions concerning task requirements and performance expectations. The effectiveness of these messages contributes to subordinates' job satisfaction and quality of work. Subordinates want interaction with their supervisors and, in fact, are more likely to seek informal help from their supervisors than from peers or their own subordinates.

Research on supervisor-subordinate communication reports a "positivity bias" in upward communication. Paul Krivonos (1982) has summarized many of the findings about upward communication in the following four categories: (1) subordinates tend to distort upward information, saying what they think will please their supervisors; (2) subordinates tend to filter information and tell their supervisors what they, the subordinates, want them to know; (3) subordinates often tell supervisors what they think the supervisor wants to hear; and (4) subordinates tend to pass personally favorable information to supervisors while not transmitting information that reflects negatively on themselves.

The work of Kathleen Krone (1992) suggests that subordinates who are most likely to attempt to influence their supervisors report having high control over their work and high participation in decision making. Supervisors with empowered (control over work and decisions) subordinates are more likely to ask subordinates for their opinions, and subordinates believe their upward influence is likely to be successful. Eric Eisenberg and H. L. Goodall (1993) reference the work of Patricia Riley and Eric Eisenberg when they suggest:

> The primary skill individuals must cultivate in managing their boss is advocacy—the process of championing ideas, proposals, actions, or people to those above you in the organization. Advocacy requires learning how to read your superior's needs and preferences, and designing persuasive arguments that are most likely to accomplish your goals. The advocacy approach differs sharply from traditional views of superior-subordinate communication, which emphasize the importance of subordinate compliance and dramaturgy, of playing the good underling, and making your boss look good. A number of factors are involved in becoming a successful advocate.
>     1. Plan.
>     2. Determine why your boss should care to listen.
>     3. Tailor your arguments to your boss's style and characteristics.
>     4. Assess prior technical knowledge.
>     5. Build coalitions.
>     6. Hone your communication skills. (p. 230)

John Athanassiades (1973) has found that upward distortion is more likely to occur if the subordinate has advancement aspirations and has some degree of insecurity in his or her job. In a classic study, William Read (1962) reported that trust was a major factor supporting accuracy in upward communication. Furthermore, subordinate mobility aspirations and supervisory ability to influence mobility aspirations lowered trust levels and interfered with accurate upward communication. Karlene Roberts and Charles O'Reilly (1974) have reported that trust in a supervisor is the most important factor for open, upward communication, more important than mobility aspirations of the subordinate or perceptions of the influence of the supervisor. In a more recent work Janet Fulk and Sirish Mani (1986) have suggested that the perception of supervisors' downward communication, or the extent to which supervisors are perceived as actively withholding information, influences the accuracy of upward messages. The more the supervisor withholds, the more subordinates withhold and distort. In general, we can say that if trust levels between supervisors and subordinates are low, and if subordinates have mobility aspirations that they believe their supervisors can influence, there is likely to be a positivity bias that distorts upward communication.

We can certainly see why individuals want to be positively perceived by their supervisors, but we can also readily understand that a bias for positive upward communication may not be effective for the organization. When a positivity bias distorts upward communication, supervisors may not receive timely information about problems. Thus, needed information about innovation and change may be slow in coming, particularly if the supervisor is perceived as resistant to new ideas. Trust between supervisors and subordinates is the key to improving accurate communication and reversing the possible negative effects of a positivity bias. And trust is established through the communication competencies that both parties bring to relationships. In other words, the knowledge, sensitivity, skills, and values exhibited by both supervisors and subordinates contribute to the quality of relationships and to ultimate effectiveness.

The relationship between a supervisor and a subordinate is influenced not only by the amount of openness and support between the two but also by the amount of influence the supervisor has in satisfying the subordinate's needs. Much research supports the notion that subordinates base upward influence messages on their perception of how their supervisor attempts to influence them, the ability or power of the supervisor to influence others positively on behalf of his or her subordinates, and the perception on the part of subordinates about whether or not upward influence will indeed affect organizational decisions.

One of the important characteristics of supervisor-subordinate communication is the frequent gap in information and understanding between what the supervisor perceives and what a subordinate believes to be true. Supervisors and subordinates frequently differ on such important issues as basic job duties, performance expectations, amount and quality of communication exchange, and desirability of subordinate participation in decision making. John Hatfield, Richard Huseman, and Edward Miles (1987) reported that supervisors overestimate, according to subordinates, the amount of positive verbal recognition they give. In addition, supervisors report giving less negative feedback than their subordinates report receiving. Finally, the greater the perceived gap in verbal recognition, the lower the subordinate's satisfaction with supervision and overall job satisfaction. Eric Eisenberg, Peter Monge, and Richard Farace (1984) have reported that supervisors and subordinates are more likely to evaluate each other highly when agreement or similarity between personal attitudes and predicted attitudes about the communication rules of others is high.

Another type of relationship frequently developed between supervisors and subordinates is the mentor-to-mentee relationship. This relationship is based on mutual trust and respect and the desire of the mentor (usually a supervisor/manager or another person higher in position or senior in longevity with the organization than the mentee) to assist in career development for a specific individual. The mentor engages in coaching and advice extending beyond immediate job requirements to include information on how to be viewed as a successful contributor to the organization and how to make decisions likely to result in favorable organizational recognition. Research consistently has supported the importance of mentoring for career advancement. Unfortunately, much of this research suggests that mentors are most likely to select for mentoring those individuals who are similar to the mentor. These findings present challenges with an increasingly diverse work force.

After being exposed to some significant findings from the research on supervisor-subordinate relationships, how would you advise Sally and Dave? Describe the adequacy of the performance expectations she has established. How can she build trust with Dave? What should Dave do? Think about any supervisor-subordinate relationships in which you have been involved. How candid were you in upward communication? Describe what trust means to you.

## Peers

Although secondary in importance to supervisor-subordinate relationships, peer relationships are an important part of an individual's organizational experiences. Relationships with peers are characterized by both task and social interaction: peers communicate job information, advice, evaluation of performance, and personal feedback. Peers help us "learn the ropes" and identify with the organization. Peers are members of a work group to which an individual belongs. Peers also are members of other groups at the same approximate structural level within the organization as well as individuals who are internal customers of a product or service produced by a given work group. Simply put, peers are all organizational members of approximately the same organizational structure, role, and responsibility levels.

Few research studies have focused on the one-to-one aspect of peer relationships. The studies that do exist, however, support the importance of peer interactions for providing integration, or a sense of belonging, in organizational life. For example, individuals who are high in communication apprehension are less likely than others either to send or to receive integrative messages at the peer level. These same individuals also report less communication participation overall than their peers and lower overall communication satisfaction. On the other hand, individuals who have been promoted to management and those who expect vertical mobility are more likely than others to have developed a sense of belonging with their peers and organization.

Beverly Davenport Sypher and Theodore Zorn Jr. (1987) described how peers evaluate each other in terms of liked and disliked coworkers. Liked coworkers were most frequently depicted as considerate, personable, and exhibiting integrity-related behaviors. The higher in the organization the employee and the more he or she had mobility aspirations, the more ability to influence was wanted from liked peers. Lack of integrity led the list of descriptors for disliked coworkers, followed by self-centered and insecure behaviors. The Sypher and Zorn research specifically addresses the importance in peer relationships of the sensitivity and value components for communication competency.

In recent work, Patricia Sias and Daniel Cahill (1998) explored factors and communication changes associated with the development of workplace friendships among peers. Sias and Cahill explain:

> We found that peer friendships experienced three primary transitions: from coworker/acquaintance-to-friend, friend-to-close friend, and close friend-to-almost

best friend. The coworker-to-friend transition was perceived to be caused primarily by working together in close proximity, sharing common ground, and extra-organizational socializing. Communication at this transition became broader, yet remained relatively superficial. The friend-to-close friend transition was associated primarily with problems in one's personal and work experiences. Communication at this transition became broader, more intimate, and less cautious. The close friend-to-almost best friend transition was associated primarily with life events, work-related problems, and the passage of time. Communication became less cautious and more intimate. (p. 273)

Peers exchange information about job requirements, provide social support, and are in a position to give advice without formally evaluating performance. They can help one another solve problems and determine what approaches are best with particular supervisors. Dave Green, for example, hopes that John will be able to clarify his first assignment from Sally. Dave has positive expectations about his interactions with John. Peer relationships, however, are not always as positive as the one Dave and John share.

Peers can withhold important information from one another, contributing to a variety of problems. In an exit interview conducted in a highly successful West Coast research and development lab, one computer engineer claimed that both of his peers were aware that the line of reasoning he was using for his design had been previously rejected by their manager. Neither peer shared that information, permitting the engineer to pursue six months of research with a high likelihood of failure. When asked why the manager did not know of the line of inquiry the engineer was pursuing, the engineer replied that his peers had advised him to be somewhat vague with his manager, a person who rarely examined the specifics of the projects under his direction. Was the engineer set up to fail? Although not clear from the interview, his peer relationships were certainly destructive and probably contributed to an organizational performance that did not reflect his abilities or the needs of the company.

## Customers and Vendors

Individuals also form important interpersonal communication relationships with internal and external customers as well as vendors or suppliers of the organization. These relationships are based initially on task concerns but frequently emerge into social-support relationships as well. Customer and vendor relationships are based on exchanges of information about products, services, timing, delivery, quality, and cost. These relationships often are established through telemediated channels but remain important to the goals of all the parties involved in the relationship. Supervisors and peers frequently provide advice about these relationships, and individuals often are evaluated based on the satisfaction and production related to communication exchanges with customers and vendors. As the marketplace becomes more diverse and international, communication with customers and vendors will require increasingly complex competencies.

## TRUST AND INTERPERSONAL RELATIONSHIPS

Most people consider trust a critical factor in all types of interpersonal relationships, including those established in organizations. Although a somewhat ambiguous term, trust can be viewed as positive expectations about the behavior of others based on roles, relationships, experiences, and interdependencies. In work that Kathleen Ellis, Ruggero Cesaria, and I have conducted (Shockley-Zalabak, Ellis, and Cesaria, 2000), we discuss the central role that organizational communication plays in the behavioral dimensions of trust. The work we reviewed generally supports (1) accurate information, (2) explanations for decisions, and (3) openness as communication behaviors affecting perceptions of trustworthiness and overall job satisfaction. Information flow has the strongest relationship with trust in supervisor. Adequate explanations and timely feedback on decisions are associated with higher levels of trust, as is communication that is accurate and forthcoming. Managers and supervisors who freely exchanged thoughts and ideas with their employees enhanced overall perceptions of trust. Research generally supports a concept that describes trust in overall organizational policies, processes, and programs as predictive of trust in top management. Perceptions of trust also are related to confidence that employees express in the competence of organizational leadership. This competence refers to leadership not only at the top management level, but also at the supervisory and coworker levels. Here workers judge whether their supervisors and coworkers are competent and therefore trustworthy. At a peer and group level, the perception of competence and trust among peers and their leaders predicts the completion of goals for effective group outcomes. As we form interpersonal relationships, we make evaluations about the trustworthiness of others while understanding that they are forming similar perceptions of us. Fully competent organizational members learn to think about their behaviors in terms of whether they contribute to or detract from building trust.

## TECHNOLOGY AND INTERPERSONAL RELATIONSHIPS

Most of the discussion to this point has talked about interpersonal relationships with people with whom we have face-to-face interactions. Although these relationships are vitally important, they are not the only interpersonal relationships important for our organizational experiences. Technology has changed and is changing literally all types of relationships in which we engage. We no longer work only with those with whom we have face-to-face contact. We work across time zones, different languages, cultural differences, and geographic locations. We work with people without extensive information about their backgrounds, values, or experiences. We are expected to work effectively with others, using a variety of communications technologies. For organizations today and more tomorrow, basic communication competencies include abilities to use electronic mail, computers, voice mail, fax machines, the Internet and World Wide Web, group decision support systems (GDSS), a variety of management information systems, computer and video conferencing, and a host of older technologies such as the telephone.

The selection of one communication medium over another has been linked to whether or not the medium has the ability to support immediate feedback, can provide verbal and nonverbal information, uses natural language, and exhibits a personal focus. Using these criteria, face-to-face communication can be described as rich in information. Rich channels are more likely to be used for ambiguous and important messages, whereas channels low in richness are better suited to deal with unambiguous tasks. As you would expect, most telemediated channels rate relatively low in media richness.

**Teleworkers**
Individuals who work at home or in other than organizationally owned or controlled spaces.

More and more of us regularly use e-mail to exchange messages about tasks and social information. For a growing number of **teleworkers** (individuals who work at home or in other than organizationally owned or controlled spaces), telemediated communication is their primary process for establishing relationships, working on task-related concerns, and communicating the results of their work. Research suggests that for teleworkers, e-mail carries task information but contains more messages (than for workers in organizationally controlled physical space) about social/relational issues, innovation/suggestions, and grapevine information. How teleworkers develop relationships and relate to the organization is of increasing importance. Craig Scott and C. Erik Timmerman (1999) report that teleworkers who spend approximately 50 percent of their time as virtual employees are more likely to identify with the organization and its values than those who telecommute more frequently. Nicolle Ellison (1999) reports that traditional managerial paradigms are challenged by arrangements wherein employees work primarily off site. Ellison found that telework seemed to exacerbate tensions between organizational subcultures and between managers and employees. Employee and supervisor trust remained an issue. Teleworkers, more than their less "virtual" counterparts, socialized with clients, friends, and family as contrasted to coworkers.

All types of interpersonal relationships are affected by technology. Teleworkers submit work mostly without daily close supervision by management. Technology use in general promotes less face-to-face interaction. Working across time zones and geographies also means working across cultures and languages and with those with whom we have very little personal experience. Trust becomes increasingly important to virtual environments because we must act, perform, and behave without the cues with which we are most familiar. Although the nature of these changes requires further exploration, it is fair to say that technology will change the types of interpersonal relationships we form and how we evaluate these relationships for effectiveness.

## INCREASING INTERPERSONAL EFFECTIVENESS

Thus far, intrapersonal and interpersonal experiences common in organizational life have been examined, in an attempt to understand how motivation influences communication behavior and how dyadic relationships are formed and shaped through communication. The importance of our own personal communication competency and our perception of the competency of others as it relates to satisfaction with interpersonal relationships and overall job satisfaction have been described. Yet the specific skills that individuals can use to improve communication effectiveness have not been identified. Now comes a discussion of the importance of valuing diversity, active listening, and descriptive message strategies.

## Valuing Diversity

### Barriers and Positive Approaches

Understanding that the work force is diverse does not automatically give us the ability to relate effectively to that diversity. In fact, most of us have had uncomfortable interactions with people who seemed to discount us and our abilities. We in turn have probably left others with that same sense of uneasy concern. Lea Stewart (1993), in describing Barbara Walker's work at Digital Equipment Corporation, provides a model of valuing differences based on four key principles:

> (1) People work best when they feel valued; (2) people feel most valued when they believe that their individual and group differences have been taken into account; (3) the ability to learn from people regarded as different is the key to becoming fully empowered; and (4) when people feel valued and empowered, they are able to build relationships in which they work together interdependently and synergistically. . . . In this conceptualization, people participate in a process in which they examine their own beliefs and stereotypes about individual and group differences. This process leads individuals through five steps: (1) stripping away stereotypes; (2) learning to listen and probe for the differences in people's assumptions; (3) building authentic and significant relationships with people one regards as different; (4) enhancing personal empowerment; and (5) exploring and identifying group differences. (pp. 3–4)

**Valuing diversity**
Ability to understand and appreciate the contributions that differences in people can make to organizations.

As we consider our personal communication competency, we can increase our effectiveness by understanding barriers to **valuing diversity** and positive approaches helpful in increasing understanding.

Several important barriers to valuing diversity help explain problems that frequently occur among men and women of differing ages, ethnicity, race, and values. For each barrier there are positive approaches that can improve effectiveness. The following discussion of barriers and positive approaches help us examine our personal behaviors and better understand others.

*Barrier One: Preconceptions and beliefs that foster inaccurate information and confusion between perceptions of behaviors and actual behaviors*
Carl Carmichael (1988) described the impact of beliefs that foster inaccurate information when he discussed cultural communication, which "has perpetuated

myths of aging that have become so widely accepted they are all but impossible to change, even in the face of recent scientific evidence to the contrary. Consider a few salient examples and check your own beliefs in each case: When people get old, they can expect increased memory loss. You can't teach an old dog new tricks. Intelligence declines in old age." Carmichael goes on to explain that these beliefs persist despite gerontological research that disputes their accuracy. These beliefs have obvious implications for organizations with a growing number of workers past age forty. Are training classes populated with people of all ages, or are younger workers given preference? Who has the most opportunity to influence decisions? How might beliefs and preconceptions about aging block organizational effectiveness?

Judy Pearson (1988) has illustrated how we confuse perceptions and reality when men and women behave similarly in organizations but are evaluated differently. Specifically, Pearson stated, "We may view a given behavior of a woman as negative, but we may judge the same behavior to be positive when a man exhibits it. For instance, a businesswoman may be labeled 'aggressive, pushy, and argumentative,' whereas her male counterpart who exhibits the same behavior may be viewed as 'ambitious, assertive, and independent.'"

*Positive Approach: Personalize knowledge and perceptions*
We can learn to separate our preconceptions, beliefs, and attitudes from actual behaviors. We can continually open our awareness to new information and new ways of understanding others. We can understand that knowledge is individual in nature and that others may legitimately view what is factual or correct very differently from us. As Brent Ruben (1988) has so aptly suggested, "People who recognize that their values, beliefs, attitudes, knowledge, and opinions are their own—and not necessarily shared by others—often find it easier to form productive relationships than persons who believe they know The Truth, and strive to 'sell' their own perceptions, knowledge, skills, and values to others." In our organizational relationships we can learn to describe what is accomplished, the merit of an idea, or the quantity of work performed. We can consciously separate, or personalize, these descriptions from beliefs about people of a given age, sex, race, or ethnic group.

*Barrier Two: Stereotypes that limit the potential contributions of individuals based on their membership in a group or class*
Stereotypes simplify our ability to understand the world by making predictions about people based on the group or class to which they most obviously belong. Stereotypes emerge from basic, widely believed characteristics of a given group. Although stereotyping in a diverse environment makes the world more predictable and deceptively approachable, in and of itself stereotyping invites inaccuracy and undervalues diversity. Stereotypes emerge not only about specific groups or classes of people but also about who should be more powerful, exhibit dominance in interrelationships, and generally engage in social control. Edith Folb (1988) has described the "top dog" stereotype of our society: "Within the United

States, those most likely to hold and control positions of real—not token—power and those who have the greatest potential ease of access to power and high status are still generally white, male, able-bodied, heterosexual, and youthful in appearance if not in age." Put simply, stereotypes give us a false aura of similarity and predictability that limits individual potential.

*Positive Approach: Tolerance for ambiguity*
Learning to tolerate and value ambiguity is the positive counterpart to the negative effects of stereotyping. An attitude of tolerating ambiguity accepts as normal an environment that requires us to know people as individuals, not as members of a group or class. A tolerance for ambiguity is a sensitivity competency important as we enter new situations of all types. Frustration and discomfort may be normal reactions to ambiguity, but the sorting through and making sense of diverse relationships is an essential characteristic for interpersonal effectiveness. Ruben (1988) has suggested that tolerance for ambiguity and tolerance for the lack of control one senses in new situations substantially assist efforts to integrate into new environments successfully.

*Barrier Three: Prejudices that produce negative emotional reactions to others*
According to Richard Brislin (1988), "When people react negatively to others on an emotional basis, with an absence of direct contact or factual material about the others, the people are said to behave according to prejudice." Prejudice arises from beliefs that given groups of people are generally inferior or that a given group is interfering with important basic values. Prejudice is associated with discomfort about the unfamiliar and associated with behaviors we personally find offensive. The chances that are we have all had prejudices at one time or another. We react emotionally and negatively to others without accurate information or even direct personal contact. Prejudiced behavior can be overt, as in refusal to work with a given group of people, or subtle, as in appearing to accept an individual as equal while carefully controlling the amount of influence he or she can exert in any given situation. Prejudice limits interpersonal relationships by arbitrarily devaluing groups of individuals based on negative emotional reactions. In addition, as previously discussed, anything that hampers effective communication limits organizational effectiveness.

*Positive Approach: Nonjudgmentalness*
We all want to feel valued as individuals. Prejudice, or prejudging on the basis of the group to which we obviously belong, robs us of our individuality and limits effective interpersonal relationships. Nonjudgmentalness, or the positive opposite of prejudice, is exhibited by people who give others an opportunity to explain themselves. Nonjudgmental people base their reactions—whether positive or negative—on explanations, not group membership. Nonjudgmentalness requires active listening (a skill discussed later in this chapter) and a willingness to base our evaluations on what Ruben (1988) has described as "a reasonably complete understanding of the other's point of view. When persons believe they have been fully and

attentively listened to, they are generally much more receptive to hearing reactions—whether positive or negative."

*Barrier Four: Stylistic differences in personal communication that inhibit interpersonal relationships*
We all have style, personal and individual expressions of attitudes about ourselves and our culture. We speak, dress, and behave nonverbally with personal style influenced by culture. We develop vocabulary, syntax, idioms, slang, and dialects reflecting both our past and our present. Our speech style has been developed within the context of our background. What we view as appropriate and effective is a result of our evaluation of our past and present experiences. The same is true for our dress and nonverbal behaviors. Although we may recognize how our style develops, many of us remain uncomfortable with others who have differing styles. Some people appear aggressive and threatening when they are reflecting their own culturally acceptable behaviors. Others physically stand too close, invading our personal space. We move away, signaling a form of disrespect we do not intend. When others are enthusiastic in speech we may consider them illogical, based on our preference for details. We become uncomfortable with each other and thereby limit our interpersonal effectiveness. Style differences frequently block the substance of what we can contribute to each other.

*Positive Approach: Display of respect*
A display of respect for differences begins with the attitude that differences are desirable. Respect includes specific recognition that although stylistic differences are normal, they are a possible source of misunderstanding. A display of respect includes active listening and nonverbal behaviors that encourage interactions with others. A display of respect also includes monitoring our own behaviors to minimize misunderstanding of our intentions. A display of respect is a sensitivity competency based on a genuine valuing of diversity.

The barriers and positive approaches just discussed are obviously not the only ones important for interpersonal effectiveness. What other barriers have you observed? How might they be applied to the organizational setting? Next, some of the specific communication skills necessary for valuing diversity and establishing effective interpersonal relationships within organizations are considered.

**Active listening**
Processes of hearing, assigning meaning, and verifying our interpretations. Increases the accuracy of message reception, enabling responses based on what was said, not on what might have been said.

# Active Listening

## Myths and Barriers
Listening is as fundamental to effective communication as talking. It is important in organizations. Supervisors talk and incorrectly assume subordinates are listening; groups engage in lively debate, hearing each other but not arriving at similar meanings; organizational members argue without understanding that they support essentially the same position.

Several important myths about listening and barriers to **active listening** help explain the ineffectiveness described in our examples. The following discussion of myths about listening and barriers to active listening help us understand our personal listening habits and the listening habits of others.

*Myth One: Listening and hearing are the same thing*
Fact: Hearing is the physiological process in which sound waves strike the eardrum, creating vibrations for transmission to the brain. Listening extends the physiological process to the assignment of meaning to sounds. Listening is therefore essential for message decoding.

*Myth Two: Listening and hearing are physiological processes*
Fact: Hearing is a natural physiological process, but effective listening extends the physiological process of hearing into the skill of accurate decoding and assignment of meaning. In fact, more people speak well than listen well, although what we choose to say in most situations is a result of our listening skill.

*Myth Three: Everyone listening to the same message receives the same message*
Fact: Because listening involves individual decoding and assignment of meaning, listening will be different for everyone.

In addition to myths that confuse listening and hearing, several important barriers to effective listening (the act of receiving and interpreting communication) have been identified. First described by Ralph Nichols (Nichols and Stevens, 1957), listening barriers are important for understanding individual habits that interfere with accurate message reception.

*Barrier One: Labeling communicators and subjects as uninteresting or unimportant*
Although at times these labels may be accurate, many of us determine early in an interaction or presentation that we don't understand the subject, don't like the person, or find little of interest or importance in the message. We then tune out the speaker and spend our time thinking about other matters. By not listening to the message we have no way to assess accurately the value of what we might have heard.

*Barrier Two: Emotionally resisting messages*
Often we react quickly to emotionally charged words or subjects. Internally we think of ways to respond to the speaker and argue our position. In this process we often quit listening to what is being said. We make judgments and respond to those judgments as if the speaker's position was accurately known to us. Criticisms from supervisors and peers often are met with emotional listening resistance. We hear only the negatives and do not attend to offers of help or ways to improve our performance. We are overstimulated and do not accurately receive messages that could help us grow and develop.

*Barrier Three: Criticizing personal style rather than messages*
We often find ourselves criticizing the way a message is presented and ignoring its content or value. We don't like the message being "read" to us, we find the speaker

lacking in experience, or we don't care for the negative tone of the boss. Our listening focuses on delivery and approach. Stylistic elements rather than content capture our attention.

*Barrier Four: Failing to identify listening distractions*
Believe it or not, listening for facts can be distracting. Trying to listen accurately for a series of facts is not only difficult but also frequently distracts from the overall meaning of the message. Taking notes can distract from meaning, as can attempts to memorize what we are hearing. Physical noise, interruptions, and unidentified sounds also contribute to ineffective listening.

*Barrier Five: Faking attention*
Many of us get into the habit of faking attention whether the speaker is interesting or not. We have a lot on our minds and use our listening time for reflecting. We develop behaviors such as head nodding and eye contact that are designed to make the speaker believe we are listening. In reality we have tuned in to our own special world. At times we are not even aware that we have begun to fake attention. Most of us can recall a time when we intended to listen and suddenly realized that we had not heard a word. Obviously, we miss most of the message and reduce our chances for accurate communication.

*Barrier Six: Misusing thought speed and speech speed differential*
We can think three to four times faster than we talk. Thus, we have time for our minds to wander as we attempt to listen. For most people, the thought speed and speech speed difference is not used to increase listening effectiveness but to think of other subjects while another person is speaking. We sometimes think of our own response, we think of subjects unrelated to the speaker's message, and we use the time to jump from subject to subject. Listening experts tell us our time would be better spent in internally restating the speaker's message, drawing analogies and examples related to the subject, and determining what questions to ask. In other words, effective listeners use the differential time to make sure they understand the message.

## Guidelines for Good Listening

Active listening includes the processes of hearing, assigning meaning, and verifying our interpretations. Skill in active listening supports effective communication by increasing the accuracy of message reception. Accurate message reception in turn enables better responses, responses based on what was said, not on what we think might have been said.

Active listening begins with an attitude about our role in the communication process. A positive active listening attitude begins with a genuine concern for understanding messages as others intend, to sense meaning from another person's point of view. This attitude includes empathy for others and a willingness to control our emotions to facilitate mutual understanding. Skillful active listeners control mental arguments, avoid jumping to assumptions and conclusions, and are careful not to stereotype others.

Active listeners stop talking long enough to hear what others have to say. When others have finished talking, active listeners frequently paraphrase or feed back what they have understood. They allow people to verify the accuracy of those perceptions or to explain what inaccuracies exist. Active listeners use questions for meaning clarification and do not interrupt attempts to explain ideas or positions.

Active listeners summarize main points and evaluate facts and evidence before responding. Thus, the skill of active listening is as important for disagreements as for agreements. This skill is practiced to foster understanding of another's position, not necessarily to generate agreement with that position. In fact most communication scholars argue that an individual is in a better position to disagree if he or she has accurately understood the meaning of another's ideas.

## Descriptive Messages

By now you are aware that none of us ever fully experiences another person's meaning. Instead, we interpret that meaning through communication. The message strategies and tactics we adopt are our attempts to make our meanings understandable to others. Thus, it is important to develop message skills that help others accurately interpret our meanings.

**Descriptive messages**

Messages characterized by ownership of perceptions and conclusions and language that presents facts, events, and circumstances all parties in communication are likely to observe or experience personally.

**Descriptive messages** can help us accurately exchange information with others. In organizations we frequently communicate with people with whom we have little in common and little or no personal relationship; they don't know us and we don't know them. Yet our ability to be understood is crucial to our performance and contributes to the functioning of our organization. Descriptive messages can help us accurately exchange information with supervisors, peers, and subordinates as well as with those with whom we have little regular contact.

Descriptive messages are characterized by two basic tactics: **message ownership** and **descriptive language.** Message ownership refers to the ability to "own" our perceptions and conclusions without undue reference to others or attempts at blame. Descriptive language describes rather than evaluates and does so in language that presents facts, events, and circumstances all parties are likely to observe or experience personally.

**Message ownership**

Attempts to communicate verbally individual perceptions and feelings without attempting to establish blame or find unnecessary corroboration.

When I "own" my own messages, I verbally communicate my personal perceptions and feelings without attempting to establish blame or find unnecessary corroboration. The use of the pronoun *I* replaces the you message so often associated with blame. The pronoun *I* also replaces vague ownership references such as *we, some,* and *they.* Figure 5.5 illustrates effective and ineffective message ownership tactics.

**Descriptive language**

Language choice based on facts, events, and behavior as opposed to language choice describing attitudes, blame, or other subjective and vague concepts.

Descriptive language is used to describe what all parties to the communication can reasonably be expected to observe. Those

**FIGURE 5.5    Message Ownership Tactics**

| EFFECTIVE | INEFFECTIVE |
| --- | --- |
| I am angry with you. | You always make me mad. |
| I don't understand the technical terms you are using. They seem to me to be specific to engineering. I am not an engineer. | You're talking like an engineer. |
| I am responsible to do this job as part of our contractual agreement. | You have problems with authority. |
| I am telling you directly and honestly what my findings are. | You are being a bit paranoid. |
| I need this specific information to complete this report. | How do you expect me to do my job without adequate information? |
| I am concerned about the level of costs on Project X. | We think costs are running wild on Project X. |
| I am worried about the mistakes in your last report. | Some of us think you haven't been yourself lately. |

using descriptive language avoid evaluation by choosing facts and observable behavior over interpretations of facts and behaviors. Descriptive-language users talk about facts, events, and behavior, not attitudes, blame, or other subjective and vague concepts. In other words, descriptive-language use tells what is needed, what happened, or what is in question. This statement is not to say that effective communication never evaluates behavior; rather, descriptive-language use is based on the assumption that it is difficult to exchange accurate information about the adequacy (good or bad) of facts and behaviors until all parties understand the specific facts or behaviors of reference. For example, when an important report is late and departments are in conflict, chances are the conflicting individuals can agree that the report must have a new due date. It is less likely that these same individuals will similarly interpret who caused the delay and who should bear the most responsibility and blame. From an organizational point of view, completion of the report is the primary goal of the communication. Of secondary consideration is agreement on blame for the failure.

Descriptive messages combine tactics of message ownership with selection of descriptive language and can be both statements and questions. They are useful for summarizing during active listening. Figure 5.6 presents effective and ineffective examples of descriptive messages.

# SUMMARY

An individual's organizational experiences result from the attitudes, beliefs, preferences, and abilities the individual brings to the organization, how the organization

**FIGURE 5.6   Descriptive Messages**

| EFFECTIVE | INEFFECTIVE |
|---|---|
| I need information for cost overruns for ____ product to finish my audit report by ____ date. | You were to have provided me all the information necessary to finish this report on the costs. |
| Which part of the cost overrun data is not being submitted? Can you tell me why that particular information seems inappropriate to you? | Why don't you understand my request? What do you mean my request for information is not appropriate? |
| I do not have a response to my memo of ____ date requesting ____ data. | You are not being straightforward with the agency. |
| My position suggests that I need A, B, and C to prepare the report. I understand that you are willing to give me A and C but not B. Is that correct? | I know what I need to finish the report and so do you, but you are not willing to give it to me. |

seeks to influence the individual, and the types of relationships an individual develops. An individual's communication experiences are related to quality and quantity of job performance, job satisfaction, and communication satisfaction.

The intrapersonal experience of individuals in organizations is composed of personal needs, predispositions for behavior, communication competencies, and expectations. Personal needs, commonly referred to as motivation, have been described by Maslow, Herzberg, Skinner, Salancik, and Pfeffer. Maslow (1954) contended that individuals behave so as to increase or avoid a decrease in need satisfaction. Maslow described needs in an ascending hierarchy beginning with physiological needs and followed by safety and security needs, love and social belonging, esteem and prestige, and self-actualization. Herzberg (1966) contended that satisfaction and dissatisfaction are not polar opposites, that what produces dissatisfaction in the work environment, if corrected, will not necessarily produce satisfaction or motivation. His research suggested that environmental factors (hygiene factors) influence dissatisfaction and that motivational factors are work itself, achievement, growth and responsibility, recognition, and advancement. Skinner (1953) believed that behavior is motivated or reinforced through positive feedback or tangible rewards. Salancik and Pfeffer (1978) proposed that needs and attitudes are determined by the information available to people at the time they express the attitude or need.

Predispositions for organizational communication behaviors are personally held preferences for particular types of communication situations or behavior. Communication apprehension—an individual's level of fear or anxiety associated with either real or anticipated communication with others—influences a wide variety of organizational outcomes, as do preferences for leadership and conflict behaviors. Perceptions of communication competency can be described as an overall summation of preferences and predispositions for organizational communication behaviors.

The paid work force of today and tomorrow is characterized by a diversity of people that is only expected to increase as we begin the twenty-first century. Not only is the work force increasingly diversified by women, minorities, and immigrants, but also the overall aging of workers, the increased participation by the physically challenged, and the resulting differences in communication style and values all stimulate our abilities to form effective interpersonal relationships. Interpersonal relationships in organizations are formed for important task and social considerations. Unlike our personal relationships, the organization actually structures for us many interpersonal encounters necessary for task accomplishment. We are attracted to others based on both physical and personality characteristics. As fully competent organizational members, we must not limit ourselves to the similar but must be open to establishing satisfying and effective interpersonal relationships with both similar and dissimilar others.

The relationship an individual develops with his or her supervisor is one of the most important of the primary communication experiences in organizational life. In certain circumstances this relationship is subject to a positivity bias in upward communication. Peers also are an important source of information and support. Communication experiences with supervisors and peers are related to how well individuals perform and their overall measures of satisfaction.

Interpersonal effectiveness can be achieved through valuing diversity, active listening, and message ownership and descriptive language. These skills contribute to communication competency for interpersonal communication.

---

# WORKSHOP

1. Write a letter to a hypothetical new employer describing how best to motivate you. Describe the working environment that you would find personally motivational. After your letter is completed, compare it with the various motivational theories described in this chapter. Which theory or theories can be applied to your letter?

2. You and another member of your class (preferably someone you do not know well) should take turns describing what you find important in a work environment. This exchange should take ten minutes. Each of you can ask questions of the other. At the end of ten minutes, complete the following What Do People Really Want? rankings. Rank your preferences and what you believe to be the preferences of your partner. After both rankings are complete, you and your partner should exchange ranking sheets and discuss on what basis rankings are made. (See pp. 176–177.)

3. Anita Foeman provides an essay, "Colorblindness and the Organizational Mystique," for discussion. (See pp. 177–179.)

4. "The Marketing Department Has a Diversity Issue" case by Amy Martz and Anita Foeman asks you to think about what you have learned about valuing diversity and apply it to a specific problem faced by the marketing department of a medium-sized credit union. (See pp. 179–181.)

5. The following essay, "Are We So Different We Can't Work Together?" provides a thought-provoking description of cultural differences that influence how individuals are accepted in work environments. The essay stimulates thought about the characteristics of our own culture that influence our relationships with those of another culture. (See pp. 181–182).

6. To build skills and practical experience with the technique of active listening, select a controversial issue appropriate to the class (an issue that students raise or one that relates directly to work problems is recommended). Form groups of six students each. Two volunteers from each group should represent opposing opinions on the issue. The remaining group members should form a circle around the two volunteers. The only rule that must be followed is that before either volunteer responds to the other, the listener must state to the other's satisfaction what the speaker has just been saying. In other words, no replies are allowed until the speaker is satisfied that the listener can restate the original message. With the group observing, the two members should proceed to discuss the issue. Group members are to act as monitors and may intervene if the rule has been violated. After ten minutes of discussion, the class should describe how active listening influenced the issue under consideration. (Alternative exercise form: All members of the class can participate in the activity by forming pairs of participants for issue discussion.)

## What Do People Really Want?

For the following ten work-related items, you will develop a ranking (1–10) of their importance to you and project how the person with whom you have been interacting will rank the items. You will then compare your self-rankings with your partner's projection of your rankings and compare your projections with his or her self-rankings. Discuss the similarities and differences in rankings.

Remember, rank what is important to you and what you believe is important to your partner in a work environment.

| | MY PERSONAL RANKING | MY PARTNER'S RANKING OF ME |
|---|---|---|
| 1. Sensitivity to personal problems | _____ | _____ |
| 2. Interesting work | _____ | _____ |
| 3. Salary | _____ | _____ |
| 4. Job security | _____ | _____ |
| 5. Loyalty of company to employees | _____ | _____ |
| 6. Tactful and constructive criticism | _____ | _____ |
| 7. Appreciation for work | _____ | _____ |
| 8. A sense of belonging | _____ | _____ |
| 9. Good working conditions | _____ | _____ |
| 10. Opportunities for advancement | _____ | _____ |

|                                           | MY RANKING OF MY PARTNER | MY PARTNER'S SELF-RANKING |
| ----------------------------------------- | ------------------------ | ------------------------- |
| 1. Sensitivity to personal problems       | _____              | _____               |
| 2. Interesting work                       | _____              | _____               |
| 3. Salary                                 | _____              | _____               |
| 4. Job security                           | _____              | _____               |
| 5. Loyalty of company to employees        | _____              | _____               |
| 6. Tactful and constructive criticism     | _____              | _____               |
| 7. Appreciation for work                  | _____              | _____               |
| 8. A sense of belonging                   | _____              | _____               |
| 9. Good working conditions                | _____              | _____               |
| 10. Opportunities for advancement         | _____              | _____               |

## Colorblindness and the Organizational Mystique

### Anita Foeman, Ph.D.[1]

Many have struggled with the complexities of addressing human diversity in American organizations. As theory in the area of organizational communication continues to evolve, students and practitioners alike search not only to explain the phenomena they see in organizations, but also for instruction for how to process and respond to what they experience as part of organizational life.

Earlier generations have dealt with the issue of diversity by aspiring to be colorblind. And, in fact, to the extent that they believed their alternatives to be colorblindness versus rampant racial (or other) stereotyping, their attempts were noble. Yet the struggle to be colorblind is futile. Humans are categorizing animals. Indeed, our ability to use language is based on our capacity to categorize things and ideas. The belief that we could ever view all people as exactly the same, regardless of race, gender, ability, or other variation, is probably naive. The belief that we already see one another as "simply human and exactly alike" is self-deception. When driving to work on a crowded highway, one has only to be cut off in traffic by another motorist to realize how quickly and easily epithets of difference can pop to mind.

In addition to seeing overt physical differences among people, however, we are faced with the fact that different people behave and experience reality differently as well. Our beliefs about what is appropriate behavior are tightly tied to our different cultural group experiences. We cannot escape the cultural nature of our communication behavior. Cross-cultural researchers Gudykunst and Ting-Toomey assert that although it is possible to respond to others based solely on their groupness, it is not

---

[1]Anita Foeman, Ph.D., received her doctorate from Temple University in organizational communication in 1982. Her research explores the communication styles of marginalized organizational members. Foeman provides consultation services to a variety of academic, corporate, and social service agencies. Her work has been published in *Communication Education, Communication Quarterly, Journal of Negro Education,* and other journals.

possible to interact with others based only on individual, idiosyncratic factors. As students of communication we fundamentally agree that all behavior exists in a context. To pretend through feigned colorblindness that varying cultural contexts do not exist is to believe that communication can exist in a vacuum.

So what do we really mean when we speak of "colorblindness"? Often, when individuals suggest that they are colorblind they are, in fact, making a tacit "deal" with their cocommunicator. The deal is this, "I will pretend that I do not see you as different if you behave in ways that make me feel comfortable and help me to believe that you are like me." In most instances, the person who is capable of "negotiating" such an arrangement is the person in power and the one who has the energy and force of the status quo on his or her side.

Unfortunately, in the making of such a deal, a person who is deemed different is generally left with two interpretive alternatives: either believing that there is something so awful about being who or what she or he is that the difference is not to be addressed or, alternately, that her or his needs are too insignificant to be of interest to the powerful other. The message to the less powerful is not, "we are different from one another" but rather, "you are different and difference is bad."

This arrangement may have been functional as long as the organizational structure remained controlled by homogeneous groups. Today, in an organizational world that is far more multicultural in terms of power distribution, such a deal is unlikely. Rather than causing harmony, colorblindness may cause high levels of organizational volatility.

In addition to increased levels of organizational instability, the organization limits its opportunities to tap the variety of insights necessary to meet organizational challenges. People who are different bring different insights. Non-whites, for example, are far more able to identify problems associated with the traditional ways of doing things than those who may have been entrenched in the power structure for too long. A person in a wheelchair may well have insights into the experiences of the elderly, children, and other physically challenged people in ways the nondisabled do not. Such perspectives are far from marginal. Complex problems addressed by multinational and diverse organizations operating in multifaceted societies require that the insights of former "outsiders" be utilized. When we identify people as unimportant and expendable, we miss the brilliance that comes from their differences.

The alternative to being colorblind is not stereotyping as we may have once assumed. In fact, colorblindness and stereotyping are the two sides of the same coin of intolerance. The opposite of blinding ourselves to diversity is celebrating it, using it, and growing from it. Toward that end, I would make two preliminary suggestions regarding improved attention to diversity in all organizations.

First, we can begin with the assumption that diversity is good and to be explored. Often we address issues of diversity only when they present themselves in the context of a conflict situation. At such time organizational decision makers may feel so mired in the conflict itself that a positive exploration of diversity is all but impossible. Exploration of diversity that is not based on conflict should be a part of all managerial training and ultimately training at all levels of the organization. Training should include a wide range of diversity themes (race, gender, age, ability, somatypes, etc.), and the contributions of all members should be encouraged and treasured.

Second, we can encourage an attitude of respectful inquiry in our diversity work. We can avoid projecting an attitude that some differences are off limits. Through our discussions of organizational case studies (or real-life cases) organizational members should be encouraged to ask questions regarding the context of behaviors and avoid immediately making assessments based on cultural homogeneity. We can begin our analysis of cases with the assumptions that all identified individuals are sane, well-meaning, and doing the best that they can with the resources they feel they possess. When we assume these things, the nature of our questions to one another will change dramatically, and questions based on beliefs that others are "radical," "crazy," "myopic," "self-centered," or simply "stupid" will tend to fall away.

Part of the challenge is to keep in mind the notion that culture is the context for communication and not communication itself. What we seek in examining human diversity is not a simplistic view of the world based on cultural clichés but rather a rich understanding of how unique individuals respond to a variety of cultural challenges. Such knowledge may be very useful in adding to our organizational options. Through a process of questioning and listening we may become more adept and comfortable with identifying and discussing difference and solving organizational problems.

I encourage all students of organizational communication to seek materials that discuss the multicultural nature of organizations. These materials help us learn to extract the very best from ourselves and others. There is much to be gained in such a venture.

## The Marketing Department Has a Diversity Issue

### Amy Martz, Ph.D.[2], and Anita Foeman, Ph.D.

You are Director of Marketing for a medium-sized credit union. You have four employees in your department—three white women (Shannon, Gail, and Valerie) and an African-American man (Curtis)—who often work together as a team on various projects. You evaluate such efforts as a whole, giving no one individual more "credit" than the others. The newest member of the team is Curtis, who has been in the department for three months. Recently you have become aware of tensions between Curtis and the three female team members. Both Curtis and Shannon have spoken to you about interpersonal problems developing in the team.

From Curtis's perspective, it seems that the women are trying to dominate all projects. They decide on the division of labor (usually giving him what he perceives

[2]Dr. Amy Martz received her Ph.D. from Penn State University. She currently teaches organizational communication, communication theory, and small-group communication courses. She also works with interested groups in the areas of managing diversity, organizational change, and conflict management. Her research interests lie in the areas of unethical organizational decision making and organizational culture.

to be the minimal part); they ignore suggestions when he makes them. They rarely ask his opinion. According to Curtis, Valerie, who is pregnant, has been the center of the women's discussion since he has arrived in the department, and Curtis feels that the three women are inconsiderate in discussing what he experiences as inappropriate work or social conversation in his presence. Further, the women frequently commiserate about barriers they experience in business (the lack of a family-leave program, the glass ceiling, etc.) that make their professional lives less than completely fulfilling. They have not once asked him how he is faring as the lone black man in his area of expertise at the agency. Once, in fact, when he returned excited from a special advancement workshop, the women ignored his return and almost seemed resentful that he had sought to improve his professional life. Several times the three women have been out to lunch together and on a few occasions they have made work decisions over their lunch without conferring with Curtis. When at work, Curtis feels that the women barely acknowledge his presence in meetings and rarely make eye contact with him. Finally, when he does work hard on his part of a project, the women evaluate him using much harsher criteria than they apply to their own work.

On the other hand, from Shannon's perspective, it seems that Curtis has trouble taking direction and constructive criticism from the women, who technically are more experienced and have seniority over him. Curtis often stares off into space, looking detached and distracted when they attempt to engage him. When someone asks Curtis to take a piece of a project, he is unenthusiastic in his response and usually turns the work in late. Further, just last month, during a particularly busy period, Curtis took off a day and a half to attend an advancement workshop cosponsored by the organization and the Black Professionals Alliance. When he is in the office, Curtis never volunteers for any work or asks for a specific task that may interest him. The work he does accomplish, Shannon claims, must be dramatically adjusted to fit into the overall project. Finally, on the several occasions when one of the female team members has tried to offer suggestions, he has become defensive and raised his voice to an unacceptably loud level in response.

Yesterday, Curtis came into your office and told you that he will be accepting a lateral appointment with one of your competitors. Should Curtis choose to leave, the next person in line for his position is a young white man.

What, as director of the department, should you do? In developing your response, keep the following questions in mind.

1. How could both these accounts be accurate? Try to track the factors that could make Curtis see the situation the way he sees it. Do the same with the factors that could make Shannon, Gail, and Valerie see the situation as they do.
2. Do traditional, stereotypical beliefs about white/black or male/female communication patterns play a role in the widely divergent perspectives offered by Shannon and Curtis? If so, identify them. How can you handle the situation to work through such barriers?
3. What areas of agreement and similarity might you be able to identify for these individuals?

4. Are there strategies Curtis could have used upon his introduction to the team to improve his chances of acceptance? Identify them.
5. Are there strategies Shannon, Gail, and Valerie could have used upon Curtis's introduction to the team to improve his chances of succeeding in the group? Identify them.
6. If Curtis does leave, how might you prepare for a new member to enter the group?

## Are We So Different We Can't Work Together?

### Adelina M. Gomez, Ph.D.[3]

John Smith, a black supervisor of predominantly white employees, in response to the question "How do you think your subordinates see you as a manager?" said, "In this particular agency, they see me as being low on the power chain even though I am their supervisor. They know they can challenge certain things I ask them to do because there are certain higher level supervisors who are white and who will listen to them and often countermand my decisions, even though they have disregarded the chain of command. This has caused me some supervisory problems in terms of controlling the employees and it has an impact on respect. I do not believe that they feel they have to be as loyal to me as they are to those above me. Therefore, I am ineffective as a supervisor. So I personally feel they see me as a convenience-type supervisor, someone they tolerate probably because I am black."

———————

Leo Marquez is a Hispanic manager who complains that the cultural differences among his subordinates often create problems in work-related situations when he has to talk to any of them about deficiencies in their work. He explained, "It is easier for me to talk to other Hispanics and Anglos than it is for me to talk to blacks. They usually become defensive when I bring to their attention the mistakes in their work. I try to talk to them in a manner that is not construed as offensive or racist. I have learned to be careful that a black does not feel that I am singling him out because he is black."

———————

Manager Maria Torres has expressed serious concerns about the problems that arise in managing culturally diverse groups. She argues that because 98 percent of the top-level managers in her agency are white males, they are not sensitive to the needs and concerns of minorities, much less those of women. She indicated that there are few, if any, minorities who are in top-grade management levels that are

[3]Adelina M. Gomez, associate professor of communication at the University of Colorado, Colorado Springs, holds B.A. and M.A. degrees from Western New Mexico University and a Ph.D. in communication from the University of Colorado. Her research and teaching interests include intercultural communication, comparisons of management behaviors across cultures, family communication, and public speaking. Gomez is an active consultant for both public and private sector organizations.

the policy-making positions. She explained, "A few male minorities are promoted to a certain grade level where they are usually dead-ended; women seldom are promoted. I am an exception, and although I am as capable as any man here, I believe mine was a token promotion. There is a strong need to remind white men about this inequity because it seems that no women or minorities will be promoted soon. I address the issue every chance I can. I do it in oversight reports and in supervisory and sensitivity training. I try very hard to get it across to them but to no avail."

She explained that there are serious problems because the buddy system and the selection process work predominantly for white men as they climb the ladder. She concluded, "These men seldom take minority men under their wing and we know they will certainly not take women!"

---

These three real-life case studies demonstrate some serious organizational problems that often go unrecognized even today. Although management programs have made great strides in preparing employees to be effective managers, significant weaknesses exist when these programs fail to recognize that we all have cultural identities and that culturally diverse groups may experience stressful working relations because of those cultural differences.

When people have little understanding of their own culture, it is unlikely they will understand other cultures, thus increasing the chances of communication barriers developing. All cultures have unique values that influence how individuals of those cultures interpret the world around them. It is from these values that attitudes and beliefs are derived that influence the communication process.

When people begin to understand who they are, culturally speaking, then they can proceed to the next stage of increasing their knowledge of other cultures. They can begin to understand how cultural differences influence such dimensions of an individual's working experiences as conflict management, leadership, and decision making. They can begin to make more sense of another person's behavior that may be strongly influenced by his or her culture.

Although some cultures share more similarities than differences, it is the differences that are misunderstood and precipitate culturally related problems. For this reason, we should focus on the problems that can occur in the overgeneralizations often made with regard to cultures. These overgeneralizations usually result in patterns of stereotyping, especially with regard to behaviors. Effective communication training supports the need for flexible attitudes and behaviors based on acknowledgment of healthy cultural diversity. In reality, effective communication training recognizes that cultural differences within our organizations are as important to sound relationships as they are to our society as a whole.

### QUESTIONS FOR DISCUSSION

1. Select one of these case studies and analyze the problem by addressing the role of cultural differences and how they may have contributed to the existing situation.

2. "Equality," "wisdom," and "a comfortable life" are examples of cultural values. What attitudes do you have that stem from these values, and where did they originate?

3. List four characteristics about your own culture that help you to understand the behaviors of someone from a different culture.

# REFERENCES AND SUGGESTED READINGS

Albrecht, T. L. and B. Hall. 1991. Relational and content differences between elites and outsiders in innovation networks. *Human Communication Research* 17: 535–561.

Amason, P., M. Allen, and S. Holmes. 1999. Social support and acculturative stress in the multicultural workplace. *Journal of Applied Communication Research* 27: 310–334.

Athanassiades, J. 1973. The distortion of upward communication in hierarchical organizations. *Academy of Management Journal* 16: 207–226.

Baird, J. E., Jr. 1977. *The dynamics of organizational communication.* New York: Harper and Row.

Booth-Butterfield, M., and S. Butterfield. 1986. Effects of evaluation, task structure, trait-CA, and reticence on state-CA and behavioral disruption in dyadic settings. *Communication Monographs* 53(2): 144–159.

Brislin, R. W. 1988. Prejudice in intercultural communication. In *Intercultural communication: A reader,* eds. L. Samovar and R. Porter, 339–344. Belmont, CA: Wadsworth.

Carmichael, C. W. 1988. Intercultural perspectives of aging. In *Intercultural communication: A reader,* eds. L. Samovar and R. Porter, 139–147. Belmont, CA: Wadsworth.

Cox, T. 1993. *Cultural diversity in organizations.* San Francisco: Berrett-Koehler.

Cummings, H. W., L. W. Long, and M. L. Lewis. 1983. *Managing communication in organizations: An introduction.* Dubuque, IA: Gorsuch Scarisbrick.

Daly, J. A., and J. C. McCroskey. 1975. Occupational desirability and choice as a function of communication apprehension. *Journal of Counseling Psychology* 22(4): 309–313.

Dansereau, F., and S. Markham. 1987. Superior-subordinate communication: Multiple levels of analysis. In *Handbook of organizational communication,* eds. F. Jablin, L. Putnam, K. Roberts, and L. Porter, 343–388. Newbury Park, CA: Sage.

DeVito, J. A. 1988. *Human communication: the basic course.* 4th eds. New York: Harper and Row.

DeWine, S., and F. Barone. 1984. *Employee communication and role stress: Enhancement or sabotage of the organizational climate?* Paper presented to the Organizational Communication Division of the International Communication Association Convention, May, San Francisco.

Downs, C., and T. Hain. 1982. Productivity and communication. In *Communication yearbook 5,* ed. M. Burgoon, 435–453. New Brunswick, NJ: Transaction Books.

Downs, C. W., and M. D. Hazen. 1977. A factor analytic study of communication satisfaction. *Journal of Business Communication* 14: 63–73.

Eisenberg, E., and H. L. Goodall, Jr. 1993. *Organizational communication: Balancing creativity and constraint.* New York: St. Martin's.

Eisenberg, E., P. Monge, and R. Farace. 1984. Coorientation of communication rules in managerial dyads. *Human Communication Research* 11: 261–271.

Ellison, N. 1999. *Dispersed work environments: A case study in communication technology and organizational culture.* Paper presented at the International Communication Association Convention, May, San Francisco.

Falcione, R., J. McCroskey, and J. Daly. 1977. Job satisfaction as a function of employees' communication apprehension, self-esteem, and perceptions of their immediate supervisor. In *Communication yearbook 1,* ed. B. D. Ruben, 363–376. New Brunswick, NJ: Transaction Books.

Farace, R. V., P. R. Monge, and H. M. Russell, 1977. *Communicating and organizing.* Reading, MA: Addison-Wesley.

Folb, E. A. 1988. Who's got the room at the top? Issues of dominance and nondominance in intra-cultural communication. In *Intercultural communication: A reader,* eds. L. Samovar and R. Porter, 121–130. Belmont, CA: Wadsworth.

Fulk, J., and S. Mani. 1986. Distortion of communication in hierarchical relationships. In *Communication yearbook 9,* ed. M. McLaughlin, 483–510. Newbury Park, CA: Sage.

Goldhaber, G., M. Yates, D. Porter, and R. Lesniak. 1978. Organizational communication. *Human Communication Research* 5(1): 76–96.

Granovetter, M. 1973. The strength of weak ties. *American Journal of Sociology* 78: 1360–1380.

Harris, P., and R. Moran. 1996. *Managing cultural differences: Leadership strategies for a new world of business.* Houston, TX.: Gulf.

Hatfield, J., R. Huseman, and E. Miles. 1987. Perceptual differences in verbal recognition and relative job satisfaction. *Communication Research Reports* 4: 8–13.

Herzberg, F. 1966. *Work and the nature of man.* Cleveland, OH: World.

Jablin, F. M. 1978. Message-response and openness in superior-subordinate communication. In *Communication yearbook 2,* ed. B. D. Ruben, 293–309. New Brunswick, NJ: Transaction Books.

Johnston, W. 1987. *Workforce 2000.* Indianapolis, IN: Hudson Institute.

Ketrow, S. 1992. *Cultural diversity and organizational communication: The gender perspective.* Paper presented to the Applied Communication Section of the Speech Communication Association Convention, October, Chicago.

Krivonos, P. D. 1982. Distortion of subordinate to superior communication in organizational settings. *Central States Speech Journal* 33(1): 345–352.

Krone, K. 1992. *Communicative and relational consequences of centralized authority structures.* Paper presented at the Speech Communication Association Convention, October, Chicago.

Lee, J. 1997. Leader-member exchange, the "Pelz effect," and cooperative communication. *Management Communication Quarterly* 11(2): 266–287.

Maslow, A. 1954. *Motivation and personality.* New York: Harper and Row.

McCroskey, J. C. 1982. *An introduction to rhetorical communication.* 4th ed. Englewood Cliffs, NJ: Prentice Hall.

McGee, G., J. Goodson, and J. Cashman. 1987. Job stress and job dissatisfaction: Influence of contextual factors. *Psychological Reports* 61(2): 367–375.

McCroskey, J. C., and V. P. Richmond. 1979. The impact of communication apprehension on individuals in organizations. *Communication Quarterly* 27(3): 55–61.

Miller, K. I., and P. R. Monge. 1985. Social information and employee anxiety about organizational change. *Human Communication Research* 11(3): 365–386.

Monge, P., and N. Contractor. 2001. Emergence of communication networks. In *The new handbook of organizational communication: Advances in theory, research, and methods,* eds. F. Jablin and L. Putnam, 440–502. Thousand Oaks, CA.: Sage.

Nichols, R., and L. Stevens. 1957. *Are you listening?* New York: McGraw-Hill.

Pace, R. W. 1983. *Organizational communication: Foundations for human resource development.* Englewood Cliffs, NJ: Prentice Hall.

Pearson, J. C. 1988. Gender and communication: Sex is more than a three-letter word. In *Intercultural communication: A reader,* eds. L. Samovar and R. Porter, 154–162. Belmont, CA: Wadsworth.

Pelz, D. 1952. Influence: A key to effective leadership in the first line supervisor. *Personnel* 29: 209–217.

Pincus, J. D. 1986. Communication satisfaction, job satisfaction, and job performance. *Human Communication Research* 12(3): 395–419.

Ray, E. 1993. When the links become chains: Considering dysfunctions of supportive communication in the workplace. *Communication Monographs* 60(1): 106–111.

Read, W. 1962. Upward communication in industrial hierarchies. *Human Relations* 15: 3–15.

Richetto, G. M. 1969. *Source credibility and personal influence in three contexts: A study of dyadic communication in a complex aerospace organization.* Unpublished doctoral dissertation, Purdue University, Lafayette, IN.

Richetto, G. M. 1977. Organizational communication theory and research: An overview. In *Communication yearbook 1*, ed. B. D. Ruben, 331–346. New Brunswick, NJ: Transaction Books.

Roberts, K., and C. O'Reilly. 1974. Measuring organizational communication. *Journal of Applied Psychology* 59(3): 321–326.

Ruben, B. D. 1988. Human communication and cross-cultural effectiveness. In *Intercultural communication: A reader*, eds. L. Samovar and R. Porter, 331–339. Belmont, CA: Wadsworth.

Salancik, G., and J. Pfeffer. 1977. An examination of need-satisfaction models of job attitudes. *Administrative Science Quarterly* 22: 427–456.

Salancik, G., and J. Pfeffer. 1978. A social information processing approach to job attitudes and task design. *Administrative Science Quarterly* 23: 224–253.

Scott, M. D., J. C. McCroskey, and M. F. Sheahan. 1978. Measuring communication apprehension. *Journal of Communication* 28: 104–111.

Scott, C., and C. E. Timmerman. 1999. *Communication technology: Use and multiple workplace identifications among organizational teleworkers with varied degrees of virtuality.* Paper presented at the International Communication Association Convention, May, San Francisco.

Shah, P. 1998. Who are employees' social referents? Using a network perspective to determine referent others. *Academy of Management Journal* 41(3): 249–268.

Shockley-Zalabak, P., K. Ellis, and R. Cesaria. 2000. *Measuring organizational trust.* San Francisco: International Association of Business Communicators.

Shockley-Zalabak, P., and D. Morley. 1984. High apprehensives within the organization: How and with whom do they talk? *Communication Research Reports* 1(1): 97–103.

Sias, P., and D. Cahill. 1998. From coworkers to friends: The development of peer friendships in the workplace. *Western Journal of Communication* 62(3): 273–299.

Skinner, B. F. 1953. *Science and human behavior.* New York: Macmillan.

Smith, A. F., and S. A. Hellweg. 1985. *Work and supervisor satisfaction as a function of subordinate perceptions of communication competence of self and supervisor.* Paper presented to the Organizational Communication Division of the International Communication Association Convention, May, Honolulu, HI.

Smith, P. C., L. M. Kendall, and C. L. Hulin. 1969. *The measurement of satisfaction in work and retirement.* Chicago: Rand McNally.

Snavely, W., and J. McNeill. 1985. *A path analytic study of the impact of organizational and interpersonal stressors on job tension, satisfaction, and turnover propensity.* Paper presented to the Organizational Communication Division of the International Communication Association Convention, May, Honolulu, HI.

Snyder, R. A., and J. H. Morris. 1984. Organizational communication and performance. *Journal of Applied Psychology* 69(3): 461–465.

Stewart, L. 1993. *Ethical issues in organizational diversity.* Paper presented at the International Communication Association Annual Conference, May, Washington, DC.

Stohl, C. 1995. *Organizational communication: Connectedness in action.* Thousand Oaks, CA: Sage.

Sypher, B. D., and T. E. Zorn Jr. 1987. *Individual differences and construct system content in descriptions of liked and disliked coworkers.* Paper presented to the Organizational Communication Division of the International Communication Association Convention, May, Montreal.

Tompkins, P., and G. Cheney. 1983. Account analysis of organizations: Decision making and identification. In *Communication and organizations: An interpretive approach*, eds. L. Putnam and M. Pacanowsky, 123–146. Beverly Hills, CA: Sage.

Waldron, V., and M. Hunt. 1992. Hierarchical level, length, and quality of supervisory relationship as predictors of subordinates' use of maintenance tactics. *Communication Reports* 5(2): 82–89.

Wilson, G. L., H. L. Goodall, Jr., and C. L. Waagen. 1986. *Organizational Communicaiton.* New York: Harper and Row.

# CHAPTER SIX

# GROUPS IN ORGANIZATIONS

---

**DEVELOPING COMPETENCIES THROUGH . . .**

**KNOWLEDGE**

Identifying types of groups in organizations

Describing small-group experiences of individuals in organizations

Describing group development

Describing the team-based organization

**SENSITIVITY**

Relating individual communication behaviors to effective participation in groups

Understanding positive and negative participation behaviors

Evaluating personal skills for group participation

**SKILLS**

Practicing effective group participation

Practicing analysis capabilities

**VALUES**

Relating group effectiveness to individual participation behaviors

Identifying responsibilities for self-managing groups

Understanding the concept of workplace democracy

■ ■ ■ ■ ■

## DAVE GREEN'S SMALL-GROUP EXPERIENCES

Dave had been at AMX for over three months. He would be glad when his first presentation to Sally and the group was behind him. It wasn't that they had not been helpful. The weekly planning meetings Sally held with the team were useful, and he was beginning to get more familiar with what to expect. John was clearly the leader. He talked more than any of the others, at least when Sally was present. The staff meetings usually began with an overall progress report of the week's activities, with some attention given to any problems encountered since the last meeting. Dave had observed that few serious difficulties were aired during the meetings. He wasn't sure if the others approached Sally for individual problem solving. As for him, he had not experienced a serious problem, except not knowing what Sally expected. John had helped with clarifying expectations on more than one occasion. The staff meetings were the forums for formal presentation of researched materials. Dave had observed two such presentations in the last three months. Next week was his turn, and he expected that the group would be supportive.

In addition to the staff meetings, the research team met informally about once every two weeks. Again, John seemed to call and run the meetings. Dave was not sure how the others felt about John's leadership but assumed that both Ralph and Susan supported him. At two of these meetings Dave had been a little uncomfortable with being assigned some work from John. He wasn't quite sure what, if anything, to do about the assignments. After all, John seemed an accepted informal leader and John had been personally supportive of Dave.

## INTRODUCTION

Peer relationships are more frequently discussed as small-group rather than as one-on-one organizational experiences. Most individuals in organizations spend considerable time in groups. Membership in work, problem-solving, and social support groups is common and influences how we experience organizational life. Dave Green is the new member of his team. His new job gives him formal membership in the group. He hopes that he will become part of an informal social group, but AMX as an organization won't make that happen. Dave's social support network will depend on his informal relationships at AMX.

Most of us have memberships in multiple groups. Families, work organizations, athletic teams, friendships, and volunteer groups are only a few **small-group experiences** in which most of us are involved. We join these groups in different ways and for different reasons. In our organizational lives, our jobs often define membership in certain groups. Our skills and visibility within the organization may determine membership in other types of groups, and our interpersonal relationships determine the extent of our membership in social support networks. In this chapter the types of primary group relationships in organizations and the roles individuals play in

**Small-group experiences**
Individual involvement in the formal and informal groups formed within organizations for task or social support.

these groups are explored, then Dave Green's reflections on his early group experiences are examined.

This chapter is designed to contribute to *knowledge* competencies by discussing groups common to most organizations, identifying individual experiences in groups, and describing group development. *Sensitivity competencies* are fostered by relating individual participation to group effectiveness, distinguishing between positive and negative participation behaviors, and evaluating personal communication skills for participation. *Skills* are developed by practicing positive participation behaviors and analyzing transcripts and group participation. Finally, *values* are developed by relating group effectiveness to individual participation behaviors and by identifying responsibilities for self-managing groups.

## SMALL-GROUP EXPERIENCES

Dave Green became a member of Sally Johnson's staff by virtue of his new job assignment. His first three months on the job have helped him learn about how the group works, what the expectations are, how issues are handled, and what his role or roles will be. Dave is also a member of an informal work group unofficially led by John. This group also has informal rules and operating procedures. He is less clear about his responsibilities to John but in general finds the group supportive and helpful. Dave's AMX experiences are common to most organizations. Some of the groups to which we belong are formally structured with specific goals, rules, and procedures. Others are more informal, blending task and social roles, and still others serve a purely social support function.

Organizations have many different types of formal and informal groups. Work teams, quality teams, sales teams, problem-solving groups, management teams, and unions are only a few examples of formally structured organizational groups. Informal groups come together for social events, athletic competition, coffee breaks, gripe sessions, and a variety of other purposes. Both types of groups are important for individual task accomplishment and social support.

We talk about groups as if they are easily described and recognized, but what exactly is a group? How do we identify group members and the types of activities in which groups actually engage? John Baird (1977) has defined a group as "a collection of more than two persons who perceive themselves as a group, possess a common fate, have organizational structure, and communicate over time to achieve personal and group goals." This definition places communication relationships at the core of group activity. As such, groups can be understood in terms of how they are formed and structured, how individuals understand their dependence on one another, and how members communicate.

Organizations form groups to fulfill a variety of organizational needs. Work groups are formed for maximum task efficiency and effectiveness. Problem-solving groups address ongoing organizational issues as well as emergencies. Groups meet regularly to review organizational operations and make future plans, to negotiate labor-management agreements, to respond to financial crises or unusual pressure from competition. Groups such as quality teams are formed to examine systematically new and better ways of doing things. The underlying assumption is that the efforts of numbers of individuals exceed individual efforts requiring energy and creativity for either completing tasks or examining issues.

Groups also contribute to establishing the shared realities of the organization. Expectations about member conduct can be found in most groups. Members communicate expectations to new members and evaluate behavior as either conforming to or disregarding the group rules. Dave is learning the communication rules of his work team. For example, he is learning that John expects to be the informal leader and that apparently Ralph and Susan accept this situation. Dave is attempting to determine whether the lack of problem discussion in staff meetings is a communication rule or the absence of any real problems during his tenure with AMX. He is also trying to determine what the group expects to be discussed in group settings and what should be handled privately with Sally. These rules and others become the realities Dave shares with his work team.

The next several sections of this chapter help us to understand Dave's experiences by describing the types of groups commonly formed in organizations, experiences individuals have in groups, and how groups develop. Finally, how we can increase effective group participation by working individually and cooperatively is discussed.

## TYPES OF GROUPS

Organizations have many different types of formal and informal groups for important task and social considerations. Relationships in primary work groups between supervisors and subordinates and among peers have been discussed. Most of us will have multiple group memberships in addition to our primary work team. Some of the specific types of groups common to organizations are identified next.

**Primary work team**
Group to which an individual is assigned upon organizational entry.

### Primary Work Teams

The first group assigned to us when we enter an organization is our **primary work team.** What we have been hired to do places us structurally within the organization and identifies our supervisor and related peer group. Work teams vary in size and formality. Some will work closely together, whereas others exchange infrequent information. Carl Larson and Frank LaFasto (1989) have identified three common features of competent work-team members: (1) the possession of essential skills and abilities, (2) a strong desire to contribute, and (3) the capability of collaborating effectively.

In research on effective teams, Larson and LaFasto found that effective work teams had members whose technical abilities were relevant to the team's objectives and who valued commitment and contributions to the team. Effective teams were characterized by the understanding of individual members concerning the relationship of their personal efforts to team effectiveness. Finally, Larson and LaFasto reported: "A consistent response . . . was the importance of selecting team members capable of working well with others. The emphasis in their responses was on capability. It was noted, repeatedly, that some people are capable of dealing with others in a collaborative fashion, and some are not." Larson and LaFasto concluded that their data collected from effective teams strongly suggested that people who could not collaborate should be removed from team efforts.

John Cragan and David Wright (1986) have identified some of the different types of work teams we are likely to encounter. Their descriptions of long-standing work groups, project teams, and "prefab" work groups help us to understand the different team structures organized to meet particular work needs. **Long-standing teams,** for example, are formed when the overall responsibilities of the team change slowly with time and when team membership can be expected to remain relatively stable. Long-standing work teams have well-defined organizational responsibilities, enabling selection of new team members based on qualifications previously identified as important for the group. Dave Green is joining such a group at AMX. The training function is well established and is expected to continue over time. AMX has experience with the types of people who are successful in training and development jobs. As such they have developed a list of qualifications they believe new members of the department should possess. Dave Green matches their initial expectations and enters a relatively long-standing group.

**Long-standing teams**
Relatively permanent groups of individuals organized for task accomplishment.

University departments are examples of long-standing teams. Although advances in knowledge change the content of courses, the general responsibilities for teaching, research, and service remain. Our government is another long-standing example. Congress, state and local governments, the Supreme Court, the presidency, and numerous other entities are examples of groups established by law but supported by the customs of the society as a whole. In most organizations personnel, financial, legal, and overall management responsibilities are carried out by long-standing teams. Long-standing teams develop ways of doing things that not only make qualifications for new members clear but also identify expected behaviors for members. Long-standing teams have the strength of team history and practical experience. They can, however, limit creativity and change when group traditions block rapid adaptation to new circumstances.

**Project teams**
Work groups established for the duration of a specific assignment.

**Project teams** are formed with highly specialized individuals to accomplish a specific project in a fixed period of time. These teams have specific goals, such as the design of a new product or the integration of technologies across the organization. Project teams are commonly used in high-technology industries for the research and design of products and processes. Their formation is based on the technical expertise needed for a given line of inquiry. Project teams draw membership from other teams in the organization, and assignments may be viewed as temporary or relatively permanent, depending on the needs of the project. Project teams have been part of the space program for many years and are common in telecommunications, electronic, computer, and research-based industries. Because of the nature of their formation, project teams do not have the history and traditions of long-standing work groups. They must quickly clarify goals, roles, and responsibilities in order to establish working relationships necessary to meet project guidelines and timetables. The formation of project teams permits an organization to respond rapidly to changing markets. Team members, however, may have difficulty in establishing trust and mutually satisfying working relationships when pressured by deadlines and the technical complexity of a challenging assignment. In recent research on project teams, Karen Brown, T. D. Klastorin, and Janet Valluzzi (1990) report that high-performing project teams more than their less successful counterparts were characterized by lower opinions of peers at the beginning of the project and were more valuing of technical expertise. Their results indicate that project teams that begin with harmonious interpersonal relations may not perform as well as those that experience early disharmonies. Information exchange throughout the duration of the project, however, is linked to ultimate success. Robert Keller (1994), in his work with research and development project teams, found that the more challenging (nonroutine) the team's assignment, the more prevalent the requirement for high information processing to achieve project quality.

**Prefab group**
Work group designed and structured for frequent replacement of members. Prefab groups have detailed individual assignments requiring limited experience to produce specified products.

Whereas project teams are associated with high-technology research and development efforts, the **prefab group** is the invention of the U.S. service industry. As Cragan and Wright (1986) have described the prefabricated group, "the job descriptions of this type of work group have been meticulously defined and rigidly structured so that a collection of people with no previous experience of working together can quickly form a work group that will produce a predictable level of productivity. Fast-food chains in the United States of America are the most obvious examples of industries that use prefab groups." The prefab group is efficient and predictable. Behavior expectations are specifically and clearly established. The group is designed to produce an average level of production and not expected to solve problems, introduce creativity into the process, or adapt to new situations. Prefab groups are best utilized for the production of goods and services but are not appropriate to meet problem-solving needs.

**Self-managing team**
A small number of people with complementary skills who are committed to a common purpose, have a defined set of performance goals, and execute an approach for which they hold themselves accountable.

**Self-managing teams** are formed to give individual team members more responsibility, authority, and accountability for their work. Jon Katzenbach and Douglas Smith (1993) define a team as "a small number of people with complementary skills who are committed to a common purpose, set of performance goals, and approach for which they hold themselves accountable." The growth of the numbers of self-managing teams in organizations is a result of the need to reduce management layers and the realization that high-performing teams potentially can outproduce work groups in more traditional hierarchical structures. Support is found throughout numerous organizations for the assertion that teams outperform individuals, particularly when multiple skills and experiences are required. Individual performance is frequently enhanced within a climate of group goals. Katzenbach and Smith contend, "Hierarchy and teams go together almost as well as teams and performance. Teams, in fact, are the best way to integrate across structural boundaries and to both design and energize core processes." Self-managing teams usually schedule their own work, cross-train team members, troubleshoot process and product problems, set evaluation criteria, conduct peer evaluation, and recommend product and process improvements. Clay Carr (1992) suggests that teams are most likely to succeed when they have clear, worthwhile, and compelling goals and when team members understand that they are expected to commit themselves to these goals. Carr's work also supports the notion that teams must be rewarded for team, not individual, success. When John Court right, Gail Fairhurst, and Edna Rogers (1989) compared traditional hierarchical structures with self-managing teams, they found that the self-managing environments were characterized by a variety of question-and-answer combinations, conversational elaboration, and a lack of managerial orders and commands. In contrast, competitive interchanges, interruptions, and statements of nonsupport typified interaction in the more traditional hierarchies. James Barker and Phillip Tompkins (1993) report that workers in self-managed teams tend to identify more strongly with their team than with their company, particularly in terms of loyalty.

## Directional Groups

Another category of important groups in organizations are those groups that are formally charged and structured to provide overall direction for the organization. Management teams, standing committees, and boards of directors are examples of groups empowered both structurally and legally to develop vision and policy for the organization. Generally viewed as powerful organizational groups, **directional groups** are responsible for review of the plans and performance of most other units within the organization. Directional groups establish policy and are generally considered responsible for both the oversight and the performance of the organization.

**Directional groups**
Groups formally charged and structured to provide overall direction and oversight of the organization.

Directional groups, frequently referred to as executive teams, set strategic direction for the organization and often must seek approval of another directional group, the board of directors, to implement that direction. A recent example from a Fortune 50 (corporation in the top fifty in dollar volume in the United States) illustrates the significance of the directional group. The chief executive officer and executive team of this large computer company launched an e-business initiative with the approval of the board of directors. The initiative included the purchase of another company known for technical expertise in e-business. The results were marginal, resulting in a drop in stock prices and market analysts questioning basic leadership decisions. Within five months the chief executive officer and several members of the executive team submitted their resignations, and the board of directors quickly moved to replace leadership with senior executives responsible for the product lines that had formerly been the long-standing strengths of the corporation. This type of experience is common for members of directional groups based on the significant influence they have for major organizational decisions.

Directional groups frequently are criticized for their failure to fully understand organizational issues or to make timely decisions in the best interest of the organization and its various stakeholders. Directional groups often are composed of representatives from various constituencies both within and outside the organization and come to decisions representing various and often opposing interests. Directional groups frequently are dependent on effective leadership to establish processes that support decision making. Directional groups usually are less dependent on the personal communication competencies of individual members than they are on the information-seeking and communication processes that the group adopts for problem solving and decision making.

**Quality teams**
Groups charged with responding to quality or quantity problems and to issues raised by management.

## Quality Teams

**Quality teams** is the name applied to a specific application of group problem solving that has gained popularity in the United States recently. The term *quality team* is applied to a group that meets regularly to identify and propose solutions to problems affecting product or process quality. Although the use of problem-solving teams began as early as the turn of the twentieth century, the emphasis on quality teams as we know it today began after World War II when Edward Deming introduced his statistical quality-control methods to Japanese management. By the early 1970s over six million Japanese workers were participating in what was initially called quality circles, or attempts to have line workers and leaders spend voluntary time solving product quality problems. The success of quality circles in Japan and increasing concerns for product quality in the United States have generated intense interest in this participative process of quality control.

Typically, quality teams are groups of volunteers who work in the same general area with the same general technology. Groups are led by supervisors or elected group members and are charged with responding to quality or quantity problems and to issues raised by management. Emphasis is placed on training quality circle members in group dynamics, problem solving, communication, and quality control. Quality teams are formed around the idea that groups can more quickly and effectively identify problems and propose solutions; that workers at all levels want to participate in problem solving, not just task implementation; and that innovations proposed at all levels within organizations can improve quality and productivity. Quality teams have made documented improvements in productivity. They must, however, be supported by access to useful information for problem solving and by genuine management responsiveness to change.

Quality teams have been used frequently in manufacturing situations and are credited with many improvements in the American automobile industry in the

1980s and 1990s. Quality teams are used regularly in health care settings and are associated with cost reductions in the financial transactions processing industry.

Marshall Scott Poole (2000) and his colleagues have investigated the adoption of quality improvement initiatives by intact teams (teams with the same overall goals as quality teams but formed with members of an ongoing work group). Their work in an integrated health care system indicates that quality improvements are most successful when the work groups enjoy a good deal of autonomy in their work, have high task variability, and task interdependence. When interaction styles support creativity and efficiency, attitudes toward quality initiatives are more positive and implementation efforts increase.

## Task Force Groups

**Task force groups**
Groups of individuals with diverse specialties and group memberships who are charged with accomplishing a specifically designed task or project.

**Task force groups** are formed to bring together individuals with technical specialties, and who are members of other organizational groups, to accomplish a specifically designed task or project. Like project groups, task force groups are formed around the technical specialties of their members. Unlike project teams, task force groups generally do not create products or implement processes but plan the initiation of projects or organizational changes. Simply put, task force groups are study groups charged with making recommendations. A task force may research and evaluate how to restructure organizational responsibilities. Recently, for example, a major high-technology firm was unable to recruit successfully approximately 60 percent of the job applicants to whom they made offers. In their concern for recruiting effectiveness, top management formed a task force to study recruiting responsibilities and make recommendations for changes. Membership of the task force was selected from all organizational groups with any recruiting responsibility. The task force was given specific responsibilities by management and a time frame in which to present conclusions. Task force groups have the advantage of focused responsibilities and potential membership from qualified individuals throughout the organization. They frequently face challenges, however, because individual members may seek to protect the position of their primary work groups. Task force groups are generally more successful when members agree that change is needed and when they work cooperatively for organizational versus subgroup goals.

## Steering Committees

**Steering committees**
Groups of individuals with diverse specialties and group memberships who are charged with implementing organizational plans, processes, or change.

**Steering committees** resemble task force groups in the composition of their memberships, but what task force groups recommend, steering committees implement. Formed with diverse organizational membership, steering committees implement organizational plans, processes, or change. Whereas the task force might recommend a new recruiting process for the high-technology firm, a steering committee might be formed to implement recommendations and monitor the process of the new plan. Steering committees literally steer the progress of a plan, goal, issue, or program. They give organizations the advantage of broad participation in the oversight of a project. Steering committees have been criticized, however, as rubber-stamp groups in which no one takes definite responsibility, permitting the best-laid plans to miss the mark or actually fail. Research suggests that authority and responsibility to bring about change are critical for successful steering committees.

## Focus Groups

**Focus groups**
Collections of individuals who have familiarity with a problem or issue and are asked in a somewhat non-structured format to describe the issue and make recommendations; formed to discuss problems but not to take responsibility for final recommendations or implementation of change.

Like quality teams, **focus groups** represent a technique gaining in organizational use. Focus groups are collections of individuals who are familiar with a problem or issue and are asked in a somewhat unstructured format to describe the issue and any recommendations they might have. Focus groups have been used by advertising and marketing organizations to understand consumer preferences, identify effective message strategies, and evaluate potential new products. The successful use of focus groups in advertising and marketing has stimulated their application to numerous other organizational issues. Focus groups are formed to discuss problems, not to take responsibility for final recommendations or implementation of change. Focus groups can be used to gather information and get reactions quickly to proposed courses of action. The groups are frequently formed to identify new types of training needs, assess employee morale, uncover poorly defined problems, and make policy recommendations. They provide excellent information when made up of individuals with adequate concern for or information about the subject for discussion. On occasion, focus group members have voiced frustration about not knowing the outcome of their efforts. Forward-thinking companies, when using employee focus groups, are careful to provide feedback mechanisms.

## Geographically Diverse Teams

**Geographically diverse groups**
Groups of individuals who form a work team but are separated in distance and linked through technology.

Sometimes referred to as networked teams, **geographically diverse teams** are emerging to link people together across time zones, distance, language, and a variety of other personal and organizational circumstances. Geographically diverse teams communicate using networked computers, video, and audio connections. Geographically diverse teams include individuals who work out of their homes (commonly called telecommuters) as well as individuals separated by miles and even continents.

Sales, transaction processing, manufacturing, and service support functions increasingly are organized as geographically diverse teams. Although many of the same issues apply as with other organizational groups, geographically diverse teams are heavily dependent on technology and the ability of group members to solve complex problems without face-to-face interaction. Many organizations, however, are finding that geographically diverse teams need some face-to-face meeting. For example, one large computer manufacturer using teams with membership in a variety of countries brings team members together quarterly to discuss problems and operating norms and to work on issues brought about by their geographic separation. Most of us will experience working in geographically diverse groups over the next several years. This reality underscores the importance of a combination of human and technological communication competencies.

**Social support groups**
Formed as subgroups of larger task groups or among people with similar organizational interests; function to stimulate trust and cohesiveness among group members.

## Social Support Groups

Work teams, quality teams, task forces, steering committees, and focus groups can all be **social support groups.** Formed for task considerations, most continuous groups provide informal social support to group members. Social support groups form as subgroups of larger task groups among people with similar organizational interests and among friends. They have few formal task responsibilities as such but often support task accomplishment by stimulating trust and cohesiveness among group members. Social support group membership has been associated with organizational and communication satisfaction and competency. Individuals apprehensive about communication are less likely to be members of diverse social support groups and are more likely than others to work in relative isolation. Those comfortable with their communication competencies are more likely to be involved in diverse groups and are more likely than their more highly apprehensive counterparts to exhibit communication and job satisfaction.

As you can readily see, groups are important for our organizational experiences. In many cases, our competencies will be evaluated through our group participation. The next section of this chapter describes a growing application of groups in organizations—the team-based structure.

## THE TEAM-BASED ORGANIZATION

Based on the successful use of teams in a variety of industries, one of the fastest growing of all contemporary organizational changes is the move to team-based structures. Characterized as a "flat organization" with fewer managers and supervisors than a traditional hierarchy, the **team-based organization** is composed of a variety of teams with defined responsibilities and accountabilities for which managers provide mostly indirect supervision. Self-managing teams discussed earlier in this chapter are the cornerstone of the team-based structure.

**Team-based organization**
Organizational structures with fewer managers and networks of self-managing teams.

The growing number of team-based organizations is in direct response to increased global competitiveness requiring overhead reductions and increased productivity. A by-product of this need to improve competitive positioning is the potential in the team-based structure (but not necessarily the reality) of a more mature treatment of the work force. In other words, the opportunity to work in self-managing teams and team-based organizations replaces the close supervision of hierarchies with individuals and groups who self-monitor, innovate, and produce quality work with little or no supervision.

Team-based organizations and the concept of teamwork frequently are confused. The term *team-based organization* refers to a structural change from hierarchy to flat and often networked configurations of teams. Teamwork is the ability of individuals to work collaboratively together. Teamwork is required for successful team-based structures, but teamwork also is important for hierarchy. Team-based organizations alter the way in which work is organized, supervised, and rewarded, whereas teamwork is the interactional process through which work is accomplished.

Over 70 percent of major corporations today have team-based structures in parts of their operations. Many small organizations also use team organizational forms. Research indicates team-based organizations generally outperform more hierarchically organized structures in terms of product and service output, less absenteeism, fewer industrial accidents, more worker flexibility, quality improvements, and overall employee job satisfaction. Michael Hackman and Craig Johnson (2000) report research covering fifteen years that describes team-based structures as more innovative, able to share information, involved, and task-skilled than more traditional organizational structures. Examples include AT&T Credit Corporation, where teams process eight hundred lease applications per day as contrasted to four hundred per day before the team structure; Corning, where teams are credited with decreasing defect rates from 1,800 parts per million to 9 parts per million; Federal Express, with a reduction in service errors by 13 percent in one year; and General Mills, with 40 percent more productivity in factories with team-based structures compared with traditional factories. Some estimate that by the year 2010 over 75 percent of the work force will participate in a team-based structure. Needless to say, the implications of this change will affect most of us and will be a challenge to our ability to work effectively in groups.

A useful way to understand a team-based organization is to examine four important aspects of organizational life: goals, roles, relationships, and processes. In both team-based structures and hierarchies, overall goals guide all aspects of work. In a hierarchy, management generally is responsible for goal setting with limited input from workers. In the team-based organization, the overall business goals of the organization are established by management, but work unit goals are established by team members who monitor their own results. Numerous examples exist of teams establishing goals that exceed the productivity of their counterparts in hierarchies. A team-based organization requires a more diverse role set from individual team members. For example, team members not only set productivity and quality goals, but they monitor and report results, conduct team meetings, provide feedback to team members, problem solve, evaluate performance, and provide input on needed process or product changes. In essence, team members assume many of the supervision responsibilities formerly residing with management. In a team-based structure relationships with customers, vendors, and others in the organization are managed directly by the team, whereas in a hierarchy supervisors and managers are charged with initiating change and providing communication links throughout the organization. Finally, processes such as conflict management, problem solving, decision making, and leadership become team member responsibilities more so than in more closely supervised models. Again, these processes require highly developed communication competencies from all team members. In a recent national employer survey, team skills were listed as a major requirement for college graduates and also a major deficiency as employers evaluated their new college hires.

Team skills usually are divided into two categories: task and maintenance roles. Task roles represent the processes in which the team engages to achieve its goals, whereas maintenance roles deal with literally maintaining the ability of the team to work together. Task roles include problem analysis, idea generation, idea evaluation, abstract ideas/vision identification, solution generation, solution implementation, goal setting, agenda making, discussion clarification, disagreement identification, and consensus identification. Maintenance roles include group participation, group climate, and conflict management. Later sections of this chapter have more discussion about task and maintenance roles and increasing participation effectiveness.

The team-based organization with its use of self-directed work teams is not without issues and concerns. First, working in a self-directed work team requires a complex mixture of competencies both technical and communicative. Many technically capable people report difficulty adapting to providing and receiving peer feedback. In addition, career advancement is less well understood in team-based organizations than in hierarchies with more established paths to increasing responsibility and associated prestige. The question of who gets credit for what is an issue as well as whether team members are adequately compensated by the organization for their contributions to increased competitiveness. Critics also charge that team-based structures have a potential for exploitation based on continual pressures to increase productivity.

Of particular importance to the subject of this text are the issues in teams surrounding participation. Paul W. Mulvey, John Veiga, and Priscilla Elsass (1996) have studied self-limiting behavior in teams when individuals either surrender their positions or withhold effort, a process they call "raising a white flag." Mulvey, Veiga, and Elsass report that the top six reasons for self-limiting behaviors are (1) the presence of someone with expertise, (2) the presentation of a compelling argument, (3) lacking confidence in one's ability, (4) an unimportant or meaningless decision, (5) pressure from others to conform to the team's decision, and (6) a dysfunctional decision-making climate. These issues and others are fundamental to the functioning of teams and to individual satisfaction with the work unit. They also are linked to the next issue for the discussion: workplace democracy. In fact, self-directed work teams and new organizational structures only add to concerns for genuine worker participation.

## Workplace Democracy

George Cheney (1995) describes **workplace democracy** as a

> system of governance which truly values individual goals and feelings (e.g., equitable remuneration, the pursuit of enriching work and the right to express oneself) as well as typically organizational problems (e.g., effectiveness and efficiency, reflectively conceived), which actively fosters the connection between those two sets of concerns by encouraging individual contributions to important organizational choices, and which allows for the ongoing modification of the organization's activities and policies by the group. (pp. 170-171)

Workplace democracy, as described by Cheney, may or may not be found in team-based organizations. In fact, few organizations incorporate practices that fully support all aspects of his definition. The rise of employee-owned organizations, worker cooperatives, and employee stock ownership plans begins to address democracy issues. Clearly, globalization, change, innovation, and increased competitive pressures are closely linked to genuinely valuing people for their contributions. It is fair to conclude that organizations are challenged to increase employee input on a wide variety of issues that not only affect the work directly but all aspects of organizational life. Communication processes are at the heart of these challenges.

## INDIVIDUALS IN GROUPS

In the discussion of how individuals experience organizations, predispositions or preferences for organizational communication behaviors that are related to occupation choice, job satisfaction, productivity, and a variety of other organizational outcomes were described. The importance of communication apprehension, leadership and conflict preferences, and perceptions of communication competencies was emphasized. As you might expect, these predispositions or preferences for communication also are influential as we work in groups.

John Brilhart and Gloria Galanes (1989) have suggested that "the most important resource a small group has is its members: their knowledge, attitudes, and skills. How well they work together toward a common goal depends partly on the attitudes they have toward themselves, each other, the group, and the information and ideas presented." Brilhart and Galanes have contended that the sense of responsibility for the success of the group that each individual brings to group efforts is what promotes group effectiveness.

Generally speaking, the more positive we feel about our personal communication competencies, the better able we are to work in groups successfully. Moreover, when we respect the competencies of others, we consider the time and energy invested in group experiences to be worthwhile. We all have attended a meeting or served on a committee that we evaluated as a waste of time. Think for a moment about that group and the commitment of individual members. Think about the knowledge, sensitivity, skills, and values each brought to the effort. What conclusions can you draw from your experience? Now recall a more positive group effort. What made the difference? How were your individual contributions affected?

We all bring our previous experiences and backgrounds to group participation. As our work force and markets become increasingly diverse, an important component of our personal communication competency is the ability to work effectively in groups with those who have differing backgrounds from our own. As Taylor Cox Jr. (1993) suggests:

> It is important to acknowledge that all members of organizations, not just members of minority groups, have salient group identities. To the extent that gender affects organizational experience, it affects both men and women. To the extent that racioethnic identity has effects, it affects Whites and non-Whites. If accountants are disdained in favor of engineers, both engineers and accountants are affected. Appreciation of this simple fact, that we all have group identities which affect our own behavior and how others treat us, is a vital step toward building personal competence for working in diverse groups. (p. 61)

**Rhetorical sensitivity**
Quality that describes individual acceptance of personal complexity, avoidance of communicative rigidity, interaction consciousness, appreciation of the communicability of ideas, and tolerance for inventional searching.

Brilhart and Galanes (1989) have suggested that the concept of **rhetorical sensitivity** is important for group communication. Broadly defined, rhetorical sensitivity is the ability of an individual to monitor personal communication behaviors with regard to potential consequences for other group members. Five components of rhetorical sensitivity are identified by Brilhart and Galanes as especially relevant to group communication: (1) acceptance of personal complexity, (2) avoidance of communicative rigidity, (3) interaction consciousness, (4) appreciation of the communicability of ideas, and (5) tolerance for inventional searching.

Acceptance of personal complexity is a sensitivity competency that recognizes and values the diversity of people in a group. When individuals value diversity, they are likely to avoid communicative rigidity and to use a variety of speaking and interacting patterns based on the needs of the situation. Dave Green is an excellent example. In the past Dave has been a leader in most of his school groups. He has frequently contributed ideas and set directions. At AMX Dave is the junior member of an experienced group. His participation patterns are different because of his sensitivity to the needs of the new situation. He realizes that he does not fully understand the personal complexity of his new work team, although he values their willingness to help him.

Interaction consciousness refers to the awareness an individual brings to the process of interaction. How can ideas be presented? What support do others need? What is the balance between aggressiveness and passivity or argumentativeness and acquiescence? Along with sensitivity to interactions comes appreciation for the communicability of ideas or an awareness of when expressing ideas and feelings facilitates goal achievement. We all have been in situations when an idea, although valuable in and of itself, made no real contribution to the issue at hand.

The rhetorically sensitive individual weighs the appropriateness of expressions as they relate to the purpose of the situation. Finally, the rhetorically sensitive individual understands that many approaches may be effective in the expression of an idea or feeling and, based on this belief, attempts to engage others in interactions. This sensitivity is referred to as tolerance for inventional searching.

# GROUP DEVELOPMENT

Previously it was said that the organization actually structures many of the groups to which we belong. Although certainly accurate, this notion of group formation only begins to help us understand how groups evolve and develop. We can be more effective group participants when we become familiar with stages of group development and how groups generate norms and roles. In addition, it is important to consider specific influences on group participation such as prestige and climate.

## Group Stages

Groups have both socioemotional and task concerns. Group members must become acquainted, learn about each other, and usually move from impersonal to somewhat interpersonal relationships. Group members also recognize that there is a job to do or an assignment to accomplish. These socioemotional and task concerns need attention as groups form; move through production, performing, or decision phases; and adjourn or recycle to new issues or problems.

**Group stages**
Concept that groups progress through sequences such as formation, production, resolution, and dissolution; frequently described as forming, storming, norming, performing, and adjourning.

Researchers generally suggest that groups progress through a series of **group stages** that begin with formation. During formation members work out interpersonal concerns or tensions and establish relationships necessary for enough stability to permit task efforts. Groups move from formation to production phases, that is, an emphasis on task-related behaviors such as idea generation or problem solving. These production phases have been variously referred to as decision emergence, confrontation, compromise and harmony, and performing. The labels are not as important as the concept that as the group matures, a variety of communication processes—idea generation, conflict, problem solving, decision making, compromise—become typical of group interactions. The effectiveness of these interactions is directly related to the effectiveness of group outcomes, both task and socioemotional. Following production, groups move toward resolution, the phase when problems are more readily resolved and the group is productive with less overall expenditure of energy than in earlier phases. Resolution can precede the actual dissolving of groups formed for a specific and not ongoing purpose.

Bruce Tuckman and Mary Ann Jensen (1977) have provided a frequently used five-stage description of task group development. Their first stage, forming, includes the establishment of new relationships and the tension associated with entering new situations. The second stage, storming, is characterized by individuals reacting to the demands of the situation, questioning authority, and developing enough comfort to be themselves. Norming is described as the third stage, in which the group establishes general ways of doing things that are particular to the group and can be described as rules for behavior. The next stage, performing, finds group members working on the task as they have previously worked on relationship formation. Finally, when the task nears completion, group members, in what is called the adjourning phase, bring closure to both task and interpersonal issues.

It is important to understand that these stages or phases, regardless of the labels associated with them, are meant to describe groups moving through a developmental process. As with any other type of development process, the stages are not distinct and do not necessarily progress in a fixed sequence. They do, however, provide an overall model to help us understand the variety of communication behaviors we experience in the numerous organizational groups in which we are likely to become members.

Dave Green is joining a work group that has been together for some time. In a very real sense his membership may influence the group to reform to include the new member. Obviously, the others know each other well. Their sense of tension with one another is predictably less than the tension of coming to know Dave. Dave, on the other hand, must establish new relationships with Sally, John, Ralph, and Susan. His tension is probably the highest in the group as he attempts to absorb the most new information. Dave is experiencing the reality of group membership in organizations. Often we will find ourselves the new member of a long-standing group. At other times we will be assigned to group projects in which all members are new. At times we will be responsible for forming groups for important task and social considerations.

Dave is anxious to understand the expectations of Sally and the others in his work group. He has observed that very little conflict is voiced in group meetings. He is attempting to know whether this is a behavior expectation of the group—a norm—or whether few potentially conflicting issues have come before his group in the short period of his membership. Dave is concerned, as we all are in new groups, about the expectations the group holds and how the members will evaluate him. Simply put, Dave is concerned about AMX norms.

**Group norms**
Unwritten behavior rules, ways of doing things, that groups develop over time. Norms reflect what groups deem desirable and can be said to be cultural beliefs about effectiveness or appropriateness.

**Group norms** are unwritten behavior rules, ways of doing things, that groups develop over time, usually through tacit rather than explicit approval. Norms reflect what the group deems desirable, and they can be said to be cultural beliefs about effectiveness or appropriateness. Groups have general norms that apply to all members and role-specific norms that apply to individual members in such roles as leader, secretary, information collector, and critic. Generally speaking, group members disapprove and sometimes punish members who violate norms. We can only imagine what might occur if Dave Green openly disagreed with John in one of Sally's staff meetings. We don't know if the absence of conflict is an AMX norm, but we suspect that based on his observations, Dave will be cautious in initiating conflict. Dave is essentially attempting to establish his role in the group by understanding its norms or expectations. Based on the competencies Dave brings to the group, that role will emerge and will be worked out in relationship to other group members.

## Group Communication Roles

Previously, organizational communication as the construction of the multiple realities and cultures of organizations was described. We can also observe communication activities in groups as they contribute to shared group realities and culture. One way is by examining the roles group members enact and how these roles are encouraged or discouraged in the group.

Individuals assume different roles in groups. As a newcomer to the AMX team, Dave has a task role but also a newcomer role. Probably at first Dave's group will expect less from his task role because he is a newcomer who does not yet know the ropes. Dave can probably get more help from the group while he is still a newcomer than when the group believes that he has had enough time to become socialized and make an equal contribution.

Dave also brings to his group predispositions for a variety of communication behaviors. His predispositions and his communication roles will interact with the predispositions and roles of other group members to create the shared realities of the group.

Kenneth Benne and Paul Sheats (1948) have developed three important classifications of **group communication roles:** group task roles, group maintenance roles, and self-centered roles. **Task roles** help groups accomplish goals, whereas **maintenance roles** promote social support among group members. **Self-centered roles** support individual goals and may or may not be compatible with overall group goals and relationships. An understanding of individual communication roles is useful for determining how groups work and for identifying personal roles and skills that contribute to improved competency for group interaction.

Following is an adaptation of the Benne and Sheats role classification with examples of role statements taken from transcripts of staff meetings at a major national retailer.

**Group communication roles**
Task, maintenance, and self-centered categories for description of behaviors that individuals exhibit in groups.

**Task roles**
Communication roles that help groups accomplish goals.

**Maintenance roles**
Communication roles that promote social support among group members.

**Self-centered roles**
Communication roles that support individuals' goals and may or may not be compatible with overall group goals and relationships.

### GROUP TASK ROLES

1. *Initiator:* makes suggestions, contributes new ideas, recommends goals and procedures, speculates about approaches. "I don't think we should be bound by what we did last year for the Fourth of July sale. After all, the competition knows all that. Let's brainstorm for a few minutes about a new approach."

2. *Information requestor:* asks for facts, asks for experiences and comparisons, asks for new ideas, seeks clarification of expectations and information. "Do we know what our three major

competitors are planning for the Fourth? I think it's important to find out, especially after our strong showing last year."

3. *Information giver:* submits facts, experiences, identifies relevant data, makes comparisons. "We were first in sales over the Fourth, but we kept locations adjacent to public parks open at least two hours longer than our competitors. Our profit picture was influenced by additional operating overhead."

4. *Procedure facilitator:* takes notes, records ideas, distributes handouts, guides group to agenda. "I will gladly record all our ideas while we brainstorm."

5. *Opinion requestor:* seeks opinions, values, beliefs of others, speculations about courses of action. "I know we aren't ready to make a final commitment to a promotion. If we had all the money we need, which of the proposals would fit your best guess of an ideal Fourth promotion?"

6. *Opinion giver:* gives opinions, expresses values and beliefs, gives speculations about courses of action or direction. "I think we ought to go with the television campaign. I don't have all the cost estimates, but I think that gets us the most overall visibility."

7. *Clarifier:* explains ideas and elaborates; describes expectations, illustrates ideas, coordinates relationships between ideas and information. "I want to make sure we all understand. We need to compare cost projections for both types of promotions and then compare with sales projections."

8. *Summarizer-evaluator:* restates ideas and describes relationships, criticizes accomplishments, details agreements and differences. "I believe it is fair to say we have agreed on the need for a new promotion for this Fourth of July. We have agreed that it is between the TV campaign and a major celebrity event for the big stores. We will need to have full presentations on both ideas for the next meeting."

### GROUP MAINTENANCE ROLES

1. *Social supporter:* expresses togetherness, encourages others, gives praise, suggests solidarity. "I think we have a really good group here. Of course, we don't always agree, but our track record is really impressive."

2. *Harmonizer:* mediates and reconciles differences, suggests areas of agreement between disagreeing members, suggests positive ways to explore differences. "John and Sally both have good points about possible promotions. Let's ask them both to present their ideas and identify possible ways of combining the best from both promotions."

3. *Tension reliever:* relaxes others, changes subjects, jokes, admits mistakes. "Let's not worry so much about this point. After all, we can't make as big a mistake as we did for the Thanksgiving promotion. None of us got fired over that. We can take ourselves too seriously if we aren't careful."

4. *Energizer:* stimulates group activity, seeks group action. "Look, we need to decide what we are going to do next. Facts are nice, but we can't have a paralysis of indecision."

5. *Leader:* takes personal responsibility, represents group to others, determines agenda. "I will take personal responsibility to confront our advertising

agency. They need to keep us better informed. I will put them on the agenda for our next meeting."

6. *Follower:* goes along with the group, accepts others' ideas, supports group decisions, listens to others. "You senior managers have the experience. Whatever you decide is fine with me."

7. *Compromiser:* seeks a middle position in disagreement, supports both task and people issues, gives up some of own position. "I think we can find a middle ground on this problem. It is possible to do TV and have a celebrity at one or two of the big stores. This combination might be better than either idea by itself."

8. *Gatekeeper:* asks opinions of nonparticipants, prevents dominance by others, facilitates overall interaction. "We haven't heard from John. Let's be quiet and hear what he has to say."

### SELF-CENTERED ROLES

1. *Negative blocker:* gives negative responses to most ideas, is negative about any positive solutions, raises continuous objections. "Look, I have told you over and over again that what we decide doesn't make any difference. The advertising department controls the promotions; our ideas don't matter."

2. *Dominator:* controls through interruptions, superiority of tone, and length of conversational control. "What you are saying isn't very important. I believe that I know best what we should do."

3. *Attacker:* is aggressive to achieve personal status, expresses disapproval, is critical of status of other. "Look, you are the manager of a small store that isn't all that successful. I would keep my mouth shut if I were you."

4. *Clown:* disrupts with jokes and other diverting behavior, brings up tangents, refuses to take ideas seriously. "We don't have a problem, we need to let the good times roll. You take all this too seriously. When I was with [names a competitor] we really knew how to party when all the managers got together."

Generally speaking, group task and maintenance roles are considered productive for group interaction, whereas self-centered roles are destructive and contribute to ineffectiveness. Chances are, however, that most of us engage in all these roles at one time or another. Communication competency for group settings is related to our ability to identify the roles we are likely to use and to analyze group needs in order to use these roles for effective problem solving.

Although the roles we have just described are frequently observed in organizational groups, they by no means represent all the possible communication roles. You can probably add to the list from your group experiences. Which communication roles are you likely to fulfill? Does your answer differ depending on the group in which you find yourself? If so, why? If not, why not? The transcript of a small-group problem-solving session in Figure 6.1 was taken from a staff meeting in the personnel department of a major computer manufacturer. As you read the transcript, try to determine the roles of the individual participants. Try also to determine whether or not these roles contribute to productive group outcomes.

## FIGURE 6.1   Group Problem-Solving Transcript

*Jane* (department manager): I think we had better get started. We have a lot to do to get ready to announce the new training plan.

*Sally* (senior trainer): Jane, I'm not sure everyone in the group really understands our plans. I think that before we decide how to introduce the program to the division we need to make sure that everyone in personnel is thoroughly familiar with what we intend to do.

*Jane:* That's a good point. How much information do the rest of you have?

*John* (compensation specialist): I just know we are going to plan a training program for each employee, but I have been on vacation and don't know much more than that.

*Henry* (recruiter): Look, I don't think each of us can be expected to know all the details. I think we should stick to our original plan and decide how a division-wide announcement should be made. The rest of us are too busy to understand all the details.

*Sally to Henry*: I think you're very wrong. Especially in your job, you can actually attract people to this company with the type of ongoing training we are proposing.

*Kathy* (benefits administration): Sally, maybe you could describe the type of training our department will receive. That might help us understand the general concept.

*Jane:* Sally, I do think an overview of the program would be helpful. We do, however, have to decide on the timing of the division-wide announcement.

[Sally explains the basics of the new training program to the staff (narrative not included).]

*Frank* (employee representative): I think it sounds like a very impressive program, but I wonder if we can really pull it off. Remember the time we decided to computerize all the records and start the year with a new payroll process? We were crazy. Who made that decision, anyway? Does anyone remember? Let's not have another Kent Smith [employee who left the company following the record computerization project].

*Sally to Frank:* This one is not another Kent Smith project. I resent you implying that it is. A lot of hard work and planning have gone into identifying training opportunities that will help all our employees. I think you should keep an open mind.

*Jane:* Does anyone else have any questions about the program?

*Kathy:* Well, I think we need to move in this direction. What ideas do you need from us to make the division announcement?

*Sally:* Thanks, Kathy. First of all, we need to know the timing of major communications from your individual areas to all employees. We don't want too much new information going out at once.

Try to identify the roles individuals played in the dialogue (see the following list). Can you determine which individuals work more cooperatively than others? Is there a leader? Are important roles missing? How would you describe this group?

**FIGURE 6.1    Continued**

| Task Roles | Maintenance Roles | Self-Centered Roles |
| --- | --- | --- |
| Initiator | Social supporter | Negative blocker |
| Information requestor | Harmonizer | Dominator |
| Information giver | Tension reliever | Attacker |
| Procedure facilitator | Energizer | Clown |
| Opinion requestor | Leader | |
| Opinion giver | Follower | |
| Clarifier | Compromiser | |
| Summarizer-evaluator | Gatekeeper | |

## Influences on Group Members

Stages of group development, norms, and group communication roles do not fully explain some of the subtle influences on our group experiences. Why are we more comfortable in some groups than others? What makes one group more prestigious than another? Why is it that certain group memberships help our career and others hinder professional success? How can we determine the difference?

There are no definite answers to these questions. Generally speaking, we are most comfortable in groups in which group goals and our individual goals are compatible. When our personal needs are met, we are more likely to attempt to meet the needs of others and to exhibit cohesive behavior within the group. We are attracted to remain in the comfort of the group.

Most of us are also attracted to groups with high prestige or in which we have prestige. Conventional wisdom suggests that prestige contributes to career success. The culture of an organization communicates which groups are prestigious and which are not. Prestigious groups usually have more authority, responsibility, and risk associated with their efforts. Those with confidence in their communication and task competencies will be attracted to such groups, whereas those with lower estimations of themselves will avoid membership in such visible groups.

Additionally group participation is influenced by the overall climate of a group, the degree of interaction among group members, and the overall size of the group. Rodney Napier and Matti Gershenfeld (1989) have suggested that group members are more attracted to groups in which the climate is characterized by commitment to the group, compatibility among members, more cooperative than competitive behaviors, and expectations that work will be evaluated on a team versus individual performance basis. Finally, groups are more attractive as participation among members increases and the overall size of the group remains relatively small. In addition, Napier and Gershenfeld have identified influences that they believe block effectiveness: domination of single members, negatively critical norms, vested interests of individual members, changing group membership resulting in less compatible relationships, and problems of physical space. Janet Fulk (1993) extends our thinking about the powerful influences of group membership for individual behavior with her study of technology adoption and use. Fulk found that an individual's attraction to the group was related to the use of technology. In her study of e-mail use, Fulk found that technology-related attitudes and behaviors were stronger when individuals were highly attracted to their work groups.

Leadership, problem-solving processes, and conflict affect our group experiences. Whether or not conflict is effectively handled may determine whether we wish to continue membership in a given group. Leadership may determine whether any actual work gets done or whether members are recognized for their contributions. Problem-solving processes determine the task effectiveness of organizational groups. Conflict processes in groups, leadership and management communication, and problem solving and decision making are the specific subjects of the next three chapters in this text. In each of these chapters, emphasis is placed on how leadership, problem-solving processes, and conflict affect both individual and group effectiveness.

## INCREASING GROUP PARTICIPATION EFFECTIVENESS

The importance of a variety of groups for organizational life has already been discussed. How individuals bring attitudes about themselves, others, groups, and information to group membership has been described. The types of groups common in organizational life, how groups develop, the group communication roles that emerge, and general influences on group members have been examined. Recent research supports the importance of group participation processes. For example, Michael Mayer (1998) investigated specific behaviors perceived by group members to improve decision making. Mayer found that people believe decisions are most likely to be of high quality when group members participate fully in the process, when the group climate is characterized by the presence of respectful behaviors and the absence of negative socioemotional behaviors, and when information and solutions offered in groups are analyzed by group members. Renee Heath and Patricia Sias (1999) reported communication practices supportive of a collaborative spirit, namely shared mission and shared power. Communication associated with creating a shared mission included discussion of the mission, affirmation, testimony, and pride statements. Communication associated with sharing power included use of a consent process, barter and negotiating behavior, provision of equal opportunity, soliciting others' input, and rotating leadership responsibilities. It is safe to conclude that effective organizational participation includes participation in groups.

The question now becomes how we can evaluate our competencies for group participation. What types of behaviors are most productive? What should be avoided? Are there particular communication skills we should develop for group effectiveness? Finally, can we identify general guidelines for effective group participation? The next section of this chapter seeks to increase our effectiveness by identifying positive and negative group participation behaviors, describing communication skills necessary for effective participation, and concluding with guidelines for effective group participation.

The positive behaviors, skills, and guidelines discussed are based on the emerging concept of self-managing groups. In our fast-paced information society, less emphasis is placed on layers of management control and more on innovation and creativity at all organizational levels. The increasing use of project teams, quality teams, focus groups, task forces, and steering committees attests to the notion that organizations are seeking teams of people who can be self-motivated and self-directed. The concept of self-managing teams speaks to the need for broad-based responsibility from all team members and underscores our need to develop effective personal participation behaviors. With fewer managers, more complex decisions, more information, and less time to respond, teams in organizations will increasingly be required to manage information and change while effectively managing themselves.

## Negative Participation Behaviors

Each individual brings to group participation preferences for behavior. Research on group participation permits us to generalize about counterproductive individual behaviors.

### NEGATIVE BEHAVIORS

1. Argue stubbornly for your own ideas, positions, and conclusions. Make sure all members know exactly where you stand, and resist modifying or changing your views. Do not bother to listen actively to opposing viewpoints because of the rightness of your position.
2. Suppress differences of opinion and conflict. Use formal techniques such as agendas or majority rule to quiet opposition. Don't encourage others to express controversial opinions, and make sure the group considers only safe topics.
3. Work for quick agreement. Extended problem analysis and solution generation may contribute to dissent. Don't worry about "groupthink" because, after all, you are a group and everyone should support the same viewpoint.
4. If a stalemate occurs, pit one person against another so that there are clear winners and losers. This action will return the group to action and discourage others from blocking progress.
5. Use your power position to get others to agree with you. Don't hesitate to "pull rank" or threaten sanctions to preserve your ability to influence others.

## Positive Participation Behaviors

The following positive participation behaviors have been adapted from the work of John Cragan and David Wright (1986) and others. As you review these positive behaviors, try to decide which are the most important and what additional guidelines you would suggest.

### POSITIVE BEHAVIORS

1. Be prepared and informed when in decision-making and problem-solving groups. Review relevant materials before meetings, ask for additional needed information, formulate ideas, help with physical arrangements, encourage other team members. Contributions to meetings should be based on knowledge about the topic, agenda, and facts that bear directly on the problem.

2. Exhibit cooperative and open-minded behaviors that encourage participation by all involved. In a group work setting, group goals have important priority. Cooperation includes encouraging participation and encouraging listening and the clarification of meanings among group members. Cooperation also includes speaking with receivers in mind (concerning both content and style) to minimize message distortion. Groups tend to work best when all members accept a collective responsibility for productive outcomes.

3. Value diverse opinions and people. Promote differing ideas, challenge team members to offer alternative views, support disagreement, and encourage broad participation.

4. Contribute ideas and seek information. Willingly risk ideas and opinions, ask for criticism, ask for opinions, support participation, and discourage negative evaluation.

5. Attempt to remain rational, and thoughtfully evaluate all information. Effective participation includes analyzing our own logic as well as the logic of others. Effective members exhibit enough patience for this examination to be possible. Effective members recognize that good decisions are based on good information subjected to solid reasoning and evaluation.

6. Observe the participation process of the group. Members have not only a contribution responsibility but also a process responsibility for helping all members to participate thoughtfully. Those not speaking are in a position to observe when the group is straying from its goals or when silent members are not being given an opportunity for participation. Observation is also important for subtle cues that suggest some members may be holding important reservations that will ultimately affect their commitment.

7. Actively participate as well as observe. Active participants who seek active participation from others set a tone in the group that encourages good decision making and problem solving.

8. Stress group productivity: Encourage group members, note past successes, identify group strengths, and remember group responsibilities.

9. Avoid "role ruts." Use diverse communication roles, encourage diversity among team members, and share roles with others.

10. Avoid self-centered roles. Identify disruptive behaviors, self-monitor behavior, and give feedback to those exhibiting self-centered roles.

11. Ease tensions. Facilitate positive expressions of differences, support people, evaluate ideas, and stress cooperation.
12. Support leadership. Help leaders accomplish goals, and share leadership when necessary.
13. Build group pride. Create traditions, symbols, and slogans; celebrate work, progress, and success; and celebrate interpersonal relationships.
14. Produce results. Take responsibility for group outcomes, encourage responsibility from team members, and focus on effectiveness.

## Communication Skills for Effective Participation

Self-managing group members assume roles and responsibilities in task and maintenance areas. Earlier group communication roles in task, maintenance, and self-centered categories were described. Now comes an examination of how, as we assume group roles, we will engage in task and maintenance behaviors using a variety of communication skills. Effective group members learn to think strategically about the tactics they use to achieve overall excellence from group efforts. Figure 6.2 describes a variety of communication skills and their desired results. In the Workshop section of this chapter you have an opportunity to evaluate your own skill development in each of these areas.

# SUMMARY

An individual's small-group experiences result from the attitudes, beliefs, preferences, and abilities the individual brings to a variety of groups and the overall effectiveness of group participation behaviors. Organizations form groups to fulfill diverse organizational needs. The underlying assumption is that the efforts of numbers of individuals exceed individual efforts either for completing tasks or for examining issues requiring energy and creativity.

Effective groups have essential skills and abilities, a strong desire by members to contribute, and the capability of collaborating effectively. The first group assigned to us when we enter an organization is our primary work team. Primary work teams have been described as long-standing work teams, project teams, prefab groups, and self-managing teams. Directional groups are groups formally charged and structured to provide overall direction and oversight of the organization. Quality teams are groups of workers from the same general area or related technology who meet regularly to identify and propose solutions to problems affecting product or process quality. Task force groups are formed to bring together individuals with technical specialties who are members of other organizational groups to accomplish a specifically designed task or project. Steering committees resemble task forces in composition but are formed for the implementation of projects or to steer the progress of a plan, goal, issue, or program. Focus groups help organizations quickly understand issues and programs through use of unstructured formats. Focus groups are not charged with final

**FIGURE 6.2  Communication Skills, Descriptions, and Results**

| SKILL | DESCRIPTION | PURPOSE |
|---|---|---|
| 1. Initiating | Introduces ideas, directions; calls for action | To increase productivity, include expertise, and pace the group process |
| 2. Questioning | Asks for ideas, analysis, and exploration; seeks participation | To generate information, stimulate thinking, and increase overall participation |
| 3. Interpreting | Offers explanations for self and others' verbalizations and behaviors | To provide expanded perspective and clarify meaning |
| 4. Suggesting | Offers ideas, advice, information, and tentative direction | To provide group directions and explore alternatives |
| 5. Facilitating | Asks for participation, reminds of agenda and goals, organizes group activities | To promote effective participation among group members and stimulate good problem solving |
| 6. Evaluating | Appraises and critiques ideas and group process | To stimulate quality decisions/solutions and promote effective group processes |
| 7. Giving feedback | States reactions to ideas and group processes | To open the communication process and develop self-awareness of others |
| 8. Clarifying | Attempts to explain messages for maximum understanding at both the feeling and thinking levels | To improve message understanding for entire group |
| 9. Summarizing | States all important elements of the group process | To give overall direction and facilitate group process |
| 10. Terminating | Brings a group session to a close | To finalize decisions, summarize disagreements and agreements, and establish follow-up responsibilities |
| 11. Active listening | Attends to verbal and nonverbal communication and feeds back to speaker a summary of what was understood | To seek understanding and clarify meaning for self and others |
| 12. Confronting | Challenges others to eliminate discrepancies between words and actions, produce ideas, or manage personal behavior | To promote critical evaluation of ideas, open honest communication, eliminate destructive behavior, and encourage participation |
| 13. Positive blocking | Stops counterproductive individual or group behaviors | To provide for effective overall group process and good problem solving |

**FIGURE 6.2  Continued**

| | | |
|---|---|---|
| 14. Modeling | Demonstrates through personal behavior desired group behaviors | To give examples of effective behaviors for others to follow |
| 15. Reflecting feelings and supporting | Communicates understanding of feelings and encourages and reinforces participation | To develop trust and an atmosphere in which all feel free to participate and disagree |
| 16. Empathizing | Verbally identifies with the frame of reference of others | To develop trust and encourage group understanding of similarities and differences |

recommendations or implementation planning. Geographically diverse teams are work groups formed with team members separated geographically and linked through technology. Geographically diverse groups are challenged to work effectively across time zones, language barriers, and a variety of other obstacles to problem solving. Finally, social support groups form across all types of formally structured groups and in less structured ways. Individuals comfortable with their communication competencies are more likely to be involved in diverse groups and are more likely than their more highly apprehensive counterparts to exhibit communication and job satisfaction.

The team-based organization is a widespread organizational form used to increase overall competitiveness. Team-based organizations have fewer managers and are generally considered more productive than their hierarchical counterparts. Team-based organizations are challenged by issues of worker participation, rewards, and career issues. Finally, the need for increasing employee involvement and participation raises important concerns about the concept of workplace democracy or the valuing of individual goals and feelings about issues of primary concern to employees.

The most important resource a group has is its members. Working relationships in groups result from the attitudes we have about ourselves, our attitudes about others, our beliefs about groups in general, and our concern for inquiry. Generally speaking, the more positively we feel about our personal communication competencies, the better able we are to work in groups successfully. Our rhetorical sensitivity, important for group communication, is related to (1) acceptance of personal complexity, (2) avoidance of communicative rigidity, (3) interaction consciousness, (4) appreciation of the communicability of ideas, and (5) tolerance for inventional searching.

Groups have both socioemotional and task concerns. Researchers generally suggest that groups progress through a series of stages that begin with formation, move to production, and finally to resolution and dissolution. A frequently used five-stage description of task group development is forming, storming, norming, performing, and adjourning. It is important to understand that these stages or phases are meant to describe groups moving through a developmental process generally.

Norms are unwritten behavior rules, ways of doing things, that groups develop over time. Norms reflect what the group deems desirable and can be said to be cultural beliefs about effectiveness or appropriateness. Groups have general norms that apply to all members and role-specific norms that apply to individual members. Individuals assume different roles in groups. Generally speaking, three important classifications of group communication roles can be described: group task roles, group maintenance roles, and self-centered roles. Task roles help groups accomplish goals, and maintenance roles promote social support among group members. Self-centered roles support individual goals and may or may not be compatible with overall group goals and relationships. Most frequently, we are attracted to groups in which our individual goals and group goals are compatible; prestige is high; the climate is characterized by commitment to the group, compatibility among members, and team versus individual work; and the size of the group remains relatively small.

The concept of self-managing teams emerging in a fast-paced information society speaks to the need for broad-based responsibility from all team members and underscores the need to develop effective personal participation behaviors. Self-managing groups exhibit roles and take responsibility in task and maintenance areas. Finally, guidelines for effective group participation include individual participation requirements, valuing of diverse opinions and people, avoidance of role ruts and self-centered roles, and a concern for the group and its results.

# WORKSHOP

1. Identifying effective and ineffective communication roles in groups helps us to understand our own behavior and the behavior of others. Read the Group Communication Roles section that follows, and attempt to identify the communication roles used by John, Henry, Tim, Mary, and Mike. (See pp. 215–216.)

2. Form groups of six members each and select a topic of mutual interest for discussion. One member of the group will become a nonparticipating observer. Select a topic for which a group recommendation for action can be made. The group will be given fifteen minutes for discussion. Although consensus is not required, each group should attempt to reach one or two recommendations for the issue that most members can support. During the discussion the appointed observer will fill out the observation form that follows. At the conclusion of the discussion, each participating member also should fill out the form from his or her memory of communication skills exhibited by each group member. The assigned nonparticipant discusses his or her observations with the group, followed by general discussion of all observations. (See p. 217.)

3. Membership in organizational groups is more diverse than ever before. Most acknowledge that this diversity can be a group strength, but many groups continue to report difficulties based on ethnic, racial, age, gender, and cultural differences among other characteristics. Dr. Anita Foeman's essay, "Cre-

ating a Diversity Program," provides an opportunity to think about how groups can improve their own awareness and ability to value and work productively with diversity. After you read the essay, you and others in your class can design a diversity program for a campus organization, for your class, or for a particular work group. (See pp. 217–220.)

4. Using the *Identification of Group Communication Skills* form on page 217 for a research guide, visit a public meeting (city council, club or organization, student government, etc.). Record each participant's name across the top of the form. As the meeting progresses, identify with a small check in the appropriate box the various skills that individuals use during the course of the meeting. Also record any notes that will help you to determine the effectiveness or ineffectiveness of each participant. Following the meeting compare your notes with the total checks in each skill box. What type of a profile was established for the most effective participants? How did the less effective members behave? What do these observations tell about participation skills?

## Group Communication Roles

Read the following transcript of a typical group meeting that could occur in any organization.[1] Identify the various communication roles used by the group members. Which individuals demonstrate more effective roles? What might members do differently to improve their communication?

The group members: John, Henry, Tim, Mary, Mike

The problem: Planning the development of an improved employee policy manual

Communication roles: Task, maintenance, self-centered

### The Transcript

**John:**  I know you'll all agree that it's an honor to be chosen to be on this committee. And as you know, my background is primarily in personnel, so I'll be glad to take primary responsibility for a first rewrite on the manual.

**Henry:**  That's good of you, John, but before moving too quickly to a rewrite, I'd like to hear some general ideas for improving the manual from all the members of our committee. Policy for the employees is a matter of importance to all of us.

**Tim:**  Hey, you two, either of your suggestions would work well. John, if you want to do a rewrite, it might save us all plenty of time, but then again,

[1]Prepared by Sherwyn P. Morreale.

it might also be good to base your rewrite on ideas from other committee members.

**Mary:**    True, Tim, but the main point we want to keep in mind is that we, as a committee, want to write a new manual that will act as a model for other companies, something we can all be proud to have worked on.

**Mike:**    You're right, Mary, that's the spirit. We're all in agreement on doing the best possible job. I'd sure like to hear everybody's thoughts regarding the two possibilities we can now consider. Do you all think we should begin with a rewrite from John? Or should we begin with the manual we've got? Or are there other possible ways to go that we should consider?

**John:**    Listen, because our time is limited today, why don't I go ahead with just a simple rough draft of a rewrite. Then I'll get a copy of it to each group member before our next meeting. We can go from there.

**Tim:**    Sounds great to me. You'll be saving all of us time and energy. When's the next meeting?

**Henry:**    Saving time is always a good idea. I'm with you 100 percent, Tim, but I'm a little concerned about our committee being a group that forgets to look before it leaps. Before we adjourn today, why don't we go out and come in again on this one. Let's talk it through a little more.

**Mary:**    Okay, Henry, do you think we should take more time right now and have everyone present what they think this rewrite should focus on? I'd like to hear some more ideas from everyone also. It may be our ideas will be a little different, or we may really disagree on just how the rewrite should be done.

**Henry:**    True, but the best final manual is going to be a product of some friendly disagreeing. So how does everybody see it? Where do we go with this rewrite job?

**Mary:**    I think the best thing to do, at this point, is for each of us to draw up a list of the best things we see in our present manual, plus a list of its weakest points. Then together we can do a summary list of what to keep and what to improve.

**John:**    That sounds good, from a creativity point of view, but time counts here, and unless I can get on the rewrite soon, my schedule might tighten up. Then I might not have time to do a rewrite at all.

**Tim:**    Then maybe we need to prepare these lists as quickly as possible and get them right to John. Whichever way, though, it'll work well. We seem to know how to work together on a job like this one.

**Henry:**    We don't need to make a decision here on how to proceed. Let's have each person put their ideas out for, say, five minutes each. Then we can take a vote on what to do.

## Identification of Group Communication Skills

| SKILLS USED | NAMES OF GROUP MEMBERS | | | | | |
|---|---|---|---|---|---|---|
| Initiating | | | | | | |
| Questioning | | | | | | |
| Interpreting | | | | | | |
| Suggesting | | | | | | |
| Facilitating | | | | | | |
| Evaluating | | | | | | |
| Giving feedback | | | | | | |
| Clarifying | | | | | | |
| Summarizing | | | | | | |
| Terminating | | | | | | |
| Active listening | | | | | | |
| Confronting | | | | | | |
| Positive blocking | | | | | | |
| Modeling | | | | | | |
| Reflecting feeling and support | | | | | | |
| Empathizing | | | | | | |

## Creating a Diversity Program

### Anita Foeman, Ph.D.

Have you ever had a conflict or misunderstanding with another person when you believed that race (or some other cultural difference) was at the heart of your disagreement? In a world that is quickly becoming more diverse, such experiences will likely be more commonplace. Yet while the challenges of dealing with diversity are great, the potential payoffs for interacting well with a variety of people can be even greater.

Many organizations have begun to employ organizational trainers who can help them effectively utilize and coordinate the skills of people who are different. Diversity training has been a part of the American work scene at least since the 1960s, but the patterns of training have begun to shift, partly because our society has changed and partly because the focus of diversity training is different today.

In the past, diversity training usually had very narrow, situation specific aims like implementing a school bussing program or integrating a public housing project. Today, training is often geared broadly toward helping people adjust to a multicultural workplace and society. Further, issues between whites and blacks tended to drive past programs. Today, gender, sexuality, age, ability, and a variety of other ethnic concerns are included under the heading of diversity.

Of course, the effectiveness of any training is tied to the fit between the approach selected and the goals sought. A typical goal of diversity training today is to encourage people to discuss their feelings so as to demystify sensitive topics such as race or sexual orientation. At the other end of the spectrum, training may attempt to change individuals' attitudes, beliefs, and, most importantly, behaviors relative to other groups. Some training seeks to change the behaviors of marginalized members so they will fit better into mainstream culture. Other training attempts to encourage insiders to increase their level of acceptance of people with whom they are unfamiliar. Most programs attempt some combination of the two.

Three primary models have been used to achieve these types of goals. The oldest appears to be the didactic model in which the primary training mechanism is lecture. Most often the underlying belief is that telling people about others will create a knowledge base and encourage respect for that group. The drawbacks of this approach are several. First, the learner-participant is usually provided only one person's view of reality. Therefore, the training is only as strong as the presenter. If consciously or unconsciously the presenter provides images of different groups that are inaccurate, stereotypical, overly romantic, or otherwise inconsistent with the reality of participants, the impact of training can be limited. A second drawback is that participants are not provided an opportunity to test interpersonal skills that may be suggested in didactic training. Therefore, training may not functionally provide an opportunity for change. Third, the didactic model, with its conventional format, even while espousing respect for diversity, may reinforce traditional ways of teaching and knowing. And finally, oftentimes when presenters address sensitive or controversial issues, such as institutional racism or the wooden leg syndrome (when a person uses his or her difference as an excuse for nonperformance), listeners may become defensive and feel stifled in their ability to respond to what they hear as accusations, and thus become angered and shut down.

An alternative to the didactic model is the experiential model. This approach depends primarily on participants sharing their personal experiences to encourage sensitivity to one another. Research has confirmed that attitude change does come about as the result of such training. Critics warn, however, that the goal of increased liking across cultural lines is not necessarily valid. They argue that people in power often like nonthreatening others. Liking and social power are quite different, critics contend. And, in fact, in many experiential programs, people who have typically been considered different are asked to explain themselves, whereas those in power rarely explore their feelings of betterness and privilege. So, beyond bringing about arguably irrelevant change, the experiential model may do harm in that it may encourage a pattern in which the historically excluded are placed in the position of teaching and expunging the guilt of the privileged while their own concerns are left unaddressed.

The groupwork model attempts to meet the challenge of providing a socially responsible intervention that also maintains a strong interpersonal dimension. In groupwork, the facilitator attempts to infuse information into group exchange to create an adequate context for interaction. This model makes use of films, news articles, and other materials to help guide conversation and encourage understanding of the variety of viewpoints represented in the group. The strength of this model is that it both attempts to validate individual feelings and to highlight institutional realities. For example, this approach allows that it is important to acknowledge that, as some workshop participants argue, "Everyone has been discriminated against at one time or other." Yet it also drives home the point that some groups have been subjected to systematic and sanctioned oppression over centuries (as in the legal mistreatment and warehousing of severely disabled citizens). Another strength of this model is that it provides a forum for addressing current events (the Rodney King incident, the gay ban in the military, the Senator Packwood scandal, the Americans with Disabilities Act, etc.) that color organizational climate. Last, the groupwork model allows participants to explore their own meanings and note how outside influences define them and their responses to others.

Although the groupwork model is emerging as a strong training option, the selection of a competent, sensitive trainer/facilitator is paramount to its success. The successful facilitator must have training in both group process and group relations as well as personal credibility in these areas. It is important that a trainer be willing to share with participants her or his orientation toward training and diversity along with personal background where relevant. Feelings about human diversity are often powerful. Participants have the right to know that the person who is leading them into rather uncomfortable waters is caring and knows what she or he is doing.

The participant group should also be selected carefully. The best groups generally represent a variety of perspectives and interest areas. A skilled trainer (just as the skilled manager) is able to identify and positively exploit the diversity within even an apparently homogeneous group. The details of training as well as the number of participants must be adjusted to the particular makeup of the group and training conditions. One training program may take the form of a semester-long college class while another, a week-long off-site corporate program.

There are a variety of activities trainers can use in designing programs. They range from encouraging participants to keep logs or diaries of the comments they hear about others among their friends and colleagues to activities in which participants draw pictures of themselves in relation to other groups they have encountered. Many source materials are available for trainer use.

We can all begin our own diversity program by exploring our own feelings about diversity. We can ask ourselves how we feel about the issues we face every day: How do we feel about interracial couples on campus, or about older, nontraditional students in our classes, or the treatment of students with disabilities? What do we say when we overhear homophobic or racist remarks? Have we ever reinforced a pattern that female students usually get the role of secretary in small group projects? Do women on campus expect men to pay for everything on dates and then refer to all men as "dogs" or "jerks"? And, ultimately, what would our ideal world be like and who would be a part of it?

In addition to asking questions, consider placing yourself in situations that give you contact with people who are different from you. Try to learn more about others' perspectives. Begin to create a context in your own life in which conversations of difference and diversity take on a positive and comfortable tone. Perhaps the next time you find yourself in a misunderstanding based on human difference you will be able comfortably and with sincerity to ask, "Why do you think we see this situation differently? Can we talk about how we can find a solution we can both live with?"

# REFERENCES AND SUGGESTED READINGS

Baird, J. E., Jr. 1977. *The dynamics of organizational communication.* New York: Harper and Row.

Barker, J., and P. Tompkins. 1993. *Organizations, teams, control, and identification.* Paper presented at the Speech Communication Association Convention, November, Miami, FL.

Bantz, C. 1993. Cultural diversity and group cross-cultural team research. *Journal of Applied Communication Research* 21(1): 1–20.

Benne, K., and P. Sheats. 1948. Functional roles of group members. *Journal of Social Issues* 4(2): 41–49.

Brilhart, J. K., and G. J. Galanes. 1989. *Effective group discussion.* 6th ed. Dubuque, IA: Brown.

Brown, K., T. D. Klastorin, and J. Valluzzi. 1990. Project performance and the liability of group harmony. *IEEE Transactions on Engineering Management* 37(2): 117–125.

Carr, C. 1992. Planning priorities for empowered teams. *Journal of Business Strategy* 13(5): 43–47.

Cartwright, D., and A. Zander. 1968. *Group dynamics research and theory.* 3d ed. New York: Harper and Row.

Cheney, G. 1995. Democracy in the workplace: Theory and practice from the perspective of communication. *Journal of Applied Communication Research* 23, 167–200.

Courtright, J., G. Fairhurst, and E. Rogers. 1989. Interaction patterns in organic and mechanistic systems. *Academy of Management Journal* 32(4): 773–802.

Cox, T., Jr. 1993. *Cultural diversity in organizations.* San Francisco: Berrett-Koehler.

Cragan, J., and D. Wright. 1986. *Communication in small group discussions.* 2d ed. St. Paul, MN: West.

Fulk, J. 1993. Social construction of communication technology. *Academy of Management Journal* 36(5): 921–950.

Hackman, M. Z., and C. E. Johnson. 2000. *Leadership: A communication perspective.* Prospect Heights, IL: Waveland.

Heath, R. G., and P. M. Sias. 1999. Communicating spirit in a collaborative alliance. *Journal of Applied Communication Research* 27: 356–376.

Katzenbach, J., and D. Smith. 1993. *The wisdom of teams.* Boston: Harvard Business School Press.

Keller, R. 1994. Technology-information processing fit and the performance of R&D project groups: A test of contingency theory. *Academy of Management Journal* 37(1): 167–179.

Larson, C. E., and F. M. LaFasto. 1989. *TeamWork: What must go right/What can go wrong.* Newbury Park, CA: Sage.

Mayer, Michael. 1998. Behaviors leading to more effective decisions in small groups embedded in organizations. *Communication Reports* 2(2): 123–132.

Mulvey, P. W., J. F. Veiga, and P. M. Elsass. 1996. When teammates raise a white flag. *Academy of Management Executive* 10(1): 40–49.

Napier, R. W., and M. K. Gershenfeld. 1989. *Groups: Theory and experience.* Boston: Houghton Mifflin.

Poole, M. S., K. Real, L. Alston, B. Beal, F. Villamaria, J. Wunsch, A. Vedlitz, and T. Dacin. 2000. *Participation in quality improvement in work groups II: A longitudinal study of structural and communication process explanations in a managed care setting.* Paper presented at the International Communication Association Convention, May, Acapulco, Mexico.

Tuckman, B. W., and M. A. C. Jensen. 1977. Stages of small-group development revisited. *Group and Organization Studies* 2(4): 419–427.

# CHAPTER SEVEN

# LEADERSHIP AND MANAGEMENT COMMUNICATION

## DEVELOPING COMPETENCIES THROUGH . . .

### KNOWLEDGE

Describing leadership from trait, style, situational, and transformational approaches

Distinguishing between leadership and management

### SENSITIVITY

Clarifying a personal theory of leadership

Understanding leadership styles, strategic objectives, and tactics

### SKILLS

Assessing leadership strategies and tactics

Practicing analysis capabilities and skills using cases, transcripts of meetings, and group activities

### VALUES

Relating leadership to organizational excellence

Understanding need for leadership from all organizational members

Describing principled and ethical leadership

■ ■ ■ ■ ■

## THE CASE OF THE INVISIBLE MANAGER

John Mitchell was a superior engineer who was widely known throughout Invest Corporation for his ability to solve creatively highly complex technical problems. No one had been surprised when John was promoted approximately a year ago to laboratory manager at Invest's main research and development facility. What was surprising were the complaints from the lab that nothing was getting done. Senior lab members were particularly vocal about John's insistence on knowing every detail of their decisions before letting them move forward. They also complained about their inability to get to see him and the days on end that went by with no word from him about decisions.

Although acknowledging John's technical brilliance, several members of the lab management team openly questioned whether John would ever be a leader or even understood the difference between engineering responsibilities and those of management. John responded that his technical abilities were the type of leadership the lab needed. He believed that if intelligent people were doing their jobs, they did not need close personal contact with their managers. John viewed leadership as a purely technical contribution and was amazed that some of his top engineers were doubting his contributions. He could hardly believe they had labeled him their "Invisible Manager."

## INTRODUCTION

Is John right in his view of leadership? Is superior technical ability the type of leadership that a management team really needs? Can both John and his managers be right? How can we define management and leadership responsibilities?

In his new position John is faced with a test of his beliefs about leadership and management. He contends that technical contributions are the essence of his leadership. To make complex technical decisions, he requires large amounts of detail, and the sheer volume of work has delayed his response to his managers. He believes delay is justified to improve the technical capabilities of the laboratory. He disagrees that leaders and managers need to stay in close personal contact with subordinates. John, however, is on a collision course with a capable group of senior lab managers. They disagree that his approach is working or that he is even exhibiting leadership. How would you help John and his managers? What does he need to understand to resolve this important problem?

Most of us have seen leadership and management situations similar to the one in which the laboratory is involved. We have been members of a group in which the leader and group members were at odds over the way a project should be accomplished. We have experienced frustration when someone like a teacher or a doctor had information or a service we needed but was not available for an appointment. We have been delayed in making plans while waiting for the decisions of others. We are influenced in all aspects of our lives by leadership or the need for leadership. Most of us act as both leaders and followers in our families, at work, and in the political and social organizations of which we are a part.

Think about the most effective leader with whom you have had direct contact. How did this person behave? What were his or her communication competencies? Now think specifically about an ineffective leader. Describe his or her behavior and communication competencies. Most of us have been influenced by leaders and have fulfilled leadership roles without giving detailed consideration to how leadership works and the competencies necessary for effectiveness. To develop communication competencies for leadership, we need to understand the importance of leadership and management communication, how leadership and management have been described, where leadership and management can differ, the determinants of leadership effectiveness, and constructive communication strategies and tactics for leadership.

This chapter is designed to contribute to *knowledge* by demonstrating the importance of leadership and management communication; distinguishing between the two; and understanding them by describing trait, style, situational, and transformational approaches. *Sensitivity* competencies are developed by identifying individual preferences and styles for leadership and by becoming familiar with commonly used strategies and tactics. Sensitivity competencies also are influenced by self-analysis of leadership experiences. Sensitivity competencies, in turn, influence the use of strategic and tactical communication *skills*. *Value* competencies are encouraged by describing the importance of leadership for organizational excellence, identifying determinants of leadership effectiveness, and associating leadership with overall interpersonal communication competency. Value competencies are reflected in the choice of skills for leadership.

Finally, all four competencies—knowledge, sensitivity, skills, and values—are applied to competency practice through self-analysis and case study.

# THE IMPORTANCE OF LEADERSHIP AND MANAGEMENT COMMUNICATION

Leadership and management communication affect nearly all aspects of organizational life. Leaders help guide individuals, groups, and entire organizations in establishing goals and sustaining action to support goals. Managers fulfill specific organizationally assigned roles designed to direct and evaluate the work of others. Managers are expected to be leaders, although not all managers exhibit leadership behaviors. In fact, leadership communication can come from virtually anyone in the organization, with the effectiveness of leadership and management communication directly relating to organizational success and work satisfaction.

What exactly is meant by leadership and management communication? There are literally hundreds of definitions of what leaders do and what is considered to be leadership. Chances are our personal definition of leadership may vary from that of our friends and may even change from situation to situation. We might call an individual a leader, for example, because of the person's election to the presidency of a particular organization. At another time we might say that that same individual is not a leader because he or she does not exhibit leadership behaviors expected from the president. In other words, we expected leadership from the legitimate position of the presidency, but when the president does not exhibit leadership behaviors, we say that the president is not a leader.

**Leadership**
Process for guiding individuals, groups, and entire organizations in establishing goals and sustaining action to support goals.

**Management**
Responsibility, specifically assigned by the organization, to direct and evaluate the work of others.

**Leadership** takes place through communication. Leaders communicate about needed change, translate intentions into reality, propose new strategies, and help sustain action to support decisions. Leadership communication is a process of influence whereby leaders attempt to convince followers to attain specific goals or broad organizational outcomes. The ability to influence is based on the leader's position, credibility to a follower group, analysis and technical skills, and overall communication competence. People can be assigned the position of leader, but leadership occurs not from the assignment itself but through communication behaviors in interactions with others.

**Management** fulfills specifically defined roles designed to facilitate work to support organizational goals. Managers are given legitimate power to influence the behavior of subordinates. They are charged with obtaining routine compliance with the operating procedures and expectations of the organization. It is hoped, of course, that managers can exceed routine compliance and instill in subordinates a desire for excellence that goes beyond merely acceptable performance. Whether resulting in routine compliance or a desire for excellence, managerial influence occurs through human communication. Based on the formal superior-subordinate relationships, managerial communication is directed to work assignments, work evaluation, needed changes, and all other aspects of directing organizational action for goal achievement.

Both leadership and management communication are powerful organizational influences. Communication relationships between managers and subordinates influence innovation, decision making, work satisfaction, and perceptions of organizational climate. In work that Kathy Ellis and I have done (Ellis and Schockley-Zalabak, 1999), leadership and management communication were strongly related to both trust in individuals within the organization and overall organizational trust. Jaesub Lee (2000) reports that the perceived quality of leader-member exchanges significantly affected perceptions of organizational rewards and fairness in a variety of processes. For example, individuals reporting low-quality leader-member exchanges (LMXs) also reported deficiencies in both formal and informal organizational rewards as well as less fairness in organizational processes than individuals with more positive communication exchanges with their leaders. Alicia Marshall and Cynthia Stohl (1993) found "two communicative activities that significantly contribute to one's level of organizational knowledge: cultivating strong relationships with managers and engaging in various leadership activities over time. These findings add to our understanding of what, in particular, may directly influence information flow, lead to a diverse knowledge base, and ultimately enhance workers' performance."

Leadership communication, whether exhibited by managers or other influential organizational members, becomes the vision of the organization that directs and redirects all organizational activity. As Warren Bennis and Burt Nanus (1985) suggest, "effective leadership can move organizations from current to future states, create visions of potential opportunities for organizations, instill within employees commitment to change, and instill new cultures and strategies in organizations that mobilize and focus energy and resources."

Leadership and management communication is part of the sense-making activities of the organization. It helps members develop priorities and determine what is needed by the organization. It influences decision making, transmits communication rules, and contributes to the shared realities that become the organization's culture or cultures. As such, leadership and management communication charts the course of action for the organization. The effectiveness of this communication is therefore central to organizational excellence.

## THEORIES OF LEADERSHIP AND MANAGEMENT

Thousands of articles have been written about leadership and management. We talk about the need for leadership in our communities, in the organizations in which we work, and in government. Yet trying to describe how leadership and management work and how they should work remains a difficult and often controversial task. Are leaders born with leadership talents? What styles do successful leaders employ? Are some people simply in the right time and place to assume leadership responsibility? What type of leader is John Mitchell (from the beginning of this chapter)? What type of manager? Is there a difference? What can we do to increase our leadership effectiveness?

Theories of leadership and management describe leaders and managers in terms of personal traits or characteristics, preferences for leadership styles or approaches, and responsiveness to leadership requirements in specific situations. Before trait, style, situational, and transformational theories of leadership are explored, please complete the leadership experience exercise in Figure 7.1. The exercise will give you a profile of some of your attitudes and experiences with leadership that you can compare with major theories of leadership and management.

You now have before you an assessment of your personal theory of leadership. As you begin to evaluate major theories of leadership and management, think about your own personal theory and what is needed for leadership effectiveness.

### Trait Approaches

Early theories of effective leadership assumed that leaders had innate traits that made them effective. That is, great leaders were considered to be born with the ability for leadership. This theory of the "great man" first surfaced in the writings of the early Greeks and Romans and is prevalent today among those who believe that leadership cannot be developed, that you either have leadership qualities or not.

Over eighty-five years of research has attempted to define traits or personality characteristics that best predict the effective leader. Lists of desirable traits have

**FIGURE 7.1** **Leadership Experiences**

The following twenty-one statements have been used to describe leadership and leaders. Following them are four incomplete sentences that begin "My experience with leadership and leaders has taught me that . . . " For each of the four incomplete sentences, select from among the following twenty-one statements the five that best reflect your experiences with leadership and leaders. Statements may be used to complete more than one incomplete sentence.

**STATEMENTS DESCRIBING LEADERS AND LEADERSHIP**

1. Leaders are *born*.
2. Leadership *ability* can be *developed*.
3. Leaders are high in *intelligence*.
4. Leaders take *initiative*.
5. Leaders *deviate* from norms.
6. Leaders have *good communication* skills.
7. Leaders are in the *right place* at the right time.
8. Leaders are *democratic*.
9. Leaders are *autocratic*.
10. Leaders are *risk takers*.
11. Leaders take a *hands-off* approach.
12. Leadership is *situation specific*.
13. Leaders *block ideas* and *punish opposition*.
14. Leaders *seek ideas* and *encourage disagreement*.
15. Leaders *ignore conflict*.
16. Leaders *solicit feedback*.
17. Leaders are *outcome oriented*.
18. Leaders *share praise*.
19. Leaders *set goals*.
20. Leaders *blame* those who fail.
21. Leaders *control* their followers.

My experience with leadership and leaders has taught me that effective . . .
1.
2.
3.
4.
5.

My experience with leadership and leaders has taught me that ineffective . . .
1.
2.
3.
4.
5.

## FIGURE 7.1    Continued

My experience with leadership and leaders has taught me that the most important aspects of leadership are . . .

1.
2.
3.
4.
5.

My experience with leadership and leaders has taught me that the least important aspects of leadership are . . .

1.
2.
3.
4.
5.

What type of person and situation does your personal leadership theory describe? Compare your theory to the ones you will now study in Chapter 7.

---

**Trait approach**
Theory of leadership that assumed that leaders possessed innate traits that made them effective; commonly referred to as the "great man" theory.

numbered approximately eighty characteristics, but the **trait approach** has failed to define clearly a stable set of characteristics associated with effective leadership. Even the concept of what is effective remains open to question.

Ronald Applbaum and colleagues (1974) suggest that effective leaders are higher in intelligence than other group members, are able to adapt to changing situations, and are willing to deviate more than other group members from traditions and norms, all contributing to the perception of others that the individual is a leader. These researchers suggest that "perhaps leadership is not so much a function of deviancy as it is a function of knowing how much and when to deviate."

Applbaum and his colleagues' observations reflect the findings of Ralph Stogdill and Alvin Coons (1957), which suggest that leaders more than others are higher in intelligence, scholarship, responsibility, participation, and socioeconomic status. Keith Davis (1967) suggests that intelligence, social maturity (being emotionally stable with a good self-concept), initiative, and human relations abilities affect leadership. He does caution, however, that we really do not understand cause-and-effect relationships between traits and effective leadership.

When we study group leaders who emerge on their own rather than being appointed or elected, we find relatively low communication apprehension and a willingness to participate verbally in group activities. Those not emerging as leaders are more likely to exhibit communication behaviors that include rigidity, authoritarian statements, and generally offensive verbalizations.

Despite the importance of intelligence, communication ability, and situational adaptation, the approach of identifying traits has generally failed to explain effective leadership. This approach simply does not provide a comprehensive explanation of how leaders interact with followers and meet the needs of specific circumstances.

To illustrate the difficulty of establishing a trait approach for leadership, identify two leaders you would characterize as effective. Describe their personality traits and characteristics in relation to the groups they lead. Now identify two leaders whose effectiveness you question. What traits and characteristics do they exhibit? Do your effective and ineffective leaders share similar characteristics? How do they differ? What leadership traits do you exhibit? How effective are these characteristics?

## Style Approaches

**Style approach**
Theories that attempt to identify a range of general approaches leaders use to achieve goals. The approaches are thought to be based on a leader's assumptions about what motivates people to accomplish goals.

The **style approach** theories for understanding leadership attempt to identify a range of general approaches leaders use to influence goal achievement. These approaches are theorized to be based on the leader's assumptions about what motivates people to accomplish goals. Particular approaches also are thought to reflect complex relationships among the personal characteristics of the leader (i.e., communication competencies, communication apprehension, and internal motivational forces), the requirements of the situation at hand, and the resources over which the leader and followers have control or influence.

Chief among the style theories is the autocratic-to-democratic continuum first proposed by Ralph White and Ronald Lippitt (1960). This continuum suggests that leadership can be understood as ranging in behavior from autocratic to democratic. The three primary styles identified are autocratic, democratic, and laissez-faire.

**Autocratic**
Style of leader or manager who makes decisions with little influence from others.

The **autocratic** leader or manager makes decisions with little influence from others. This leader tells others what to do and usually enforces sanctions against those who choose not to comply. The autocratic leader views followers as essential for goal achievement but usually feels little responsibility for subordinate needs and relationships. Some research suggests that autocratically led groups produce more in quantity than democratically led groups but that the quality of output is better when more democracy is practiced.

We have all been involved with autocratic leaders. Can you identify a successful autocratic leader and one who is not so successful? What makes the difference? Is there a best time for autocratic management? What do you lose in the process of being an autocrat?

**Democratic**
Style of leader or manager who involves followers in decision making.

**Democratic** leaders involve followers in decision making. They assume creativity will be greater and there will be more broad-based support for goals if participation is high. Democratic leaders assume followers are able to participate in decision making. These leaders therefore attempt to generate a climate in which problem solving can take place while interpersonal relationships are preserved.

Democratic leaders, as do autocrats, both succeed and fail. Now identify a successful democratic leader and one who is not so successful. As you did for the autocrats, attempt to determine the difference. What made the approach work for one and not the other? From your personal leadership profile, attempt to place your theory on the autocratic-to-democratic continuum.

**Laissez-faire**

Style of leader or manager who behaves as a nonleader. Individuals and groups are expected to make their own decisions because of a hands-off approach from the leader.

The **laissez-faire** leader is really an example of a nonleader. This leader expects individuals and groups to make their own decisions. The laissez-faire leader takes a hands-off approach and contributes information only when asked by group members. This leader shows little direct concern for individuals or goals. Groups can succeed with laissez-faire leaders. Their success, however, depends greatly on the abilities of the group and the willingness to work with little or no leadership. Have you ever been in a group with laissez-faire leadership? What happened? How did you feel about that type of working experience?

Robert Tannenbaum and Warren Schmidt (1958) have expanded the concept of the autocratic-to-democratic continuum by describing it in terms of the use of authority by the leader and the area of freedom for subordinates. Figure 7.2

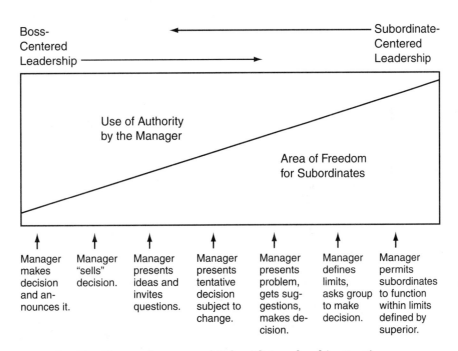

**FIGURE 7.2    The Tannenbaum and Schmidt Leadership Continuum**

illustrates the conception of what happens when leadership moves through the continuum from autocratic to democratic. As you can see, the autocratic end of the continuum is characterized by the manager using authority to make and announce decisions with little decision-making input from subordinates. As the approach to leading becomes more democratic, more input from subordinates is asked for and utilized.

How would you describe John Mitchell on this continuum? What are his basic assumptions about people? How are those assumptions reflected? If you were advising John, where should he be on the leadership continuum?

Perhaps the best known of the style theories for leadership and management is the one proposed in 1964 and updated through 1985 by Robert Blake and Jane Mouton. The Blake and Mouton Managerial Grid® suggests that leadership styles or approaches are based on two central dimensions: concern for relationships with people and concern for task production. The balances leaders and managers make between these dimensions have become known as the leadership styles of impoverished, middle-of-the-road (organization man), country club, task (authority-obedience), and team management. Figure 7.3 illustrates

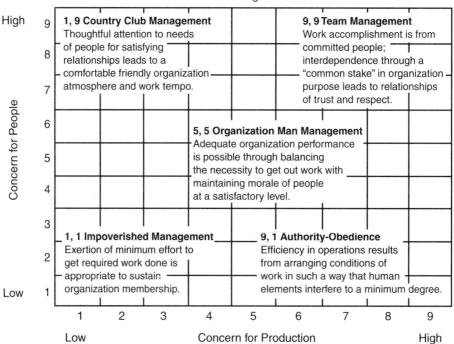

The Managerial Grid®

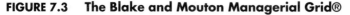

**FIGURE 7.3    The Blake and Mouton Managerial Grid®**

From *The Managerial Grid III: The Key to Leadership Excellence*, by Robert R. Blake and Jane Srygley Mouton. Houston, TX: Gulf Publishing Company, copyright 1985, p. 12. Reproduced by permission.

the Managerial Grid® styles with the two dimensions of concern for people and concern for task.

**Impoverished management**

Leadership style characterized by a low concern for interpersonal relationships and task accomplishment.

## Impoverished Management (1, 1)

**Impoverished management** is characterized by low concern for interpersonal relationships and task accomplishment. The impoverished leader makes few attempts to influence people toward task or goal achievement. This leader frequently dislikes leadership responsibilities and lets others take responsibility that rightfully belongs to the leader. This leader often is uncomfortable with leadership and intellectually resists the need for it. Many impoverished leaders are excellent technically; they have been promoted to supervision or management because of strong technical skills. Technical skills, however, do not prepare them for managing people or letting others accomplish tasks that the leaders themselves have been used to doing. Impoverished leaders may even think that if people would do their jobs, there would be little real need for leadership. Such leaders are most often found in legitimate or formal leadership positions rather than in emergent positions as the choice of a group of peers. These leaders may be primarily responsible for the failure of a group, yet they can rarely claim much credit for a group's success. Groups with impoverished leaders often succeed despite the leader and through the emergent leadership of other group members.

**Middle-of-the-road management**

Style of leader who balances task and people concerns; commonly referred to as compromise management or leadership.

## Middle-of-the-Road (Organization Man) Management (5, 5)

As Figure 7.3 suggests, **middle-of-the-road management** balances task and people concerns. Sometimes referred to as compromise leadership, the middle-of-the-road leader negotiates and compromises to achieve workable agreements and directions for action. This leader is more concerned with practical versus excellent solutions. The middle-of-the-road leader will seek the "middle" position to maintain a group where everyone has some stake in the decision. The compromise positions of middle-of-the-road leaders have been criticized as Band-Aids on the wounds of more serious problems. Critics suggest that middle-of-the-road leadership provides short-term solutions guaranteeing long-term problems. Middle-of-the-road leaders are frequently found in middle (or "organization man") management, where compromise between the needs of subordinates and top management seems inevitable. In fact, the difficult position of middle management has often been referred to as the sandwich position because of the pressures from below (subordinates) and from above (top management), pressures that often result in the need for compromise.

## Country Club Management (1, 9)

Figure 7.3 shows that **country club management** places the emphasis on interpersonal relationships at the expense of goal achievement. The country club leader wants to be liked and to have a group of followers who feel supported by

**Country club management**
Style of leader or manager who emphasizes interpersonal relationships at the expense of goal achievement.

the leader. This leader provides an interpersonal relationship bond that is low on task emphasis and high in interpersonal support. Country club leaders may want the task accomplished but will not take steps to emphasize this element to others if group members are not highly task oriented. Country club managers are frequently observed doing the work of their subordinates rather than insisting that their subordinates exhibit high standards of performance. These managers may not develop the abilities of their subordinates. They may, however, lead successful groups when group members themselves have high task motivation and only require interpersonal support to maintain motivation.

**Task management**
Style of leader or manager who is concerned with goals or task achievement while exhibiting little concern for personal relationships; commonly referred to as autocratic leadership.

## Task (Authority-Obedience) Management (9, 1)

Often referred to as autocratic leadership, the **task management** leader is concerned with goals or task achievement and exhibits little concern for personal relationships. This leader makes decisions and expects compliance. He or she often enforces decisions with little subordinate input and is willing to defend his or her position when necessary. Task leaders often exhibit win/lose conflict style preferences. The task leader values efficiency and will make quick and timely decisions. Task leadership, as do other approaches, requires having appropriate information on which to make good decisions, but by showing low concern for people, such leaders may alienate others to the point that they withhold information that might improve decision making. Task leadership, however, may be appropriate when a group is hopelessly deadlocked on an issue and someone needs to take responsibility for making a decision. Furthermore, surveys of top management in leading U.S. companies indicate that task leadership is a prevalent style preference among highly influential managers.

**Team management**
Team leadership or management is the theoretical ideal. Team leaders exhibit high concern for both task and interpersonal relationships by emphasizing goal accomplishment while supporting people.

## Team Management (9, 9)

As can be seen from Figure 7.3, **team management** is the theoretical ideal. Exhibiting high concern for both task and interpersonal relationships, team leaders emphasize goal accomplishment while supporting people. Team leadership fosters a sense of "we" with high performance standards. This leadership shares decision making and strives for problem solving designed to solve rather than postpone problems. Team leaders respect differing points of view and value diversity as long as all contribute to the group effort. Team leaders, however, must have capable and willing team members for successful efforts. Although the style is highly desirable, team leaders depend on team followers for their style of leadership to work. Team members who support each other but who do not have enough ability or information to work on problems will not be able to produce a high-quality decision. In other words, willingness to be a team member does not ensure a solid team, and team leadership only produces excellent results with a capable team.

To understand the styles approach to leadership better, identify a series of leaders with whom you have had contact and who exhibited each of these five approaches. Try to determine how you reacted to each and how effective his or her leadership was. From your own experiences, what determines whether a particular style is effective or ineffective?

**Situational approaches**
Leadership theories that explore how leaders interact with followers and the requirements of a particular environment.

## Situational Approaches

Both the trait and style approaches failed to describe comprehensively why particular approaches would work in one set of circumstances and fail in another. In response to this difficulty, **situational approaches,** or contingency approaches, were developed to understand better how leaders interact with followers and the requirements of a particular environment.

In 1967, Fred Fiedler pioneered understanding leadership styles based on the concept of contingencies. He suggested that leader effectiveness could be evaluated only in relationship to how style choices related to contingencies in particular situations. Task and interpersonal relationships were important, but also to be considered were the leader's power position and how rewards and punishment were handled. Sometimes powerful leaders had good follower relationships to accomplish well-defined tasks, a favorable condition for leadership. At other times the leader's power position was in question, with an ambiguous goal to accomplish. In the latter circumstance, leader-member relationships could become strained, generating an overall unfavorable condition. According to Fiedler, the approach or style an effective leader chose depended on a combination of task, relationship, power, and situational contingencies.

Building on the work of Blake and Mouton, Paul Hersey and Kenneth Blanchard (1977) proposed a concept of leadership that suggested that the appropriateness and effectiveness of leadership behaviors could not be determined by the specific behavior of the leader but by the appropriateness of the behavior in a particular situation. Hersey and Blanchard's Situational Leadership theory postulated that effectiveness of a particular leader was related to the leader's selection of behavior appropriate to the maturity level of the follower group. Maturity was based on achievement-motivation, ability, education, experience, and the willingness to participate responsibly in goal-oriented activity. In other words, the maturity level of the follower group was the primary factor that determined an effective leadership style. Hersey and Blanchard described situational leadership as dependent on concern for relationships, concern for task, and concern for maturity of followers. They saw four general styles of situational leadership: telling, selling, participating, and delegating. Figure 7.4 depicts the Hersey and Blanchard situational grid.

As you can tell from Figure 7.4, the telling style has high task and low relationship emphases and is best used with immature followers. The leader defines what should be done and instructs followers in how to accomplish well-established goals or tasks.

Situational Leadership Model

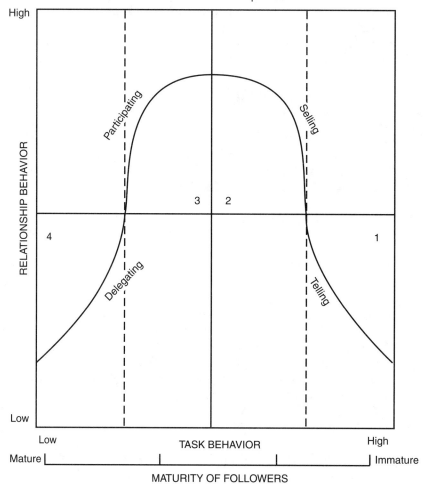

**FIGURE 7.4    The Hersey and Blanchard Concept of Situational Leadership**

P. Hersey and K. Blanchard, *Management of Organizational Behavior: Utilizing Human Resources,* 3d ed., 1977, p. 322. Adapted by permission of Prentice-Hall, Inc., Englewood Cliffs, NJ.

The selling style also has high task emphasis, but it has a higher relationship emphasis than the telling style. The selling style is characterized by the leader's attempt to convince followers of the importance of the goal and the leader's definition of how the goal is to be accomplished. The selling style is appropriate for a follower group mature enough to accept some responsibility for decisions and actions.

Unlike the team style of Blake and Mouton, the participating style in Figure 7.4 has high relationship and low task emphases to stimulate the creativity of a mature group of followers. The leader supports relationships and encourages participation in decision making because followers are sufficiently mature to contribute to good decisions and support decisions with appropriate action.

The final style, delegating, has low task and low relationship emphases based on high follower maturity. In other words, the leader lets followers take responsibility for decisions and actions based on a maturity level sufficient for that responsibility. The leader actually passes leadership to the group in the delegating style.

Based on the Hersey and Blanchard description of effective leadership, a mature follower group with considerable experience in a particular set of circumstances may become an immature group when faced with new challenges. An effective leader would therefore be required to delegate under the first circumstance and possibly return to the telling style when circumstances change.

As an example of how situational leadership might be applied, consider the case of an advertising account team in transition from one account to another. The creative group—artists, writers, and producers—was very familiar with the products manufactured by their former client. They knew how the products worked, what their advantages were over major competitors, and how to produce budget-effective commercials the client liked. When the client was sold to a major competitor, the needs of the situation changed. The entire creative team was transferred to the new owner's account with only limited responsibility to their old product line. In fact, the assignment was to integrate the old product line with the new owner's products. Quality advantages, pricing structure, client tastes, and budgets were all changed. The talent of the creative staff remained the same, but the changing assignment contributed to less "maturity" in the group. The account executive supervisor could no longer use a delegating style under dramatically changed circumstances. Although not reverting to the extreme of the telling style, the group's supervisor used a selling style to bring about quickly needed changes without losing the account to other agencies. That the account stayed with the same creative team despite a change in client ownership attested to the flexibility of the manager and the appropriate application of a leadership style reflecting changing business needs. Leadership effectiveness, from the situational perspective, can be described as style selection appropriate to the needs of followers in a particular circumstance. With this approach, situational analysis becomes as important as task and relationship behavior.

## Transformational Approaches

**Transformational approaches**
Leadership theories that explore how leaders motivate followers by personal example, through appeals to higher-level needs, and by the establishment of vision.

The trait, style, and situational approaches discussed all focus on the leader's interactions or transactions with followers. Implied in these approaches is the leader's ability to motivate followers through situational understanding and the control of rewards and (in some cases) punishments. **Transformational approaches** to leadership suggest that inspirational leadership goes beyond the transaction between leaders and followers and literally transforms or changes situations and circumstances through personal example and the rhetorical capability for establishing vision. Michael Hackman and Craig Johnson (1991) explain:

> In the past decade, the Transformational Approach has emerged as a new perspective for understanding and explaining leadership. The Transformational Approach was first outlined by James MacGregor Burns. Burns compared traditional leadership, which he labeled as "transactional," with a more "complex" and "potent" type of leadership he called "transforming." The motivational appeals of the transactional leader are designed to satisfy basic human needs. The motivational appeals of the transformational leader go beyond basic needs in an attempt to satisfy a follower's higher level needs. . . . Transformational leadership is empowering and inspirational; it elevates leaders and followers to higher levels of motivation and morality. (p. 60, 63)

Hackman and Johnson, in summarizing research on transformational leaders, conclude that five primary characteristics appear in one form or another. Transformational leaders are creative, interactive, visionary, empowering, and passionate. In the Workshop section of this chapter, Hackman and Johnson contribute an essay expanding these five characteristics.

J. Kevin Barge (1994) provides evidence that transformational leaders encourage extra effort from followers. Barge suggests, "Taken as a whole, the research indicates that transformational leadership is more capable than transactional leadership at empowering employees and at generating higher levels of employee commitment, satisfaction, and motivation." Transformational leaders are characterized as providing a sense of vision and mission, as having the capability to inspire through communication of high expectations, as stimulating the use of intelligence for problem solving, and as providing personal attention and coaching for followers. Barge underscores the importance of communication for transformational leadership:

> Here the combination of individualized attention and charismatic leadership emphasizes the creative function of communication. The transformational leader must assess the unique qualities of the situation and then select from a large repertoire of communication skills, rather than rely on a predetermined set of such techniques. Effective leaders model desired behavior and articulate a vision through their rhetorical and persuasive skills. The ability to compose a message that is not only clear but also visionary and inspiring requires a sophisticated use of communicative skills. Transformational leadership cannot be scripted; its success depends to a great extent on the leader's ability to create novel communication messages, especially crafted for particular individuals, at a particular place, and at a given time. (p. 57)

Bennis (1992) suggests that the transforming of the globe calls for a new type of leader, the chief executive officer (CEO) who becomes the chief transformation officer (CTO). Bennis bases the new leadership paradigm on alignment, creation, and **empowerment.** According to Bennis,

> Today's leader needs to align the resources of the organization, particularly the human ones, creating a sense of shared objectives worthy of people's support and

**Empowerment**
Process of giving employees the maximum amount of power to do a job as they see fit; includes both responsibility and accountability for work performed.

even dedication. . . . Today's leader must create an organizational culture where ideas come through unhampered by people who are fearful. Such leaders are committed to problem-finding, not just problem-solving. They embrace error, even failure, because they know it will teach them more than success. . . . That overused word from the '60s—empowerment—involves the sense people have that they are at the center of things rather than on the periphery. In an effectively led organization everyone feels he or she contributes to its success. Empowered individuals believe that their actions have significance and meaning. Empowered people have discretion, but also obligations. (pp. 50–51)

Lionel Topaz (1989/1990) underscores the importance of empowerment, which he describes as giving employees the maximum amount of power to do a job as they see fit. Topaz contends that empowered employees require an organizational culture that is led by a vision, uses data to understand customer needs, has a willingness to make mistakes, shares accurate and timely information throughout the organization, and bases rewards on personal achievement or meaningful group achievement.

**Dispersed leadership**
Leadership responsibilities broadly distributed throughout the organization.

**SuperLeadership**
The process of leading others to lead themselves.

The concepts of transformation and empowerment are moving rapidly beyond notions of what happens between leaders and followers. A newer approach, sometimes referred to as **dispersed leadership,** is characterized by leaders attempting to develop leadership in others. Charles Manz and Henry Sims (1989) provide a view of this dispersed transformational approach, SuperLeadership. Simply put, **SuperLeadership** is the art of leading others to lead themselves. SuperLeaders create SuperFollowers, who become skilled self-leaders. The fundamentals of SuperLeadership include (1) establishing a vision, (2) defining goals for the leader and for the followers, (3) reinforcing individuals for good performance, (4) using constructive contingent reprimands, (5) managing and facilitating change, (6) enhancing the self-efficacy of followers, and (7) using models to teach desired and appropriate behaviors. SuperLeaders use self-management as a basis for leadership and deliberately act as models for followers. SuperLeaders encourage followers to self-set goals, create positive thought patterns, develop leadership through rewards, treat mistakes as learning opportunities, promote self-managed teams, and promote a self-leadership culture.

Sims and Peter Lorenzi (1992) summarize the potential of SuperLeadership:

*Effective organizational performance results from the interaction of the thoughts and actions of employees and managers—the practice of leadership. Empowerment of all employees is the new paradigm for organizations. Learning to work (and think) effectively requires an ongoing attention to (1) the long-term development of the manager and employee, and (2) the short-term performance of employees and managers. The achievement of a culture of self-leadership through SuperLeadership expresses our vision of the new leadership paradigm. (p. 304)*

Much of the discussion about transformational approaches is based on the rapid changes that organizations are currently experiencing and will continue to experience in the twenty-first century. As discussed in previous chapters, the increasing diversity within organizations and the diversity of customers and markets is fundamental to organizational change. Taylor Cox Jr. (1993), stressing diversity as a dimension of the transformational approach, suggests that managing diversity is at the core of leadership today. Cox contends:

> By managing diversity I mean planning and implementing organizational systems and practices to manage people so that the potential advantages of diversity are maximized while its potential disadvantages are minimized. Further, I view the goal of managing diversity as maximizing the ability of all employees to contribute to organizational goals and to achieve their full potential unhindered by group identities such as gender, race, nationality, age, and departmental affiliation. (p. 11)

Rosita Daskal Albert (1992) describes this leadership imperative:

> A new awareness is emerging that U.S. organizations need to understand and manage with a polycultural environment, both internally and externally, both at home and abroad. . . . Cultural factors and cultural differences may be just as important—and in some instances perhaps even more important—domestically as they are when American managers meet with their counterparts abroad. At times, the degree of cultural difference may be greater, and the consequences of communication may be more enduring domestically than internationally. (p. 75)

In a linking of transformational leadership approaches to the concepts of new science first discussed in Chapter 4, Margaret Wheatley (1992) describes the natural organizing phenomena in the physical world and suggests that the power of guiding principles or values is the natural organizing phenomena of the organizational world. She links these concepts to leadership:

> These ideas speak with a simple clarity to issues of effective leadership. They bring us back to the importance of simple governing principles: guiding visions, strong values, organizational beliefs—the few rules individuals can use to shape their own behavior. The leader's task is to communicate them, to keep them ever-present and clear, and then allow individuals in the system their random, sometimes chaotic-looking meanderings. (p. 133)

Using the concept of the strange attractor as an organizing principle, Wheatley identifies meaning as a powerful strange attractor for organizations. She concludes that when purpose is clear and compelling that, although behaviors among individuals will differ, trust can be placed in behaviors staying within the bounds of supporting the purpose of the organization. Wheatley describes her view of leadership derived from concepts of new science:

> Leadership skills have also taken on a relational slant. Leaders are being encouraged to include stakeholders, to evoke followership, to empower others. Earlier,

when we focused on tasks, and people were the annoying inconvenience, we thought about "situational" leadership—how the situation could affect our choice of styles. A different understanding of leadership has emerged recently. Leadership is always dependent on the context, but the context is established by the relationships we value. We cannot hope to influence any situation without respect for the complex network of people who contribute to our organizations. Is this a fad? Or is it the web of the universe becoming felt in our work lives? (pp. 144–145)

How would you describe John Mitchell's leadership from the style, situational, or transformational perspective? Describe the assumptions John makes about his subordinates. Also describe the overall situation in which John is expected to provide leadership. If you were advising John, which of the theories would you use? Why?

Trait, style, situational, and transformational approaches to understanding leadership and management communication have been described. By now you have probably recognized that these approaches are complementary, each building on the other. In other words, the approaches for studying leadership are simply different ways of attempting to describe how leadership occurs. We look at the traits, styles, and the circumstances in which a particular leader influences his or her group. We use our trait, style, situational, and transformational approaches together to help explain why a particular leadership effort was successful or how the effort might have been more effective. We are not trait, style, or situational leaders but leaders who exhibit traits, styles, and reactions to specific situations. The approaches just studied should help us evaluate our own efforts and better understand the efforts of others.

Throughout the discussion leadership has been described as a responsibility of managers as well as an influence process that engages those other than managers. Now come important distinctions between leadership and management communication. Keep in mind, however, that whereas managers need to be leaders, excellent organizations require leadership from all organizational positions.

## DISTINCTIONS BETWEEN LEADERSHIP AND MANAGEMENT

Bennis and Nanus (1985) make important distinctions between leaders and managers when they suggest:

> The problem with many organizations, and especially the ones that are failing, is that they tend to be overmanaged and underled. They may excel in the ability to handle the daily routine, yet never question whether the routine should be done at all. There is a profound difference between management and leadership, and both are important. "To manage" means "to bring about, to accomplish, to have charge of or responsibility for, to conduct." "Leading" is "influencing, guiding in direction, course, action, opinion." The distinction is crucial. Managers are people who do things right and leaders are people who do the right thing. The difference may be

summarized as activities of vision and judgment—effectiveness versus activities of mastering routines—efficiency. (p. 21)

Bennis and Nanus further contend that the vision leaders provide is the clearest of all distinctions between leaders and managers. To provide vision requires marshaling the "spiritual and emotional" resources of the organization as reflected in its values, commitment, and aspirations. Management, on the other hand, is charged with directing the physical resources of the organization, its people, machines, and products. Competent managers can get work done efficiently, but excellence comes from leaders who inspire followers to emotional involvement with work and their organization. Bennis and Nanus state, "Great leaders often inspire their followers to high levels of achievement by showing them how their work contributes to worthwhile ends. It is an emotional appeal to some of the most fundamental human needs—the need to be important, to make a difference, to feel useful, to be a part of a successful and worthwhile enterprise."

The increasing complexity of an information society places new demands on leaders and managers. The sheer volume of information available for organizational decision making complicates the development of organizational vision and the direction of organizational activities. This volume of information, when coupled with fast-paced technological changes, puts a new emphasis on the need for leadership from diverse organizational positions. In a complicated information society, the development of vision and the generation of emotional commitment to the work and values of an organization can no longer rest solely with leaders at the top of the organization or with the management team that directs organizational activity.

Put simply, the information society requires leadership from diverse organizational positions. Managers will continue to fulfill specific organizational roles for the direction of work. It is hoped that those in the role of manager will also provide leadership and generate commitment to the values of the organization. The management role, however, represents the formal organizational hierarchy and as such is deeply involved in efficiently planning and implementing what the organization has decided to do. Put another way, managers are responsible for generating enough stability for efficient work to be accomplished. Leaders, on the other hand, are responsible for generating enough change continually to adapt to new circumstances. Thus, the competencies for effective leaders and managers are not the same. Complex organizations need leadership exhibited by those who identify emerging problems and opportunities, whether they fulfill the role of manager or not.

We can readily understand how a manager becomes a leader when inspiring subordinates to excellent performance. What we do not as readily see is the leadership role of the subordinate who identifies a needed work change, a possible new product, or an improved service opportunity and proceeds to influence others to share that vision of an improved organization. This subordinate's assumption of leadership responsibility is highly desirable for the fast-paced information age.

## LEADERSHIP AND MANAGEMENT CHALLENGES

The new leadership and management challenges are not without internal contradictions. On the one hand, the imperative is to move to group and team self-leadership; on the other hand, if necessary, leaders are exhorted to singularly risk the future to motivate follower commitment. Leadership is described as both a lonely and a highly participative endeavor. The increasing complexity of an information society places new demands on leaders and managers. Ellen Van Velsor and Jean Brittain Leslie (1995), in reviewing studies of why executives derail (have negative outcomes), identified four primary themes enduring over time and across countries. According to Van Velsor and Leslie, executives derail because they are challenged by (1) problems with interpersonal relationships, (2) failure to meet business objectives, (3) failure to build and lead a team, and (4) inability to change or adapt during a transition. Think about your own leadership competencies as you read about major challenges facing leaders of today and tomorrow.

### Changing Organizational Forms

Fast-paced change is the order of the day and a fundamental leadership challenge. Bennis (1992) contends that "the organizations of the future will be networks, clusters, cross-functional teams, temporary systems, ad hoc task forces, lattices, modules, matrices—almost anything but pyramids." Many describe the organizations of the twenty-first century as borderless and boundaryless.

The "middleless" organization is the new organizational design. Fewer managers with larger spans of control characterize organizational hierarchies in almost all industries. Work teams are given higher degrees of autonomy and control over immediate work situations. The goals are to increase competitiveness and improve employee morale. Traditional responsibilities of managers are replaced by passing power and control to lower levels in the organization. Managers become facilitators, coaches, teachers, and experts, whereas previously they may have been controllers, directors, planners, and rewarders. The new responsibilities are roles, not new organizational positions. Advances in communications technology give rise to the concept of networked teams and the technology form (T-form) organization. Leaders and managers must learn how to contribute to teams of people who may not be in the same geographic location and who work face-to-face only on rare occasions if at all. The T-form organization challenges leaders and managers to concentrate on using technology to design electronic work flows, production automation, technological matrixing and leveling, and virtual components.

Leaders also are faced with the fluid nature of the formal organization. Mergers with other organizations change processes, policies, markets, and leadership responsibilities. Acquisitions of other companies or product lines provide similar challenges. Michael Hammer (1996) contends that a historic chain reaction is under way, forcing deep changes in management structure, strategic planning, and financial structures precipitated by the rise of the demanding customer. This shift in focus from investors to customers is the force behind the process-centered organization. Hammer suggests:

> A customer focus forces an emphasis on results, hence on the processes that produce results, hence on developing a structure that centers on processes and on fashioning a culture that supports them. . . . This means that "paternalistic management" gives way to "candid leadership." The company no longer "manages" its people; the term reeks of passivity, of victimization, of abdication of personal responsibility. Leadership, by contrast, provides people with the vision, motivation, and context they need to succeed. But it demands action and responsibility on everyone's part. (pp. 13–14)

For the most part, educational background and past work experiences do not prepare leadership for the magnitude of these organizational changes.

## Global Changes

Sims and Lorenzi (1992) provide a thoughtful discussion of several global issues affecting leadership challenges today. Sims and Lorenzi describe economic challenges that include (1) increasing competition among firms on a global basis; (2) emphasis on speed, service, and information, a mandate for flexibility and change in organizations; (3) creative and conceptual demands of a computer-based work setting, with great opportunities for value-added labor; and (4) the economic necessity of embracing previously un(der)employed workers. Sims and Lorenzi believe leaders must deal with the changing socioeconomic status and demographics of employees with a need for more training, flexibility, and lifelong learning. Employees will demand greater participation in management decisions, including a shifting emphasis on teams, skill-based pay, and employee-management cooperation. Gain sharing, profit sharing, and other attempts will be made to encourage and reward productivity. Finally, leaders and managers will help to design flatter, more decentralized organizations, with greater employee need for self-management and concomitant accountability. Rosabeth Moss Kanter (1996), in reference to changing organizations and the world economy, calls for partnering within and across organizations. According to Kanter, leaders must share and spread leadership and become learning-oriented. Leaders will come to see the community as a whole system and they will continually enlarge their network.

Alvin Toffler and Heidi Toffler (1994) suggest that the world economy is undergoing its deepest restructuring since the Industrial Revolution. As Philip Harris and Robert Moran (1996) explain: "Advances in telecommunications and mass transportation, and the breaking down of national borders and cultures have led to the emergence of a global, information-oriented culture. . . . Within the cultures of our civilizations, there is a universal microculture of work and that is changing worldwide as well." Doug Jung and Bruce Avolio (1999) suggest that leaders must understand cultural differences to stimulate high-quality individual or group performance. They discuss the differences between individualist and collectivist cultures in which people in individualist cultures are expected to be more motivated to satisfy their own self-interests and personal goals, whereas in collectivist cultures the strong tendency is to support organizational values and norms. They suggest that leadership will need to understand employee cultural orientations to make important decisions about a variety of organizational communication processes ranging from problem solving and decision making to conflict management.

## High-Speed Management

The challenges described by Sims, Lorenzi, Kanter, and others are literally transforming a variety of leadership and managerial processes. Donald Cushman and Sarah King (1993) have termed some of these new processes high-speed management. High-speed management has as its goal the achievement and maintenance of sustainable competitive advantage through innovative, flexible, adaptive, efficient, and rapid response to environmental change. Cushman and King argue that breakthroughs in information and communication technologies, increased world trade, and a volatile business characterized by rapidly changing technology have all contributed to a new perspective on leadership and management. Cushman and King describe a high-speed management system:

> Innovative management refers not only to product development, but to innovation in corporate structure, human resources utilization, outsourcing, inventory control, manufacturing, marketing, servicing, and competitive position. Adaptive management refers to an organization's appropriate adjustment to change in employee values, customer tastes, investor interests, government regulations, the availability of global economic resources, and the strategic position of competitors. Flexible management refers to the capacity of an organization to expand, contract, and shift direction on products and competitive strategy; to assimilate acquisitions, joint ventures, and coalitions; and to excise unproductive or underproductive units. Efficient management refers to maintaining the industry lead in world-class products, productivity, investors' equity, return on investment, employee satisfaction, customer support, product quality, and serviceability. Rapid response management refers to setting and maintaining the industry standard in speed of response to environmental change. (pp. 215–216)

Although the concept of high-speed management has both supporters and detractors, few challenge the notion that rapid and constant change is clearly a central issue for leaders and managers.

## High-Participation Processes

Organizations of today and tomorrow are faced more than before with understanding the concept of multiple stakeholders and how their participation in all aspects of organizational life contributes to a variety of organizational outcomes. Stanley Deetz (1993) describes stakeholders (groups with organizational interests) as consumers, workers, investors, suppliers, host communities, general society, and the world ecological community. The managing process or coordination of these groups contributes to what Deetz calls outcome interests: goods and services, income distribution, use of resources, environmental effects, economic stability, labor force development, lifestyles, profits, personal identities, and child-rearing practices. Regardless of the precise understanding of who is a stakeholder and the variety of potential outcome interests, a clear pattern of high-involvement participation is emerging for marketplace competitiveness and to meet a variety of stakeholder needs and demands. Leaders and managers are directly challenged to both address and generate these high-participation processes.

Some have referred to the imperative to generate high-participation processes as the total-quality paradigm. Richard Blackburn and Benson Rosen (1993) describe a total-quality paradigm as based on collective efforts, cross-functional work, coaching and enabling, customer satisfaction, and product and service quality. Blackburn and Rosen suggest this paradigm is characterized by multidirectional communication, team goals, customer review of performance, team-based rewards, promotion based on group facilitation, autonomous work teams, empowerment, and innovation, among other factors. Autocratic leadership is replaced by coaching and enabling, and the role of the individual leader gives way to leadership responsibilities broadly dispersed within groups and teams. Edward Lawler III (1994) suggests there are important differences between the total-quality paradigm, sometimes referred to as total quality management (TQM), and employee involvement, or, as it is often called, empowerment. Lawler explains:

> Both the TQM and the employee involvement approach emphasize the importance of managerial behavior and leadership. Nevertheless, there is a difference between what is expected of a senior manager in the employee involvement approach and what is expected in the TQM approach. The TQM approach seems to place more emphasis on managers engaging in typical managerial behavior such as monitoring performance, improving work methods and work procedures, receiving input, processing suggestions, and facilitating the implementation of suggestions. Employee involvement programs emphasize the leadership aspect of the manager's job. They stress vision, moving power to individuals lower in the organization, and acting as a facilitator of the work of others. (p. 73)

John Zenger and colleagues (1993) stress five principles of leadership important for the new high-participation environments. They believe effective leaders (1) focus on the issue not the person, (2) maintain the self-confidence of others, (3) maintain constructive relationships, (4) take the initiative to make things better, and (5) lead by example. Creating and sustaining teams requires intensive planning and persistent follow-through. The role of the leader is not to dictate solutions to problems, but to help the team begin to solve them.

## DETERMINANTS OF LEADERSHIP EFFECTIVENESS

Thus far, whether leaders are born or can be developed, what traits are associated with effective leadership, how leadership styles relate to the maturity of followers and to particular leadership situations, and how leadership contributes to establishing organizational vision have been discussed. Throughout the discussion the contention has been that both leadership and management are enacted through human communication. With this perspective now comes an examination of how communication competencies, influence (power bases), and analysis abilities contribute to leadership effectiveness.

## Communication Competencies as Determinants of Leadership Effectiveness

A recurring theme throughout this text has been that communication competence is necessary for organizational excellence. Knowledge, sensitivity, skills, and values must all be understood and developed for both individuals and entire organizations to be effective in our emerging information era. Nowhere is communication competency more important than when individuals are attempting to lead and establish vision and direction for organizations.

Research on managerial effectiveness and perceptions of effectiveness supports the importance of communication competence. In the famous works of Chris Argyris (1962), Peter Drucker (1966), and Bennis and Nanus (1985), communication effectiveness is described as a central element for overall managerial effectiveness. Communication encoding, decoding, and interaction capabilities are described as factors necessary for communication and overall managerial competence.

## Predispositions for Leadership Communication

As previously discussed, the knowledge, sensitivity, skills, and values we bring to particular situations powerfully influence our behavior choices. Whether or not we choose to attempt leadership is related to our assessment of our own competencies, the needs of the situation, the receptivity of a follower group, and our potential ability to influence (power).

Those high in anxiety about communication, for example, are less likely to engage in leadership attempts than those lower in communication apprehension. Highly task-oriented individuals are more likely to adopt leadership styles reflecting task emphasis, whereas those preferring close interpersonal relationships are more likely to adopt styles reflecting their concern for people. Return for a moment to Figures 7.3 and 7.4. Although the grids in these figures represent behavioral approaches used for leadership and management, they can also be understood as preferences individuals bring to leadership and managerial situations. Concern for task and people relationships, when coupled with an assessment of follower maturity, influences behavior choices in specific circumstances. Yet concerns for task and people relationships, follower maturity, personal assessments of communication competence, and assessments of influence or power positions are also reflected in our predispositions for leadership communication, predispositions that subsequently influence strategic objectives and tactical choices.

## Strategic Communication Objectives for Leadership

Strategic objectives for leadership communication can be described as the general game plans leaders employ for conducting communication based on personal preferences or predispositions and on assessments of the probable outcomes within particular contexts. Tactics are the specific behavior choices made by leaders to influence followers in specific situations and to support overall strategies.

Autocratic strategies are used by leaders who seek to have followers implement decisions with little or no follower input. John Mitchell can decide that the current complaints at Invest Corporation call for autocratic strategies. He can announce that he will continue to determine when decisions will be made and that his technical decisions will not be subject to question. He can choose to ignore complaints that he is "invisible" and continue to view leadership as a technical contribution. These autocratic strategies are possible as long as top management supports him.

John also has choices among more participative strategies. He can encourage senior lab members to suggest ways in which he can work with them in a team atmosphere. He can compromise about the number of details he will handle personally and the amount of time he is taking to make decisions. He can seek to establish more open and supportive relationships to become a more "visible" manager. Finally, John can use avoidance or laissez-faire strategies and ignore the complaints he is hearing. He has the avoidance option because of his legitimate power position as laboratory manager. He can ignore much of the discontent as long as he retains the support of senior management.

John's selection of strategies is related to his assessment of what is needed for leadership and his assessment of whether individuals need leadership. As you will recall, John believes leadership is primarily a technical responsibility and that intelligent people do not need close personal contact to do their jobs. These assumptions will influence what happens next at Invest.

Howard Gardner (1995), in his portraits of outstanding twentieth-century leaders, identifies what he calls constants of leadership with significant communication implications. Gardner suggests that leaders must have a central story or message. The story must assist in creating a sense of group identity that is inclusive and encourages individuals to think of themselves as part of a broader community. He describes how leaders such as Martin Luther King Jr. benefited from building on previous stories by synthesizing them in new ways. Gardner also describes the relationship between the leader and what he calls the audience. This complex and dynamic interplay is based on the audience's needs and desires and the vision of the message. He uses Gandhi as an example of a leader with a steadfast concentration on the same core message while exhibiting flexibility in how it is presented. Finally, the credibility of the leader is based on whether or not the creator of the message actually embodies or lives the story through personal example.

In a recent extensive study of some ninety outstanding leaders, Bennis and Nanus (1985) identified four major strategies or competencies that all 90 leaders seemed to exhibit: (1) management of attention through vision, (2) meaning through communication, (3) trust through positioning, and (4) deployment of self through positive self-regard.

The outstanding leaders of the Bennis and Nanus study commanded the attention of their followers and organizations by establishing and communicating a *vision* about where the organization should go, what it should be, and what was needed to achieve it. As Bennis and Nanus suggest, "All ninety people interviewed had an agenda, an unparalleled concern with outcome. The visions these various leaders conveyed seemed to bring about a confidence on the part of the employees, a confidence that instilled in them a belief that they were capable of performing the necessary acts." Bennis and Nanus further suggested that successful leaders not only caught the attention of others but also paid attention to others, underscoring the essential interactional relationship between leaders and followers.

The second strategy, the management of meaning through *communication,* relates to the conscious effort the leaders made to communicate so that their meanings would become the meanings of every organizational level. These excellent leaders were concerned not only with what should be done but also with how to develop messages that conveyed that vision. Bennis and Nanus state, "Getting the message across unequivocally at every level is an absolute key. Basically it is what the creative process is all about and what, once again, separates the managers from the leaders." Management of meaning rests on well-developed communication competencies and an understanding of the process of organizational communication. Without competencies and process understanding, effective leadership is problematic.

*Trust* as a strategy is hard to define. Bennis and Nanus describe trust as the "glue that maintains organizational integrity." The leaders in the Bennis and Nanus study were trusted (although not always liked) because they were constant, predictable, and reliable. They positioned themselves as worthy of trust by exhibiting personal stability even while encouraging change and innovation. They helped their organizations develop a sense of identity (culture) and integrity (trust). This sense of direction is considered by Bennis and Nanus to be fundamental to their effectiveness.

Finally, the effective leaders in the study liked themselves and other people. They did not focus on failure but viewed mistakes as learning opportunities and challenges. They were like famed tight-rope walker Karl Wallenda, who, until shortly before the fall that claimed his life, always focused on walking, never on falling. Bennis and Nanus contend that the Wallenda factor in leadership is the ability to focus on success, not on failure, and to frame behavior in terms of the goal, not in terms of every detail of the process.

The strategy of positive self-regard and regard for others is closely related to the description of developing communication competencies (knowledge, sensitivity, skills, and values) for organizational excellence. The relationship between regard and developing communication competencies is made clear when Bennis and Nanus sum up positive self-regard as three major factors: "knowledge of one's strengths, the capacity to nurture and develop those strengths, and the ability to discern the fit between one's strengths and weaknesses and the organization's needs." They continue:

> In the case of our ninety leaders, they used five key skills: (1) The ability to accept people as they are, not as you would like them to be. . . . (2) The capacity to approach relationships and problems in terms of the present rather than the past. . . . (3) The ability to treat those who are close to you with the same courteous attention that you extend to strangers and casual acquaintances. . . . (4) The ability to trust others, even if the risk seems great. . . . (5) The ability to do without constant approval and recognition from others. (pp. 66–67)

Bennis (1999) concludes that leaders must learn to develop a social architecture that encourages incredibly bright people to work together successfully and to engage in creativity. Leaders must constantly reinvent their organizations and learn to deploy work forces so that rather than downsizing they are creating new opportunities. Finally, Bennis believes tomorrow's leaders will have to learn how to create an environment that actually embraces changes not as a threat but as an opportunity.

Research by Eric Eisenberg (1984) lends support to the Bennis and Nanus contention that generating vision is an important leadership responsibility. Eisenberg proposes strategic ambiguity as an organizational communication strategy that promotes unity while maintaining sufficient individual freedom to ensure flexibility, creativity, and change. Eisenberg argues that divergent organizational goals cannot always be resolved through the development of specific consensus from all organizational members. He proposes that

> ambiguity is used strategically to foster agreement on abstractions without limiting specific interpretations. . . . Focusing on organizational symbolism casts leadership in a new light as well. While a primary responsibility of leaders is to make meanings for followers . . . and to infuse employees with values and purpose . . . the process of doing so is less one of consensus-making and more one of using language strategically to express values at a level of abstraction at which agreement can occur. . . . Effective leaders use ambiguity strategically to encourage creativity and guard against the acceptance of one standard way of viewing organizational reality. (p. 231)

Organizational goal and mission statements, communication rules, and organizational stories and myths are all examples of strategic ambiguity influenced by leaders. An excellent example of strategic ambiguity (vision) comes from the recurring theme to "do what's right, not what's written" of a certain large computer manufacturer. What's "right" is subject to varying interpretations across the organization. The leadership imperative, however, is to take action and personal responsibility, a value with high consensus even though specific interpretations often vary dramatically. In fact, conflict frequently occurs in this generally healthy organization over "what is right" and "who should decide."

The work of Gail Fairhurst, Stephen Green, and B. Kay Snavely (1984) supports the Bennis and Nanus contention that trust and positive self-regard and regard for others are important leadership strategies. In their study of managerial attempts to control poor performance among subordinates, they found that the strategy of using positive face (maintaining an approval of the subordinate's self-image) was positively related to performance improvement. Also, the involvement (trusting) of subordinates in decisions about performance improvement was positively associated with longer periods of time between problem recurrence. These findings suggest that positive self-regard and regard for others can contribute to improved performance and that trusting subordinates by involving them in behavior change decisions improves the quality of and commitment to solutions.

So far, autocratic, participative, and laissez-faire or avoidance strategies for leadership have been discussed. Strategies for the communication of vision, management of meaning through communication, management of trust, and management of positive self-regard and regard for others have been described. Now comes a description of specific communication tactics used for each of these strategic orientations.

## Communication Tactics for Leadership

Leadership tactics can be described as the communication behaviors used to support authoritarian, participative, and avoidance preferences as well as to establish vision, manage meaning, generate trust, and communicate regard and success orientations. Specific tactics are influenced by individual preferences and strategies, by communication competencies of leaders and followers, and by overall organizational values and expectations about how leadership works. Military organizations, for example, encourage authoritarian leadership, whereas organizations involved in research and development of new products usually stress more participative styles. Still others reflect a mix of leadership approaches representing the diversity of people and personalities who work together. It is important to understand that as with most tactics, the choice of specific leadership tactics illustrates the interactive nature of relationships. Both leaders and followers are involved in complex tactical interactions influenced by individual preferences and strategic objectives as well as the needs of a particular situation.

It is not possible to list or define all the communication tactics available to potential leaders. It is useful for our personal sensitivity and our skill development, however, to identify several frequently used communication tactics. Figure 7.5 presents excerpts from group problem-solving situations in which the identified group leader illustrates a particular leadership tactic. Each example is accompanied by a description of the tactic it represents, and tactics are grouped into authoritarian, participative, avoidance, vision-setting, meaning-management, trust-generating, and positive regard and success categories.

**FIGURE 7.5   Communication Tactics for Leadership**

| ORGANIZATIONAL NARRATIVE | LEADERSHIP TACTICS |
|---|---|
| *Authoritarian Tactics* | |
| "The seriousness of the problem leaves little room for continuing to think about new ideas. I believe I know what we should do and am willing to take the responsibility." | 1. *Blocking ideas* by establishing responsibility |
| "We will first assign new sales territories, then we will put one senior salesperson in each territory, and then we will establish sales quotas." | 2. *Controlling the process* of events |
| "I have decided we will stop development of the Henderson project. I think our direction is in Richardson Heights." | 3. *Announcing goals* without consultation |
| "I expected you to be on my team. You can forget about my support come budget time, and you know you need that." | 4. *Punishing opposition* through sanctions or withholding support |
| *Participative Tactics* | |
| "To make the best decision we need everyone's ideas. I don't want anyone to think that he or she doesn't have a say." | 1. *Seeking ideas* from all involved |
| "We need to make a decision on the budget, and I want everyone to have ample time to participate. Therefore, we will each spend fifteen minutes on our initial presentations." | 2. *Facilitating group processes* that encourage participation |
| "Look, I'm glad you will disagree with me. That is the only way we will have a good solution." | 3. *Encouraging disagreement* when constructive and solution oriented |
| "I think opening the store at Third and Franklin is a good idea, but I need your honesty with any reservations you may have." | 4. *Seeking idea evaluation* |
| "I believe that we all agree that the new product line will work. We can easily say to stock minimum quantity of each appliance in the group." | 5. *Verbalizing consensus* among group members |
| *Avoidance Tactics* | |
| "I don't think we have any real disagreements in this group." | 1. *Ignoring conflict* even when obvious |
| "Look, we have spent enough time on this problem. I don't think it is as important as you think. Let's move on." | 2. *Changing subject* when disagreements or difficulty seem likely |

**FIGURE 7.5   Continued**

"Whatever you want to do is fine with me. You all definitely know best."

3. *Agreeing with others* to avoid conflict or new ideas

"Look, I shouldn't have to ask you to do this. It is your job. I am not going to be a baby-sitter. You can take the consequences yourself."

4. *Refusing responsibility* for motivating others to action

*Vision-Setting Tactics*

"I believe we can make our bowl game the Super Bowl of college football."

1. *Visualizing abstract ideas* by symbolic association

"I want us to move from number five to number two during the next three months. I know with a sales force like all you that it is only a matter of time."

2. *Stating desired outcomes* without undue emphasis on details

"To start performing like a team we have to start acting like a team. That's why I called you here today."

3. *Articulating reasons* for actions and goals

*Meaning-Management Tactics*

"I have talked about what I see ahead. I now need to know how you think that affects each group represented here today."

1. *Soliciting feedback* to understand message clarity and impact

"Our course of action is a little like putting our own person on the moon. Awe, courage, pride, all are part of this achievement we have just experienced."

2. *Generating symbolism* to interpret events and accomplishments

"I want everyone to hear this change at the same time. Schedule me to personally meet with each shift."

3. *Managing messages* to support exchanges of meaning

*Trust-Generating Tactics*

"I told you the truth about the layoffs. I know it wasn't popular, but you can trust what I am now going to say. The layoffs are behind us, but we still have considerable belt tightening to do."

1. *Communicating constancy* by linking present messages to past actions

"People are the most important resource this company has. For that reason I am asking all you and all the management team to take a 10 percent pay cut so that no one will have to be without a job."

2. *Identifying values* and relating values to needed action

"I am asking each department head to meet with me over the next few months. I want to know what is going on and have people free to come to me."

3. *Encouraging access* through planned communication interaction

*(continued)*

**FIGURE 7.5    Continued**

*Positive Regard and Success Tactics*

"I know you consider this move a mistake. I consider that you have learned a valuable lesson."

1. *Providing support* for individual effort

"This is the best new product release this company has ever produced."

2. *Offering praise* for efforts

"Look, we are all in this together. It doesn't matter as much whose fault it was as what we need to do next."

3. *Avoiding blame* and seeking solutions

"I know the economy is troubled, but this gives us a chance to really see what we are worth. After all, anyone can be successful when things are going well. The mark of excellence is now."

4. *Identifying challenges and opportunities* when others see problems

## Power Bases for Leaders

Preferences for leadership, strategic objectives, and communication tactics all contribute to how leaders influence followers. Yet behaviors alone do not adequately explain how one individual is recognized as a leader whereas another is not. We have all seen individuals who are recognized as leaders exhibit almost identical behaviors to those who never achieve leadership recognition. Frequently the difference in who is a leader and who is not is a subtle matter of credibility, a credibility that enables one person to be more influential than another. This credibility is commonly referred to as power or the **power bases** of the leader.

**Power bases**
Influence an individual has over another as a result of dependency on the powerful person. Power bases are commonly identified as legitimate, reward, coercive, referent, expert, and connection.

The concept of power can best be understood as an interactive process. In other words, power does not exist in a vacuum but rather as people interact with one another. From this perspective power can be understood as the influence an individual has over another as a result of dependency on the powerful person. To understand this interaction it is helpful to think about some of the power bases available to leaders. John French and Bertram Raven (1968) have given a useful description of five power types: legitimate, reward, coercive, referent, and expert. Connection power is also discussed.

**Legitimate power**
Power emerging from the positions, titles, or roles people occupy.

**Legitimate power** comes from the positions, titles, or roles people occupy. Supervisors have legitimate power over subordinates. As such, certain rights and responsibilities are legitimately defined and generally understood by group members. Disagreement can surround the ability of the legitimate leader, yet most agree that certain leadership responsibilities accompany the position. For example, virtually every president of the United States has supporters and critics, yet despite these diverse opinions few would disagree that the individual is legitimately the president.

**Reward power** is based on the leader's control and distribution of tangible and intangible reward resources. A leader can influence with the promise of rewards only as long as those rewards are within the leader's control and perceived by followers as rewarding. Many people attempt to influence with rewards that others do not find important or influential. Many supervisors believe, for example, that money is the primary reward for good performance, although considerable research suggests that communication contact with supervisors is one of the most sought-after of all subordinate rewards. Interestingly enough, communication interaction is more often controlled by supervisors than money or other tangible benefits.

**Coercive power** can be understood as the sanctions or punishments within the control of the leader. Coercive power is the ability to punish for not complying with influence attempts. To be effective, coercive power must not be threatened beyond what the leader is willing to administer. We have all seen people lose credibility by threatening sanctions or punishments that were not within the control of the one making the threats. Although reward power can be exercised by virtually anyone, coercive power is related to the role or legitimate position an individual occupies. For example, a peer can threaten to get another peer fired, but although unpleasant, the threat is generally not considered coercive power. When a supervisor makes the same threat, though, the influence attempt takes on an entirely different meaning.

**Referent power** is a result of others identifying with the leader. It is a power base that is only indirectly related to the leader's overt influence attempts. Referent power comes from the desire of others to use the leader as a reference or from others seeking to imitate the leader's behaviors with or without the leader's desire for them to do so. Referent power results from actions of the leader, yet the leader cannot directly exercise referent power; instead, it is assigned by others.

**Expert or information power** rests on what the leader knows as a result of organizational interaction or areas of technical specialty. As such, expert power does not require legitimate power for the expert to be influential. Expert power can be used without coercive power and often contributes to the development of referent power Expert power is considered to be important for organizational excellence and is ideally the basis of effective influence attempts.

**Connection power** is the influence leaders have as a result of who they know and the support they have from others in the organization. Generally conceived of as support from others in power, connection power also comes from followers. Supervisors and

---

**Reward power**
Power based on the leader's control and distribution of tangible and intangible resources.

**Coercive power**
Power based on the sanctions or punishments within the control of the leader.

**Referent power**
Power based on others identifying with the leader.

**Expert or information power**
Power based on information the leader knows as a result of organizational interaction or areas of technical specialty.

**Connection power**
Power resulting from who the leader knows and the support he or she has from others in the organization.

managers, for example, are generally in better influence positions when follower "connections" are supportive. In turn, group members are more influential when their leaders are "connected" to others in the organization. Connection power is understood by observing communication networks and how individuals are linked throughout the organization.

## Situational Analysis for Leadership

Understanding the situations or circumstances requiring leadership is fundamental for effectiveness. The ability to assess thoughtfully the requirements of the problem and the group attempting its solutions contributes to the selection of effective strategies and tactics for leadership.

The ability to communicate vision is related to the ability to generate vision based on sound problem analysis. Communicating outcomes is related to knowing where an organization should go and having a concept of how it can get there. In other words, good problem-solving and analysis skills are fundamental for effective leadership. Analysis skills help define problems, generate solutions, and contribute to the selection of influence strategies appropriate for leadership. Analysis skills cannot be separated from influence strategies for effectiveness. The individual who thoroughly understands a problem may not be able to influence others if communication strategies and tactics are carelessly chosen. On the other hand, we have concern for individuals who are so adept at persuasive communication that they convince groups to follow courses of action that are ill conceived or ill advised.

John Mitchell's experience at Invest is a good example. Chances are John has the technical expertise to lead the laboratory to significant technical accomplishments. No one doubts his ability to analyze technical problems. Yet John is close to failure as the manager of the laboratory. His situational analysis is only partially complete. He understands the technical direction he wants but has not communicated his vision to others and does not see any need for that type of sales pitch. John's communication behaviors do not reflect his technical excellence. His dilemma illustrates what can happen when problem analysis is not coupled with appropriate communication behaviors.

## INCREASING LEADERSHIP EFFECTIVENESS

The communication competencies needed to increase leadership capabilities can be described as an expansion of those competencies necessary for interpersonal and conflict management effectiveness. The knowledge, sensitivity, skills, and values identified and developed in previous chapters are all important for effective leadership, especially if we take the position that organizations need leadership from all position levels.

As previously suggested, effective leaders understand the problems facing their group and have skill in helping diverse individuals approach common problems. Effective leaders participate in group efforts and encourage others to participate by being open-minded and exhibiting supportive behaviors. Effective leaders consult others and express sensitivity for disagreement. Effective leaders, however, will help groups make decisions when consensus is unlikely. Finally, effective leaders empower others by sharing success and credit.

Self-awareness is a key to leadership effectiveness. Understanding personal preferences, behaviors, and problem situations is fundamental to discovering why some leadership efforts succeed while others fail. Return for a moment to your personal theory of leadership. What does it tell you about your personal leadership strengths and weaknesses? What competencies need further development? When have you been most successful?

Next, in an effort to help you increase your leadership effectiveness, an important concept of principled leadership is described; task, procedural, and interpersonal leadership responsibilities are described; and leadership in group settings by identifying barriers to effective group decision making and by proposing how to plan for leadership in a group setting is discussed. Finally, knowledge, sensitivity, skill, and value competencies are applied in the Workshop section of the chapter.

**Principled leadership**
Leadership that provides a consistent message, has a perspective for unleashing talent, practices ego suppression, and creates leaders.

## Principled Leadership

In their extensive study of successful teams, Carl Larson and Frank LaFasto (1989) identified **principled leadership** as one of the core characteristics of why successful teams develop. According to Larson and LaFasto, principled leadership provides a consistent message, has a perspective for unleashing talent, practices ego suppression, and creates leaders.

Larson and LaFasto found that "effective team leaders begin by establishing a vision of the future. In the most common language, this need was articulated as the clear, elevating goal. . . . The goal, or vision, is seen as worthwhile, making team members eager to be a part of its achievement." In other words, principled leadership establishes and communicates a vision that creates change by unleashing the talent of team members.

In thinking about increasing our own leadership effectiveness, we question what qualities and behaviors are most likely to generate this commitment to vision and overall leadership success. The work of Larson and LaFasto provides insight:

> A content analysis of our research data yielded a consistent message that focused on how team leaders generated enthusiasm, a bias for action, and a commitment to the team's objective among team members. The single most distinguishing feature of the effective leaders in our data base was their ability to establish, and lead by, guiding principles. These principles represented day-to-day performance standards. They represented what all team members, including the team leader, should expect from one another on a day-to-day basis. The principles identified by our sample

created three natural categories of expectations: (1) what the team should expect of the team leader; (2) what the team leader should expect from each team member, and each team member should expect from one another; and (3) leadership principles that established a supportive decision-making climate in which team members could take risks. (pp. 122–123)

Figure 7.6 summarizes the principles identified by Larson and LaFasto.

Not only did the successful leaders of the Larson and LaFasto work unleash talent through the use of guiding principles, but they also suppressed individual ego displays for themselves and the team. Team members were active participants in shaping the destiny of the team, and this active participation contributed to leadership not only for the team but also within the team. In sum it can be said that effective leadership promotes the development of leadership in others. Think for a moment about your own leadership attempts. Which of the Larson and LaFasto principles did you use? Which were missing? Would you add others to the list? Next we consider how effective leaders use principled leadership for task, procedural, and interpersonal responsibilities.

## Identifying Constructive Communication Behaviors for Leadership

Gail Fairhurst and Robert Sarr (1996) describe the "art of framing" as managing the language of leadership. Fairhurst and Sarr contend that the intricacies of communication and the difficulties of conveying even a simple message to an organization are challenges for leaders. They propose that framing a message is like framing a picture. When framing is successful the message gains impact and minimizes distortions. Leaders have constructive framing opportunities in the following general areas: task, procedural, and interpersonal responsibilities.

### Task Responsibilities

Whether leading a major corporation or leading a group in a class project, leaders have task, procedural, and interpersonal responsibilities. In the task area, leaders are responsible for facilitating problem analysis, idea generation, idea evaluation, solution generation, and decision implementation. Leaders need to stimulate creativity and urge people to push the boundaries of their thinking. Effective leaders encourage team members to listen actively to others and expand good ideas. Leaders are responsible for promoting focused and in-depth investigation of ideas and critically evaluating all aspects of a problem. Leaders help the group address the accuracy of their information, evaluate information sources, apply information carefully to defined problems, and develop solution criteria. Review the guiding principles in Figure 7.6. Which of the principles would you apply to task responsibilities? What types of communication skills are required? Can you understand the importance of communication competency for effective leadership?

**FIGURE 7.6** **Principled Leadership**

**TEAM LEADER PRINCIPLES**

1. Avoid compromising the team's objective with political issues.
2. Exhibit personal commitment to our team's goal.
3. Do not dilute the team's efforts with too many priorities.
4. Be fair and impartial toward all team members.
5. Be willing to confront and resolve issues associated with inadequate performance by team members.
6. Be open to new ideas and information from team members.

**TEAM MEMBER PRINCIPLES**

1. Demonstrate a realistic understanding of one's role and accountabilities.
2. Demonstrate objective and fact-based judgments.
3. Collaborate effectively with other team members.
4. Make the team goal a higher priority than any personal objective.
5. Demonstrate a willingness to devote whatever effort is necessary to achieve team success.
6. Be willing to share information, perceptions, and feedback openly.
7. Provide help to other team members when needed and appropriate.
8. Demonstrate high standards of excellence.
9. Stand behind and support team decisions.
10. Demonstrate courage of conviction by directly confronting important issues.
11. Demonstrate leadership in ways that contribute to the team's success.
12. Respond constructively to feedback from others.

**TEAM LEADER BEHAVIORS FOR DECISION MAKING**

1. Trust team members with meaningful levels of responsibility.
2. Give team members the necessary autonomy to achieve results.
3. Present challenging opportunities that stretch the individual abilities of team members.
4. Recognize and reward superior performance.
5. Stand behind the team and support it.

## Procedural Responsibilities

Leaders also are responsible for procedures such as goal setting, agenda making, discussion clarification, and both consensus and disagreement identification. Leaders must be able to introduce ideas, give directions, and call for action. They ask for ideas and the participation of team members. Leaders remind groups of agendas and goals and generally organize group activities. Leaders actively listen as well as offer explanations for their own and others' verbalizations and behaviors. Recall the description in Chapter 6 of communication skills important for group participation. All these skills and more apply to leadership responsibilities. In effect, leaders and team members alike must develop key interaction process skills for effective group efforts. Again review the guiding principles in Figure 7.6. Which of the principles apply to procedural responsibilities? What might you add?

### Interpersonal Responsibilities

Finally, leaders make significant contributions to the interpersonal dynamics of groups. Leaders contribute to participation, group climate, and conflict management. As Larson and LaFasto (1989) have suggested, effective leaders generate an environment in which team members can achieve excellence because they have the confidence to take risks. Confidence to take risks comes from the supportive climate of effective interpersonal relationships. Leaders are responsible for reflecting feelings and supporting others, empathizing, and stopping personal attacks or other counterproductive individual or group behaviors. What guiding principles should a leader adopt for interpersonal responsibilities? What skills are most important?

In summary we can say that leaders affect how the task is accomplished, how people are supported within the group, and what processes and procedures the group uses to achieve its objectives. Group members also share these responsibilities, but the leader remains influential in guiding task, procedural, and interpersonal contributions.

## SUMMARY

Leadership and management communication affect nearly all aspects of organizational life. Leaders help guide individuals, groups, and entire organizations in establishing goals and sustaining action to support goals. Managers fulfill organizationally assigned roles and are expected to be leaders, but leadership can come from virtually any organizational position. Theories of leadership and management emphasize traits such as intelligence, social maturity, initiative, and human relations abilities. Style theories emphasize authoritarian, democratic, and laissez-faire behaviors and frequently use such categories as impoverished, middle-of-the-road, country club, task, and team leadership. Situational approaches build on style theories by emphasizing an interaction among leadership style, maturity of followers, and needs of a particular situation. Transformational approaches emphasize understanding of particular situations with the establishment of vision important to motivate workers to high levels of achievement. Distinctions can be made between leadership and management. Managers need to be leaders, but organizations in the information society need leaders in diverse organizational positions. Strategic objectives for leadership include authoritarian, participative, and avoidance approaches. Research suggests that excellent leaders use strategies that manage attention through vision, meaning through communication, trust through positioning, and deployment of self through positive self-regard and an emphasis on success. In addition, leaders adopt specific communication tactics that support these strategic objectives.

The ability to influence others is related to the power bases of leaders. Power bases are commonly described as legitimate, reward, coercive, referent, expert or information, and connection power. Situational analyses along with strategies, tactics, and power bases determine leadership effectiveness. Leadership effectiveness is increased by understanding the guiding principles for principled leadership and understanding leadership responsibilities in task, procedural, and interpersonal areas.

# WORKSHOP

1. In groups of six, identify by name examples of effective and ineffective leaders. Describe the behaviors of your effective leaders. Describe the behaviors of those you believe were ineffective. Discuss the similarities and differences in your list.

2. Practicing a variety of communication tactics helps to build both oral and analysis skills. The Leadership Team Exercise that follows (see pp. 259–261) is designed for participants to use a variety of communication tactics and then analyze their influence on the decision-making process.

3. As you know from reading this chapter, transformational approaches to leadership are among the newest of the theories used to describe leadership. In "Leadership That Transforms," Michael Hackman and Craig Johnson help us understand this important approach to leadership. Read their comments and be prepared to discuss them and offer your own opinions. (See pp. 262–265.)

4. Interview three leaders of your choice. Ask them about their personal theories of leadership. What do they see as the challenges facing leaders of today and tomorrow? Summarize your findings either in writing or in an oral report for class discussion.

5. Use the group tactics chart that follows. Select a group meeting for observation. Enter the names of group members across the top of the chart. As you observe the meeting, identify with a check mark the tactics each individual uses. If a tactic is used more than once, put multiple checks in the appropriate box. After the meeting, develop a profile of tactics used by each member and an overall profile of the numbers of times each tactic was used within the group. Then describe your observation of the overall effectiveness of the meeting. Describe how the balance of the tactics utilized contributed to the meeting's outcomes.

## The Leadership Team Exercise

The class is divided into teams of seven members each. The following list of communication tactics used during leadership situations is written on small cards or pieces of paper. Each member of the groups draws a card that assigns a range of tactics the member will use during the decision-making exercise. Individuals are aware of the tactics they personally are to use and do not know what tactic cards others have drawn.

### INFORMATION FOR THE TACTIC CARDS
1. You are to use authoritarian tactics such as blocking ideas, controlling the process, announcing your goals, and punishing opposition.
2. You are to use participative tactics such as seeking ideas, facilitating group processes, encouraging disagreement, seeking idea evaluation, and verbalizing consensus.
3. You are to use avoidance tactics such as ignoring conflict, changing subjects, agreeing with others, and refusing responsibility.
4. You are to use vision-setting tactics such as visualizing abstract ideas, stating desired outcomes, and articulating reasons for actions and goals.
5. You are to use meaning-management tactics such as soliciting feedback, generating symbolism, and managing messages to support exchanges of meaning.
6. You are to use trust-generating tactics such as communicating constancy by linking present messages to past actions, identifying values, and encouraging access to all group members.
7. You are to use positive regard and success tactics by providing support, offering praise, avoiding blame, and identifying challenges and opportunities.

In addition to specific tactic assignments, each group member will attempt to identify the tactics used by other group members during the activity. A group tactics chart is provided for recording impressions during group discussion. The information generated on the chart will be discussed when the exercise is complete.

## Group Tactics Chart

**TACTICS USED**                        *Names of Group Members*

*Authoritarian*
  Blocking ideas
  Controlling process
  Announcing goals
  Punishing others

*Participative*
  Seeking ideas
  Facilitating
  Encouraging disagreement
  Seeking idea evaluation
  Verbalizing consensus

| **TACTICS USED** | | | *Names of Group Members* | | | | |

**Avoidance**
Ignoring conflict
Changing subjects
Agreeing with others
Refusing responsibility

| | | | | | | |
|---|---|---|---|---|---|---|
| | | | | | | |
| | | | | | | |
| | | | | | | |

**Vision setting**
Visualizing abstract ideas
Stating desired outcomes
Articulating reasons

| | | | | | | |
|---|---|---|---|---|---|---|
| | | | | | | |
| | | | | | | |

**Meaning management**
Soliciting feedback
Generating symbolism
Managing meaning

| | | | | | | |
|---|---|---|---|---|---|---|
| | | | | | | |
| | | | | | | |

**Trust**
Communicating constancy
Identifying values
Encouraging access

| | | | | | | |
|---|---|---|---|---|---|---|
| | | | | | | |
| | | | | | | |

**Positive regard/success**
Providing support
Offering praise
Avoiding blame
Identifying challenges

| | | | | | | |
|---|---|---|---|---|---|---|
| | | | | | | |
| | | | | | | |
| | | | | | | |

## The Situation

Your group of seven is a policy committee appointed to make a recommendation about the position your company should take on an important issue. The committee has never worked together before, and members are unaware of the styles each brings to the group. The problem for the committee is to recommend what type of position the company should take on drug and alcohol abuse by all employees, for hourly workers through top management.

The committee will have fifteen minutes to discuss the new policy. When the time is up, committee members will complete their forms, attempting to identify the use of various tactics by group members. Each member also will attempt to identify the general tactic assignments of all other members.

Discussion should follow, comparing the tactic identification forms and relating various tactics to the effective development or lack of development of the policy.

## Leadership That Transforms

### Michael Z. Hackman, Ph.D.[1] and Craig Johnson, Ph.D.[2]

In recent years, scholars from a variety of disciplines have studied the behavior of extraordinary leaders to determine what these individuals have in common. The search for common characteristics of highly effective leaders has led researchers to conclude that outstanding leaders not only move followers to action, but also transform followers into leaders themselves. This model for understanding and explaining leadership has been called the transformational approach. Under transformational leadership, followers are motivated to work harder, to become more sensitive to moral and ethical issues, and to think and act like leaders. As a result, organizational climate and productivity often dramatically improve.

Lee Iacocca is one example of a transformational leader who had a significant impact on his organization's performance. The Chrysler Corporation was nearly bankrupt when Iacocca became the company's president. Iacocca persuaded employees to produce higher quality products. At the same time, he convinced customers and federal officials that the company would survive. Soon, Chrysler regained its profitability, repaying government loans ahead of schedule. Other examples of transformational leaders include the late Bill Hewlett and Dave Packard of Hewlett-Packard; Michael Eisner, CEO of Disney; Anita Roddick, founder and managing director of Body Shop cosmetics stores; and Jeff Bezos, founder and driving force behind Internet giant Amazon.com.

What are the common characteristics shared by these leaders? In nearly all the classification systems of transformational leadership, five common characteristics appear. Research suggests that transformational leaders are creative, interactive, visionary, empowering, and passionate.

### Creative

Transformational leaders recognize that satisfaction with the status quo poses a serious threat to an organization's survival. Resting on past achievements can blind members to new opportunities and potential problems, and as organizations such as Montgomery Ward, IBM, and Netscape have discovered, the most successful organizations are often in the most danger. As one observer notes, "Nothing fails like success."

Transformational leaders act as problem finders who sense gaps between what is and what ought to be. They seek out new markets, products, clients, and customers that can help the organization grow and prosper.

[1]Michael Z. Hackman is a professor and chair in the Department of Communication at the University of Colorado at Colorado Springs. He received his Ph.D. in speech communication from the University of Denver. His research interests include leadership communication, human communication theory, and instructional communication.

[2]Craig Johnson is professor and chair of the Department of Communication and codirector of the Leadership Studies Program at George Fox College. He received his Ph.D. in speech communication from the University of Denver. His research interests include leadership communication, creativity, and leadership ethics.

In addition to acting as problem finders, transformational leaders foster an atmosphere encouraging experimentation and innovation. Toleration of failure is the key element of a creative climate. Transformational leaders believe failure is an important tool because those who do not fail are neither trying nor learning.

A company recognized as one of the most innovative in the world, 3M, is an example of how important it is for an organization to foster creativity. At 3M, employees are rewarded for creative success but are not punished for creative failure. Any mistake is tolerated at 3M as long as it is an original mistake. According to 3M executive Allen Jacobson, "Outsiders say we are very lenient in rewarding failure."

Actually, 3M is very insightful in realizing that nothing inhibits creativity like the fear of punishment for failure. More than 60 percent of new product ideas developed at 3M ultimately fail. Yet successes like the Post-it Note (those adhesive-backed note pads found in virtually every office in the world) more than compensate for 3M's product failures. Sales of Post-it Notes alone generate over $300 million per year for 3M.

The Post-it Note, like so many products at 3M, was developed by using materials from a failed venture. The original compound for the adhesive on the back of the Post-it Note was initially considered a failure. The adhesive compound was deemed useless because of its limited adherence to other objects, the very quality that made that adhesive a success in the Post-it Note!

*Interactive*

Extraordinary leadership is the product of extraordinary communication. Transformational leaders are masterful communicators able to articulate and define ideas and concepts that escape others. Transformational leaders spend much of their time talking with followers. They walk the shop floor or the office suite shaking hands, joking, asking questions, providing information, and most of all listening. Extraordinary leaders do not hole up in corporate offices.

One organization that embodies the transformational philosophy is Johnsonville Foods of Sheboygan, Wisconsin. At Johnsonville, traditional organizational structure was replaced by self-directed work teams. Middle managers adopted the leadership roles of coordinators and coaches rather than the traditional roles of supervisor and disciplinarian. These leaders were made responsible for teaching team members how to lead themselves more effectively. They coaxed, cajoled, encouraged, challenged, offered advice, and inspired team members. In short, the primary job responsibility of organizational leaders at Johnsonville Foods became one of interacting with team members. Another organization that emphasizes interaction is AT&T. CEO Mike Armstrong brings together the company's top executives each Monday for a day-long meeting. To keep an organization on track the key is to "communicate, communicate, communicate," explains Armstrong.

*Visionary*

Communicating a vision to followers may well be the most important act of the transformational leader. A vision is a concise statement or description of where the organization is headed. Compelling visions provide a sense of purpose and encourage commitment. Followers achieve more and make more ethical decisions when they pursue a worthy goal.

In a study of ninety transformational leaders from government, education, music, business, and sport, Warren Bennis and Burt Nanus found that the leaders spent a good deal of time talking with employees, clients, other leaders, and consultants before developing a vision for their organization. Leaders carefully studied their organization's past, to determine the reasons for success and failures; the present, to determine current strengths, weaknesses, and resources; and the future, to identify possible long-term social, political, and environmental changes. The leaders then interpreted the information to construct a realistic vision that fit the norms of the group and inspired followers to put forth more effort.

To be compelling a vision must be both desirable and attainable. According to Harvard professor John Kotter, an effective vision is specific enough to provide real guidance to people yet vague enough to encourage initiative and remain relevant under a variety of conditions. If a vision is too specific, the vision may leave followers floundering when achieved.

An example of a vision statement too specific was President John Kennedy's vision of NASA stated in 1962. Kennedy defined NASA's vision as "landing a man on the moon and returning him safely to earth before this decade is out." When a vision this specific is achieved (as it was in 1969), followers may feel a sense of confusion regarding what to do next (as NASA did in the 1970s and 1980s).

More effective vision statements offer general guiding philosophies without detailing a specific end result. The following vision statements are examples of well-conceived organizational visions:

| | |
|---|---|
| Apple Computer | To make a contribution to the world by making tools for the mind that advance humankind |
| Bristol-Myers Squibb | To extend and enhance human life by providing the highest-quality health and personal care products |
| Disney Corporation | To make people happy |

These vision statements provide a general philosophy that guides the actions of members of the organization.

### Empowering

Transformational leaders know how to give power away and how to make others feel powerful. Transformational leaders give followers access to the funds, materials, authority, and information needed to complete tasks and to develop new ideas.

These leaders allow others to make decisions rather than insisting on making all the decisions themselves.

Along with distributing power throughout the organization, transformational leaders help followers believe in their own abilities. Psychologist Albert Bandura refers to believing in one's own abilities as the efficacy expectation. Followers who believe in their abilities to deal with people, events, and situations encountered in the organization are those who have a sense of self-efficacy. These individuals are more likely to take initiative and persist in the face of difficult circumstances than those followers who have little or no sense of self-efficacy. Transformational leaders build followers' perceptions of self-efficacy by providing positive emotional support, particularly during times of stress, by offering words of encouragement, by modeling successful performance, and by structuring tasks so followers experience initial successes that build their expectations for future triumphs.

Max DePree, former CEO of the Herman Miller furniture company, goes so far as to suggest that leaders act as servants to their followers. As DePree explains, "The first responsibility of the leader is to define reality. The last is to say thank you. In between the two, the leader must become a servant and a debtor." As such, followers are empowered to complete the tasks assigned to them. The leader serves followers by providing necessary resources and encouragement to allow for the completion of assignments in the most productive manner. In the words of Jan Carlzon, the president of Scandinavian Airline Systems, "If you're not serving the customer, you'd better be serving someone who is."

### Passionate

Transformational leaders are passionately committed to their work. They love their jobs and have a great deal of affection for the people with whom they work. This passion and personal enthusiasm motivates others to perform to their highest levels as well. Transformational leaders are able to encourage others because they first and foremost encourage themselves.

This type of passion is exemplified in a story related by Fred Smith, CEO of Federal Express. The story involves the actions of a Federal Express courier. The courier persisted in scanning and loading customers' packages even though the building was shaking and stairways were collapsing because of an earthquake. The courier struggled to carry the shipment down nine flights of rubble-filled stairs to a waiting van and drove to the airport just in time for the shipment to be loaded onto a waiting plane. Such passion is a reflection of the organization and its leaders.

By demonstrating the characteristics of transformational leaders, individuals can begin to transform themselves and their organizations. By encouraging creativity, fostering open communication, demonstrating forward thinking, sharing responsibility, and exhibiting commitment, leaders can construct organizations prepared to meet the challenges of the future.

# REFERENCES AND SUGGESTED READINGS

Albert, R. D. 1992. Polycultural perspectives on organizational communication. *Management Communication Quarterly* 6(1): 74–84.

Applbaum, R. L., E. M. Bodaken, K. K. Sereno, and K. W. Anatol. 1974. *The process of group communication.* Chicago: Science Research.

Argyris, C. 1962. *Interpersonal competence and organizational effectiveness.* Homewood, IL: Dorsey Press.

Bacon, C. C., and W. R. Ullmann. 1986. *Dimensions of interpersonal communication competence, communication accuracy, as predictors of managerial performance and job satisfaction.* Paper presented at the Speech Communication Association Convention, November, Chicago.

Barge, J. K. 1994. *Leadership: Communication skills for organizations and groups.* New York: St. Martin's.

Bennis, W. 1992. Leading change. *USC Business,* winter/spring: 47–51.

Bennis, W. 1999. Becoming a leader of leaders. In *Rethinking the future,* ed. R. Gibson, 148–162. London: Nicholas Brealey.

Bennis, W., and B. Nanus. 1985. *Leaders: The strategies for taking charge.* New York: Harper and Row.

Blackburn, R., and B. Rosen. 1993. Total quality and human resources management: Lessons learned from Baldrige award-winning companies. *Academy of Management Executive* 7(3): 49–66.

Blake, R. R., and J. S. Mouton. 1964. *The managerial grid.* Houston, TX: Gulf.

Blake, R. R., and J. S. Mouton. 1985. *The managerial grid III: The key to leadership excellence.* Houston, TX: Gulf.

Corey, G. 1985. *Theory and practice of group counseling.* 2d ed. Monterey, CA: Brooks/Cole.

Cox, T., Jr. 1993. *Cultural diversity in organizations.* San Francisco: Berrett-Koehler.

Cushman, D., and S. King. 1993. High-speed management: A revolution in organizational communication in the 1990s. *Communication yearbook* 16, ed. S. Deetz, 209–236. Newbury Park, CA: Sage.

Davis, K. 1967. *Human relations at work.* New York: McGraw-Hill.

Deetz, S. 1993. *The negotiative organization: Building responsive and responsible workplaces.* Paper available through the Center for Negotiation and Conflict Resolution, Rutgers University, Newark.

Dobbins, G. H., and S. J. Zaccaro. 1986. The effects of group cohesion and leader behavior on subordinate satisfaction. *Group and Organization Studies* 11(3): 203–219.

Drucker, P. 1966. *The effective manager.* New York: Harper and Row.

Eisenberg, E. M. 1984. Ambiguity as strategy in organizational communication. *Communication Monographs* 51: 227–242.

Ellis, K. and P. Shockley-Zalabak. 1999. *Communicating with management: Relating trust to job satisfaction and organizational effectiveness.* Paper presented at the National Communication Association Convention, November, Seattle, WA.

Fairhurst, G. 2001. Dualisms in leadership research. In *The new handbook of organizational communication: Advances in theory, research, and methods,* eds. F. Jablin and L. Putnam, 379–439. Thousand Oaks, CA.: Sage.

Fairhurst, G. T., and R. A. Saar. (1996). *The art of framing: Managing the language of leadership.* San Francisco: Jossey-Bass.

Fairhurst, G. T., S. G. Green, and B. K. Snavely. 1984. Face support in controlling poor performance. *Human Communication Research* 11(2): 272–295.

Fiedler, F. 1967. *A theory of leadership effectiveness.* New York: McGraw-Hill.

French, J., and B. Raven. 1968. The bases of social power. In *Group dynamics,* eds. D. Cartwright and A. Zander, 259–268. New York: Harper and Row.

Gardner, H. (1995). *Leading minds.* New York: Basic Books.

Geier, J. 1967. A trait approach to the study of leadership in small groups. *Journal of Communication* 17: 316–323.

Hackman, M., and C. Johnson. 1991. *Leadership: A communication perspective.* Prospect Heights, IL: Waveland.

Hammer, M. 1996. Beyond reengineering. *Executive Excellence* 13(8): 13–14.

Harris, P. and R. Moran. 1996. *Managing cultural differences: Leadership strategies for a new world of business.* Houston, TX: Gulf.

Hesselbein, F., M. Goldsmith, and R. Beckhard, eds. 1996. *The leader of the future.* San Francisco: Jossey-Bass.

Hersey, P., and K. Blanchard. 1974. So you want to know your leadership style? *Training and Development Journal* 28(2): 22–37.

Hersey, P., and K. Blanchard. 1977. *Management of organizational behavior: Utilizing human resources.* 3d ed. Englewood Cliffs, NJ: Prentice Hall.

Jung, D., and B. Avolio. 1999. Effects of leadership style and followers' cultural orientation on performance in group and individual task conditions. *Academy of Management Journal* 42(2): 208–218.

Kanter, R. M. 1996. World-class leaders: The power of partnering. In *The leader of the future,* eds. F. Hesselbein, M. Goldsmith, and R. Beckhard, 89–98. San Francisco: Jossey-Bass.

Kelleher, D., P. Finestone, and A. Lowy. 1986. Managerial learning: First notes from an unstudied frontier. *Group and Organization Studies* 11(3): 169–202.

Larson, C., and F. LaFasto. 1989. *TeamWork: What must go right/What can go wrong.* Newbury Park, CA: Sage.

Lawler, E. E., III. 1994. Total quality management and employee involvement: Are they compatible? *Academy of Management Executive* 8(1): 68–76.

Lee, J. 2000. *Leader-member exchange, perceived organizational justice, and cooperative communication.* Paper presented at the National Communication Association Convention, November, Seattle, WA.

Manz, C. 1986. Self-leadership: Toward an expanded theory of self-influence processes in organizations. *Academy of Management Review* 11: 585–600.

Manz, C., and H. Sims. 1989. *SuperLeadership: Leading others to lead themselves.* New York: Prentice Hall.

Marshall, A. A., and C. Stohl. 1993. Being "in the know" in a participative management system. *Management Communication Quarterly* 6(4): 372–404.

Peppers, L., and J. Ryan. 1986. Discrepancies between actual and aspired self: A comparison of leaders and nonleaders. *Group and Organization Studies* 11(3): 220–228.

Shockley-Zalabak, P. 1994. *Understanding organizational communication: Cases, commentaries, and conversations.* White Plains, NY: Longman.

Sims, H., Jr., and P. Lorenzi. 1992. *The new leadership paradigm.* Newbury Park, CA: Sage.

Skaret, D. J., and N. S. Bruning. 1986. Attitudes about the work group: An added moderator of the relationship between leader behavior and job satisfaction. *Group and Organization Studies* 11(3): 254–279.

Snavely, W. B., and E. V. Walters. 1983. Differences in communication competence among administrator social styles. *Journal of Applied Communication Research* 11(2): 120–135.

Soares, E. J., and L. J. Chase. 1985. *Communication elements of managerial competence.* Paper presented at the International Communication Association Convention, May, Honolulu, HI.

Stogdill, R. M., and A. E. Coons. 1957. *Leader behavior: Its description and measurement.* Research monograph No. 88. Columbus: Bureau of Business Research, Ohio State University.

Tannenbaum, R., and W. Schmidt. 1958. How to choose a leadership pattern. *Harvard Business Review* 36: 95–101.

Toffler, A., and H. Toffler. 1994. *War and anti-war: Survival at the dawn of the twenty-first century.* New York: Bantam Books/Doubleday Del.

Topaz, L. 1989/1990. Empowerment—Human resource management in the 90's. *Management Quarterly* 30(4): 3–8.

Van Velsor, E., and J. B. Leslie. 1995. Why executives derail: Perspectives across time and cultures. *Academy of Management Executive* 9(4): 62–72.

Wheatley, M. 1992. *Leadership and the new science.* San Francisco: Berrett-Koehler.

White, R., and R. Lippitt. 1960. *Autocracy and democracy: An experimental inquiry.* New York: Harper and Row.

Zenger, J., E. Musselwhite, K. Hurson, and C. Perrin. 1993. *Leading teams: Mastering the new role.* Homewood, IL: Business One Irwin.

# CHAPTER EIGHT

# PARTICIPATING IN ORGANIZATIONS
## Developing Critical Organizational Communication Competencies

---

DEVELOPING COMPETENCIES THROUGH . . .

**KNOWLEDGE**

Distinguishing between decision making and problem solving

Describing problem-solving processes

Describing types of organizational interviews

Describing types of organizational presentations

Describing types of organizational communications technologies

**SENSITIVITY**

Understanding individual and organizational influences and barriers for decision making and problem solving

Considering the organizational and personal impact of interviews, presentations, and use of technology

**SKILLS**

Applying analysis capabilities to group interactions and case studies

Assessing individual communication competency needs

Practicing analysis capabilities for interviews and presentations

## VALUES

Relating decision making and problem solving to excellence

Understanding effective communication as essential to decision making and problem solving

Understanding the importance of individual communication competencies for organizational participation

Relating effective interviews, presentations, and use of technologies to overall organizational effectiveness

■ ■ ■ ■ ■

## THE DECISIONS, PROBLEMS, MORE DECISIONS CASE

Joan Murphy had an important and exciting dilemma. She had been offered management training positions by two of the top retailers in the country. When she had interviewed, Joan had been hoping to get an offer from one of the two, but in her wildest dreams she had not expected to hear from both. The two companies were making similar financial offers; both were in the Midwest, where she hoped to stay; and both were reported to have excellent training programs with fast promotional progress. Both alternatives were attractive. How should she decide?

Joan went to work for Dayton Retailers. The decision had been a difficult one, requiring considerable weighing of various alternatives. She felt good about Dayton and hoped they liked her work. Joan did not, however, feel comfortable with some of the behaviors being exhibited by others in her management training group. Joan knew that at least two of her peers in the training program were having other friends at Dayton complete their project assignments. To make matters worse, the two were getting the highest praise in the class and seemed likely to get the best assignments when the courses were over. Joan didn't think that was fair or good for Dayton. She questioned what she should do, especially when others might view her complaints as simply trying to get ahead. Joan decided to work very hard on her final presentation for the management training course to demonstrate to the trainers and the trainees as well what her capabilities were.

Joan's assignment to the Ridgefield Shopping Center was terrific. To be put in charge of Junior Sportswear in a thriving store was quite a plum. Her only difficulty was caused by department remodeling, which limited space to bring in new, competitive lines. Three new lines had been proposed, but space limitations permitted the stocking of only one of the three. Joan had called a meeting of the junior sportswear buyers, the top salespeople from the floor, and the floor manager to attempt to decide which of the three would be best. Joan began to think about how the group should approach the decision.

After several successful months at Ridgefield, Joan was transferred to Glencrest, a store that was struggling. Although she knew this position was a real learning

*(continued)*

opportunity, Joan was sorry to leave Ridgefield and the wonderful group of people with whom she was working. Joan also knew that the staff of Glencrest was anything but happy to have her come. The manager Joan was replacing had been popular, and the staff were not pleased at the changes management was making. They appeared to be especially apprehensive about the new computerized inventory system due for installation. Joan knew the staff did not dislike her personally but were unhappy about management's statement that the store would have to establish a better track record or suffer staff and merchandise reductions. Joan's first responsibilities were to change the sales promotions schedules for the next several months and to get the new inventory system running. She needed the cooperation of her new staff and their advice on how to develop a promotions plan that could hope to increase sales in the struggling store. After all, she did not know this market area nearly as well as Ridgefield. Joan thought about the type of group she would form for solving the Glencrest problems. She decided to interview each staff member individually to learn more about them and to understand what they might contribute to changes at Glencrest.

## INTRODUCTION

Joan Murphy is engaged in using communication competencies common to all types of organizational situations. Her interviewing skills resulted in two jobs offers. She has an individual decision to make when she must choose between these alternatives. She encounters a problem when peers in her training group violate ethical standards of conduct, potentially positioning them for superior job assignments. She must prepare a final presentation for her management training course. In her first assignment, Joan must work with a group of people charged with deciding among three competitive lines. Finally, she is responsible for attempting to bring together a team that is capable of solving a sales problem while introducing new workplace technology.

The decisions Joan makes and the effectiveness of the problem solving in which she engages not only will affect her personal career but also will influence the success of Dayton Retailers. Indeed, it is fair to say that decision making, problem solving, interpersonal and small-group interactions, and presentations can be described as guiding processes for all organizational functioning. In this chapter decision making and problem solving are defined, various types of organizational interviews are discussed, and important characteristics of organizational presentations, including training or educational presentations, are described. In addition, the chapter describes competencies important for the use of communications technologies. Competencies are built through a variety of decision-making and problem-solving cases, and interviewing and presentational competencies are developed through an understanding of basic preparation strategies coupled with practice opportunities. Finally, you will be asked to examine the technologies that you believe will be most important for communicating within the organizations of today and tomorrow.

This chapter is designed to develop *knowledge* by identifying critical communication competencies for participation in organizations. The competencies developed include decision making, problem solving, interviewing, presentations, and communications technologies. *Sensitivity* is encouraged through awareness of individual and organizational influences for decision making and problem solving and by considering ethical and credibility issues for interviewing and presentations. *Skills* are increased through decision-making and problem-solving practice, interviewing experiences, and preparation for presentations. *Values* are influenced by relating quality decisions and problem solving to overall organizational effectiveness and encouraging an understanding of the importance of ethical and credible individual behaviors during all types of organizational interactions including interviews and formal presentations. Finally, all four competencies—knowledge, sensitivity, skills, and values—interact during analysis and practice opportunities.

## DEFINING DECISION MAKING AND PROBLEM SOLVING

**Decision making**
Process of choosing from among several alternatives.

**Problem solving**
Multistage process for moving an issue, situation, or state from an undesirable to a more desirable condition.

**Decision making** is the process of choosing from among several alternatives, whereas **problem solving** is a multistage process for moving an issue, situation, or state from an undesirable to a more desirable condition. Although problem solving includes decision making, decision making and problem solving are not one and the same process. Decision making depends on individuals and groups choosing from among known alternatives. Problem solving is the process by which individuals and groups generate alternatives and evaluate those alternatives in light of the identified problem.

Joan Murphy is engaged in both individual and group decision making and problem solving. Joan and her coworkers have alternatives from which to choose as well as sales problems to attempt to understand and correct. The decision-making and problem-solving processes in which they are engaged require them to take risks. These risks ultimately will contribute to the effectiveness of Dayton Retailers.

All decision making and problem solving involve a level of risk. Decisions, whether as choices from among well-defined alternatives or the result of complex problem solving, are desired courses of action before the results of the action are known. Unknown results represent risk. The level of risk is related to the importance of the decision: more risk generally is associated with more important decisions. In other words, the more that can go well as a result of a good decision, the more that can usually go wrong if that decision fails.

Joan Murphy is faced with a high-risk situation as she moves to the Glencrest store. Sales are down and the manager she is replacing was popular with her subordinates. If Joan is successful, the store will have an increase in sales and Dayton management will view her efforts favorably. Joan has a lot to gain, and so does Dayton. If her decision-making and problem-solving efforts are ineffective, the store faces staff and merchandise reductions and Joan's own career may be damaged. A good decision-making process will not guarantee success, but a poor process will almost certainly contribute to failure. Thus, both individual and group decision-making and problem-solving capabilities influence personal and organizational effectiveness. The following sections in this chapter describe important influences and methods for decision making and problem solving and discuss a variety of problem-solving processes.

## INFLUENCES FOR DECISION MAKING AND PROBLEM SOLVING

Four primary factors influence individual and group decision making and problem solving. (See Figure 8.1.) These factors—organizational culture, decision/problem issues, technical competencies, and communication competencies—influence the methods used for problem solving, the quality of decisions made, and the satisfaction participants feel with decision-making and problem-solving processes.

### Culture

Most scholars agree that central to the notion of organizational culture are the decision-making processes in which organizational members engage. As Phillip Tompkins and George Cheney (1983) have pointed out, "the examination of the decision-making process provides a means of tapping the mutual influences of people and organizations." Indeed, the very activity of organizing can be described as synonymous with the decision-making process. Organizing can be seen as a conscious limitation of alternatives and therefore decision making. It is this limitation of alternatives (decisions) that becomes the shared realities of the organization or its culture.

Organizational cultures influence the methods of decision making. Some organizations expect leaders to make and announce decisions. The military, for example, does not depend on majority rule or consensus decision making for determining plans of action. The university, on the other hand, has a long tradition of consensus decision making at all organizational levels. Some organizations expect individuals to make decisions about their jobs or areas of responsibility without notifying others or seeking extensive input. Other organizations emphasize notification of others of intended plans or actions even if such actions are not expected to affect those being notified. Particular organizations may value broad participation in decision making, whereas others may emphasize limited access to decision makers. It is appropriate to conclude that the methods and levels of participation desired for decision making and problem solving are reflections of organizational values and culture.

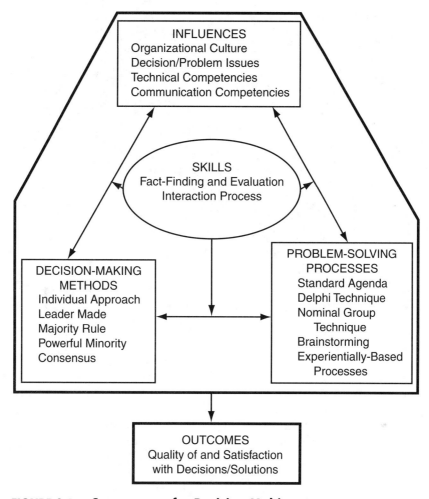

**FIGURE 8.1   Components for Decision Making and Problem Solving**

## The Decision/Problem Issue

The nature of a problem also influences decision making and problem solving. Is the problem highly complex? Does the organization have available resources to understand the problem? How important is this decision or solution to organizational effectiveness? Has the organization previously attempted to solve this type of dilemma? Complexity, resources, importance, and previous experience concerning problems all influence how individuals and organizations approach decisions. Complex problems may require more extensive involvement, a higher level of participation, more thoroughness, and greater resources than do less complex problems. The importance of the decision or problem may influence who is responsible and how much time is allocated for decision making.

## Communication Competency

Throughout this text the need for communication competency has been continually described. Many of the competencies discussed relate to effective decision making and problem solving. What motivates us and what we believe motivates others influences the quality of our decision-making participation. Our perception of our personal competencies and our predispositions for communication help determine how and when we engage in individual and group decision making. Our interpersonal effectiveness contributes to whether we can influence others during problem solving. Our comfort or discomfort with conflict may determine whether we will contribute information if others are likely to disagree. In addition to our individual participation, the communication competencies of others influence the quality of decision making. Individuals who fail to participate even though they have needed information lower the quality of problem solving. Because decision making and problem solving occur through human communication, the ability and willingness of all involved to engage in quality participation influence the ultimate quality of decisions.

## Technical Competency

The final factor to influence decision making and problem solving is technical competency. Do individuals involved in decision making have the technical background or competencies necessary to approach the problem thoughtfully? Are decision makers aware of the best available information on which to base their evaluations? Has the group been formed with a distribution of appropriate technical skills? Excellence in decision making requires a communication process that supports excellence and appropriate technical backgrounds or information. Most of us have attended meetings in which we were willing to participate and yet found that we had no relevant information for the problem at hand. We had to depend on others for our understanding. That dependence probably worked as long as other group members brought appropriate technical competencies to the decision. All too often, however, groups make important decisions without a full range of available information.

# METHODS FOR DECISION MAKING AND PROBLEM SOLVING

Influenced by culture, the issue at hand, and communication and technical competencies, organizational members choose from among a variety of methods and processes for decision making and problem solving. The following methods—individual approach, leader mandate, majority rule, powerful minority, and consensus—are described to illustrate the diversity of options available for individuals, groups, or entire organizations. It is important to note that in the twenty-first century, the emphasis on decision making and problem solving is rapidly shifting from an individual to a group or team responsibility. The emphasis on group/team problem solving and decision making increasingly asks those who will actually implement a decision to make that decision. In the past managers characteristically made decisions that were carried out at least one organizational level removed from the manager.

## Individual Approaches

Individuals and groups engage in decision making and problem solving with a variety of methods and approaches. Individuals make decisions with a range of involvement from others. At times they come to important decisions without others even knowing that a decision is being considered. An individual may decide to apply for a promotion, leave a company, or go back to school based on very private evaluations of alternatives. At other times individual decisions result from extensive interaction with others. An individual, for example, may seek feedback from peers, supervisors, or professional advisors to determine needed skill improvements. A supervisor may have discussions with other supervisors in an effort to solve a performance problem, or a supervisor may work directly with the subordinates in question. In any event, individual decision makers have the option to consider their alternatives alone or with others.

## Leader Mandate

Groups also come to decisions with a variety of methods. When a group is hopelessly deadlocked, for example, a leader may make a decision and announce the decision to the group. The authority of the leadership position may be sufficient to enforce the decision without regard to disagreements. Some leaders prefer this method of decision making and only use group members to gather information

**Leader-made decision**
Leader of a group makes a decision and announces the decision to the group.

from which the leader will arrive at the final decision. Decisions made in this fashion may or may not be of high quality. Research suggests, however, that **leader-made decisions** frequently have less group commitment than decisions in which members are more actively involved.

## Majority Rule

Majority rule is a common method for decision making. When more than 50 percent of a group agree, a decision is reached. Some groups reach majority agreement informally, whereas others, such as legislative bodies, have operating rules and procedures that govern majority decisions. Although faster

**Majority-rule decision**
When more than 50 percent of a group agree, a decision has been reached.

than moving a group to true consensus, the majority-rule method may not adequately account for the views of the minority. **Majority-rule decisions** can be high in quality, but they can also ignore central issues of concern.

**Powerful-minority decision**
Process for decision making occurring when group membership is characterized by unequal distribution of power among members. Those members who have the most power (although in the numerical minority) are in a position to assume decision-making responsibility.

## Powerful Minority

Although used less frequently than majority vote, the **powerful-minority decision** is another way groups can make decisions. When group membership is characterized by unequal distribution of power among members, those members who have the most power (although in the numerical minority) are in a position to assume decision-making responsibility. The powerful-minority method can be effective when the minority members have the best information on which to base the decision. This method fails, however, if other-than-expert power drives the decision. Examples of failure of the powerful-minority method can be found in organizational resistance to change. Longtime organizational members who control decision making through seniority and position level may retard needed changes by ignoring the expert opinions of other group members with less organizational power and influence.

**Consensus**
Method for decision making that results in all members agreeing on what is best and supporting the group decision.

## Consensus

The **consensus** method results in a decision all members can agree is best and all can support. As John Brilhart (1986) suggests, "When a true consensus has been reached, the result is usually a superior quality decision, a high level of member satisfaction with it, and acceptance of the result." The consensus method may take more time than other methods, unless considerable agreement existed at the beginning of the process. The consensus method does not rest with everyone completely agreeing but with everyone reaching a level of agreement sufficient for decision support. Brilhart states: "Unanimity—the state of perfect consensus in which every group member believes that the decision achieved is the best that could be made—is not at all common. But if all members accept that a consensus may require compromise and collaboration, all will usually support it even though it is not the decision some might have preferred."

# BARRIERS TO EFFECTIVE DECISION MAKING AND PROBLEM SOLVING

Throughout the text a variety of knowledge, sensitivity, skill, and value competencies important for organizational effectiveness have been developed. Individual experiences in organizations have been described, and positive and negative group participation behaviors have been identified. The importance of leadership and management communication has been discussed. In general, it is fair to say, the important roles, relationships, and responsibilities that relate to organizational decision making and problem solving, the subject of this chapter, have been explored.

We all have participated in groups that made bad decisions or failed to solve real problems. Think for a moment about those groups. Can you identify any particular barriers to effectiveness? What would you do differently if you were to meet again?

Barriers to effective decision making and problem solving can be described in organizational task, procedural, and interpersonal areas. It is important for our knowledge and sensitivity competency development for us to understand what commonly goes wrong during problem solving even when individuals have the best of intentions.

## Organizational Barriers

With virtually all types of organizations engaging in problem solving and decision making and with 80 to 90 percent of Fortune 500 companies using a variety of group decision-making processes, it is surprising to many that the American Management Association has estimated that only about 50 percent of organizational decisions are ever implemented. The reasons are diverse, but two—no commitment to the decision and a lack of resources—are among the most prominent. Numerous research studies have highlighted the importance of multiple and divergent points of view for effective organizational decision making. Elizabeth Morrison and Frances Milliken (2000) argue that there are powerful forces in many organizations that cause widespread withholding of information about potential problems contributing to poor decision making. They refer to these barriers as producing organizational silence. Morrison and Milliken suggest that dynamics giving rise to organizational silence include beliefs by top management that employees are self-interested, that management knows best, and that unity is good and dissent is bad. Organizational silence can retard change and development, inhibit effective decision making, and contribute to low commitment and trust. Organizational structures and policies that become decision-making barriers include centralization of decision making and a lack of formal upward feedback mechanisms. Organizational silence is promoted when managers fear negative feedback, reject or respond negatively to dissent, and do not solicit information about negative feedback.

## Task Barriers

Groups make poor decisions when they short-circuit problem analysis. One of the most important barriers to problem-solving effectiveness is an inadequate description of problems. Group members frequently jump to solutions that appeal to them rather than work toward solutions better suited to the complexity of the issues. In addition, both individuals and groups have been known to overestimate the positive benefits of a chosen alternative while rejecting accurate or valid information in favor of more popular but flawed data.

## Procedural Barriers

Groups also make poor decisions when role ambiguity contributes to confusion about responsibilities, process, or leadership. Who is responsible for what, how decisions are to be made, and what authority resides in the group are all procedural questions that when inadequately answered contribute to ineffective group decisions. The lack of agendas, too much or too little time for meetings, and a variety of other procedural issues are related to low-quality decisions.

## Interpersonal Barriers

We have all observed or participated in interpersonal conflict that blocked effective decision making. We know from experience that poor leadership or a variety of self-centered or ego-centered behaviors can negatively influence any group. What we may not see is that group cohesion—too much to too little—can influence the quality of decisions. There are potential dangers from groupthink, or conformity behaviors that suspend critical thinking. It is important also to recognize that too little group cohesion can leave members distrustful and afraid to risk the best of their thinking. In addition, influential group members have been known to override the logic of others, leading to poor choices. Others discount the contributions of some group members and engage in disagreement behaviors without describing the substance of the disagreement.

Needless to say, so far only the major barriers to effective problem solving and decision making have been identified. What additional barriers can you identify? How can you advise a group to avoid the more serious ones?

# PROBLEM-SOLVING PROCESSES

A variety of processes can be identified for both individual and group problem solving. These processes help individuals and groups move from problem identification to determination of action appropriate for problem needs. Although these processes include numerous decision-making activities, they are described as problem-solving processes because of their focus on moving situations, issues, or problems from undesirable to more desirable states. Although decision making occurs during problem solving, problem-solving processes include numerous other stages. The Standard Agenda, brainstorming, the Delphi Technique, and nominal group process approaches to problem solving are described next. The goal of all these group-process designs and others not covered in this text is creative decisions that will contribute to organizational excellence. Which process is most appropriate depends on the needs of the problem, the competencies—both technical and communication—of all involved, the culture of the organization, and a variety of other situation-specific concerns.

## The Standard Agenda: A Rational Model

The **Standard Agenda** is a group application of what John Dewey (1910) identified as reflective thinking necessary for individual problem solving. It can apply to both individuals and groups. Julia Wood, Gerald Phillips, and Douglas Pedersen (1986) suggest that the Standard Agenda can be described as follows:

**Standard Agenda**
Process for decision making based on reflective thinking, beginning with understanding the charge, and followed by understanding and phrasing the question, fact-finding, setting criteria and limitations, discovering and selecting solutions, and preparing and presenting the final report.

**THE DIAGNOSTIC PHASE**

1. *Understanding the charge.* Why is the group in existence? What is it to do? What form does its output take? Who gets it? What is to be done with it?
2. *Understanding and phrasing the question.* What, precisely, is the group to examine or inquire about? What do the words in the question mean? Are all technical words and issues clear to the members?
3. *Fact-finding.* What are the symptoms of the problem? What is the cause of the symptoms? What is happening that should not be happening? What is not happening that should be happening? Who is suffering from the situation? How badly? What will happen if the situation is not remedied? How must the question be modified in light of fact-finding?
4. *Setting criteria and limitations.* What is possible (as opposed to desirable)? What are the legal, moral, financial, practical, and logistical limits on decision making? What would a solution look like? What would be happening that is not now happening? What will stop happening?

**THE SOLUTION PHASE**

5. *Discovering and selecting solutions.* What are the alternatives? How does each meet the goals? How do they measure up against the limitations? Which provides more of what is wanted with the least new harm? Which one should be selected? Who is to do what about what, when, and where and with what projected effect, and how will it be paid for? What evaluation plan can be used to measure the effectiveness of the solution?
6. *Preparing and presenting the final report.* What must be written down? What must be said? When, where, and to whom? How can the final report be most persuasively presented?

**Brainstorming**
Technique for generating ideas for problem solving based on methods that break away from linear and controlled processes. The process encourages maximum idea generation in a short period of time.

# Brainstorming

One of the most used and popular processes for generating ideas for problem solving is **brainstorming.** In use for over thirty years, the technique breaks away from linear and controlled processes and seeks creative thinking based on four basic rules: (1) criticism is not appropriate during idea generation; (2) all ideas are welcome (the more absurd, the better); (3) quantity is wanted (the more ideas, the better); and (4) combinations and alterations of ideas are sought (improve on the ideas of others and combine them). Brainstorming is often used to help understand or diagnose a problem and to elicit ideas when groups are in an alternative- or solution-generation phase. Brainstorming is used as a process in and of itself and often within the framework of the Standard Agenda. It reduces dependency on single powerful or influential individuals by encouraging broad participation without negative evaluation. Brainstorming also encourages a maximum output in a short period of time.

Brainstorming has evolved over the past several years to include the use of metaphors and fantasy chaining—sometimes referred to as synectics—to generate new ideas. Metaphors are used to stimulate innovation and creativity while attempting to link seemingly unrelated concepts through their potential connections and relationships. Fantasy chaining is a form of brainstorming that uses a spontaneously emerging story or drama to help a group unfold or describe a situation or problem. Group members build on the ideas of others to develop a chain of events. Ideas for the problem at hand come from the collectively generated fiction of the group. A popular brainstorming approach that uses both metaphors and fantasy chaining is synectics. Synectics generally refers to a facilitated process through which group members explore problems in terms of what the problem is also like and how it can best be described. A synectics approach might guide a group in understanding an air traffic control system by understanding how schools of fish swim without bumping into one another. Regardless of the specifics of the approach, brainstorming is designed to produce innovative thinking to assist in developing new views of problems as well as numerous alternative solutions.

## The Delphi Technique

**Delphi technique**
Process of group problem solving conducted through written response and critique of situations and the responses to those situations; designed to balance the influence of strong personalities.

The **Delphi technique** for solving group problems is designed to balance the influence of strong personalities on the problem-solving process. This technique is group problem solving conducted through written response and critique of situations and the responses to those situations. A group leader, referred to as a *charging authority*, forms the group and directs its activities through written correspondence. As Gerald Wilson, H. L. Goodall, and Christopher Waagen (1986) suggest: "By limiting the group communication format to written memos, and by channelling all communication directly between each member and the charging authority, the Delphi technique works through the centralized direction of the charging authority. Group members never know the rest of the group unless the charging authority reveals their identities."

Problem definition or decision alternatives and group membership are defined by the charging authority. Thus, the effectiveness of the Delphi technique rests largely with the leader's understanding of the issues, ability to communicate those issues to others, and capability in selecting competent group members. Once members are selected and the task is defined, each member is asked to respond directly to the leader, describing his or her position or offering solution strategies. The charging authority then responds to members with all the positions taken by each member. Group members, in turn, respond by continuing support for their original position, modifying that position in light of reviewing the positions of others, or changing their original position as a result of additional information. Written correspondence continues to be circulated until the group reaches a consensus.

The Delphi technique is designed to equalize power among group members and minimize the importance of oral communication skills. Written communication skills, however, replace oral skills in importance and influence. The Delphi technique is useful for problem solving when group members are in diverse geographic locations. A modification of the technique frequently occurs in organizations when managers circulate for comments correspondence concerning policy changes, new procedures, or a variety of other subjects. This modified Delphi technique is not based on member anonymity, nor does it require responses from all potential participants. The modified Delphi technique is a way of gathering feedback on problems and solutions without seeking full consensus. The major concern with a pure Delphi technique is the responsibility placed on the leader for problem definition and membership selection. This technique, however, does require members to articulate their positions in writing without undue influence from powerful others.

Group Decision Support Systems (GDSS), a form of the Delphi technique, function to provide balanced communication for decision making and problem solving. GDSS use networked computers with software capable of organizing a variety of decision inputs provided anonymously by group members. Group members are usually in a computer-equipped room where GDSS are used to facilitate a discussion or decision around a set of issues or problems. As with other versions of the Delphi technique, the goal is to increase participation without the influence of individual influence or power positions.

**Nominal group process**
Problem-solving process combining individual and group idea generation. Individuals contribute first in writing, and then the group discusses and decides.

## Nominal Group Process

**Nominal group process** is a combination of individual and group idea generation. Based on the assumption that each individual and group idea has value, a nominal group process begins with individuals silently writing down their ideas. Ideas are reported to the group at large for discussion, clarification, and usually a preliminary vote or decision. Discussion of issues occurs again, and a final decision vote is taken. The process is especially helpful for people who are fearful of free-wheeling discussions of ideas or among groups in which tension levels have previously been high.

**Experientially-based processes**
Processes reflecting bounded rationality contributing to satisficing, or the generation of decisions that are good enough if not the best. Processes use a variety of past experiences, emotional reactions, and knowledge and beliefs in producing decisions often not possible with more strictly rational approaches.

## Experientially-Based Processes

In Chapter 4 the James March, Richard Cyert, and Herbert Simon concept of bounded rationality was introduced as a way to understand information processing and decision making. The concept of bounded rationality assumed that people intend to be rational, but with limited information-processing capacity, human decision making is based on selective perception and therefore exhibits "limited" rationality. Simon argued that individuals often make organizational decisions even though realizing that their decisions are based on partial information. Simon called this process "satisficing," or the making of decisions with the hope the decisions will be good enough if not the very best. This satisficing approach frequently uses individuals' past experiences and is mindful of organizational precedents developed while handling similar problems. We all bring to our decision-making efforts masses of facts, techniques, values, knowledge, beliefs, and awareness of outcomes of previous decisions. We use intuition, feelings, fears, hopes, power relationships, and a variety of other personal and organizational concerns to select positions and courses of action. We know that the fully rational or ideal solution often is simply not available or possible. We call these processes experientially based decisions.

# INCREASING DECISION-MAKING AND PROBLEM-SOLVING EFFECTIVENESS

Effective problem solving and decision making require individuals and groups to use a broad range of communication and technical competencies. In the next section of this chapter, the focus is on two types of skills necessary for problem solving: interaction process and fact-finding and evaluation skills. These communication competencies, coupled with competencies developed in previous chapters, form a basis for increasing our decision-making and problem-solving effectiveness.

**Interaction process skills**
Skills based on an understanding of the communication process; an awareness of individual predispositions, strategies, and tactics in a variety of circumstances; and knowledge and sensitivity for decision making and problem solving.

## Interaction Process Skills

Previously, individual strategies and tactics for effectiveness have been discussed. Yet to be described, however, are **interaction process skills** that relate to effectiveness for decision making and problem solving. Interaction process skills are based on an understanding of the communication process; an awareness of individual predispositions, strategies, and tactics in a variety of circumstances; and knowledge and sensitivity for decision-making and problem-solving processes. Interaction process skills help individuals and groups structure problem-solving discussions, exhibit productive individual behaviors, and avoid behaviors destructive to effective decision making and problem solving.

Brilhart (1986) has identified seven general principles for structuring effective problem-solving discussions:

1. Focus on the problem before thinking and talking about how to solve it.
2. Begin with a single, unambiguous problem question.
3. Develop a thorough statement of the problem analysis. Map the problem thoroughly (who, what, why, when, where, and how).
4. Be sure that the group members agree on criteria or ways of measuring the adequacy of decisions/solutions.

5. Resist evaluation/judgment when gathering ideas/solutions.
6. Avoid groupthink (conformity to the beliefs of the group or its leaders) through constructive disagreement.
7. Verbally plan for implementation and follow-up solutions.

These seven principles closely resemble the Standard Agenda discussed earlier in this chapter. There are, however, important distinctions. The Standard Agenda is a process for reflective thinking about problems designed to encourage workable solutions to which groups are committed. The seven principles for structuring group discussion are communication strategies and tactics that support the reflective thinking process. For example, the interaction principle of focusing on the problem before solutions refers to group member and leadership responsibilities to direct conversation toward problem definition and diagnosis without allowing members to jump ahead with recommendations for solutions. Obviously, the principle supports reflective-thinking processes, but it should be understood as a communication responsibility. Groups can intend to think reflectively about problems and still stray from that goal by engaging in and supporting communication behaviors that make their intended process less than effective. The principle of beginning with a single unambiguous question relates not only to developing a problem statement but also to the use of communication strategies and tactics such as questioning and active listening to determine whether the question contains levels of ambiguity for some group members. The communication skill is not just the formulation of a question statement but the ability to probe to discover what all group members understand as a result of the statement.

Interaction process skills can both restrict and assist in unleashing creativity during decision making and problem solving. Gay Lumsden and Donald Lumsden (1993) suggest that group interactions can contribute to mind locks or rigid assumptions about what individuals or groups should be. When interaction supports rigid mind locks, creativity shuts down. Lumsden and Lumsden give examples of Roger von Oech's Mind Locks:

1. The right answer.
2. That's not logical.
3. Follow the rules.
4. Be practical.
5. Avoid ambiguity.
6. To err is wrong.
7. Play is frivolous.
8. That's not my area.
9. Don't be foolish.
10. I'm not creative.

Lumsden and Lumsden recommend that group interactions be characterized by encouraging playfulness; by agreeing not to judge people or ideas; by engaging in a search for different, even bizarre, idea relationships; and by consciously breaking down barriers.

In work by Randy Hirokawa and Kathryn Rost (1992), the importance of interaction process skills is underscored in their proposed "vigilant interaction theory." Hirokawa and Rost propose that effective groups pay particular attention to process and specifically attend to assessing the nature of the task, assessing their standards for evaluation, assessing the strengths of their various alternatives, and finally assessing the negatives of their various alternatives.

## Fact-Finding and Evaluation Skills

We make decisions based on our evaluation of the information that bears on the decision. We solve problems based on information about the problem and decisions about the adequacy of our solutions. Furthermore, we base complex decisions on the information available to us, whether or not it is the best information. It is therefore fair to say that the quality of information we bring to decision-making and problem-solving processes directly influences the quality of our decisions and solutions.

To illustrate, let's assume for a moment that careful planning has gone into our long-awaited vacation. We've contacted several airlines and have selected what appears to be the best fare. We have asked friends about a possible hotel and selected the one most often recommended. We arrive at our destination and are pleased with our accommodations. The newspaper in our hotel room, however, is advertising air fares to the resort area, and these fares are at least $100 less than we paid. We also find that although our hotel is very nice, there are other charming inns that give a better view of the mountains. Suddenly, our well-laid plans begin to seem inadequate; we are unsure of our choices. How did that happen with all our careful planning? The answer is relatively simple. We made decisions about our flights and hotel reservations without all the available information. We simply did not have a comprehensive awareness of our alternatives. Our initial fact-finding was inadequate.

Lumsden and Lumsden (1993) identify four general categories of questions we can ask as we fact-find and evaluate information for problem solving and decision making. Lumsden and Lumsden suggest that we ask questions of fact, questions of value, questions of policy, and questions of prediction. Questions of fact help us understand how things can be measured or proved and whether our answer can be represented in numbers, historical records, empirical research, or expert testimony. Questions of value address the degree of significance of the issue or problem and assist us in prioritizing concepts and actions. Questions of value also relate problems and issues to moral, ethical, and value criteria. Questions of policy address what should be done. Both value and fact questions are subsumed in questions of policy when we are seeking actions as solutions to problems. Finally, questions of prediction are used to apply **fact-finding and evaluation skills** to seek to determine the future state of a problem or issue.

**Fact-finding and evaluation skills**
Skills that assist in the discovery and criticism of information used in problem solving and decision making.

## Information Criteria

How can we evaluate the information we need? What criteria are important for our fact-finding and evaluation skills? Dennis Gouran (1979) suggests that three characteristics of information should be considered in forming our decision-making rules: relevancy, sufficiency, and plausibility. *Relevancy* refers to the extent to which information bears directly on the matter for decision. In the case of our airline reservations, the fare information acquired was relevant but did not meet the second necessary characteristic, *sufficiency*. Sufficiency refers to the amount of information necessary to establish positions or claims, or to verify what is likely to be correct. The fare schedules acquired were relevant but did not represent all of the possible fares from airlines flying our desired route. Thus, the failure to meet the sufficiency criterion cost us over $100. Finally, *plausibility*, or the extent to which information is credible, also influences our decision. Again, our rate information was credible. The airline we chose sold us the ticket for the stated price. Even though we had relevant plausible information, however, the lack of a comprehensive set of fare schedules (sufficiency) causes us concern about our decision. The same might be said for our hotel selection. We gathered relevant and plausible information but did not have a full set of alternatives from which to choose.

Relevancy, sufficiency, and plausibility of information affect not only individual decisions but also the quality of group efforts. The fact-finding abilities of all involved in decision making influence the effectiveness of decisions and how satisfied individuals and entire organizations are with decision making and problem solving.

Fact-finding also includes locating information in files, libraries, archives, reports, and a variety of other documents. Librarians, computer searches, the Internet, and catalogue files are only a few of the resources used to identify information sources. Much to the surprise of many students, research skills previously applied to term papers and other similar reports are valuable organizational skills when decision making and problem solving require data collection. As stated earlier, the complex information age brings more potential information to bear on problems than at any previous period in human history. This sheer volume of information complicates the fact-finding process and makes our ability to locate and evaluate data of increasing importance.

■ ■ ■ ■ ■

## THE SPENDING MORE TO SAVE MORE PRESENTATION CASE

Nancy Winslow was concerned about next week's manufacturing staff meeting. She had wanted to be scheduled to talk to management about her training plan and budget but not necessarily in such a potentially difficult setting. Nancy had just been notified that she was to make a formal presentation justifying her request for $200,000 to train assembly workers on new equipment, including new messaging systems for work scheduling. The new equipment and communications technologies required

*(continued)*

improved reading comprehension, keyboarding, and mathematics skills. Nancy knew from her interviews with the affected workers that the need for skills training was great, but she was also aware that several influential managers opposed spending training time and money and favored replacing the most deficient employees. Nancy had hoped to convince the manufacturing manager of her plan before meeting with his staff. Now it was obvious that she would not have that opportunity and could expect serious challenges to her proposal.

Nancy began to think about the recent interviews and needs assessment she had conducted among assembly workers. Their responses and the production data supported her training proposal, yet her findings were not designed to demonstrate whether training was a better investment than hiring new employees. Nancy wondered if she should interview someone in finance to support her point of view or leave that decision for the manufacturing management staff. The memo indicated that she was to have approximately twenty minutes to present her plan, including a preliminary training design, with an additional hour for questions and answers. Nancy did not mind presenting her information but wondered exactly what her presentation goals should be. She felt uncomfortable about attempting to persuade management to train versus replace workers, although she strongly believed that training was a better solution. She also was nervous about the "grilling" questions she could expect from at least two members of the staff. Nancy was apprehensive as she began to prepare her material. What information should she collect? What information should she present? Was something missing? How could she plan to respond to tough questions and challenges?

Nancy is facing a typical organizational situation requiring data collection, interviewing, and presentation skills. She must convince management of her training plan and, in so doing, will influence what happens to the employment future of several assembly workers. She wants to do a good job not only for the assembly workers but also for her reputation with the manufacturing staff. Nancy is experiencing what most of us can expect in our work lives. We will be asked to gather information and to make presentations about our work, and we will be challenged by those who may disagree with the position we represent. The decision at hand and our professional reputations will be affected by the competencies we bring to these situations.

Think about some of your experiences with interviewing, training, and presentations. What went through your mind as you began to prepare? Do you believe your current skills are adequately developed for most organizational situations?

The chances are that most of us have concerns about our interviewing, training, and presentation capabilities as well as our ability to use and understand new communications technologies. We realize that unlike the somewhat structured evaluation of our abilities during school, at work we will continually have to demonstrate our abilities by explaining and supporting our positions during both formal and informal presentations and with the use of technology.

## INTERVIEWS IN ORGANIZATIONS

Interviews are a fact of life for just about everyone. We interview to get a job, we interview others who want to work with us, we receive performance feedback during interviews with the boss, we give performance feedback to others, and we gather information through interviews. Interviews are important communication activities requiring careful preparation and skilled execution. In this section types of organizational interviews are discussed and suggestions for preparing for interviews are offered. Specifically, the informational interview, employment interview, performance-appraisal interview, complaint interview, counseling interview, and media interview are described.

## Informational Interview

**Informational interview**
Interview to gather data for problem solving and decision making.

Information gathering takes place through **informational interviews.** The adequacy of our information-gathering capabilities is measured by our ability to gather relevant, sufficient, and plausible data from others and to identify sources where needed information is likely to be found. Interviews are a primary source of information. They are conducted to provide needed information or to verify perceptions of a problem. Ideally, informational interviews are conducted with individuals who can plausibly be expected to have the needed facts and perceptions.

Whether they are informal or highly structured exchanges, informational interviews begin with careful planning. Planning is based on what we want to know, on who has that information, and in what form we are likely to find it. What we need to know emerges during our problem definition and our examination of the limits of our current information. We do not use interviews to gather information we already have unless there is some disagreement about its credibility.

What we need to know is influenced by our ability to define the limits of what we do not know. Although it sounds like a play on words, the concept is very important to decision making and problem solving. One of the limitations many of us exhibit during information gathering is the tendency to define what is needed in terms of what we know exists. We often do not seek enough open-ended information that may be relevant to our problem. In our vacation example, we knew we needed a nice hotel. We did not even consider our desire for a good view of the mountains in our fact-finding. We limited our fact-finding to what we knew to expect and inadvertently eliminated a highly desirable alternative.

After broadly identifying what we need to know, effective fact-finders locate sources likely to have that information. Fact-finders are faced with deciding who or what source is most accessible and who will be willing to give the needed information. Does one person have the data for our problem? Should we take a representative sample of individuals who can be expected to be affected by the problem? How precise do our sampling techniques need to be? These questions and others help fact-finders focus their efforts to find information sources appropriate for decision making and problem solving.

Once sources have been identified, the fact-finder proceeds to establish a general format for data collection. If an interview is to be conducted, the interviewer thinks about questions to ask and determines how responses will be documented for later evaluation. If written data are to be reviewed, the fact-finder decides how much will be recorded and in what format. This preparation for data collection enables the fact-finder to make better use of time spent with the interviewee or other relevant sources.

When conducting an informational interview with another person, the interviewer must establish rapport and explain the purpose of data collection activities. During this phase of the interview, the fact-finder should establish personal credibility by introducing himself or herself, identifying the organization, and relating facts or circumstances that link the requested information to the purposes at hand. In other words, respondents are more likely to be cooperative if fact-finders introduce themselves with credentials and establish a need for the type of questions to be asked.

Once the interview begins, the fact-finder becomes concerned with framing questions that are clear and will elicit the desired information from the interviewee. Robert Kahn and Charles Cannell (1964) suggest five principles that contribute to success during the questioning phase.

1. Use language appropriate to the respondent.
2. Be sure the questions are clearly related to the purpose of the interview.
3. Be certain the informant has the information you want.
4. Avoid questions that are overly complex.
5. Avoid questions that ask the respondent to violate a social norm.

These suggestions are similar to numerous other concepts of interpersonal effectiveness. Kahn and Cannell are suggesting that successful interviewers adopt a receiver orientation, continually monitoring whether the interviewee understands the line of questioning and whether the interviewer is placing the interviewee in a situation where truthful response is difficult. A communication consultant seeking information from employees about a supervisory problem, for example, may need to be careful to ensure employee anonymity in order to gather information employees think may not be safe for management to hear. The consultant must understand what employees really think, not a filtered version, to make effective recommendations. Rapport and careful selection of questions are fundamental to gathering this important but sensitive information. Interviewers must know whether interviewees want credit for their remarks or anonymity. Interviewers also must carefully monitor potential bias in the remarks of interview subjects. The ability to evaluate information continually for relevancy, sufficiency, and plausibility is necessary for fact-finders to gather information that supports effective decision making and problem solving.

Effective fact-finders frequently close informational interviews by asking for any additional information the respondent would care to offer. Interviewers also ask subjects what they have not been asking that they should have explored. These questions and others give interviewees an opportunity to add information the fact-finder may not have known existed. This step can be as important to effective solutions as information previously identified as important.

John Baird (1977) well summarizes an effective atmosphere for an informational interview:

> The informational interview should create opportunity and willingness. Respondents give only the information they have an opportunity to give. If our questions do not provide them the opportunity, the information is lost. In addition, respondents give only the information they are willing to give. . . . Through careful selection of topics, questions, and respondents, coupled with skillful questioning, both opportunity and willingness can be maximized. (p. 141)

**Employment interview**
An exchange of questions between an individual seeking employment and the individuals responsible for evaluating job applicants.

## The Employment Interview

When you are seeking a job, the **employment interview** provides an opportunity to determine if the match between you and a particular job is right. Employment interviews allow you to demonstrate that you are the best person for a job, while at the same time allowing an employer to give you an accurate description of the job. When you are the interviewer, you are responsible for evaluating the responses of potential employees while accurately describing the position and your organization.

When you are the interviewee, you want to provide information about yourself that demonstrates you would be a valuable and productive member of the organization. At the same time, the employment interview provides you with an opportunity to obtain specific information about the job and the organization in which you are interested. This information will be very important to help you make an informed decision on whether to accept or reject the job if it is offered to you.

**Performance-appraisal interview**
Exchange about job performance between a supervisor/manager and an individual contributor.

## The Performance-Appraisal Interview

Once an individual is employed in an organization or becomes responsible for the supervision of others in the organization, the **performance-appraisal interview** becomes one of the most important communication events that contribute to individual development and overall organizational performance. Although formats vary extensively with specific organizational appraisal systems, the general purpose of the performance-appraisal interview is to exchange between a supervisor/manager and an individual contributor information about the adequacy of performance and to establish needs for development. Constance Staley and Robert Staley (1992) suggest that the performance-appraisal interview is an opportunity to

> let your subordinates know what you think of their performance, discover your subordinates' views of their performance, praise and encourage positive trends, point out desired changes, strengthen organizational commitment, point out opportunities for advancement, and keep a record of progress over time. (p. 305)

Although often described as an anxiety-producing experience, the effective performance-appraisal interview is essential to competency development. Individual contributors can learn about others' perceptions of their performance, and managers/supervisors can learn about needs that individual contributors have to perform more effectively and develop additional expertise. Performance issues, however, are reported by both managers and individual contributors to be difficult to discuss, often leading to general statements and faint or insincere utterances of praise. When we avoid needed feedback because of our apprehension or lack of communication skills, we are limiting individual development and contributing to overall organizational ineffectiveness.

**Complaint interview**
Question-and-answer exchange dealing with grievances or disciplinary actions.

## The Complaint Interview

The **complaint interview** is of two general types, the grievance interview or the disciplinary interview. Both types deal with organizational problems, and the effectiveness of these exchanges contributes directly to problem-solving and organizational performance. The grievance interview is designed for individuals to express specific problems to those who have legitimate organizational responsibility for dealing with the issues related to the grievance. The grievance interview can deal with issues ranging from work dissatisfaction to various forms of inappropriate behaviors such as discrimination, racism, or harassment. Grievance interviews are both informal and formal. Formal grievance interviews usually follow organizationally specific published procedures. Although difficult in nature, grievance interviews can support productive problem solving, especially when they are conducted shortly after a problem becomes troublesome.

The disciplinary interview confronts a violation of organizational rules, norms, and performance expectations. Generally, the disciplinary interview occurs between a supervisor and an individual contributor and frequently follows organizational procedures for disciplinary action. The disciplinary interview provides specific remedies for stated problems. Again, when conducted effectively, the disciplinary exchange can improve individual performance and in many cases prevent more serious action such as suspension, demotion, or termination. It is easy to understand why effective communication is crucial in both the grievance and disciplinary interviews.

**Counseling interview**
Question-and-answer exchange with individuals seeking advice from other organizational members.

## The Counseling Interview

Occurring between supervisors and individual contributors and among peers, the **counseling interview** involves an individual seeking advice and assistance from another organizational member or members. Topics included in the counseling exchange include work performance, work-related interpersonal conflicts, and personal problems. People seeking counseling are asking others to provide support and assistance with problems. Empathetic listening is important during this exchange. Depending on the nature of the problem, it may be important to remember the limitations of your individual qualifications to offer advice. Referring individuals to professional assistance should be encouraged for certain types of problems. As discovered in Chapter 9 on organizational conflict, it is important for individuals who must make changes to generate those changes themselves without other people imposing solutions. The counseling interview is always a balance between fixing problems and helping others generate their own commitment and solution strategies.

**Media interview**
Question-and-answer exchange between members of the press and an organizational representative.

## The Media Interview

Many communication professionals represent their organizations or departments with statements to the press. The public relations professional, for example, is responsible for answering press inquiries and for assisting others in the organization to provide needed information in a manner that reflects favorably on the organization. Many other organizational members, however, are called on to talk with the press about new product developments, services, union/management issues, and a host of other topics. Generally speaking, **media interviews** are most successful when you can formulate a clear objective for your statements with a limited number of key assertions. Supporting data such as anecdotes, analogies, facts, or simple statistics enhance understanding. The media interview reflects on you individually but also is a powerful contributor to the overall reputation of the organization.

## INCREASING INTERVIEW EFFECTIVENESS

Preparation is the key to effectiveness for all the types of interviews described. We are responsible for developing objectives for each interview and formulating questions and statements that will assist us in achieving those objectives. This section of the chapter provides recommendations for increasing the effectiveness of one specific type of interview, the employment interview.

Effective employment interviewing involves preparation and practice. To be prepared for an employment interview you must acquire knowledge about yourself, about the job, and about the employer in which you are interested. You will need the following information about an organization prior to your interview:

The typical duties and salary range for the job in which you are interested.

The background of the organization. (How long has it been in operation? What is the outlook for its future?)

The products or services the organization produces.

The vision and goals of the organization.

Any specific problems or issues that might be of concern to the organization.

You also should be prepared to provide concise but descriptive answers to the following types of questions:

Tell me about yourself.

Why are you interested in working for this company?

Why have you chosen this particular field?

Why should we hire you?

What are your long-range goals?

What is your greatest strength?

What is your greatest weakness?

Describe a specific example of a work goal you have achieved.

Describe how you have handled a difficult situation at work.

For a complete listing of the most frequently asked employment interview questions, see the Workshop section at the end of this chapter.

A final phase of your preparation involves gathering information about the person or persons who will interview you. Try to use your networks or other sources to gain information about the individual who will conduct your employment interview. If you have difficulty gathering information about the person who will interview you, simply rely on your preparation and research concerning the job and the organization to help you effectively perform in the interview.

Practice is vital to successful interviewing. Role playing is a valuable method for improving your interviewing skills. Enlist your family, friends, or coworkers to help you practice. Avoid being overly self-critical, but spend some extra practice time working on any weaknesses you identify.

Not only is what you actually say during the course of an interview very important but so are the way you look, act, and deal with the physical environment. Nonverbal factors are significant in making a positive first impression. Your first communication with an interviewer occurs through nonverbal channels. Before you say anything, your appearance, body movements, and management of the physical environment influence the interviewer's opinion of you. There are cultural differences and organizational differences in appropriate nonverbal behaviors and management of the physical environment during an interview. Your own self-awareness and your ability to accurately perceive the environment in which the interview takes place will assist you in presenting yourself effectively.

An employment interview is a dialogue between you and the interviewer. Your verbal responses give information about you to the interviewer. These responses, plus impressions gained from nonverbal behavior, influence decisions about your potential employment.

Keep in mind that most of the people who interview you are not professional interviewers. They are likely to be as concerned about the interview as you are. The interviewer's credibility may be on the line. He or she can't afford to make a hiring mistake and must get answers to basic questions. Help the interviewer by providing as much information as possible. Realize that during the course of the interview, the interviewer must decide whether you can do the job, whether you have a good work attitude and can get along with others in the organization, whether you have any character flaws or problems that will cause tension on the job, and whether you are qualified.

During the employment interview, you should do more than just answer questions. You should use this time to get answers to the questions you have concerning the job you are considering. For example, any of the following questions are appropriate during an employment interview.

What are the specific duties and responsibilities of the job?

Could you describe a typical day or week in this position?

What are the training and educational opportunities?

How have those who have had this job in the past advanced in the organization?

What are the organization's future plans and goals?

What are some examples of the best results produced by people in this job?

It is the interviewer's responsibility to close the interview. You should be prepared to summarize how your skills, interests, experiences, and goals would contribute to the job. Also you should be prepared to provide references and usually a résumé.

## PRESENTATIONS IN ORGANIZATIONS

Most jobs today, and more in the future, will require employees to give presentations. We are asked to describe to management the status of a project. We train other organizational members on the use of equipment or a process. We report conclusions from our team meeting. Organizations in our information society depend more than ever before on individuals transferring information through **presentational speaking.** Blue-collar workers and executives alike make presentations as part of their regular job responsibilities. Presentations are used in organizations to train, inform, critique plans of action, and persuade others to support decisions. Our ability to present material effectively contributes to our organizational credibility and influences the progress of our careers.

**Presentational speaking**
Speaking in organizations that is designed to educate, inform, or persuade.

Surveys of top management in major organizations consistently suggest that employees have deficiencies in presentation skills. Companies annually spend thousands of dollars developing oral competencies. Fully competent organizational members face the reality that they will be asked to give speeches and that others will evaluate their overall effectiveness and the quality of their efforts.

Many people dread presentations. Highly apprehensive individuals will avoid job responsibilities requiring talking before groups, and when that happens, both the individual and the organization lose. Excellent organizations need contributions from all members. When fear blocks an individual from contributing, the individual loses an ability to influence decisions, and the organization loses a valuable resource.

Once we become aware of the likelihood and importance of making presentations in organizations, we start thinking about how to develop our own competencies. We ask questions about what to expect in professional settings and how to evaluate our current skills. A discussion of general characteristics of business presentations will answer some of these questions.

Generally, business presentations occur on the business site with a topic chosen to fit a particular problem or issue. Topics are specific, and speakers are expected to adhere to announced agendas. Presenters are expected to respect time constraints while effectively covering important and often complex details. Unlike many public speaking settings, the audience is usually known to the speaker and may be composed of peers, subordinates, and managers. In other words, the speaker will probably be involved in a continuing working relationship with members of the audience. Furthermore, most audience members will attend presentations as part of their job requirements.

Organizational presentations are characterized by a high degree of audience involvement. The presenter is frequently interrupted with questions and at times challenged on positions or technical information. Both the audience and the presenter accept responsibility for information exchange. Most effective organizational presenters are skilled at both clear and concise presentation of information and the handling of audience interactions.

The audience holds the presenter responsible for preparation and topic expertise. In fact, the overall organizational credibility of an individual can be adversely affected if he or she does not adequately prepare or presents information not credible to the audience. In public speaking, the speaker's efforts at decentering are often subtle and understated, whereas in presentational speaking, the audience members expect the presenter to demonstrate an effort to address their specific points of view and needs overtly.

Organizational presentations are usually less spontaneous than presentations designed for public settings. More detail intensive, organizational presentations frequently use computer-assisted (visual and audio) supporting materials and audience handouts. Those skilled in business presentations become familiar and comfortable with a variety of technologies important for enhancing understanding and retention of information. Overhead projectors, video playback machines, tape equipment, computers, teleconferencing equipment, and other devices are all used for business presentations.

Finally, most organizational presenters must respond to questions and answers during and following presentations. The ability to respond to questions influences the credibility of the information transmitted and may contribute as much as the formal presentation to overall effectiveness. As Nancy Winslow begins to prepare for her presentation to the manufacturing staff, she considers what information they currently have about the skill level of assembly workers. She prepares visuals to detail her budget. She is considering gathering data to compare training costs to the costs of hiring new, more skillful employees. In addition, she is thinking about how she can answer managers who do not believe that training skill-deficient employees will meet the organization's needs.

Nancy currently works with most of the managers to whom she will make the presentation. She knows that her credibility will be on the line because she is advocating a position that at least two powerful members of the group oppose. How would you advise Nancy to prepare? Should she attempt to persuade the group to her position or simply make them aware of all of their options? What responsibility does she have to the assembly workers? What responsibility does she have to herself? The next several sections of this chapter describe the types of presentation options that Nancy has and make specific recommendations for increasing her effectiveness.

## TYPES OF ORGANIZATIONAL PRESENTATIONS

Organizational presentations can be divided into three broad types: training/ educational, informational, and persuasive. Training or educational presentations literally teach others information relevant to the organization. Informational presentations transmit knowledge from one organizational member or unit to another, and persuasive presentations are aimed at helping the organization solve problems or make decisions. Many presentations will be combinations of all three, requiring competent organizational presenters to develop skills in educating, informing, and persuading.

**Training/educational presentations**
Presentations that literally teach organizational members their jobs. Instructions and training are common examples.

### Training/Educational Presentations

**Training/educational presentations** literally teach organizational members their jobs. Groups of people are trained in new processes, interpersonal relations, communication skills, or new technologies. Presentations are designed to help others use the information that the presenter has learned and is responsible for transmitting to others. Giving instructions is perhaps the most common form of an educational presentation. In either a group or individual setting, the presenter is responsible for organizing information clearly and concisely to enable others to meet the expectations of an assignment or task. Giving instructions may be the most frequent of all educational presentations. When given effectively, instructions can contribute to the overall productivity of the organization. Instructions that fail to convey effective information cost organizations money in mistakes, poor-quality decisions, frustration of employees, and a variety of other, less obvious ways.

Educational presentations also include technical training, basic skills training, interpersonal development and management training, and introductions of new concepts or technologies. These presentations are typically several hours in length and include diverse types of audience participation. Educational presentations that train or introduce new concepts require competency in holding people's attention over a period of time while providing material in enough detail to generate understanding. Educational presentations are specific career responsibilities in a variety of jobs (see Chapter 11 for a more complete description) and temporary responsibilities of those with expertise in a particular area. As your educational experiences in your school will almost certainly confirm, some presenters are better than others in generating understanding. Think about a time when you were part of an effective training program. What did your instructor do well? How might you use your observations to build your skills? Now think of a time when you were not pleased with the results of your training. What made the difference? Can your observations help you understand what to avoid?

**Informational presentations**
Presentations focused on providing the most current information available. Common examples are management briefings, checkpoint meetings, and technical reports.

## Informational Presentations

Information is the life blood of organizations. Problems surface through information exchanges, and problem solving occurs as individuals and organizations seek to discover information alternatives on which to base decisions. Earlier the importance of relevant, sufficient, and plausible information for problem solving and decision making was discussed. Now comes a description of the role that **informational presentations** play in generating that information.

Informational presentations occur in a variety of organizational settings. Managers brief their subordinates on organizational policy. Individual contributors brief management on the status of a work project. A project team may review for management staff the technical problems associated with product design. Although similar to educational presentations, informational presentations are focused on providing the most current information available, as opposed to teaching the audience new information. Unlike educational presentations, which frequently assume that the audience has minimal familiarity with the topic, most informational presentations assume a reasonable degree of subject familiarity by the audience. In fact, many organizational presentations that are primarily of an informational nature will begin from the point of the last information exchange rather than the beginning of the project or issue. A common example of this type of informational presentation is the checkpoint meeting, in which an individual or team will report on the status of a project based on progress from the last checkpoint. Although introductions in these presentations frequently summarize the project, little attention is paid to details previously communicated.

Management teams request informational presentations to solve problems and make decisions. Nancy Winslow is asked to bring information to the manufacturing management staff of her organization. They need to make important decisions about assembly-line workers. She is considering expanding their request to attempt to persuade them to her point of view, yet her basic assignment is to inform them with relevant, sufficient, and plausible information.

**Persuasive presentations**
Presentations that attempt to influence the problem solving or decision making of the organization. Common examples are sales presentations, action recommendations, and resource requests.

# Persuasive Presentations

If Nancy Winslow decides to attempt to influence the decision of the manufacturing staff, she will be engaged in persuasive communication. She will seek to influence the attitudes and beliefs of others by the arguments she makes. She will attempt to get manufacturing managers to interpret her data as she does and support her recommended training plan. Organizational members frequently are requested to make recommendations. In a very basic sense, recommending a course of action is a persuasive process.

**Persuasive presentations** are made to request resources, gain approval of an idea, sell a product or process, convince others to make changes, gain support for a course of action, and critique the efforts of others. Persuasive presentations are focused on getting an audience to adopt the point of view of the presenter based on relevant, plausible, and sufficient arguments. These presentations guide the audience to the conclusions the presenter favors. They ask for support, for business, for change, and make a variety of other requests.

Persuasive presentations in organizations are usually task related and contain more factual support than is common in other settings. Essentially, persuasive presentations are asking for a decision from the audience that supports the intentions of the presenter. Effective presenters realize that for a persuasive presentation to be successful, they must not only understand what information their audience is likely to have on the topic but also consider relevant attitudes and issues. Nancy Winslow, for example, is aware that two powerful managers generally oppose training and prefer to replace deficient workers. This awareness will drive her strategies if she decides to try to persuade the manufacturing staff. If that opposition were not present, her presentation might be organized very differently. Given her knowledge of the manufacturing managers, what advice would you give Nancy? Can she afford to ignore these two managers? Should she state her opinion but make no real effort to change their minds? What would you do if you were Nancy?

There are ethical implications in Nancy's concerns. She is concerned about the assembly workers. She can choose information for her presentation that primarily supports her training request, or she could let the managers develop their own data on replacement costs. She has a number of other options based on her evaluation of what is right and wrong in this context. Regardless of what she chooses, Nancy is engaged in making decisions that will affect her credibility with the manufacturing management staff.

# INCREASING PRESENTATION EFFECTIVENESS

Thus far, the importance of presentational speaking in organizations has been discussed and a variety of types of common organizational presentations have been described. Now comes an attempt to identify ways in which individual competencies can be developed for presentational speaking.

## Increasing Credibility

Although credibility evaluations rest with audiences, we can enhance the likelihood of a positive response if we consciously think about how to describe ourselves, our intentions, and our concerns. We can begin by considering what our initial credibility is likely to be with a particular group. What do they know about our background? How much have we interacted before? What were the results of previous exchanges? If our task competence or subject expertise is unknown to an audience, we may want to begin by briefly describing our training or experience. If our expertise is known but our position controversial, we may want to cite research and stress the competence of our sources. In addition, we can avoid needlessly calling attention to our inadequacies.

In many organizational settings, questions and challenges to presenters are common and appropriate for decision making. We can usually increase our credibility by stressing our fairness, demonstrating that we have examined various alternatives, not just the ones we are recommending. We can stress our concern for enduring values such as quality, creativity, or team play. We can stress our similarity with an audience in terms of beliefs, attitudes, values, and goals. We can point to our long-term consistency and demonstrate our concern for others through non-defensive behaviors during questioning and challenges. In general, we can increase our credibility by demonstrating that we support the welfare of the group or organization, not just our own concerns. Finally, we are more likely to be perceived as credible if we present a positive orientation to the situation, are assertive, and are generally enthusiastic.

**Audience analysis**
Assessment of what receivers are interested in, what they know, what their attitudes and values are, what they are wanted to know, what the speaker's probable credibility is, and what format will be most effective.

## Audience and Context Analysis

When thinking about establishing personal credibility, we began to think specifically about our audience and the context or circumstances of our presentation. Earlier, effective communication as resulting from meanings being understood among people as accurately as possible was described. This base of interpersonal communication obviously remains true for the presentation. How can we ensure that the results of our problem-solving or work accomplishments are best represented to those who have a need to know? Who are our potential audiences, and what do we want them to do? Effective presentations reflect good **audience analysis.**

At times, the audience will be a management team who will grant final authority or resources to implement the proposed solution. They must be convinced by our presentations of what we expect to achieve by our solutions or particular courses of action. At other times, we will be announcing decisions to people who are affected by them. In this case, the decision implementation and how it affects the receiver may be more important than any explanation of our decision process.

## Preparation of Material

After questions about the potential audience have been satisfactorily answered, we can proceed to the selection of material for presentation. Selection of material depends on audience analysis and the assignment at hand. We select material with relevancy, sufficiency, and plausibility criteria. These criteria must be met for us individually before we can make projections about how they can be met for our expected audiences. Once material has been selected, we begin the organizing process. Material can be organized in a variety of formats.

After decisions are made about the material to be included and the organizational sequence, introductions and conclusions should be developed. Introductions attract audience attention, establish credibility for the presenter or presenters, and clarify the purpose of the presentation. As with all other presentational decisions, introductions are most effective when careful consideration is given to the needs and interests of the audience. It is very difficult to capture attention if the introduction to a presentation is poorly planned.

Conclusions, particularly crucial to the success of presentations, summarize the key elements in the presentation and restate and call for needed action on the part of audience members. Effective conclusions leave the audience with a short and concrete summary of what the presenter has decided is most important to know. Conclusions are last impressions and influential in setting the tone for what happens next. Sometimes conclusions return to introductions to emphasize how the presentation has met the goals established then. At other times, the conclusion focuses on the needed action from the audience and solicits questions to gain more direct involvement.

## Preparation for Presenting

So far, the discussion has been about preparing material for presentations and coping with anxiety. In either case the word preparation is the key. Preparation generally increases effectiveness and helps us manage most presentational situations.

Personal preparation for presenting includes rehearsing the speech, working with visual aids, preparing notes, and timing the presentation. In addition, it is a good idea to check specific details in the room scheduled for your presentation and to arrive early to confirm arrangements. Personal preparation also includes selecting clothing that is appropriate for the occasion and comfortable for the presenter. A rule commonly recommended is that you never wear new clothing or new shoes for a presentation. Anything that introduces newness or uncertainty should be reserved for less stressful situations.

Many organizational presentations are prepared and presented by teams or groups of individuals. Many of you may have worked on a group project for which certain team members did not adhere to their allotted presentation time, making life miserable for other presenters. Groups need to rehearse and time presentations just as much as individuals do. In addition, team presentations are most effective when all team members have tightly coordinated information so that segments of the presentation are not unnecessarily repeated.

## Handling Participation

Previously, the frequency and importance of audience participation during most organizational presentations and the necessity to respond to differing ideas and challenges have been discussed. Not yet described are some basic ways to handle audience participation.

Effective presenters anticipate lines of questions they might get from their audience. They not only prepare the formal presentation but also practice answers to expected questions or challenges. Effective presenters learn to analyze questions and ask for necessary clarification before responding. If a group is relatively large, repeating a question so that all can hear increases the perception that the speaker is interested in the audience and in answering the questions.

Effective presenters respond to all audience members and control domination attempts from one or two individuals. Effective presenters also ask the audience for ideas or critiques. At times skilled presenters have questions for their audience to increase ownership of a decision or position. Perhaps most important, effective presenters maintain supportive, nondefensive behaviors that encourage a sense of "we," or belonging with the audience. This sense of "we" is especially important in ongoing organizational relationships.

# COMMUNICATIONS TECHNOLOGY IN ORGANIZATIONS

Throughout the text individuals working with others and participating in organizational life have been discussed and changing and emerging challenges have been described. Nowhere will our communication competencies be more challenged than by the increasing use of information technologies in all types of organizations. Most of us are familiar with voice messaging, facsimile-transmission (fax) machines, basic word processing with computers, e-mail, and the Internet. Fewer of us are regular users of teleconferencing, desktop publishing, spreadsheets, graphics, GDSS, and high-powered statistical and data manipulation programs. Yet for most users of this text, all these technologies and more will be normal and required ways of participating in organizational life. Moreover, we will be required to continually learn and relearn sophisticated communications technologies so as to perform the basic functions of our jobs.

Ronald Rice and Urs Gattiker (2001) describe computer-mediated communications and information systems:

> CISs [computer information systems] combine four major components. *Computing* allows processing of content and structuring of communication participation. *Telecommunication networks* allow access and connectivity to many others and to vari-

eties of information across space and time. *Information or communication resources range from databases to communities of potential participants. Digitization of content* allows the integration and exchange of multiple communication modes—such as graphics, video, sound, text—across multiple media and distribution networks. . . . Such systems include, for example, audiotex; automatic teller machines (ATMs) that are redesigned as information services terminals; cellular phones and pagers; collaborative systems such as screen-sharing and joint document preparation; computer bulletin boards; computer conferencing; conversational and workflow processors; cyberphones; decision support systems with communication components; desktop publishing and document distribution; multimedia desktop conferencing and screen-sharing; electronic document interchange (EDI); electronic mail; facsimile; gophers/World Wide Web; group support systems and other groupware; home shopping and banking; hypertext and hypermedia; intelligent telephone systems; Internet listservers; local area networks; mobile personal communication devices; multimedia computing; on-line and portable databases; optical media such as CD-ROM and lasercards; optically scanned and networked documents; personal information assistants; personal locator badges; presentation devices such as computer screen projectors; telephone services such as call forwarding, redial until delivery, or automatically transferring a pager message to one's voice messaging system; teletext; video teleconferencing; videotex; virtual reality and cyberspace; voice mail; wide area networks; and word processing. (pp. 545–546)

Rice and Gattiker go on to suggest that CISs have some potential to resolve problems of traditional bureaucracies by reducing organizational complexity, hierarchical structures, and facilitating a better sense of member opinions through increasing participation and democratic interaction. In addition, CISs are important to the restructuring of interorganizational interactions.

Janet Fulk and Lori Collins-Jarvis (2001) identify new and highly sophisticated electronic meeting support widely available to organizations. They describe "three generic categories of meeting technologies. *Teleconferencing* includes meetings held through audioconferencing and videoconferencing systems. *Computer conferencing* allows multiple participants to interact by contributing to an ongoing computer file accessible to all. *Group support systems* (GSSs) supplement computer conferencing with information management capabilities, decision support tools, graphics displays, and meeting process management software." These technologies permit both synchronous and asynchronous work among individuals in diverse time zones and locations.

The potential to work in geographically diverse teams or telecommute exists in many organizations today. Communicating by e-mail, in chat rooms, with threaded discussions, and through teleconference unites people across not only miles but also cultures and languages. The time to contemplate responses is shortened as technology collapses the time float generated when messages are sent by land or air transportation. In addition, technology permits the examination of a volume of information unknown to all previous members of the work force.

Face-to-face communication potentially can be reduced with increased use of e-mail and fax machines. The ease of electronic communication has been known to contribute to ill-conceived messages hastily developed and transmitted. Competent communicators using electronic channels will need to learn to monitor their responses, deciding wisely when more reflection or the reaction of face-to-face interaction is needed. With the new technologies we do not have to work the same hours as those with whom we interact, or even work in traditional offices. More of us will work from our homes than at any period since the Industrial Revolution. Homes routinely will be equipped with modem connections, fax machines, and portable teleconferencing units. All forms of wireless communications will increase. We will engage in gathering information and making decisions with people we know less well while working with media that both distance us from others and bring us in more immediate contact across space and time.

## Preparation for Communications Technology

Perhaps the most important preparation for our rapidly changing technological environments is an attitudinal preparation, the understanding that we may never completely master the technologies we use and that change will bring about the necessity of lifelong learning. The good news is that research consistently demonstrates that, as we go through our careers, we are capable of new learning and increased competencies with the machines of today and those projected for the future.

In addition to accepting as normal that our learning does not stop with formal education but is an ongoing part of our organizational lives, we can prepare for communications technology by availing ourselves of opportunities to experience as many diverse applications of technologies as are readily available. Most schools and public libraries have a variety of computer as well as teleconferencing capabilities. In addition, most work organizations and more in the future will provide basic training for a variety of specific applications. It is important when we think about preparing for participation in the organizations of the future to consider how we can develop competencies in communications technology that will support the human communication competencies that we continue to develop.

## SUMMARY

Decision making is the process of choosing from among several alternatives, and problem solving is a multistage process for moving an issue, situation, or state from an undesirable to a more desirable condition. Groups make decisions and solve problems through a variety of methods, including leader mandate, majority rule, powerful minority influence, and consensus. Organizational culture, the problem itself, technical competencies, and communication competencies all influence decision-making and problem-solving processes. Barriers to problem solving can be identified in organizational, task, procedural, and interpersonal areas. Problem-solving processes include the Standard Agenda, brainstorming, Delphi technique, nominal group process, and a variety of experientially-based processes. Each represents a different process for solving problems and different interpretations of how groups come to decisions. Decision-making and problem-solving effectiveness can be increased by developing fact-finding and evaluation skills.

Participating in organizations requires competencies in interviewing, presentations, and a variety of communications technologies. We interview to get a job, we interview others who want to work with us, we receive performance feedback during interviews with the boss, we give performance feedback to others, we experience grievances or disciplinary actions, we ask for help, and we meet with the media. The informational interview, employment interview, performance-appraisal interview, complaint interview, counseling interview, and media interview are some of the major types of organizational interviews. Interview effectiveness is improved with extensive preparation and practice.

Most jobs today, and more in the future, will require employees to give presentations. Blue-collar workers and executives alike make presentations designed to educate, inform, or persuade. Surveys of top management consistently suggest that employees are deficient in presentation skills, and fully competent organization members realize that speaking before groups is part of most job responsibilities. Organizational presentations usually occur on the business site, with topics focused on specific problems or issues. Most presentations are made to groups with whom the presenter has an ongoing working relationship, and both the presenter and the audience are responsible for information exchange. Organizational presentations are characterized by a high degree of interactivity between the presenter and an audience that generally has considerable familiarity with the subject. Organizational presentations can be divided into three broad types: training/educational, informational, and persuasive. Audience and context analysis helps us make decisions about establishing credibility as well as the selection of material and actual organization of the presentation. Preparation of material includes the selection of content and organizational sequences based on the goals of the presentation. Group presentations have the same requirements, with additional emphasis on group content and timing coordination. Effective presenters encourage audience participation with supportive, nondefensive behaviors. Questions are answered honestly and directly, with emphasis on establishing a sense of belonging with the audience.

Nowhere will our communication competencies be more challenged than by the increasing use of information technologies in all types of organizations. We will be required to continually learn and relearn sophisticated communications technologies to perform the basic functions of our jobs. Technology will change the way in which we work, in time, geography, culture, location, and many other ways. The most important preparation for our technological futures may well be an attitude supporting lifelong learning. Communications competencies with technology will support human communication competencies.

# WORKSHOP

1. You have been studying a variety of approaches to decision making and problem solving. You will now be asked to assume the position of training manager for Food Service Industries. As training manager you are responsible for making a series of routine business decisions. You are returning from your annual vacation and find a number of decision items in your e-mail. For each item, describe what you would

do and what criteria you are using for each decision. Small groups or the class as a whole will compare and discuss responses. (See pp. 305–307.)

2. To illustrate similarities and differences in decision-making and problem-solving approaches among class members, select a current problem familiar to class members. (Cases and question 1 are also appropriate for this activity.) Divide the entire class into groups of six members each. Each group will appoint one member to be a facilitator. All groups need flip-chart paper and markers. Each group will have fifteen minutes to find possible solutions for the problem. (All solutions are taken, even if other group members disagree.) At the end of fifteen minutes each group will spend five minutes choosing their top three solutions (through consensus or majority vote). The top three solutions will be recorded on flip-chart paper and posted for the entire class to review. Each group facilitator reads the top three to the entire class. The class then goes "shopping" for ten minutes. Shopping is simply walking around the room and recording any solution that individual group members believe is especially productive. Groups again convene for twenty minutes. Group members begin by adding from shopping any solutions they want discussed. Within the allotted twenty minutes each group will rank their top two solutions one and two. Facilitators again record these decisions on flip-chart paper, post the findings, and report to the entire class. Discussion follows about the process and the similarities and differences in solutions.

3. The following are among the most frequently asked questions during employment interviews. Either individually or in role-playing teams, develop and practice answers to these questions. Take turns playing the role of the interviewer and interviewee.

   a. Tell me about yourself.
   b. Describe yourself.
   c. Have you done this type of work before?
   d. Why do you want to work here?
   e. Why are you interested in this job?
   f. What are your salary requirements?
   g. Why would you be better for this job than anyone else?
   h. What are your major strengths?
   i. What are your major weaknesses?
   j. What are your immediate employment goals?
   k. What are your long-term employment goals?
   l. What kinds of machines/technology can you use?
   m. How did you get along with your coworkers, supervisor, clients, or customers in your last job?
   n. What kind of people do you work with best?
   o. What kind of work environment do you prefer?
   p. How do you feel about: pressure, deadlines, travel, relocating, overtime, or weekend work?
   q. What makes you lose your temper?
   r. What do you like to do in your spare time?

    **s.**   What would you like to accomplish if you were hired for this job?

    **t.**   What are the toughest problems you have faced, and how did you handle them?

    **u.**   What kinds of decisions are most difficult for you?

    **v.**   What have you learned from your previous experiences?

    **w.**  Describe a specific problem you have handled well.

    **x.**   Describe an example of a situation that you did not handle well. What have you learned from that experience?

    **y.**   What do you want to know about this organization?

    **z.**   Why should we hire you?

4. Identifying your presentational strengths and weaknesses is a good way to improve your presentational abilities. List five presentational strengths you currently practice. List five presentational weaknesses. In small groups discuss what you can do to improve the weaknesses. Describe how your strengths were developed and how they might be used to work on weaknesses.

5. Divide the class into groups of five members each. Ask each group to develop a list of three national figures, all of whom the group can support as sincere and believable. Each group should be prepared to describe why they selected these individuals. Compare lists and discuss reasons for selection.

6. Individually or in small groups, identify individuals who might be credible for each of the following subjects: health, fashion, entertainment, politics, music, football, social change, and business. Discuss why they are credible to you.

## The Training Manager of Food Service Industries E-Mail Exercise

Instructions: You have been away on your annual vacation. On your return, the following items have been printed from your e-mail and marked with a priority stamp by your secretary. For each item, describe what you would do next. Can you make an immediate decision? What additional information do you need? Are you going to involve other people? Describe your criteria for each decision.

### Item 1

> To: YOUR NAME, Training Manager for Food Service Industries
> From: Mike Barnes, Vice President of Major Accounts
>
>     I have just received two complaints about one of our newest salespersons. Topco Foods and Bestway both said Jim Johnson was rude and did not effectively represent our product line. I thought he had just been in one of your training sessions. How would you evaluate his performance? Please advise immediately.

## Item 2

> To: YOUR NAME, Training Manager for Food Service Industries
> From: Jane Connors, Chair, Community Service Speakers Bureau, Chamber of Commerce
>
> We know your company is an active and vital member of this community. As chair of the Speakers Bureau for our Community Outreach program, I would like to invite you to give a motivational talk on leadership at our September banquet. Mike Barnes of your company recommended you and felt you were just the person to do the job. Our program goes to press next week, so we need your response as soon as possible.

## Item 3

> To: All Department Heads
> From: Finance
>
> Because of a downturn in our profit projections for the next quarter, each department is being asked to reduce its fourth quarter budget by 2 percent. Because each department's spending authority is established through finance, we need a list of those items or events you want to eliminate. Thank you very much for your cooperation in this matter. This list should be in our office no later than Friday.

## Item 4

> To: YOUR NAME
> From: Jerry Masters, Head of Manufacturing Services
>
> I have a problem and know you can help. We have hired six new people for our new manufacturing process group. We had not budgeted any training courses for the six, because we did not anticipate starting the group before the first of next year. Company policy requires me to schedule them for new employee orientation, but I don't have the training funds available to reimburse your department. Please advise how I should handle this situation.

## Item 5

Dear YOUR NAME

I was in your June 4th class on managing poor performance. I tried everything you said and now am really in a mess. In fact, the subordinate in question has gone to my manager and made a formal complaint. I just want you to know that I told my manager it was all your fault and they should really look at what people are taught in those supervision classes.

Sincerely,
John Price

# REFERENCES AND SUGGESTED READINGS

Baird, J. E., Jr. 1977. *The dynamics of organizational communication.* New York: Harper and Row.

Baird, J. E., Jr. 1981. *Speaking for results: Communication by objectives.* New York: Harper and Row.

Baird, J. E., Jr. 1982. *Positive personnel practices, quality circles leader's manual.* Prospect Heights, IL: Waveland Press.

Brilhart, J. K. 1986. *Effective group discussion.* 5th ed. Dubuque, IA: Brown.

Cummings, H. W., L. W. Long, and M. L. Lewis. 1983. *Managing communication in organizations: An introduction.* Dubuque, IA: Gorsuch Scarisbrick.

Dance, F. E. X. 1987. What do you mean presentational speaking? *Management Communication Quarterly* 1(2): 260–271.

DeVito, J. A. 1984. *The elements of public speaking.* 2d ed. New York: Harper and Row.

Dewey, J. 1910. *How we think.* Boston: Heath.

Fisher, B. A. 1980. *Small group decision making.* 2d ed. New York: McGraw-Hill.

Fulk, J., and L. Collins-Jarvis. 2001. Wired meetings: Technological mediation of organizational gatherings. In *The new handbook of organizational communication: Advances in theory, research, and methods,* eds. F. Jablin and L. Putnam, 624–663. Thousand Oaks, CA.: Sage.

Gouran, D. S. 1979. *Making decisions in groups: Choices and consequences.* Glenview, IL: Scott, Foresman.

Harris, T. L., and W. E. Schwahn. 1961. *Selected readings on the learning process.* New York: Oxford University Press.

Hirokawa, R. 1988. Group communication and decision-making performance: A continued test of the functional perspective. *Human Communication Research* 14(4): 487–515.

Hirokawa, R., and K. Rost. 1992. Effective group decision making in organizations. *Management Communication Quarterly* 5: 267–288.

Jones, S. E., D. C. Barnlund, and F. S. Haiman. 1980. *The dynamics of discussion communication in small groups.* New York: Harper and Row.

Kahn, R., and C. Cannell. 1964. *The dynamics of interviewing.* New York: Wiley.

Kelly, L., L. Lederman, and G. Phillips. 1989. *Communicating in the workplace: A guide to business and professional speaking.* New York: Harper & Row.

Kepner, C. H., and B. B. Tregoe. 1965. *The rational manager.* New York: McGrawHill.

Larson, C. E. 1969. Forms of analysis and small group problem-solving. *Speech Monographs* 36: 452–455.

Lumsden, G., and D. Lumsden. 1993. *Communicating in groups and teams.* Belmont, CA: Wadsworth.

Morrison, E., and F. Milliken. 2000. Organizational silence: A barrier to change and development in a pluralistic world. *The Academy of Management Review* 25 (4): 706–725.

Phillips, G. M. 1982. *Communicating in organizations.* New York: Macmillan.

Rice, R., and U. Gattiker. 2001. New media and organizational structuring. In *The new handbook of organizational communication: Advances in theory, research, and methods,* eds. F. Jablin and L. Putnam, 544–581. Thousand Oaks, CA.: Sage.

Scheidel, T., and L. Crowell. 1964. Idea development in small discussion groups. *Quarterly Journal of Speech* 50: 140–145.

Simon, H. A. 1960. *The new science of management decision.* New York: Harper and Row.

Staley, C. C., and R. S. Staley. 1992. *Communicating in business and the professions: The inside word.* Belmont, CA: Wadsworth.

Tompkins, P., and G. Cheney. 1983. Account analysis of organizations: Decision making and identification. In *Communication and organizations: An interpretive approach,* eds. L. Putnam and M. Pacanowsky, 123–146. Beverly Hills, CA: Sage.

Wilson, G. L., H. L. Goodall, Jr., and C. L. Waagen. 1986. *Organizational communication.* New York: Harper and Row.

Wood, J. T., G. M. Phillips, and D. J. Pedersen. 1986. *Group discussion: A practical guide to participation and leadership.* 2d ed. New York: Harper and Row.

# CHAPTER NINE

# ORGANIZATIONAL CONFLICT
## Communicating for Effectiveness

---

## DEVELOPING COMPETENCIES THROUGH . . .

### KNOWLEDGE

Defining and describing organizational conflict
Identifying conflict episodes
Describing contexts for conflict
Describing causes for conflict

### SENSITIVITY

Understanding individual conflict styles and strategic objectives
Understanding group conflict approaches
Distinguishing between productive and counterproductive
  conflicts
Identifying supportive communication climates
Understanding emotion and conflict
Understanding ethical abuses during conflict

### SKILLS

Assessing communication tactics used during conflict
Developing a problem-solving process for conflict
Practicing analysis capabilities

### VALUES

Developing personal awareness for conflict
Understanding individual responsibilities for productive conflict
Clarifying ethical conflict behaviors

# THE MIDDLESEX INSURANCE COMPANY CASE

John Fellows was excited to be named manager of the highly respected claims division for a major midwestern insurance company. John's experience in the insurance business was varied, and at age thirty-three he had just completed extensive training on a new computer system the company hoped would eventually reduce escalating overhead costs. John was aware that at least two members of his new department had applied for the job he was assuming, and he believed the company had placed him in the position partly to avoid making a choice between two competent peers.

John's initial month in the claims office of Middlesex was productive, confirming what he had been told about the competence of department personnel. Even the former applicants for his job, Joan and Tom, were cooperative and helpful. As a result of these early successes, John decided to move forward quickly with a plan to train personnel and install a new computer system. His immediate manager expressed concern that he was moving too fast without being thoroughly familiar with the department.

Following his staff meeting announcement of training schedules for all employees, John was surprised and somewhat irritated when Joan complained that he was moving too quickly before understanding department procedures. John decided that Joan probably had not really accepted his promotion into the job she wanted. This feeling seemed to be confirmed when Tom came to John and suggested there was reason to be concerned about the morale of the department with all the upcoming changes. Tom even hinted that three key people were considering asking for transfers. Although Tom did not say so, John was sure that Joan was at the bottom of the trouble.

John decided to confront Joan with her lack of support for this major corporate project. Joan became defensive and denied she was resisting the change: in fact, she claimed that John's misunderstanding of her concerns proved her point. To Joan, John simply was moving too fast and would create problems in systems about which he knew very little. John left the encounter wondering if maybe he had made a mistake about Joan, about Tom, or about his decision.

# INTRODUCTION

Are John and Joan engaged in organizational conflict, or is it a personal problem? Is the new computer system the issue? Is the issue John's approach? How is Tom involved? More important, what would you do if you were John, Joan, or Tom?

As a new manager, John is faced with a real test of his communication competency. Also, he is dealing with how important and inevitable conflict is in organizational life. What John decides will affect Joan, the entire department, and possibly his future career. How would you help John decide? What does he need to understand to be an effective manager of the claims division?

Although we may not have had John and Joan's specific problem, most of us have been involved in numerous conflicts and have been faced, as John is, with important decisions. Students have conflicts with teachers over grades. Families argue about issues of responsibility or money. Coworkers have negative feelings when particular individuals carry more of the work load than others. All are examples of conflicts that test our understanding and abilities.

It is important before you read further to think specifically about some of the conflicts that have been meaningful to you. What were the issues? Who was involved? What happened? For most of us it is easier to decide what John should do in the claims division than to make decisions when we are directly involved. Yet as John and Joan discovered, conflict is an inevitable part of our daily interactions.

Certainly if we are to be competent organizational communicators, we will be confronted with the need to solve problems effectively during conflict. To develop communication competencies for conflict, it is necessary to understand what conflict is, how it works, what role it plays in organizational functioning, and finally how individuals within organizations influence conflict outcomes.

This chapter is designed to contribute to *knowledge* by defining the concept of conflict, describing its various contexts and causes, and developing an analysis framework for understanding its process. Knowledge competencies will in turn help develop analysis skills for specific situations. *Sensitivity* competencies are developed by identifying individual and group predispositions and style preferences for conflict, by becoming familiar with strategies and tactics commonly used in conflicts, and by describing emotion during conflict. Sensitivity competencies influence the use of verbal and problem-solving process *skills* appropriate for each individual and the conflict at hand.

*Value competencies* are developed by exploring productive consequences of conflict, identifying supportive climates for conflict, and clarifying ethical conflict behaviors. As would be expected, value competencies are reflected in the use of ethical and supportive skills during conflict.

Finally, all four competencies—knowledge, sensitivity, skills, and values—are applied to the development of a problem-solving process for conflict and to competency practice through case analysis.

## DEFINING AND DESCRIBING CONFLICT PROCESSES
### Defining Conflict

**Conflict**
Process that occurs when individuals, small groups, or organizations perceive or experience frustration in attaining goals and concerns.

**Conflict** can be described as a process that occurs when individuals, small groups, or organizations perceive or experience frustration in attaining goals and concerns. At times this frustration is the result of a struggle over differing values or scarce rewards, whereas other times the central issue is the status or power of involved individuals. Regardless of the reasons, for all conflict participants the process includes perceptions, emotions, behaviors, and outcomes.

**Conflict context**
Any organizational setting where there are two or more competing responses to a single event or circumstance.

# Conflict Contexts

Researchers H. Wayland Cummings, Larry Long, and Michael Lewis (1983) have suggested that conflict can occur in any organizational setting in which there are two or more competing responses to a single event. In other words, conflict can occur in any context: intrapersonal, interpersonal, small group, intergroup, or organization-wide or between the organization and its broader environment.

The **conflict context** influences the conflict symptoms, behaviors, and outcomes. Intrapersonal conflict, for example, is not readily observable through overt behaviors; an individual experiencing internal conflict may not discuss the problem. Yet he or she may be observed to be under pressure or generally in a bad mood. These observations are indirect symptoms of the intrapersonal conflict. When John begins to wonder about his assumptions regarding Tom and Joan and to doubt his decision about the computer system, he may begin to experience intrapersonal conflict common to us all when our perceptions differ from those around us and when our judgments are called into question. Furthermore, because John is the manager, it will be difficult for him to take a wait-and-see attitude while letting others resolve the problem.

The conflict between John and Joan is a good example of the interpersonal context for organizational conflict. John is excited about his job and the opportunity to put into practice his training on the new system. Although he can understand that Joan wanted his job, he isn't prepared for her resistance to change. He believes that she is frustrated because she was not promoted and thus discounts her concerns about his lack of understanding of the department. He also links Tom's warning about people leaving the claims area to an attempt by Joan to undermine his efforts. Joan, on the other hand, sees John as another example of a powerful manager moving too quickly without sufficient background. In addition, neither really trusts the other's motives. Chances are that what happens next between John and Joan not only will affect their relationship but also will influence productivity throughout the department.

As in the interpersonal setting, conflict in the small-group context can be observed through behaviors during the conflict and by the conflict's lasting effects. The productive or destructive outcomes of conflict often are evidenced in the amount of group cohesion and productivity a team exhibits long after the actual conflict has ended. An example comes from a large West Coast electronics firm where four of ten senior research scientists left the organization within a period of fourteen months. The ten scientists had been together on a successful project for more than six years when two in the group disagreed with the direction a new product was to take. The two refused to negotiate a settlement and ordered their two principal assistants to pursue a line of research not supported by other team members. The remainder of the team approached project management with the problem and asked for resolution. Management refused to intervene, fearing alienation of the entire group if forced to take sides. Over a period of weeks, a once-productive team ceased to work together, and four key members began to look for new employment. The technical merits of the disagreement were never resolved, and in effect the team ceased to exist.

The contexts for organizational conflict are not limited, however, to interpersonal or small-group exchanges. Two separate organizational units may conflict over priorities in providing resources to one another, or an entire organization may appear to be in conflict over the fairness of pay and benefit plans. The organization-wide context, in actuality, is interpersonal, small-group, and intergroup conflict simultaneously addressing the same event or issue. Finally, the context of the organization's conflict with others—its competition, the public, the stockholders, the government—illustrates both how complex and how necessary conflict is for organizational functioning. U.S. automobiles and foreign competition, airline and oil company mergers, concern for nuclear accidents and hazardous waste disposal, and competitive approaches to advertising and marketing are only a few examples of conflicts between organizations and their environment.

**Causes of conflict**
Causes include scarce resources, deception, change, incivility, aggression, stress, burnout, emotional labor, relationships of all types, preferences, and past experiences.

## Conflict Causes

Circumstances contributing to conflict and the **causes of conflict** become common as the pace of organizational change intensifies. Adapting to global competition and changes in local situations is accomplished with scarce resources, both financial and human. Competition for resources exists between units within organizations, among individuals with differing agendas, and between and among organizations. Heavy workloads put conflicting time demands on employees at all organizational levels. The increasing complexity of organizational life generates conflicts, as does the use of increasingly sophisticated technologies. You can read daily news accounts of pressures to cut costs while improving performance whether the organization is in the private or public sector. Changes in organizational structure, mergers, alliances, and the regulatory environment all contribute to both individual and organization-wide conflict. Some contend that the increase in part-time and temporary workers generates conflict among peers because of the continuous turnover in skills experienced in the work group. Others view management turnover during change as introducing ambiguity that in turn produces conflict.

How organizations handle and value dissent during decision making contributes to norms of how to handle conflict. Organizations encouraging dissent during decision making generally experience more productive conflict than their counterparts valuing little disagreement and limited participation. In addition, all organizations have as employees, customers, or vendors or are in alliances with people who exhibit difficult behaviors contributing to conflict. One of the most frequent types of conflict you will encounter in organizations is working with people who engage in backstabbing, demonstrations of helplessness, excuses for nonperformance, and procrastination. Dealing with difficult people is indeed one of the most frequent tests of our organizational conflict management skills.

The conditions and causes of conflict discussed so far contribute to what many describe as a rise in incivility in the workplace and in some cases increased aggression and violence. Workplace civility has generally been conceptualized as courteous treatment of coworkers and other contacts. It includes treating others with dignity, regarding others' feelings, and using social norms of mutual respect. Incivility, on the other hand, is characterized by intents to harm either specific individuals or the organization. Incivility manifests itself in behaviors that demean the dignity of others and violate broad social norms of mutual respect. Civility and incivility take place through human communication interaction and overt behaviors. As Lynne Andersson and Christine Pearson (1999) explain:

> The need for civility becomes even greater when the interactions among people increase in complexity and frequency. . . . We face the growing challenge of relationships mediated by high-tech, asynchronous, global interaction. With history as counsel, one might assume a need for increased civility in forging and reconciling increasingly complex interactions. Yet, despite the implicit need for increasingly civil interaction, a recent poll of the American public revealed that 90 percent of the respondents think incivility is a serious problem . . . business has started to reflect the informality of society at large. . . . As the complexity of workplace interaction increases, discourteous behavior has more nuances: there are a greater number of ways to show disregard for fellow workers. (p. 452–453)

Also contributing to the opportunity for conflict are the various ways in which deception occurs within organizations. Anne Hubbell and Caryn Medved (2000) describe three perspectives: information distortion, strategic ambiguity, and complete distortion or lying. Information distortion is a process of modifying messages to receivers. Earlier was a discussion of how distortion occurs as messages move throughout the organization. Whether intentional or not, distortion contributes to differing perspectives and opportunities for conflict. The second perspective, strategic ambiguity, focuses on the purposeful use of vague language so that receivers can interpret a message from diverse perspectives. Again, although ambiguous messages may permit more people with differing views to identify with a particular position, the lack of common understanding has the potential for conflict. A recent example comes from a national clothing retailer. The chief executive officer (CEO) announced a major e-business initiative designed to transform the competitive position of the company. Reactions from senior managers were both enthusiastic and explosive. Some interpreted the message as a signal to move the somewhat traditional organization in new and exciting directions, but others voiced the opinion that the CEO was directing focus away from their core markets and customers. Finally, lies, deceit, deception, and concealment are behaviors with obvious potential to produce conflict. They often can be characterized as serious ethical abuses.

Certain types of jobs are characterized by the conflicting and stressful situations that are a routine part of the work. For example, leaders are charged with bringing about change and often encounter serious disagreements about courses of appropriate action. Other jobs require people to respond directly to emergencies and crises, whether from customers, the public at large, or within their specific organizations. Still others must adopt a service attitude even in the face of abusive behavior. Arlie Hochschild (1983) has used the term *emotional labor* to describe the work performed by those whose jobs involve a high degree of personal contact and who are expected to produce an emotional state, such as pleasure, gratitude, or self-esteem in the people with whom they deal.

With the overall growth of the service-based economy, Geoff Anderson (1993) claims that an increasing percentage of the work force will engage in some degree of emotional labor. Sales representatives, bill collectors, service complaint representatives, telemarketers, and flight attendants all fall within this category. These jobs and others require a separation of "true self" feelings from those that are expected to be expressed when in contact with the public. Hochschild (1983) contends that these emotional labor jobs require regulated emotion because they entail voice or face contact with the public, require the workers to produce a specific emotional state or reaction in the customer, and are regulated by employer control of the emotional activities of the employee. All you need to do to understand the potential conflict in these jobs is to think back to a time when you had a disagreement with a sales clerk or someone in a customer service position. How did you react? How did they respond? Was it a conflict or a normal routine business interaction? What makes the difference?

All the factors discussed are related to stress and the associated concept of burnout. Katherine Miller (1999) conceptualizes workplace stress as a process in which certain aspects of the environment create strains on individuals contributing to negative psychological, physiological, and organizational outcomes. The term *burnout* refers to the literal wearing out from the pressures of a situation or a job. Communication strategies associated with coping with stress and burnout include participation in decision making, receiving social support from peers and supervisors, and engaging in productive conflict. Try to identify times when you have experienced stress or burnout. Where these times or situations related to conflict?

Needless to say, daily organizational life is filled with conflicts in a variety of contexts. The results for individuals or entire organizations rest, however, not with whether conflict occurs but with the appropriateness of conflict behaviors and the effectiveness of conflict outcomes.

**Conflict episodes**
Descriptions of the complex interactions of both individual and group perceptions, emotions, behaviors, and outcomes during conflict.

## Conflict Episodes

Knowing what conflict is, why it happens, and in what context it occurs contributes to our understanding of conflict as a complex interaction of both individual and group perceptions, emotions, behaviors, and outcomes. These complex interactions frequently are viewed as a process researchers describe as **conflict episodes.** Scholar Louis Pondy (1967) has provided a particularly useful understanding of episodes as five basic conflict stages: (1) latent conflict, (2) perceived conflict, (3) felt conflict, (4) manifest conflict, and (5) conflict aftermath. These stages are seen as influencing each other, and the total interaction determines whether the conflict is productive or counterproductive. The stages help us visualize conflict as a process and analyze specific conflicts from a process perspective.

## Latent Conflict

**Latent conflict**
Underlying conditions in organizations and individual relationships that have the potential for conflict.

**Latent conflict** refers to underlying conditions in organizations and individual relationships that have the potential for conflict. For example, decisions about responsibility and authority, control of resources, goals, and activities in the pursuit of goals are all necessary for organizational functioning, yet few, if any, organizations make these decisions with the total agreement of all members. In other words, the daily functioning of the organization generates disagreement and conflict.

When John became the new manager of the Middlesex claims department, his appointment over two qualified applicants—Tom and Joan—can be considered a latent conflict condition. Furthermore, the introduction of the new computer system, as with any organizational change, has the potential for conflict. From the individual perspective, John, Tom, and Joan fulfill multiple roles in the department. These multiple roles may carry different and sometimes incompatible requirements, again underlying conditions for conflict. A supervisor, for example, may genuinely encourage a subordinate group to be open about mistakes. That same supervisor may work for a manager who is critical of mistakes and harsh in the treatment of those who make them. What the supervisor wants from the subordinate group is very different from what the supervisor, in the role of subordinate, sees as rewarded behavior. These incompatible requirements are underlying, or latent, conflict conditions.

It is important to understand that latent conflict conditions always exist in one form or another, although they may or may not produce conflict. Communication competence develops from being able to recognize latent conditions without assuming that conflict will automatically result.

## Perceived Conflict

**Perceived conflict**
Awareness of individuals or groups that differences exist.

Although latent conflict conditions always exist, individuals, work groups, or entire organizations may not see goals, individual roles, resources, or authority decisions as conflict producing. When conditions of high agreement and mutual satisfaction exist, organizational members are unlikely to view latent conflict conditions as anything other than routine decisions necessary for smooth organizational functioning. Most organizations, however, have disagreements about even routine decisions. Who gets a promotion, which approach is best to achieve a sales goal, or how individual performance is to be evaluated are examples of decisions frequently subject to differing viewpoints and misunderstandings. When individuals or groups become aware these differences exist, they are in the **perceived conflict** stage of an episode.

It is important to recognize that in this stage, overt conflict has not occurred, only the perception of significant frustrating differences. Also in this stage, it is possible that only one person in a relationship or situation will perceive a potential conflict. Problems between supervisors and subordinates arise, for example, when a supervisor sees a performance problem that the subordinate does not. Likewise, a subordinate may define the lack of supervisory feedback as a problem, whereas the supervisor believes additional communication is unnecessary. These perceptual differences are characteristic of the perceived conflict stage.

The ability to analyze thoughtfully is very important in this stage. Think about your relationship with a person who is important to you and try to recall a time when you became aware that a significant difference was possible between you. What were the cues to the difference? What assumptions were you making? How did you think the difference might alter your relationship? Was the other person aware of the problem? Were his or her perceptions of the situation similar to yours? The perceptions we form as we face significant differences with others are crucial to the process of conflict because those perceptions shape and influence the next two stages, which hinge on emotions and behaviors.

**Felt conflict**

Emotional impact the perception of conflict has on potential conflict participants.

## Felt Conflict

Closely linked to the perceived conflict stage is **felt conflict,** the emotional impact the perception of conflict has on potential conflict participants. This stage precedes actual conflict behaviors and is important to behavior because it represents the merger of our perceptions and emotional reactions. It is at the felt conflict stage that we conceptualize or define probable outcomes should an actual conflict occur; in other words, it is our ego-investment stage.

Our perception of the importance of the problem, our motives and the motives of others, and the varying abilities and relative power positions of those involved all contribute to the emotional impact, or the felt conflict. For most of us, seeing a possible difference with a coworker is a different emotional experience from seeing that same possible difference with the boss; it is not that the difference with the boss is necessarily worse, only that the relationships are different. The emotional impact of the problem is linked to the value we place on the specific relationship. Put another way, the felt conflict stage is an expansion of the perceived conflict stage. Perceptions are intensified by our emotional reactions to the potential conflict. Think again about the personal situation you identified for the perceived conflict stage. How did your emotional reaction influence your behavior? What was most important to you as you considered what was going to happen? Were you aware of consciously considering your behavior choices?

## Manifest Conflict

The **manifest conflict** stage has been referred to as the "action time" of conflict or the time "when the lid blows off and we really get down to business." The manifest conflict stage consists of conflicting behaviors: problem solving, open aggression, covert action, or numerous other possibilities. In this stage, communication behavior is

**Manifest conflict**
Actual conflict behaviors: problem solving, open aggression, covert action, and numerous other possibilities; influential for determining the productivity of the conflict and the way conflict participants will interact in the future.

influenced by participants' conflict preferences, perceptions of rules of interaction, power relationships, roles, and skills and abilities. All too often it is this manifest stage that we recognize as conflict, without realizing the powerful influence of previous stages.

Actual conflict behaviors—manifest conflict—are influential in determining the productivity of the conflict and the way conflict participants will interact in the future. Are all sides of the issue heard? Does power and influence decide what happens? How are people treated when their ideas are rejected? Group conflicts in which all members are treated with respect, for example, frequently result in decisions group members can support. On the other hand, when groups engage in personal attacks or use coercive power to enforce decisions, a very different result is predictable. Although both groups may reach reasonable decisions related to specific problems, the chances of continuing group support may be reduced if individual members feel discounted or threatened. These discounted members may contribute to future disagreements that are covert and unproductive.

Think about your personal experiences. Recall a conflict that you believe was resolved productively. How did you behave? How did others behave? Was the decision a good one? How did you feel several days later? Next, recall a conflict that left you frustrated and concerned. How did this situation differ from your more productive experience? What can be learned from contrasting the two? What competencies do you think are most important for the manifest conflict stage?

**Conflict aftermath**
Result of the complex interactions of latent conditions, perceived conflict, felt conflict, and manifest conflict.

## Conflict Aftermath

The **conflict aftermath** (outcomes) stage is a result of the complex interactions of latent conditions, perceived conflict, felt conflict, and manifest conflict. Put simply, this stage is what happens—in terms of both issues and relationships—as a result of the other four stages. It is the stage in which we evaluate the conflict as productive or counterproductive.

Although most of us fear conflict, contemporary thinking suggests that it can be productive as well as counterproductive. Although the contemporary view acknowledges that conflict outcomes can disrupt communication, produce psychological scars, and disrupt individual relationships, groups, or even entire organizations, the view also holds that conflict permits individuals and organizations to develop new ideas and approaches and to become actively involved in necessary change. In fact, communication scholar Brent Ruben (1978) contends that "conflict is not only essential to the growth, change, and evolution of living systems, but it is, as well, a system's primary defense against stagnation, detachment, entropy, and eventual extinction." When applied to organizations, conflict is an essential process for continued operation. Without conflict, organizations stagnate and die.

From a practical point of view, conflict outcomes influence the quality of decisions in organizations and consume large amounts of organizational resources. Managers spend from 20 to 40 percent of their time handling conflict. Practicing managers also report that managing conflict continues to become more important to organizational effectiveness. Although it is certainly obvious from this examination of conflict processes within various contexts, an often underestimated reality is the important role of individual behaviors in organizational conflict.

Many people who communicate effectively under harmonious conditions lose the ability to influence others and contribute to good decision making because they communicate poorly during conflict. Evidence suggests that personal experiences with organizational conflict influence how satisfied and productive organizational members are. In essence, fully effective organization members must exhibit communication competency under conflicting conditions and must contribute to productive outcomes both for themselves and the organization as a whole.

## THE INDIVIDUAL IN ORGANIZATIONAL CONFLICT

Organizations bring together diverse individuals, some of whom approach conflict as you would and others with very different preferences. The various predispositions, skills, and abilities of individuals in organizations influence how organizational conflict occurs. Sensitivity to these differences is central to becoming a competent communicator within a complex environment.

Sensitivity to our own preferences and behaviors helps us develop sensitivity to differences among people. One of the best ways to develop that sensitivity is to examine our own preferences in conflicts that have been important to us. The self-report questionnaire in Figure 9.1 should be completed and scored before you study the material about conflict styles, objectives, and tactics. This questionnaire is designed to increase your awareness of your individual preferences and predispositions for conflict. Scoring forms and profile interpretations are located on pages 348–349. Score your profile before studying the remainder of the chapter.

On completing the questionnaire in Figure 9.1, you will have short profiles of three conflicts you saw as important to you. These profiles are organized around conflict scholar Kenneth Thomas's (1976) basic components of individual conflict behavior: orientation/style, strategic objectives, and tactics. You will want to refer to your profiles as each of the behavior components is discussed.

*Orientations*, or predispositions, for conflict are the balances individuals try to make between satisfying their personal needs and goals and satisfying the needs and goals of others in the conflict. These orientations or predispositions are commonly referred to as conflict *styles*. *Strategic objectives* are a combination of balancing the individual preferences for conflict styles with what the individual sees as feasible outcomes in a particular situation. Behavior choices, known as *tactics*, are specific communication choices that are influenced by both orientation and style and strategic objectives.

### Orientations/Predispositions/Styles

Prominent conflict researchers such as Leonard Berkowitz (1962), Robert Blake and Jane Mouton (1964), Jay Hall (1969), and Kenneth Thomas (1976, 1988) all support

**FIGURE 9.1    Personal Profile of Conflict Predispositions, Strategies, and Tactics**

Before attempting to answer the following questions about your preferences and behaviors during conflict, list three conflicts that have been important to you.

1. The conflict was with _____
   about_____.
   It was generally productive/counterproductive. (circle one)

2. The conflict was with _____
   about_____.
   It was generally productive/counterproductive. (circle one)

3. The conflict was with _____
   about_____.
   It was generally productive/counterproductive. (circle one)

Based on your memory of these conflicts and others, respond to the following questions about preferences for conflict behaviors.

Circle the number that indicates whether you strongly agree (4), are inclined to agree (3), are inclined to disagree (2), or strongly disagree (1) with each of the following statements.

| | | | | |
|---|---|---|---|---|
| 1. When problems arise I prefer to let others take the responsibility for solving them. | 4 | 3 | 2 | 1 |
| 2. I believe a middle ground can be reached in most conflicts. | 4 | 3 | 2 | 1 |
| 3. I like everyone to be able to say what they think even if they don't agree with me. | 4 | 3 | 2 | 1 |
| 4. I can be firm in pursuing what I think is right. | 4 | 3 | 2 | 1 |
| 5. I try to reduce tension with others, to take people's minds off their problems. | 4 | 3 | 2 | 1 |
| 6. Usually it is best to postpone trying to talk to someone when he or she is upset. | 4 | 3 | 2 | 1 |
| 7. Talking about feelings and issues is important in conflict. | 4 | 3 | 2 | 1 |
| 8. I like people to be willing to give some if I will also. | 4 | 3 | 2 | 1 |
| 9. The goal must come first; conflict is inevitable and some people just can't take it. | 4 | 3 | 2 | 1 |
| 10. When people are upset, I am more concerned about their feelings than any particular problem. | 4 | 3 | 2 | 1 |
| 11. I don't like to be in unpleasant or tense situations. | 4 | 3 | 2 | 1 |
| 12. I like to win my points. | 4 | 3 | 2 | 1 |
| 13. Most conflicts are subject to compromise. | 4 | 3 | 2 | 1 |
| 14. Everyone should share in the gains and bear some of the losses. | 4 | 3 | 2 | 1 |
| 15. I will not contradict others if I believe that it will make them unhappy. | 4 | 3 | 2 | 1 |

**FIGURE 9.1    Continued**

| | | | | |
|---|---|---|---|---|
| 16. I offer solutions and ask others for solutions. | 4 | 3 | 2 | 1 |
| 17. I prefer to have everyone who is affected involved in solving a conflict. | 4 | 3 | 2 | 1 |
| 18. Believing disagreements can destroy effectiveness, I encourage others to stay with more agreeable subjects. | 4 | 3 | 2 | 1 |
| 19. I go after what I want, even if that makes others uncomfortable. | 4 | 3 | 2 | 1 |
| 20. Differences usually aren't important enough to worry about. | 4 | 3 | 2 | 1 |
| 21. I don't like to make other people feel bad by disagreeing. | 4 | 3 | 2 | 1 |
| 22. I think the best solutions come when everyone participates and has concern for others. | 4 | 3 | 2 | 1 |
| 23. I want others to know where I stand and will convince them of the rightness of my position. | 4 | 3 | 2 | 1 |
| 24. Confrontation can be managed if we seek middle ground. | 4 | 3 | 2 | 1 |
| 25. I try to help others be at ease, even if that means not pressing my point. | 4 | 3 | 2 | 1 |

Again remembering the important conflicts you identified, circle a number ranging from 1 (never) to 5 (always) to describe your behaviors during conflict.

| | Never | | Average | | Always |
|---|---|---|---|---|---|
| 1. Name calling | 1 | 2 | 3 | 4 | 5 |
| 2. Postponing the discussion | 1 | 2 | 3 | 4 | 5 |
| 3. Proposing compromise | 1 | 2 | 3 | 4 | 5 |
| 4. Expressing concern for others | 1 | 2 | 3 | 4 | 5 |
| 5. Expressing concern for facts | 1 | 2 | 3 | 4 | 5 |
| 6. Proposing areas of agreement | 1 | 2 | 3 | 4 | 5 |
| 7. Making threats | 1 | 2 | 3 | 4 | 5 |
| 8. Silence | 1 | 2 | 3 | 4 | 5 |
| 9. Adding issues to the original conflict | 1 | 2 | 3 | 4 | 5 |
| 10. Denying the conflict | 1 | 2 | 3 | 4 | 5 |
| 11. Supporting friends even if disagreeing | 1 | 2 | 3 | 4 | 5 |
| 12. Proposing solutions | 1 | 2 | 3 | 4 | 5 |
| 13. Agreeing to solutions | 1 | 2 | 3 | 4 | 5 |
| 14. Using formal rules to suppress conflict (voting, parliamentary procedure, etc.) | 1 | 2 | 3 | 4 | 5 |
| 15. Overpowering competition | 1 | 2 | 3 | 4 | 5 |
| 16. Describing gains and losses | 1 | 2 | 3 | 4 | 5 |

**Orientations/ predispositions**
Behavioral preferences for handling conflict; frequently described as avoidance, competition, compromise, accommodation, and collaboration.

the notion that individuals have behavioral **orientations/predispositions** or styles for handling conflict. Researchers further conclude that individuals have an order of preference among the styles that ultimately influences communication choices. In other words, an individual has a dominant or most preferred style, but when that style seems inappropriate in a given situation or does not work, the individual may go to the next preference in the hierarchy, and so on. The self-assessment you just completed identified the hierarchy you used in the specific conflicts you remembered. Refer back to that hierarchy as we explore what these various styles mean. Think about the accuracy of your profile and whether it is an effective one for you.

Conflict styles frequently are described as five basic orientations based on the balance between satisfying individual needs and goals and satisfying the needs and goals of others in the conflict. Figure 9.2 depicts the five styles—avoidance, competition, compromise, accommodation, and collaboration—on a two-dimensional grid with individual goals/assertiveness and concern for other/cooperativeness dimensions.

**Avoidance**
Style of individuals who, as a result of their preferences, are unlikely to pursue their own goals and needs or to support relationships and the goals and needs of others during conflict.

## Avoidance

Individuals preferring the **avoidance** style are unlikely to pursue their own goals and needs or to support relationships and the goals and needs of others during conflict. Conflict makes them very uncomfortable and often fearful. Although avoiders may have a genuine concern for goals and relationships, they do not see conflict as a positive solution. Avoiders may cope well during times of harmony but refrain—often both psychologically and physically—from participating in conflict situations.

Where was the avoidance style in your personal hierarchy? Can you identify friends or family who have this preference? How would you describe the impact of avoiders on decision making and on long-term relationships? The question of impact is especially important for organizations. Although most people agree that individuals within organizations have important preferences, organizations employ people to use their skills and abilities, the best of their thinking. When an individual avoids participating in decisions subject to conflict, the organization may lose important information that the individual is essentially responsible for contributing.

**Competition**
Preference for emphasizing personal goals and needs without considering the opinions or needs of others in the conflict.

## Competition

The individual who prefers **competition** approaches conflict by emphasizing personal goals and needs without considering the opinions or needs of others in the conflict. Competitive individuals often conceptualize conflict as win/lose and prefer to view themselves as winners. This orientation can block good problem solving, particularly if the competitive person needs input on a decision. On a more positive note, when a group is hopelessly deadlocked, competitors often

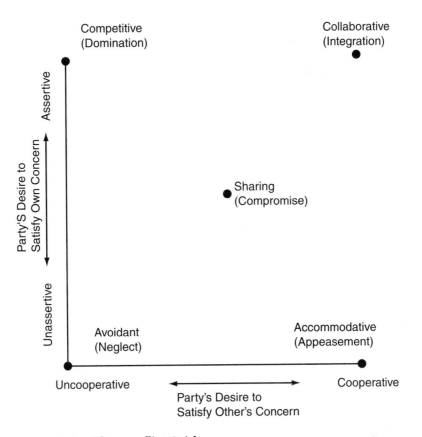

**FIGURE 9.2   The Conflict Grid**

K. Thomas, "Conflict and Conflict Management," in *The Handbook of Industrial and Organizational Psychology*, ed. M. Dunnette, 1976, p. 900. Reproduced by permission of John Wiley & Sons, Inc.

believe it is their responsibility to make a decision and to take responsibility for that decision. Given ability appropriate to the problem, this approach can be organizationally effective.

How often do you use the competitive approach? How effective has it been? Can you visualize a competitor and an avoider in a conflicting situation? What would you predict will occur? Sensitivity to the impact of the competitive approach is especially important because this style can be both abusive or exactly what the organization needs. The strong competitor can be guilty of discounting other good ideas and personally attacking others in order to remain a winner. When an avoider and a competitor disagree, the competitor usually wins, with little or no resistance; but this win is good for the organization only if the competitor was right and had all the appropriate information. Can you think of a time when you really had the best information, even if others disagreed? What type of behavior was needed for an effective decision? How important was it to pursue your point of view? The competitor runs the risk of competing for the sake of competing. The competitor can, however, make a decision when others are hopelessly deadlocked. The potential positives and negatives from the competitive style illustrate the need for the sensitivity competency in communication. Competent communicators are sensitive to their preferences and the appropriateness of applying them to specific situations. In this case, competency involves knowing when competitiveness is needed and when it is counterproductive.

**Compromise**

Preference during conflict for balancing people concerns with task issues and exhibiting give and take or negotiation behaviors.

## Compromise

Compromisers prefer to balance people concerns with task issues and often approach conflict with a give and take attitude that contributes to negotiation. Compromisers engage in give and take toward a goal or desired outcome in order to resolve the conflict situation. Most of us can identify numerous times when conflict was managed through **compromise.** Compromise works because all parties can minimize losses while establishing some gains. Indeed, organizations frequently encourage compromise, and it has become a preferred orientation in many decision-making groups.

A word of caution is appropriate, however. Have you ever been involved in a compromise that didn't really work, and the problem surfaced again? Did the compromise represent good problem solving, or was it just a convenient and comfortable way out of conflict? As with the competitive approach, a preference for compromise should be matched to the needs of the situation. Individuals who are willing to compromise can help organizations make a decision from among various conflicting viewpoints. If that decision does not represent thorough problem solving and allows the issue to resurface, however, the compromise orientation should have been avoided. Look again at your profile. How important is compromise to you? How effective has it been?

**Accommodation**

Preference for conflict associated with the sacrifice of personal goals to maintain relationships.

## Accommodation

People who want to be liked, have high affiliative needs, or genuinely are concerned for the needs of others often prefer an accommodative approach to conflict. **Accommodation** is characterized by the sacrifice of personal goals to maintain relationships or in some cases to maintain peace or the lack of conflict whether or not the relationship is maintained over the long term. This style can provide important support to groups engaged in making difficult decisions, but it also encourages the accommodative individual to abandon issue, goal, or task input when others appear to disagree.

Naturally, most of us want to be liked. Again, though, the issue is organizational effectiveness. Is the accommodative individual withholding an opinion to maintain a relationship with his or her boss or coworkers? How important is that opinion to what happens in the work group? Does the accommodative style keep the individual from being a good contributor, or is his or her real contribution the support of others? These are difficult questions requiring both sensitivity and good analysis skills. Think again about the conflicts you identified in your profile. Was accommodation a preference for you or others? How did the accommodative approach work? Should it be used again?

**Collaboration**

Preference for ideally balancing people and task concerns during conflict.

## Collaboration

When you examine Figure 9.2, the collaborative style is clearly seen as the ideal because this approach influences individuals to work for goals, to examine issues thoughtfully, and to be task oriented while supporting others to do the same. On the other hand, **collaboration** is the most difficult of all the styles to actually use for strategic objectives and tactical behaviors. Individuals who prefer collaboration can only behave collaboratively when others assume a collaborative orientation and have enough task or goal information to solve the problem thoroughly.

Where was the collaborative preference in your hierarchy? Can you see why conflict researchers believe this approach has more merit than avoidance, compromise, competition, or accommodation? Now think back to the specific conflicts you used in your self-analysis. Were these problems handled collaboratively? If these problems were not handled collaboratively, describe what might have been managed differently. Also, return to John's problem at Middlesex Insurance. Try to determine what John can do to establish a collaborative approach to his problem with Joan.

## Strategic Objectives

As Thomas (1976) has suggested, individuals' strategic objectives in conflict are determined not only by orientations or preferences for conflict styles but also by assessments of the probable outcomes of behavior within particular contexts. Specifically, strategic objectives are determined by matching general preferences for particular conflict styles with assessments of the risks involved in a particular situation. In addition, as Charles Conrad (1985) has pointed out, strategic choices are made not only with individual preferences in mind but also with consideration of the communication strategies used by others involved in the conflict. Organizational role, power positions, previous experiences, and the importance of specific issues all contribute to the strategic objectives adopted by conflict participants.

A strategic choice is, according to Gerald Phillips and Nancy Metzger (1976), a "planned method of conducting operations" so as to structure the conflict in one of four strategic directions: escalation, reduction, maintenance, or avoidance. As Joyce Hocker and William Wilmot (1991) have suggested, "strategies are the large, general game plans in conflicts, and tactics are the moves made to advance the conflict in the strategic direction that the participants informally and implicitly work out among themselves."

In the Middlesex Insurance case, as John reflects on his problem with Joan, he is beginning to establish strategic objectives. His personal preferences and decisions will affect whether the conflict escalates, reduces, stays at the present level, or is avoided. For example, if John chooses to escalate the conflict, he can announce that his training schedule will be initiated as announced and that those not in agreement can look for work in other departments. If John has good analysis skills, he can predict that this action will probably anger Joan and possibly others. He cannot know with certainty what Joan's reaction will be, but he can assume that conflict escalation is the probable outcome. John might attempt to escalate the conflict if he really wanted Joan and the others to leave, but his analysis ability probably will tell him that he may be viewed with suspicion if competent people leave a department soon after he becomes manager.

On the other hand, John might attempt to reduce the conflict by asking Joan to help him understand her objections to the timetable for training. He would then be in a position to decide whether her objections were based on department operations or were primarily due to his promotion.

John could attempt to maintain the conflict at its present level by acknowledging that he and Joan have differences. He can suggest that he will try his new ideas while being willing to listen to her objections if there are problems. John will have difficulty in choosing the strategic objective of avoidance because he and Joan have already voiced opposing views. He can, of course, back off his training schedule and not make further reference to their disagreement.

Regardless of what John decides, the result is determined by all those involved in the situation. John's strategic objective is based on his desired outcome and his best estimate of the reaction of Joan and others. His individual preferences, past experiences, and overall competency with conflict will influence his decisions and contribute to whether the outcomes are productive for the Middlesex Insurance claims department.

## Communication Tactics in Conflict

Conflict tactics can be described as communication behaviors that attempt to move the conflict toward escalation, reduction, maintenance at the present level, or avoidance. The tactics adopted are influenced by individual conflict preferences and strategies and by overall organizational values about how conflict is supposed to work. For example, powerful individuals frequently use competitive and confrontational tactics, whereas individuals apprehensive about communicating use more avoidance tactics. Some organizations encourage open debate and disagreement, whereas others insist on disagreement only if there are no personal attacks or displays of anger. Still others discourage overt conflict of any type. In any case, the exchanges of communication tactics among conflict participants illustrate the interactive nature of conflict, with outcomes related to complex tactical interactions as well as orientations and strategic objectives.

Although it is impossible to list or define all the possible tactics available to conflict participants, it is important for our personal sensitivity and also for our verbal skills to identify frequently used conflict tactics. Figure 9.3 presents excerpts from actual organizational conflicts. Each example is accompanied by a description of the tactic it represents. Tactics are grouped into the following categories: tactics

## FIGURE 9.3 Communication Tactics for Conflict

| ORGANIZATIONAL NARRATIVE | CONFLICT TACTIC |
|---|---|

### Tactics for Conflict Escalation

"You have a bad attitude or you wouldn't do such sloppy and unprofessional work."

1. *Applying evaluative labels* to individuals or issues

"I know you don't want to work this out. Six months ago you weren't willing to give us the extra people for the [manufacturing] line. I can't imagine that it is any different now."

2. *Expanding the conflict* at hand to related problems or old unsettled disputes

"It's not just me. Every member of this department thinks you are wrong. We just can't make the deadlines you keep establishing."

3. *Forming alliances* and making them known in an attempt to overpower competitors

"I don't intend to be surrounded by people who make trouble for me. You get this machine fixed this time or you can cause trouble for someone else."

4. *Making threats* with or without control of sanctions or outcomes

"I don't want to work with John on this project. You can give me Mary or Sam but not John."

5. Deliberately *limiting the choices* of others

"I know we agreed to work this out between us, but I went to Ralph [both people's supervisor]. Your team just doesn't have the workload that mine does, and he has got to create some justice."

6. *Breaking previously agreed-upon rules* of behavior for the specific relationship

### Tactics for Conflict Avoidance

(Supervisor to subordinate not recommended for promotion) "Being upset about Mary getting the job isn't going to help. Let's talk about it when you're feeling better. You just need to be patient and wait for another opportunity."

1. *Delaying* or procrastinating in addressing conflicting issues

(Top manager to unhappy employee) "I understand that you think your boss is unfair—and I know we have an open-door policy—but when you have a grievance you are to go to personnel and file a formal report. I will look at the issue only after you have followed proper channels."

2. *Using formal rules,* rank, seniority, majority rule, and other means of controlling processes to constrain the behavior of conflicting parties

"This issue is simply not a problem. I am not angry with you and you have no right to be mad at me. I am going to continue to believe nothing is wrong."

3. *Denying* the existence of a conflict

*(continued)*

**FIGURE 9.3    Continued**

"I know it was important to get two more people on the night shift, and I know you really need them, but I believe that you can maintain your production level. More people would help, but your group is good and I know they can continue to do the job."

4. *Fogging the issue* by acceptance of part of the concern while ignoring other important concerns

## Tactics for Conflict Maintenance

"The only way we are going to meet this deadline is to work together. It doesn't matter right now who got us into this mess. If we don't deliver to the customer on time, we will all get blamed."

1. Describing what all parties have to *gain and lose*

(Two managers before a board of directors meeting) "No, I won't make matters worse. I have always supported you in the directors meeting. I will continue to do that even though you know I think this is not the way to go."

2. Agreeing to *honor long-term relationship* rules

"Look, I think the way you have been behaving is inconsiderate of your fellow workers, but maybe I don't have all the facts and I certainly don't know how you are feeling."

3. Combining both *escalation and reduction tactics*

"I believe we can agree that this level of budget is all we are going to have to spend between us. I will look at my travel plans if you will consider your expenditures for part-time secretarial support services."

4. *Proposing areas of agreement* and areas for compromise

## Tactics for Conflict Reduction

"Now, changing the entire computer system is a major departure from our current operations. I think we need to think first of who has what type of training and how we can approach bringing people up to speed without destroying our work schedules. We then can approach purchasing and installing the new system."

1. Identifying *numerous manageable issues* and suggesting approaching "smaller" concerns

"I know we are upset that John promised we would get these shipments out over the holiday, but if we are to present our case and be listened to, we must not personally attack John or remind him that this is the second time in six months that has happened."

2. Describing *behaviors and outcomes to be avoided* during the conflict

**FIGURE 9.3    Continued**

"Obviously the report has to be corrected. I'm concerned about the amount of time that is going to take and how fatigued you must be, but I am also concerned about how we got so much inaccurate information to begin with."

3.  Exhibiting concern *for both facts and feelings*

"Perhaps I was wrong to believe that we should hire another account executive before secretarial support staff. I will consider a part-time secretarial type along with the new exec."

4.  Offering *compromises* from original positions

for conflict escalation, tactics for conflict avoidance, tactics for conflict maintenance, and tactics for conflict reduction. Strategic objectives and tactics have been summarized from the research of Hocker and Wilmot (1991), Conrad (1985), and Joseph Folger, Marshall Scott Poole, and Randall Stutman (1993).

Organizational conflicts are characterized by the frequent use of all these tactics and many more. Furthermore, organizational life brings us all in contact with individuals who have vastly different conflict styles, strategic objectives, and tactical approaches. These differences can either contribute to productive conflict or be a primary reason that conflict is destructive, resulting in bad decisions and, ultimately, additional conflict.

Figure 9.3 identifies frequently used conflict communication tactics through short excerpts from transcripts of organizational conflict. To further develop your sensitivity and skills for tactic identification, Figure 9.4 provides a more detailed transcript of an organizational conflict. As you read the transcript, try to identify tactics used for escalation, avoidance, maintenance, or reduction. Also, identify and describe any tactics not previously listed in Figure 9.3. Finally, as you read the transcript, think about tactics you use and tactics you have observed.

Before leaving the topic of conflict predispositions, strategies, and tactics, some words of caution are important. Although it is useful to understand our own preferences and behaviors, research reported by Hocker and Wilmot (1991) indicates that most of us are prone to see ourselves as trying to solve problems while other people are using control or aggressive approaches. In other words, we are likely to view our efforts more positively than those with whom we are in conflict. In addition, emphasis on style, strategy, and tactic choices may block us from understanding that conflict is an interactional, dynamic process with others. We will be less capable of productive approaches if we, as Folger, Poole, and Stutman (1993) suggest, overemphasize a consistent, specific orientation toward conflict. Finally, most of our style, strategy, and tactics research has been conducted in the United States or Great Britain and has been carried out with majority groups. We know much less about preferences and orientations in cultures that are more group oriented than individualistic. We have just begun to think through the implications of an increasingly diverse work force and multiculturalism for organizational conflict and conflict management. As

**FIGURE 9.4   Transcript of an Organizational Conflict**

Mary is in conversation with her subordinate, Dan. This conversation is Dan's second warning about tardiness and absenteeism. Dan contends that he does more work than others on the maintenance crew. Mary knows that Dan is a good worker but cannot tolerate his abuses of company policy.

> **Mary:**   Dan, you know why I asked you to come in this morning. We talked about your problem last month, and I thought you intended to improve. Yet when I checked the monthly time report it shows you were late four times and used two more sick-leave days. That tells me you didn't take our conversation very seriously. Dan, your work is good, but your attitude isn't. I can't tolerate any more of this behavior.
>
> **Dan:**   Yeah, I know we talked last month, and I did intend to get here on time, but my car is old, and anyway, I always get all my work done. I work twice as hard as Fred. I wish you would do something about that instead of always being on my back.
>
> **Mary:**   Now, Dan, Fred is not the issue; you are.
>
> **Dan:**   Well, Fred and several of the others should be. I'm in here defending myself when I do better work than most of the crew. You aren't fair!
>
> **Mary:**   Dan, I acknowledge that your work is good, but the company policy is important. You can't keep being late and running out of your sick leave by April or May of each year. What am I going to do with you? I really would hate to have to use a formal warning. You do know what that is?
>
> **Dan:**   Yeah, I know about formal warnings. I guess I can watch it a little better. The problem is, I still think that my working harder than the others should count for something.
>
> **Mary:**   Well, Dan, your good work could count for something if you didn't have these other problems. If you ever want to make more money or be a supervisor, you are going to have to be here on time and support company policy.
>
> **Dan:**   Well, I suppose you're right, but I still don't like it.
>
> **Mary:**   Dan, the choice is yours. If the report next month is not better, I am going to put you on warning.
>
> **Dan:**   [Under his breath] Okay, okay, but I still don't think it's fair.

such, understanding cultural context and the limitations of any set of descriptive categories becomes an important sensitivity for productive conflict behaviors.

## Emotion during Conflict

In thinking about styles, strategic objectives, and tactics for conflict, it is possible to overlook the importance of emotion and the reality that conflict stirs emotions in almost everyone. Tricia Jones (1997) describes emotion as having three components: cognitive, physiological, and behavioral. The cognitive component of emotion involves the appraisal of situations that in turn invoke emotional responses. The physiological component involves the embodied experiences that literally radiate throughout the body as ongoing lived experiences. Finally, the expressive component of emotion is what we do—the behavioral response—as an expression of the cognitive and physiological experience. Jones argues that conflict is emotionally defined, in other words, events that cause conflict are by definition events that elicit emotion. She relates emotion to conflict strategies and tactics by suggesting that our emotional definitions of conflict impact our orientations, what we believe should occur during conflict, and our actual behavior. This view of the importance of emotional communication during conflict can help us understand our personal responses to conflict as well as approaches taken in a variety of organizational circumstances.

Anger, generally described as a very strong emotion, is a frequent response in most organizations. Anger occurs when individuals experience humiliation, receive verbal abuse, are ignored when trying to engage in contributions or disagreements, or encounter a host of other emotion-producing interactions. Responses to anger include silence, stress, aggression, and both productive and negative conflict behaviors. Anger can stimulate creativity, but it also has been related to poor-quality work, chronic absenteeism, and even theft of company property. Although expressions of anger can be constructive and appropriate, anger displays often are associated with the types of conflict behaviors many of us fear and seek to avoid. Can you remember a time when anger contributed to how you reacted in a conflict? Was it productive? If not, how did you respond later to your own anger? What role do you believe anger plays in organizational conflict?

Earlier we talked about jobs with high components of emotional labor or controlled emotional expressions and their potential for contributing to conflict. Unlike anger displays, which are associated rightly or wrongly with volatile conflict, the conflict experienced by those in jobs with high emotional labor components often is suppressed and surfaces in much less direct ways. Some have characterized these mostly high-visibility service jobs as contributing to workers' inability to recognize their own private feelings. Flight attendants have used the phrase "go robot" to describe their public behaviors. Vince Waldron and Kathy Krone (1991) reported personal costs associated with the suppression of emotion, which included suppressed disagreements, reduced upward information flow, and the loss of voice or the sense of being heard and responded to within the organization. Although anger and emotional suppression are somewhat different processes, we can readily see how they both become important emotional experiences for individuals and how both relate to many types of organizational conflict.

Given the pressure of today's workplace and what many consider unhealthy and unproductive approaches to conflict that focus solely on rationality, the concept of emotion in the workplace and in conflict takes on new meaning. Linda Putnam and Dennis Mumby (1993) have proposed the concept of bounded emotion as a way to think about the problem of emotional control in organizations. Bounded emotionality encourages the expression of a wider range of emotions than is usually condoned in traditional organizations while stressing the importance of maintaining interpersonally sensitive, variable boundaries between what is felt and what is expressed. In other words, many believe it is time to value emotion and the feelings, sensations, and affective responses to organizational situations that emotion brings. This valuing can benefit individuals and also a variety of organizational processes, including conflict processes.

The recognition of the importance of emotion in conflict is in direct opposition to those who believe we should only discuss major points of disagreement if we all can be "rational" and "logical." The reality of emotion is part of the fabric of organizational life. Think about times you have observed emotional displays in organizations. What happened? How did you react? Do some organizations have rules for how emotion is to be expressed? Are some emotional expressions more valued than others? For example, are anger and crying treated in the same manner? What makes the difference? Finally, think about conflicts where you have "lived emotion" and try to remember how that experience influenced your behavior.

## GROUPS IN ORGANIZATIONAL CONFLICT

In Chapter 6 the importance of groups for organizational functioning was described and many of the types of groups we will probably join were discussed. Now the specifics about some of the reasons for group conflict and a variety of approaches for conflict management are described.

Most of us have been in groups in which tensions and conflict made us uncomfortable or blocked problem solving. It is hoped that most of us also belonged to groups in which conflict contributed to new and better ways of doing things, actually strengthening the group's ability to work together. Think for a moment about these experiences. What made the difference? How did you feel and behave in these differing circumstances?

### Group Members in Conflict

Earlier were described a variety of orientations, predispositions, and styles; strategic objectives; communication tactics for conflict; and the importance of emotion. As you would expect, all these factors and more can contribute to conflict when diverse individuals participate in groups. Group members also play task, maintenance, and self-centered roles. In Chapter 6 was discussed the generally negative influence of self-centered roles and the need for balance in task and maintenance behaviors. It is easy to understand why self-centered roles and inappropriate balances of task and maintenance roles are a possible source of group conflict. In addition, although most organizations talk about the importance of teamwork, rewards usually recognize individual versus group efforts. Members of a work team, for example, will be asked to collaborate, yet each knows that merit salary increases will reflect how they compare to each other, not how they produce as a group. This seeming contradiction is another source of work group conflict.

Conflict styles generally have been studied as specific to individuals. Much of the earlier discussion took that focus. Tim Kuhn and Marshall Scott Poole (2000) provide an expansion of the individual approach when they consider conflict styles at the group level "as a typical interaction pattern a group enacts when members deal with oppositions and disagreements." According to Kuhn and Poole, these group styles are "embodied in group norms about how to handle disagreements. . . . The process of norm formation is complex and depends on the particular combination of individual styles that exists in a group and on the resources available to members to influence others to adopt and maintain a particular stylistic choice." Kuhn and Poole use the categories of avoidance, distributive, and integrative styles to access the effect of conflict styles on group decision making effectiveness. Avoidance styles describe behavior that minimizes addressing the conflict. A distributive style, much like the competitive style, uses a confrontive approach, with one party or group essentially giving in to another. The integrative approach is characterized by cooperative and collaborative behaviors to pursue mutually positive resolutions. Building on previous work that has related decision making quality and effectiveness to groups using competing interpretations about issues and synthesizing these interpretations into a decision the group can accept, Kuhn and Poole sought to determine if groups develop norms regarding how they will manage conflicts that carry over to affect other activities, such as decision making, even when these activities do not involve open conflict. After studying several teams over a period of time, Kuhn and Poole concluded that groups that developed integrative conflict management styles made more effective decisions than groups that used confrontation and avoidance. Groups that did not develop a stable conflict style were also less effective than groups with integrative styles.

## Procedural Conflict

Most types of organizational groups conflict over procedures or ways of doing things. How the group is organized, the process of decision making, who accepts responsibility, or what happens when responsibilities are not carried out can all contribute to tension and conflict within groups. Most of you have experienced this procedural conflict when preparing a project for a class. Some group members preferred majority rule, others worked for genuine consensus, and still others attempted to force their positions or opinions on the entire group.

## Interpersonal Issues

One of the most common types of group conflict emerges when all members do not fairly or equally perform their responsibilities or make contributions to the group. The necessity to "carry" a member of the team raises tension and disrupts group cohesiveness. Groups also have interpersonal power clashes among members who seek influence and control. Powerful members produce conflict when attempting to force group members to take sides in essentially interpersonal disputes. We have all observed two individuals disagreeing or disparaging one another in front of the group. We often suspect that their disagreements have little or nothing to do with the issues at hand but reflect ongoing difficulties in the relationship. Unfortunately, they introduce tension and counterproductive behaviors into what might otherwise be an effective setting.

## Substantive Issues

The very reason for forming groups in organizations can contribute to group conflict. Organizations should use the energy of diverse individuals to establish effective ways of doing things or to challenge existing processes in favor of new and better efforts. In effect, organizations should encourage conflicts of ideas that contribute to excellence. Individuals normally and productively can differ about positions, interests, approaches, or problems. Groups can therefore be expected to have conflicts over issues, ideas, or tasks.

**Groupthink**
Tendency of groups to suspend critical thinking and too quickly adopt proposed solutions.

## Groupthink

As is true in interpersonal conflict, group conflict can range from highly productive to counterproductive. Most of us have been present at a meeting where displays of anger blocked effective problem solving. If we think carefully about our group experiences, however, we probably can remember a time when surface harmony also blocked problem-solving effectiveness.

Surface harmony, or the absence of productive conflict, can block group effectiveness when critical thinking is absent, resulting in ill-conceived courses of action. Irving Janis (1983) has called the surface harmony frequently associated with highly cohesive groups **groupthink,** or the tendency of groups to suspend critical thinking and to adopt proposed solutions too quickly. Groups in danger of groupthink overestimate their own capabilities, seek information that supports their point of view, and avoid or discount contradictory ideas. Have you ever participated in groupthink? What happened? How can group members decide if they genuinely agree or are exhibiting groupthink tendencies? A discussion of a format for productive conflict provides some possible answers.

## Group Conflict Management Processes

Group conflict is so important in organizations that a variety of processes for management have become commonplace. These processes are typically described as negotiation, bargaining, mediation, forcing, and arbitration. Although this chapter does not describe each of these processes in detail, your awareness that they are frequently used becomes part of your knowledge competency for group participation.

**Negotiation**
Broad conflict management process involving discussions between and among individuals who are interdependent and need to come together for a decision or course of action; frequently associated with the need to compromise effectively.

**Negotiation** is a common process in groups. Generally speaking, negotiation can be understood as a broad process involving discussions between and among individuals who are interdependent and need to come together for a decision or course of action. Groups negotiate procedures and issues with expected give and take among members. The negotiation process is frequently associated with the need to compromise effectively. The next section of this chapter describes a concept of principled negotiation that supports productive conflict.

**Bargaining** is a more structured form of negotiations. Bargaining usually involves the presentation of fairly specific proposals for the purpose of achieving a working agreement on particular issues. You are probably familiar with collective bargaining as it applies to labor and management group interactions. Yet bargaining has numerous other organizational applications. At budget time, groups may be asked to present very specific proposals for money. Representatives from each group may be asked to negotiate or bargain for fixed resources. In some cases the rules for these exchanges will be well defined, whereas in others the process is more open-ended. Regardless of the formality, bargaining is an established conflict resolution procedure in many organizations.

**Mediation** is another possible group conflict management process. In mediation a designated individual guides the negotiations or bargaining efforts of the groups in conflict. Mediation is used when negotiations are deadlocked or tensions so high that a designated leader is desirable. When mediation fails, the designated leader frequently has to rely on forcing or making a decision that the group must accept. Obviously, for mediation or forcing to be effective, the designated leader must have credibility with the opposing factions and responsibility and authority appropriate to the task. Generally speaking, mediators are members of the group or organization involved in the process.

Finally, when negotiation, bargaining, or mediation fails, organizations can manage group conflict with **third-party arbitration.** Arbitration usually involves an outside negotiator who resolves differences with formally established procedures. Labor-management disputes have been subjects of arbitration, as have a variety of legally related cases. Arbitration frequently results in ill will because of the forced nature of resolving the conflict.

Fortunately most of us will work in groups that manage conflict through collaboration and negotiation. We know from experience that effectiveness is more likely to occur when group members voluntarily solve their own disputes than when leaders or an outside individual must take charge. Therefore, the need is to develop an understanding of how to engage in conflict productively. The next section of this chapter returns to the earlier discussion of power and relates power processes to organizational conflict.

## Power and Organizational Conflict

The concept of power was first discussed in Chapter 3. The discussion of conflict is an excellent time to return to this important organizational process because perceptions of power and its uses continually influence all aspects of organizational conflict. The organizational structure itself represents how formal power is

**Bargaining**
Structured form of negotiations usually involving the presentation of fairly specific proposals for the purpose of achieving a working agreement on particular issues.

**Mediation**
Use of a designated individual for guiding the negotiations or bargaining efforts of groups in conflict.

**Third-party arbitration**
Conflict management process involving an outside negotiator who resolves differences based on formally established procedures.

intended to work. The organizational chart defines for the formal power structure who has the right to overrule whom and who makes decisions and resolves disagreements when collaboration or compromise break down. Formal power relationships rarely explain, however, the complexity of organizational conflict. Informal leaders, coalitions of individuals with special relationships, politics, and assumptions of superiority all influence conflict processes. We see individuals and groups with excellent ideas submitting to the ideas of more powerful organizational members and groups. This "raising the white flag" affects decision making and also structures future relationships. We observe what we call power plays in all types of organizational situations. Power plays can be described as tactics which make explicit how power should be viewed in particular circumstances in order to preserve the position of the person or persons making the "play." Technical and communicative expertise become sources of power as well as resources within the control of individuals. Information is an increasingly important organizational resource. Information resides with individuals throughout the organization, contributing to the dynamic and shifting nature of power. Our perceptions of our own power and the power of others will influence the approaches we choose during conflict. Both the wise use and the abuse of power influence how conflicts occur and what happens during conflict. Think about conflicts you have observed or in which you have been involved. How was power used? How did power influence what happened?

Although power use during conflict can be productive, power often is associated with behaviors that marginalize others and attempt to maintain the status and position of the person or persons exercising power. In the next section the special and important abuses of power come up in the discussion of sexual harassment, discrimination, and ethical abuses as special forms of organizational conflict.

## SPECIAL TYPES OF ORGANIZATIONAL CONFLICT: SEXUAL HARASSMENT, DISCRIMINATION, ETHICAL ABUSES

Although sexual harassment, discrimination, and numerous types of ethical abuses all have legal consequences beyond the scope of this conflict discussion, they also can be viewed as important types of organizational conflicts. Virtually all organizations have policies prohibiting sexual harassment, discrimination, and ethical abuses, yet the prevalence of these actions impacts literally thousands of workers each year. The impact on individuals can be severe, but less well understood is the impact these negative conflicts have on the overall effectiveness of organizations.

**Sexual harassment** is an important example of power abuse that generates negative conflict. Gerald Pepper (1995) provides a useful definition of this conflict-producing abuse:

**Sexual harassment**
Situation in which one person persists in behaving in a way that offends the sexual morals of another or creates employment conditions based on sexual relationships.

Sexual harassment refers to situations in which one person persists in behaving in a way that offends the sexual morals of another or creates an expectation on the part of the harassed that his or her employment conditions are subject to change if the victim does not respond as the harasser desires. Harassment can also take the form of an overall working environment that is permeated with offensive behavior or materials. Sexual harassment may be physical or psychological, may occur between same- or different-sex individuals, may happen to both women and men, and is not a condition of hierarchical level. (p. 149)

The number of individuals who experience workplace sexual harassment is difficult to determine, but research estimates range from 40 percent to as high as over 90 percent of all female workers. Estimates for abuse of men is less well documented. Sexual harassment is communicated through inappropriate verbal and nonverbal displays as well as the display of offensive objects in the workplace. Inappropriate verbal acts range from compliments with sexual overtones to terms of endearment not reflective of the workplace relationship. Nonverbal behaviors range from gestures with sexual inferences to physical acts of touching, fondling, stroking, or generally using physical presence to create a hostile environment. Displays of objects include posters or calendars with sexually explicit photos as well as use of the Internet and other communications technologies to bring sexually explicit material into the workplace. Sexual harassment includes the communication of the need to submit to sexual advances as a basis of continued employment or as a condition of advancement. Finally, harassers frequently instill fear of retaliation for reporting sexual harassment. All these behaviors occur within organizations and with customers and vendors as well.

Although sexual harassment is illegal and not supported by organizational policies, well-developed communication skills provide the most readily available assistance for women and men experiencing this abusive conflict. Harassment conflict rarely is resolved without direct intervention ranging from confronting the harasser to reporting concerns to supervisors and those charged with handling grievances. Unfortunately, many women and men have been culturally conditioned to believe that many of the behaviors we have been describing are normal and acceptable communication. Nevertheless, the impact of this type of abusive behavior both limits individual potential and satisfaction as well as overall organizational effectiveness. Have you experienced sexual harassment? Have you participated in any of the above-described behaviors? How would you describe your current abilities to confront workplace sexual harassment?

**Discrimination**
Exclusion of individuals or groups based on personal characteristics not associated with competence or performance.

**Discrimination** in the workplace is both a legal and cultural issue. Discrimination can be defined as the systematic exclusion of individuals based on characteristics such as race, ethnicity, gender, or age. Sometimes referred to as labor market discrimination, discrimination in the workplace is based on personal characteristics of workers that are not related to productivity. As with sexual harassment, discrimination is illegal, and most organizations take public stands against a variety of discriminatory practices. The experiences of women, racial and ethnic minorities, and older workers provide evidence of the continuing presence of conflicts because of discrimination. Women and racial and ethnic minorities continue to make less money than their white male counterparts in similar jobs, and the presence of the "glass ceiling" (the level above which women and minorities are not typically promoted) remains for most upper management and leadership positions.

Bias can begin with hiring and selection processes. Job postings often require experience and backgrounds that have little or no relationship to the ability of applicants to perform the job. Often experience and or educational requirements favor members of the majority population in an organization. Hiring decisions often favor close friends, relatives, or college connections, whereas promotions may come as a result of seniority over competence or ignoring seniority in favor of preferences for "younger" people. The potential for conflict is obvious. When competence is not the criteria for hiring and promotion, frustration and anger are understandable responses from those who are continually "outsiders."

Pepper (1995) helps us understand subtle discrimination that can reside in the culture of the organization. Pepper contends:

> Women and minorities in the workplace can profitably be understood as "marginal persons." The marginal person suffers the consequences of having no firm footing. The lack of a peer or reference group, coupled with the hostility or rejection or conditional acceptance of the desired reference group leaves the marginal person feeling as though he or she is only a peripheral participant.
>
> Marginality offers an interesting clarification, if not a replacement, for existing theories that attempt to explain the slow progress that minorities and women have made in the workplace. Rather than relying on explanations like differences in socialization, or patriarchal organizational environments, the theory of marginality is a communication-based explanation for discrimination. It is predicated on the assumption that the marginal person, an intercultural sojourner of sorts, will continually have to wrestle with the rejection of the group left behind and the resistance of the group desired. (p. 240)

The theory of marginality focuses on the conflicts that marginalized people face with both their old and new groups. For example, research supports the difficulty of many women who are promoted from among their peers to positions of leadership. Women, more than their male counterparts, often face resistance from their former peers and hostility at worst and a lack of assistance at best from the leadership group to which they have been promoted.

The last category of special types of organizational conflict—ethical abuses—incorporates issues of sexual harassment and discrimination along with numerous other abuses in day-to-day organizational life. Dalmar Fisher (1993) identifies six major areas in which ethical abuses can occur as organizations relate to their external environments: (1) products, (2) advertising, (3) finance and accounting, (4) pricing, (5) international operations, and (6) ecology. These issues and others are what Fisher describes as corporate social responsibility. He goes on to identify (1) working conditions, (2) due process and fair treatment of employees, (3) personnel policies and procedures, (4) design of work, and (5) free speech as issues with potential for ethical abuse within organizations.

Convictions of individuals for ethical abuses such as insider trading, embezzlement, sexual harassment, and discrimination are at an all-time high. In addition, research suggests that well over 50 percent of all employees have been pressured by their organizations to engage in what they consider unethical behaviors.

**Whistleblowing**
Reporting unethical behaviors to those who can do something about them.

Employees increasingly are reporting ethical abuses to those in positions of power. These reporting behaviors frequently are referred to as **whistleblowing,** or the disclosure of illegal and unethical behaviors to those who can do something about them. Reporting unethical behavior is conflicting and a complicated ethical issue. Should the whistleblower report his or her finding internally and wait for results, or should the whistleblower go directly to the public? The answers are not simple. The decisions individuals make about either the knowledge of or participating in ethical abuses will not only influence their own career satisfaction but also directly affect the performance of the organization.

It is fair to say that we all will be faced by one or more of these negative conflict-producing situations. How we will respond is related to our knowledge, sensitivity, skills, and values. In other words, communication competency in its broadest sense will contribute to our ability to handle these special types of organizational conflict. The next section of this chapter contributes to our competencies by describing supportive climates, ethical behaviors, and principled negotiation for conflict. The section concludes with guidelines for productive conflict and a recommended format for productive problem solving during conflict.

## PRODUCTIVELY ENGAGING IN CONFLICT

Thus far this chapter has been exploring what conflict is, how it works, and what role individuals and groups play in the process. Specifically, the chapter has attempted to develop knowledge, sensitivity, and skills important for communication competence during conflict. The underlying assumption for this development has been that conflict can be productive and can make a valuable contribution to individuals and organizations. In other words, not only is conflict inevitable, but also, when productively managed, it is often desirable.

Before thinking specifically about possible positive outcomes of conflict, review again the conflicts you identified earlier in this chapter and the Middlesex Insurance case. Were there positive outcomes from your personal conflicts? What do John and the entire department have to gain from productive resolution of their problem? How was conflict valuable in either your personal experiences or the Middlesex Insurance case?

In general it can be said that a major value of conflict is its stimulus for creativity. Conflict with others forces us to evaluate and assess issues and problems. When productively managed, this evaluation can stimulate new and creative solutions that may not have emerged without competing perspectives. For example, most of us have habitual or routine ways of doing things. Frequently we do not even think about new approaches until someone challenges our effectiveness. Productive conflict can help keep us from getting in a rut. Conflict can restructure our relationships, a fact many of us fear and resist. Yet conflict can bring relationships up to date and strengthen them by addressing underlying problems and working for solutions. Both individually and organizationally, productive conflict can help us analyze goals and find effective means of achieving them.

When we adopt the perspective that conflict can be valuable, we then begin to focus our knowledge, sensitivity, and skills toward conflict as a productive process. We think about what atmosphere is best for conflict, what contributes to ethical behaviors during conflict, and finally what types of problem-solving processes support productive conflict outcomes.

## Supportive Climates, Ethical Behaviors, and Principled Negotiation

Creating an environment in which individuals feel secure and encouraged to seek good solutions is a difficult yet important task. The quality of the problem-solving environment is closely linked to considerations of what constitutes ethical communication behaviors during conflict. This subtle but critical relationship between **supportive climates** and the quality of human interaction is well described by Paul Keller and Charles Brown (1968) in their interpersonal ethic for communication. Keller and Brown suggest that people will be able to reach their potential only when they are psychologically free—not fearful of disagreement—and when their beliefs, opinions, and values are acceptable in their interactions with others.

**Supportive climates**
Organizational environments in which individuals feel secure and encouraged to seek good solutions; characterized by problem description, problem orientation, spontaneity, empathy, equality, and provisionalism.

Organizations annually spend millions of dollars training personnel in problem solving and conflict management with the hope that this training will contribute to productive organizational outcomes. Yet the outcomes from conflict often are influenced not only by the skills and abilities of the individual conflict participants but also by the overall organizational climate, which contributes to either supportiveness or defensiveness.

Organizational climates that produce defensiveness are characterized by inaccurate perceptions of motives, values, and emotions of those in conflict. Jack Gibb (1982), in a classic study of behaviors individuals perceive as threatening, discovered that "increases in defensive behavior were correlated positively with losses in efficiency in communication. Specifically, distortions became greater when defensive states existed in the groups." Gibb concluded that there are characteristic behaviors of defensive groups that are distinctly different from the characteristic behaviors in supportive groups.

### Evaluation versus Problem Description

Defensive climates are described by Gibb as being evaluative, whereas supportive environments are characterized by problem description. The supervisor who identifies the "bad attitude" or "low commitment" of a subordinate may not fully understand how this evaluative approach contributes to a predictably defensive subordinate reaction. On the other hand, the supervisor who describes concern for a subordinate's absenteeism is describing a problem both the supervisor and subordinate can readily observe and approach, very different from the subjective assessment of attitudes. In summary, the descriptive approach attempts to fit our words as nearly as possible to our experience of reality through descriptive, nonjudgmental terms and by avoiding strong, emotion-laden words.

### Control versus Problem Orientation

Defensiveness also is produced through attempts to control the behavior and responses of others. Although enforcing compliance may get short-term results, it rarely builds long-term commitment. Problem orientation is the supportive climate opposite to control. Specifically, problem orientation assumes a collaborative approach to solutions with particular emphasis on the participation of those being asked to make behavior changes. One of the more difficult tasks for many new managers is to encourage participation from those who either need to make behavior changes or are most affected by them. Inexperienced managers frequently learn that attempts to control subordinate behaviors result in the need for time-consuming behavior monitoring. Their more experienced counterparts have learned that subordinates are more likely to keep commitments in which they participate.

Most of us can understand the problem orientation approach in our own behavior. Try to determine when your commitment is greater: when you participate in a decision or when that decision is made for you. For most of us the answer is relatively simple: we put more time and energy into our own commitments.

### Strategy versus Spontaneity

Although we all operate from strategic objectives in conflict, defensiveness is produced when we are perceived by others to be engaging in manipulative behaviors. Organizational strategies for "selling" unpopular decisions often produce a defensiveness based on the belief that manipulation is a fundamental form of disrespect. Spontaneity, the opposite of strategy, is reflected in behaviors that make real motives plain and generate a trust that straightforward and honest interactions are taking place. This trust level is fundamental for long-term effectiveness. In fact, Warren Bennis and Burt Nanus (1985), in their research on leaders, suggest that trust in their constancy is one of the fundamental distinguishing characteristics of highly successful leaders. Furthermore, as Joseph DeVito (1986) suggests, straightforward and honest interactions (spontaneity) facilitate the individual's freedom of choice through accurate information, a requirement in his view for ethical interpersonal communication.

### Neutrality versus Empathy

Gibb (1982) found that productive groups empathically supported their members rather than assuming a rational neutrality based on "pure" objectivity. Productive groups also were characterized by the acceptance of others with different values and beliefs. This empathic support is closely related to the Keller and Brown (1968) notion of an interpersonal ethic for communication based on psychological free-dom to express opinions and beliefs. Thinking again about our personal behavior, most of us would agree that it is more comfortable to express disagreement when we know we will be thoughtfully heard than when we expect personal attack or discounting. Also, for most of us, constructively expressing disagreement is more likely to occur when we feel supported in our right to do so.

### Superiority versus Equality

In general, defensive groups are more likely than supportive groups to have mem-bers intent on asserting superiority and exhibiting an unwillingness to participate equally in problem solving. In fact, defensive climates are often characterized by individuals believing that they really do not have enough in common with others to make communication possible. Although differences in individuals exist, sup-portive individuals and groups stress commonalities while respecting numerous and diverse contributions to solutions.

### Certainty versus Provisionalism

Defensive groups, more than their supportive counterparts, are likely to have members who are certain and dogmatic about their positions. Supportive individ-uals are more provisional or open to experimentation in behavior, attitudes, and ideas. The provisional individual is investigative and problem oriented rather than polarized into either-or positions. The provisional approach seeks numerous alter-natives so as to find the most appropriate solution to a given problem. Again, this support for the generation of alternatives is fundamental to individual choice and ethical communication.

### Ethical Communication Behaviors

The supportive conditions as described by Gibb (1982) are closely aligned to notions of ethical conflict behaviors as described by Gary Kreps and Barbara Thornton (1984). Specifically, Kreps and Thornton believe that ethical conflict behaviors are exhibited when the individual stays with the issue at hand without hidden agendas; constructs reasonable, logical arguments rather than arguments designed to discount and devalue others; and keeps an open mind to new ideas while avoiding a win-at-all-costs attitude. In other words, ethical communication behaviors generate an environment in which individuals have freedom of expres-sion and also have adequate information to make free, informed choices. Put another way, the value of productive conflict is to stimulate creativity in individu-als, groups, and organizations. That creativity is most likely to emerge if we are personally safe, if we are open to many suggestions and viewpoints, and if we hon-estly seek the best solution from among numerous alternatives.

### Principled Negotiation

Principled negotiation is based on ethical communication behaviors and support-ive climates. Introduced by Roger Fisher and William Ury (Fisher, Ury, and Pat-ton, 1991), principled negotiation is a strategy for groups of individuals in conflict to express their needs and search for alternatives that meet diverse needs. The strategy supports ethical behavior by separating people from the problem and focusing on interests, not positions. Group members are asked to develop options for mutual gain based on mutual interests. In addition, objective criteria are used to evaluate options so that all parties to the conflict can determine the fairness of decisions.

Principled negotiation is based on the assumption that we should express disagreements and react to them with a spirit of inquiry and supportiveness rather than defensiveness. During principled negotiations, group members express concern for one another even when issue and position disagreements are obvious. Groups engaging in principled negotiation describe needs and interests in common and avoid rigid, polarized positions. Using common needs and interests as a basis, groups develop options that can be evaluated with agreed-on objective criteria. Once evaluation has been completed, groups engaging in principled negotiation can arrive at decisions with a high likelihood of broad support.

## GUIDELINES FOR PRODUCTIVE CONFLICT

The following guidelines are presented to help you think about your personal participation in conflict. As you read, consider how each of the guidelines relates to your recent experiences during conflict and what guidelines you might add.

*Monitor your personal behavior and the behavior of others for signs of destructive conflict.* What are you and others doing to contribute to destructive conflict? Folger, Poole, and Stutman (1993) have developed useful symptoms of escalation or avoidance cycles. Avoidance behaviors include marked decrease in commitment to solving the problem; quick acceptance of a suggested solution; avoidance of raising controversial aspects of any issue; people stop listening; discussion stays on safe aspects of the issue; little new information is exchanged; no plans are made to implement solutions; and evidence for claims or positions is not challenged. Escalation behaviors include dogmatically arguing for the same position; taking longer than anticipated to deal with issues; threats used to win arguments; mounting tension; nothing being solved despite hard work; hostile nonverbal communication; sarcastic behavior to relieve tension; and arguments over trivial issues. Consider these behaviors and other pertinent situations as you monitor your own experiences.

*Identify common goals and interests between people or in groups.* Try to think about problems in terms of common interests and goals. Avoid thinking about concrete positions and focus on common needs, desires, concerns, or fears. In organizations, legitimate and constructive disagreement often occurs about ways to implement solutions or to achieve goals. Identifying common interests and goals helps people avoid blaming and identifying other people as the problem. When people are the problem, it is important to learn to deal directly with the individual or individuals involved and not let "people conflict" contribute to poor organizational decisions.

*Develop norms to work on problems.* Norms or rules of behavior during a problem discussion can contribute to productive conflict by assisting individuals to identify how they will work on the problems with behaviors likely to facilitate informed decisions. Frequently adopted norms include (1) everyone in the group being responsible to assist everyone else in presenting individual opinions; (2) avoiding win/lose statements; (3) avoiding suppression of differences by using procedures such as voting, averaging, and formal rules; (4) avoiding quick solutions; (5) making decisions only after alternative perspectives have been discussed; and (6) supporting differences of opinion and valuing diverse contributions for effectiveness.

*Focus on mutual gain.* Identify what everyone has to gain from productively solving the conflict. State how everyone can benefit from working on the problem. Test proposed ideas against the criteria of mutual gain. Effective conflict resolution is more likely if opposing parties can see how their interests are protected. Avoid thinking that there is only one right answer and that if the opposing party benefits, you must therefore lose or not benefit. Develop the habit of thinking creatively in terms of mutual gain.

## A Process for Productive Conflict

Individuals who observe or participate in productive conflicts frequently characterize them as good problem-solving processes. Indeed, that is exactly what productive conflict is. Earlier in the chapter, conflict was defined as frustration stimulated by competing responses or alternatives to a particular situation. When that frustration is resolved to the mutual satisfaction of involved parties and to the needs of the issue, good problem solving has occurred. The following process for productive conflict is a basic problem-solving format. Based on the concepts of supportive climates, ethical behaviors, and principled negotiation, it is designed to integrate all of our competencies—knowledge, sensitivity, skills, and values—into a productive conflict management process.

## The Process

### Self-Analysis of the Issues

When we are experiencing perceived and felt conflict, the time is right to do an in-depth self-analysis about the problem. Can we describe the conflict in terms that represent observable behaviors or events to all parties? What are the limits of our understanding of the problem? What types of solutions can we propose? Who needs to change or make a decision? What can we support in resolution strategies, and what types of results are clearly not acceptable? Also, what are the power issues, roles, and relationships of the parties involved? Finally, what are our personal responsibilities for this conflict?

### Setting a Meeting to Work on the Problem

Productive conflict occurs in a climate in which all participants feel supported. The setting of the meeting beforehand and the environment of the meeting itself are critical to this supportive climate. Generally speaking, all parties involved in conflict should be notified in advance about the issue for discussion. Although that will sometimes produce anticipation stress, mental preparation can occur only when everyone knows the agenda. Also, the emotional impact of conflict can be lessened and trust levels increased when people don't feel surprised by a conflict. Commitment to agreements is greater if parties have time to think about the problem and their input and limits. In addition, the meeting environment should be conducive to the free exchange of ideas, usually private and on relatively neutral ground. Individuals using the power position of their private offices may actually inhibit real problem solving. Finally, adequate time for full discussion should be allotted, with the timing of the meeting as convenient as possible for all participants.

## Defining the Problem

Effective conflict outcomes occur in solving the basic problem rather than finding solutions to surface issues or discovering vastly differing descriptions of the problem. Conflict participants should be encouraged to define the problem fully before any discussion of solution strategies. Problems often are poorly described because of underlying tension in the setting and a desire to get the confrontation over with as soon as possible. Clarification of the problem—through self-disclosure and active questioning—is essential to productive problem solving.

## Developing Solutions

We are often relieved to be "getting through this problem" and neglect to look comprehensively at approaches and solutions. In the development of solutions it is important to think broadly about all alternatives, even those that seem to have little immediate merit. Better and longer-lasting solutions will emerge from broad rather than narrow perspectives of alternatives. All conflict participants should be encouraged to participate in solution generation. In fact, if a critically involved party to a dispute cannot offer a single solution, it may be better to adjourn the meeting temporarily and let that person consider what he or she might suggest. Forcing a decision on a nonparticipative individual may result in little commitment or sometimes actual sabotage of the solution. Ultimately, of course, action must be taken. All parties however, must recognize the potential impact of a decision with varying ranges of agreement and commitment.

## Narrowing the Choices for Action

Decisions should be discussed in light of the defined problem issues. Often decisions made with broad agreement fail because the participants have not linked their intended actions to the actual problem. If behavior change is required on the part of some but not all participants, particular care should be taken that the affected individuals participate in narrowing the choices for action. They should be encouraged to select options to which they can commit, although these options can be rejected by others if they do not meet acceptable standards. When individuals who need to change their behavior make commitments to change that they have helped generate, the long-term possibilities for successful conflict resolution have been enhanced.

## Committing to Solutions

Agreeing on a solution or approach to the problem should occur only after the parties assess how that solution addresses the identified problem, whether individuals can support the decision, if those most affected have participated in the decision, and whether the solution is workable and can be implemented. Commitment to the solution comes through developing an implementation plan. Who is going to do what and in what time frame? How is the solution going to be evaluated? Is everyone clear about what we think this solution will accomplish and also what it cannot do? Finally, can we predict from this experience whether we have a solution that will work? If so, what were the keys to this outcome? If not, what were the barriers we could not surmount?

## Monitoring the Process

A real key to long-term conflict management is effective implementation of agreed-on solutions. Effective conflict outcomes are encouraged when participants establish how they will monitor the implementation plan and when they will meet again to assess how it is working. This follow-up builds accountability into the process and also allows for celebration when solutions are working and meeting problem needs. This closure on the process also establishes a framework for revisiting an issue for which the solution—even if faithfully implemented—still does not satisfy the real needs of the conflict.

Although no process, set of skills, or body of knowledge will free individuals, groups, or entire organizations from the reality of conflict, the knowledge, sensitivities, skills, and values of conflict participants directly influence the productivity of conflict outcomes. Effective organizational communicators know they bear responsibilities to monitor continually their own abilities and support that process for others. In particular, effective conflict outcomes help individuals improve their organizational relationships and are an important organizational mechanism for good decision making and adaptation to change.

## SUMMARY

Conflict occurs when individuals, groups, or entire organizations perceive or experience frustration in the attainment of goals. Described as an episode, the conflict process has the stages of (1) latent conflict, (2) perceived conflict, (3) felt conflict, (4) manifest conflict, and (5) conflict aftermath. Conflict episodes occur in intrapersonal, interpersonal, small-group, organization-wide, and organization-to-environment contexts. Regardless of context, participants interact in conflict with their individual preferences or styles, strategic orientations, and tactical communication behaviors. Conflict styles are described as five basic orientations based on the balance between satisfying individual needs and goals and satisfying the needs and goals of others in the conflict. These five most commonly referred to styles are avoidance, competition, compromise, accommodation, and collaboration. Strategic objectives are determined by preferences for conflict styles and by assessment of the probable outcomes of behavior within particular contexts. Strategic objectives structure the conflict in one of four strategic directions: escalation, reduction, maintenance, or avoidance. Conflict tactics are communication behaviors that attempt to move the conflict toward escalation, reduction, maintenance at the present level, or avoidance. The tactics adopted are influenced by conflict preferences and strategies and by overall organizational values. Emotion is a critical part of conflict processes.

Group conflict is common in organizations. Individual characteristics, group conflict styles, procedures, interpersonal issues, substantive issues, and group-think all contribute to productive and counterproductive group conflict. Organizations manage conflict with negotiation, bargaining, mediation or forcing, and third-party arbitration. The use of a variety of power processes is prevalent during conflict. Negative and abusive workplace conflicts include sexual harassment, discrimination, and ethical abuses. Conflict outcomes are more likely to be productive if parties in conflict foster supportive rather than defensive climates. Supportive climates are characterized by problem orientation, spontaneity, empathy, equality, provisionalism, and ethical communication behaviors. Principled negotiation is a strategy for group conflict based on supportive climates and ethical behaviors.

A process for constructive conflict can be used to integrate all our competencies: knowledge, sensitivity, skills, and values. The format includes self-analysis of the issues, setting a meeting to work on the problem, defining the problem, developing solutions, narrowing the choices for action, committing to solutions, and monitoring the process. In summary, productive conflict requires competent communicators who can effectively solve problems in a variety of organizational circumstances.

# WORKSHOP

1. To put into practice the various competencies this chapter has begun to develop, read The New Career Development Program That Ruins Careers case, which follows. (See pp. 349–351.) After studying the case, can you describe the events in terms of a conflict episode? What were the predispositions and styles of the principal participants? Did Denise and John have similar strategic objectives? Examine the conflict narrative and establish which tactics were used. Finally—and this is the most challenging part of the assignment—generate for Jane a specific format for productive conflict management. Generate this format with both supportive climates and ethical behaviors in mind. Be prepared to present your format to the class and role-play how Jane should handle her meetings with Denise and John.

2. Develop a list of outcomes from conflicts that have been important to you. Divide the list into productive and counterproductive outcomes. What kinds of behaviors made the difference? What does this list tell you about your role in conflict?

3. Interview an individual in a high-emotion labor job. Ask that person to describe their reactions to required emotional control. Ask them to describe the types of conflicts they experience and how they manage them.

4. Attend a public meeting where the issue for discussion is likely to produce conflict. Record the strategies and tactics used by each participant. Describe the effectiveness of the outcomes. Attempt to assess how the conflict behaviors influenced the outcomes.

## Personal Profile of Conflict Predispositions, Strategies, and Tactics Scoring Form: Style Predispositions

1. Total your scores from questions numbered 1, 6, 11, 18, 20.                                                       A. _____

2. Total your scores from questions numbered 2, 8, 13, 14, 24.                                                       B. _____

3. Total your scores from questions numbered 3, 7, 16, 17, 22.                                                       C. _____

4. Total your scores from questions numbered 4, 9, 12, 19, 23.                                                       D. _____

5. Total your scores from questions numbered 5, 10, 15, 21, 25.                                                       E. _____

Your scores represent a rank ordering of your preferences or predispositions for five conflict styles: (A) avoidance, (B) compromise, (C) collaboration, (D) competition, and (E) accommodation. Your highest number represents your first preference, and so on down the line. It is possible that you gave two styles the same score. This indicates that you have little difference in preference between the two. List your style preferences in order from most preferred to least preferred.

First choice        _____

Second choice       _____

Third choice        _____

Fourth choice       _____

Fifth choice        _____

These styles are discussed in detail as you study Chapter 9.

## Scoring Form: Strategies and Tactics

1. Total your scores from questions numbered 1, 7, 9, 15, and divide by 4.                                           A. _____

2. Total your scores from questions numbered 2, 8, 10, 14, and divide by 4.                                          B. _____

3. Total your scores from questions numbered 3, 6, 11, 16, and divide by 4.                                          C. _____

4. Total your scores from questions numbered 4, 5, 12, 13, and divide by 4.                                          D. _____

Your scores represent your average use of a variety of conflict tactics grouped into the four general conflict strategies of (A) escalation, (B) avoidance, (C) maintenance, and (D) reduction. Compare your average use figure with the scale: 1 = Never; 3 = Average; and 5 = Always.

Now return to Chapter 9 where preferences and orientations, strategies, and tactics are discussed in detail.

■ ■ ■ ■ ■ ▬▬▬▬▬▬▬▬▬▬▬▬▬▬▬▬▬▬▬▬▬▬▬▬▬▬▬

## THE NEW CAREER DEVELOPMENT PROGRAM THAT RUINS CAREERS

The training department of AMEX Corporation was well respected for the quality of programs its staff developed and regularly presented to the over 10,000 AMEX employees. Department members were always ready for new challenges and prided themselves on developing the best training programs in the industry.

Jane Johnson, director of the AMEX training department, was excited that her presentation to top management had been well received. She believed, along with her senior staff, that the AMEX career development program was out of date and needed new materials and a new training format. The changes she and her staff wanted to make would cost around $100,000, requiring management approval and agreement that the program was a top priority for the coming year. The new career development program would be the first such program to be made available to all 10,000 employees.

During her first staff meeting following the management presentation, Jane became aware that although all four senior staff members agreed on the importance of the program, there was little agreement on who should have the lead responsibility and how other work responsibilities should be divided to provide time for program development. Although no open disagreement had been voiced, Jane came away from the meeting with the sense that she had considerable work to do to determine how project assignments might best meet the needs of the entire group.

Jane believed that Denise Giles, her senior staff member in charge of management development programs, had the best experience for the job. Denise had been with AMEX for over seven years and had developed, staffed, and implemented seven new programs for managers at all levels in AMEX. Her program evaluations were consistently outstanding, and top management held her work in high regard. Yet Jane also knew that John Martin, senior staff member in charge of manufacturing training programs, wanted the assignment. John had less overall program experience than Denise, but the work he had done in quality training was truly outstanding. In fact, he had been asked to lead a workshop describing his program at the International Manufacturers Convention in London. Jane was proud of John and believed he had an outstanding future in training and development. The other two senior staff members, Jill and Roger, had not yet introduced their first programs. Although able trainers and good program managers, neither had the development and writing experience necessary for the career development project.

Jane decided to devote her next staff meeting to a discussion of project allocations for the coming year. She was not prepared for the tenseness she felt as the meeting began.

> **Jane:** As you know, today's agenda deals with our program planning for the next year. Obviously, if we are to undertake the career development project, we will have to evaluate work loads on all our projects. I would also like expressions of interest in which parts of the career development project each of you would like and ideas on what type of team should be established to

*(continued)*

manage its development. As we talk, please keep in mind not only your own interests but also the strengths and overall workloads of each of your individual staffs.

**Denise:** Jane, this issue is troublesome for us as a group. We all want the career development program to work, but we know it takes one lead person, not all four of us working independently.

**John:** Denise is right. One of us has to head up the group and be responsible for the lead. I guess I should say right now that I want to take that lead responsibility. I have worked with the largest group (manufacturing) in all AMEX and believe that experience qualifies me for developing a program that reaches large numbers of diverse people. My manufacturing folks represent almost 6,500 of our total employment.

**Denise:** (In a tense voice) I don't think we should be declaring who wants the job until we decide how the project might ideally be developed with all our other responsibilities.

**Roger:** Well, I think we need to get down to facts. Neither Jill nor I have the experience to lead the project and we know it. Everyone knows the lead job is between Denise and John. We can't really divide the other work and decide how we can support the project until we choose a leader.

**Jill:** Roger is right. I would love to lead the project but with about five years more experience.

**John:** Well, I just stated that I want the lead job and that I think my experience is best suited to the job. What do you think, Denise?

**Denise:** I think this is an unprofessional way for us to be entering into this decision. After all, the final decision is Jane's and she should not be forced to choose this way. Her agenda was a discussion of project assignments, not announcing who would take the lead assignment. Isn't that right, Jane?

**Jane:** Yes, that was the agenda, but I am not adverse to hearing what each of you really wants to do. Denise, how do you feel about the lead role?

**Denise:** How do I feel? How can you ask me that? I am the senior member of this team. Everyone expects me to lead this project. If I don't get the job it will be a slap in the face. Sure, John has done a great job in manufacturing, but what about the management programs? They may reach fewer people, but the people they do reach drive the entire company. What about that experience? Frankly, I resent being put on the spot. This issue is not for general discussion. It is (to Jane) your responsibility to make that decision.

**John:** Denise, you are doing it again. I have never raised this point before, but you just won't confront things openly. Sure, you have a good record, but I am willing to say openly that I want the job, not just expect someone to hand me the assignment. It is too important to give it to someone just because they expect it.

**Jane:** Wait a minute, you are both out of line. We are going to adjourn this meeting right now and I will see both of you individually later in the day. We will meet again as a staff tomorrow morning.

**Denise:** (Under her breath as she leaves the room) This career development project is already ruining some careers.

### QUESTIONS FOR DISCUSSION
1. What conflict preferences do we see in the case?
2. What strategies and tactics are in use?
3. What can Jane do to resolve this conflict?
4. How is emotion contributing to this conflict?

# REFERENCES AND SUGGESTED READINGS

Anderson, G. 1993. Emotions and work in a lifestyle occupation. *Journal of European Industrial Training* 17(5): 10–14.

Andersson, L., and C. Pearson. 1999. Tit for tat? The spiraling effect of incivility in the workplace. *Academy of Management Review* 24(3): 452–471.

Bennis, W., and B. Nanus. 1985. *Leaders: The strategies for taking charge.* New York: Harper and Row.

Berkowitz, L. 1962. *Aggression: A social psychological analysis.* New York: McGraw-Hill.

Blake, R., and J. Mouton. 1964. *The managerial grid.* Houston, TX: Gulf.

Brilhart, J., and G. Galanes. 1989. *Effective group discussion.* Dubuque, IA: Brown.

Canary, D., and B. Spitzberg. 1987. Appropriateness and effectiveness perceptions of conflict strategies. *Human Communication Research* 14(1): 93–118.

Conrad, C. 1985. *Strategic organizational communication: Cultures, situations, and adaptation.* New York: Holt, Rinehart and Winston.

Cummings, H. W., L. W. Long, and M. L. Lewis. 1983. *Managing communication in organizations: An introduction.* Dubuque, IA: Gorsuch Scarisbrick.

DeVito, J. A. 1986. *The interpersonal communication book.* 4th ed. New York: Harper and Row.

Fisher, D. 1993. *Communication in organizations.* 2d ed. St. Paul, MN: West.

Fisher, R., W. Ury, and B. Patton. 1991. *Getting to yes.* New York: Penguin.

Folger, J., M. Poole, and R. Stutman. 1993. *Working through conflict.* New York: HarperCollins.

Gibb, J. 1982. Defensive communication. In *Bridges not walls,* ed. J. Stewart, 235–240. New York: Random House.

Hall, J. 1969. *Conflict management survey: A survey of one's characteristic reaction and handling of conflicts between himself and others.* Conroe, TX: Teleometrics International.

Hochschild, A. 1983. *The managed heart.* Berkeley: University of California Press.

Hocker, J., and W. Wilmot. 1991. *Interpersonal conflict.* Dubuque, IA: Brown.

Hubbell, A. and C. Medved. 2000. "*When I had to lie to my boss, I said something like this . . . " The validation of a typology of organizational deception.* Paper presented at the annual meeting of the International Communication Association, May, Acapulco, Mexico.

Janis, I. 1983. *Groupthink: Psychological studies of policy decisions and fiascoes.* 2d ed. Boston: Houghton Mifflin.

Jones, T. S. 1997. *Emotional communication in conflict: Essence and impact.* Paper presented at the National Communication Association Convention, November, Chicago.

Keller, P. W., and C. T. Brown. 1968. An interpersonal ethic for communication. *Journal of Communication* 18(1): 73–81.

Kreps, G., and B. Thornton. 1984. *Health communication: Theory and practice.* White Plains, NY: Longman.

Kuhn, T., and M. Poole. 2000. Do conflict management styles affect group decision making? *Human Communication Research* 26(4): 558–590.

Martin, J., K. Knopoff, and C. Beckman. 1998. An alternative to bureaucratic impersonality and emotional labor: Bounded emotionality at the body shop. *Administrative Science Quarterly* 43(2): 429–469.

Miller, K. 1999. *Organizational communication.* Belmont, CA: Wadsworth.

Morris, J., and D. Feldman. 1996. The dimensions, antecedents, and consequences of emotional labor. *Academy of Management Review* 21(4): 986–1010.

Morris, J. and D. Feldman. 1997. Managing emotions in the workplace. *Journal of Management Issues* 9(3): 257–274.

Mumby, D., and L. Putnam. 1992. The politics of emotion: A feminist reading of bounded rationality. *Academy of Management Review* 17: 465–486.

Pepper, G. 1995. *Communicating in organizations: A cultural approach.* New York: McGraw-Hill.

Phillips, G., and N. Metzger. 1976. *Intimate communication.* Boston: Allyn and Bacon.

Pondy, L. 1966. A systems theory of organizational conflict. *Academy of Management Journal* 9: 246–256.

Pondy, L. 1967. Organizational conflict: Concepts and models. *Administrative Science Quarterly* 12: 296–320.

Putnam, L., and D. Mumby. 1993. Organizations, emotion, and the myth of rationality. In *Emotion in organizations,* ed. S. Fineman, 36–57. London: Sage.

Putnam, L., and M. Poole. 1987. Conflict and negotiation. In *Handbook of organizational communication,* eds. F. Jablin, L. Putnam, K. Roberts, and L. Porter, 549–599. Newbury Park, CA: Sage.

Ray, E. B., and G. B. Ray. 1986. Teaching conflict management skills in corporate training: A perspective-taking approach. *Communication Education* 35(3): 288–306.

Ruben, B. 1978. Communication and conflict: A system theoretic perspective. *Quarterly Journal of Speech* 64: 202–210.

Shockley-Zalabak, P. 1984. Current conflict management training: An examination of practices in ten large American organizations. *Group and Organization Studies* 9: 491–507.

Thomas, K. 1976. Conflict and conflict management. In *The handbook of industrial and organizational psychology,* ed. M. Dunnette, 889–935. Chicago: Rand McNally.

Thomas, K. 1988. The conflict-handling modes: Toward more precise theory. *Management Communication Quarterly* 1(3): 430–436.

Thomas, K., and R. Kilmann. 1975. The social desirability variable in organizational research: An alternative explanation for reported findings. *Academy of Management Journal* 18: 741–752.

Thomas, K., and W. Schmidt. 1976. A survey of managerial interests with respect to conflict. *Academy of Management Journal* 19(2): 315–318.

Waldron, V., and K. Krone 1991. The experience and expression of emotion in the workplace: A study of a corrections organization. *Management Communication Quarterly* 4: 287–309.

Walton, R., and J. Dutton. 1969. The management of interdepartmental conflict: A model and review. *Administrative Science Quarterly* 14: 73–84.

# CHAPTER TEN

# STRATEGIC ORGANIZATIONAL COMMUNICATION

## Professional Applications of Organizational Communication

**DEVELOPING COMPETENCIES THROUGH . . .**

### KNOWLEDGE

Describing strategic organizational communication

Defining the role of the professional communicator in strategic organizational communication

Describing leading planned change and organizational development

### SENSITIVITY

Understanding the complexity of strategic organizational communication

Developing an awareness of professional responsibilities for strategic organizational communication and the leadership of change

### SKILLS

Using analysis capabilities to select options for case problems

Assessing personal skills related to professional communication responsibilities

**VALUES**

Relating strategic communication to ethical and value issues
faced by organizations

Understanding value dimensions of professional communication
responsibilities

■ ■ ■ ■ ■ ▬▬▬▬▬▬▬▬▬▬▬▬▬▬▬▬▬▬▬▬

## THE PRESS AND THE STOCKHOLDERS WANT TO KNOW CASE

Linda Thomas and Brad Youngren were almost speechless. Their meeting with Jane
Bevins, president of Ostern Corporation, was not what they had expected. They knew
that there was big trouble but nothing as complex as this problem and with so many
multiple issues. Linda and Brad sat down to determine what to do next. It would be
only a matter of hours before the press would be calling. They had to figure out how
to approach public announcements and get more specialized information to their
stockholders as well. Linda called Ostern's corporate attorneys and asked for an
emergency meeting. She and Brad began to make a list of all their options.

As communication professionals in the Corporate Communications/External
Relations department of Ostern Corporation, a publicly traded, mid-size, medical
software manufacturer noted for its excellent software programs for hospital and
medical practice offices, Linda and Brad are challenged to handle the public
announcements of a serious earnings loss, the firing of a popular senior vice president, and the filing of a major lawsuit against Ostern. In their tenure at Ostern, a situation like this one had never happened. Until recently sales growth had averaged 200
percent per year, with the most recent year end figures topping one billion. Stock
prices had increased 40 percent since the first public stock offering, and confidence
was high in the company's future. Linda and Brad were faced with determining how
to use past credibility to help with the present situation.

Jane Bevins had laid it on the line. Mike Mitchell, the senior vice president in
charge of software development, had taken shortcuts with Hospital Manager 99, a
major upgrade of the Manager Programs used by over 2,000 hospital systems
throughout the country. Worse yet, conversion to the upgrade, which had begun in
the last quarter and was continuing, had created serious trouble in some five hundred
hospitals. Software flaws were creating major scheduling and inventory mistakes as
well as billing errors. Interwest Hospitals, the largest chain of hospitals using the Hospital Manager programs, had notified Jane that they would file a lawsuit against
Ostern asking for damages due to problems with the upgrade. If that were not bad
enough, Jane told Linda and Brad that her internal investigation indicated that Mike
had subcontracted work on the upgrade to vendors in which he had substantial personal investments. Vendors who had helped with the initial release of Hospital Manager were not even contacted for bids to work on the revisions. Jane cautioned that
this information must not be used publicly, but she wanted Linda and Brad to know
that she had no choice but to instantly terminate Mike. The lawsuit from Interwest

was to be filed on Monday, and Monday also was the day to release the most negative quarterly earnings figures in Ostern's history. Jane told Linda and Brad she believed a loss in one quarter, although not desirable, was not the major problem. What the public would learn was that Ostern had a loss, had fired a senior vice president, and was to be sued by its most important customer. Jane asked Linda and Brad to return later in the day to discuss options and approaches to handling the press, detail how to communicate with stockholders, and recommend processes for internal announcements to management and employees.

## INTRODUCTION

Linda and Brad are faced with a difficult situation that will challenge their professional expertise as well as influence what happens next at Ostern. The positive environment within which Ostern has been operating is changing rapidly. What appears to be an internal ethical and legal problem with a senior official has resulted in significant problems with a new product release. Not only has the release created a negative earnings environment, but a major customer with high industry visibility has been so seriously damaged that they are instituting legal action to deal with their losses. Linda and Brad will be faced with developing communication messages to announce quarterly earnings to stockholders and the press, to announce the departure of Mike Mitchell, and to respond to concerns about the lawsuit. They must consider the overall reputation of Ostern, legal issues surrounding both the lawsuit and the termination of Mitchell, and a host of other issues including internal employee reactions. Linda and Brad are faced with an environment that is rapidly changing, with conflicting needs for information. Their communication efforts have ethical and value implications, and what they do will in part contribute to the future of Ostern. Linda and Brad are engaged in creating recommendations for strategic organizational communication.

In previous chapters the complexities of interpersonal and group communication within organizations were explored. Ways to increase awareness of our interactions and to develop critical competencies for participating in organizations were discussed. This chapter turns to the competencies required for participating in external communications, communicating with those who are outside the organization. Communications, both internal and external, are considered in the context of overall strategic communication planning. The ways in which communication professionals analyze situations and select and implement communication strategies—in other words, their professional and strategic application of organizational communication—are explored. A strategic planning model is discussed, and the roles of public relations and marketing in strategic management are explored. The chapter also addresses the role of the communication professional in the leadership of organizational change.

*Knowledge* competencies are developed through defining and describing various aspects of strategic organizational communication and the management of planned change and development. *Sensitivity* is encouraged by exploring the multiple audiences and needs for strategic organizational communication and examining the potential impact of planned change and development. *Skills* are practiced through case and situation analysis. Finally, *values* are influenced by exploring the ethical implications of strategic organizational communication and planned change.

## DESCRIBING STRATEGIC ORGANIZATIONAL COMMUNICATION

In today's rapidly changing business environment, cohesive, integrated communications are gaining recognition as a means of developing competitive advantage and of allowing an organization to adapt quickly to evolving needs and demands. Professionally developed organizational communication increasingly is part of overall strategic planning and action.

**Strategic organizational communication**
Transactional processes in which organizational messages are deliberately generated; are based on environmental data, analysis, and strategy selection; and are guided by organizational objectives.

What is **strategic organizational communication?** Charles Conrad (1994) states, "strategic organizational communication involves the ability to analyze a situation, select appropriate communication strategies, and enact those strategies effectively." Strategic communication is therefore goal-oriented, based on knowledge, and is a result of considered, deliberate decisions.

Tom Daniels, Barry Spiker, and Michael Papa (1997) describe another view, one in which strategic communications are controlled by those who control organizational resources, the management. Daniels, Spiker, and Papa explain that strategic communications, although generated by numerous individuals and groups within an organization, usually consist of messages selected by management and tend to reflect management objectives and biases. Although sometimes mistaken as one-way communication (originating with management), strategic communication is in fact a two-way, transactional process. Information is received by management from organizational members and the external environment, and in turn messages are sent by management to involved parties. It is a dynamic interaction.

Phillip Clampitt, Robert DeKoch, and Thomas Cashman (2000) describe communication strategy as "the macro-level choices and tradeoffs executives make, based on their organizational goals and judgments about others' reactions, which serve as a basis for action." Clampitt, DeKoch, and Cashman contend that organizational leadership faces continuing pressing problems such as retaining quality employees, combating organizational cynicism, and creating a dynamic, evolving workplace. They suggest: "A communication strategy can provide a hedge against employee cynicism by ensuring that dissenting opinions about decisions, practices, or policies are appropriately channeled. A well-developed communication strategy also cultivates the kind of environment more accepting of change and innovation." They go on to describe efforts at 3M to cultivate seeds of innovation by routinely recording and telling stories about breakthrough products, processes, and ideas.

Within the context of this chapter, strategic communication to encompass most of the elements discussed above are considered. Strategic organizational communication is regarded as transactional processes in which organizational messages are deliberately generated; are based on environmental data, analysis, and strategy selection; and are guided by organizational objectives.

## Perspectives on Strategic Organizational Communication

Historically, many organizations have viewed various strategic communication functions—such as internal communications with employees, public relations, and marketing—as largely isolated operations. These activities have often been planned and implemented by separate departments, with limited coordination or communication among functions. In addition, a predominant view of the strategic communication process has been described as an inside-out approach in which the organization is seen as the initiator of the communication process. This orientation is a one-way communication model, beginning with an organizational objective, which is transformed into communication objectives, and then culminating with action on the part of the audience, the individuals to whom the communication was directed.

There is a major shift occurring regarding the underlying assumptions and processes of strategic organizational communication. Research has indicated it is more effective to view strategic communications from an outside-in perspective. This orientation recognizes the importance of an organization's environment and the need for organizations to be aware of changing environmental conditions. The orientation challenges notions of fixed organizational boundaries and permits a view which blurs distinctions between internal and external interactions. This view is supportive of the George Cheney and Lars Christensen (2001) description of internal and external communication as interrelated dimensions of organizational sense making.

Outside-in planning begins with an analysis of the organizational environment. By taking environmental conditions into account, communications can be designed more effectively and can be targeted more accurately to meet the needs of various organizational **stakeholders,** those individuals and groups who have an interest or "stake" in the organization and are able to influence the organization's ability to meet its goals. In addition, outside-in planning is concerned with more than just disseminating messages. Because this approach is based on getting to know the interests and needs of various stakeholders, it cultivates the tools required to build long-term relationships with stakeholders. Unlike the traditional inside-out model, outside-in planning lays the foundation for ongoing communication between an organization and its stakeholders.

**Stakeholders**
Individuals and groups who have an interest in the organization and are able to influence the organization's ability to meet its goals.

Communication strategy differs from communication tactics. A strategic communication goal may be to foster better interdepartmental and vendor communication. Numerous tactics such as job rotations, regular meetings, or teleconferencing may be used in support of the goal. Strategy involves choice. What issues are the most important? What issues can or should be ignored? Who should present what? Why should it become a major theme? When is the best timing for communication? Strategy also involves anticipating the reactions of others and planning with those reactions in mind. Strategy becomes the basis for action. Communication tactics are the actions—both planned and otherwise—that determine whether or not the strategic objective is realized.

A number of environmental factors have contributed to the growing acceptance of a more integrated strategic approach to communication. Corporate downsizing and reengineering have flattened organizations, breaking down structural barriers and involving cross-functions and greater numbers of individuals in decision making and planning. Global competitive markets have forced corporations to become more customer-oriented, resulting in targeted communications designed to reach specific groups of people rather than a mass audience. The numbers of communication channels have increased as technologies such as digital television, e-commerce, wireless communications, and the Internet have become commonplace. We are bombarded with messages from all fronts, making integrated communications more likely to be effective in a splintered, information-overloaded world.

## THE ORGANIZATION AND ITS ENVIRONMENT

Chapter 4 discussed how Integrated Perspectives theories acknowledge the importance of the interaction between an organization and its environment. An outside-in approach to strategic communication also values this dynamic relationship. As contemporary organizational environments become increasingly complex, new technologies are changing the ways in which organizations communicate and conduct business. Globalization is occurring due to advances in communications and transportation, rapidly transitioning political climates, and the lifting of trade restrictions.

As Cheney and Christensen (2001) suggest:

> In the corporate landscape of today, the issue of identity is closely tied up with the ways organizations organize their "world" in terms of communication. To begin with, the key communication elements of source, message, and receiver are all much more complicated and less easily distinguished than in prior periods. As many organizations have come to realize, the principal management problem in today's marketplace of goods and ideas is not so much to provide commodities and services or to take stands on the salient issues of the day, but to do these things with a certain distinctiveness that allows the organization to create and legitimize itself, its particular "profile," and its advantageous position. This quest for visibility has

made disciplines such as public relations, issue management, marketing, and advertising chief architects of organizational identity. (pp. 241–242)

Today's rapidly changing business climate and its competitive customer-orientation require a high degree of interaction with what are described in the next section as multiple publics.

**Publics**
A small or large group of stakeholders with interests and needs relative to a particular organization.

## Multiple Publics

When studying an organization's environment, it is helpful to identify its various **publics.** As defined by Scott Cutlip, Allen Center, and Glen Broom (1985), a public is "a group of individuals tied together by some common bond of interest and sharing a sense of commonness. It may be a small or a large group; it may be a majority or a minority group. . . . There is an infinite number of smaller publics within the general public. . . . Each issue, problem, or interest creates its own public." Every organization has multiple publics. Publics also may be thought of as groups of stakeholders. The changing interests, needs, and actions of publics, or stakeholders, must be considered when planning organizational strategy. Linda and Brad are very aware of the multiple publics who are interested in Ostern's problems. Stockholders, the media, customers, employees, vendors, and others all have questions about what has happened at Ostern and what Ostern will do in the future. Yet their questions are not the same. Linda and Brad are charged with understanding the needs of these various stakeholders and creating communication exchanges to meet diverse expectations.

Edward Lawler and Jay Galbraith (1994) propose a number of characteristics they believe put an organization at risk of becoming a corporate "dinosaur—of becoming so cumbersome and highly adapted to its historical environment that it cannot respond to today's rapidly changing climate." One of these characteristics is "lack of contact with the customer and the environment," which leads organizational members to focus on internal processes rather than on how to best satisfy customer or stakeholder needs. Another risky characteristic is the attitude "If it ain't broke, don't fix it." This cultural rule encourages employees to stick with the status quo instead of recognizing that customer needs change or that there is benefit in looking to the future and considering innovation. Maintaining a high degree of stakeholder contact and a willingness and ability to adapt are critical to long-term organizational success.

An organization's view of its position in its environment also affects its ability to respond to environmental changes. Bill Richardson (1995) suggests that organizations have a tendency "to operate from a basis of inappropriate paradigms about their strength in an environment and their 'natural' right to provide the goods and services they have traditionally provided to that environment. In modern, powerful and hostile environments, this is an inappropriate mindset and a recipe for organizational decline and failure." Organizations need to match their paradigms and planning systems to their environments.

# Environmental Scanning

Because the environment is rich with useful information, many organizations routinely monitor or scan the environment for data to help shape business strategy. **Environmental scanning** is "the acquisition and use of information about events and trends in an organization's external environment, the knowledge of which would assist management in planning the organization's future courses of action" (Auster and Choo, 1994).

Although most senior managers recognize the value of environmental scanning, many organizations do not participate in systematic scanning efforts. The frequency and intensity of scanning activities vary greatly among organizations. Some organizations passively receive external information, while others actively search it out. Information may be gathered informally or sporadically through members' interactions with professional organizations, attendance at off-site training sessions or conferences, or scanning newspapers and journals. Public relations and marketing specialists often compile external data through formal activities such as market research. Some organizations have even established large, complex systems or units whose sole purpose is to scan the environment. The most aggressive organizations use an intrusive approach, actually probing the environment by testing or manipulating it and observing the reaction (Fisher, 1993). Despite the variation in method, most experts would agree that to be effective, some structure must be established to facilitate the process. In fact, it appears that organizations that have adopted systematic approaches exhibit higher growth and greater profitability than those without structured systems (Subramanian, Fernandez, and Harper, 1993).

Eric Eisenberg and H. L. Goodall (1997) point out that boundary spanners, or organizational members who have direct contact with the public (such as salespeople or customer service representatives), can play an important role in gathering external data. "Boundary spanners serve at least three main functions: (1) They can access the opinions of people outside of the organization and use that information to guide organizational decision making; (2) their awareness of subtle trends in the environment can serve as a warning to the system for environmental jolts; and (3) they serve as important representatives of the organization to its environment." Effective organizations find ways to use information gained through boundary spanning activities.

Environmental scanning should encompass all factors likely to influence the organization, now and in the future. Such scanning usually begins with identifying internal and external stakeholders and their interests and needs. Broader scanning can point out trends and events in the competitive, economic, technological, political, social, cultural, ecological, and demographic arenas. These data may be used to forecast and strategize for the short- and long-term.

One difficult aspect of environmental scanning, and one at which many companies fail, is the process of distributing the information to appropriate organizational members. Computer databases and information systems are important tools for organizing, retrieving, and disseminating data.

The interpretation of information also presents challenges. Data must be evaluated, filtered, and interpreted to construct meaning. Many organizations do not have methods in place for systematically interpreting data. Richard Daft and Karl Weick (1984) propose that two factors influence an organization's process of data interpretation: how actively or passively the organization scans its environment and whether or not the organization assumes the environment to be "analyzable," or understandable. In other words, the organization's assumptions about and interactions with its surroundings play a role in its ability to influence the environment and in how it interprets the data it receives.

Although we have described environmental scanning primarily as a process of monitoring the external environment, successful organizations also are aware of the events, trends, and cultural conditions that exist within the organization. Members who have responsibility for external scanning often scan internally, as well. The compilation of these data can provide a rich pool of information to help guide the organization.

## STRATEGIC MANAGEMENT

**Strategic management**
The process of formulating and implementing an organizational plan of action.

Environmental information is useful only if considered in light of its relationship to and impact on organizational activities. Through the practice of **strategic management,** external information converges with other factors to shape organizational decisions and actions. Strategic management is the process of formulating and implementing an organizational plan of action, a roadmap of sorts that sets direction and guides the organization among alternative courses. The purpose of strategic planning is to strengthen the organization's competitive position.

Many of today's ideas about strategic management have their roots in the 1960s in the pioneering work of Harvard Business School's Kenneth Andrews and C. Roland Christensen. Andrews (1971) expanded on their work in his seminal book, *The Concept of Corporate Strategy.* Andrews described strategy development as beginning with an assessment of environmental conditions and trends and the organization's internal capabilities and resources. This information could be used to determine a match between the organization's qualifications and its environment. From the area of intersection (the best match of opportunity and resources), strategy was created. Andrews defined strategy as "the pattern of major objectives, purposes, or goals and essential policies and plans for achieving those goals, stated in such a way as to define what business the company is in or is to be in and the kind of company it is or is to be." Strategic management seeks to create competitive advantage by using the organization's unique qualifications to pursue opportunities existing in the environment.

**SWOT**
Strengths, weaknesses, opportunities, and threats identified for strategic planning.

Andrew's model has come to be known by the acronym **SWOT:** strengths, weaknesses, opportunities, threats. In practice, the SWOT model represents these activities: the organization identifies its strengths and weaknesses as well as the opportunities and threats existing in the external environment; this information is used to design a strategy that will create competitive advantage; the strategy is implemented with consistent, coordinated, organization-wide effort. Designing and implementing all aspects of the business to support the strategy is known as strategic alignment.

Although Andrews defined strategy in rather broad terms, over the years the concept of strategy has developed to hold more precise meanings in different contexts, such as competitive strategy, business strategy, corporate strategy, and operating strategy. For the purposes of this discussion of strategic organizational communication, the focus is on the development of competitive strategy. Competitive strategy is often described as the unique quality or competence an organization has to offer, the one that will create competitive advantage. Eisenberg and Goodall (1997) suggest this straightforward definition: "a (competitive) strategy is a clear statement of why customers should choose a company's products or services over those of competing companies."

Bruce Henderson (1991) describes the relationship between competition and strategy:

> Competitors that make their living in the same way cannot coexist. . . . Each must be different enough to have a unique advantage. The continued existence of a number of competitors is proof per se that their advantages over each other are mutually exclusive. They may look alike, but they are different species. . . . Strategy is a deliberate search for a plan of action that will develop a business's competitive advantage and compound it. . . . The objective is to enlarge the scope of your advantage, which can happen only at someone else's expense. (pp. 4–5)

There are several common competitive approaches. One strategy is to be the low-cost leader in an industry, such as Wal-Mart in discount retailing. Other companies select differentiation strategies, designed to provide a unique feature within a product or service repertoire. For example, L.L. Bean offers their mail-order customers an unconditional, 100 percent satisfaction guarantee. Other differentiation strategies may be focused on superior technical support, custom-order manufacture, excellent customer service, spare parts availability, or any of a long list of special features. Other companies, such as Rolls Royce, differentiate by appealing to a narrow market niche (for example, those willing to pay premium prices for world-class products).

Over the years, many individuals have elaborated on and refined Andrews's strategic planning model. Many have specified in greater detail the various aspects of strategic planning. Most of the models are still based on the SWOT analysis and contain, in some form or another, the following phases: (1) scanning and interpreting the internal and external environments; (2) formulating a mission, or vision for the future, and transforming it into specific objectives; (3) developing strategy and implementing supporting programs; and (4) monitoring, reviewing and revising the plan and its implementation.

Although the SWOT model remains a dominant one, it is not without its critics. Henry Mintzberg (1990, 1991, 1994) has criticized the approach for its formalization of strategic planning as a detailed and detached prescriptive process. Traditional models, such as SWOT, tend to emphasize planning, or thinking, before implementation, or action. The tasks of planning managers tend to be separated from those of operating managers. Mintzberg suggests that it is artificial to separate thinking and acting into separate phases. Actions influence thoughts, and thoughts influence actions; the two are intimately connected. Not only can strategies be formulated, but they sometimes emerge from a pattern of actions. "Various people can interact and so develop a pattern that becomes a strategy. . . . Strategies can develop in all kinds of unusual ways, as people interact, mutually adjust, learn from each other, conflict, and develop consensus" (Mintzberg, 1990). Mintzberg also writes, "The implication that thinking stops when the strategy is decided on—at least the broad thinking of senior management, once an articulated strategy has been handed over to others for implementation—discourages adaptation of the strategy." Strategies are sometimes best developed gradually, so the wisdom gained from experience may be allowed to shape decisions.

An important element of strategic management is the accurate and consistent communication of strategy to internal and external stakeholders. Although all organizational activities are involved in supporting strategy in one way or another, two functions carry a major responsibility for strategy communication and implementation: public relations and marketing.

## STRATEGIC ORGANIZATIONAL COMMUNICATION

Clampitt, DeKoch, and Cashman (2000) describe an effective communication strategy as having the following characteristics: (1) linking to organizational goals, (2) legitimizing certain issues and delegitimizing others, (3) shaping organizational memory, (4) making sense of the confusing and ambiguous, (5) providing a proper point of identity, and (6) continuously evolving. Further, they suggest that communication strategy should be developed through a discover, create, and assess process. Discover refers to discerning critical issues within the context of specific circumstances. Create includes the process of establishing goals, developing strategy, and selecting tactics for communication, and the assess phase refers to the actual implementation of strategy and its evaluation.

**Public relations**

Strategic organizational communication involving an organization's image, internal communication, public affairs and issues management, media relations, and crisis management.

## Public Relations

There has been little agreement over the years regarding the definition of **public relations.** In many ways, it has been a profession in search of a clear identity. Public relations, or PR, is viewed by some as one of several narrow functions, including employee communications, publicity, public affairs, media relations, or marketing support. Others see public relations as representing a broader group of activities, even encompassing all the communication activities of an organization.

There also has been little agreement regarding the purposes of public relations. In years past, public relations was widely viewed as a means of one-way, persuasive communication. Although the perception of PR as "the art of influence" remains prevalent, many contemporary definitions have emerged promoting a more mutually beneficial, two-way interaction between an organization and its publics. For example, S. Cutlip, A. H. Center, and G. M. Broom (1985) define public relations as "the management function that identifies, establishes, and maintains mutually beneficial relationships between an organization and the various publics on whom its success or failure depends."

According to James Grunig (1992), his five-year study to determine the characteristics of excellent public relations programs has shown that excellent programs are based on symmetrical, or two-way, communication presuppositions. Symmetrical public relations is "a tool by which organizations and competing groups in a pluralistic system interact to manage conflict for the benefit of all." Grunig (1990) argues that not only is a symmetrical approach more effective, but it is also "more ethical and socially responsible." Rather than focusing solely on the needs of the organization, symmetrical public relations builds mutually beneficial relationships that are more likely to be sustained over the long term.

Clarke Caywood (1997) explains how public relations, more than other functions, strengthens the outside-in perspective of an organization by building and integrating stakeholder relationships. Public relations professionals foster new relationships with valuable stakeholders and maintain and enhance the reputations of . . . [the] organization with stakeholders and audiences who are familiar with the organization. . . . More than other professions, public relations strengthens the outside-in perspective of an organization through its managed relationships with many stakeholder groups inside and outside the organizational boundaries."

Although public relations encompasses the full range of communication between an organization and its publics, a major PR function that receives a lot of attention is that of image building. Other specific public relations activities include the management of internal communications, public affairs and public issues, media relations, and communication during organizational crises.

## Managing an Organization's Image or Reputation

To many, the phrase image building carries negative connotations of deceit and manipulation. Public relations professional Leonard Saffir (1992) explains:

> Some PR professionals deplore the word "image" because it is so often misused. They complain that too many clients think of PR people as super manipulators who can create images that bedazzle the public into buying weak stories or inferior products. Image building is a legitimate topic for a discussion of public relations. It is, to a considerable extent, what PR people do. The trouble comes when PR professionals and clients, alike, misunderstand the term. "Imaging" may involve sharpening perceptions, broadening them, or, in some cases, changing them. Imaging is

not the building of illusions or the blurring of minds so the truth cannot be perceived. In thinking about images, clients and professionals should talk about skillfull projection or real qualities, not the construction of something imaginary. The best approach is to take it as a given that the substance is there before anybody goes to work bringing out the image. (p. 130)

As Grunig (1992) points out:

Public relations practitioners use the term image to refer to many different concepts, such as reputation, perception, attitude, message, attributes, evaluation, cognition, perception, credibility, support, belief, communication, or relationship. The average person sees image as the opposite of reality. In everyday language, images are projected, manipulated, polished, and tarnished. We believe the only escape from this confusion is not to use the term. Instead, we prefer to use one of the more precise terms to which image refers—such as reputation, perception, or evaluation. (p. 33)

In light of the ambiguity of the term, this discussion of "image" focuses on the building and managing of an organization's reputation. For many public relations professionals, reputation management is a major responsibility and a function that is considered critical to an organization's success. As Graham (1997) reported:

A 1994 Opinion Research Corporation survey showed that 90 percent of the business executives polled (two-fifths of whom were senior executives) agreed strongly that a company's reputation is a vital corporate asset that must be maintained as carefully as any other asset. . . . The poll also indicated that most executives believe a good corporate image has a direct impact on a company's profitability by influencing the buying decisions of consumers." (p. 274)

What are the factors that influence corporate reputations? Most organizations attempt to shape their reputations by drawing the attention of stakeholders to favorable qualities. Reputations, however, are dependent on much more than information communicated by the organization itself. In fact, they can be quite different than those intended. Stakeholders receive information about an organization from a variety of sources, and multiple factors come into play as stakeholders construct their views. Charles Fombrun and Mark Shanley (1990) suggest the following factors play a role: "information about firms' relative structural positions within organizational fields, specifically using market and accounting signals indicating performance, institutional signals indicating conformity to social norms, and strategy signals indicating strategic postures." Mary Anne Moffitt (1994) argues that "image is determined by the intersection, or articulation, of multiple factors [such as] the receiver's personal experiences of gender, work, family, race, economic class; the messages produced by the organization; and the various cultural and historical factors present in the environment."

It is important to recognize that not only do multiple factors play a role in forming reputations, but that organizations have multiple, and sometimes conflicting, reputations. Each individual stakeholder forms opinions based on unique factors. Moffitt explains, "Each individual can have unique and different images based on the unique intersection and combination of these factors" (personal experiences, organizational messages, environmental factors). Even a single individual "can hold multiple ever-changing, positive and negative images" of an organization, based on the contexts of different experiences. The construction of reputation is clearly a complex process.

Grunig (1993) suggests that many public relations professionals are preoccupied with image, which he views as only superficial symbolism. An emphasis on image can cause professionals to lose sight of the need to build substantive behavioral relationships between organizations and their publics. He argues for more attention given to managing ongoing, interactive relationships with stakeholders, which are required for long-term organizational success.

Any discussion of image or reputation building should consider the ethical implications inherent in the process. Is the image portrayed a true reflection of the company? Does the company in fact provide quality products or services? Organizations are challenged to ensure that public relations not only make people think well of organizations, but that they think well because the reputations are deserved.

**Internal communications**
Planned and formalized communication prepared and disseminated by communication professionals to internal organizational members.

# Internal Communications

**Internal communications,** sometimes referred to as employee communications, are often managed by public relations departments. In most organizations employees are considered an important public. Organizations are increasingly recognizing the value of building with employees long-term relationships based on mutual satisfaction.

There is an important distinction between the types of internal communication discussed here and the management of internal communications. Most of the communication discussed in earlier chapters occurs during the daily interactions of organizational members. The function of internal communications, by contrast, although often dealing with the subject matter of daily interactions, is planned and formalized communication prepared and disseminated by communication professionals to and for internal organizational members.

Internal communications specialists may be involved in a wide range of activities: seeking input from employees through surveys, interviews, meetings, or other methods; communicating the organization's mission, objectives, strategies, and programs through training activities or the preparation and dissemination of newsletters, manuals, pamphlets, and other publications; establishing formalized structures to improve the quality and flow of organizational communication; and in general managing all communications designed to help the organization achieve its strategic objectives.

It is important to point out that although many organizations house the internal communications function within the public relations department, that is not always the case. Internal communications may be managed by human relations, corporate communications, or other management functions.

**Public affairs and issues management**
Shaping of public opinion regarding social and political issues important to an organization.

# Public Affairs and Issues Management

**Public affairs and issues management** involve the shaping of public opinion regarding social and political issues important to an organization. Public affairs departments "concern themselves with 'corporate citizenship' and public policy—political education for employees, civic service by employees and managers, and cooperation in the development of home communities. Public affairs specialists serve as liaisons between their organizations and governmental units, implement community improvement programs, encourage political participation via campaign contributions and votes, and participate in voluntary organizations and fund raising" (Cutlip, Center, and Broom, 1985).

Issues management, a proactive function of public affairs, involves foreseeing emerging public policy issues and responding with strategies to resolve issues of importance to the organization. The strategies may be aimed at creating organizational or environmental change. "The purpose of issues management is to help organizations anticipate social, economic, and political issues. By doing so, the goal is to develop and manage programs that respond to those environmental changes with potential impact on organizational relationships with concerned publics" (Cutlip, Center, and Broom, 1985). An example from a city council dispute with land developers can help describe issues management. The city council of a medium-sized midwestern community voted to permit land development of a beautiful wooded site used for many years as a recreation area by local residents. The land was not designated as a park although some efforts had been made by citizens to encourage the council to purchase the land for open space and parks. Following the council's vote for development, an active citizens' campaign attempted to block development efforts. Developers, anticipating citizen protest, mounted their own efforts, focusing not on the particular land in question but on the overall value of development to the community. Press conferences, direct mail, and advertising were all used to describe responsible growth and the need for sensitive development of beautiful land. Citizens responded with letter-writing and telephone campaigns citing examples of questionable development activities. In addition, citizens, using a somewhat obscure statute, collected signatures for a citywide vote on development. Council was forced to call an election. The outcome—developers were permitted to build but were required to leave a significant amount of the property without houses—was a compromise. Observers believe that the developer's campaign—an example of issues management—was the primary reason they were able to continue with their plans. Citizens criticized the outcome, alleging that developers bought the issue by spending amounts of money the citizens could not hope to raise.

Rogene Buccholz (1988) suggests that "public issues emerge in our society because values change or because corporations operate in ways that conflict with existing values. Either condition is sufficient to generate pressures on our institutions by causing a gap between public expectations and institutional performance." Issues management specialists work toward resolving these conflicts.

Grunig (1990, 1992) argues that if excellent public relations are practiced (described as symmetrical and aimed at building long-term, mutually beneficial relationships between an organization and its publics), few problems will develop into "issues" because they will be handled in earlier interactions with publics. Grunig (1992) believes that "publics make issues out of problems that have not been resolved." Grunig suggests that organizations identify and manage problems before they develop into issues in the public policy arena.

Public policies are sometimes described as having a life cycle. Issues management strategies should be selected that are appropriate to each stage of the cycle. The first phase of the public policy life cycle is the formation of public opinion. During this stage, the organization may become involved in the public discussion by advocating positions through press releases, media interviews, advertising, newsletters, or other appropriate strategies. During the second stage, a policy has been proposed and is under consideration for legislation. The participants in the discussion now include legislators. The organization may attempt to influence the legislative process through lobbying, coalition building, or making contributions to political parties. In the third stage, the legislation has been enacted; the public policy has become law. An organization must now deal with governmental regulators charged with monitoring and enforcing compliance with the law. The organization may choose from any number of strategies, including cooperation, taking a position of noncompliance, or challenging regulations through the court system. Recognizing the various life stages of public policies can help issues management professionals select appropriate and effective strategies to influence their environments (Buccholz, 1988).

Raymond Ewing (1997) offers a seven-step model of the issues management process: (1) issue identification, or scanning the social and political environments for emerging issues; (2) issue analysis, or projecting how an issue will affect the organization; (3) development of a corporate policy position on an issue; (4) development of specific action plans to deal with issues; (5) implementation of action plans and communication of the organization's positions on issues; (6) review of the results, including public reactions, objections, negotiations, and organizational adjustments; and (7) continued focus on the issue "until it is resolved in a manner the company can live with during the current phase of the issue's life."

Ewing also describes the relationship between the two functions of issues management and strategic planning:

> Issues management and strategic planning together form the planning platform on which CEOs and their senior management team can stand to strategically manage their organizations.
>
> While issues management focusses on public policy research, foresight, and planning for the organization, strategic planning is concerned with business research, foresight, and planning for the organization. The first is concerned with policy planning; the second is concerned with profit planning. . . .
>
> Issues management is concerned with plans that groups outside the corporation are making in the sociopolitical and economic environment (the public policy

process) that would impact the corporation's future and viability. It is also concerned with the outside plans it must make to counteract or support the plans of others as the corporation seeks to participate in the public policy process where the issues will be resolved. . . .

Strategic planning is primarily concerned with the corporation's internal planning for its own business future, as it seeks to meet and beat its competitors in the economic arena.

Both issues management and strategic planning use similar techniques, share research, and reinforce each other in support of the organization's bottom line. (pp. 178–179)

## Media Relations

**Media relations**
Working with the media on behalf of an organization.

Media relations professionals Richard Kosmicki and Frederick Bona (1996) describe the practice of **media relations:**

As a practitioner of media relations, you serve three masters. One is your company, non-profit organization, or, if you work in an agency, your client. The second is the print and electronic media. The third is the various publics who receive their information from the media. You are responsible to all three—yet you have little or no authority to influence or make final decisions. So, it takes great skill and experience to accommodate these three masters. In fact, if you're a smart communicator, you'll treat the media, print and electronic, as well as you treat your employer, client, and the audiences the media serves. (p. 59)

Those who serve only one, such as their organization or client, usually wind up on the media's "drop dead" list. Serving all three masters equally well may be the most formidable challenge in public relations. (p. 75)

Media relations specialists are often the gatekeepers between their organizations and the media. "The interests of the organization and those of the journalist frequently clash. . . . Organizations want news reported in a favorable manner that will promote their objectives and will not cause them trouble; the news media want news that will interest readers and viewers" (Cutlip, Center, and Broom, 1985). Yet, despite a relationship that appears adversarial, the media relations specialist and the journalist function in a mutually dependent manner. This dependency offers the practitioner an opportunity to communicate important facts and the organization's point of view.

Effective media relations are important for strategic organizational communication. According to Thomas L. Harris (1991), the general public "continues to believe what is seen in the local and trade papers and broadcast on the evening news. Publicity has the impact of a respected third-party endorsement. . . . Media relations heightens the impact of other communications efforts."

It is important for media relations specialists to become familiar with the nature of the various media and to understand the needs of the press and their range of approaches. From newspapers to magazines, the Internet to network or cable television, each medium has its own style, scope, and audience. For example, a trade magazine is likely to target an industry audience with an in-depth article or case study; national television tends to focus on breaking news and to communicate to a broader audience (depending on the program) using visuals and sound bites. Likewise, the demands on a journalist vary somewhat based on the medium and the size and resources of his or her employer. The length of time allowed to research and develop a story, deadline frequency, and the availability of support staff all affect the manner in which journalists function. The media relations specialist can increase the likelihood of press coverage by understanding journalists' needs and providing them with information that is timely, interesting, newsworthy, and presented in a straightforward and useable format. Knowing the various media and their methods and approaches can be invaluable in effectively establishing press contacts and managing media relations efforts.

Cutlip, Center, and Broom (1985) suggest a number of guidelines, originally developed by Chester Burger, for communicating effectively with the media. One important suggestion is to talk from the viewpoint of the public's interest, not the organization's interest. Others include, tell the truth, even if it hurts, and do not exaggerate the facts. Overall, Cutlip, Center, and Broom advise adhering to the "five f's—dealing with journalists and program producers in a manner that is fast, factual, frank, fair, and friendly."

**Crisis management**
Use of public relations to minimize harm to the organization in emergency situations that could cause irreparable damage.

## Crisis Management

Sooner or later, most organizations face crises requiring major strategic communication efforts. Dalmar Fisher (1993) describes **crisis management** as "the use of public relations to minimize harm to the organization in emergency situations that could cause irreparable damage." Crisis management is a public relations challenge, demanding decision making and action under extreme stress and a high degree of public scrutiny. Accidents such as an airline crash, product failures or recalls, the untimely death of an important leader, allegations of fraud or illegality, and a host of other possible occurrences can be described as organizational crises.

A number of characteristics are typical of crises. According to public relations practitioner Jonathan Dedmon (1996), a crisis is a situation of major importance and visibility that presents elevated risk for the organization. Crises tend to evolve rapidly and in unpredictable ways, to require extraordinary levels of communication and to create strong and lasting public impressions. A crisis holds the potential to influence an organization's ability to fulfill its mission. Crisis management efforts are generally directed at minimizing damage to the organization's reputation and limiting its legal liability. These efforts typically, but not always, are managed by media relations specialists in conjunction with legal advice.

A 1993 study of public reaction to crises showed that crises do in fact damage reputations. Kurt P. Stocker (1997) summarizes the findings: "(1) The larger the crisis, the longer the public remembers. (2) How the company behaved influenced the public reaction. The pubic became angry if the organization denied responsibility or appeared to be slow, inaccurate or self-serving in its response. (3) Eyewitnesses and third parties are believed. Company spokespersons . . . are not credible. (4) A damaged reputation affects the customer's decision to purchase." Stocker adds support to this final conclusion by reporting that "the largest single segment of [crisis-associated] costs is market costs—the cost of lost sales, either through damaged products or damaged reputation." Because the actions of the organization have a direct influence on its reputation and ultimately on its customers' willingness to do business, it is paramount the organization prepare itself to handle potential crises. The choices made during crises will impact the organization for a long time to come.

A common mistake made during crises is an overall lack of action or communication. Although many executives feel reluctant to confront the press, it is important to use the media to communicate the organization's messages. If the organization fails to respond to media requests, the void will be filled with information from other sources. Being the first to tell the story allows the organization to define the situation and to develop a favorable public impression regarding its handling of the event.

Many organizations prepare for potential crises by designing a crisis management plan. Plans frequently include the following (compiled from Saffir, 1992; Stocker, 1997; and Dedmon, 1996):

- A statement of the principles (or approach) to be applied in dealing with a crisis. Kurt Stocker suggests that the statement "summarize the company's philosophies and ethics, and delineate what the company plans to 'protect'" in the event of a crisis (for example, the reputation of the company, the bottom line, the current management, the brand). Clarification of overall principles and policies provides a basis for decision making throughout the crisis.
- A comprehensive list of the kinds of crises that may occur. The crises most likely to occur will vary, of course, depending on the nature of the organization. Crises are generally of the following types: environmental, public health/safety, financial/business, natural disasters, human-caused disasters, criminal malfeasance by executives/employees, civil suits, or governmental actions.
- Formation of a crisis team. Generally, a member of senior management heads up the team, with other members chosen as needed for their expertise. Members might include specialists in the following areas: communications, legal, human resources, medical, research, operations, technology, safety, security, transportation, government affairs. Spokespersons should be designated and trained; other responsibilities may be defined. Contact information for team members should be readily available.
- Establishment of a crisis center (for example, an existing conference room) that is outfitted with communications equipment and any other materials or supplies that might be needed (written materials regarding the crisis plan, contact lists, stationery, portable communications equipment).

- A list of the key audiences, including adversaries, and an assessment of each.
- An analysis of resources for the crisis plan.
- A statement of media guidelines, describing the organization's general media policies and suggestions for communicating effectively with the media.
- Advance preparation of materials that might be needed, such as background information on the organization.
- Establishment of a "network alert system." Ongoing, open communications should be established with departments and employees throughout the organization so that regular dialogue can occur regarding potential problems, and that, when possible, action can be taken to avert crises. Ongoing communications with external stakeholders also serves as an early warning system.

Rehearsal of the plan is generally recommended, especially by enacting a simulation of a crisis scenario. It is also suggested that the plan be periodically reviewed and revised.

Crisis managers should be aware that different publics may require different crisis strategies. Employees, shareholders, and customers will probably be affected differently, and their needs and expectations will vary. These considerations should be taken into account when developing crisis plans. Given the high-risk nature of crisis management and the potential for long-term, irreparable damage to the organization, crisis management has become an important aspect of public relations.

**Marketing**

Strategic organizational communication that is directed at bringing about an exchange between an organization and a customer.

## Marketing

Like the various public relations functions, **marketing** is a management process that bears major responsibility for communicating and implementing strategy. Perhaps because public relations and marketing share this responsibility, and both are involved in communicating with external publics, there is often confusion regarding their specific organizational roles. Public relations is sometimes considered part of the marketing department, or vice versa. In many organizations the two are viewed as separate but complementary functions. There is currently a trend toward integrating the two to form the most comprehensive and effective means of communicating with an organization's many publics. This trend of integrated marketing communication is discussed later in this chapter.

Marketing, unlike public relations, is usually directed at bringing about an exchange between an organization and a customer. Marketing can be thought of as "a social and managerial process by which individuals and groups obtain what they need and want through creating and exchanging products and value with others" (Kotler and Armstrong, 1996). Marketing management involves analyzing markets and then planning, implementing, and monitoring programs designed to create and maintain these exchanges.

Philip Kotler and Gary Armstrong (1996) explain the relationship between marketing planning and strategic planning:

[Marketing planning] supports company strategic planning with more detailed planning for specific marketing opportunities. . . . There is much overlap between overall company strategy and marketing strategy. Marketing looks at consumer needs and the company's ability to satisfy them; these same factors guide the company mission and objectives. Most company strategy planning deals with marketing variables—market share, market development, growth—and it is sometimes hard to separate strategic planning from marketing planning. In fact, some companies refer to their strategic planning as "strategic market planning." Marketing plays a key role in the company's strategic planning in several ways. First, marketing provides a guiding philosophy—the marketing concept—which suggests company strategy should revolve around serving the needs of important consumer groups. Second, marketing provides inputs to strategic planners by helping to identify attractive market opportunities and by assessing the firm's potential to take advantage of them. Finally, within individual business units, marketing designs strategies for reaching the unit's objectives. (pp. 36, 43)

In the most effective organizations, marketing, public relations, strategic planning, and all other functions work together to develop and achieve strategic objectives and ultimately to serve the needs of customers.

## Traditional Marketing Approaches

During the economic boom of the 1950s and 1960s, companies focused on mass producing goods for the lowest cost and in turn selling these products to mass markets. In general, the demand for goods was high, and within industries there were fewer companies competing for market share. There were plenty of customers to go around. Organizations tended to be product-oriented, rather than customer-oriented. As Don Schultz, Stanley Tannenbaum, and Robert Lauterborn (1992) explain, "The manufacturer decided to make a product because it could, priced it to cover costs and to yield as much profit as possible, placed it on store shelves through the distribution chain it still dominated, and promoted it shamelessly." Given the high-growth economy, this approach was successful for many organizations.

The advent of television and its rapid proliferation offered companies a convenient way to promote products and services to mass audiences. Mass advertising, especially via television, became the focus of most marketing programs. Early on, the television audience was largely viewed as one homogeneous group of typical American families.

From this situation, a dominant marketing orientation emerged. Many companies operated from a top-down, inside-out perspective. The emphasis was on producing and selling goods, with little attention given to customer needs or satisfaction. Consumers were viewed as members of a mass, undifferentiated audience. Marketers focused on promoting existing products to achieve profits through sales volume. Advertising messages were directed at moving the customer toward the culminating act of making a purchase. Marketing success was measured by the number of transactions (purchases) made.

## Marketing Today: The Customer Is Central

Today, the customer has become a central figure in marketing planning. Economic and cultural factors have contributed to this shift in perspective. A fiercely competitive business environment requires organizations to work hard to attract and retain customers. The population is increasingly diverse. As customers become more sophisticated, they are more likely to demand products and services that meet their specific needs and wants. Today's consumers also tend to be more skeptical regarding advertisers' claims. The marketing process has become much more complex, and most organizations have realized that to survive, delivering value and satisfaction to their customers is key.

In response to this customer focus (sometimes referred to as market-driven focus), many organizations have adopted an outside-in marketing orientation, which involves knowing the needs of customers first, then designing products or services and marketing strategies based on consumer needs and wants. Rather than viewing customers as members of a mass audience, organizations usually segment audiences into targeted markets consisting of individuals who share common characteristics and interests. Although mass advertising still plays a major role in most marketing plans, it is now targeted to specific markets, and overall its role is decreasing. Other more targeted marketing approaches, such as telemarketing, are on the rise. The general trend is a movement from broadcasting (attempts to reach a mass audience) to what is referred to as narrowcasting (targeting specific subsets of consumers).

Companies also have realized that to remain competitive, they must not only attract new customers but retain current ones. The goal of this newer marketing perspective is not the single transaction, or sale of goods or services, but the building and maintaining of ongoing relationships with satisfied customers. Philip Kotler and Gary Armstrong (1996) point out that the focus on lasting relationships makes economic sense because "it costs five times as much to attract a new customer as it does to keep a current customer satisfied." Many companies now understand that, over the course of a lifetime, the value of a single customer can be extremely high. It is well worth the effort to ensure outstanding customer satisfaction.

## The Marketing Mix

A well-designed marketing plan coordinates multiple elements that have been designed to work together to achieve marketing goals. There are numerous tools available to the marketer; the blend of these tools is referred to as the marketing mix. The tools fall into four categories, known as the four Ps: *product* decisions (such as quality, design, packaging, services); *pricing* decisions (price, discounts, credit terms); *place* decisions (distribution channels, or the system for providing convenient access to products); and *promotion* decisions (advertising, personal selling, sales promotion, or public relations).

The focus here is on promotional tools because promotion encompasses many important communication activities in the marketing field. Promotion refers to the "activities that communicate the merits of the product and persuade customers to buy it" (Kotler and Armstrong, 1996). Promotion is designed to inform, persuade, and remind the target audience.

A common framework used to achieve promotional objectives is the AIDA model. AIDA suggests four sequential aspects of an effective promotional message: attracting *attention,* holding *interest,* creating *desire,* and obtaining *action* (a purchase) (Kotler and Armstrong, 1996). Although few promotional messages actually bring about all these reactions, messages that are considered well-designed have these customer reactions as goals.

Marketing professionals select from a range of promotional tools, including advertising, personal selling, sales promotion, or public relations strategies. Advertising is a mass-communication strategy and is by nature impersonal. It may be transmitted via television, radio, newspapers, magazines, Internet, direct mail, or any other form of mass media. Personal selling involves interpersonal communication, which can occur face to face or over the telephone (known as telemarketing). Sales promotion refers to strategies that offer added value or incentives to purchase. For example, tools for sales promotion include contests, coupons, bonuses, and free samples. Public relations also offers unique strategies to the mix of promotional tools. Favorable publicity about a company or product tends to be more credible than advertising and may even have the effect of a third-party endorsement. A successful marketing program coordinates the various promotional tools with product, price, and place strategies to create an effective marketing mix.

Direct marketing is the fastest growing form of marketing. "Direct marketing consists of direct communications with carefully targeted consumers to obtain an immediate response" (Kotler and Armstrong, 1996). Direct marketing techniques include direct mail and catalog marketing, telemarketing, television marketing (infomercials or home shopping programs), and on-line shopping. Direct marketing provides avenues for customer feedback and is designed to encourage an immediate purchase response. As the trend toward narrowcasting advances, direct marketing strategies are playing an increasing role in the overall marketing mix.

## The Emergence of Integrated Marketing Communications

**Integrated marketing communications**

Process of managing all sources of information about a product that behaviorally moves the customer toward a sale and maintains customer loyalty.

During the 1990s, **integrated marketing communications** (IMC) emerged as a growing approach to the marketing process. Integrated marketing communications is defined by Northwestern University's Medill School of Journalism as "the process of managing all sources of information about a product which behaviorally moves the customer toward a sale and maintains customer loyalty" (Thomas Harris, 1997).

IMC proponents stress the importance of building a multichannel, integrated communications strategy that communicates a single, unified message to a customer. According to Thomas Harris (1997):

> The process [of IMC] is based on the benefits of synergy and the assumption that the whole is greater than the sum of its parts. Thomas Duncan, director of the integrated marketing communications graduate program at the University of Colorado, says: "When all brand and corporate messages are strategically coordinated, the effect is greater than when advertising, sales promotion, marketing, PR, packaging, etc., are planned and executed independently, with each area competing for budgets and power and, in some cases, sending out conflicting messages." (p. 91)

Recent trends toward customer-focused, outside-in planning are also at the core of the integrated marketing communications orientation. IMC proponents, viewing the customer as central, seek to better understand customers: how to identify and track their needs, wants, and buying behaviors. They look for ways to increase customer satisfaction by building long-term relationships through two-way communications with customers. Communication tactics are derived from analyses of consumer behaviors. Through IMC, customers are not only viewed as members of narrow market segments, they are recognized to be individuals. IMC embraces the emerging trend toward one-on-one marketing (Schultz, Tannenbaum, and Lauterborn, 1992).

Why should communications be integrated? Integrated marketing communications researchers study how people take in, process, store, and use information about products and services. This research suggests that "marketing communications messages that are not recognizable, are not related to each other, conflict with what has already been stored [in the consumer's mind], or are simply unrelated or unimportant to the person simply will not be processed" (Schultz, Tannenbaum, and Lauterborn, 1992). In a world where we are constantly bombarded by information, it becomes necessary for marketers to do all they can to ensure that their messages are processed by consumers. Matching messages to consumer needs and integrating communications into a single message are important ways to increase the likelihood that marketing messages will be processed.

## Relationship Marketing and the Use of Marketing Databases

The practice of using transactional communication to build long-term relationships with customers is known as relationship marketing. In relationship marketing, "there is a relationship between the buyer and the seller that normally results from interchanges and exchanges of information and things of mutual value" (Schultz, Tannenbaum, Lauterborn, 1992). Advances in information technology allow companies to compile information about their customers that is necessary for maintaining ongoing relationships. As companies attempt to learn more about their customers to better serve their needs, they are employing computerized databases to store, organize, and retrieve consumer data.

Organizations gather customer information in numerous ways. Marketers may directly solicit responses from consumers through telemarketing, toll-free phone numbers, warranty cards, or direct mail pieces. Data from sweepstakes entries and magazine subscriptions are compiled. Companies also may track a customer's purchasing history by scanning the UPC codes on products that are purchased, supplying data on the buying behaviors of an individual or household. This information is compiled in a computerized marketing database and can later be used to target communications to specific audiences. Kotler and Armstrong (1996) cite a 1994 survey that "found that more than one-half of all large consumer products companies are currently building such databases." A marketing database is considered an important tool of integrated marketing communications.

The proliferation of database marketing is accompanied by a growing concern about invasion of privacy. Kotler and Armstrong (1996) explain:

> Many critics worry that marketers may know too much about consumers' lives, and that they may use this knowledge to take unfair advantage of consumers. At some point, they claim, the extensive use of databases intrudes on consumer privacy. . . . In a recent survey of consumers, 78 percent of respondents said that they were concerned about threats to their personal privacy. . . . Left untended, such problems will lead to increasingly negative consumer attitudes, lower response rates, and calls for greater state and federal legislation to further restrict direct marketing practices. (pp. 485–486)

This is an exciting and challenging time for professionals in the field of marketing. Changes in the marketing environment, advances in communications technology, and the development of new marketing tools and approaches all converge to create a dynamic and evolving profession.

# ETHICAL ISSUES IN STRATEGIC ORGANIZATIONAL COMMUNICATION

As with all the forms and processes of organizational communication discussed so far, strategic organizational communication encompasses important ethical issues. In the Ostern case, Linda and Brad are dealing with a critical ethical abuse as well as the ethical implications of the options they recommend to Jane Bevins. Although we each have personal responsibilities for the ethics of our individual behaviors, the communication professional engaging in strategic communication efforts is combining personal responsibility with the broader concept of organizational ethical responsibilities.

Cheney and Christensen (2001) provide an important description of ethical-moral issues related to strategic organizational communication. Cheney and

Christensen identify seven broad issues with ethical, moral, and even legal implications resulting from planned communication: (1) the posited character or integrity of the source of the message, (2) the defensibility of a particular message, (3) the legitimacy of a pattern or campaign of messages, (4) the practical impact of a message or the cumulative effect of a series of messages, (5) the openness of the structure of communication between an organization and its publics/audiences, (6) the articulation/representation of genuine public interests, and (7) the question of shared responsibility.

We have all questioned the truth of particular organizational messages. Advertising claims often are exaggerated with consumer complaints frequently hidden from public scrutiny. Think of a time when you questioned the accuracy or truthfulness of an advertising message, thought that an organization was covering up product problems, or simply did not know who was believable when making a product or service choice. We think not only about individual integrity but the credibility of the organization as a whole. Strategic organizational communication is an intentional effort to shape our perceptions. Themes selected for marketing, advertising, and crisis management may focus or frame an issue away from the product or service to a more generally accepted societal good. For example, messages from tobacco, liquor, and gun manufacturers often emphasis freedom, individuality, fun, or fear over more specific product advantages or features. These ethical issues and a host of others underscore the shared responsibility between organizations and consumers for the ethical-moral evaluation of messages and their potential influence.

With the increasing complexity of organizational environments and the growing awareness of the importance of strategic communication with its ethical and legal impacts, strategic organizational communication positions in public relations and marketing represent important career options for organizational communication majors. These options and others are discussed in Chapter 11 to help as you continue to think about your skills and interests as related to the requirements of professional organizational communication. Internal and external communications positions, however, are not the only ones where communication professionals make significant contributions to organizational change. In the next section, the management of development and change and the responsibilities of those engaged in these important organizational processes are discussed.

## THE MANAGEMENT OF DEVELOPMENT AND CHANGE

Inherent in most of the career options in Chapter 11 is the responsibility of communication professionals to help organizations identify needed change and develop strategies and tactics appropriate for productive change. Because of the rapid changes associated with an information-rich society, increasing importance is being attached to organizational positions responsible for guiding and directing change and development. The public relations and marketing positions discussed in the previous sections of this chapter are directly or indirectly associated with identifying, conceptualizing, introducing, teaching, and evaluating change. Thus, helping organizations develop and change is a primary professional application of organizational communication competencies.

**Organizational development**
Educational strategies intended to change the beliefs, attitudes, values, and structure of organizations.

The management of development and change goes beyond public relations and marketing. Warren Bennis (1969) suggests that **organizational development** is needed for dealing with continuing change and can be described as a complex educational strategy. Educational strategies are designed to promote organizational change so that adaptation to new technologies, markets, and challenges, and the rate of change itself can take place.

Fundamental to the Bennis notion of organizational development is the ability to identify needed change, to develop educational strategies (internal communication, training, publications, advertising, public relations) that help bring about change, and to evaluate the results of these efforts. When in Chapter 11 the responsibilities and skills required for most of the communication career options are discussed, you will see that problem identification, design of educational strategies, and evaluation techniques are primary responsibilities for communication professionals.

**Human resource development**
Sets of activities that prepare employees to perform their current jobs more effectively; to assume different positions in the organization; or to move into jobs, positions, and careers that are not yet defined.

Closely aligned with Bennis's description of organizational development is Wayne Pace's definition of **human resource development.** Pace (1983) suggests that human resource development "refers to a set of activities that prepare employees to perform their current jobs more effectively, to assume different positions in the organization, or to move into jobs, positions, and careers that are yet unidentified and undefined." Pace contends that the importance of human resource development rests on seven basic assumptions:

(1) That human beings are important in their own right as resources to achieve organizational goals; (2) that human beings have the right to be satisfied with ways in which they contribute to the organization; (3) that changing conditions, environment, markets, and resource demands necessitate the continual preparation of human beings to assume different positions; (4) that human beings do not come to the organization with all of the knowledge and skills they need to fulfill any and every demand placed upon them; (5) that a pool of developing workers, supervisors, and managers constitute a body of individuals who can help meet future human resource needs; (6) that development constitutes more than technical training, but involves an understanding of human behavior, how people respond and relate to one another, how human beings contribute to organizational productivity as well as to their own well-being; and (7) that the quality of work life is a legitimate and valuable concern of human beings in all areas of development. (p. 3)

Peter Senge (1998) contends that the increasing interdependency of the world requires change and new learning: "We have to develop a sense of connectedness, a sense of working together as part of a system, where each part of the system is affecting and being affected by the others, and where the whole is greater than the sum of the parts." Senge believes that the learning organization will develop capacities for change and learning not found in traditional organizations.

John Kotter (1998) describes an eight-stage process for creating major change through successful organizational transformation. Kotter contends:

> It starts off with pushing the urgency rate up. What people have to do is to start focusing attention on performance data and on industry data. In other words, they've got to look objectively at how the organization is doing, and at where the industry is going, in the hope that by getting enough people looking at the real situation, those people will either become convinced that there is a crisis, or they will begin to see some major opportunities that they hadn't seen before. In either case the urgency rate goes up, and all of a sudden you've got an opportunity to get things going.
>
> The next step is to form an appropriate guiding coalition, a group that has enough power to lead the change effort. Then you've got to develop a vision, and a strategy for achieving it, and you've got to communicate that vision effectively to the whole organization. You've got to empower people to change systems and structures that stand in the way of the vision. And you've got to create some short-term wins, so that employees can begin to see visible improvements, and they can be recognized and rewarded for their part in those improvements.
>
> Next it's a question of consolidating the credibility from those short-term wins to produce even more change. And finally, you must ensure that it is all institutionalized into a new culture. (pp. 170–171)

Both internal and external communication specialists have professional responsibilities for organizational and human resource development and organizational change processes. Whether as an employee of the organization or as an external consultant, communication specialists collect and evaluate data, interpret data to those responsible for decision making, develop processes and plans for solutions, and evaluate the results of change and development efforts.

The manner in which communication specialists provide these professional services can be described by three general models: purchase, doctor-patient, and process. Each model reflects different assumptions about the role of the communication specialist; the abilities of individuals, departments, or entire organizations to define their own problems; and who has responsibility for problem solving.

**Purchase model**
Consulting model in which the organization relates to the specialist by requesting particular services to meet a need the specialist has not been involved with identifying.

## The Purchase Model

In the **purchase model,** the organization relates to communication specialists, whether they are organizational employees or external consultants, by requesting particular services to meet a need the specialist has not been involved with identifying. The communication professional may be requested to conduct a training class, write a news release, or design a publication announcing a new policy. The parties requesting the specialist's services assume they understand their own needs and have identified the specialist as capable of meeting those needs. In other words, they are purchasing the desired services. This model can be an efficient use of resources if the assignment is well defined and the specialist capable of implementing the desired request. This model is ineffective, however, when the client does not thoroughly understand the problem or requests of the specialist services beyond the specialist's scope of responsibility or capability.

**Doctor-patient model**
Consulting model in which the organization expects the specialist to diagnose problems and prescribe solutions.

## The Doctor-Patient Model

The **doctor-patient model** is based on assumptions very different from the purchase model. In the doctor-patient model, the communication professional acts in much the same manner as a medical doctor who examines patients, identifies their symptoms, and prescribes treatment. In the organizational setting, the doctor-patient model requires the communication specialist to examine symptoms of organizational problems and prescribe appropriate solutions to meet the identified problems. As in the purchase model, the results are effective if the specialist has abilities appropriate to the task and if the organization readily accepts the diagnosis and treatment. One of the primary problems with the doctor-patient model is in the lack of organizational acceptance of proposed solutions when organizational members have little or no input into the process.

**Process model**
Consulting model in which the organization and specialist work jointly to diagnose problems and generate solutions.

## The Process Model

The **process model** for organizational development finds members of the organization working hand in hand with the communication professional to identify problems, propose solutions, implement action, and evaluate results. In the process model, the communication specialist is responsible for guiding organizational members through inquiry and problem solving. The basic assumptions underlying the model are that organizational members are more likely to be committed to solutions they have helped generate and that the talents of the specialist are best used when working directly with those affected by the problem.

## Planned Development and Change

Regardless of the model or models from which the communication professional works, four basic activities occur in the process of planned development and change: data collection; data evaluation; planning and implementation of development, solutions, and change; and evaluation of results. The effectiveness of each of these activities contributes to the overall effectiveness of development and change. Although the activities are closely related to one another, they each require unique skills for effective performance.

## Data Collection

Primary techniques for data collection include questionnaires, audits, interviews, performance data, cost analysis, and trained observation. Each technique can yield useful information, and often the techniques are combined to provide a more comprehensive understanding of potential problems and issues.

Questionnaires contain open-ended or closed questions. Entire populations may be asked to respond, or sampling techniques may be used to survey part of a population from which to generalize the results. For questionnaire data to be useful in planned change, questions must be relevant, well framed, and valid, with respondents representing a population who can be expected to understand the problem.

Organizational communication auditing is a particular type of questionnaire currently gaining in credibility and use. Such auditing is the periodic examination of important communication activities such as message-sending and message-receiving activities as they relate to important organizational outcomes. Numerous audit instruments exist and numerous others are tailored for particular organizations. Audits are used to design communication strategies, assess needs, and evaluate practices. Regardless of the procedure used, organizational communication specialists are expected to understand auditing's basic principles and to be able to use the approach as part of planned change activities.

Interviews can contribute a rich amount of data important for change and development. Whether from informal or tightly scheduled interviews, interview data can expand understanding of complex problems and identify resistance to organizational change. Interviewing requires problem knowledge, the ability to be understood by others, the ability to understand others, and skills for meaningful interpretation of interview results.

Questionnaires and interviews are techniques that gather data the organization does not already have. Other data, called performance data, exist as a result of the daily operation of the organization. These performance data come from sales reports, turnover rates, employee absenteeism, quarterly profit statements, and a host of other routine organizational measures. These data all too often are not thoughtfully used along with questionnaire and survey data to better understand needs. Communication specialists often find such performance data useful to substantiate or expand understanding of problems identified with questionnaire and interview techniques.

Gathering data about the cost of a problem also contributes to directing action toward solutions. Cost analysis may range from determining a ratio of return on an advertising campaign to assessing the dollar value of employee time spent in meetings as compared to the value derived from decisions made in meetings. Cost analysis is based on the assumption that communication behavior has both human and financial consequences. From this perspective, a seemingly inexpensive training program that fails to explain an important concept is costly. Gerald Wilson, H. L. Goodall, and Christopher Waagen (1986) propose a six-step process for analyzing communication costs in task behaviors:

1. Describe the task to be costed in terms of behaviors.
2. Identify behaviors involving communication.
3. Describe communication network coordinating communication behaviors.
4. Determine the time spent by each person involved with the task in various communication functions.
5. Value time spent by each person.
6. Compute total cost of communication for the task.

Although cost analysis can be used to determine the cost efficiency of particular types of communication (television commercials or newspaper advertising), the primary purpose of collecting cost data is to understand the financial consequences of the event, task, or behavior within the broader context of what the organization needs. Thus, communication cost analysis frequently becomes the responsibility of the communication specialist.

Finally, trained observation is a valid technique for data collection. The communication specialist, either as a participant-observer or as an observer alone, may collect data about group processes such as decision making and problem solving. Specialists assess the effectiveness of training approaches by observing participant interactions and abilities to perform behaviors proposed during training. Skilled observation can also uncover information not previously known to the organization and therefore difficult to collect in formal questionnaires or interviews. One communication specialist's observation, for example, discovered unexpected resistance to a new policy eliminating an eating area near a production line. Although the organization provided an attractive alternative area, employees were disgruntled. Observation of the displeasure led the specialist to investigate further, finding that the production manager had increased the number of breaks per shift for each employee but had reduced the amount of time for each break. The quality assurance manager, concerned with removing food from the product assembly area, had moved the new break area further from the production line, requiring more walking time per break. The two changes, each well founded, were not compatible.

## Data Evaluation

Once data are collected, evaluation and interpretation begin. In the case of questionnaires and audits, answers are tabulated and statistical analysis is used to develop a numerical description of the issues or problems under consideration. The use of appropriate statistical tests, an understanding of the limits of particular tests, and an ability to translate the numerical data into the essence of the problem are important in data evaluation. Interviews are coded to discover recurring themes or identify unique problems and creative solutions. When interview and survey data are collected for the same general problem area, data are examined for convergence, that is, whether the two forms of data yield essentially the same understanding of the problem. When they do, the specialist has added confidence in the accuracy of the findings. When findings are dissimilar, additional data may be needed to understand discrepancies.

Cost analysis data are used to evaluate communication efficiency and effectiveness and to understand the financial impact of issues and problems. These data may be used to make decisions about the amounts of organizational resources needed for change and development. Cost data also contribute to a better understanding of questionnaire and interview results. Finally, observation data are used to confirm understanding from other data, stimulate the identification of additional data needs, and bring subtle yet often crucial interpretation to data collected with more formal techniques.

Once data have been analyzed, the communication professional is responsible for interpreting data to those involved in developing solutions and making decisions about change. Data interpretation must therefore fit the needs of the proposed audience while thoughtfully and honestly reflecting the findings. This feedback stage can be especially difficult if the specialist has data that may not meet with the approval of key decision makers.

A dilemma faced by a communication consultant in a large East Coast manufacturing plant illustrates this problem. The consultant was hired to help management understand why several key supervisors had requested transfers to other divisions within the organization. Also, turnover rates for the plant exceeded the company average and absenteeism was at an all-time high. Management was perplexed because of the longtime excellent reputation of their division and the recent installation of new state-of-the-art manufacturing equipment designed to improve both quality and quantity of output. Data collected by the consultant revealed that supervisors were asking to leave because they did not trust the motives of management with regard to the new equipment. Many supervisors, and a significant number of workers as well, believed management was planning to use technology to eliminate jobs or at best to reduce advancement opportunities by requiring fewer and fewer lead positions on the manufacturing line. Many of the top supervisors were young and wanted to continue their career advancement, which they believed to be jeopardized by management planning. The consultant knew that management would not be pleased with these findings, although the findings accurately reflected the data. The consultant was faced with the problem of presenting findings for maximum problem understanding while facilitating management to generate a solution.

A communication professional is concerned with how to facilitate understanding without placing blame and with how to generate commitment for a problem solution. This component of the change process can be especially difficult for the internal communication consultant who may gain his or her primary visibility with management during the discussion of difficult problems. The ability to be effective in this type of circumstance requires careful planning and broad-based communication competency.

Data are reported in written and oral form. Raw data and interpretations of data are identified and carefully separated. Interpretations are labeled for source and basis. Limitations of data also are specified. Frequently, reports will contain only portions of a data set. Decisions about what data to include are based on relevancy to the problem, the audience for the report, and the audience's ability to use data for problem solving. Reports identify the existence of additional data should the people involved need more detailed information.

## Planning and Implementing Solutions

The planning and implementing of needed change come about in diverse ways. At times the communication professional is charged with the responsibility to develop and propose plans for change that are subject to management approval. At other times the specialist may be charged with developing and implementing plans as part of regular job responsibilities. For example, communication professionals frequently are responsible for determining organizational training needs and providing training services appropriate to those needs. In other types of problem situations, the communication professional may act as a group facilitator, with others responsible for decision making and problem solving.

The communication professional is most likely to be involved with the following types of change activities: policy changes, process changes, training and development activities, and advising and counseling. Although the responsibility and level of involvement for each activity will vary from organization to organization, these primary change activities are fundamental for organizations to improve their adapting, coping, and problem-solving capabilities.

*Policy* refers to formally established decisions about organizational operating procedures. Organizations have personnel policies, financial policies, and customer service policies, to name just a few. For policies to be effective, they must reflect not only what the organization does but also what the organization should be doing. Effective organizations have dynamic policies that reflect changes in changing environments. Communication professionals are involved in developing personnel policies, customer relations policies, policies that govern relationships with suppliers to the organization, advertising and public relations policies, and policies that prescribe what information will be available to all organization members.

Communication professionals also involve themselves in needed *process changes*. Performance appraisal, meetings, decision making, and problem solving are only a few examples of organizational processes in which communication professionals develop plans for training organizational members in their effective use or make recommendations for process improvements.

*Training and development activities* are formal education strategies to help organizations perform more effectively. As already discussed, training is a primary responsibility for communication professionals. Effective training can help individuals and entire organizations develop better self-awareness, incorporate the use of new skills and processes, and adapt to the changing needs of dynamic environments. Training also is used to transmit organizational beliefs, attitudes, and values. As such, training reflects organizational culture and becomes part of the shared realities of organizational members.

Policy, processes, and training and development activities are generally somewhat formally structured and part of the planned operation of the organization. *Advising and counseling activities* are both formal and informal responsibilities of the communication professional. Personnel liaisons, for example, meet regularly with departments and department managers to provide advice and counsel. Counseling may examine specific behaviors, include improved ways of doing things, or focus on career development. Communication professionals, however, are frequently sought for informal advice about human relations problems and personal dilemmas organizational members face. The ability to understand and represent both the interests of the individual and the organization requires sensitivity and strong interpersonal communication skills. Effective advice and counseling help individuals reach good decisions and improve behaviors, both vital processes to organizational adaptation and change. This advising and counseling role is especially important in organizations undergoing rapid change. When individuals are asked to acquire new skills and face somewhat uncertain futures, they may need assistance in planning their personal response to the circumstances around them. The communication professional can assist the entire organization in developing flexibility for an information-rich society by individually helping members maximize their personal coping mechanisms.

## Evaluating Results

Changes in policies, processes, training and developmental activities, and advising and counseling are part of the ongoing process of organizational life. Almost everyone, however, recognizes that change for the sake of change may or may not be organizationally effective. The final component of the change and development process, therefore, is the evaluation of the results.

Change can be evaluated in a number of ways and with a number of different criteria. Organizations frequently use performance measures such as profit and loss, sales quotas, manufacturing output, quality defects, and employee turnover to measure change. When a sales and profit problem has been caused by quality defects on the manufacturing line, the effectiveness of improvement efforts is measured against previous sales, profit, and defects figures.

Many organizational change efforts, however, are not directly linked to quantifiable measures of performance. Attempts to generate increased teamwork, for example, although ultimately related to profit and loss figures, cannot be immediately measured in terms of dollars and cents. Evaluation of this somewhat subjective problem can be established by looking for changes in the data that identified the problem. Data gathered by one consultant identifying a teamwork problem indicated that instead of peers and supervisors working together to solve problems, supervisors routinely went to managers for decisions they should have been making themselves. The consultant evaluated whether her team-building efforts had generated improvement by determining whether managers were still being asked as frequently for solutions. Effectiveness of teamwork efforts also was evaluated by asking the supervisors themselves how they felt about change efforts. Thus, trained observation can also be important in the evaluation of change efforts not suitable for direct performance measures.

Finally, additional data collection serves a useful role in the evaluation of change. Questionnaires, auditing, interviews, and the other techniques discussed in the data-collection phase of change can be used to determine the effects of educational strategies for organizational development and change. In one very real sense, evaluation is not the end of the change process but instead is the way the process begins again. The evaluation of change gives us a new organizational point of reference from which additional change efforts can occur. Figure 10.1 illustrates how the four components of the change process can be visualized as a cyclical process, with evaluation efforts influencing subsequent data collection and problem identification.

Most researchers and business practitioners agree that the rate of change in organizational life will continue to escalate as we come fully into the information age. If these predictions continue to prove true, organizational communication competencies will be increasingly desirable for those responsible for organizational decision making and problem solving. Professional positions for managing change will continue to be important, but managing change will increasingly become

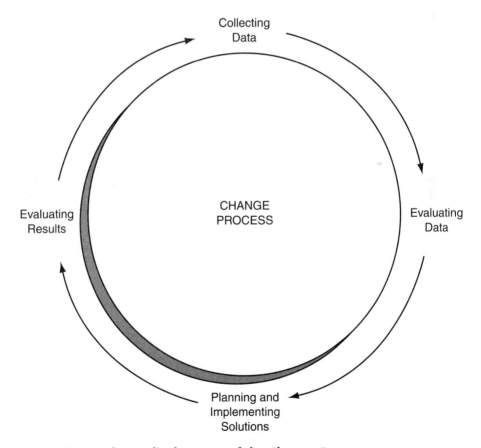

**FIGURE 10.1   The Cyclical Nature of the Change Process**

everyone's responsibility. Indeed, the challenges of change in an information-rich society suggest the growing importance of communication professionals for effective organizations of the future.

## SUMMARY

Strategic organizational communication can be described as transactional communication processes in which organizational messages are deliberately generated, are based on environmental data, analysis and strategy selection, and are guided by organizational objectives. Strategic organizational communication messages usually are developed by communication professionals. Organizations increasingly are integrating communication functions to create coordinated, complementary messages. Strategic organizational communication is based in part on environmental information and an understanding of the concepts of multiple publics and stakeholders. Strategic management is the process of formulating and implementing an organizational plan of action. Public relations and marketing are two types of strategic organizational communication functions which support strategic organizational direction. Little agreement exists whether public relations is a specific set of functions or whether it encompasses all of the communication activities of an organization. Public relations functions frequently include image management, internal communication, public affairs and issues management, media relations, and crisis management. In broad terms, most agree public relations is responsible in part for managing an organization's image or reputation. Internal communication refers to communication with employees and is frequently a responsibility of the public relations function.

Public affairs and issues management involve the shaping of public opinion regarding social and political issues important to the organization. Media relations involves working with the media on behalf of an organization. Media specialists are responsible to their organizations, the media, and the publics who seek information from the media. Crisis management protocols are developed to communicate during organizational crises. Marketing is the management communication process directed at bringing about an exchange between an organization and a customer. Integrated marketing communications is growing in importance, stressing strategy that communicates a single, unified message to a customer. In addition to public relations and marketing, the management of planned development and change is a responsibility of communication professionals. Organizational development is described as educational strategies designed to promote organizational change so that adaptation to new technologies, markets, and challenges, and the rate of change itself can take place. Models for intervention in organizations include the purchase model, the doctor-patient model, and the process model. Planned development and change are based on data collection, data evaluation, planning and implementing solutions, and evaluating results.

# WORKSHOP

1. Using all the media at your disposal, including the Internet, identify a variety of marketing and public relations approaches. Bring several examples to class for discussion.

2. Locate at least two examples of crisis communication efforts. Prepare to present them to your class.

3. In groups of four, describe the image or reputation of your school. Groups should report to the class as a whole. Compare similarities. What were the differences?

4. Discuss the ethical dimensions of public relations and marketing.

5. In the Communication Professional at Work Activity, organizational situations are presented that require the services of a communication professional. You are the professional consultant chosen to work with these organizations. (See pp. 389–390.)

6. Susan Bowick, in an essay entitled "Communication as a Management Tool," describes a Hewlett-Packard communication strategy to deal with change. Read her "change strategy" and discuss it with your class. (See pp. 390–392.)

## The Communication Professional at Work Activity

Each of the following organizational situations will result in a request for the services of a communication professional. As you read each case, try to determine which of the consulting models you would recommend and what types of data must be collected to initiate the change cycle.

■ ■ ■ ■ ■

## JANE EDWARDS'S PROBLEM EMPLOYEE

Jane Edwards was proud of the people who worked for her in the data-processing department. They were capable and had shown a great deal of commitment and creativity during the last few difficult months of program expansion. With such a positive performance by the entire department, Jane could hardly believe the reports she was getting about George Jones. He was one of her most capable programmers. Could he really have been responsible for major errors in the new program? Did he really walk away last Friday, threatening never to come back? Should she go to him directly? Jane decides to contact her personnel liaison, Jim Hillis. She wants to know how Jim can help her understand what, if anything, is happening to George.

### QUESTIONS FOR DISCUSSION
1. What model is Jane putting in place to work with Jim?
2. What data does Jane have?
3. If you were Jim, what data would you need to help with Jane's problem?

■ ■ ■ ■ ■ ▬▬▬▬▬▬▬▬▬▬▬▬▬▬▬▬▬▬▬▬▬▬▬▬▬▬▬

## THE CASE OF THE POORLY WRITTEN MANUAL

John Howard was shaking his head as he left the meeting with his boss, Joe French. Joe was right; the new technical manual was simply not up to the company's standards. Yes, he had told Joe that there were three new people in the test group, but that was no excuse. The three apparently were simply not capable writers; they may be capable product engineers, but their writing was terrible. John called the training department and asked for Susan Harris. Could Susan schedule his three new employees in her next technical writing course?

### QUESTIONS FOR DISCUSSION
1. What model is John putting into place to work with Susan?
2. What are his assumptions in making this decision?
3. Is this an appropriate approach for solving his problem?

■ ■ ■ ■ ■ ▬▬▬▬▬▬▬▬▬▬▬▬▬▬▬▬▬▬▬▬▬▬▬▬▬▬▬

## THE TRANSITION OF STANLEY MANUFACTURING

Stanley Manufacturing has enjoyed a fine reputation in the small home-appliance industry. Since its beginning some sixty years ago, Stanley has prided itself on maintaining a family atmosphere for its employees, who are expected to stay with Stanley for their entire working careers. Times have changed, though. Stanley's management team sees profits being eroded and more and more competitors using innovative manufacturing processes, enabling them to produce a quality product at a price lower than the Stanley line. Stanley's management team understands that Stanley Manufacturing must undergo major changes to regain a prominent position in the market. They decide to hire a consultant external to the Stanley organization to help them begin a change process.

### QUESTIONS FOR DISCUSSION
1. Which model is the Stanley management team putting in place?
2. If you were the consultant, what type of data would you collect?
3. How would you involve people in the Stanley organization?
4. Can an external person be useful in this situation?

## Communication as a Management Tool

### Susan Bowick[1]

The notion that part of a manager's job is talking to people in his or her organization is certainly not revolutionary. Walk into any bookstore in America today, and

---

[1]Susan Bowick was personnel manager at the Lake Stevens Instrument Division of Hewlett-Packard Company when she wrote this essay. Bowick currently is vice president of Personnel with Hewlett-Packard in Palo Alto, California.

you will see shelves of books that focus on performing the managerial job more effectively. Much of the information in current management literature deals with the importance of translating a manager's vision into a clear agenda, with priorities that employees can readily understand.

Robert Waterman Jr., coauthor of *In Search of Excellence*, the bestseller on well-managed companies, notes, "In all our basic research, C.E.O.s were constantly telling us that you can't reiterate your corporate vision and goals enough. It's just amazing how fast people lost direction and wandered from the basics." Effective corporate leaders also understand the power of infectious enthusiasm. "If a company's in deep yogurt," says Waterman, "a good policeman can turn it around. But to make it a great company requires a cheerleader."

The importance of having a strong communications philosophy has been brought home to me many times as a manager at Hewlett-Packard Company. Being part of the high-tech business sector means constant change. The Lake Stevens Instrument Division of HP is no exception, as the management team quickly evolved business strategy from one traditional instrument product line (which employees knew well and loved!) to four different product lines. The future of our business was with new products and new customers that were not understood by employees. This change created lots of apprehension about why the new strategic direction was necessary, who was responsible for the decisions that propelled us into the new business, and most important, the uncertainty individual employees experienced as they tried to figure out what their role might be in the new scheme of things.

In the midst of the changing business strategy, I noticed some interesting phenomena taking place. Much of the panic and uncertainty being felt by employees was based on a lack of information. In the absence of accurate, current information, employees were creating information by speculating and sharing what information was available. Employees were acting on this information without verifying the accuracy of it. The grapevine was humming, but with the wrong tune.

After looking at the communication occurring within the organization, the reasons behind much of the uncertainty became clear. Most managers were communicating within their departments but, sure enough, managers were talking about lots of different things. Managers were choosing various times and ways to communicate. What was being said reflected individual views and priorities, so a cohesive business picture was just about impossible to sort out. It became apparent that if we wanted employees to support the organization through the change in business strategy, the management team needed to take the lead in communicating more information to employees.

Our business needed a way to answer employees' questions. We needed our employees to be able to count on hearing information on a regular basis. All employees in the organization needed to hear a consistent message, not just a few people close enough to the decisions to be "in the know." Individual managers needed to do a better job explaining overall business strategy, then translating that into specific plans for each department. And we needed to figure out what information employees wanted to hear. The managerial role in communicating had just become more complex than any of us had realized!

**FIGURE 10.2    HP Lake Stevens Instrument Division's Communication Matrix**

| AUDIENCES | MESSAGE CONTENT | WHEN | HOW | WHO | MEASUREMENT OF EFFECTIVENESS |
|---|---|---|---|---|---|
| All LSID employees | Division objectives, current year (emphasize LSID tactical plans, why, when, link to long-term strategies) <br><br> Communicate current results, new LSID issues | Quarterly | Quarterly communica- tion sessions | Division manager | Employee interviews <br><br> Number of questions received about business direction |
| Manager/ supervisor "leaders of change" | LSID strategic direction, key organizational issues, visibility into planning process and resource allocation <br><br> Emphasize why and relationship to other functional areas | At least two times/year or as needed | LSID management meeting | Division manager and functional managers | Questionnaire at end of meetings <br><br> Number of questions from employees |
| Each functional area | Impact of above on functional area | Monthly, or as needed | Coffee talks, crackerbarrels | Functional managers | Multi-level management survey (MLMS) results for goals, orderly work planning, upward communication |
| | Plans to manage within functional area <br><br> Department results, issues | | Department meetings | | Does department have tactical plans linked to strategy? Have those plans been presented to all employees? |

Matrix from *Soper Hill Views*—LSID Publication. Reprinted with permission.

The communication challenge was treated as any other business problem to be solved. We developed an objective and designed a communication program that specified the who, when, and what of sharing our business strategy with employees. Ways to measure the effectiveness of the communication were also defined. The matrix in Figure 10.2 became the Lake Stevens Instrument Divisions' communications strategy.

The expected result is being achieved. Employees are hearing consistent, frequent information. We have asked for feedback from employees about the communication and found out that there are no William Jennings Bryans among us, so the entire senior management team is taking a class to become more effective presenters. The role of manager as communicator is taken seriously.

# REFERENCES AND SUGGESTED READINGS

Andrews, K. R. 1971. *The concept of corporate strategy.* Homewood, IL: Irwin.
Auster, E., and C. W. Choo. 1994. How senior managers acquire and use information in environmental scanning. *Information Processing and Management* 30: 607–618.
Bennis, W. 1969. *Organization development: Its nature, origins, and prospects.* Reading, MA: Addison-Wesley.
Bennis, W., K. Benne, R. Chin, and K. Corey. 1976. *The planning of change.* 3d ed. New York: Holt, Rinehart and Winston.
Buccholz, R. A. 1988. Adjusting corporations to the realities of public interests and policy. In *Strategic issues management,* ed. R. L. Heath, pp. 50–72. San Francisco: Jossey-Bass.
Caywood, C. L. (ed.) 1997. *The handbook of strategic public relations and integrated communications.* New York: McGraw-Hill.
Cheney, G., and L. Christensen. 2001. Organizational identity: Linkages between internal and external communication. In *The new handbook of organizational communication: Advances in theory, research, and methods,* eds. F. Jablin and L. Putnam, pp. 231–269. Thousand Oaks, CA: Sage.
Clampitt, P., R. DeKoch, and T. Cashman. 2000. A strategy for communicating about uncertainty. *Academy of Management Executive* 14 (4): 41–57.
Conrad, C. 1994. *Strategic organizational communication: Toward the 21st century.* Orlando, FL: Harcourt, Brace.
Cutlip, S. M., A. H. Center, and G. M. Broom. 1985. *Effective public relations.* 6th ed. Englewood Cliffs, NJ: Prentice Hall.
Daft, R. L., and K. E. Weick. 1984. Toward a model of organizations as interpretation systems. *Academy of Management Review* 9: 284–295.
Daniels, T. D., B. K. Spiker, and M. J. Papa. 1997. *Perspectives on organizational communication.* Madison, WI: Brown and Benchmark.
Dedmon, J. (1996). Thinking the unthinkable: Crisis communications. In *Dartnell's public relations handbook,* ed. R. L. Dilenschneider, pp. 206–225.
DeWine, S. 1994. *The consultant's craft.* New York: St. Martin's.
Eisenberg, E. M., and H. L. Goodall. 1997. *Organizational communication: Balancing creativity and constraint.* New York: St. Martin's.
Ewing, R. P. 1997. Issues management: Managing trends through the issues life cycle. In *Handbook of strategic public relations and integrated communications,* ed. C. L. Caywood, pp. 173–188. New York: McGraw-Hill.
Fisher, D. 1993. *Communication in organizations.* Minneapolis, MN: West.
Fombrun, C., and M. Shanley. 1990. What's in a name? Reputation building and corporate strategy. *Academy of Management Journal* 33: 233–258.

French, W. L., and C. H. Bell. 1973. *Organization development: Behavioral science interventions for organization improvement.* Englewood Cliffs, NJ: Prentice Hall.

Goldhaber, G. M. 1986. *Organizational communication.* 4th ed. Dubuque, IA: Brown.

Graham, J. D. 1997. Making the CEO the chief communications officer: Counseling senior management. In *Handbook of strategic public relations and integrated communications,* ed. C. L. Caywood, pp. 274–285. New York: McGraw-Hill.

Grunig, J. E. 1990. Theory and practice of interactive media relations. *Public Relations Quarterly* 35(3): 18–23.

Grunig, J. E. 1992. *Excellence in public relations and communication management.* Hillsdale, NJ: Lawrence Erlbaum.

Grunig, J. E. 1993. Image and substance: from symbolic to behavior relationships. *Public Relations Review* 19: 121–139.

Harris, T. L. 1991. *The marketers' guide to public relations.* New York: Wiley.

Harris, T. L. 1997. Integrated marketing public relations. In *Handbook of strategic public relations and integrated communications,* ed. C. L. Caywood, pp. 90–105. New York: McGraw-Hill.

Henderson, B. D. 1991. The Origin of strategy. In *Strategy: Seeking and securing competitive advantage,* eds. C. A. Montgomery and M. E. Porter, pp. 3–9. Boston: Harvard Business School.

Kosmicki, R., and F. Bona. 1996. Media relations: How to relate to the press. In *Dartnell's public relations handbook,* ed. R. L. Dilenschneider, pp. 58–75. Chicago: Dartnell.

Kotler, P., and G. Armstrong. 1996. *Principles of marketing.* Englewood Cliffs, NJ: Prentice Hall.

Kotter, J. 1998. Cultures and coalitions. In *Rethinking the future,* ed. R. Gibson, pp. 164–178. London: Nicholas Brealey.

Lamb, C., J. Hair, and C. McDaniel. 1992. *Principles of marketing.* Cincinnati, OH: South-Western.

Lawler, E. E., and J. R. Galbraith. 1994. Avoiding the corporate dinosaur syndrome. *Organizational Dynamics* 23: 5–17.

Mintzberg, H. 1990. Strategy formation: Schools of thought. In *Perspectives on strategic management,* ed. J. W. Frederickson, pp. 105–235. New York: Harper Business.

Mintzberg, H. 1991. Crafting strategy. In *Strategy: Seeking and securing competitive advantage,* eds. C. A. Montgomery and M. E. Porter, pp. 403–420. Boston: Harvard Business School.

Mintzberg, H. 1994. *The rise and fall of strategic planning.* New York: Free Press.

Moffitt, M. A. 1994. Collapsing and integrating concepts of "public" and "image" into a new theory. *Public Relations Review* 20: 159–170.

Pace, W. 1983. *Organizational communication: Foundations for human resource development.* Englewood Cliffs, NJ: Prentice Hall.

Richardson, B. 1995. The politically aware leader: Understanding the need to match paradigms and planning systems to powerful, "turbulent fields" environment. *Leadership and Organization Development Journal* 16(2): 27–35.

Saffir, L. 1992. *Power public relations.* Lincolnwood, IL: NTC Business Books.

Schein, E. H. 1969. *Process consultation: Its role in organization development.* Reading, MA: Addison-Wesley.

Schultz, D. E. 1995. The many views of integrated marketing communications. In *The AMA marketing encyclopedia: Issues and trends shaping the future,* ed. J. Heilbrunn, pp. 190–194. Chicago: American Marketing Association.

Schultz, D. E., S. Tannenbaum, and R. Lauterborn. 1992. *Integrated marketing communications.* Lincolnwood, IL: NTC Business Books.

Senge, P. 1998. Through the eye of the needle. In *Rethinking the future,* ed. R. Gibson, pp. 123–146. London: Nicholas Brealey.

Stocker, K. P. 1997. A strategic approach to crisis management. In *Handbook of strategic public relations and integrated communications,* ed. C. L. Caywood, pp. 189–203. New York: McGraw-Hill.

Subramanian, R., N. Fernandez, and E. Harper. 1993. Environmental scanning in U.S. companies: their nature and their relationship to performance. *Management International Review* 33: 271–286.

Wilson, G. L., H. L. Goodall, Jr., and C. L. Waagen. 1986. *Organizational communication.* New York: Harper & Row.

# CHAPTER ELEVEN

■ ■ ■ ■ ■

# APPLICATIONS OF ORGANIZATIONAL COMMUNICATION

## DEVELOPING COMPETENCIES THROUGH . . .

### KNOWLEDGE
Describing influences for career decisions

Identifying career option areas and educational preparation for organizational communication

Describing twenty-first century careers

### SENSITIVITY
Developing awareness of personal influences for career decisions

Understanding employment matching

### SKILLS
Assessing individual career development needs

Practicing analysis capabilities for career decisions

### VALUES
Relating personal and organizational values to employment matching

Understanding continuous change as important for careers

■ ■ ■ ■ ■ ▬▬▬▬▬▬▬▬▬▬▬▬▬▬▬▬▬▬▬▬▬▬▬▬▬▬▬▬▬▬▬▬▬▬▬▬

# THE "WHERE DO WE GO FROM HERE?" CASE

As John walked toward the student union to join his friends Jill and George, he thought about his round of upcoming interviews. Jill, George, and John were all scheduled for several of the same companies, and he knew they were concerned as well. Being almost ready to graduate had some advantages, but this job-search thing was tough. Not only was John trying to determine what were good companies and how to sell himself to them, but also he was thinking about what parts of the country he would like and how it was going to feel to leave his friends. He hadn't realized it was going to be that difficult. Well, at least he wasn't alone; Jill and George were having some of the same problems, too.

As Jill waited for John and George, she began to rehearse mentally questions and answers for her upcoming interviews. Six companies scheduled in the next two days will put her skills to the test. Jill is wondering if John and George are right about taking the offer with the best salary. What else should she be considering, and what about cost of living in various parts of the country? The companies she will talk with in the next two days are in four different states several hundred miles apart. What other considerations should she make?

John and George enter the union at the same time and spot Jill.

**George:**   Sorry I'm late, I went by the library to check the annual report of Randel Corporation. John was right that their expansion has been slowing for the last two years. I will probably not consider them as seriously as I thought.

**Jill:**   George, are you sure that is an appropriate approach? You have really liked the type of job that Randel is describing; growth certainly isn't everything. What do you think, John?

**John:**   I have been thinking that we should all take the best salary offer, but I am beginning to have second thoughts. How much consideration should we give to where we want to live and the type of products and services the company produces? I have interviews scheduled with a defense contractor, computer manufacturer, retail chain, and that government job. They all need training specialists, and I think I qualify for what they want, but they do very different things.

**Jill:**   I was just sitting here thinking about what factors are most important to me. I expected to be so excited when this time came. I can hardly believe I am fearful of making the right choice.

# INTRODUCTION

John, Jill, and George are experiencing the concerns of many of us when we begin to make important decisions about the beginning of our careers. What company would be best? What factors deserve the most weight in our decision? Which choice will work best in the long term? We almost need a crystal ball to help us find answers.

Our concerns really begin much earlier than during the job-search process. John, Jill, and George chose organizational communication as their major. As you would expect, they are thinking about job choices that will use the skills they have developed during their years in the communication program. In a real sense, their career choices began when they selected their majors and the abilities they wanted to develop with their education. The jobs they now take will reflect that overall direction and those decisions.

This chapter is designed to increase awareness of communication-related career choices. It discusses how to begin planning a career, what general career choices are available to those studying organizational communication, what skills are important, and what types of education are required. The chapter also addresses important issues influencing changing career opportunities and paradigms. Finally, the Workshop section of this chapter presents a self-analysis process helpful for career planning.

This chapter is designed to increase *knowledge* through the presentation of career options for organizational communication and through the identification of individual and organizational factors influencing careers. *Sensitivity* is developed through awareness of personal experiences influential in career choices and through identification of primary responsibilities for major career options. Analysis *skills* are practiced with the self-analysis process and by gathering data with informational interviews. *Values* are presented as important in career planning, integral to the individual and organizational relationship, and central to all professional organizational activities. Finally, knowledge, sensitivity, skills, and values are applied to our interpretation of diverse career issues.

## CHOOSING A COMMUNICATION CAREER

In one sense, all careers are communication careers. The majority of our organizational time is spent communicating, whether we select communication or a seemingly unrelated field as our primary area of emphasis. As proposed throughout this book, organizational communication competencies are important for us all, regardless of career choices. Although this chapter focuses specifically on communication careers, the factors important for selecting a communication career also are applicable to other choices and are basic for understanding both individual and organizational needs.

Careers are the sum total of our job experiences over time. Careers involve decisions about personal interests, aptitudes, educational preparation, and the match of our individual competencies to the needs of particular organizations. Career planning should begin while pursuing our education and continue throughout our work lives and even into retirement. We usually think of career planning as it relates to paid employment, but in reality career planning is the process by which we plan to use our competencies as they relate to all types of work environments. As such, careers are best understood as an integral part of our total lives.

**Employment match**
When individual competencies match organizational competencies and the individual becomes a working member of the organization.

How, then, should we begin to plan our careers? Put simply, an **employment match** between an individual and an employer occurs when individual competencies match organizational competencies and the individual becomes a working member of the organization. This notion of an employment match is important for understanding how individuals select jobs and how organizations select individuals for employment. Awareness of these factors is necessary for effective career planning.

## Knowledge for Employment Matching

Individuals base job and career choices on what they know is available and usually with incomplete understanding of all that is possible. We gather occupational information from past experiences, the people around us, exposure during education, the media, and in a variety of less systematic ways. Sometimes we are aware of skill and educational requirements associated with particular occupations, whereas at other times we have only a vague understanding of what competencies are required in a given profession. Individuals also have general knowledge that applies to almost all occupations. The depth and breadth of this general knowledge contributes to occupational flexibility, or the ability to fit oneself for a variety of job positions. General knowledge includes communication competencies, organizing abilities, time-management skills, critical-thinking abilities, and decision-making capabilities.

Organizations develop knowledge about the functional requirements they need in specific occupational categories. A human resource development position may carry similar responsibilities from organization to organization, but a specific human resource development position will have specific job requirements. A human resource position in one organization might require extensive training experience, whereas a similar position in another company would not include the training responsibility. In addition, organizations require the general knowledge base that we previously described for individuals. Indeed, one of the difficulties for most organizations during interviews is assessing the somewhat subjective, yet critically important, areas of general knowledge exhibited by job applicants. Research on who is promoted into top management in U.S. corporations suggests that general knowledge in communication and decision making may be more important for long-term advancement than most technical skills.

## Sensitivity for Employment Matching

Individuals bring a variety of expectations to the job-search process. Salary, position responsibilities, and advancement opportunities are only a few of the expectations individuals seek to clarify in interviews. Individuals also have expectations about how employees should be treated and the type of work environment that is personally desirable. We have been oriented to work by our family experiences, by those who have acted as role models for us, and by our previous work experiences.

Research indicates that we are likely to be influenced in occupational choices by direct contact with individuals in specific occupations and advice from individuals personally close to us. It is therefore not unusual to find similar occupational choices—such as law, medicine, and education—made by several members of one family. These orientations, however, can be limiting. A woman, for example, who is surrounded by those who believe her best occupational choice is teaching may or may not consider other possible alternatives suitable for her abilities. That is not to say the teaching profession would be inappropriate, but to the extent it is a stereotypical expectation (a choice appropriate for women), her potential may be limited. The same is true for men. Occupational expectations of parents and influential role models can both encourage and restrict the range of possibilities considered when making educational and career choices.

Self-awareness also is an important sensitivity for career choices. What types of competencies do we bring to an employment situation? What competencies remain in need of development? What are our preferences regarding work? How do our communication, conflict, and leadership preferences influence career choices and the jobs in which we will be comfortable and productive? How well do we know ourselves and our needs?

Organizations are sensitive to finding employees who meet their expectations. Organizations develop work norms and behavior expectations they believe contribute to productivity in their particular environments. Some organizations, for example, expect workers to put in numerous hours of overtime. In an interview, the answers a prospective employee gives to questions about work and time commitments may be pivotal to the organization's assessment of the prospect's future. Organizations also develop sensitivities to changing markets and environmental needs that require new skills and abilities from their work force. In today's labor market, most organizations expect computer competencies from prospective employees; not too long ago there was only marginal concern for computer skills.

## Skills for Employment Matching

Individuals bring a variety of technical qualifications to their job search. The technical qualifications an individual develops should support occupational choices because technical qualifications or the lack thereof limit choice. We know that without certain skills we cannot consider certain occupations. Only the rare individual will attempt to land a computer programming job without having technical preparation on computers. Unfortunately, far more individuals attempt to occupy communication jobs without the training or background appropriate for these responsibilities. Because we have all been "communicating" for as long as we can remember, many take for granted the technical preparation necessary for excellence in communication jobs. Yet our technical preparation is fundamental to success in the job search and in the job itself.

Our ability to translate our knowledge, sensitivity, skills, and values to a prospective employer will in large measure determine the types of jobs we are offered. Few job interviews begin with an objective test of the skills and abilities of applicants. Most organizations rely on communication exchanges—interviews, résumés, letters of application—for initial if not final screening of potential employees.

Individuals bring their technical qualifications to the job search in hopes of matching those qualifications with the organization's technical requirements. Rarely, however, is there a perfect match. Organizations generally seek the best available match between an individual's technical background and the technical requirements of a particular job. Organizations also weigh the applicant's general knowledge in communication, decision making, critical thinking, time management, and leadership. They make judgments about the current skill level of the applicant and the amount of training time necessary for the applicant to become a productive employee. Just as the individual must be able to communicate adequately his or her abilities, organizations attempt to define for the applicant the needed requirements of the job and any additional relevant information. This match between abilities and requirements is fundamental for the employment match to work successfully.

## Values for Employment Matching

As in all other aspects of our life, values are a central factor in career decisions. What is important to us and what we find desirable, interesting, and stimulating all relate to the values we hold. Our career interests are reflections of our value systems. The socioeconomic goals we hope our employment will support are a product of a complex set of values that have developed throughout our life experiences. Even our achievement aspirations can be described as an extension of our personal value systems. Understanding what is important to us should guide overall career choices as well as decisions about whether or not specific jobs meet our needs. One of the most common employment mistakes is the acceptance of a job because it represents a good financial offer, regardless of whether the job is of interest and supports other needs. A good offer in the fullest sense is an offer that helps us support our value system.

Organizations also have value systems. Earlier the text referred to the importance of organizational culture and values. Cultures help to define what is expected and valued within particular organizations. Products, services, resource allocations, and development interests all reflect the values of organizations. As do individuals, organizations have socioeconomic goals and overall achievement aspirations. For a successful employment match, the individual's values and the organization's values need to be in harmony, if not in all respects, at least in those areas central to job performance.

An individual should begin career planning with the concept that jobs and ultimately careers are continual matches of individual knowledge, sensitivity, skills, and values with organizational knowledge, sensitivity, skills, and values. The success of these matches for both individuals and organizations begins with the ability to define and articulate competencies, a process fundamental for effective organizational communication. To assist in your planning, an extensive Self-Analysis for Career Planning activity is provided in the Workshop section of this chapter.

# CAREER CHOICES IN ORGANIZATIONAL COMMUNICATION

The growth in communication career choices continues, as does the increase in numbers of students studying communication. This growth in opportunity and the diversity of potential jobs contribute to the difficulty of describing exactly what an organizational communication major is qualified to do. R. Wayne Pace and Don Faules (1994) provide a useful overall description:

> They apply their knowledge in public contact positions in organizations, such as sales, marketing, public relations, advertising, fund raising, and community affairs; . . . they may apply their knowledge in development positions in organizations, such as counseling, career development, organization development, internal consulting, technical training, and management development, as well as general management (both line and staff) positions. (p. 358)

Pace and Faules (1994) go on to suggest that job opportunities exist for communication professionals in every major employment sector, including health care, manufacturing, retailing, banking, construction, communications, transportation, agriculture and forestry, military, education, beverages, chemicals and pharmaceuticals, computer and data processing, energy and petroleum, hospitality and recreation, insurance, justice systems, utilities, government, and the consulting and training industry.

Figure 11.1 identifies eight major career option areas and job titles within each area for those planning careers in organizational communication. As each of the eight areas is described in terms of job responsibilities and required skills, think about your self-analysis and what you will need to know to select a communication career.

**Internal communication careers**

Work within an organization to assist management in employee and management communication, coordinate a variety of training activities, coordinate internal communication media, facilitate team building, and develop numerous other communication activities.

## Internal Communication

Options in **internal communication careers** for those studying organizational communication initially were compiled by a committee for the International Communication Association Organizational Communication Division (Petrie, Thompson, Rogers, and Goldhaber, 1975). This initial collection has expanded over the years, emphasizing the increasing importance of organizational communication for a variety of internal communication positions. A synthesis of these collections suggests that those working in internal communication jobs have the following types of responsibilities:

**1.** Provide consultation, assistance, and guidance to management on matters relating to employee and management communication; coordinate employee communication programs and activities; coordinate publishing of regular employee media; advise, coordinate, and conduct attitudinal and other polls among employees; provide editorial and publishing services; produce, edit, and distribute special publications.

**FIGURE 11.1   Career Options in Organizational Communication**

| OPTION AREA | JOB TITLES |
| --- | --- |
| Internal communication | Human resource specialist<br>Training and development specialist<br>Personnel liaison<br>Internal publications coordinator<br>Internal communication specialist<br>Organizational development specialist<br>Internal consultant<br>Labor negotiator<br>Recruiter |
| External communications | Advertising specialist<br>Public relations coordinator<br>Webmaster<br>Industrial media producer/director<br>Technical writer<br>Telecommunications coordinator<br>Editor<br>Scriptwriter<br>Video editor<br>Audio editor<br>Videographer<br>Community affairs coordinator<br>Government affairs coordinator<br>Marketing specialist<br>Technical writer |
| Sales | Account representative<br>Retail salesperson<br>Marketing specialist<br>Media salesperson<br>Advertising salesperson<br>Real estate, insurance, products, etc.<br>  salesperson |
| Human services | Fund-raiser<br>Counselor<br>Career development specialist<br>Program specialist |
| Education | Teacher/professor<br>Administrator |
| Research/information management | Associate<br>Business analyst<br>Content research<br>Marketing research analyst<br>Social science specialist<br>Instructional design Web-specialist |

**FIGURE 11.1    Continued**

| | |
|---|---|
| Management | Trainee |
| | Section/branch manager |
| | Store manager |
| | Regional manager |
| | Corporate staff |
| | Sales manager |
| | Personnel director |
| | Media manager |
| | Advertising manager |
| | Human resource development manager |
| | Corporate communications manager |
| Consultant (external to employing organization) | Organizational development specialist |
| | Human resource development specialist |
| | Trainer |
| | Analyst |

**2.** Develop and maintain informational unit to serve the needs of senior management and the communication department.

**3.** Develop, coordinate, and implement small-group, face-to-face communication programs to facilitate team building, problem identification, and problem solving.

Internal communication specialists must have extensive backgrounds in interpersonal and organizational communication with an emphasis on human relations. These specialists are familiar with principles of instructional design, can evaluate the designs of others, can plan and implement their own programs, and have well-developed presentational skills. In addition to speaking skills, internal communication jobs require good listening skills and an ability to write clearly. They also may be required to understand technical print production for internal publication responsibilities. They must be able to analyze data and must be skilled in a variety of data-gathering techniques. Most internal communication specialists are required to have a basic understanding of statistics and the use of computers.

**External communications careers**
Responsibility for external public relations activities; corporate advertising; community, shareholder, financial, and government relations; corporate literature, sales promotions, and special productions.

## External Communications

The ICA report and more recent reviews identify the following responsibilities common among those with **external communications careers:**

Are responsible for a full range of external public relations activities: corporate advertising; community, shareholder, financial, and government relations; produce corporate literature, sales promotions, marketing, and special productions.

Direct and coordinate all activity in the development, implementation, and administration of a corporate identification system covering all aspects of visual communication, material, and media.

Have administrative responsibility for public relations and development departments.

External communications specialists also may be responsible for community relations, telecommunications systems, and the public relations contacts for specific individuals within or related to the corporation.

External communications specialists may be required to have a broad range of journalism and media production skills. These specialists design and produce media in addition to supervising others (such as advertising agencies) in the design of corporate identifications ranging from logos and television commercials to e-commerce and Internet applications. They understand the fundamentals of public relations and have skills in written communication and audience analysis. Some external communications jobs require financial background to direct public relations efforts in financial markets.

**Sales careers**
Representing products and services to potential customers.

## Sales

Those with **sales careers** represent products and services to potential customers. Sales responsibilities include preparing sales presentations, analyzing the market or audience, soliciting accounts, making sales presentations, taking and handling orders, and servicing accounts. Those in sales positions are primary representatives of the organization to its external public.

Salespeople need abilities in interpersonal and organizational communication, market analysis, and the preparation and presentation of both oral and written materials. Sales positions also frequently require technical ability appropriate to specific products or services and a basic understanding of budgeting, costing, and accounting procedures.

**Human service careers**
Responsibility for fund-raising, grant writing, and other formal budget justification processes. Human service professionals engage in counseling, design, administration, and evaluation of programs; they also engage in responsibilities similar to internal communication careers.

## Human Services

**Human service careers** generally involve nonprofit or government organizations. Job responsibilities include fund-raising through public solicitation of funds, grant writing, and other formal budget justification processes. Human service specialists may engage in individual counseling on subjects ranging from managing personal finances to job-search skills. They design, administer, and evaluate a full range of programs that provide human services.

In addition to those job titles listed in Figure 11.1 for human service specialists, many of the job titles listed for the internal communication option also apply. In fact, the skills required for internal communication positions also are needed in the human service area. In addition to those skills common for both internal communication and human service positions, human service jobs may require knowledge of direct mail, persuasive appeals in fund-raising, cost accounting, budgeting, and program evaluation.

**Careers in education**
Teaching in high schools, junior colleges, and universities.

## Education

**Careers in education** require professional certification and advanced degrees. Those with communication backgrounds teach primarily at high school, junior college, and college and university levels. Job responsibilities include instructional design and development, presentation of educational materials, evaluation of student performance, and individual counseling and guidance. Educational administration opportunities exist in colleges and universities, elementary and secondary schools, preschools, day care centers, and in religious education.

In addition to professional certification required for high school teachers and elementary and high school administrators, teachers need interpersonal, small-group, and organizational communication abilities. Listening is a necessary skill, as is the ability to speak and write well. Graduate degrees are required for almost everyone entering the field of education. A master's degree is necessary for elementary and secondary education positions, and a doctorate is required for most postsecondary and administrative positions. Educators are responsible for developing expertise in particular subjects, for conducting research, and for presenting material appropriate to these subjects. Educational administrators also need skills in finance, personnel management, and public relations.

**Research and information management careers**
Responsibility for the design and development of research programs to support the ongoing activities of the organization or to chart a course of change; responsibility for the acquisition and interpretation of information and the selection of technologies to support decision making and e-commerce.

## Research: Information Management

Those with **research and information management careers** are responsible for the design and development of research programs to support the ongoing activities of the organization or to chart a course of change. Research specialists conduct interviews and surveys, evaluate data, commission data collection, and coordinate research forums. These specialists are involved in business-trend analysis, marketing and demographic research, and a broad range of social science applications to organizational life. They evaluate organizational performance with both qualitative and quantitative measures.

Depending on the focus of the position, research specialists are required to exhibit capabilities in social scientific research methods, marketing research, and financial analysis. Research specialists must understand data collection and evaluation procedures. They must be familiar with needs-analysis techniques and a variety of types of data interpretation. Research specialists also are responsible for interpreting their findings to the organization, which requires good skills for oral and written presentations. By far the majority of research positions require extensive knowledge of statistics and computers.

Information management is an emerging job title in all types of organizations. Information managers literally manage information the way other managers manage people. Information managers are responsible for identifying sources of information, recommending technologies appropriate for organizational use, subscribing to diverse databases, creating databases, conducting database searches, and organizing information for easy access to support decision making. Information managers may assist with instructional design for computer-based training and contribute to e-commerce development and implementation. Information management jobs require many of the same skills as those needed for more basic research. Generally speaking, information management jobs couple an understanding of basic principles of organizational communication with fairly detailed knowledge of information retrieval technologies.

**Management careers**
Responsibility for planning, coordinating, supervising, and controlling many of the activities of the organization.

## Management

People with **management careers** are responsible for planning, coordinating, supervising, and controlling many of the activities described in the other career options. Managers guide and direct subordinates to achieve organizational goals. Thus, managers involve themselves in a variety of personnel activities such as interviewing, hiring, performance evaluation, and employee goal setting. Managers also help to direct the activities of the organization through the use of both human and material resources. They perform communication activities to guide and direct subordinates, solicit subordinate feedback, and exchange information with other management levels and the organization's public. Managers fulfill the formal organizational role of coordinating information and activities.

Managers are generally required to have at least basic technical skills in the areas in which they manage. Advertising managers, for example, usually bring to their positions technical knowledge about media production. Managers need interpersonal, small-group, and organizational communication competencies. They should be able to listen, think critically, lead group decision making and problem solving, and generally speak and write well. Managers also may be required to exhibit competence in business management, finance, economics, and law.

**Consulting careers**
Work as an external advisor to organizations to identify problems, evaluate performance, find solutions, and implement a wide variety of change activities.

## Consulting

Those with **consulting careers** are hired by organizations to provide expertise either not in existence in the organization or more objectively supplied by someone not directly employed by the organization. Consultants help organizations identify problems, evaluate performance, find problem solutions, and implement a wide variety of change activities. Consultants design data-collection activities, collect and evaluate data, and make recommendations for organizational improvements. Consultants design, conduct, and evaluate training programs. Typical topics for such programs include interpersonal communication, small-group processes, leadership, conflict management, and problem-solving processes. Consultants also prepare a variety of written reports summarizing assignment findings.

Consultants combine many of the skills required for internal communication and research positions. They must be able to assess quickly the quality of information they are receiving and establish working relationships appropriate for their assigned responsibilities. Consultants need awareness of interpersonal, group, and organizational communication processes as well as the ability to effectively seek information both orally and in writing. Graduate degrees and extensive work experience are desirable for consulting positions.

## Additional Options for Organizational Communication

Many other career options exist for those who study organizational communication. Those described here are but a few of the possibilities.

### Preprofessional and Combination Options

Organizational communication backgrounds frequently are used as preprofessional preparation for training in law, social work, and business. Many of the competencies developed in an organizational communication program are favorably evaluated for entrance into a wide range of graduate programs, including, of course, graduate programs in communication. Numerous students have creatively combined organizational communication competencies with other interests such as engineering, medicine, art, or science.

### Organizational Communication and Technology

Individuals who have combined organizational communication with a variety of technical specialties will find a growing number of employment opportunities. Instructional design for Internet or computer-based training, GDSS use, web-based sales and marketing, Internet-based research, and a variety of other emerging technology uses all require individuals within organizations to develop material and translate that material into a variety of technological forms. The need for content development appropriate to emerging technologies is a largely unmet need in which organizational communication students can participate. The organizational communication major who has a desire to work with computers and video and acquires an understanding of instructional design will find a wide variety of interesting employment opportunities available.

## EDUCATIONAL PREPARATION FOR ORGANIZATIONAL COMMUNICATION CAREERS

Educational preparation for organizational communication careers is most often based on a broad liberal arts background with particular emphasis on a combination of theory and practical courses. Developing competencies for the career options described here begins with an overview of the human communication process, an introduction to basic concepts and theories in organizational communication, and an understanding of how theories of organizations relate to human communication. The first part of this text was designed to introduce you to these concepts.

Preparation for a communication career also requires development of oral skills for interpersonal, small-group, and public settings. Basic research methods and statistics are essential for evaluating and collecting data, a responsibility of many communication positions.

For those selecting internal communication, human service, and research options, particular emphasis should be placed on social science courses that contribute to understanding human behavior and research techniques appropriate for behavioral-science data collection and interpretation. Preparation for external communications positions is found in journalism, technical writing, public relations, and media production courses.

Courses in instructional design are important for those in education, training, and consulting. Understanding how to develop effective learning situations requires a mix of theory and practice courses and opportunities.

Those entering sales and management positions can benefit from courses in interpersonal communication, persuasion, interviewing, small-group processes, and conflict management. These option areas are also supported by courses in business management, finance, and economics.

As stated earlier, most of the option areas also require a basic understanding of statistics and computers. In fact, leading organizational recruiters suggest that communication professionals can best prepare themselves for good entry-level positions if they have competencies in organizational communication accompanied by special skills in video production, computers, statistics, or program design and evaluation.

For most students today, educational preparation will not stop with an undergraduate degree. Many students will continue through graduate programs, and most will participate in continuing education, whether or not in the pursuit of a formal degree. Our fast-paced information age requires flexibility and change not only from organizations but also from us all. Part of the ability to make necessary changes comes from identifying how educational preparation strengthens our competencies and enables us to be productive members of the organizations for which we work.

## CAREERS IN THE TWENTY-FIRST CENTURY

Throughout this text has been described a technologically linked, global environment characterized by rapid change. Nowhere is that change more evident than in the notion of what it means to have a career and what can be expected in thinking about careers in the twenty-first century. Although no one really can predict the future with precision, a number of current developments point to a shift from the career paradigm of the last several decades to a more person-centered versus organization-centered concept of careers. The next section contrasts old and new career paradigms, describes the protean career of the twenty-first century, identifies career skills associated with new organizational forms, and raises issues for team-based careers. As you read, think about what this means for your planning. How can you create opportunities that are of special importance to you?

## Old versus New Career Paradigms

Michael Arthur, Priscilla Claman, and Robert DeFillippi (1995) contrast new versus old career paradigms in five broad categories: (1) discrete exchange versus the mutual loyalty contract, (2) occupational excellence versus the one-employer focus, (3) organizational empowerment versus the top-down firm, (4) regional advantage versus the fortress firm, and (5) project versus corporate allegiance. According to Arthur, Claman, and DeFillippi, the old career paradigm implied mutual loyalty between employees and organizations. Employee compliance was rewarded with job security. Job rewards were deferred to the future, and career opportunities were mostly standardized and prescribed by the firm. Employees often expected to stay with one organization for an entire career, and reliance was on the organization to specify jobs and their associated occupational skill base. Employees were expected to identify with their particular firm and forgo general development in favor of firm-specific learning. In the top-down firm, management set strategic direction and defined competitiveness, and the corporate agenda generally discouraged independent enterprise. The fortress firm meant there was little identification with other regional firms, which were generally viewed as competitors. Finally, corporate allegiance meant that project goals were subordinated to corporate policy and organizational constraints. Loyalty to the work group was expected, and the organization formed a distinct boundary within which careers were expected to be pursued.

The new career paradigm is described very differently. The concept of discrete exchange means

> explicit exchange of specified rewards in return for task performance, basing job rewards on the current market value of the work being performed, engaging in disclosure and re-negotiation on both sides as the employment relationship unfolds, and exercising flexibility as each party's interests and market circumstances change. Occupational excellence means performance of current jobs in return for developing new occupational expertise; employees identifying with and focusing on what is happening in their adopted occupation; emphasizing occupational skill and development over the local demands of any particular firm; getting training in anticipation of future job opportunities; and having training lead jobs. (Arthur, Claman, and DeFillippi, 1995, p. 13)

Organizational empowerment is described as strategic positioning dispersed to separate business units with everyone responsible for adding value. Business units are encouraged to cultivate their own markets. Regional advantage means building alliances and interdependence with clusters of organizations including competitors. Work and careers are boundaryless. Individuals move in and out of firms and work as consultants. The project becomes primary, and a successful outcome of the project is considered more important than holding the project team together.

The differences between these two paradigms have enormous implications for careers. The old paradigm emphasizes stability, the new flexibility and constant change. The old was more dependent on organizational planning, the new emphasizes individual initiative. Most observers believe the twenty-first century will see a blend of both perspectives, but even with the blend, there will be increasing reliance on individual responsibility to plan for job and career transitions.

**Protean careers**
Careers characterized by lifelong changes and continual learning.

## Protean Careers

Douglas Hall (1996) describes the **protean career:**

> The career of the 21st century will be protean, a career that is driven by the person, not the organization, and that will be reinvented by the person from time to time, as the person and the environment change. (This term is derived from the Greek god Proteus, who could change shape at will.) (p. 8)

Hall describes the goal of the protean career as psychological success. The career is managed by the individual and is a lifelong series of changes and continuous learning. A profile of success is the ability to learn, to move from job security to employability, to think not in terms of organizational careers but protean careers and from the work self to the whole self. Training becomes an ongoing reality of employability and vertical mobility—moving up—is replaced by moving across and between organizations. Hall and others contend that these changes can bring more life satisfaction than the more paternalistic careers of the past. Critics express concern, however, that the lack of commitment from the organization and the overall flexibility required for the "new career" is problematic and difficult for most to conceive.

## Twenty-First-Century Organizational Forms and Career Skills

Throughout this text competencies important for organizational participation have been described. We have identified many of the specific competencies and skills needed in the twenty-first century. You have been exploring your own skills and thinking about development needs. Next career skills associated with two emerging organizational forms, networks and cellular organizations, are described.

Chapter 4 described a variety of theoretical approaches to organizing. Traditional hierarchies were examined and changes over time were explored, including approaches to organizing based on new scientific concepts. It was learned that functional, hierarchical structures permitted organization-wide standardization important for early mass production. Later, divisional structures gained popularity in response to the need for market expansion and customization. Divisions standardized, and multiple divisions within a given organization permitted customization. As the movement from standardization to customization matured, the matrix organization emerged. Matrix organizations were developed to serve both stable and emerging markets by producing differentiated, standard products in one or more divisions while also transferring resources from profitable units into project groups designing future-oriented projects or services.

**Networked organization**

Partners or alliances across groups and organizations to leverage the best possible resources for a given project.

## Networked Organization

The late 1970s was the beginning of the **networked organization.** Brent Allred, Charles Snow, and Raymond Miles (1996) describe the rise of the networked form:

> Intense international and domestic competition left many large traditional organizations slow to respond to global threats and opportunities. For example, the planning and coordinating efficiencies achieved by the global matrix organization were frequently offset by the unyielding bureaucracy it created. The extensive vertical and horizontal integration of previous decades increased the market clout of many companies, but when speed and flexibility were needed, traditional structures became burdensome. . . . To become more competitive, corporations downsized, delayered, and outsourced many functions during the 1980s. In innovative companies such as Nike, Motorola, and Novell, a new form of organization was emerging, called the network. Similar to a computer network, network organizations linked independent firms to provide the critical expertise needed for specific projects or manufacturing, and marketing a product, various complementary firms were networked to provide the most efficient service at each of these stages. . . . Network firms are able to achieve maximum leverage of their core competencies by relying on their external or internal partners to perform other activities on the value chain. (pp. 19–20)

Allred, Snow, and Miles go on to describe the core competencies for the networked organization (p. 21):

- Referral skills rely on the ability to analyze a problem and prescribe a solution within the network firm and across its partners. The traditional mentality of do it all yourself has given way to a focus on doing only what you do best. Thus, in a network, when a problem or opportunity is recognized, members are able to determine who has the best ability to address or pursue it. Referrals are made such that the best resources are brought to bear on all situations, including the use of resources outside the current network.
- Partnering skills refer to the capacity to conceptualize, negotiate, and implement mutually beneficial outcomes. Many network organizations are multifirm, so managers within the network must know how to connect other

firms' resources quickly and effectively to their own such that both parties benefit.

■ Relationship management involves giving high priority to the needs and preferences of key customers and partners. In dynamic multifirm networks, in which company participation may be periodic, relationships among past, present, and potential customers and partners must be carefully maintained.

**Cellular organization**
Collaborative but not considered permanent association of professionals working together for a specific project or service.

## Cellular Organization

The minimalist organizations forecast for the twenty-first century are a further evolution of what has begun with the networked form. Careers in traditional organizations involve climbing a vertical ladder, network careers move across organizations, and the **cellular organization** does not involve hierarchies at all. In the cellular organization success does not equate to the concept of success as advancement through vertical or horizontal mobility. Allred, Snow, and Miles (1996) explain:

> A cellular organization is made up of cells (self-managing teams, autonomous business units, etc.) that could exist on their own, but that by interacting with other cells can produce a more potent and competent organism. Common knowledge and information are shared by all the cells in a manner, akin to human DNA, that reflects heredity and guides development. . . . In the cellular firm, the organization functions not as an employer but as a facilitating mechanism to promote the application and enhancement of the knowledge-intensive skills of its membership. The firm has some of the key properties of the classical guilds and professional associations, such as sharing knowledge and accepting responsibility for member competency and performance. Within the cellular organization, members take full charge of their own careers, enjoying the learning opportunities provided by their own initiatives and those of their fellow members. An agreed set of norms promotes full self-governance as well as professional allegiance. (pp. 21–22)

The skills needed for the cellular organization include a knowledge-based technical specialty as in the past but much more attention to cross-functional and international experience. Collaborative leadership and self-management skills also are of particular importance for the cellular organization.

Regardless of the specific form of the organization of the future, the challenges are evident. For us all, becoming and staying competent will be a lifelong pursuit. The importance of understanding personal competencies and how to continually expand and develop skills for the future will remain a personal challenge throughout our career.

## Team-Based Careers

As we are beginning the twenty-first century, more and more of us will work in teams. A new model of career development is emerging because of these experiences. Put simply, career development in teams can be described as the responsibility of the entire team. Team members serve as role models for each other, and team members usually determine both team and individual development needs and training opportunities. Individual members cross-train and move laterally within and across teams. Advancement usually is based on competency level, with more advanced team members responsible not only for task contribution but training and development of newer team members. Rewards are based on both team and individual results. As discussed in earlier chapters, communication competency is at the heart of a successful team-based career.

## SUMMARY

Careers are the sum of our job experiences over time. Careers involve decisions about personal interests, aptitudes, educational preparation, and the match of our individual competencies to the needs of particular organizations. This employment match is based on the knowledge, sensitivity, skills, and values of both the individual and the employing organization. Self-analysis helps generate awareness of influences for our occupational choices and can be used to develop important criteria for career planning. Self-awareness in turn can help us evaluate the major career options in organizational communication: internal communication, external communications, sales, human services, education, research, management, and consulting. Each of these areas requires educational preparation and a diverse set of communication skills.

Individuals will assume increasing responsibility for career and job transitions in the twenty-first century. In protean careers, individuals can expect to manage their own careers, which will include a lifelong series of changes and the need for continuous learning. New organizational forms—networked and cellular organizations—will place new emphasis on participation competencies, international experience, and personal traits of flexibility and adaptability. Finally, team-based careers will emphasize the success of entire teams as well as individuals.

## WORKSHOP

### Self-Analysis for Career Planning

1. The purposes of a self-analysis are to help you understand personal influences on career choices, to identify achievements valuable to you, to define skills used in important achievements, and to make projections of the type of career and lifestyle you desire. Your self-analysis is designed to guide decisions about competency development and to identify any limitations in occupational choices you may have inadvertently created for yourself. Figure 11.2 summarizes the self-analysis activity. Your individual work sheet follows on pages 417–419.

**FIGURE 11.2   Summary of Self-Analysis Activities for Career Planning**

1. Identify specific individuals who have been influential in shaping your concept of work and occupational choice.

   What have they told you about possibilities?
   How satisfied are they with their work?
   How would they profile a successful person?
   What occupations have they suggested to you?
   What occupations do they not suggest for you?

2. Describe your ideal occupation in terms of responsibilities, skills, and measures of success.

3. Compare your "perfect occupation" with messages from those who have influenced you.

4. Define four important achievements with skills used for each achievement and values satisfied. Identify common skills used and values satisfied among the achievements. List ten skills and ten values that seem to be predictive of achievement and satisfaction for you.

5. Write a narrative describing your desired lifestyle for a five-year span following your formal education. How should this narrative influence your career choices?

6. Make ten statements about your current career planning. Identify ten questions you need answered for career planning.

## Influences on Career Choices

Identify by name those individuals who have been most influential in helping you form expectations about work, occupations, and achievements. What have these individuals told you about what is possible? How satisfied are they with their work? How would they profile the successful person? What types of occupations have they suggested you should pursue? What have they told you is a waste of time?

After you have identified important "work" messages from those around you, write a one-paragraph description of your ideal occupation. Include the responsibilities the occupation entails, the skills the occupation uses, and how individuals in this occupation will know if they are successful.

Next, compare your "perfect" occupation paragraph with your answers to questions about how key people have influenced your occupational choices. Can you see their influence in your "perfect" occupation? If so, how? If not, what other influences have contributed to your selection?

## Identification of Achievement Skills and Values

The next portion of your self-analysis requires careful reflection. Identify four major achievements in your life. These achievements must have one important quality: they must be very personally important. Others may have considered the

achievements you identify as significant, but that is not the most important quali-
fication. The achievements you choose should be of high personal value, regardless of external evaluation. In fact, it is common for an achievement in this category
to be something of which few others are aware. These four achievements also must
be achievements in which your personal efforts were primary contributions. Many
people might say, for example, that they consider their family life to be an achievement, and of course it may be. For purposes of this activity, however, writing a
poem, building a piece of furniture, conquering your fear of public speaking, or
learning to use a computer are better examples of achievements for which you
have had primary responsibility. Once the achievements have been identified, list
the skills and abilities you used in these achievements and the values each achievement satisfied. (A partial skill and value list is provided in Figure 11.3.)

When you have listed important achievements, skills, and values, identify
those skills and values that have contributed to more than one of your achievements. You are beginning to identify through this activity those skills and values
that have been most important to you over time. Which additional skills should be
on your "most important" list? Which additional values? Next, list ten skills and

## FIGURE 11.3 Partial Skills and Values List

**PARTIAL SKILLS LIST**

| | | |
|---|---|---|
| mathematical | administrative | documentation |
| analytical | planning | speaking |
| creative | organizational | financial |
| managerial | writing | graphic |
| communication | artistic | team building |
| persuasive | athletic | motivational |
| listening | research | teaching |
| decision making | problem solving | delegation |

**PARTIAL VALUES LIST**

| | | |
|---|---|---|
| security | family happiness | power |
| geographic location | wisdom | expertness |
| justice | autonomy | love |
| humanitarianism | leadership | aesthetics |
| recognition | honesty | service |
| enjoyment | self-actualization | health |
| achievement | material wealth | knowledge |
| prestige | emotional well-being | religion |
| fame | social | creative |

values you believe are most likely to contribute to a sense of personal achievement. This list, if thoughtfully constructed, should be influential in career planning and occupational choice.

### Describing a Desired Lifestyle

Next, write a one-page narrative describing all aspects of your most desired lifestyle for the five years immediately following completion of your education. Describe where you think you want to live, what leisure activities you envision, what family and social relationships you prefer, and how work relates to these choices.

Include in your narrative a desired level of income and any other important choices you want to consider. (We are not attempting to suggest that it is possible to define perfectly all these issues, but general themes can usually be discovered.) What do these preferences say about your choice of work? Should they be considerations in your career planning? What other influences are important?

### Identifying Current Status of Career Planning

After completing all the analysis activities, list ten statements you can make about the status of your current career planning. These statements should relate to choices you have already made, skills you want to use in your future occupation, and values you want to satisfy through work. Finally, develop ten questions you want answered as a result of your self-examination. What do you need to know about occupational choices? How can you find out? Who would be good information sources? Much of what was discussed in Chapter 8 about decision making and problem solving should be used to help you examine your personal career planning needs.

2. One way to make decisions about educational preparation for your future employment is to think about what you want to be able to present to a prospective employer on your résumé. The following résumé development exercise first presents basic information about résumé preparation, followed by suggestions for you to individualize information about you. (See pp. 419–421.)

3. Locate five advertisements requiring communication competencies in each of three newspapers: (1) your local paper, (2) a national paper such as the *Wall Street Journal* or the *Washington Post* national edition, and (3) a paper from a major city other than the one in which you live. Also search the Internet. Compare the advertisements. Identify the skills and experiences wanted by potential employers. What are the salary ranges? How can you prepare yourself for these opportunities?

4. Select the communication career option area (or areas) that interests you most. Identify a local professional who is employed in this career area. Develop a list of questions you would like answered. Make an appointment and interview this person. Report your findings to the class. (This activity can be accomplished in pairs or teams. The exercise is more meaningful if all eight option areas are reported to the class.)

5. Dr. Don Morley reflects on communication careers in his essay "So What Are You Doing after Graduation? Some Reflections of a Former Xerox Salesperson." Have you considered sales as a communication career? Should you? (See pages 422–424.)

6. Select a particular organization in which you are interested and to whom you might want to apply in the future. Research this organization on the Internet. Report your findings during a class discussion.

7. Contact your college or university placement office. Determine what type of on-line job-search services are available. Browse these on-line services to determine how they can be useful for your job-search strategies. Make a list of any web sites you visit, including a description of the types of services provided by each. Which sites will be most useful to you?

## Work Sheet and Example of Self-Analysis Activities for Career Planning

NAME _____

Achievements are observable results of individual skills in action. Achievements that have lasting importance normally satisfy key values in an individual's life. This exercise is designed to help you identify both skills and values that have contributed to your personal achievements. Identification of important skills and values is a fundamental step in successful career and life planning.

*Instructions.* Read the instruction for each activity, reflect on it, and then write your response. Be as brief or extensive as you like.

1. Identify specific individuals who have been influential in shaping your concept of work and occupational choice.
     What have they told you about possibilities?
     How satisfied are they with their work?
     How would they profile a successful person?
     What occupations have they suggested for you?
     What occupations do they not suggest for you?

2. Describe your ideal occupation in terms of responsibilities, skills, and measurement of success.

**3.** Compare your perfect occupation to messages from those who have influenced you (exercises 1 and 2).

**4.** Identify and list four important achievements, skills used for each achievement, and values satisfied. Identify common skills used and values satisfied among the achievements. List ten skills and ten values that seem to be predictive for you of achievement.

ACHIEVEMENTS              SKILLS USED              VALUES SATISFIED

COMMON SKILLS USED                    COMMON VALUES SATISFIED

TEN SKILLS PREDICTIVE OF ACHIEVEMENT/TEN VALUES PREDICTIVE OF ACHIEVEMENT

**5.** Write a narrative describing your desired lifestyle for a five-year span after your education is complete. How should this narrative influence your occupational/career choices?

6. Identify ten statements you can make today about your current career planning. Identify ten questions you need answered for career planning.

| TEN STATEMENTS | TEN QUESTIONS |
|---|---|
| 1. | 1. |
| 2. | 2. |
| 3. | 3. |
| 4. | 4. |
| 5. | 5. |
| 6. | 6. |
| 7. | 7. |
| 8. | 8. |
| 9. | 9. |
| 10. | 10. |

## Résumé Development Exercise

A résumé is a well-prepared description of your accomplishments, skills, and experiences written to address the needs of potential employers. Résumé formats are numerous, with the most common described as the chronological résumé (Figure 11.4) and the functional résumé (Figure 11.5).

## The Chronological Résumé

A traditional chronological résumé begins with your work experiences listed in reverse chronological order, beginning with your most recent job. Dates of employment are included as well as names of employers, job titles, and duties or responsibilities. Other relevant information such as education is included. The chronological résumé tells people what your work experience is and is best used when you have consistent experience that applies to your current job applications.

## The Functional Résumé

A functional résumé describes work objectives, skills, accomplishments, and education when applicable. Skills, experiences, and accomplishments are grouped according to the skills of the functions they represent. The following words represent common categories for functional résumés: Administration, Bookkeeping, Communication, Computer Use, Coordination, Customer Relations/Service, Data Entry, Editing, Facilitating, Human Resource Management, Inventory Control, Management, Marketing, Negotiation, Nursing, Office Support, Problem Solving, Production, Promotion, Public Speaking, Quality Control, Record Keeping, Reporting, Sales, Supervision, Team Building, and Writing.

The functional résumé is most frequently used by new entrants to the job market, recent college graduates, and those changing career fields.

## Résumé Questionnaire

1. Describe your work objectives.
2. What types of organizations are you considering?
3. Develop a list of your paid work experiences. Describe your responsibilities and accomplishments.

**FIGURE 11.4   Chronological Résumé Sample**

---

Jan Waxton
5050 Warton Lane
Minneapolis, Minnesota 74329
(405) 598-8333

OBJECTIVE: Position in training department in major organization or consulting firm.

WORK EXPERIENCE:

| 1996 to Present | Arby's Restaurants, Minneapolis, MN<br>Shift Supervisor |

Supervised eight employees per shift. Delivered corporate training programs. Compiled weekly sales reports. Conducted annual performance reviews. Promoted twice in three years.

| 1994 | IBM Corporation, Minneapolis, MN<br>Human Resource Intern |

Developed research summary for design of organizational change training program. Report used by design team for new training program.

RELEVANT EXPERIENCE:

| 1995 to Present | YMCA Volunteers, Minneapolis, MN   Volunteer Trainer |

Designed and delivered YMCA Leadership Course for over 200 volunteers. Delivered over 25 orientation presentations.

| 1998 to 2000 | United Church of Christ, Minneapolis, MN<br>Youth Services Volunteer |

Designed and delivered Leadership Class for over 100 Youth Fellowship participants. Led over 15 other classes.

| 1997 to 1999 | Memorial Hospital, Minneapolis, MN<br>Volunteer Trainer |

Designed and delivered Leadership Class for over 50 volunteers.

EDUCATION:

B.A.—University of Minnesota
    Major: Organizational Communication
    Minor: Human Resource Management

REFERENCES:
    Available on request

---

4. Identify your most important skills. Group them as they relate to your work objectives.
5. Assess your volunteer and college activities. How can they be used to provide additional relevant experience?

**FIGURE 11.5    Functional Résumé Sample**

Jan Waxton
5050 Warton Lane
Minneapolis, Minnesota 74329
(405) 598-8333

OBJECTIVE: Position in training department in major organization or consulting firm.

SKILLS:

Training:
Designed and delivered leadership programs for three non-profit organizations. Received excellent evaluations over a two-year period.

Researched organizational change for design team in a major electronics corporation training department. Research used by design team for introduction of new training program.

Delivered training for new employees in a food-service franchise. Received excellent evaluations and two promotions over a three-year period.

Supervision:
Supervised up to eight employees per shift in a food-service franchise. Received performance appraisals exceeding expectations over a three-year period.

Writing:
Compiled weekly sales reports for management. Reports forwarded to franchise headquarters without alterations over a three-year period.

Developed research summary for design of organizational change training program. Research summary utilized by design team for training outline.

Conducted annual performance appraisal for food-service employees from compilation of weekly reports into overall written narratives for annual reviews. No review reports returned with negative comments over a three-year period.

Public Speaking:
Delivered over 50 presentations on behalf of two nonprofit organizations. Received excellent evaluations over a five-year period.

EDUCATION:
B.A.—University of Minnesota
    Major: Organizational Communication
    Minor: Human Resource Management

REFERENCES:
Available on request

6. What should you do now to improve the résumé you will soon prepare for an employer?
7. Prepare a sample résumé.
8. Ask others to critique your efforts and make suggestions for additions.

## So What Are You Doing after Graduation? Some Reflections of a Former Xerox Salesperson

### Donald D. Morley, Ph.D.[1]

In the spring of my senior year, the not-so-sudden realization set in that I was about to graduate and had to find a job. Armed with a soon-to-be-granted bachelor's degree in communication and a desire not to be chained to a nine-to-five desk job, I decided that something in the area of sales might be a logical choice. In retrospect, it was a good choice for a substantial number of communication graduates. The problem is that very few communication majors know much about (1) the different types of sales positions that exist, (2) how to find a good entry-level sales position, and (3) how to minimize the pitfalls that await the new sales representative. This essay offers some reflective advice on these issues.

All too often the mention of "sales representative" conjures up a stereotypic image of a pushy, arm-twisting, aggressive person. At the mention of sales as a possible career, one student replied that she did not even like salespeople, much less want to become one. Although the stereotype is at least partially accurate, few people recognize that sales jobs vary a great deal in the amount of assertiveness or push required of the sales representative.

The major determinant of required assertiveness is the type of sales. Outside retail sales, where the salesperson seeks out a customer who is the ultimate consumer of the product or service, requires the type of salesperson that can (1) be creative in locating and identifying the prospective customers within the territory; (2) convince high-level people within the organization who don't really want to talk to them to do so; (3) get around receptionists whose job is to greet others but to keep you away from their bosses; and (4) be dynamic, trustworthy, competent, confident, and persuasive enough within minutes to close the order successfully or at least close for some intermediate step leading to an order. In short, we are talking about a comparatively aggressive salesperson with a rare combination of abilities. Because outside retail sales is a difficult high-pressure business, salespeople generally command substantial commissions.

Wholesale and industrial sales representatives stand in sharp contrast to outside retail representatives. Unlike the retail salesperson, whose products are more often than not perceived by customers to be increased overhead, the wholesale representative supplies customers with products or materials the customer will eventually resell for profit. This being the case, prospective customers are more likely to hear out the salesperson in anticipation that the transaction will be mutually profitable. Furthermore, because the product is resold, these sales representatives have repeated contact with their customers and selling per se becomes more a process of servicing accounts than trying to talk someone into buying something.

---

[1]After receiving his bachelor's degree in communication, Donald Morley was a sales representative for Xerox Corporation. After leaving Xerox he received his master's degree and Ph.D. in communication and currently is a professor of communication at the University of Colorado at Colorado Springs. His major teaching and research interests are in persuasion, organizational communication, and research methods.

Like the retail sales representative, the wholesale representative must be creative in identifying prospective customers within his or her territory and must be good at developing small "foot-in-the-door" accounts into substantial profitable accounts. Even more than the retail sales representative, these representatives need to be highly organized, excellent recordkeepers, excellent time managers, and in short must give their customers the impression that they are on top of everything because they are on top of everything.

Assuming that you are interested in sales, just how do you find a good sales job? Every newspaper in every city is full of advertisements for sales representatives. Many promise fun, excitement, hundred-thousand-dollar-plus incomes, and products that sell themselves. Unless you just fell off the turnip truck, however, you know nobody is going to pay you a hundred thousand dollars to sell something that sells itself. In fact, only a small percentage of the sales positions advertised in newspapers are worth looking into. The reason is that there seems to be an unwritten rule among sales professionals that the true salesperson is an actively creative person who finds a sales position in the same way he or she finds potential customers. So how do you find and recognize a good sales position?

First, get involved in the community and network. When a company treats its salespeople right, only a few openings will arise, and when they do the word tends to spread informally. Second, recognize that the first product you will sell is yourself, and that's also probably the most expensive product you'll ever sell. Xerox, for example, estimated that it cost more than forty thousand dollars to hire and train a new sales representative. If you look around your home, work, and environment in general you will realize that the potential list of companies that will "buy you" is enormous. Every product and service that you look at has been sold by somebody a multitude of times. While you're looking around, write out a list of companies for which you might want to work and research them. I find it perplexing that students will spend over forty hours in the library doing research for a term paper, but not even forty minutes researching a potential job. In addition to library research, talk to people who already sell for the company. For example, I recently ran into a factory representative for a well-known manufacturer of camping equipment. Within a short time I learned that he had been with the company over twenty-five years, was very happy with his job, made a great deal more money than a university professor, and that the president of the company personally interviewed and hired all the factory representatives. And yet I doubt that the thought of selling for this particular company, and hundreds of others like it, ever occurs to many people on the job market. In contrast, the big-name companies such as Xerox are flooded with applications, hire only a few, and have a persistent tone of "You're replaceable."

Once you know a fair amount about some companies, go after them. If they say they are not interested, go after them again. After all, sales requires a degree of tasteful persistence, and an initially uninterested sales manager might start seeing that you have what it takes.

There are a number of sales jobs, however, that you should avoid. I call them sink-or-swim positions. Essentially, these companies are ones that put little time, effort, and money into training their salespeople. If they need five good sales representatives, they hire a hundred, knowing full well they will fire ninety-five of them within a year. I was once offered a headhunter fee by a life insurance broker for every college graduate that I sent him. He made it clear that he was out to hire as many as he could, because he knew that only a few of them would work out and they all could at least sell life insurance to their family and friends before he had to let them go. I never sent him anybody. In short, take a good hard look at what the company is going to invest in you before you invest in them.

Even after you've landed a good sales position, a number of pitfalls await you, the major one being that you don't sell enough to make a good living, or worse yet, keep your job. It is hoped your selection of the right company, good training, and hard creative work will go a long way in avoiding this pitfall. The organizational structure of most sales divisions, however, tends to foster a self-fulfilling prophecy for success or failure. It works something like this scene: your immediate sales manager's income and performance depend on how you and the rest of the sales team perform. In turn, the district manager's performance evaluations depend on how well the sales managers do, and so on up the organizational hierarchy. Although generally a good system, what happens is that this mutual dependency causes organizational superiors to assign their best sales territories to what they perceive to be their best salespeople and the lesser territories to what they perceive to be their weaker salespeople. As a result, the prophecy is fulfilled when the good sales representative outsells the weak ones. The lesson is simple: be perceived as a strong sales representative. Dress and act professionally, make sure your accomplishments are known, do not dwell on your failures, and most important, be positive. Managers will not entrust a major accounts package to people who fail to display the confidence and optimism that they not only can do the job but also can do it better.

Professional salespeople are not peddlers and charlatans. Rather, they perform a valuable service to the people and organizations to whom they sell, while earning themselves a good income. Before anyone looks down at sales as a career, they would be well advised to remember that Lee Iacocca started his career in sales and that much of what he learned in those early days was pivotal in preventing the demise of Chrysler Corporation.

### QUESTIONS FOR DISCUSSION

1. The author points to the problem of how the organizational structure of most marketing divisions results in a self-fulfilling prophecy. What are some alternatives that might avoid this problem? What are their advantages and disadvantages?

2. Even if you do not choose to go into sales, you will someday have to market yourself. What ideas do you have about finding a prospective employer and convincing that company to hire you?

---

# REFERENCES AND SUGGESTED READINGS

Allred, B. B., C. C. Snow, and R. E. Miles 1996. Characteristics of managerial careers in the twenty-first century. *Academy of Management Executive* 10(4): 17–27.

Arthur, M. B., P. H. Claman, and R. J. DeFillippi. 1995. Intelligent enterprise, intelligent careers. *Academy of Management Executive* 9(4): 7–20.

Bennis, W. 1969. *Organization development: Its nature, origins, and prospects.* Reading, MA: Addison-Wesley.

Bennis, W., K. Benne, R. Chin, and K. Corey. 1976. *The planning of change.* 3d ed. New York: Holt, Rinehart and Winston.

DeWine, S. 1994. *The consultant's craft.* New York: St. Martin's.

French, W. L., and C. H. Bell. 1973. *Organization development: Behavioral science interventions for organization improvement.* Englewood Cliffs, NJ: Prentice Hall.

Goldhaber, G. M. 1986. *Organizational communication.* 4th ed. Dubuque, IA: Brown.

Hall, D. T. 1996. Protean careers of the twenty-first century. *Academy of Management Executive* 10(4): 8–16.

Miles, R. E., C. C. Snow, J. A. Mathews, G. Miles, and H. J. Coleman Jr. 1997. *Organizing in the knowledge age: Anticipating the cellular form.* 11(4): 7–24.

Pace, W. 1983. *Organizational communication: Foundations for human resource development.* Englewood Cliffs, NJ: Prentice Hall.

Pace, R. W., and D. F. Faules. 1994. *Organizational communication.* 3d ed. Englewood Cliffs, NJ: Prentice Hall.

Petrie, C., E. Thompson, D. Rogers, and G. Goldhaber. 1975. *Report of the ad hoc committee on manpower resources.* Report prepared for the Division IV meeting of the International Communication Association, April, Chicago.

Schein, E. H. 1969. *Process consultation: Its role in organization development.* Reading, MA: Addison-Wesley.

Wilson, G. L., H. L. Goodall Jr., and C. L. Waagen. 1986. *Organizational communication.* New York: Harper and Row.

# CHAPTER TWELVE

# ORGANIZATIONAL COMMUNICATION

## Values and Ethical Communication Behaviors

---

## DEVELOPING COMPETENCIES THROUGH . . .

### KNOWLEDGE

Describing individual and organizational values

Defining ethical communication

Identifying criteria for the evaluation of ethical communication behaviors

### SENSITIVITY

Awareness of our personal value systems

Understanding the complexity of ethical dilemmas

Distinguishing between what we would do and what we should do

### SKILLS

Assessing personal value systems and behaviors

Applying skills to case and dilemma analysis

### VALUES

Relating values to individual behavior and organizational effectiveness

Understanding ethical behavior as contributing to choice, growth, and development

■ ■ ■ ■ ■

## THE PRESIDENTIAL FACT-FINDING (WITCH-HUNT?) CASE

Alyne Carter was surprised to receive a call requesting her to come to the office of the president of Melton Corporation. Alyne had never had an appointment with the president, and she was concerned about what he wanted to discuss. The president was relatively new to Melton, and rumor had it that the board of directors had hired him as a "hatchet" man to terminate some long-term Melton managers who were associated with the failure of one of Melton's major land-development projects. Alyne's boss, Jim Johnson, had received criticism from some board members, although he was not directly involved with the development project.

Melton had a long history of being a good place to work, with open communication and support for taking risks, even though risks sometimes resulted in failures. Management at Melton had traditionally believed that their speculative land-development business would be most successful if they developed properties other companies had chosen to ignore. The strategy had generally worked, with the Briarwood project a major and important exception. The failure of Briarwood and the loss of several million dollars had upset important board members and had contributed to the resignation of Melton's president.

Alyne Carter did not work on the development side of Melton's business. She reported directly to the vice president in charge of personnel and human resource development, Jim Johnson. Alyne and Jim had a good working relationship based on mutual trust and admiration. Alyne was concerned when she heard criticism of Jim as well as the general rumors that people were going to be fired. The upcoming meeting with the new president increased her fears.

When Alyne left the meeting, she knew her concerns were real. The discussion with the new president had confused her and had left her wondering what to do. Although he had been perfectly pleasant, she knew he was looking for information to use against her boss. The president had begun the meeting by asking her to describe her work at Melton. He then said he needed to ask her some hypothetical questions about her department's management, recruitment, and promotional practices. Following several general questions, the president said that the rest of their conversation must stay within his office. He then proceeded to ask her if pressure had come from certain managers to hire several key individuals thought to be responsible for bad decisions in the Briarwood project. The president specifically asked if Jim Johnson had approved her hiring recommendations and whether any of her recommendations had been reversed in the last six months. Alyne attempted to answer the questions directly, although she felt as if she were walking into some unknown trap. She wished she had called Jim to tell him she had been asked to see the president. He might have been able to give her some insight about what was going on. The president closed the meeting by again suggesting that their conversation was not to leave the room. He also made a somewhat vague reference to his responsibility to make unpopular changes in the best interest of Melton. He said he hoped that she would understand and realize he had to do his job in the best way he saw fit.

Alyne could not believe that this type of meeting had taken place at Melton. The rumors about a hatchet man certainly seemed correct. She knew she had been told not to talk about her discussion with the president, but she thought that Jim should know. Was it unethical to break her promise to the president? Where did she owe her loyalty? Was the president engaged in fact-finding or in a witch-hunt?

# INTRODUCTION

Alyne Carter is faced with a question of values and ethics. She has inadvertently become involved in a communication situation that makes her uncomfortable and violates what she believes to be basic Melton company values. Alyne has been told by the president of Melton that their conversation should be kept in confidence, yet she believes that her boss, Jim Johnson, should know about the president's fact-finding and veiled threats of future action. Alyne is caught between respecting directions from the president and valuing her loyalty to her boss. She has to decide about her values in this situation and what constitutes ethical behavior. Part of her decision will be based on a determination of whether Melton's president has engaged her in unethical communication.

Although an uncomfortable situation, Alyne's dilemma unfortunately is repeated hundreds of times a day in all sizes and types of organizations. Individual and organizational values clash, making determinations of ethical behavior difficult. Organizational values appear to change, leaving employees perplexed about what communication behaviors are valued and what behaviors should no longer be exhibited. Individual organizational members try to determine whether personal ethics and business ethics can or should mix.

This chapter is designed to help you think about how values and ethics influence human communication within organizations. The chapter also introduces you to value and ethical dilemmas commonly encountered by communication professionals. The chapter attempts to contribute to the development of *knowledge* by defining values and ethics, identifying individual and organizational values, and establishing frameworks for evaluating ethical communication behaviors. *Sensitivity* is developed for relationships among organizational cultures, values, ethics, and decision making. Analysis *skills* are practiced through personal assessment of values, by identifying value themes in organizational philosophy statements, and by evaluating ethical behaviors in typical organizational communication situations. *Values* development is encouraged through an understanding of the importance to organizations of personal and organizational value systems and through discussions of the role of ethical communication behaviors for communication competency and effectiveness. All four competencies—knowledge, sensitivity, skills, and values—are applied to a case study, practical examples of value and ethical dilemmas, a decision-making simulation, and the development of a personal values and ethics statement for organizational communication.

# VALUES IN ORGANIZATIONAL COMMUNICATION

Although most of us frequently use the word *value*, we often do not stop and thoughtfully consider what the concept really means to us. If asked, could you readily identify your value system for others? How did it develop? Who or what has influenced your choices? How does your value system influence your communication behaviors?

**Value**

Concept that refers to the relative worth of a quality or object.

Generally speaking, **value** refers to the relative worth of a quality or object. Value is what makes something desirable or undesirable. Values are subjective assessments. As Joseph DeVito (1976) suggests:

> A value is an organized system of attitudes. If, for example, we have a cluster of favorable attitudes pertaining to various issues relating to freedom of speech, then we might say that one of our values is that of free speech. In another sense, a value is an organizing system for attitudes. If we have a particular value, say financial success, then this will give us guidelines for developing and forming attitudes. Thus, we will have favorable attitudes toward high-paying jobs, marrying into a wealthy family, and inheriting money because of the value we place on financial success. Values also provide us with guidelines for behavior; in effect, they direct our behavior so that it is consistent with the achievement of the values of goals we have. (p. 416)

Richard Johannesen, in his important book *Ethics in Human Communication* (1983), states that "values can be viewed as conceptions of The Good or The Desirable that motivate human behavior and that function as criteria in our making of choices and judgments." Family belonging, achievement, financial security, prestige, and hard work are all values that have some degree of importance for most of us. Johannesen and others suggest that the importance of our personal values influences a wide variety of our decision-making activities and behavior choices. In other words, we are more likely to make choices that support our value systems than choices that will not. Let us say that financial security is a strong value for an individual. When faced with a choice of jobs, chances are the individual will carefully examine each organization for potential financial and job security. The job applicant who values financial security may well take a lower salary offer with a well-established company over a higher-paying offer from a new, high-risk venture. Another job seeker with different values, possibly adventure and excitement, might choose the newer company simply for the potential risk and uncertain future.

Values therefore become part of complex attitude sets that influence our behavior and the behavior of all those with whom we interact. What we value guides not only our personal choices but also our perceptions of the worth of others. We are more likely, for example, to evaluate highly someone who holds the same hard-work value we do than someone who finds work distasteful, with personal gratification a more important value. We may even call this person lazy and worthless, a negative value label.

Before reading further in this chapter, stop for a few minutes and attempt to describe your personal value system. What are your priorities? Have you ever stopped to think about their influence on your activities and your evaluations of others? Think about how your personal values may influence your communication behavior.

## Organizational Value Systems

Part of the unique sense of a place called organizational culture develops from the values held in common by organizational members. Leonard Goodstein (1983) goes so far as to suggest that

> many persons who are seriously interested in organizational behavior now believe that organizations are best regarded as cultures, with all that the term "cultures," in an anthropological sense, implies. In my opinion, the most important implication of this position is that organizations, like persons, have values and that these values are integrated into some coherent value system. (pp. 203–204)

Milton Rokeach (1973) has defined a value system as "an enduring organization of beliefs concerning preferable modes of conduct or end-states of existence along a continuum of relative importance." Based on the Rokeach definition, Goodstein (1983) contends that "in any organization, the members generally have a set of beliefs about what is appropriate and inappropriate organizational behavior. Furthermore, these beliefs can be ordered in importance in a reliable fashion by the members of the organization." In other words, organizational value systems help organizational members to understand what the organization holds as important and how the unique sense of the place should influence their personal decision making and behavior.

Terrence Deal and Allen Kennedy (1982) describe organizational values as "the bedrock of any corporate culture" and link value systems to overall organizational effectiveness. They state:

> As the essence of a company's philosophy for achieving success, values provide a sense of common direction for all employees and guidelines for their day-to-day behavior. These formulas for success determine (and occasionally arise from) the types of corporate heroes, and the myths, rituals, and ceremonies of the culture. In fact, we think that often companies succeed because their employees can identify, embrace, and act on the values of the organization. (p. 21)

Values are part of the shared realities generated through organizational communication. These shared values are reflected in organizational myths, stories, mission statements, physical surroundings, slogans, decision making, and thematic and tactical communication rules, to identify but a few of the ways in which organizational members encounter organizational values. Indeed, it is fair to say that organizational values are transmitted, maintained, and changed through organizational communication processes.

As described in Chapter 3, thematic communication rules are general prescriptions of behavior reflecting the values and beliefs of the organization. Tactical rules prescribe specific behaviors as related to the more general value themes. In fact, several tactical rules may evolve from one general thematic rule. One example was of a Midwest computer manufacturer with a strong value theme of "Communicate your commitment to the company." Based on that value theme, employees reported tactical rules, including "Come in on Saturday to finish up, but make sure you tell someone," "Complain about how tough the challenge really is," and "Use the term *family* to refer to the company." These tactical rules supported an important value theme in that particular company. Employees exhibiting compliance with thematic and tactical rules were generally considered to have been well socialized into the organization and supportive of its values.

In addition to thematic and tactical communication rules, stories, and myths, organizational values are seen in the decisions members make. Deal and Kennedy (1982) suggest that "if employees know what their company stands for, if they know what standards they are to uphold, then they are much more likely to make decisions that will support those standards." Research conducted by David Palmer, John Veiga, and Jay Vora (1981) supports the important link between values and decision making. They found that "value profiles were relatively successful in predicting managers' decision preferences and in providing further evidence of the linkage between personal values and decision making." In other words, an individual's value system, when coupled with the more general value system of the organization, influences the decisions individual organizational members will make. Deal and Kennedy contend that "shaping and enhancing values can become the most important job a manager can do." They further suggest that successful companies stand for something (clearly communicated values), that managers put effort into shaping and fine-tuning values, and that values are shared realities at all organization levels.

Organizational values not only influence the behaviors of current members but also contribute to the type of person who gets hired and the types of career experiences employees are likely to have. Some organizations value very specific types of educational backgrounds, whereas others are more likely to look for particular work experiences. Some organizations value promotion from within, whereas their counterparts never fill important vacancies from among existing employees. During times of economic difficulty, organizations valuing long-term commitment to their employees may reduce work hours or salaries for everyone rather than lay off a portion of their work force. Other organizations with less employee-centered values may decide that layoffs are the most efficient and effective way to deal with a business downturn. Arguments can be made for either position. The values of the organizations, however, are likely to guide the alternatives even considered by their respective management teams.

## Organizational Values and Diversity

There is a danger, of course, in thinking about organizations as having singular sets of values reflecting the closely held beliefs of all organizational members. Within an organization diverse functions, leadership, and histories all contribute to differences in what is desirable and important. Differences in values within and between organizations are only expected to increase. As discussed throughout this book, the diversity of the work force combined with the forces of internationalization not only bring new challenges for working together and new organizational forms but also contribute to value diversity within organizations.

David Strubler (1993) provides an interesting illustration of value diversity within organizations in his study of what he calls hybrid companies for which large numbers of Japanese and Americans work together either in the United States or in Japan. Strubler suggests that the cultural and value dimensions of context, face saving, and truth can help us understand how value differences within and between organizations contribute to potential misunderstanding and difficulty. According to Strubler, the Japanese, coming from a high context culture, have a high volume of commonly shared information that makes implicit communication more desirable than more explicit information exchanges. By contrast, in the United States, generally low context culture is heavily dependent on explicit information exchange, often supported by extensive written documentation. In addition, although both cultures are concerned with face saving, the Japanese generally place a higher imperative on face-saving behaviors than do Americans. Strubler relates:

> Consequently, high face-saving cultures view indirect (implicit) communication as preserving one's sense of dignity. Open argumentation in Japanese culture is considered unethical. Low face-saving cultures such as found in the U.S. view indirectness as unethical and typically favor argumentation as a method of settling difficulties. . . . In low context cultures, an emphasis is placed on the explicit written or spoken word. Truth is objective and absolute. When truth is violated (someone does not keep his or her word) guilt is experienced. In high context cultures, an emphasis is placed on relational (harmonious) communication. (p. 12)

Both Japanese and American cultures recognize the subjective and objective nature of truth, but value differences frequently have been observed, as when Strubler (1993) describes: "Japanese often accuse Americans of being brash. Americans accuse Japanese of being deceitful. Often there is a failure to understand one another's cultural imperatives." Obviously, these types of cultural and value differences extend to numerous types of international work settings. Competent communicators therefore begin to appreciate their personal responsibilities to understand how value differences may influence a variety of important organizational communication settings.

Diversity in values does not occur solely in the international business environment. As the work force includes increasingly diverse cultural groups, organizations, often attempting to have their own distinct value systems, will increasingly reflect value differences and similarities across groups. These value differences and similarities are important for both individuals and organizations.

**Value congruence**
The similarity between individual and organizational values.

A large body of research, for example, continues to demonstrate that **value congruence** (the similarity between individual and organizational values) between employees and their organizations has a significant affect on organizational commitment, employee work satisfaction, and turnover. Taylor Cox (1993), in his work on cultural diversity in organizations, describes the importance of understanding this dynamic of value congruence. Cox states:

The message . . . of value congruence may seem somewhat ambiguous. It may seem to suggest that diversity results in lower organizational performance. However, this is only true if we make certain assumptions about organizations such as that they should seek to assimilate all entrants into a monolithic culture, which tends to produce culture clash for entering members who are different from the traditional norm. Instead, my intended message is that the importance of value congruence illustrates the need for multicultural organizations, one feature of which is that the organizational culture specifies alternatives that are equally appreciated rather than the one best way. Thus it is important to bear in mind that person-organization fit, in a cultural sense, is a function of the flexibility and inclusiveness of the organization as well as the individual. (p. 22)

Think about the values of your school. Can you describe these values in any order of priority? How do they influence the policies and procedures that you as a student are asked to follow? What kinds of formal and informal messages transmit these values to students? What values do students transmit to the administration and faculty?

Figure 12.1 provides three examples of organizational value statements. Each statement is taken from the new employee handbook of the three organizations. Without knowing anything else about these organizations, think about the value systems you believe that the messages represent.

## FIGURE 12.1   Organizational Value Statements

### COMPANY A

As a company, we want to share timely and accurate information on policies, programs, and activities. We want the information to be consistent and available to all employees. This is a goal that all managers should help to achieve. The company believes communication about our business creates a motivated and creative work force.

### COMPANY B

The mission of Company B is as follows: Command, control, and support the work force. Modernize the workplace. Prepare to support other divisions of the company. Train, motivate, and maintain individual capabilities. Provide a motivated environment that will attract and retain motivated and challenged workers.

### COMPANY C

Our philosophy in managing is to plan aggressively and anticipate events rather than let them drive us. Our program for our personnel must include fair compensation, appropriate benefits and working conditions, and an opportunity for advancement based on skills and ability. Our company will endeavor to participate in and offer educational programs necessary to ensure the qualified training of personnel, with a primary emphasis on improving customer service. All of these efforts are adopted to support our goal of excellence.

Which of the three most closely fits your personal value system? Which least fits your values? Would value statements such as these make a difference in the organizations for which you would want to work? If so, why? If not, why not?

## Individual Values

Although the discussion has been on organizational value systems, organizations are really groups of individuals working together in goal-directed activities. Thus, organizational value systems are a collective interpretation of the values individual organizational members share in common. As Goodstein (1983) suggests:

> In the final analysis, we are talking about the values and beliefs of individuals. Organizational values are the modal or general values that are espoused by most of the organization's members and the ones that are put forward as representing "organizational truths." New members are recruited into the organization by their willingness to accept these "truths," and much of the focus of organizational socialization is to shape these values and beliefs. (p. 204).

Numerous other organizational researchers have come to believe, as does Goodstein, that the more similar organizational and individual values are, the more likely the individual is to identify positively with the organization. In other words, a closeness between "this way is the way I believe things are" and "this way is the way I believe things should be" generally means that the individual is satisfied with the organization and can personally commit to organizational values and beliefs. One of the difficulties, of course, is thoughtfully understanding the real values of an organization before one becomes a member. The process of matching individual and organizational values also is complicated by the lack of individual understanding of how value systems relate to work life. (As you will recall, the self-analysis exercises for career planning located in Chapter 11 were designed to help you think about your values as they might relate to career and job selection.)

### Value Orientations
Personal values have been discussed in a variety of ways. Gordon Allport, Philip Vernon, and Gardner Lindzey (1960) suggest that personal values can be described in terms of six orientations: theoretical, economic, aesthetic, social, political, and religious. Theoretical values focus on the discovery of truth, knowledge, and order, whereas economic values focus on the useful and practical and on material acquisition. Aesthetic values are expressed in our concerns for artistic experiences and in our desire for form and harmony. Social values are expressed in our relationships with others and our love and service commitments. Political values relate to needs for power, influence, leadership, and domination, and religious values are expressed in needs for unity and meaningful relationships to the world.

**Terminal values**
Concerns for end states of existence or desirable goals.

**Instrumental values**
Desirable behaviors or modes of conduct that are related to and influence terminal values.

## Terminal and Instrumental Values

Rokeach's (1973) value survey identifies terminal and instrumental values. **Terminal values** can be viewed as concern for "end states of existence," or desirable goals, and **instrumental values** are desirable behaviors or modes of conduct that are related to and influence terminal values. The terminal values that Rokeach identifies are a comfortable life; an exciting life; a sense of accomplishment; a world at peace; a world of beauty, equality, family security, freedom, happiness, inner harmony, and mature love; national security; pleasure; salvation; self-respect; social recognition; true friendship; and wisdom. Instrumental values are the qualities of being ambitious, broad-minded, capable, cheerful, clean, courageous, forgiving, helpful, honest, imaginative, independent, intellectual, logical, loving, obedient, polite, responsible, and self-controlled.

A possible relationship between terminal and instrumental values can be illustrated through the example of someone with a high priority on the terminal value of accomplishment and instrumental values of being ambitious, capable, imaginative, intellectual, logical, and self-controlled. That is not to suggest, of course, that these are the only instrumental values that go hand in hand with a sense of accomplishment. Obviously, there could be others. Terminal values, however, are generally accompanied by combinations of instrumental values that individuals perceive to be harmonious.

## Work Values

The personal values discussed apply to all aspects of our lives, not just the time we spend in organizations. Until recently few attempts have been made to explore personal values as they specifically apply to work environments. Roger Howe, Maynard Howe, and Mark Mindell (1982) identify five value dimensions that they believe affect our organizational lives: locus of control, self-esteem, tolerance of ambiguity, social judgment, and risk taking.

**Locus of control**
Value we place as organizational members on connections between our efforts and the success or failure of the organization.

**Locus of control** refers to the value we place as organizational members on connections between our efforts and the success or failure of the organization. In other words, do we value personal control over success or failure, or do we value an organizational environment in which circumstances beyond our control contribute to success or failure? Do we, for example, want to be personally responsible for meeting sales quotas, or do we prefer to provide support to others who have the final quota responsibility? Our locus of control value also relates to whether we value organizational advancement as a result of our own efforts (personal control) or as the result of luck, politics, or random selection (external control).

**Self-esteem**
Value we place on recognition for work, positive feedback, and the use of our contributions.

The **self-esteem** dimension relates to the value we place on recognition for work, positive feedback, and the use of our contributions. This value represents our concern for being trusted and perceived as making worthwhile contributions to the organization.

**Tolerance of ambiguity**
Value or importance we place on structured or unstructured work environments.

**Social judgment**
Value we place on the feelings of others and our general assumptions about why people work.

**Risk taking**
Value that explores the importance we place on quick rather than deliberative action and whether we prefer our own sense of job fulfillment as opposed to job security.

**Tolerance of ambiguity** as a value refers to the importance we place on structured or unstructured work environments. Our preference for one right answer or our comfort with a variety of possible approaches for decision making relates to the level of ambiguity we personally value. Those with a low tolerance for ambiguity may value one right answer and structured environments, whereas those higher in tolerance for ambiguity may prefer less structure and more opportunity for creative and diverse approaches.

The value we place on the feelings of others and our general assumptions about why people work can be described as our **social judgment.** Our concerns for sensitivity, empathy, and social insight are related to the importance we place on working relationships with others.

**Risk taking** concerns the importance we place on quick rather than deliberative action and whether we prefer our own sense of job fulfillment as opposed to job security. Our risk-taking value influences the degree of security we require in work situations, our tolerance for ambiguity in decision making, and whether we are willing to attempt tasks we have not previously encountered or have few qualifications for accomplishing.

Figure 12.2 summarizes the three value approaches that have been described. After reviewing these lists, consider which additional values you would add. Which of the three approaches best represents your personal value system? Could the three be combined?

## APPRAISING YOUR INDIVIDUAL VALUE SYSTEM

Understanding what is important to us and what our values are contributes to our ability to identify the careers and organizations in which we can be most productive and satisfied. Personal value assessment also helps us identify the ways values influence behaviors and evaluations of whether communication is ethical or not. Before beginning to explore ethics in organizational communication, a self-analysis of personal values is provided to give you insight into your value system. This assessment exercise is based on the assumption that consistent behaviors reflect value systems. Our approach in Figure 12.3 is by no means the only valid measure of a value system. This scale is presented as a useful way to begin to think about the relationship of values and behaviors. As you complete the appraisal, consider additional questions that might be asked and additional values not represented in the appraisal. The scoring form for your appraisal is located on page 460.

## ETHICS IN ORGANIZATIONAL COMMUNICATION

### Making Ethical Decisions

According to Gerald Cavanagh, Dennis Moberg, and Manuel Velasquez (1990), research in the area of ethics has emerged from three fundamental moral

**FIGURE 12.2   Three Approaches to Describing Personal Values**

| VALUE ORIENTATIONS | WORK VALUE DIMENSIONS |
|---|---|
| Theoretical | Locus of control |
|   Truth |   Internal |
|   Rationale |   External |
|   Order | Self-esteem |
|   Knowledge |   Recognition |
| Economic |   Trust |
|   Material acquisition |   Worth |
|   Usefulness | Tolerance of ambiguity |
|   Pragmatism |   Structured work |
| Aesthetic |   Unstructured work |
|   Artistry | Social judgment |
|   Harmony |   Assumptions about others |
|   Form |   Interpersonal sensitivity |
| Social | Risk taking |
|   Love |   Action oriented |
|   Concern for others |   Uncertainty as challenging |
|   Service | |
| Political | |
|   Power | |
|   Influence | |
|   Domination | |
|   Leadership | |

*Rokeach Terminal and Instrumental Values*

| TERMINAL VALUES | INSTRUMENTAL VALUES |
|---|---|
| A comfortable life | Ambitious |
| An exciting life | Broad-minded |
| A sense of accomplishment | Capable |
| A world at peace | Cheerful |
| A world of beauty | Clean |
| Equality | Courageous |
| Family security | Forgiving |
| Freedom | Helpful |
| Happiness | Honest |
| Inner harmony | Imaginative |
| Mature love | Independent |
| National security | Intellectual |
| Pleasure | Logical |
| Salvation | Loving |
| Self-respect | Obedient |
| Social recognition | Polite |
| True friendship | Responsible |
| Wisdom | Self-controlled |

**FIGURE 12.3**   **Values Appraisal Exercise**

*Instructions:* Read the following twenty-four statements, which indicate six defined values. Circle the number for each question that is most descriptive of you. Use this scale:

4 = definitely true
3 = mostly true
2 = undecided whether statement is true or false
1 = mostly false
0 = definitely false

1. I intend to retire by age fifty with enough money to live the good life.   4   3   2   1   0
2. I take pleasure in decision making, particularly when other individuals are involved.   4   3   2   1   0
3. I enjoy now, or have enjoyed in the past, a close relationship with one or both of my parents.   4   3   2   1   0
4. I especially enjoy and appreciate beauty and beautiful objects, events, or things.   4   3   2   1   0
5. I enjoy creating projects of my own.   4   3   2   1   0
6. I feel a rich life has many friends and much friendship in it.   4   3   2   1   0
7. I am most valuable to clubs and groups when I am an officer rather than just a member of the group.   4   3   2   1   0
8. I enjoy both giving and going to parties.   4   3   2   1   0
9. I would choose a class in art, drawing, or sculpture over a class in math.   4   3   2   1   0
10. I think holidays should be spent with family and close relatives.   4   3   2   1   0
11. I like fine things and have expensive tastes.   4   3   2   1   0
12. I think decorating one's apartment or house is a fun thing to do.   4   3   2   1   0
13. I expect to earn more money than the common person on the street.   4   3   2   1   0
14. I take pleasure in buying special gifts for members of my family.   4   3   2   1   0
15. I am often considered a take-charge type of person in small groups and organizations.   4   3   2   1   0
16. Had I the talent, I would write, draw, or create art of some kind.   4   3   2   1   0
17. I have a close friend with whom I talk about almost everything.   4   3   2   1   0
18. I enjoy owning good music, literature, and artwork.   4   3   2   1   0

**FIGURE 12.3   Continued**

| | | | | | |
|---|---|---|---|---|---|
| 19. I think it is good and fun to make something out of nothing. | 4 | 3 | 2 | 1 | 0 |
| 20. I agree with the phrase that money can't buy happiness but it sure makes life much more comfortable. | 4 | 3 | 2 | 1 | 0 |
| 21. I think that spending time with one's family is an activity that is both necessary and enjoyable. | 4 | 3 | 2 | 1 | 0 |
| 22. I often have to aid those close to me in making choices regarding both important and unimportant things in life. | 4 | 3 | 2 | 1 | 0 |
| 23. I would give up sleep in order to spend time with some good friends. | 4 | 3 | 2 | 1 | 0 |
| 24. When I see a new building or house, I first think about how it looks and then how it will be used. | 4 | 3 | 2 | 1 | 0 |

This scale was prepared and tested by Sherwyn P. Morreale.

perspectives.[1] Each theory evaluates the morality of an action based on certain criteria. First, there is utilitarian theory that evaluates behavior based on outcomes or consequences for those involved. Second, there is the theory of rights that emphasizes individuals' entitlements or privileges as members of a society. Finally, there is a theory of justice that emphasizes balance or equity. These three perspectives are a product of our cultural values, what we as a society agree on as right and wrong. It is important to note, especially in light of global business interests, that other cultures may have differing values that define morally acceptable actions. Thus, ethics is not a concrete science. Even in our own culture, solutions to moral dilemmas are not always clear. The three perspectives have the potential to be contradictory with each other.

**Utilitarian Theory**
Utilitarian theory rests on the principle that our actions are judged by their consequences or outcomes. The statement "the ends justify the means" is often used to describe this philosophical viewpoint. Utilitarianism charges decision makers with determining the various possible outcomes in a given situation and then determining which will benefit the greatest number of individuals. To illustrate, several years ago there was a textile factory in New England that was destroyed by fire. This business employed many people in the area. Individuals were, of course, concerned that the company would relocate elsewhere rather than rebuild. Even if the company did rebuild, the employees were worried about how they would live in the meantime. The owners of the organization announced that they planned to

[1]This section was prepared by Maryanne Wanca-Thibault.

rebuild in the same place and offered to pay workers during the downtime with the stipulation that they come back to work at the factory once the construction was complete. Thus, an entire community dependent on a key industry was spared economic disaster.

Was this moral behavior on the part of the owners of the organization? Of course it was. They could have perhaps moved the company to another city or even another country to save on rebuilding costs. What makes this an ethical decision is that the owners evaluated what would be best for the greatest number of individuals, not just the organization, and then took the related action.

## Theory of Rights

The theory of moral rights asserts that all individuals have certain unalienable rights that are defined by society and that these rights must be respected in all situations, including the workplace. The most familiar rights for Americans are those found in the U.S. Constitution's Bill of Rights. Cavanagh, Moberg, and Velasquez (1990) suggest the following as commonly accepted basic moral rights:

1. *The right of free consent.* Individuals have the right to be treated only as they freely consent to be treated.
2. *The right to privacy.* Individuals have a right to a private life outside the purview of the public.
3. *The right to freedom of conscience.* Individuals have the right to refuse to do anything that goes against their moral or religious beliefs.
4. *The right of free speech.* Individuals have the right to speak freely as long as what they say does not violate other's rights.
5. *The right to due process.* Individuals have a right to a fair and impartial hearing to avoid a violation of their rights.

This theory is fairly easy to use as a guideline if individuals agree that we all have the same entitlements. Unlike utilitarian theory that has to weigh the effects of the decision for the majority, the theory of rights is more clear cut. That is, if a right is being violated, the action is not ethical. For example, because the use of e-mail has increased exponentially, there have been instances when employers have monitored employees' messages unbeknownst to employees. There is currently no law that guides an employer in this practice (although several court cases are providing some direction), but there have been judgments made regarding the moral implications of the practice that are based in part on the theory of rights.

Is it ethical to monitor employees' e-mail according to the theory of rights? Most would answer that it is. Although individuals have a right to privacy, that right does not extend to their time on the job. Although monitoring one's correspondence without one's knowledge may lower trust levels, it is not unethical. An organization might even justify the practice using utilitarian theory by concluding that it would benefit the organization (the greatest number) to know what is being communicated by employees.

## Theory of Justice

The theory of justice requires that all decision makers are guided by fairness, impartiality, and equity if their actions are to be considered ethical. Thus, treatment of individuals should not be based on arbitrary characteristics, and any differential treatment should be defendable. Treatment should also be consistent and impartially enforced. For example, most organizations have experienced some form of employee reduction or downsizing. One of the ethical issues that an employer faces is deciding which departments or individuals will be let go. Some situations are less clear cut than others. Do you make the decision based on performance or seniority?

The theory of justice would consider that whatever direction you take, you must be fair, equitable, and impartial. If organizations decide they will base layoffs on seniority, they must first develop a strong reason for their decisions. Then, that criterion must be used in all firing decisions. Finally, any subsequent decisions that affect those who are laid off must apply equally to all (e.g., severance packages).

Think about an ethical decision you have had to make. Which of these perspectives did you use? Would your decision have been the same with each of the three theories? Why? Why not?

## Defining Ethics

So far, this chapter has described values as that which makes something desirable, a subjective assessment of worth that motivates human behavior and serves as a yardstick against which we measure choices. Ethics, although related to values, are the standards by which behaviors are evaluated for their morality: their rightness or wrongness. When applied to human communication, ethics are the moral principles that guide our judgments about the good and bad, right and wrong, of communication, not just communication effectiveness or efficiency.

Johannesen (1983) helps make the distinction between values and ethics:

> Concepts such as material success, individualism, efficiency, thrift, freedom, courage, hard work, prudence, competition, patriotism, compromise, and punctuality all are value standards that have varying degrees of potency in contemporary American culture. But we probably would not view them primarily as ethical standards of right and wrong. Ethical judgments focus more precisely on degrees of rightness and wrongness in human behavior. In condemning someone for being inefficient, conformist, extravagant, lazy, or late, we probably would not also be claiming they are unethical. However, standards such as honesty, truthfulness, fairness, and humaneness usually are used in making ethical judgments of rightness and wrongness in human behavior. (p. 1)

From this perspective it is fair to say that our values influence what we will determine is ethical. Values, however, are our measures of importance, whereas ethics represent our judgments about right and wrong. This close relationship between importance and right and wrong is thought to be a powerful influence on our behavior and how we evaluate the behavior of others.

## Defining Ethical Communication

Is it ever ethical to tell a lie? Am I being ethical if I deliberately withhold information I know you need but have not asked for directly? Should I compliment a person to be pleasant, even though the compliment may be insincere? Is it ethical to withhold from my boss information about a mistake I have made? How honest should someone be in giving criticism to another? Chances are you have had to answer several of these questions in your personal determination of ethical communication behaviors. Daily we come into contact with situations requiring us to make judgments or choices about what is right, ethical, or moral. In the case of a compliment, we may spend little time debating what is ethical, whereas a decision to withhold information from the boss requires serious consideration and considerable worry.

We all face the question of trying to decide what is ethical communication behavior. Our answers to ethical questions are based on our communication competencies—knowledge, sensitivity, skills, and values—and are related to our overall communication effectiveness. As previously discussed, ethical communication is an important prerequisite for effectiveness both for individuals and entire organizations.

**Choice making**
Selection of options based on knowledge of alternatives.

Ronald Arnett (1985), in synthesizing the status of ethics scholarship in communication, points to communication behaviors that support **choice making** as a "central component in the ethics of communication." DeVito (1976), in contrasting ethical and unethical communications, suggests that ethical communication supports individual choice based on accurate information about alternatives. Unethical communication prevents individuals from acquiring needed information important for choices. Examples of unethical behaviors include lying, extreme emotional appeals, and preventing communication.

Thomas Nilsen (1966) describes communication he believes to be morally right as that which provides the listener with the information needed to make a choice and the reasoning that would make a rational decision possible; it must then help the listener to make the most reasonable choice. As Arnett's (1985) status of ethics scholarship suggests, although there is disagreement about what is ethical, there is consensus about the centrality of choice making for ethical communication.

Paul Keller and Charles Brown (1968) suggest that ethical communication fosters conditions for growth and development. Keller (1981) further contends that it is possible to be committed to a position while at the same time remaining open to new information. This openness to new information is viewed as fundamental for growth and development. Ethical communication can also be described as based on values that support the innate worth of individuals. Communication is ethical when it values the essential dignity of human beings and supports the ability of individuals to realize their full potential. Christopher Lyle Johnstone (1993) suggests, "In communication that is ethically sound, the conversations in which we participate—our own inquiries—are always open-ended and inconclusive. While human participation in such conversations may be universal, the meanings of those dialogues are particular and emergent. None of us possess the 'truth.' It is to be found in the 'becoming' of dialogue." Whether ethical communication is described as supporting informed choice making, contributing to growth and development, or valuing the innate worth of human beings, it depends on individuals taking responsibility for personal behaviors. This personal responsibility underscores the importance of developing criteria or guidelines for ethical communication behaviors.

## Influences for Ethical Organizational Communication

Individual value systems, organizational value systems and cultures, and the standards of given professions all influence the ethics of organizational communication. Employees have individual value systems and make individual judgments about the rightness or wrongness of communication behavior. Even in organizations in which openness is encouraged, an individual employee may choose not to notify a supervisor of a serious mistake. The individual judges this behavior as ethical because of his or her intent to correct the problem. The employee's supervisor, on the other hand, may consider it unethical to withhold information that could affect the productivity of the group. An absolute judgment about the rightness or wrongness of the employee's behavior is difficult. It is possible to understand, however, that individual and organizational values can differ, contributing to differing interpretations of ethical behavior.

Organizational communication also is influenced by ethical standards of particular professions. In fact, developing ethical standards is central to any concept of professionalism, and according to Gordon Lippitt and Ronald Lippitt (1978), every profession has found it necessary to establish a code of ethics. Codes of ethics help individuals define behavior within a profession, articulate relationships between professionals and those with whom they come in contact, provide protection to users of the professionals' services against abuses of professionalism, and guide advancement in the state of knowledge in a discipline. The importance of ethical standards for the communication professional is underscored by W. Charles Redding (1979), who described the impact of consultants on the careers or earning capacities of large numbers of individuals. Specifically, Redding contended that irreparable damage can be done in these high-risk consultant-client situations. Jo Sprague and Lucy Freedman (1984) underscore this concern with the argument that professional consultants should be bound by a code of ethics as rigorous as all other members of the helping professions. Redding (1991), in a continuation of his earlier concerns, categorizes common organizational messages that he classifies as unethical. Redding concluded that coercive, destructive, deceptive, intrusive, secretive, and manipulative messages all violate important ethical standards.

Formal codes of ethics such as those that guide the medical and legal professions are not as common in the communications professions. Codes of ethics for journalists do exist but codes are yet to be developed for the more general organizational communication professions.

Particular emphasis has been placed on developing ethical standards for the communication consultant. Behaviors related to client contact, skill representation, establishment of fees for services, handling of client information, and termination of the client-consultant relationship are all subject to standards of ethics. Sue DeWine (1994), describing the work of Wexley and Latham, identifies major categories of behaviors considered improper or unethical for training and development professionals. DeWine writes:

> They include: lack of professional development, violation of confidences, use of cure-all programs, dishonest evaluation of program outcomes, failure to give credit, and abusive treatment of trainees. It is easy for a consultant to assume that having been trained in communication, management, personnel, psychology, etc., he or she can diagnose the corporate ailment before consulting with the patient. This is as foolhardy as the physician who makes a diagnosis over the telephone and then prescribes medication without seeing the patient. (p. 358)

With specific emphasis on the training responsibility for communication professionals, Redding (1979) has proposed the following guidelines for all training activities:

1. Respect for the integrity of the individual trainee
2. Providing opportunity for self-actualization
3. Encouraging the exercise of critical faculties
4. Devoting explicit attention to ethical problems and issues
5. Concern for long-term development of trainees

These guidelines suggest that not only the content of the training but also the presentational approaches and overall responses to trainees should foster an environment in which trainees will explore, think critically, and examine alternatives.

## Evaluating Ethical Behavior

Most of us do not continually think about evaluating our own behavior and the behaviors of others along ethical lines. We do, however, tend to make conscious ethical evaluations when in doubt about what we should do or when the behaviors of others cause us concern about the rightness or wrongness of their actions. An important part of our communication competency is therefore determining how we should approach evaluating ethical communication behaviors.

Karl Wallace (1955) has developed a set of guidelines for the evaluation of behavior that he first applied to our political system and that Rebecca Rubin and Jess Yoder (1985, 14–15) have extended to the assessment of communication skills in an educational setting. These guidelines are appropriate for consideration in most organizational communication situations.

**Habit of search**
Ethical communication that willingly explores the complexity of any issue or problem.

**Habit of justice**
Ethical communication that presents information as openly and fairly as possible with concern for message distortion.

**Habit of public versus private motivations**
Ethical communication based on sharing sources of information, special opinions, motivations, or biases that may influence positions.

**Habit of respect for dissent**
Ethical communication that encourages opposing viewpoints and arguments.

1. The **habit of search.** Ethical communication willingly explores the complexity of any issue or problem. This exploration requires generating valid information and evaluating new and often controversial findings.
2. The **habit of justice.** Ethical communication presents information as openly and fairly as possible and with concern for message distortion. Not only is information accurate, but information is also presented for maximum understanding. When we receive and evaluate information, the habit of justice requires that we examine our own evaluation criteria and potential biases that contribute to distortion in meaning.
3. The **habit of public versus private motivations.** Ethical communication is based on sharing sources of information, special opinions, motivations, or biases that may influence our position. Hidden agendas are discouraged for both message senders and receivers.
4. The **habit of respect for dissent.** Ethical communication not only allows but also encourages opposing viewpoints and arguments. This habit of respect for dissent in an open environment supports generation of the best ideas through thoughtful examination, disagreement, and new idea presentation.

When applied to the organizational setting, these guidelines suggest that individuals and groups are engaging in ethical communication behaviors when they thoughtfully analyze problems and issues, are open to diverse types and sources of information, conduct their deliberations openly without hidden agendas, and not only respect differing viewpoints but also encourage disagreement and dissent to produce superior ideas and solutions. From this perspective, unethical organizational communication behavior suppresses the examination of issues, withholds relevant information to pursue personal interests or motivations, and uses dissent to press for personal rather than organizational advantage.

Lea Stewart (1993, 6–7) has developed a preliminary conceptualization of a multicultural organization that values ethics by:

*Fostering organizational dialogue.* Johannesen . . . contends that "the essential movement in dialogue, according to Buber, is turning toward, outgoing to, and reaching for the other. And a basic element in dialogue is 'seeing the other' or 'experiencing the other side.'"

*Embracing multiple discourses.* Organizational conflict may arise because of the multiple discourses of diverse organizational members. . . . Addressing this conflict ethically means recognizing its growth potential.

*Empowering all employees.* Employees should be empowered to make decisions about work that they are most familiar with and provide meaningful input to management.

*Leading by "walking the talk."* A leader's personal commitment to diversity should be based on both economic and moral considerations.

*Developing interpersonal communication skills of managers.* Managers need to be more inclusive in their decision making. They need to clearly communicate expectations, ask questions to increase their understanding, listen and show empathy, develop clarity across cultures and language differences, and provide ongoing feedback with sensitivity to individual differences.

*Encouraging employees to understand themselves.* Because of this (our) multiple group membership, we need to understand the groups to which we belong before we can communicate effectively with members of other groups.

## THE ORGANIZATIONAL CONUNDRUM

The word *conundrum* refers to a problem or a puzzle. The organizational conundrums discussed here illustrate the problems and perplexing dilemmas that routinely raise ethical issues for all organizational members.

Carl Anderson (1997) identifies four organizational goals that are often framed as incompatible: economic performance, competence, the learning organization, and the organization as community. These incompatibilities are a foundation for ethical dilemmas. Economic performance refers to the goal of profit, with its inherent measurement and assumption that some organizations will succeed while others fail. Competence refers to the tangible or intangible assets that yield sustainable competitive advantage. To improve the competencies supporting efficiency, methods such as restructuring, reengineering, quality control, process redesign, and downsizing have been increasingly employed. The learning organization refers to an organization's capacity to change strategies, tactics, or performance. Anderson explains:

> Decisions affecting learning are concerned with continual improvement, meaningful criticism, individual learning and creativity, and corporate renewal. Improved strategies and tactics are invented to provide more rapid and effective responses to external threats. Learning avoids narrow and rigid dependence on precedence, unquestioning adherence to a common set of assumptions, and the trap of overconfidence that comes with success. All of these are especially necessary in highly competitive situations. (p. 28)

The organization as community refers to the respect for rights and fulfillment of duty. As Anderson (1997) suggests:

> Moral positions are congruent with economic and other positions. Decisions affecting community create situations in which people willingly cooperate for the benefit of all. A strong community frames the work of the organization in a context that elicits significant levels of trust and respect. Because of higher trust, strong com-

munities should have a clear sense of goals and purpose, attract people with a high level of commitment to these goals, improve internal integration and coordination, open communication, increase risk taking, and build leadership that relies on expertise rather than legitimate authority. (p. 28)

Anderson concludes:

These four goals are in fact interdependent. Over the long run, competence and learning are necessary to sustain economic performance. A strong community is fundamental to all three. Dilemmas occur because decisions that improve competence, learning, and performance can easily hurt community. (p. 28)

Ann Plamondon (1997) identifies organizational climates in which ethical dilemmas arise. Specifically, she describes a climate of broken organizational promises, a climate in which no one takes responsibility, a climate of denying participation and dissent, a climate requiring whistle-blowing, and a climate of cultural relativism. Broken promises occur when promises do not match organizational action. Promises of increased compensation, promotions, participation in decision making, and many other forms of desired change are often made to stimulate improvement and then are either ignored or cannot be fulfilled. Bureaucracies often encourage shifting responsibility from level to level or to no particular organizational position or person. No one is responsible for delaying needed action. "I was just following orders or policy" is a common statement used to deflect responsibility for bad decisions, poor actions, and unethical behaviors. Hierarchical structures often limit participation and dissent. Not only can this limitation contribute to poor decisions, but also it often becomes a form of control requiring employees to support decisions and actions with which they have significant disagreement. Illegal behavior in a climate of control contributes to the need for whistle-blowing, the exposure of illegal behavior to organizational outsiders. Finally, a climate of cultural relativism suggests that in a global environment, ethical behavior will be different for different cultures. Certainly cultures vary in a global environment. A belief in a climate of cultural relativism, however, has been used as defense for selling products in other countries that are banned in the U.S. as well as for engaging in questionable workplace and environmental practices. Numerous examples can be found throughout the globe of leaders engaging in practices they know will harm others or the environment with the defense that they create jobs and profits critical for economic development. Can you think of recent examples in which any of these "climates" have gained public notoriety? What are the ethical issues involved in product recalls, environmental abuses, or whistle-blowing cases? Have you ever been caught in one of these climates? What did you do? What should you have done?

Michael Hackman and Craig Johnson (2000) identify ethical dilemmas for leaders and link courageous followership with ethical responsibilities. Hackman and Johnson suggest that leaders are faced with questions of honesty, responsibility, power, and loyalty. What are the ethics of the organizational lie? Is it necessary?

At times is it needed for motivation? Have you ever encouraged someone even though you thought they might not be able to perform well? Was that a lie or a necessary motivation? Hackman and Johnson contend:

> Positions of leadership are associated with social and material power. Leaders may reap social benefits such as status, privilege, or respect as well as material benefits including salaries and other forms of compensation. Is it ethical for a leader to take advantage of his or her position to achieve personal power or prestige? Should a leader's concern always be for the good of the collective?. . . . How much responsibility does a leader bear in considering the extent to which his or her actions influence others? (p. 335)

Issues of power are always present. All leaders are faced with daily decisions about how much power to exercise with regard to followers, peers, and even those above them in a chain of command. For example, what should a leader do about asking a follower for compliance when the follower has a moral objection to the leader's request? Finally, to what extent does the leader have an ethical responsibility for supporting followers who are censured, criticized, or otherwise held publicly responsible for following courses of action the leader may have developed?

Hackman and Johnson (2000) describe as courageous followership the ethical responsibilities for those who report to leaders. They suggest that assuming responsibility for themselves and taking accountable action are ethical responsibilities. Furthermore, the courage to serve refers to the ethical responsibility of supporting leaders through hard and sometimes unglamorous work. Followers also are asked to exhibit the ethical responsibility of challenge. As Hackman and Johnson state: "Inappropriate behavior damages the relationship between leaders and followers and threatens the purpose of the organization. Leaders may break the law; scream or use demeaning language with employees; display an arrogant attitude; engage in sexual harassment; abuse drugs and alcohol; and misuse funds. Courageous followers need to confront leaders acting in a destructive manner." Hackman and Johnson discuss the courage to participate in transformation, with followers identifying what needs to be changed, providing honest feedback, suggesting resources, creating a supportive environment, modeling openness to change and empathy, and providing positive reinforcement for positive new behaviors. Finally, Hackman and Johnson discuss the courage to leave: "When leaders are unwilling to change, courageous followers may take principled action by resigning from the organization. Departure is justified when the leader's behaviors clash with the leader's self-proclaimed values or the values of the group, or when the leader degrades or endangers others."

The organizational conundrums discussed all ask in one way or another the question of whether an organization can support a core of social values, act in ethical ways, and become or stay financially successful in an increasingly complex world. George Cheney (1999) uses the term *organizational integrity* to describe whether organizations can keep to humane and democratic commitments while growing, enjoying financial success, and perhaps even becoming more centralized and bureaucratized. The issues are complex and critical. They are not easy. In addition, the conundrums include us all. The next section specifically discusses common ethical dilemmas that we frequently face in our organizational lives.

# ETHICAL DILEMMAS IN ORGANIZATIONAL COMMUNICATION

Although ethical issues can arise over virtually any type of communication, several recurring organizational communication situations have ethical implications. These situations—representing skills and abilities, communication behaviors related to money, communication behaviors related to information collection and dissemination, personal communication behaviors, communication behaviors related to technology, and planned organizational communication (internal policies and decisions and external communication)—are frequently encountered by the communication professional.

## Representing Skills and Abilities

We present our skills and abilities to potential employers when seeking a job. The way in which we communicate what we know reflects an ethical decision about fair representation of our abilities. Most of us have known someone who has told an interviewer about a skill that we knew the individual did not possess. Although we would say that this behavior is not strictly ethical, we know our friend is highly motivated and will attempt to do a good job if hired. Does this motivation make the behavior acceptable, however? What is the ethical standard we should apply?

Once hired, we may attempt to seek good assignments designed to help us advance. How do we represent our abilities as compared with others in our work group? Do we keep information about mistakes from our supervisor to appear more competent than our peers? Do we blame others for problems even though we legitimately bear part of the responsibility? How can we behave ethically and still risk what others might think about our competencies if they know we have made a major mistake?

When in a supervisory or managerial position, we are responsible for giving feedback to others about their performance. Are we hesitant to give negative information to a problem employee, thereby creating a false sense of security? Are we making an important ethical decision, or are we making a realistic appraisal that the person in question can't handle bad news and would be demoralized if we were more direct?

The representation of skills and abilities also influences problem identification. Consultants and human resource development specialists are frequently asked to help define organizational problems and propose training and related development activities for problem solution. These professionals are continually faced with the dilemma of defining a problem they may or may not have the skills to solve. When the consultant is external to the organization, defining a problem as needing skills other than those the consultant possesses costs the consultant potential earnings. The organization must hire someone else to meet its needs. On the other hand, defining the problem or need in terms of services the consultant can provide is subject to serious questions of integrity. The concerns are much the same for the internal communication professional.

An example from the development of the training plan of a major East Coast retailer can help to illustrate this dilemma. The company's personnel director, at the request of the president, designed and administered a company-wide training needs assessment survey to develop a training program for all employees. The company's previous training efforts had been sporadic and generally were in response to requests from particular departments. As a result, sales employees had received more training than any other single group. The personnel director, who specialized in sales training, was sensitive to the president's request and interpreted it as an implied criticism of his past efforts. The training survey contained twenty-four items assessing needs relating to interpersonal relationships and ten items relating to specific areas such as performance appraisal, affirmative action, and administration of company benefits. Critics of the personnel director's efforts pointed out that the organization would continue to emphasize sales training based on the content items in the survey. They noted that most of the twenty-four items relating to working relationships were items covered in courses already offered through personnel. Although a training plan and budget were established from the survey, the personnel director's credibility with some of the president's staff was eroded because of their questions about his ethics in assessing the real needs of the organization rather than the needs he was capable of meeting. In reality, the personnel director may have been correct that the items represented in the survey were the most crucial for overall needs assessment. Our example does not define for us whether or not the personnel director engaged in ethical behavior. The example illustrates the dilemma the director faced and how his behavior was subject to the ethical evaluations of others.

## Communication Behaviors Related to Money

Communication surrounding fees for services, salaries, and personal versus corporate money is subject to ethical evaluation. The communication consultant, in pricing a training program to a potential client, must base the worth of services on personal credentials, program complexity, general market value of the program, and fees the consulting organization is expecting to pay. Should a consultant, for example, charge different organizations different fees for essentially the same services? How should fees and services be described? How can the consultant establish charges for diagnosing a problem that is not fully understood? The answers to these and other questions represent decisions about ethical communication.

An ethical question is whether general salary information should be available to all employees or whether salaries should remain confidential to individual employees. The communication of performance review and wage administration information is also a management communication decision with ethical consequences. Individuals communicate their ethical standards regarding organizational money when they use expense accounts, buy services or products for the organization, and establish department budgets. One way to examine our communication behaviors relating to organizational money is to determine whether we would approve of our behavior if we were the sole owner of the company.

Many communication professionals face ethical dilemmas as a result of payment for services. It is not uncommon, for example, for a communication consultant to work simultaneously for competing organizations. Do both clients need to know that the consultant is employed by the other? Internal communication specialists encounter information concerning personal problems of employees such as alcoholism or drug abuse. Are these specialists ever entitled to withhold information from the organization that pays their salary? How should these decisions be examined? All these questions and more have ethical implications for the behaviors of individuals and for overall organizational policy.

## Communication Behaviors Related to Information Collection and Dissemination

Most communication professionals are involved in collecting organizational information. They interview, conduct surveys, facilitate meetings, advise and counsel individuals, review documents, and in a variety of other ways generate data important to the conduct of their jobs. During data-collection activities, ethical decisions are made concerning what should remain confidential, who has a need to know, how accurate the information is, and what the criteria for interpretation are. These same ethical issues are related to information dissemination. Should sensitive information be kept private, going only to affected individuals? Does a guarantee of confidentiality prohibit the use of the information, even though the organization could be improved if the information surfaced? Who has a need to know? How accurate is the information, and is it subject to varying interpretations? Most experienced professionals know their ability to handle these sensitive questions ethically contributes to their personal credibility. Even if ethical considerations were not important in and of themselves, practicing communication professionals find that the exercise of ethical standards is essential to their overall organizational effectiveness. Research on effective leaders supports this perspective. As you will recall from Chapter 7, Warren Bennis and Burt Nanus (1985) found that a characteristic of effective leaders was their ability to generate trust and behave consistently. Outstanding leaders practiced their individual standards (ethics and values) in a manner that helped others accept the challenge of their organizational vision.

## Personal Communication Behaviors

Thus far we have been talking about the ethics of organizational communication as related to specific types of organizational responsibilities. Although these areas include personal behaviors, there is yet another area of personal behavior important for consideration. This area, broadly described as our personal communication style, refers to the ethics of our individual behaviors, regardless of our job responsibilities. Do we, for example, behave autocratically, attempting to win at any cost? Is this autocratic preference ethical when it stifles the good ideas of others? Do we, as a result of high communication apprehension or a preference for conflict avoidance, refuse to participate in decision making even though we have information appropriate to the decision? When employed by the organization, is it ethical to withhold the best of our thinking? Does our style help others to examine issues critically, or do we use the power of our positions or the force of our personalities to get our own way? How can we examine the ethics of our approaches? These questions and others can be answered through self-assessment and understanding of our personal ethical standards.

## Communication Behaviors and Technology

As more and more workers use technology on a daily basis, issues about its workplace use increase. Many people today and more in the future will have desktop access to e-mail, the Internet, organizational databases, video conferencing, and a host of other programs and links. Some organizations regularly monitor the e-mail and Internet use of their employees. Others limit Internet access to only selected sites known to be associated with business needs. Still others publish policies directing the type of communication behaviors expected on e-mail and when using the Internet. Many organizations, for example, prohibit individual advertising when using company electronic resources. Others, by contrast, establish web pages for employee exchange of personal information, including the desire to sell personal property. All these issues have ethical and trust implications. Do you know anyone who uses a corporate e-mail account for personal correspondence? How much time is devoted to this activity during a workday? Is that ethical? Why? Why not? How many people use their organization's Internet provider for personal Internet access? What are the implications of these behaviors?

In addition to the various uses made of organizational technologies, ethical questions can be asked about the approach to communication we select when using telemediated channels. Research consistently supports that many will be more harsh and critical using e-mail than in face-to-face interactions. Others use e-mail to raise issues they will not raise in other forums. There are strengths and weaknesses to these approaches. The question to ask, however, is whether it is ethical to use a technology that distances us from our receivers to engage in an exchange we will not "own" in less distanced communication. How can we approach understanding this issue? What does your own personal behavior suggest?

## Planned Organizational Communication

Organizations regularly communicate a variety of policies and procedures with ethical implications. Hiring processes and decisions, promotional policies, assignment of work, and working conditions are all evaluated for their ethical consequences. Do organizations genuinely open positions and promotions to the most qualified, or are those in a close network of in-group relationships most likely to succeed? Are all employees given opportunities for development and challenging work assignments, or do entire segments of the work force have little challenge and opportunity? Are working conditions free of hazards both physically and psychologically? Are employees able to engage in free statements of their concerns and positions? The answers to these questions and others become the ethical climate of the organization.

Organizations also communicate ethical decisions to their external publics. The quality of products and services can be evaluated for ethical dimensions. Planned organizational communication such as advertising, public relations, and government and stockholder interactions is more likely to be governed by formal codes of ethics or legal standards and requirements than other aspects of organizational communication. Advertising is subject to government regulations that include ethical standards about what constitutes truth in advertising. Full disclosure of financial information is required for stockholder and government relationships, and public relations efforts are subject to ethical standards established by the journalism profession. Despite these standards, we can all think of times when we have questioned the ethics of advertising and can remember when organizations attempted to manipulate the public with less than full disclosure about products or services. The global environment is placing a special challenge on understanding ethical communication when ethical standards vary greatly across cultures.

# DEVELOPING ETHICAL STANDARDS IN ORGANIZATIONAL COMMUNICATION

We have been discussing how we can determine whether communication is ethical. We also identified some common ethical dilemmas faced by communication professionals. We have not, however, attempted to apply ethical standards to the behavior choices we can expect to encounter in organizational settings. The following shortened versions of fourteen organizational dilemmas were encountered during my consulting experiences. For each dilemma, attempt to determine what you would actually do if faced by this situation and what you should do. If what you would do and should do are different, state why. Finally, after analyzing all fourteen situations, attempt to determine what criteria you were using in applying ethical standards.

## Ethical Dilemmas in Organizational Communication

**1.** You are the newly appointed personnel director for a large beverage distributor. Your new job responsibilities include screening all applicants for promotions to management positions. Your company's usual procedure is for the personnel director to screen applicants and select the top three for further interviews with management. You also know that the president of the company does not want a woman on his personal staff. Your current decision is difficult because your most recent vacancy is on the president's personal staff and your top three applicants are female. You can send the three applicants to the president and wait to see what happens. You can rethink your selection criteria and try to have a male applicant in the top three. You can reopen the position, hoping to attract additional qualified applicants. You can confront the president about his discriminatory posture. You also have other options. What would you do? What should you do?

2.  You are part of a team of people who are involved in administering and interpreting an in-depth set of surveys designed to help managers in your company better understand how their managers and subordinates view their effectiveness. The results of the surveys are intended to be developmental, and individual members of your team will meet with each manager to interpret the results and develop action plans for improvements. You are puzzled when you see the first computer printouts of the survey results. Managers who you know are well respected and effective are receiving low scores compared with a national sample of managers from similar industries. You contact the company that compiled the results and ask questions about their sample. Your contact does not provide satisfactory information. Your peers believe you should go ahead and interpret the results to the managers. You believe the results are suspect and question whether they should be presented. Your boss believes the results should be presented. After all, corporate headquarters uses the survey with no problems. You can do as your peers want you to do. You can ask for a meeting with your peers and your boss in hopes of convincing them of your concerns. You can present the results to your group of managers and tell them you don't have much confidence in the findings. You can refuse to participate further in the program. You have other options. What would you do? What should you do?

3.  A crew member from the night shift's manufacturing group has come to you as her personnel liaison with a concern about drug use on the production line. She won't give you any specific details for fear of those involved finding out who has turned them in. She suggests that you should investigate immediately but warns against involving her in any way. She asks you not to tell the other personnel liaisons because the grapevine has it that one of them may be involved. You can go to your boss and work with her in deciding what to do next. You can try to investigate on your own. You can bring up the drug problems the plant is experiencing at a staff meeting and watch closely to see if there are any unusual reactions from your peers. You can tell your source to give you more specific information before you will do anything. You can ignore the problem because of lack of evidence. You have other options. What would you do? What should you do?

4.  You are in the training department of a large West Coast hospital. Your department is responsible for all training for nonmedical staff and management training for medical department supervisors and nursing staff. Your boss has been

in his position for twenty-two years. When asked to develop a five-year report of your department's activities, your analysis of the records shows that one consultant has been paid over $50,000 for approximately six training sessions per year. This fee schedule is more than twice what other consultants working in similar subject areas have charged the hospital. You decide to pull the consultant's file and investigate. Much to your surprise, there is no formal contract or course evaluations. You ask your boss about the consultant in question, only to be told he is none of your concern. The secretary in your department warns you that the consultant is a special friend of your boss and that you had better let the matter drop. You can forget the whole thing and finish the report. You can press your boss for more information. You can ask the secretary to help you locate the missing information. You can go to the finance department and ask for its copy of the contract. You can put this deficiency in your final report. You have other options. What would you do? What should you do?

**5.** You have overheard a conversation between your manager and the manager of a department in which your best friend is employed. From their conversation, it is apparent that your friend is not pleasing her manager and she will definitely be passed over for the promotion she badly wants. You don't want to see her hurt, and you happen to know she has a job offer from another group within your organization. Should you tell her about the conversation and urge her to take the new offer? Should you remain silent because of the manner in which you heard the information? Should you go to your boss and tell him that you accidentally overheard the conversation and are concerned because your friend might turn down a good job offer? Should you urge your friend to confront her boss? You have other options. What would you do? What should you do?

**6.** You are the lead copywriter in an advertising agency handling a major chemical products account. Your copy is frequently criticized by the chemical manufacturer's marketing director. He wants a stronger sell, even if that means omitting much of the disclaimer information associated with the safe use of the products. He contends that people buying chemicals should take individual responsibility for safety and that the company should not be required to devote scarce ad and package label space to full disclosure of the potential hazards. You realize that he may even be willing to test whether government regulating agencies will restrain his actions if he refuses to comply with industry product labeling requirements. The issue comes to a head when you receive copy proofs changed by the marketing director to omit disclosure information that you believe should remain in the new ad series. Your immediate boss is out of town on vacation and cannot be reached. You either have to let the changes go or confront the marketing director. You know he will not appreciate your interference. You can let the copy go as is. (You have documented evidence that the marketing director, not your agency, made the changes.) You can refuse to make the changes, thereby jeopardizing the account. You can ask to be removed from the account. You can go to the marketing manager's boss in the chemical company. You have other options. What would you do? What should you do?

**7.** You are a consultant specializing in management communication training programs. You have been hired by a prestigious building products manufacturer to conduct a series of programs for its top management staff. The programs go well, and you are excited about future business with other branches of the organization. The president of the company invites you to lunch and congratulates you on your work. He has recommended extending your contract and indicates that it will be the beginning of a long and mutually satisfactory relationship. He then tells you of an unwritten condition in your contract: he wants a quarterly report made directly to him on promising individuals in the branch offices. He believes your contact in the training classes will give you the opportunity to spot talent that he may have little opportunity to recognize. He insists the report should be confidential, because his personnel department would object. You can do as the president requests. You can advise him of your concerns about evaluating people during training sessions not designed for that purpose. You can object to the need for secrecy in your appraisals. You can say nothing and think about what to do next. You have other options. What would you do? What should you do?

**8.** You have received a job offer from one of your current employer's principal competitors. The offer was unsolicited and has come as a surprise. Although this type of offer is not uncommon in the advertising business, you are unsure how to respond. The vice president who is urging you to come to work for her also mentioned that one of your current employer's largest accounts is talking with her group about changing agencies. You have reason to believe that the account is pleased with your work and wonder if her offer is not aimed at increasing the chances of taking business away from your employer. So far, the vice president has not asked you any questions about the account. You are scheduled to meet her for lunch next week. Should you tell your employer that you are considering another position? Should you refuse to discuss the account in question if the vice president mentions it? How can you learn whether the offer has a hidden business agenda? Do you have a responsibility to your current employer to tell him a major account is being solicited by another firm? What would you do? What should you do?

**9.** You are the newest member of your company's field sales staff. Before being assigned to your own group of accounts, you spent three months making sales calls with experienced sales personnel. During that time, you became aware of customer complaints about quality defects in two of the six product lines you represent. The salespeople you worked with assured you that the company was aware of the problem and was working hard to lower the defective shipments. In your first solo presentation, your potential customer asks you about rumors that some of your product lines are having defect problems. He wants to know very specifically what he can expect if he places a large order. You want to make the sale. You have not investigated the extent of the defects problem or when the company expects to have it solved. You know your manager expects you to secure an order from this customer. How should you answer the customer? Can you make the sale if you admit the defects problem? What will happen if you don't? What would your manager have you do? What are your other options? What would you do? What should you do?

**10.** You are the member of a task force asked to recommend to the city council how the city's Park and Recreation Department can better serve low-income members of your community. Two members of your group believe the city government should reduce its budget, and they view your assignment as an ideal way to make that statement. You disagree. The task force is charged with making programming recommendations. The Park and Recreation Department is charged with incorporating those recommendations into their budget, which must be approved by the council. You think that increased programs for low-income areas of your community are positive and hope some of your recommendations will be part of the final report. Several of the group's members agree with you, two strongly disagree, and several are undecided. At the next-to-last task force meeting before the report is due to council, a reporter asks to interview a member of the task force in order to get a progress update. The two members with whom you have had the most disagreements are late to the meeting. Others in the group suggest you talk with the reporter. You agree, hoping for an opportunity to express your support for low-income programming. As the interview begins, you wonder whether your remarks should reflect the various perspectives present in the group or whether it is appropriate to represent your personal view. Should you tell the reporter that members both support and disapprove of increased park and recreation programming? Should you tell the reporter that the final report to council is very likely to contain a dissenting opinion and you are not sure which side of the issue will receive majority support? Will this type of dissent weaken the effectiveness of the report? Should you represent your position because the other two members are late and would have had an opportunity to speak to the press had they arrived on time? What would you do? What should you do?

**11.** You are a member of a project team charged with designing a new service support training program for your organization's 150 customer support representatives. The representatives are generally knowledgeable but resistant to a new training program. Your team members include two of your peers from the training department and two customer support representatives. The initial design meetings have been productive but you become aware that the two customer support representatives expect you and your coworkers to do the work. They will critique what you propose. Further, you know that at least one of the customer support representatives is talking with others in his work group about your ideas. You have learned that some representatives think you don't know what the work really is and can't possibly design a good program. You want the program to be good but are concerned with the rumors and lack of work from two members of your team. What would you do? What should you do?

**12.** You are a member of a self-directed work team charged with processing travel requests for over 3,000 salespeople worldwide. Your team has been praised for quality work and cost savings provided to the corporation. In fact, your group has reduced processing costs by 40 percent over previous groups. One longtime member of your team is not pulling her share of the load. Jane is excellent with her accounts but is not helping other team members when they are overloaded. Jane is popular with management and many of the sales people you support. Other team members have asked you to talk with Jane. You think that the entire team should engage in this conversation. To make matters worse, you learn that Jane, but not the rest of the team, has received a coveted customer support award. Jane has not mentioned this award to the team. What would you do? What should you do?

**13.** You are a senior member of a management team that has just learned one of its major products may have a serious electrical defect. Two consumer deaths are associated with product use. Your corporate attorneys suggest that the company must immediately deny any responsibility. Your public relations people need to issue a statement. Your manufacturing manager reports that he believes there are no problems for which the company is liable. Most of your peers want to take a strong denial position based on long-term consumer loyalty to the product in question. You remember an accident in the lab while the product was under development. The accident resulted in severe burns to two testing technicians. You are assured there is no connection. You are pressured to agree to a course of action that will permit the public relations people to issue a release supporting the product. What would you do? What should you do?

**14.** You have been asked by your boss to evaluate the e-commerce strategy the marketing department of your company is proposing. You have reason to believe that your boss doesn't really understand the proposal because she has little experience with the Internet. You don't have the experience to do the evaluation but know you must make a response within the next week. You decide to review the Internet strategies of your major competitors. To your surprise, you find that your company's marketing proposal ignores several features for customer service that all your competitors are using. When you discuss this omission with the director of marketing, he laughs at you for what he considers your lack of experience and suggests that you have no right to question his judgment. You are concerned about your lack of experience but believe you have some valid concerns. You don't want to put your boss in a bad position by opposing a proposal from another department. What would you do? What should you do?

After analyzing these examples, would you say that the behaviors you would do and should do were always the same? If they were different, what caused the difference? What contributed to similarities? Was it difficult to determine what was ethical in a given situation? Can you identify the standards you used as your criteria? As a result of these examples, can you see the relationship between competency and ethics?

## SUMMARY

Values are the subjective assessments we make about the relative worth of a quality or object. These assessments are thought to guide our behavior in making choices and judgments. Both individuals and organizations have value systems that are expressed through communication behaviors. In an organizational sense, values are part of the shared realities generated through organizational communication. These shared values are reflected in organizational myths, stories, decision making, and thematic and tactical communication rules. Individual values have been described as theoretical, economic, aesthetic, social, and political. Workplace values include concern for locus of control, self-esteem, tolerance of ambiguity, social judgment, and risk taking. Milton Rokeach has identified both terminal and instrumental values. Appraising an individual value system is important for job and career decisions. Ethics are the standards by which behaviors are evaluated for morality, for rightness or wrongness. Utilitarian, rights, and justice theories have been developed as criteria for ethical decision making. When applied to human communication, ethics are the moral principles that guide our judgments about the good and bad, the right and wrong of communication, not just communication effectiveness or efficiency. Ethical communication is an important prerequisite for communication effectiveness and has as a central focus behaviors that encourage choice making, foster conditions for growth and development, and value the innate worth of human beings. Individual and organizational value systems and the standards of a given profession all influence the ethics of organizational communication. Ethical communication can be evaluated by using Karl Wallace's criteria of the habit of search, the habit of justice, the habit of public versus private motivations, and the habit of respect for dissent. A multicultural organization that values ethics fosters organizational dialogue, embraces multiple discourses, empowers all employees, leads by "walking the talk," develops interpersonal communication skills of managers, and encourages employees to understand themselves. Finally, ethical communication results from thoughtful analysis of potential dilemmas in organizational communication.

---

# WORKSHOP

1.  Divide into groups of four or six members each and discuss the fourteen examples of ethical dilemmas presented in this chapter. Compare your individual responses with those of other group members. As a group, what would you do? What should you do?

2.  Either individually or in small groups, write a statement describing the values of your ideal organization. Describe your organization's ethical communication behaviors.

3.  Organizations A and B have differing value systems. Divide the class into groups and assign each group an organization A or organization B value system. Both organizations face the same problem. Using the stated values as a basis, each group should determine how its organization would solve the problem. Report your solutions to the class as a whole. (See p. 461.)

4.  The Coronado Youth Employment and Recreational Services Case illustrates value and ethical differences between a board of directors and an executive director. These clashes result in serious authority and responsibility problems. Describe this case in terms of values and ethics. Prepare to advise Margaret Rims and the board of directors. (See pp. 461–463.)

## Scoring the Values Appraisal Exercise

*Instructions* (Part 1). Below are the six defined values indicated by the twenty-four statements in Figure 12.3. Enter the number you circled for each statement next to the number for that statement. Then total your score for each value.

| Values: | Money | Power | Family | Aesthetic | Creative | Social |
|---|---|---|---|---|---|---|
| | 1 _____ | 2 _____ | 3 _____ | 4 _____ | 5 _____ | 6 _____ |
| | 11 _____ | 7 _____ | 10 _____ | 9 _____ | 12 _____ | 8 _____ |
| | 13 _____ | 15 _____ | 14 _____ | 18 _____ | 16 _____ | 17 _____ |
| | 20 _____ | 22 _____ | 21 _____ | 24 _____ | 19 _____ | 23 _____ |
| Totals: | _____ | _____ | _____ | _____ | _____ | _____ |

*Instructions* (Part 2). Now plot your own personal values profile. Use the preceding totals for each of the six values and plot them on the chart that follows.

| Money | Power | Family | Aesthetic | Creative | Social |
|---|---|---|---|---|---|

16 _____

15 _____

14 _____

13 _____

12 _____

11 _____

10 _____

9 _____

8 _____

7 _____

6 _____

5 _____

4 _____

3 _____

2 _____

1 _____

0 _____

## Organizational Values and Decision-Making Exercise

### ORGANIZATION A VALUE SYSTEM

*Locus of control.* Little emphasis on connection between individual efforts and the success or failure of the organization.

*Self-esteem.* Little emphasis on recognition for work or positive feedback.

*Tolerance of ambiguity.* Low tolerance for ambiguity and high support for one-right-answer approach.

*Social judgment.* Little specific concern about working relationships with others.

*Risk taking.* High need for security and deliberative action.

### ORGANIZATION B VALUE SYSTEM

*Locus of control.* High emphasis on connection between individual efforts and the success or failure of the organization.

*Self-esteem.* High emphasis on recognition for work; positive feedback.

*Tolerance of ambiguity.* High tolerance for ambiguity and low support for one-right-answer approach.

*Risk taking.* Low need for security and high support for risk taking.

## The Problem

Reducing the work force through layoffs.

## The Situation

The company for which you work is faced with a decreased demand for several of its products. As a result, the company president plans to announce and implement a 3 percent reduction in the staff of your division. The actual reduction will consist of about 50 employees from a division work force of 1,350. The layoffs could start as early as the first week of January. It is now the middle of October.

## The Assignments

Given the values of your organization, decide how you should implement this reduction in force. Your plan for implementation will be conveyed to the company president.

■ ■ ■ ■ ■ ▬▬▬▬▬▬▬▬▬▬▬▬▬▬▬▬▬▬▬▬▬▬▬▬▬▬▬

# THE CORONADO YOUTH EMPLOYMENT AND RECREATIONAL SERVICES CASE

The Youth Employment and Recreational Services (YERS) program has a long and distinguished history in Coronado, California, a growing city of 1.2 million. In recent years, however, minority community members have pressed for increased services and facilities in parts of town with substantial minority populations. These requests have created dissension and growing controversy among YERS staff and members of the board of directors.

*(continued)*

Margaret Rims was promoted to executive director of the Coronado YERS in 1993 after having been with the organization for twenty-five years. Margaret began her career in recreational development while attending Coronado University and has seen the YERS program grow from a one-person staff with limited programs in a single location to a staff of fifteen offering services at seven Coronado sites.

Over the years, Margaret Rims has been given credit for the growth of the recreation program. She has also been asked by the National Council of Youth Employment and Recreational Services to lead several regional and national workshops on recreation program development.

When Margaret Rims applied in 1993 for the position of executive director, several staff and board members were surprised because most assumed Margaret was happy in her recreational development role. Several members of the board voiced concern regarding Margaret's overall administrative qualifications, but the prevailing sentiment supported her promotion.

Margaret Rims became executive director of the Coronado YERS in the climate of mounting pressure to increase services and facilities in the heavily populated minority areas of northeast Coronado. Several local groups also questioned minority representation on the YERS staff and board. Margaret felt these pressures were best ignored. She disagreed with several members of the board and staff who urged her to develop plans to increase minority involvement.

Margaret's strongest staff support came from her friend and personnel director, Jack Smith. Jack has been YERS personnel director for eighteen years. He has not been pleased with increasing personnel requirements established by the national executive council of YERS. Specifically, he has disagreed with detailing job descriptions and the institution of grievance procedures for employees. Jack believes employers should have more latitude than these policies and procedures afford. Some minority job applicants have charged that Jack was responsible for keeping them from being employed at YERS.

In early 1994, several influential minority community members met with Margaret Rims to discuss YERS program expansion. Margaret told the group she could not recommend the expansion they desired. At the meeting, Bill Hillis, a black lawyer in Coronado, confronted Margaret with questions about Jack Smith's hiring practices. Margaret stoutly defended Jack.

The citizens group was not content with Margaret's responses. Bill Hillis contacted the YERS president, Dr. Atkins, and requested a formal meeting with the board of directors. The group, with Hillis as spokesperson, also expressed concern to national YERS officials. National YERS funds, along with membership dues, are the primary source of funding for YERS programs.

The national director of YERS contacted Dr. Atkins to express his concern. He further stated his apprehension that any publicity of the issue might adversely affect the YERS fund drive scheduled to begin within the month.

Unknown to Margaret Rims, the board of directors met with Bill Hillis and the group who originally confronted Margaret. Dr. Atkins and the board pledged support of program development in northeast Coronado and promised to look into the hiring practices directed by Jack Smith.

At the next formal meeting, the board informed Margaret of the need to include this promised expansion in 1995 planning. No specific actions were taken regarding either Jack Smith or current hiring practices. At the same meeting, the firm of Jones and Belew, certified public accountants for YERS, reported that revenues from membership were down 10 percent from the previous year and that facilities maintenance costs were increasing an unexpected 8 percent. Those board members who had originally questioned Margaret's capabilities became vocal in their criticism.

In the next few months, the division between the board and Margaret Rims became open and hostile. Dr. Atkins received reports that Margaret stated in a staff meeting that she had been at YERS before any of the board and would be there when they all were gone.

The rift flared into the open when Margaret submitted the YERS program proposal for 1995 to the board of directors. No inclusion of the promised programming in northeast Coronado was made. Margaret walked out of the meeting in anger. She refused to return telephone calls from Dr. Atkins.

Dr. Atkins called an emergency meeting of the board of directors. Sentiment ran high, and the board voted to terminate Margaret Rims. Two members objected, claiming the action was in direct violation of national YERS policy, which called for warning and probation before termination of any employee. One member further expressed concern about community reaction to terminating a twenty-five-year employee.

Community leaders openly criticized both Margaret Rims and the board. Margaret retained a lawyer and named Dr. Atkins and several members of the board in a defamation of character suit. She also claimed specific damages for loss of retirement benefits because of termination. During the initial months of 1995, membership revenues dropped by 12 percent and staff morale and productivity were extremely low. Jack Smith was believed by Dr. Atkins to be a focal point of internal disruption and a source of continuing information for Margaret Rims. Amid these problems the search for a new executive director began.

### QUESTIONS FOR DISCUSSION
1. What are the ethical and value issues in this case?
2. Describe how the flow of information throughout YERS affected the problem.
3. How would you describe this communication climate?
4. What should Margaret Rims do? What should the board do?

# REFERENCES AND SUGGESTED READINGS

Allport, G., P. Vernon, and G. Lindzey. 1960. *Study of values.* Boston: Houghton Mifflin.

Anderson, C. 1997. Values-based management. *Academy of Management Executive* 11(4): 25–46.

Arnett, R. C. 1985. *The status of ethics scholarship in speech communication journals from 1915 to 1985.* Paper presented at the Speech Communication Association Convention, November, Denver, CO.

Bennis, W., and B. Nanus. 1985. *Leaders: The strategies for taking charge.* New York: Harper and Row.

Cavanagh, G., D. Moberg, and M. Velasquez. 1990. The ethics of organizational politics. In *Foundations of organizational communication: A reader,* eds. S. Corman, S. Banks, C. Bantz, and M. Mayer, pp. 243–254. New York: Longman.

Cheney, G. 1999. *Values at work: Employee participation meets market pressure at Mondragón.* Ithaca, NY: ILR Press/Cornell.

Cox, T. 1993. *Cultural diversity in organizations.* San Francisco: Berrett-Koehler.

Deal, T. E., and A. A. Kennedy. 1982. *Corporate cultures: The rites and rituals of corporate life.* Reading, MA: Addison-Wesley.

DeVito, J. A. 1976. *The interpersonal communication book.* New York: Harper and Row.

DeVito, J. A. 1978. *Communicology: An introduction to the study of communication.* New York: Harper and Row.

DeWine, S. 1994. *The consultant's craft.* New York: St. Martin's.

Goodstein, L. D. 1983. Managers, values, and organization development. *Group and Organization Studies* 8(2): 203–220.

Hackman, M., and C. Johnson. 2000. *Leadership: A communication perspective.* Prospect Heights, IL.: Waveland.

Howe, R., M. Howe, and M. Mindell. 1982. *Management values inventory.* San Diego, CA: University Associates.

Howell, W. S., and E. G. Bormann. 1988. *The process of presentational speaking.* 2d ed. New York: Harper and Row.

Johannesen, R. L. 1983. *Ethics in human communication.* 2d ed. Prospect Heights, IL: Waveland Press.

Johnstone, C. L. 1993. *Ontological vision as ground for communication ethics: A response to the challenge of postmodernism.* Paper presented at the Speech Communication Association Convention, November, Miami.

Keller, P. W. 1981. Interpersonal dissent and the ethics of dialogue. *Communication* 6: 287–303.

Keller, P. W., and C. T. Brown. 1968. An interpersonal ethic for communication. *Journal of Communication* 18(1): 73–81.

Lippitt, G., and R. Lippitt. 1978. *The consulting process in action.* La Jolla, CA: University Associates.

Nilsen, T. R. 1966. *Ethics of speech communication.* Indianapolis: Bobbs-Merrill.

Palmer, D. D., J. F. Veiga, and J. A. Vora. 1981. Personal values in managerial decision making: Value-cluster approach in two cultures. *Group and Organization Studies* 6(2): 224–234.

Plamondon, A. 1997. Ethics in the workplace: The role of organizational communication. In *Organizational communication: Theory and behavior,* ed. P. Yuhas Byers, pp. 90–113. Boston: Allyn and Bacon.

Posner, B., J. Kouzes, and W. Schmidt. 1985. Shared values make a difference: An empirical test of corporate culture. *Human Resource Management* 24(3): 293–309.

Redding, W. C. 1979. Graduate education and the communication consultant: Playing God for a fee. *Communication Education* 28(4): 346–352.

Redding, W. C. 1984. *Professionalism in training—Guidelines for a code of ethics.* Paper presented at the Speech Communication Association Convention, November, Chicago.

Redding, W. C. 1991. *Unethical messages in the organizational context.* Paper presented at the International Communication Association Convention, May, Chicago.

Rokeach, M. 1973. *The nature of human values.* New York: Free Press.

Rubin, R., and J. Yoder. 1985. Ethical issues in the evaluation of communication behavior. *Communication Education* 34: 13–17.

Shockley-Zalabak, P., and D. Morley. 1989. Adhering to organizational culture: What does it mean? Why does it matter? *Group and Organization Studies* 14(4): 483–500.

Sprague, J., and L. Freedman. 1984. *The ethics of organization intervention.* Paper presented at the Speech Communication Association Convention, November, Chicago.

Stewart, L. 1993. *Ethical issues in organizational diversity.* Paper presented at the International Communication Association Convention, May, Washington, DC.

Strubler, D. 1993. *Ethics in hybrid Japanese/American organizations: A question of whose values.* Paper presented at the Speech Communication Association Convention, November, Miami.

Wallace, K. R. 1955. An ethical basis of communication. *Speech Teacher* 4(1): 1–9.

# PUTTING IT ALL TOGETHER

The next several pages of the text contain a self-assessment instrument and cases designed to develop communication competency by applying the theory you have been studying. The self-assessment instrument has been designed to help guide your choices about additional educational preparation and to identify areas for continuing competency development. The cases in the appendix are taken from real experiences of individuals with organizational communication responsibilities. These final pages have been designed to help you pull together the various competencies this text has been seeking to develop. You should again complete the self-assessment of competency needs that was presented in Chapter 1 (Table 1.1, repeated here as Table A.1). Compare your answers from the beginning of the course with your answers now. What have you accomplished? What remains to be done?

After you have completed your self-evaluation, compile a list of competencies you rate as highly developed. Next compile lists for those competency items rated moderately developed, somewhat limited, and needing development. What is your plan for continued growth?

## CASES

The following cases are taken from real experiences of individuals with organizational communication responsibilities. "A Conflict of Interest" and "Can Newspeople Challenge My Company?" stimulate our thinking about important issues of ethics and values, whereas "What Gets Cut?" raises both communication and decision-making concerns. "Karen Mason's Management Briefing Disaster" deals with the use of humor in organizations. The "I Thought I Gave Them Everything" case and "The Barquette Cleaning Company Case" both deal with delegation and relationships between supervisors and the employees they supervise. "Ann Cartwright, Vice President of Drummond Industries" and "The Grayson-Gerald Consulting Case" address male-female organizational issues, whereas the "The Rule Here Is to Do What Management Wants" and "Two Men—Two Issues—Two Japanese Workers" present diversity and cultural concerns to stimulate our thinking. "The Case of the Internal Communications Dilemma" identifies problems with which a communication professional must deal. "The Case of the Reluctant Team Member," "I Thought We Were a Team," "The Case of the 'Walking the Talk' Manager," and "Working Together at a Distance" address individual needs in

## TABLE A.1 Self-Assessment of Personal Development Needs

The following organizational communication competencies are presented for your self-evaluation. For each area you are asked to determine whether your present competencies are highly developed, moderately developed, somewhat limited, or needing development.

| As I complete this course I would describe my KNOWLEDGE in . . . | Highly Developed | Moderately Developed | Somewhat Limited | Needing Development |
|---|---|---|---|---|
| 1. defining and understanding organizational communication as . . . | | | | |
| 2. understanding major theories or how organizations work as . . . | | | | |
| 3. determining how an individual experiences organizational life as . . . | | | | |
| 4. describing what organizational conflict is and how it relates to productive organizations as . . . | | | | |
| 5. identifying characteristics of leadership and management communication as . . . | | | | |
| 6. understanding decision making and problem solving as . . . | | | | |
| 7. understanding strategic organizational communication as . . . | | | | |
| 8. locating career opportunities in organizational communication as . . . | | | | |
| 9. distinguishing between values and ethics in organizational communication as . . . | | | | |

**TABLE A.1** *(continued)*

| As I complete this course I would describe my SENSITIVITY to . . . | Highly Developed | Moderately Developed | Somewhat Limited | Needing Development |
|---|---|---|---|---|
| 10. my personal responsibilities for organizational communication as . . . | | | | |
| 11. how "shared realities" are generated through organizational communication as . . . | | | | |
| 12. why and how people work together as . . . | | | | |
| 13. what motivates me and what is likely to motivate others as . . . | | | | |
| 14. the importance of interpersonal relationships with supervisors, peers, and subordinates as . . . | | | | |
| 15. personal preferences for a variety of approaches to conflict as . . . | | | | |
| 16. the influence of the environment of organizations as . . . | | | | |
| 17. personal preferences for leadership and management communication as . . . | | | | |
| 18. organizational influences for decision making and problem solving as . . . | | | | |
| 19. past achievements, values, and skills that can guide career choices as . . . | | | | |
| 20. how values and ethics contribute to organizational effectiveness as . . . | | | | |

*(continued)*

**TABLE A.1** *(continued)*

| As I complete this course I would describe my SKILLS in . . . | Highly Developed | Moderately Developed | Somewhat Limited | Needing Development |
|---|---|---|---|---|
| 21. analyzing a variety of organizational problems as . . . | | | | |
| 22. developing effective organizational messages as . . . | | | | |
| 23. engaging in active listening as . . . | | | | |
| 24. contributing to supportive organizational environments as . . . | | | | |
| 25. participating in productive conflict management as . . . | | | | |
| 26. leadership communication as . . . | | | | |
| 27. leading and participating in effective group meetings as . . . | | | | |
| 28. fact-finding and evaluation as . . . | | | | |
| 29. gathering information for decision making and problem solving as . . . | | | | |
| 30. analyzing data for decision making and problem solving as . . . | | | | |
| 31. developing and making public presentations as . . . | | | | |
| 32. using a variety of communications technologies as . . . | | | | |

**TABLE A.1** *(continued)*

| As I complete this course I would describe my VALUES for . . . | Highly Developed | Moderately Developed | Somewhat Limited | Needing Development |
|---|---|---|---|---|
| 33. accepting personal responsibility for communication as . . . | | | | |
| 34. relating individual communication behavior to organizational effectiveness as . . . | | | | |
| 35. using conflict for productive outcomes as . . . | | | | |
| 36. professional applications of organizational communication as . . . | | | | |
| 37. determining how leaders and managers should behave as . . . | | | | |
| 38. influencing my career choices as . . . | | | | |
| 39. understanding organizational values, ethics, and dilemmas as . . . | | | | |

organizations, the dynamics of a team-based structure, and how people at the top of organizations view teams differently from others. "What Happened to the Value of Networking?" also addresses life in teams but from the standpoint of technologically connected groups and their difficulties in communicating and maintaining a sense of connection to the team. "Career and Personal Needs Just Don't Mix" addresses the complicated life of a dual-career couple. Finally, "The Power of Symbols: Creating Corporate Identity at Agilent Technologies" describes the use of strategic organizational communication during a major change.

## A Conflict of Interest

### Summer Kircher, CT, A.S.C.P.[1]

Gerald Burnes, M.D., is administrator of St. Vincent's Hospital Laboratory. The twenty-four-hours-a-day, seven-days-a-week operation employs 165 people. Bob

---

[1]This case was prepared by Summer Kircher (CT, A.S.C.P.), cytologist, Albany School of Medicine. Kircher was a graduate student at the University of Colorado and a research assistant in the communication department at the time the essay was written.

Warft is the lab's medical technologist. Bob holds a master's degree in business administration and oversees production, budgeting, and quality control. He reports directly to Dr. Burnes. Bob also is in regular contact with seventeen supervisors who monitor their own sections.

George Rogers is the supervisor of a small section with three employees with very specific subspecialty training. Testing and the evaluation of this group's results are shared only by members of this section and the pathologist, Dr. Burnes. George has worked for Dr. Burnes for fifteen years. Janice Pearson has been in this section, reporting to George, for six months. She is conscientious, eager, and a recent graduate of medical technology school. Janice is determined to do well, because there are few available jobs in this subspecialty.

Over the years, George and Dr. Burnes have developed a personal relationship similar to that of father and son. Their lack of objectivity with each other has created past problems when determining a diagnosis. Instead of offering two clear perspectives, they will agree to avoid a conflict. George's technical skills are good when he is attentive to details. After fifteen years at the same job, however, he has become less quality conscious then he used to be. George works fewer total hours than the other supervisors and does not keep regular hours. Also, George is the only supervisor who reports directly to Dr. Burnes. He uses their relationship to register lab complaints and personal problems.

Bob Warft does not attempt to deal with George as long as George is under Dr. Burnes's supervision and protection. Bob can only register complaints from other supervisors about George's attitude and special privileges.

Although interpersonal relationships have been strained, George's position did not seem to affect patient care. Recently, however, Janice uncovered some serious errors George had made. Janice took the cases to Dr. Burnes, who quietly corrected the diagnoses. The time lapse between the initial and the corrected diagnoses was several months. These mistakes could have serious consequences for the patients. Dr. Burnes did not formally reprimand George Rogers or take other action.

### QUESTIONS FOR DISCUSSION

1. What are the organizational communication problems in this case?
2. What should Janice do?
3. How would you advise Dr. Burnes?
4. How can this problem be prevented in the future?

## Can Newspeople Challenge My Company?

### Dr. Kim Walker[2]

John Tyler is public relations director for a midwestern power company in the process of constructing a nuclear power plant to expand customer service. Local

[2]This case was prepared by Dr. Kim Walker following his research on interactions between Illinois Power and the crew of the television program *60 Minutes*. Although the case is fictional, it addresses critical issues about the public's right to know, journalistic responsibility, and the role of the communications professional in controversial organizational situations. Walker (B.A., Millikin University; M.S., Ph.D., Southern Illinois University) is on the faculty at the University of Colorado, Colorado Springs.

residents in the areas to be served by the new nuclear plant are mixed in their reactions to the facility going up in their backyards. As a result of continuing national media coverage of nuclear power issues, local media have begun frequent coverage of the plant's progress. In particular, media attention has focused on the power company's requests to the local commerce commission for rate increases and the cost overruns and delays encountered in plant construction.

John Tyler has been advised by his board of directors that he should escalate company public relations efforts to ensure a more favorable climate for the utility as it prepares to again ask the commerce commission for a rate increase. Amid preparation of an aggressive campaign on the benefits of nuclear power, John receives a call from a network news team desiring to interview management involved with plant construction. The news team assures John of fair and balanced coverage and agrees that power company officials can tape everything the network shoots for its story.

John is worried because he knows that construction cost overruns have contributed to the utility seeking its latest rate increase. He is concerned that network reporters could use this fact to generate negative publicity, just what his management is attempting to avoid. John also knows that refusing to speak with the press can be interpreted as hiding important information to which the public has legitimate access. He also is troubled by potential conflict between his management and high journalistic standards.

### QUESTIONS FOR DISCUSSION
1. Should John agree to the interviews?
2. What might happen if he refuses?
3. How can he advise his management to deal with this situation?
4. What are the ethical and value issues involved?
5. How would you advise John to proceed?

## What Gets Cut?

### Sherwyn P. Morreale[3]

The staff of the local Club of America for Boys (CAB) council is in conflict regarding some editorial decisions on a recently completed promotional film for the CAB program. The five-person executive staff handled the production of the half-hour film, which is intended to be used to promote membership and to raise funds in the local community. Part of the film was shot at the local CAB. Several boys, who happened by chance to be African American, were shown riding horseback without the use of protective riding helmets.

The executive staff is meeting to decide how to handle the part of the film shot at the local CAB camp. The finished film has been viewed. Seven of the thirty minutes are questionable and perhaps should be edited. The portion in question is

[3]Sherwyn P. Morreale (Ph.D., University of Denver, 1989) is associate director of the National Communication Association. Her research focuses on public speaking evaluation, oral communication competency assessment, and curriculum development. Her articles have appeared in such journals as *Communication Education, Education,* and *Instructional Psychology*.

aesthetically effective but does show several boys without riding helmets. If the seven minutes are cut out, the film will be less effective and will be too short for the media purposes for which it was intended. If that portion is not edited out, however, the lack of safety gear may raise some controversy in the local community. It is almost winter, so new footage that will blend seasonally with the existing film is not possible.

Present at the staff meeting are the following five persons:

Barbara, the executive director of the staff, who was hired by an all-white board of directors, is held in low esteem by her staff. The staff resent having a female director of a boys' organization. Barbara's position is that any decision that satisfies the staff is satisfactory with her.

Gary, the camp director, has extensive camping background. He is accustomed to making all decisions for the camp himself. It is his position that the film must be edited and the questionable seven minutes cut out.

Craig, the public relations director, has extensive background in the CAB program. He grew up as a CAB and has worked professionally for this council for several years. He is sensitive to the program's public image but also values the moral standards that CAB represents. Craig is ambivalent regarding the course of action for the questionable footage.

Sam, the fund development director, also has background in the CAB program but only recently began to work for the local council. He was hired by Barbara because of his ability to raise funds for the program. He is of the opinion that cutting the film will negatively affect the fundraising efforts already planned for the upcoming year. He believes the motivation for editing the film relates to the appearance of more African American than white boys in the footage and not to safety standards or the lack of safety helmets.

William, the membership director, is the only African American staff member. He was passed over by the board of directors when Barbara was hired as executive director. He has worked for the local council for many years and was considered well qualified for the position of director. He believes that some discriminatory attitudes may be affecting the editing decision but believes the best decision for the membership drive should be made. He is not sure what that decision is.

### QUESTIONS FOR DISCUSSION
1. If you were the executive director of the CAB council, how would you proceed?
2. What are the communication issues in the case?
3. What type of decision-making process would you use?

## Karen Mason's Management Briefing Disaster

Karen was humiliated. How could they? Why did John and Shirley have it in for her? Everyone at the meeting knew she was embarrassed, and there was no telling what most of the managers thought of her.

Karen Mason was upset as a result of a practical joke her two coworkers, John and Shirley, had played on her during her first presentation at Quality Products' quarterly management meeting. They knew she was nervous and wanted to make a good impression. John and Shirley thought that putting cartoon slides in place of her opening graphs would be funny and appreciated as a good joke by both Karen and the management team. After all, they had her original slides ready to hand to her as soon as the laughter subsided. They had no way of knowing that the joke would totally unnerve her. Although everyone had laughed initially, Karen knew that most felt sorry for her as she ended up reading her remarks.

John and Shirley thought Karen was being ridiculous. Their department was known for practical jokes, and Karen should be expected to join in if she really wanted to be accepted. Neither John nor Shirley had intended to disrupt the presentation. Karen should have better control of herself.

### QUESTIONS FOR DISCUSSION
1. Does Karen have a right to be angry?
2. Is it possible that Karen doesn't have a sense of humor?
3. Are John and Shirley to blame?
4. Can it be that both points of view are correct?
5. What would you do if you were Karen, John, or Shirley?

## I Thought I Gave Them Everything

Henry Gonzales has been the manager of Quality Foods' 7th Street store for four years. Henry is considered among Quality's top managers for making the once-unprofitable store the sales leader of the company. Gonzales works hard and expects the same of all store employees. He emphasizes financial rewards for hard work and has initiated a pay incentive plan for supervisors who are able to cut costs or increase sales in their respective departments.

Henry was angry and upset when the personnel director for Quality informed him that two of his leading supervisors had requested transfers to other Quality stores. Didn't they realize they were in the best of Quality's stores and making more money than their counterparts in less profitable operations? Did they really need more of his time, as the personnel director intimated? Why should grown people need hand-holding? Didn't they recognize that he was busy and always worked for the best interests of the store and his supervisors?

Henry wondered what he should do next. He felt inclined just to let them leave and see how they would like to work under another manager. On the other hand, they were good workers. Should he talk with them? What would he say?

Henry Gonzales is like many busy managers who lose touch with the wants and needs of those who work for them.

### QUESTIONS FOR DISCUSSION
1. As you study Henry's problem, think about what you would advise Henry to do.
2. What does Henry need to know about communication competency?
3. Discuss the relationship between communication and motivation.

## Ann Cartwright, Vice President of Drummond Industries

Ann Cartwright was perplexed and disturbed by the conversation taking place in hushed tones outside her office door. Apparently Tom Jackson and Jim Jurgers, both Drummond vice presidents, didn't realize Ann's door was open and that she could hear their remarks. They were saying that Ann had been promoted to vice president of marketing because she was a woman and that the president, George Miller, was unwilling to criticize her because he didn't know how to deal with a woman on his staff.

Ann had been promoted six months ago when her longtime boss, the vice president of marketing, had retired. Ann had been successful as the manager of marketing and was widely credited with developing excellent marketing plans for several new product lines and for expanding the services of the marketing department to assist the product development group in its identification of potential new lines. Her subordinates, both male and female, liked to work for her and believed her to be fair and direct. In fact, almost everyone seemed genuinely excited and pleased when her promotion was announced.

Ann wondered what the conversation meant and what she should do. She knew she needed both men's cooperation and certainly the trust of Drummond's president. Should she confront Tom and Jim? Should she go to the president? Should she ignore the remarks and act as if nothing has happened? What, if anything, does this mean for her future?

Ann Cartwright's experience is similar to those reported by female professionals in all types of organizational positions. Although the number of female managers increases daily, acceptance into previously all-male management teams is mixed, often affecting the quality of working relationships. Think about what Ann should do. What communication competencies does Ann need to work with Tom and Jim?

### QUESTIONS FOR DISCUSSION

1. In your view, what barriers does Ann face? What barriers exist for women in organizations?
2. If you were a corporate president or CEO, what specific measures might you take to ensure equality between the sexes in your organization?
3. What can women themselves do to accelerate more favorable attitudes toward managerial women?

## The Rule Here Is to Do What Management Wants

Jim Robinson liked people on his staff to get along with each other and support group decisions. As president of Firestone Insurance, he had a history of promoting mostly white men who agreed with him. He was known for avoiding men or women who engaged in confrontation and disagreement. Jerry Douglas ought to know that. He had been the sales manager for Firestone for five years and was only lately exhibiting a level of disagreement that made Robinson uncomfortable. Also, Sally Marshall, the head of finance and Firestone's only woman manager, seemed to be siding with Douglas.

Jerry was contending that Firestone had to hire a more diverse sales staff because additional competitors had entered several of their good sales territories targeting Firestone customers with international affiliates. Unlike these competitors, Firestone's field sales staff were mostly white men with no international experience. Jim and others on his staff felt Jerry was being pessimistic and negative. Sally seemed to agree with Jerry, although she wasn't as outspoken as he was.

Jerry was disgusted with all his peers except Sally. The others knew he was right but were afraid to confront Jim. They told Jerry to be patient and said that Jim would eventually see his point of view. Jerry believed that being patient would cost Firestone considerable money and might cause them to lose key accounts currently being pursued by their competition.

Both Jim and Jerry were concerned. Neither liked what was happening. What would you advise Jim to do? Jerry?

### QUESTIONS FOR DISCUSSION

1. Describe the culture of Firestone Insurance. How does Jim's world view influence what is happening between Jim and Jerry?
2. What can Jerry do to influence Jim's thinking?

## The Barquette Cleaning Company Case

### David Gehring, B.S.[4], R. Jeffrey Ringer, Ph.D.[5]

The Barquette Cleaning Company is a small but growing manufacturer of industrial detergents and other cleaning products. Its first product—Factorub—was developed in 1914 and was originally sold to small and medium-sized factories in the Midwest. It was a popular product partly because it was a local product and partly because of the shrewd marketing techniques used by the company. The success of Factorub allowed Barquette to develop a complete line of industrial cleaning products. These products have also proven to be popular.

Within the last five years, Barquette has taken its cleansers nationwide and has been very successful. Barquette established a regional office in five regions of

---

[4]David W. Gehring is an accountant for the Minneapolis-based certified public accounting firm of Brunberg Thoresen and Associates, Ltd. He received his B.S. from St. Cloud State University. Gehring's experience includes audit and tax compliance in addition to the installation and implementation of microcomputer-based accounting systems for businesses.

[5]R. Jeffrey Ringer received his doctorate from Ohio University in 1987 in interpersonal communication theory. He is currently an associate professor of speech communication at St. Cloud State University, where he teaches courses in interpersonal and organizational communication. He has authored and coauthored several other communication case studies and exercises. His current research interests include communication among members of the boards of directors of nonprofit organizations and communication in gay male relationships.

the country and hired several salespeople for each region. Now, the company has decided to explore a new market by developing a line of cleansers for the home.

Barquette is a highly centralized organization with clearly defined job descriptions. Line workers are for the most part unskilled laborers who become fairly proficient in achieving their job tasks after only a short training period. The work is mentally and physically unchallenging, but workers don't seem to mind, and company morale is high and complaints rare. They are treated fairly and paid better than most others in the industry. Many of the other comparably sized factories in the area have been forced to lay off employees, but Barquette continues to grow. Barquette also tends to promote from within. The first line supervisors have generally come from the production workers' ranks. These first line supervisors oversee the production workers. The first line supervisors report to the general supervisors, who report directly to the vice presidents.

Barquette has always had a close tie to the local community, Barquerville. Many families have had a long history with the company. It was not uncommon for several generations (grandparents, fathers and mothers, sons and daughters) to all work at the company at the same time. Many of the other employees have a sense of loyalty to the company, although because the company is growing, there has been an influx of new employees who don't have these same feelings.

Paul Stevens is a general supervisor for Barquette. He started on the production line while he was in college. He had been a dependable, intelligent worker and was popular among the people with whom he worked. When he received his management degree he was offered a management trainee position. He was familiar with the company and had always been impressed by its management.

Paul's supervisory position was newly created as part of the firm's expansion into the new product line. The line workers and first line supervisors beneath him are very experienced for the most part, and they were recruited out of some of the company's top units.

Paul sees his promotion as an opportunity to prove his ability to his superiors. He believes that the company's current procedures are a little outdated. Most decision making comes from the top down, with low-level employees having very little input. For example, previously the general supervisors set the goals for the unit, with the production workers and first line supervisors having little or no input. Other types of decisions such as production changes and job description changes tend to be made at the top as well. Paul thinks it is time for a change. Paul has been tracking chemical waste levels within the company and believes that, although his company has a relatively low level of waste, it could be reduced even more to improve efficiency. He believes that the production workers and line supervisors, if given the opportunity, probably have a lot of suggestions on how to minimize waste, so they should be given the opportunity to develop their own plans to do so. He wants his unit to be the most progressive and efficient in the company. This opportunity is his chance to implement his ideas.

Paul decided that he would implement a form of total quality management in his unit. He would develop quality circles to encourage the line workers to examine the problems they experience and develop their own solutions for these problems. The first problem was how to reduce waste. He would also encourage group decision making by asking line supervisors to work together to form goals for the unit. He was excited about what he called his progressive approach and anxious to implement it.

Three first line supervisors report to Paul. Kari Parker is the senior of the three. Kari has worked for the company for twenty years. She started immediately after graduating from high school. For her first ten years she was a production worker. She had worked at a variety of stations and proved to be a dependable worker who learned new jobs thoroughly and followed rules closely. After ten years she was promoted to first line supervisor and has performed that job well too. Her production workers liked her because she created a sense of stability for them. She was consistent when enforcing the rules and dependable when she made promises. Unbeknownst to Paul, however, Kari was resistant to change. She liked things the way they were and tended to maintain the status quo. That is probably why her line workers liked her so much. They always knew what to expect.

Paul called Kari to his office. Because she was the line supervisor with the most seniority, he thought that it would be best to discuss some of his proposed changes with her first. After some general discussion on the new products, he got to the point.

"Kari, I think that we have the opportunity to make our unit the best in the company. With a few changes, we'll be head and shoulders above the rest of the firm."

Kari responded awkwardly. "What kind of changes are you talking about?"

Paul seemed a little surprised at Kari's defensive tone but continued, "It may seem like a lot at first, but as we go along everyone will come out for the better. Here's my plan. I'd like for you to do all the production run planning, timetables, and forecasts. That will allow me to devote my time to meeting with our suppliers and buyers. It's going to take a lot of pushing for some of them to give our company a shot. We're going up against the big boys now, and it will be tough going for a while. After I've met with our suppliers and buyers and you've finished your projections, I'd like for you to meet with the other line supervisors and set goals for our unit. I'd like you also to develop quality circles among all three production lines. I want them to have input into decisions made around here. Encourage them to think of ways to minimize waste. And, uh, I'd like you to develop an overall plan on how to improve the performance of our production workers. I'll have more details on this plan for you later this week."

Paul ended by saying, "Within a few months, Kari, we'll be the envy of this firm. We're starting at the bottom, and we're going straight to the top. Do you have any questions?"

Kari felt overwhelmed by everything Paul had asked her to do. She had grown more and more tense as the conversation continued. She responded, "No," and left quickly.

Paul noticed that she seemed a little upset but hadn't given it much concern because she left so quickly. He knew he'd be seeing her later in the week, so if anything was wrong he could check it out then. He returned to hammering out the final details of his strategy.

Kari returned to her desk feeling as if she was in over her head. She could do the production run planning, timetables, and forecasts, but she didn't know anything about quality circles, and she was used to working independently, so she didn't know if she wanted to be responsible for goal setting along with the other two line supervisors. She was encouraged to take this job with this new unit because she was so well liked by her employees and she had lots of experience. She was good at doing her job. Yet after this meeting her job seemed like a new job, and she wasn't sure if she could do it. She yearned for the security of her old job. She spent the rest of the day with her production workers.

The next morning Paul was called in to see his supervisor, Vice President Jan Cummings. It was apparent that Jan wasn't happy. As Paul sat down, she slammed down what appeared to be nearly a dozen transfer requests onto her desk. "Explain these, Paul. We've only been working on this project for a couple of months now and your senior first line supervisor and half of her production workers want out of your unit."

This case involves a supervisor who delegates to a subordinate. Consider the following questions when analyzing this situation.

### QUESTIONS FOR DISCUSSION
1. How is delegation related to communication?
2. How is the Barquette Cleaning Company structured? How does this affect delegation?
3. How did Paul give the instructions to Kari? How did the use of clichés impact the instructions?
4. Why did Kari react the way she did? Why did the production workers ask for transfers too?
5. Paul wanted to allow for more input from his subordinates. Did his behaviors contradict this desire? To what extent?
6. Why didn't Paul respond to the nonverbal behaviors he noticed in Kari? What impact did this have on the interaction?

## Two Men—Two Issues—Two Japanese Workers

### Rieko McAdams[6]

*Young Mr. Kobayashi*
It is 5:30 P.M. and all employees are still at their desks working. They will head to a bar from work, socialize, and possibly brainstorm the next project. Mr. Kobayashi thinks about his wife and a baby girl not yet six months old. He wishes to see the baby and have a relaxed evening with his wife. Mr. Kobayashi knows that he is

[6]Rieko McAdams (B.A. in organizational communication, University of Colorado at Colorado Springs), originally from Japan, teaches Japanese to American students in elementary, secondary, and postsecondary schools. Prior to moving to the United States, McAdams worked in high-level administrative positions in Japan. Her observations are based on real circumstances, although the names have been altered.

expected to go to the bar with his colleagues. He knows what his coworkers will say if he says he would like to go home to his wife. He knows what his superiors would think about him for not joining the group: no dedication, no drive, no loyalty, and henpecked. Kobayashi's company is an elite company in which employees dedicate their total lives by working long hours, socializing after work hours, and seeking to be recognized as company men. Kobayashi does not want to sell his body and soul to the company, but he also does not want to see others promoted before he is. He wants to be successful but would like to have time of his own.

### Older Mr. Kobayashi

Mr. Kobayashi, fifty-six years old and loyal to his company, believes he is being pressured to quit his job. He has worked in the same company for over thirty years. His boss believes that Mr. Kobayashi does not exhibit the enthusiasm and drive he once did. Mr. Kobayashi's salary is twice the amount of hiring two younger employees with less experience but new and creative ideas. Mr. Kobayashi has three more years until retirement and wishes to stay with the company until then. His family includes two college students in addition to his wife. His boss offers him a choice: transfer to another branch or be demoted to a lower position. Mr. Kobayashi does not wish to move to another city. He is concerned because he believes that in Japan, a man with no work is lost. Japanese people are devoted to their work, and being fired or demoted is a terrible problem for the Japanese worker. Mr. Kobayashi's boss has no performance reason to fire him, so he pressures him to quit. This type of situation is called kata-tataki-no-kei in Japanese.

#### QUESTIONS FOR DISCUSSION
1. Discuss the problems of the two men from a cultural perspective.
2. How similar are these problems between the United States and Japan?
3. What are the communication issues in the cases?

## The Grayson-Gerald Consulting Case

### Maryanne Wanca-Thibault, Ph.D.

Grayson-Gerald Consulting was founded in 1992 by Tom Grayson and Joni Gerald. Both have advanced degrees and had broad experience in the corporate world prior to their partnership. Tom, fifty-two, has a bachelor's degree in business, an M.B.A., and twenty-five years of experience as a salesperson and regional sales manager for a large telecommunications firm. Joni, thirty-five, has a Ph.D. in organizational communication and worked as a corporate trainer for the same firm for five years. During a recent downsizing Joni was let go and Tom opted for early retirement. Several months later they joined forces to provide highly technical sales and motivational training for medium- to large-sized telecommunications companies.

During the first three years of operation, they handled the client load with the help of two secretaries and a technical writer. As their client list grew, however, it became evident that they needed to hire at least two additional trainers and one support person.

Tom and Joni had always worked well together as a team, but Tom spent the majority of his time in front of the audience. He often told Joni that a predominately male sales force responds better to another man with similar experience. Because Joni had always enjoyed playing a behind-the-scenes role, she hadn't challenged Tom's philosophy. An increasing number of their clients, however, had been hiring qualified woman and were specifically requesting female consultants who might be sensitive to a variety of different issues that some of the female trainees faced.

Thus, when it came to hiring the new trainers, Joni was adamant that at least one should be a women. Tom, on the other hand, refused to even consider the most qualified woman. As the time grew near to make a final decision, their differences became a source of increasing tension. They finally decided to each present a list of their five most qualified candidates and narrow the field from there. Of course, Joni selected five very qualified women and Tom presented his list of five equally qualified men.

**QUESTIONS FOR DISCUSSION**
1. What is happening between Joni and Tom in this situation?
2. What would you suggest Joni do?
3. What would you suggest Tom do?
4. How might feminist theory be applied in this case study?

## I Thought We Were a Team

Nicki Jordan had been on a fast career track from the moment she went to work for the Federation of High School Athletes. Her drive to succeed and friendly style were exactly what the executive director, Tom Welsh, wanted. Nicki was quickly assigned to work with corporate sponsors and the Federation's board. Over the years, she became known as Tom's right hand. No one was surprised when, after Nicki had been with the organization for seven years, she was promoted to associate director and was groomed to replace Tom when he announced his pending retirement.

Nicki's first year as executive director went smoothly. She promoted her longtime colleague, Jim Masters, to her former associate director position. Jim was a highly competent accountant who had a history of working well with internal systems as well as the corporate sponsors who were the financial foundation of the Federation. In her second year as executive director, Nicki decided the growth of the Federation was such that reorganization of some of the work units was in order. She hired consultants known for their ability to understand complex organizations and develop design alternatives. She asked Jim to head the project both internally and with the consultants. Nicki was surprised when the consultants requested a private and confidential meeting. When they told her that Jim was viewed as a dictator by much of the staff, she could not believe what she was hearing. Not one person had previously raised an issue about Jim's approach. Further, Jim always told her about the positive input he received from others relative to his areas of responsibility. Were the consultants wrong? Had she missed this important information? How could she be so wrong about Jim? More important, why had no one come to her sooner?

### QUESTIONS FOR DISCUSSION
1. What should Nicki do next?
2. How can she determine for herself the accuracy of the consultants' concerns?
3. If the consultants are right about Jim, what contributed to her missing this key information?

## The Case of the Internal Communications Dilemma

You are new in the public relations department of Simplex Division of Newbury Corporation, a developer and manufacturer of educational products for young children. Your job is internal communications, and your boss, the head of public relations, has indicated that you have a major challenge before you.

The new head of Simplex Division is not trusted by many of the employees. Some grudgingly admit that Loren Marks came into a tough situation, but even his supporters say that he doesn't communicate well. During Marks's first six months, fifty employees were laid off; two long-term employees were demoted, resulting in grievances and lawsuits against Simplex; and significant dollars were moved from research and development to manufacturing to attempt to upgrade old systems presumed to be creating quality problems. Loren fired the research and development manager, a popular leader of eighteen years, and replaced him with a creative but emotional person from another division. Corporate organizational climate audits placed Simplex Division near the bottom among all Newbury divisions in employee satisfaction. Employees focused numerous negative comments on Loren Marks. Employees were also vocal about the lack of recognition, a fear of reprisal for speaking up, the use of organizational resources, and the lack of understanding their future.

### QUESTIONS FOR DISCUSSION
1. As the person responsible for internal communications, what would you do first when receiving this information?
2. How might you gather information from employees?
3. Who would you involve in planning and decision making?
4. How would you advise Loren Marks?
5. What channels would you use?
6. How would you evaluate your results?

## The Case of the Reluctant Team Member

Rhonda Jenkins had worked in the credit collection department of Bass Medical Supply Corporation for over fifteen years. The announcement that credit was converting to a team-based structure came as a shock, especially amid rumors that the company would begin another round of layoffs in the fourth quarter. Rhonda liked credit and was afraid that the teams meant reductions in credit staff, especially if what she had heard about teams increasing productivity with fewer employees was true. The decision to apply for a transfer to customer support was difficult. She hated leaving her friends but didn't trust this whole team thing. After all, she had a family to support.

After only two months in customer support, Rhonda knew she had made the right move. Three people had been terminated in credit, with no plans to replace them. Rhonda was confused and upset when she learned a team-based structure was coming to customer support, based on team successes in credit. Rhonda didn't think it was a success when people lost their jobs.

Rhonda was assigned to a team of four customer support representatives. The other three were enthusiastic about the change and eager for training to develop new skills. During training each team was asked to set initial behavior expectations for the team and begin to talk about productivity goals. Rhonda explained her concerns to her new team members. The other three told her that she was making too much out of the issues and should just get on board. Rhonda ended up confronting the trainer and the entire class with her fears. The trainer was supportive and urged Rhonda to give the team a chance. Rhonda told her team members that she just could not support the effort. She would not be disruptive, but she would not participate any more than was absolutely required to stay employed.

### QUESTIONS FOR DISCUSSION
1. How would you advise Rhonda?
2. What could her new team members do?
3. Describe the communication, change, and conflict issues in this case.

## What Happened to the Value of Networking?

Ingress Computer Corporation was noted for excellent customer service in support of its networking products used by numerous multinational corporations with operations throughout the world. Ingress's International Customer Service team was well known for rapid response in complex situations requiring problem solving across international borders. Team members were located in six countries, communicating daily through e-mail and sophisticated GDSS systems and quarterly in face-to-face meetings in Rome. Other emergency meetings were conducted via video and audio conferencing. Team leader Enrico Bardini was proud of the group he believed to be among the most knowledgeable in the industry. Bardini was surprised to receive a call from Mitchell Morgan, vice president for customer service, indicating an increase in customer complaints that suggested that his team was slow to respond when systems involving more than one country were down.

Bardini decided to ask the group to discuss complaints via e-mail and to suggest potential solutions or at least explanations for recent problems. Team members responded rapidly, and their responses left Bardini even more perplexed. Yes, customer response time had slipped. The long hours of work coupled with time zone and language differences were wearing on the capabilities of individuals who worked mostly in isolation from other Ingress employees. Some members expressed the feeling that there was little appreciation for their efforts and certainly little career growth associated with their jobs. Two team members suggested more face-to-face meetings for troubleshooting, but the other four indicated that little could be done to improve the situation. All committed to trying to shorten customer response time.

Bardini reported his findings to Moran and asked for suggestions.

### QUESTIONS FOR DISCUSSION
1. Based on everything you have learned about organizational communication, describe what may be contributing to the responses Bardini received.
2. Discuss the merits and weaknesses of technologically mediated communication.
3. Describe what you would do if you were Mitchell Moran, Bardini, or an individual team member.

## The Case of the "Walking the Talk" Manager

Jeff's move to the JDW Worldwide Service Center came as no surprise to those who had followed his career. Jeff had worked for the new top management of the center in two of his previous assignments at JDW. The only surprise was that he was to become a senior manager in a team-based organization reporting directly to Mary Sikes. Jeff was known for his personable style, but few who knew him would suggest that he was a true team player. Mary was just the opposite. She was known for supporting the team structure and contributing to strong overall results. Mary had been promoted to the director's role prior to the change in top management.

Mary expected all three of her direct reports to work collaboratively with the customer service teams. Jeff openly agreed with Mary about almost everything, although she was told by her new manager that Jeff had expressed concerns that the center did not have enough managerial controls. Her manager, Jeff's former boss, seemed to believe Jeff and appeared to question her assurance that Jeff would come to understand the real benefits of the team structure. When Mary asked Jeff if he had any concerns, he assured her he did not and was fully supportive of the direction of the center.

Mary's concern increased when the two teams reporting to Jeff posted quarterly results that were below their previous metrics. When she asked Jeff to help her understand, he suggested that the teams were not as mature as she had thought and that he needed to become more involved. Mary decided to speak directly with the teams. The conversations left her puzzled.

Mary learned that Jeff rarely met with the teams and had not talked with them about their current or previous results. They claimed he could not possibly know what they needed. When Mary confronted Jeff with her findings, he claimed the teams did not understand how much he had learned from observation and review of written performance results. Mary worried that Jeff was saying all the right things but was not really "walking his talk."

Mary spoke with her boss about her concerns. He assured her there was no cause for concern and that Mary was lucky to have Jeff on her staff. In fact, Mary's manager suggested that Jeff should be groomed to replace Mary when she was promoted.

#### QUESTIONS FOR DISCUSSION
1. How can Mary evaluate whether her concerns are valid or not?
2. What should Mary consider as she communicates with her boss and with Jeff?
3. What are the ethical and practical issues in this case?

## Working Together at a Distance

The five members of the ComSci, Inc., product development team were located in three states with only two members of the group residing in the same city. All team members worked from their homes with a variety of networked technologies, including teleconferencing. During the first year following formation of the team, two successful products were introduced, with a third near completion. Management hailed the group as representing the future of the company. It came as a shock to almost everyone at ComSci when the development team lead, John Mercer, announced he was quitting for an opportunity to work with a competitor's development group. John claimed his team was competent and cooperative, that ComSci had rewarded him adequately, and the work they had produced was first rate. He could not, however, continue to work with so little real connection to others. Management asked John to reconsider, but his decision was firm. The other four team members expressed dismay but concluded that they wanted to continue to work in a geographically dispersed team.

#### QUESTIONS FOR DISCUSSION
1. Discuss the identification and socialization issues in this case.
2. What can be done to alleviate this type of problem?
3. How can individuals and organizations assess the needs of a geographically dispersed work force?

## Career and Personal Needs Just Don't Mix

Jim and Jane Wilson rarely saw each other. Jim was a stockbroker and Jane a successful lawyer. Married since graduate school, the two were devoted to each other, to their two children, Amy and Mike, and to their careers. It was not unusual for Jim and Jane to have fewer than thirty minutes a day together, although both spent more time with Amy and Mike. Jane worried about the hurried nature of their lives, but Jim assured her they were similar to most couples they knew.

Jane had not been expected to be assigned to the computer fraud case her firm had agreed to litigate on behalf of the U.S. Justice Department. The lead role was high visibility and would engage most of her time for twelve to eighteen months. She was honored and knew this assignment would position her to become the youngest partner in the firm. Jane was not prepared for the demands of the case and found herself without a free day in the first six weeks of her assignment. Jim was supportive, but she could tell her time away from home was beginning to wear. In addition, he had major clients who wanted him to travel with them to evaluate several major investments. Jim had assumed major responsibilities for Amy and Mike. If he were to be gone for several weeks, both Jane and Jim were concerned for the children's reaction.

Jane began to feel extremely tired even in the early morning. She found herself cross with staff at work and impatient with Jim at home. She knew that stress and burnout were problems for people working on intense cases, but she believed that serious problems happened to people who were not as happy at home or as committed to work as she was. Jane was amazed when Jim sent her an urgent e-mail stating they must have an evening to talk about the pressures between their work and family life. Jane knew Jim was right but was too tired to think how she might alter what was happening.

### QUESTIONS FOR DISCUSSION
1. How would you advise Jane?
2. What would you say to Jim?
3. Can intense careers and home responsibilities mix? Discuss your answers.
4. What are the communication issues in this case?

## The Power of Symbols: Creating Corporate Identity at Agilent Technologies

### Michael Z. Hackman and Ross Campbell[7]

In March 1999, technology icon Hewlett-Packard announced its intention to split into two separate companies. The Silicon Valley giant, citing the difficulty of growing its $47 billion yearly revenue stream and the challenges of competing with smaller and often more nimble competitors, announced a plan to separate its original instrument, test and measurement, and medical equipment product lines from the newer computer and imaging businesses. The surprise announcement was generally well received by customers, shareholders, and Wall Street analysts. Many of the company's 123,500 employees, however, were anxious.

A significant challenge to the leadership team chosen for the new company revolved around the celebrated company culture known to employees as "the HP Way." Long known as a pioneer in many progressive management philosophies, including management by objectives, profit sharing, and flex time, Hewlett-Packard boasted an extremely loyal set of long-term employees. These employees had grown accustomed to consensus decision making and the often bureaucratic

---

[7]Ross Campbell is a student at the University of Colorado at Colorado Springs majoring in communication. He has worked for Hewlett-Packard and Agilent Technologies for twenty years.

infrastructure that sometimes hampered the organization's ability to compete in the fast-moving new economy. The leaders of the new company were faced with the need to quickly and effectively communicate the vision of their new enterprise. What cherished elements of the old days would remain intact? What new values needed to be instilled?

In July 1999, just four months after the announcement of the split, the new company was named Agilent Technologies. The name was derived from the notion of agility. The connection to the Hewlett-Packard heritage was made clear by the tagline, "Innovating the HP Way." Further, a starburst logo, representative of a burst of insight, was unveiled. The leadership team at Agilent Technologies effectively used myriad symbols to communicate core values, vision, and purpose. The new CEO, Ned Barnholdt, told employees, stockholders, and customers that Agilent Technologies would emphasize three core values: speed, focus, and accountability. The company vision (save lives and help people communicate) and purpose (we make the tools for the people who make dreams real) were widely communicated. The company name, logo, and initial marketing campaign were meticulously crafted to communicate the new company's identity. Internal and external communications were consistent in tone and presented the same core values, vision, and purpose.

At each major milestone of the transition, employees participated in ceremonies laden with symbolic meaning. Gifts and stock option grants were given in an effort to motivate and energize employees. The popular Hewlett-Packard culture was not abandoned, as the Innovating the HP Way tagline illustrated, but the new core values began to create a distinct identity for the new company taking shape.

The leaders at Agilent Technologies successfully completed the transition by defining the transformed company culture through the use of symbols. In a matter of months the results were apparent. Organizational behavior began to change, aligning employees with the new company's well articulated ideals and values. The thoughtful management of organizational communication reaped a huge reward. Employees at Agilent Technologies rallied behind the new organization, embracing the new corporate identity with the same enthusiasm they had exhibited for their former employer, Hewlett-Packard.

**QUESTIONS FOR DISCUSSION**
1. Describe this change in terms of strategic communication planning.
2. Why was it important that the employees leaving Hewlett-Packard for the new company should have a clear sense of the vision and purpose of Agilent Technologies?
3. Think of an organization with which you have been affiliated that has done a very good or a very poor job of communicating core values, vision, and purpose. How closely do you identify with this organization? How important are core values, vision, and purpose in building loyalty?